Fodor's

# BUCKET LIST USA

# Welcome to Bucket List USA

The trip of a lifetime is around every corner of the USA, whether you want to explore national parks, big cities, or little-known gems. Hike the Appalachian Trail or drive the Golden Gate Bridge. Surf in Hawaii or skydive in Washington. Cruise around the Statue of Liberty, ride to the top of the Gateway Arch, or uncover quirky roadside attractions, like North Dakota's Enchanted Highway. Your epic adventure from sea to shining sea begins now. As you plan your travels, please confirm that places are still open, and let us know when we need to make updates by writing to us at editors@fodors.com.

## TOP REASONS TO GO

★ **Road Trips.** It's a great American tradition to drive stretches like Highway 101 and Route 66.

★ **Wild Landscapes.** Mountain peaks, lakes, beaches, forests, and prairies all reward travelers with stunning views.

★ **History.** Monuments tell the American story, from Philly to Mount Rushmore and beyond.

★ **Adventure.** White-water rafting, hiking, skiing, and more get the blood pumping.

★ **National Parks.** Grand Canyon, Zion, Yellowstone, Glacier: check them all off the list.

★ **Cool Cities.** Get wonderfully lost among the skyscrapers of New York, Chicago, and more.

# Contents

## MAPS

Chapter 1

# EXPERIENCE BUCKET LIST USA

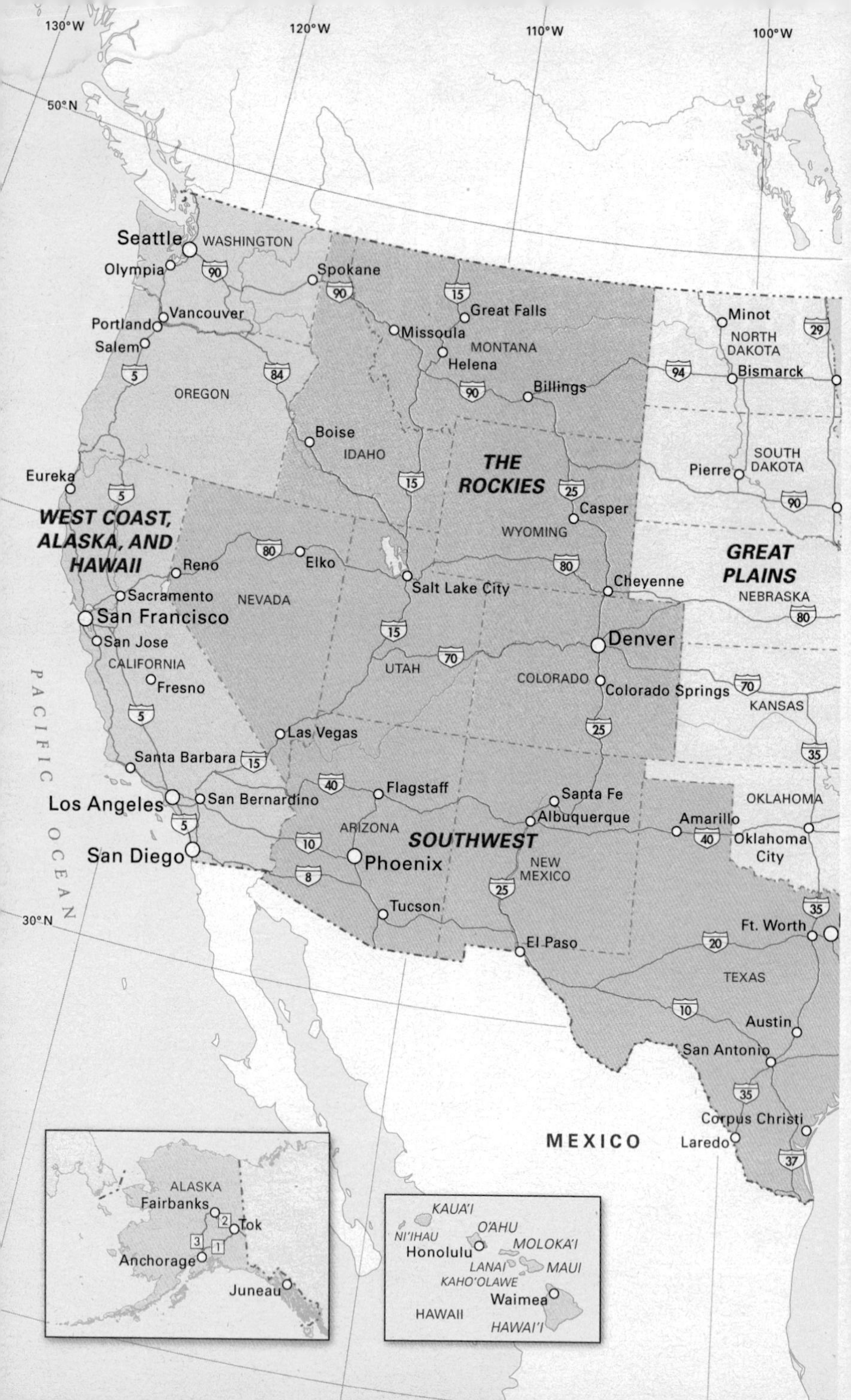

130°W
120°W
110°W
100°W
50°N
30°N
Seattle
WASHINGTON
Olympia
Spokane
Vancouver
Portland
Salem
Great Falls
Missoula
MONTANA
Helena
Minot
NORTH DAKOTA
Bismarck
Billings
OREGON
Boise
IDAHO
THE ROCKIES
SOUTH DAKOTA
Pierre
Eureka
Casper
WYOMING
WEST COAST, ALASKA, AND HAWAII
Reno
Elko
NEVADA
Salt Lake City
Cheyenne
GREAT PLAINS
NEBRASKA
Sacramento
San Francisco
San Jose
CALIFORNIA
Fresno
Denver
UTAH
COLORADO
Colorado Springs
KANSAS
Las Vegas
Santa Barbara
PACIFIC OCEAN
Los Angeles
San Bernardino
Flagstaff
Santa Fe
Albuquerque
OKLAHOMA
Amarillo
Oklahoma City
ARIZONA
SOUTHWEST
San Diego
Phoenix
NEW MEXICO
Tucson
El Paso
Ft. Worth
TEXAS
Austin
San Antonio
Corpus Christi
Laredo
MEXICO
ALASKA
Fairbanks
Tok
Anchorage
Juneau
KAUA'I
O'AHU
NI'IHAU
Honolulu
MOLOKA'I
LANAI
MAUI
KAHO'OLAWE
Waimea
HAWAII
HAWAI'I

Bucket List USA
Regional Areas
CANADA
GREAT LAKES
NEW ENGLAND
MID-ATLANTIC
SOUTHEAST
International Falls
Lake Superior
Sault Ste. Marie
Fargo
MINNESOTA
Minneapolis
St. Paul
WISCONSIN
Lake Michigan
Lake Huron
MICHIGAN
Milwaukee
Detroit
Lake Erie
Chicago
Sioux Falls
IOWA
Des Moines
Omaha
ILLINOIS
INDIANA
OHIO
Indianapolis
Cincinnati
Kansas City
Topeka
MISSOURI
St. Louis
Lake Ontario
Buffalo
Rochester
Syracuse
NEW YORK
MAINE
Augusta
Burlington
Portland
VT
NH
Boston
MA
Providence
CT
RI
Bridgeport
New York
Cleveland
PENNSYLVANIA
Pittsburgh
Philadelphia
NJ
MD
Baltimore
DE
WASHINGTON, D.C.
WEST VIRGINIA
Charleston
Richmond
Norfolk
VIRGINIA
KENTUCKY
Nashville
Knoxville
TENNESSEE
Raleigh
NORTH CAROLINA
Charlotte
Wilmington
Tulsa
ARKANSAS
Memphis
Columbia
SOUTH CAROLINA
Atlanta
GEORGIA
MISSISSIPPI
ALABAMA
Savannah
Dallas
Shreveport
Jackson
Montgomery
LOUISIANA
Jacksonville
Tallahassee
Baton Rouge
New Orleans
FLORIDA
Orlando
Houston
Tampa
Miami
ATLANTIC OCEAN
GULF OF MEXICO
BAHAMAS
Caribbean Sea
CUBA
90°W
80°W
70°W
0
200 mi
0
200 km

# Iconic Landmarks

**GOLDEN GATE BRIDGE**
Named for the mile-long strait at the mouth of San Francisco Bay that it crosses, this suspension bridge is known around the world for its graceful towers and rusty orange color. (It was originally intended to be blue and yellow, but the color of the primer stuck.) *(Ch. 7)*

**MOUNT RUSHMORE**
South Dakota's Black Hills would be famous without it, but this colossal sculpture of four presidents—Washington, Jefferson, Lincoln, and, slightly behind the other three, Theodore Roosevelt—makes them iconic. By artist Gutzon Borglum, Mount Rushmore's design changed several times before debuting in 1941. *(Ch. 6)*

**LOVE SCULPTURE**
It's amazing that in a city full of unforgettable sights—the Liberty Bell, anyone?—that the best-loved symbol of Philadelphia is Robert Indiana's red sculpture called "LOVE." It was briefly removed two years after it was installed in 1976, but the outcry from the citizenry brought it back to the City of Brotherly (and Sisterly) Love for good. *(Ch. 4)*

**STATUE OF LIBERTY**
People throw the word "iconic" around a lot these days, but New York's Statue of Liberty is perhaps the one landmark that truly represents the United States in the eyes of the world. You can visit the island, but the best way to enjoy the statue is standing on the deck of the (free) Staten Island Ferry. *(Ch. 4)*

**SPACE NEEDLE**

Built for the World's Fair in 1962, Seattle's 604-foot Space Needle is an unforgettable part of the Seattle skyline. The futuristic design was a compromise between two powerful men, one who wanted it to look like a balloon, the other like a flying saucer. *(Ch. 7)*

**EDMUND PETTUS BRIDGE**

The most potent symbol of America's civil rights struggle is this bridge outside of Selma, Alabama. In 1965, state troopers brutally attacked 400 mostly African American demonstrators peacefully marching to Montgomery. *(Ch. 5)*

**MIAMI BEACH**

More than 800 historic buildings in Miami Beach's Art Deco District make up the biggest collection of 1920s and 1930s resort architecture in the world. (Our favorite? The baby-blue, neon-lit Colony Hotel on Ocean Drive.) *(Ch. 5)*

**WASHINGTON MONUMENT**

The world is full of similarly shaped obelisks, but something about the 1884 Washington Monument—maybe its location on top of a small hill, or the ring of flags surrounding its base—inspires us. It's Washington, D.C.'s compass: east is the Capitol, north is the White House, and west is the Lincoln Memorial. *(Ch. 4)*

**GATEWAY ARCH**

The nation's tallest monument, the 630-foot St. Louis Gateway Arch treats you to sweeping views of the Mississippi River. (A futuristic tram whisks you to the top.) Don't miss the museum, which strives to weave in the stories of Native American people who lived in the region. *(Ch. 6)*

**HOLLYWOOD SIGN**

Fun fact: these 50-foot letters didn't originally spell "Hollywood." They advertised "Hollywood-land," an upscale real estate development. When they fell into disrepair, the city of Los Angeles came to its rescue with a new coat of paint, removing the last four letters in the process. *(Ch. 7)*

# National Parks

**GRAND CANYON**
You'll never forget your first visit to Arizona's Grand Canyon, gazing down at the seemingly endless expanse from the South Rim. Repeat visitors come for hiking, horseback riding, or white-water rafting. *(Ch. 8)*

**ACADIA**
It includes 17 other islands, but most visitors to this coastal paradise in Maine stick to easily accessible Mount Desert Island. Bike the carriage roads, hike lofty Cadillac Mountain, or trek to Bass Harbor Head Lighthouse. *(Ch. 3)*

**ARCHES**
It took millions of years for erosion to form the sandstone arches that give this Utah park its name. Delicate Arch is the most famous and Landscape Arch is the longest, but there are more than 2,000 others to grab your attention, making this the largest collection of natural arches in the world. *(Ch. 8)*

**OLYMPIC**
Covering 1 million acres, Washington State's jewel in the crown offers what is essentially three parks in one, with glacier-topped mountains, misty primeval forests filled with evergreens, and pristine beaches where you can set up camp and watch the waves roll in past sea stacks. *(Ch. 7)*

**GREAT SMOKY MOUNTAINS**
The country's most popular national park—partly because it sits close to large cities in Tennessee (Gatlinburg and Pigeon Forge) and North Carolina (Bryson City and Cherokee)—the Great Smoky Mountains is especially beautiful for hiking and camping in spring and fall. *(Ch. 5)*

**YELLOWSTONE**
Occupying the northwest corner of Wyoming and parts of Montana and Idaho, the country's first national park is known for the Old Faithful geyser, but it's dotted with steaming pools and bubbling mud pots, too. *(Ch. 9)*

**DEATH VALLEY**
Straddling the border of California and Nevada, Death Valley is the hottest place in the United States. It sets other records, being the driest (barely 2 inches of rain a year) and the lowest (282 feet below sea level) national park. *(Ch. 7)*

**ROCKY MOUNTAIN**
Since it's split in two by the Continental Divide, the eastern half of this Colorado park is craggy mountains, while the western half is lush, green forests. *(Ch. 9)*

**YOSEMITE**
The record-breaking granite peak of El Capitan gets star billing, but this 1,200-square-mile park in California's Sierra Nevada mountains has plenty of superlatives, including Bridalveil Fall, the country's tallest waterfall. *(Ch. 7)*

**GLACIER**
Although its glaciers are receding, Montana's most popular destination is known for more than 1 million acres of glacier-carved valleys and peaks. Hikers love the spectacular alpine mountain scenery. *(Ch. 9)*

**ZION**
Other parks offer wide-open spaces, but Utah's Zion offers breathtaking spots like the Narrows, a slot canyon that often narrows to less than 20 feet wide. Its soaring red cliffs attract casual hikers and serious rock climbers. *(Ch. 8)*

# Adventures

**CRUISING THROUGH GLACIER BAY**
Brown bears lumber along the shore of Glacier Bay while bald eagles soar overhead and sea otters swim alongside your boat. Calving glaciers and the snow-covered Fairweather Mountains complete the scene. *(Ch. 7)*

**MOUNTAIN BIKING IN MOAB**
Considered by many to be the ultimate mountain-biking experience, Slickrock Trail in Moab, Utah, is a 10-mile trek through delightful desert terrain. There are also plenty of easier rides through Moab. *(Ch. 8)*

**HIKING THE APPALACHIAN TRAIL**
Running for 2,200 miles from Georgia to Maine, the Appalachian Trail is the Holy Grail for serious hikers. Challenge yourself with the Roller Coaster, a quad-busting trek through Virginia. *(Ch. 3–5)*

**FLY-FISHING ON THE MISSOURI RIVER**
Fly-fishing doesn't get any better than in Montana, especially along the Missouri River. From June to August, the average trout—this is not a typo—is 16 inches long. *(Ch. 9)*

**BACKPACKING IN MOUNT RAINIER NATIONAL PARK**
Washington's Mt. Rainier is a magnet for backpackers, with dozens of off-the-beaten-path routes like the challenging 17-mile Mother Mountain Loop. Wildlife like chipmunks and black bears share the evergreen trails. *(Ch. 7)*

**KAYAKING SOUTH CAROLINA'S BARRIER ISLANDS**
Bottlenose dolphins follow in your wake as you kayak along the coast. You'll encounter loggerhead turtles, white-tailed deer, and even alligators (from a safe distance). *(Ch. 5)*

**SNORKELING IN THE CHANNEL ISLANDS**
The kelp forests just off the coast of California's Santa Cruz Island, one of the famous Channel Islands, make for some of the country's most seductive underwater scenery. *(Ch. 7)*

**ROCK CLIMBING IN NEW RIVER GORGE**
One of the nation's newest national parks, West Virginia's New River Gorge is already one of the most popular climbing areas in the country. The park has sheer sandstone cliffs that challenge even pros. *(Ch. 4)*

Rafting the Colorado River

**RAFTING THE COLORADO RIVER**
Riding the rapids through the Grand Canyon on the Colorado River is one of the biggest thrills imaginable. It's not all white water, though: there are long, relaxing stretches of water, where you drift amid grandiose rock formations on a multiday adventure. *(Ch. 8)*

**SNOWSHOEING IN MICHIGAN**
Michigan's Upper Peninsula is prime snowshoeing territory, especially in the towering old-growth forests of the remote Porcupine Mountains (aka "Porkies"). There's a 100-mile hut-to-hut trail where you can warm yourself up next to a wood-burning stove. Or, try the activity at Pictured Rocks National Lakeshore, also known for its ice climbing. *(Ch. 10)*

**SURFING ON THE NORTH SHORE OF OAHU**
From November to February, only experienced surfers should take on the towering waves along Oahu, Hawaii's famous North Shore. This area is often called the "seven-mile miracle" for its long stretch of breaks. *(Ch. 7)*

**SWIMMING WITH MANATEES**
Florida's gentle giants are surprisingly easy to spot from December to March, when they congregate in the warmer waters of freshwater springs. You can legally swim with them in Crystal River, and kayak with them in South Florida, but remember to respect all rules and maintain your distance. *(Ch. 5)*

**SKYDIVING IN SNOHOMISH**
Take on the ultimate bucket list activity in Snohomish, Washington, considered one of the top skydiving destinations in the world. As you soar through the fresh mountain air you can spot mini evergreens and snowcapped peaks. *(Ch. 7)*

# Historic Sites

**INDEPENDENCE HALL**
A UNESCO World Heritage site, this 18th-century landmark is where the Declaration of Independence and the Constitution were adopted. It's the centerpiece of Philadelphia's Independence National Historical Park, home to the Liberty Bell, Congress Hall, and more. *(Ch. 4)*

**CLIFF PALACE**
In Colorado's Mesa Verde National Park, this is the largest cliff dwelling in North America. Carved by Ancestral Puebloan people beneath rocky overhangs, they are extraordinarily well preserved. *(Ch. 9)*

**BILTMORE ESTATE**
The largest private house in the country, the 19th-century Biltmore Estate remains one of the most prominent mansions of the Gilded Age. It sits on 8,000 acres in Asheville, North Carolina's Blue Ridge Mountains. On view are antiques and art, 75 acres of gardens, a conservatory, landscaped grounds, and the on-site winery, the most visited one in America. *(Ch. 5)*

**THE FREEDOM TRAIL**
A bronze plaque embedded in a cobblestone street marks the beginning of Boston's Freedom Trail, which runs for more than 2 miles past some of the city's most historic American Revolutionary War–era sites, including Faneuil Hall, the Old North Church, and the Paul Revere House. *(Ch. 3)*

**AZTEC RUINS NATIONAL MONUMENT**
In New Mexico, this dazzling collection of 400 masonry buildings was constructed by the Pueblo people nearly a thousand years ago. Some are just foundations, while others are beautifully reconstructed. *(Ch. 8)*

**ELLIS ISLAND**
In the shadow of the Statue of Liberty, this tiny island in New York Harbor was once the busiest immigration center in the country. While they are here, many visitors look up ancestors who passed through. *(Ch. 4)*

**CASTILLO DE SAN MARCOS**
Construction began on St. Augustine's fortress more than three centuries ago, when the Spanish wanted to shore up their defenses in what is now known as Florida. Its waterfront perch is dazzling. *(Ch. 5)*

**EBENEZER BAPTIST CHURCH**
The Rev. Martin Luther King Jr. was pastor at this two-towered brick church in Atlanta until he was assassinated in 1968. To this day the church still has a strong focus on civil rights and racial justice. *(Ch. 5)*

**ALCATRAZ ISLAND**
On a remote island in California's San Francisco Bay, this fortresslike maximum-security prison, which held infamous criminals Al Capone and Machine Gun Kelly, was perhaps better known by its nickname, "The Rock." The open-air boat ride to the island is spectacular in itself. *(Ch. 7)*

**FORD'S THEATRE**
A history lesson come to life, this still functioning playhouse in Washington, D.C., is where Abraham Lincoln was shot. He died across the street in Peterson's Boarding House, which you can also visit. *(Ch. 4)*

**PLIMOTH PATUXET**
This living history museum in Plymouth, Massachusetts, teaches visitors about the day-to-day lives of the English settlers now known as the Pilgrims. *(Ch. 3)*

# Natural Attractions

**CRATER LAKE**
In the caldera of a dormant volcano, Oregon's brilliant blue lake has a depth of 1,943 feet, making it the deepest in the United States. It's fed by snowfall from the dramatic peaks that ring its shores. *(Ch. 7)*

**NIAGARA FALLS**
It's not the tallest (that's Angel Falls in Venezuela) or the widest (that's Khone Falls in Laos), but with more than 30 million visitors a year, Niagara, located in both New York and Canada, is by far the world's most popular waterfall. Catch a glimpse from above at Niagara Falls Observation Tower or on a boat tour. *(Ch. 4)*

**BLACK HILLS**
North America's oldest mountain range, located in South Dakota, got its name from the Lakota people, who called them Paha Sapa, or "Hills That Are Black." Bison graze in the grasslands beneath the impressive spires of Custer State Park, and sculptures of American presidents at Mount Rushmore tower over the landscape. *(Ch. 6)*

**NATURAL BRIDGE**
Sacred to the Monocan people, Virginia's 215-foot-long limestone arch makes it into the record books as the longest in North America. Thomas Jefferson called it "the most sublime of nature's works." *(Ch. 4)*

**MAMMOTH CAVE**
Although it's famous throughout Kentucky, Mammoth Cave isn't on many bucket lists. That's a shame, because these stunningly beautiful caverns make up the world's longest cave system, a wonderland for spelunking and subterranean tours. *(Ch. 5)*

**HELLS CANYON**
The deepest canyon in North America—2,000 feet deeper than the more famous Grand Canyon—this lightly traveled park sits on the border of Oregon and Idaho. Don't miss white-water rafting on the Snake River. *(Ch. 9)*

California's redwood trees

**TALL TREES GROVE**
The discovery of the world's tallest tree led to the creation of California's Redwood National Park in 1968. A moderately strenuous hike takes you to these tall wonders. *(Ch. 7)*

**KILAUEA**
Erupting almost continually since 1983, Hawaii's Kilauea is the world's most active volcanic mass. When lava pools in the Halema'uma'u crater, it's often possible to catch a glimpse on a guided hike. *(Ch. 7)*

**DENALI**
It's not hard to spot the icy slopes of Denali, North America's tallest mountain peak. It's in 6 million acres of Alaskan wilderness that's almost completely untouched, save for a single road. *(Ch. 7)*

**BAGLEY ICEFIELD**
Take to the air to see the continent's largest concentration of glaciers in Alaska's Wrangell–St. Elias. Among the record-breakers is glistening Bagley Icefield, North America's largest tidewater glacier. *(Ch. 7)*

**WHITE SANDS**
One of New Mexico's most dazzling sights, these undulating dunes of gypsum sand are the largest of their kind in the world. Some of its desert animals are found nowhere else on earth. *(Ch. 8)*

**THE EVERGLADES**
Called the "River of Grass," the Everglades is the largest mangrove forest in the Western Hemisphere. Florida's subtropical wetlands are the only place where the American alligator and crocodile coexist. *(Ch. 5)*

# Museums

**MUSEUM OF POP CULTURE**
Better known as MoPOP, this family favorite occupies an undulating building in Seattle filled with fun exhibits focusing on everything from punk rock to video games to science fiction films. *(Ch. 7)*

**GETTY MUSEUM**
No museum has a better location than the Getty, perched high on a hill overlooking Los Angeles. The modern architecture is stunning, the sculpture gardens are gorgeous, and the collection unequaled on the West Coast. *(Ch. 7)*

**ISABELLA STEWART GARDNER MUSEUM**
The art at this Boston landmark—think Rembrandt, Michelangelo, Matisse, and Sargent—is impressive, but the museum's location in a Venetian-style palazzo around a light-filled courtyard is equally enthralling. See masterpieces like Titian's *Europa* and John Singer Sargent's *El Jaleo*. *(Ch. 3)*

**AMERICAN CIVIL WAR MUSEUM**
In a former ironworks, this brilliantly realized space in Richmond, Virginia, tells the story of a pivotal time in American history: the War Between the States. The museum explores every angle imaginable, not just North and South. *(Ch. 4)*

**BIRMINGHAM CIVIL RIGHTS INSTITUTE**
Set beneath a breathtaking glass dome, this interpretive museum and research center in Birmingham, Alabama, tells the story of the ongoing struggle for racial equality in the United States and traces African Americans' struggle for equality back to the 1800s. *(Ch. 5)*

**GEORGIA O'KEEFFE MUSEUM**
Her beloved city Santa Fe, New Mexico, hosts the only museum dedicated to groundbreaking painter Georgia O'Keeffe. The pueblo-style building is the perfect backdrop for her art. *(Ch. 8)*

**NEGRO LEAGUES BASEBALL MUSEUM**
A real game changer, this Kansas City, Missouri, museum chronicles the 100-year history of this historic league, formed in 1920 because players were banned from all-white teams. *(Ch. 6)*

**UNITED STATES HOLOCAUST MUSEUM**
Washington, D.C., has dozens of museums, but none more powerful than this one telling the story of the millions murdered in World War II, and how survivors and descendants worked to change the world. *(Ch. 4)*

**METROPOLITAN MUSEUM OF ART**
You could take a week to explore this sprawling museum in New York City, which includes an Egyptian temple dating back 2,000 years and a house designed by Frank Lloyd Wright. *(Ch. 4)*

**9/11 TRIBUTE MUSEUM**
On the site of New York's Twin Towers, which were felled in a terrorist attack on September 11, 2001, this museum memorializes the event with home videos, news camera footage, and interviews with survivors. *(Ch. 4)*

**ART INSTITUTE OF CHICAGO**
It may contain modern must-sees like Pablo Picasso's *The Old Guitarist* and Grant Wood's *American Gothic*, but the vast collection here spans many eras and cultures. *(Ch. 10)*

# Festivals

**ART BASEL**
Every December, Miami becomes the center of the art world when it hosts the massive Art Basel, an international festival that also touches down in Switzerland and Hong Kong, and the swanky parties that come along with it. *(Ch. 5)*

**BURNING MAN**
Tens of thousands of avid "burners" return each summer to Nevada's Black Rock Desert for Burning Man, a "temporary metropolis dedicated to community, art, self-expression, and self-reliance." *(Ch. 8)*

**COMIC-CON**
Originally for comic book fans, San Diego's hugely popular convention has grown to include just about all pop culture. The big draw is the costumes, so be prepared to snap pics of every superhero you could imagine. *(Ch. 7)*

**NEW ORLEANS JAZZ FEST**
More formally known as the New Orleans Jazz and Heritage Festival, this annual outdoor celebration is second only to Mardi Gras in the hearts of music-loving locals. *(Ch. 5)*

**SOUTH BY SOUTHWEST**
In March, Austin, Texas, pretty much surrenders to this weeklong event that literally fills the streets with outdoor concerts by musicians of every possible genre. Indoors are film screenings and interactive media demonstrations. *(Ch. 8)*

**SUNDANCE FILM FESTIVAL**
Hollywood relocates to Park City, Utah, every winter for the world's largest independent film festival. The best inevitably end up streaming on your TV or playing at your local multiplex. *(Ch. 8)*

**TASTE OF CHICAGO**
Deep-dish pizza is delicious, but it's not the only famous food to come out of Chicago, as this annual gastronomic event makes clear. Taking over Grant Park, it's one of the city's largest events. *(Ch. 10)*

**MAINE LOBSTER FESTIVAL**
In Maine, summer isn't summer without lobster. This festival, held in the coastal community of Rockland, has a parade, cooking contests, and the crowning of the Maine Sea Goddess. *(Ch. 3)*

Coney Island Mermaid Parade

### CONEY ISLAND MERMAID PARADE

Manhattan parades might be bigger, but none of them are as fun as this Brooklyn street festival smack in the middle of Coney Island's amusement park, with thousands of mermaids, mermen, and every conceivable creature from under the sea. *(Ch. 4)*

### WAIKIKI HO'OLAULE'A

Billed as "Hawaii's largest block party," Waikiki Ho'olaule'a has become an unmissable event that celebrates the archipelago's cuisine, crafts, and culture. Four stages of entertainment are the place to watch hula, singing, and more. *(Ch. 7)*

### ALBUQUERQUE INTERNATIONAL BALLOON FIESTA

From morning to night, the skies over New Mexico are filled with every conceivable shape and color of hot air balloon. Whimsical designs include astronauts, swarms of bumble bees, and even *Star Wars* characters. *(Ch. 8)*

### OREGON SHAKESPEARE FESTIVAL

The Bard isn't the only playwright whose works are brought to life at this venerable event dating back to 1935. It now stages hundreds of performances in outdoor and indoor spaces. *(Ch. 7)*

### CHERRY BLOSSOM FESTIVAL

Every spring, thousands of cherry trees around the Jefferson Memorial and throughout all of Washington, D.C., are suddenly covered with delicate white blossoms. *(Ch. 4)*

### TELLURIDE BLUEGRASS FESTIVAL

The biggest names in bluegrass, along with a well-rounded roster of musicians from other genres, descend upon the picturesque former Colorado mining town over the annual summer solstice. *(Ch. 9)*

# Seasonal Travel

**LEAF-PEEPING**
We especially love the bright red, yellow, and orange fall leaves in Stowe and other towns in Vermont (they write songs about it, after all), but autumn is equally as lovely in the valleys of Tennessee and the aspen-covered slopes of Colorado. *(Ch. 3, 5, 9)*

**GRAPE HARVEST**
Many vineyards invite you to participate in the annual harvest festivities in Willamette Valley, Oregon, one of the most beautiful wine regions. New York's Finger Lakes region is another good choice. *(Ch. 4, 7)*

**4TH OF JULY FIREWORKS**
You might argue that the Independence Day fireworks over the nation's capital are the best, but take our word for it and join the crowds at Atlanta's beautiful Centennial Olympic Park for a showstopping display you won't soon forget. *(Ch. 5)*

**CORN MAZES**
The Richardson Adventure Farm in Spring Grove, Illinois, has perhaps the most spectacular corn maze in the country. You have to see it from above to take in the intricate design. Iowa, too, is a great place to take in corn mazes during harvest time. *(Ch. 6, 10)*

**ICE-SKATING**
Sun Valley Outdoor Ice Rink, a favorite winter destination for travelers all over Idaho, has memorable views of the undulating landscape. Duck inside to see world-class figure skaters practice. *(Ch. 9)*

**NORTHERN LIGHTS**
Alaska is the place to see swirls of green and purple dancing in the night sky. In the continental United States, it's hard to find a better place for viewing the light show of the aurora borealis than Idaho's Panhandle National Forest or Michigan's Upper Peninsula. *(Ch. 7, 9, 10)*

**SPRING TRAINING**
Baseball fans, take note: Ed Smith Stadium, in Sarasota, Florida, is a fan favorite because of the downtown location, the Spanish-style architecture, and the enthusiastic Baltimore Orioles fans. Arizona, too, is a great place to catch a ball game. *(Ch. 5, 8)*

**MARATHONS**
Spring is a favorite season for watching—or actually competing in—runs of all types. The pinnacle, of course, is the Boston Marathon, which finishes downtown. *(Ch. 3)*

Cherry blossoms in bloom

**FLOWERS**
A gift from the mayor of Tokyo, the cherry trees around the Tidal Basin in Washington, D.C., are perhaps spring's most beautiful sight. The National Cherry Blossom Festival is held in late March and early April. You can also see fields of happy yellow sunflowers each August in North Dakota, rows of colorful tulips each spring in Holland, Michigan, and Skagit Valley, and lavender each July in Sequim, Washington. *(Ch. 4, 6, 7, 10)*

**CLASSICAL CONCERTS**
Summer nights practically require spreading out a blanket, opening a bottle of wine, and listening to an orchestra play at Tanglewood, the outdoor amphitheater in Lenox, Massachusetts. Or, catch the Boston Pops Orchestra during its annual Fireworks Spectacular on the Fourth of July. *(Ch. 3)*

**CROSS-COUNTRY SKIING**
Tucked among the evergreen trees, New Hampshire's Bretton Woods Nordic Center is the largest cross-country skiing area on the East Coast. In the west, head to Rocky Mountain National Park. *(Ch. 3, 9)*

**MUSIC FESTIVALS**
There's no lack of summer music festivals on the calendar, from New York City's Governors Ball to Chicago's Lollapalooza to California's Coachella, but it's hard to deny the energy of Bonnaroo, which attracts thousands of happy campers to Manchester, Tennessee, for an epic four days of back-to-back concerts. *(Ch. 5)*

# Family-Friendly Travel

**DISNEYLAND**
Florida's Walt Disney World has many times the acreage, but for our money the original park in Anaheim, California, packs more fun into every square foot. We still love the Haunted Mansion. *(Ch. 7)*

**CHILDREN'S MUSEUM OF INDIANAPOLIS**
Dinosaurs literally burst through the walls at this beloved institution, the largest of its type in the world. It has five floors of exhibits, including fossils from an archaeological dig. *(Ch. 10)*

**BEARIZONA WILDLIFE CENTER**
There are plenty of bears on display at the drive-through nature preserve on the way to the Grand Canyon, including fearsome grizzlies, but you might find yourself enchanted by little guys like the beavers, badgers, and porcupines. Located in Williams, Arizona, it's 58 miles south of the Grand Canyon's South Rim entrance. *(Ch. 8)*

**DOLLYWOOD**
In the bustling town of Pigeon Forge, Tennessee, this country-music theme park is named for legendary singer and songwriter, Dolly Parton. Favorite attractions include Klondike Katie, a coal-fired steam engine, and the Lightning Rod roller coaster. *(Ch. 5)*

**CEDAR POINT**
Thrill-seekers flock to this venerable Ohio theme park, where the Steel Vengeance is the world's fastest and tallest hybrid roller coaster. It also has the steepest and longest drop and four inversions. *(Ch. 10)*

**COLONIAL WILLIAMSBURG**
You can walk the same streets as George Washington and Thomas Jefferson at Virginia's Colonial Williamsburg, where 18th-century structures have been lovingly restored. *(Ch. 4)*

**KENNEDY SPACE CENTER**
A thrill for young scientists, Florida's Kennedy Space Center lets you gaze in awe at the Space Shuttle Atlantis, relive the thrilling launch of Apollo 8, or talk with a real astronaut. *(Ch. 5)*

**GEORGIA AQUARIUM**
The largest of its type in the world, the Georgia Aquarium is home to 100,000 underwater creatures. It's one of the only facilities with massive whale sharks, and the playful beluga whales are adorable. *(Ch. 5)*

**ALASKA SEALIFE CENTER**
On the shores of Alaska's Resurrection Bay in Seward, this marine mammal rehabilitation facility teaches you about research on animals like puffins and sea otters, and lets you see them up close. *(Ch. 7)*

**MAUI OCEAN CENTER**
One of the world's top aquariums, Maui Ocean Center is home to Turtle Lagoon, where hefty green Hawaiian sea turtles come up for air. Also dazzling are the jellyfish and hammerhead sharks. *(Ch. 7)*

**MUSEUM OF THE ROCKIES**
The skeleton of a fully grown T. rex gives you chills at Montana's Museum of the Rockies, with one of the best collections of fossils in the country. *(Ch. 9)*

# Roadside Attractions

**CADILLAC RANCH**
Outside the Texas town of Amarillo—mentioned prominently in the song "Route 66"—is this way-out art project. The brainchild of several San Francisco hippies, it's a series of 10 spray-painted Cadillacs buried grill-first in a pasture. *(Ch. 8)*

**ELMER'S BOTTLE TREE RANCH**
In the desert town Oro Grande, California, this forest of metal and glass was a labor of love by artist Elmer Long. More than 200 metal trees hold bottles of every imaginable shape, size, and color. Long has passed on, but visitors still stop by to snap pics of the amazing sight. *(Ch. 7)*

**ENCHANTED HIGHWAY**
If you're near Regent, North Dakota, locals will steer you to this 32-mile stretch of road north of town lined with metal sculptures. Massive pheasants dash across the plain, huge grasshoppers nibble on leaves, and trout leap from imaginary streams. The gift shop in Regent sells miniature versions of the larger-than-life sculptures. *(Ch. 6)*

**JIMMY CARTER PEANUT**
Inspired by the toothy grin of the country's 39th president, this giant smiling peanut is one display in his hometown of Plains, Georgia. Made from chicken wire covered with polyurethane foam, it's proved to be a remarkably durable attraction in the middle of peanut country. *(Ch. 5)*

**WILD HORSE MONUMENT**
These 15 stallions gallop across to the top of a high plateau near Vantage, Washington. Although road signs call it the Wild Horse Monument, the real name of artist David Govedare's still-unfinished masterpiece is "Grandfather Cuts Loose the Ponies." *(Ch. 7)*

**CARHENGE**
England's prehistoric circle of standing stones is faithfully recreated in Alliance, Nebraska, except for the fact that here it's made from vintage automobiles. Just as at the original, thousands of believers congregate here whenever there's a solar eclipse. *(Ch. 6)*

**BLUE WHALE**
Rising out of its own little lake near Catoosa, Oklahoma, the Blue Whale is one of the region's most whimsical sights. Built in the 1970s as an anniversary present, it's taken on a life of its own as a tourist attraction. *(Ch. 6)*

**PAUL BUNYON AND BABE THE BLUE OX**
In the middle of the 20th century, huge statues popped up all over the Midwest to catch the eye of passing motorists. Bemidji, Minnesota, is home to the larger-than-life lumberjack and his oddly colored animal companion, built to attract tourists to the logging town. *(Ch. 10)*

**COCAINE BEAR**
We swear this is a true story: Back in 1985, a black bear in the Chattahoochee National Forest became a local hero after ingesting $15 million of cocaine that a drug dealer had jettisoned from an airplane. It died, but it was stuffed and put on display at Lexington's Kentucky for Kentucky Fun Mall. *(Ch. 5)*

**WORLD'S LARGEST GARDEN GNOME**
Iowa State University in Ames is home to this colorful fellow, who measures 15 feet tall if you count his pointy red cap. He seems right at home in Reiman Gardens. If you're in Upstate New York, the second largest, nicknamed Gnome Chomsky, is one display in the town of Kerhonkson. *(Ch. 4, 6)*

# Spectator Sports

**ROSE BOWL**
A National Historic Landmark, this storied football field in Pasadena, California, opened in 1922. Resembling a horseshoe until its southern side was completed in 1928, it has hosted five Super Bowls, two Summer Olympics, two World Cup finals, and the annual Rose Bowl Game. *(Ch. 7)*

**ARTHUR ASHE STADIUM**
The biggest tennis stadium in world, the 23,000-seat Arthur Ashe Stadium is home of the U.S. Open. The original design for the stadium, in Flushing Meadows–Corona Park, Queens, did not call for a roof, but in 2016 a dazzling retractable roof was added, giving the structure a futuristic look. *(Ch. 4)*

**BANZAI PIPELINE**
The Billabong Pipe Masters, part of surfing's Triple Crown, takes place at this world-famous spot along the coast of Oahu every December. The Banzai Pipeline (known as the Pipeline or just the Pipe to locals) is known for monster waves. *(Ch. 7)*

**FENWAY PARK**
Major-league baseball teams keep building new stadiums, but it's hard to believe any will be as beloved as Boston's Fenway Park, home of the Red Sox since 1912. Seats are at a premium atop the "Green Monster," the 37-foot left-field wall that's a goal for many batters. *(Ch. 3)*

**DAYTONA INTERNATIONAL SPEEDWAY**
Opened in 1959, this world-famous racetrack is the home of NASCAR's Daytona 500. It was an innovative design at the time, with banked corners to allow for higher speeds and better views from the stands. Its track can be configured in several different ways, depending on the race. *(Ch. 5)*

**YVETTE GIROUARD FIELD AT LAMSON PARK**
Home field of the University of Louisiana Ragin' Cajuns, this field is among the most beautiful in women's softball. It's almost among the most luxurious, with several private sky boxes for well-heeled fans. It's named for former head coach Yvette Girouard, who is the winningest coach in the history of the sport. *(Ch. 5)*

**PROVIDENCE PARK**
In Portland, Oregon, asymmetrical Providence Park was built in 1926, making it the oldest stadium in use by a major-league soccer team. Impassioned fans of the Portland Timbers wear green-and-gold scarves and are called the "Timber Army." *(Ch. 7)*

Churchill Downs

**CHURCHILL DOWNS**
Home of the Kentucky Derby, the "most exciting two minutes in sports," this Louisville landmark dating from 1875 is immediately recognizable from the twin spires above the grandstand. The Derby launched that first year, making it the longest running continuous sporting event in the United States. *(Ch. 5)*

**AUGUSTA NATIONAL GOLF CLUB**
One of the most exclusive golf courses in the world, Augusta National Golf Club in Augusta, Georgia, is home of the Masters Tournament every April. Scoring a ticket to the main event is tough, though it's a little easier to get into the lottery for practice rounds. *(Ch. 5)*

**U.S. OLYMPIC AND PARALYMPIC TRAINING CENTER**
Nicknamed Olympic City USA, Colorado Springs has the perfect climate for training throughout the year. You can tour this state-of-the-art facility or even watch figure skaters, swimmers, cyclists, and other aspiring athletes in action. Make sure to visit the U.S. Olympic Hall of Fame. *(Ch. 9)*

**WRIGLEY FIELD**
Fans love this ballpark, built in 1914 on the north side of Chicago. It's easy to see why: the iconic red marquee over the entrance, the scoreboard that's still turned by hand, and the outfield wall covered with ivy. Despite improvements over the years, it still feels like a hometown field. *(Ch. 10)*

**MADISON SQUARE GARDEN**
For basketball fans, there's no bigger draw than the home court of the New York Knicks. It's not the slickest or the best designed or the most high-tech—Brooklyn's Barclay Center beats it in all these categories—but it has such a long history that locals can't imagine catching game anywhere else. *(Ch. 4)*

# State Booze

**HIGH WEST DISTILLERY**
At the base of one of the most popular ski runs in Park City, Utah, this is the world's only ski-in distillery. It's known for its line of award-winning small-batch vodkas and whiskeys. *(Ch. 8)*

**DOGFISH HEAD BREWERY**
Milton, Delaware, is on the beer-lovers map for its funky architecture and first-rate facilities. Opt for the "Off-Centered" tour, which includes a taste of new brews that haven't been released to the public. *(Ch. 4)*

**BOULEVARD BREWING COMPANY**
For a peek behind the scenes at this Kansas City, Missouri, landmark, book the Unfiltered Tour and sip favorites like the Tank 7 American Saison. You also get to sip innovative brews that might make it on their roster. *(Ch. 6)*

**KONTOKOSTA WINERY**
East of New York City in the upscale North Fork, Kontokosta Winery is a gorgeous facility that faces the water of Long Island Sound. The tasting room is sunny and modern and has killer views. *(Ch. 4)*

**YUENGLING**
In a handsome brick building in Pottsville, Pennsylvania, D. G. Yuengling & Son is the oldest brewery in the country. Check out the hand-dug fermentation cellars and stained-glass glass ceiling in the brew house. *(Ch. 4)*

**EYRIE VINEYARDS**
The first winery to plant Pinot Noir grapes in Oregon's Willamette Valley, Eyrie Vineyards is historic. It's still a family-run business, so you'll get a warm welcome in the cozy tasting room. *(Ch. 7)*

**QUIXOTE WINERY**
A Napa Valley standout, this modern winery designed by artist and architect Friedensreich Hundertwasser has a disarmingly quirky style and serves rich Cabernets in its tasting room. *(Ch. 7)*

**KŌ HANA DISTILLERS**
The sugarcane fields around beautiful Waipahu, Hawaii, are the basis for this estate-made rum. It's the region's only farm-to-bottle distillery, so the tours are a sneak peek at a special process. *(Ch. 7)*

Wild Turkey Distillery

**WILD TURKEY DISTILLERY**
On a hillside high above the Kentucky River in Lawrenceburg, this "cathedral to bourbon" blends traditional distilling methods and a modern glass-walled tasting room with eye-popping views. It's one of many stops on the Kentucky Bourbon Trail. *(Ch. 5)*

**DUCHMAN FAMILY WINERY**
Texas Hill Country produces some stellar wines, including an array of Italian-style vintages produced here. The stone-walled villa makes this one in the rolling hills of Driftwood, Texas, one of the region's top stops. *(Ch. 8)*

**DONUM ESTATE**
Dozens of museum-quality sculptures dot the grounds at this winery, a favorite for locals in Sonoma County. Stroll through the lavender fields with a glass of Chardonnay or Pinot Noir in hand. *(Ch. 7)*

**BLACK STAR FARMS**
A curving driveway leads to this country estate in Traverse City, one of the most beautiful destinations in Michigan Wine Country. Enjoy the award-winning Riesling on the terrace or in front of a roaring fire. *(Ch. 10)*

**OLE SMOKY MOONSHINE**
You don't have to whisper anymore to find moonshine in Tennessee—you can visit the state's first legal moonshine distillery in Gatlinburg. Take a tour to see the process in action, and sample these magical mountain elixirs made with local corn in flavors like Apple Pie and Lemon Drop. *(Ch. 5)*

**SWEETWATER BREWERY**
A pair of college roommates started this now-popular craft brewery in Atlanta back in 1997, seizing an opportunity to bring West Coast brew knowledge to the Southeast. *(Ch. 5)*

## Souvenirs

**SWEETGRASS BASKETS**
A centuries-old tradition started by the Gullah Geechee people of the Carolinas, descendants of enslaved people from Africa, these intricately woven baskets are the most popular gift item in South Carolina. Charleston City Market is a great place to shop for them.

**ROSEBUD LIP BALM**
You can still sample soothing salves and ointments at the century-old Rosebud Building in Woodsboro, Maryland. If you can't make it for a visit, pick up a tube of the luscious lip balm at any pharmacy. It's a must to avoid dry or cracked lips in wintertime.

**CRYSTAL HOT SAUCE**
Louisiana residents have strong opinions about the best hot sauce in the state, and there are many. Some swear by Tabasco, even though it cheats a bit by not using aged red cayenne peppers (though its factory earns points for its location on the lush, wild Avery Island). However, Crystal is the best seller, and simply the best.

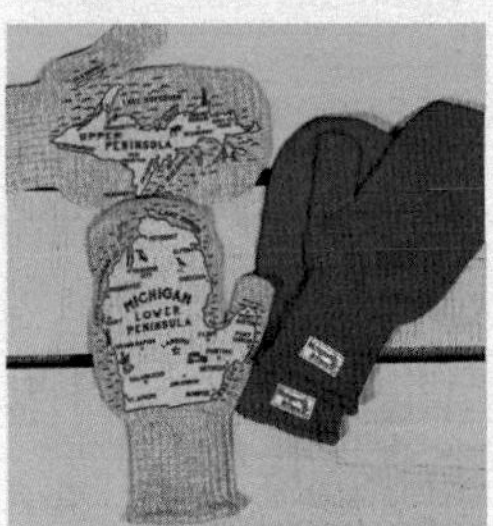


**STATE-SHAPED MITTENS**
Michigan and Wisconsin are locked in a bruising battle over who has the most adorable mittens. We love the ones emblazoned with a map of either state, and they'll surely keep you warm in a Great Lakes winter.

**SHRIVER'S SALTWATER TAFFY**
The oldest business on the boardwalk in Ocean City, New Jersey, is this confectionary. The best flavors to try are banana (look for the yellow with an orange stripe) and watermelon (green with a red center).

**PETERBORO PICNIC HAMPER**
Made in New Hampshire, these baskets made of sturdy Appalachian white ash are perfect for packing a picnic lunch for your hike in the White Mountains of the Granite State.

Amana Mills Wool Throw

**AMANA MILLS WOOL THROW**
Made in Iowa, these snuggly throws come in handsome plaids and stripes you'll want to keep on display. Find them at the showroom in Amana, or gift shops around the state.

**MINNETONKA MOCCASINS**
Named after nearby Lake Minnetonka, Minnesota's must-have footwear was first manufactured in 1946. The company proudly supports Native American organizations.

**HUCKLEBERRY LIQUEUR**
On a visit to Montana, you can find huckleberries in everything from ice cream to barbecue sauce. Try (and take home) the huckleberry sweet cream liqueur made at Willie's Distillery.

**GOO GOO CLUSTERS**
If you grew up in Tennessee, you grew up loving these sticky-sweet candy bars. Newcomers won't be able to resist tucking a few away in their bag for the trip back home.

**MINIATURE BASEBALL BAT**
Kentucky's Louisville Slugger Museum and Factory boasts the world's biggest baseball bat. Pick up a much smaller version in the gift shop or souvenir stands around the state.

**CACTUS SEEDS**
Arizona's giant saguaro cactus plants can grow to more than three stories tall. Grow a much smaller version at home with seeds from Desert Gatherings.

# Best Places to Spot Wildlife

**JACKSON, WYOMING**
The National Elk Refuge, home to a herd numbered in the thousands, is so close to Jackson that you could probably walk from Jackson Town Square. While you're here, you can also head to Cache Creek to spot moose. *(Ch. 9)*

**MIAMI, FLORIDA**
When someone mentions the sandy beaches of Miami, it's hard not to imagine a mass of lounge chairs and umbrellas extending to the high-tide mark. But it's not hard to find stretches of sand that are completely deserted. Barely an hour south is Biscayne National Park, where you can kayak along the mangrove-fringed coastline (manatees are frequent visitors in colder months). Half an hour farther down the coast in Key Largo is John Pennekamp Coral Reef State Park, the country's first underwater park. Snorkel around the shores in search of angelfish, parrotfish, and other colorful aquatic creatures. Head due west from Miami and you'll reach Everglades National Park, the vast "river of grass" that's home to both the American alligator and American crocodile—the only place they coexist. *(Ch. 5)*

**CORPUS CHRISTI, TEXAS**
The bustling metropolis of Corpus Christi is ringed by nature preserves, including Aransas National Wildlife Refuge to the north (home to the only flock of wild whooping cranes every winter) and Laguna Atascosa National Wildlife Refuge to the south (where you'll find stunning birds like the American white ibis). In case it's not evident, the Corpus Christi area is a bird-watcher's paradise. The coastline is part of the Central Flyway, one of the region's most important migratory routes. About 30 minutes due east is Padre Island National Seashore, where more than 380 species of birds have been spotted, including colorful tanagers, orioles, and warblers. Be on the lookout for the tricolored heron, in shades of blue, lavender, and mauve. *(Ch. 8)*

**HONOLULU, HAWAII**
Oahu is a well-known magnet for tourists—just look at the crowds along Honolulu's Waikiki Beach—but it's also one of the world's best spots for wildlife. Spinner dolphins, known for their acrobatic antics, can often be spotted from shore. They usually spend their days in Yokohama Bay and other protected waters a little over an hour away on the western edge of the island. During winter, North Pacific humpback whales can be spotted from the southern shore, especially a half hour east of Honolulu around Hanauma Bay. An ocean excursion increases your chances of spotting these gentle giants. Hawaiian green sea turtles are frequently spotted during the summer in Hanauma Bay, but their favorite spot seems to be Laniakea Beach on Oahu's northern shore. *(Ch. 7)*

Honolulu, Hawaii, dolphins

**GATLINBURG, TENNESSEE**

The Tennessee gateway to Great Smoky Mountains National Park, Gatlinburg gives you almost immediate access to the best wildlife in the region. Less than 10 minutes from the front gate is Sugarlands Visitor Center, where you might spot a wild turkey. Cades Cove Loop Road is one of the most popular destinations in the park, partly because you have a good chance of catching a glimpse of a black bear. Look for them on the hillsides and in trees foraging for food. But the park's greatest display comes in May or June, when tens of thousands of synchronous fireflies in search of mates appear at Elkmont Campground. They are the only species in North America that can blink their lights at the same time, and it's a wondrous sight. *(Ch. 5)*

**RAPID CITY, SOUTH DAKOTA**

Many travelers head to Rapid City for a glimpse of Mount Rushmore, but it is also a destination for animal lovers. In Custer State Park, half an hour south of the city, the 18-mile Wildlife Loop State Scenic Byway is the best place to see hundreds of bison. In Badlands National Park, bighorn sheep are often spotted at Pinnacles Overlook and Big Badlands Overlook. Prairie dogs are also found here, including the world's only "town" of white prairie dogs. *(Ch. 6)*

**SAN FRANCISCO, CALIFORNIA**

An hour north of San Francisco is a wildlife refuge most visitors have never heard about. Northern elephant seals were gone for 150 years, then they returned to Point Reyes National Seashore in the 1970s. Now there are thousands sunning themselves on the beaches here. Head to Elephant Seal Overlook or (more recently) Drakes Beach. About 45 minutes southeast of the city is Sunol Regional Wilderness, your best chance to spot birds of prey. Golden eagles, peregrine falcons, and kestrels all make an appearance. And just a half an hour south is Fitzgerald Marine Reserve, a favorite with kids. The tide pools hold starfish, hermit crabs, and sea anemones. *(Ch. 7)*

**GLACIER BAY, ALASKA**

A cruise through the icy waters of Alaska's Glacier Bay National Park is an animal lover's dream. From the comfort of a ship deck you'll spot seals, mountain goats, puffins, and perhaps breaching whales. In towns like Sitka, where some cruises depart, you can spot bald eagles and brown bears. *(Ch. 7)*

# Top Music Experiences

New Orleans: Jazz and Blues

It's not just musicians who go on tour—sometimes the fans are the ones who journey across the country in search of great music. Some head to tiny jazz clubs, others to stadiums with the hottest hip-hop performers. Below are a few of our favorite destinations.

**NEW ORLEANS: JAZZ AND BLUES**

A city where any night of the week you're likely to encounter dancing in the streets, New Orleans is a mecca for music lovers. Start a few blocks from the Mississippi River in Jackson Square, where street performers are a local institution. There will be more musicians a block or two north on Royal Street and Bourbon Street. This is the heart of the French Quarter, where you'll find legendary nightspots like Preservation Hall. For something a little more contemporary, head to One Eyed Jacks. To escape the crowds, head to Frenchmen Street in the nearby neighborhood of Marigny. It's three solid blocks of music venues, including standards like The Spotted Cat. If you can't decide, schedule your trip for October, when New Orleans Jazz Fest takes over the city.

**NEW YORK AND MASSACHUSETTS: CLASSICAL MUSIC**

Classical musicians don't get a summer vacation, at least not those based in the Northeast. They mostly leave the big cities and head to music festivals all over region, but especially in Upstate New York. In New York City, Lincoln Center stages one of the year's most anticipated festivals, the Mostly Mozart. Running from early July to early August, the massive annual event has grown to include both indoor and outdoor events. Barely an hour north is Caramoor, a new music festival held from mid-June to late July. It's set on a 90-acre estate at an Italianate mansion. Continuing up New York State's famed Hudson Valley is the Bard Music Festival, held during the first weeks in August. On the campus of Bard College in Annandale-on-Hudson, it mostly takes place in the dazzling Frank Gehry–designed Fisher Center for the Performing Arts. Two hours northeast is the Glimmerglass Festival, nestled between the Adirondack and Catskill mountains in Cooperstown, New York. It presents operas and musicals. Perhaps the most beautiful venue is the outdoor amphitheater at Tanglewood, in Lenox, Massachusetts. The season runs from June to August and features the Boston Symphony.

**AUSTIN: INDIE VIBES**

In March, the "live music capital of the world" of Austin, Texas, more than lives up to its name. South by Southwest fills the streets with outdoor concerts by musicians of every possible genre. (The White Stripes, Katy Perry, and Janelle Monáe didn't build up huge following until playing at SXSW.) If you're here any other time of year, you won't do better than heading to Sixth Street, meaning the five blocks of East Sixth Street between Congress Avenue and Red River

Nashville music

Street. Locals call it Dirty Sixth because of its reputation for drunken college students stumbling down the sidewalk. There are actually some great music venues here, like the Parish, where indie rockers like Grizzly Bear and Yeasayer have performed. Around the corner on Red River Street is the Mohawk, a no-frills music venue with a hip vibe and a motto of "All Are Welcome." Across the Colorado River is maybe the best-known local spot, the Continental Club. When big-name groups play Austin's bigger venues, they often unwind with a relaxed set here.

## NASHVILLE: COUNTRY FLAVOR

The main draw here is the Grand Old Opry, country music's mecca. It's a homely building—its former home in Ryan Auditorium is an architectural gem—but what comes off the stage every weekly in heavenly. It's a hike to get to, but there are plenty of smaller music venues downtown. The flashiest district is the stretch of Broadway between 1st and 5th Avenues dubbed the Honky Tonk Highway. There are so many notable concert spaces that it's hard to pick a favorite, but start with Tootsie's Orchid Lounge, a Nashville landmark where Willie Nelson used to hang out when he was an up-and-coming artist. Off the main drag are the Bluebird Café in Green Hills (Garth Brooks and Taylor Swift got their starts here) and the Station Inn in the Gulch (Vince Gill and Ricky Skaggs have played this house). When the weather's warm, Nashville heads outdoors for live music. Multiple stages are set up downtown for June's CMA Fest, a four-day festival featuring all things country. If you want to see Tennessee's answer to Coachella and Lollapalooza, head to Bonnaroo, held each June. An hour from Nashville, it's like summer camp for music lovers.

## MIAMI: LOUD AND OUTDOORS

Miami has a music scene unlike anywhere else, so it's not surprising that it has multiple annual events. Perhaps the best known is March's Ultra Music Festival, a celebration of electronic music featuring world-famous DJs held at Bayfront Park. The long-running Afro Roots Fest, held in April in North Beach, celebrates the influence of African music and culture. Rolling Loud, the massive hip-hop festival that started in Miami and now has events around the world, usually returns each spring to an outdoor venue. If you're looking for a more intimate experience, Miami has it too: try Lagniappe for jazz.

# What to Watch, Read, and Listen to

## Watch

### *THE BUCKET LIST*

Even people who've never seen this 2007 film starring Jack Nicholson and Morgan Freeman have been inspired by this story of two not-so-lovable old codgers who decide to see and do everything they've been putting off for years. (The scene at California Motor Speedway will definitely make you want to watch a race, if not drive in a race car.) It's silly and sentimental, but includes some eye-popping views of destinations that might end up on your list, too.

### *NOMADLAND*

Moviegoers are fascinated with tales of people who leave everything behind and follow their dreams. This 2021 film features Oscar-winner Francis McDormand as Fern, a down-on-her-luck woman who buys a van and joins a community of nomadic people who gather in temporary communities. It just happens to be filmed in some gorgeous spots: Nevada's Black Rock Desert, California's San Bernardino National Forest, and the austerely beautiful Badlands of South Dakota.

### *FREE SOLO*

If you have a fear of heights, then this 2019 documentary probably isn't for you. It follows legendary free climber Alex Honnold and his climbing partner Kevin Jorgeson as they decide to be the first to scale the 3,000-foot vertical rock face of El Capitan. It's a nail biter, with cameraman Jimmy Chin often making the climb beside him and worried that he might distract his friend at a critical moment and watch him "fall out of frame." The cinematography is so beautiful that you'll soon be planning your own trip to Yosemite National Park. Another great documentary about rock climbing is 2017's *The Dawn Wall*.

### *TASTE THE NATION*

Longtime *Top Chef* host Padma Lakshmi sets out on her own to discover the culinary traditions of various parts of the country, especially those whose roots here go back a generation at the most. The series is part cooking show, part travelogue, and part exploration of the immigrant experience. Most memorable is her conversation with a Thai woman whose high-end food was initially rejected by Las Vegas diners used to cheap and greasy fare. She triumphs, and so does the series.

### *EXPEDITION HAPPINESS*

In this disarming 2017 release, a couple of German free spirits (filmmaker Felix Starck, musician Selima Taibi), rehab an old school bus and hit the road to Alaska. It's less of a documentary and more of a home movie, which isn't necessarily a bad thing when the focus is the rugged mountain scenery. Oh, and we loved their very photogenic Bernese water dog named Rudi.

## Read

### *LASSOING THE SUN: A YEAR IN AMERICA'S NATIONAL PARKS*

The 100th anniversary of the national park system inspired writer Mark Woods to take a bucket list journey. He revisits many of the places he had first seen from the windows of the family station wagon when he was a child: Redwood, Yosemite, and the Grand Canyon, for starters. What starts out as a sentimental journey becomes something more when his travel-loving mother dies suddenly, and he's forced to confront bigger issues like love, loss, and the meaning of travel.

### *DRIVE-THRU DREAMS: A JOURNEY THROUGH THE HEART OF AMERICA'S FAST-FOOD KINGDOM*

Journalist Adam Chandler explores the country's complicated relationship with fast food. It starts at the industry's bootstrapping beginning, chronicling the rise of colorful characters like Kentucky Fried Chicken's Harlan Sanders, a "ham who served chicken." As he brings us up to the present, he touches on all the fast-food joints we stopped at during family road trips.

### *WILD HORSES OF CUMBERLAND ISLAND*

There's believed to have been a herd of horses on Cumberland Island, a remote spot off the Georgia coast, since they were brought over in the 16th century by Spanish conquistadors. In a project that was 10 years in the making, award-winning photographer Anouk Masson Krantz captures the majesty of these animals and the sandy dunes, sugar-white beaches, and old-growth forests of their habitat.

### *THE UNLIKELIEST BACKPACKER: FROM LONDON OFFICE DESK TO WILDERNESS*

Author Kathryn Barnes and her husband decamp from their one-bedroom London flat so that they can camp along the Pacific Crest Trail, making their way through California, Oregon, and Washington along the way. She might not be the unlikeliest of backpackers, but she was woefully unprepared. Finding her way is the book's throughline, and it's inspiring for would-be hikers.

## Listen

### LET'S GO TOGETHER

It's hard not to love this podcast, especially because it's hosted by travel writer and TV host Kellee Edwards, a licensed pilot and open-water scuba diver. Her love of travel shines through immediately. And when it comes to diversity, Edwards doesn't just talk the talk, she walks the walk: recent podcasts have focused on traveling with a trans identity, hitting the trail as a Native American, and what road-tripping means for an African American couple.

### OUT TRAVEL THE SYSTEM

We all have that friend who knows everything about travel, from what seasons offer the best deals to when to book holiday flights to how a "reverse road trip" saves you plenty of dough. (And if you don't know what a "reverse road trip" is, this podcast is for you.) Expedia's Nisreene Atassi knows just about everything, and when she doesn't she brings in experts in every field imaginable.

### WILD IDEAS WORTH HAVING

A lot of us want to hike the Appalachian Trail, but this podcast ups the ante by talking with a guy who ran the whole way and set a record. It's these kinds of interviews that make Wild Ideas Worth Living so inspiring. Host Shelby Stanger, who quit her job to pursue a more adventurous life, seems to really love talking with others who've done the same.

### EXTRA PACK OF PEANUTS

This podcast gets extra points for the cute name, as well as the extremely engaging hosts, the husband-and-wife team of Travis and Heather Sherry (or Trav and Heath, as they invariably say on the podcast). It's been running since 2013, so there are hundreds of episodes to inspire you to take that bucket list trip you've been dreaming about.

# Wacky State Laws

### DON'T ORDER A JACK AND COKE

Tennessee, Mississippi, and Kansas are dry by default, meaning local jurisdictions have to specifically authorize the sale of alcohol for it to be legal. That's why you can't open a bottle in the county where Jack Daniels is made.

### KEEP YOUR EYES ON THE ROAD

In Alabama a law bans driving while blindfolded. Kansas state law criminalizes screeching your tires. A local noise ordinance in Arkansas prohibits drivers from honking their horns outside restaurants after 9 pm. Best to stick to driving without the distractions.

### THESE STATES ARE SERIOUS ABOUT FOOD

Sending a pizza to someone who didn't order can get you a $500 fine in Louisiana. In Wisconsin—known as "America's Dairyland"—restaurants can't serve you margarine and call it butter. But luckily, it seems to be an urban myth that Oklahoma makes it illegal to take a bite out of someone else's hamburger.

### WEIRD PLACES YOU CAN'T DRINK

In Wyoming, you're not allowed to drink in a mine. In Colorado, it's while you're on top of a horse. Several states prohibit drinking while piloting a boat, but New Mexico also bans drinking while using "water skis, wakeboards, kneeboards, or similar devices."

### DON'T SLEEP WHERE YOU EAT

This one sounds hard to believe, but it's a real statute passed by the Illinois State Legislature in 1911. It's illegal for someone to sleep in a bakery, fudge shop, cheese factory, or anywhere food is prepared, served, or sold.

### NO SPITTING IN PUBLIC

In California, the Burlingame City Council passed a regulation that bans spitting in public—except, that is, unless you're on a baseball diamond. Turns out that spitting was already a misdemeanor in California, but the council wanted to take the law into their own hands. Can't say we dislike this one.

### YOU CAN GO YOUR OWN WAY

The majority of states have made marijuana legal in some way or another, including Michigan. But the state has one weird quirk in its laws: since 1927, it insists on using the archaic spelling "marihuana" in legislation.

### NO CROWD-SURFING ALLOWED

Performers in Billings, Montana, can't step off the stage during a performance. A local law stipulates that "no entertainer or performer whether male or female shall be permitted to leave any such platform or area while entertaining."

### NO SALTY LANGUAGE

In Rockville, Maryland, it's against the law to "profanely curse and swear or use obscene language upon or near any street, sidewalk, or highway." Nearby Arlington, Virginia, decided to keep a similar law on the books, even though it was repealed statewide in 2020.

### RESPECT THE INSECT

Pacific Grove, California, is intent on protecting its most famous visitors, monarch butterflies. It's illegal to "molest or interfere with, in any way, the peaceful occupancy of the monarch butterflies on their annual visit."

### IT DOESN'T RHYME WITH KANSAS

In Arkansas, it's illegal to mispronounce the name of the state. This isn't one of those antiquated laws that never got taken off the books. It was passed in 2010, and includes the following: "the sounding of the terminal 's' is an innovation to be discouraged."

Chapter 2

# GREAT ITINERARIES



Written by
Mark Sullivan

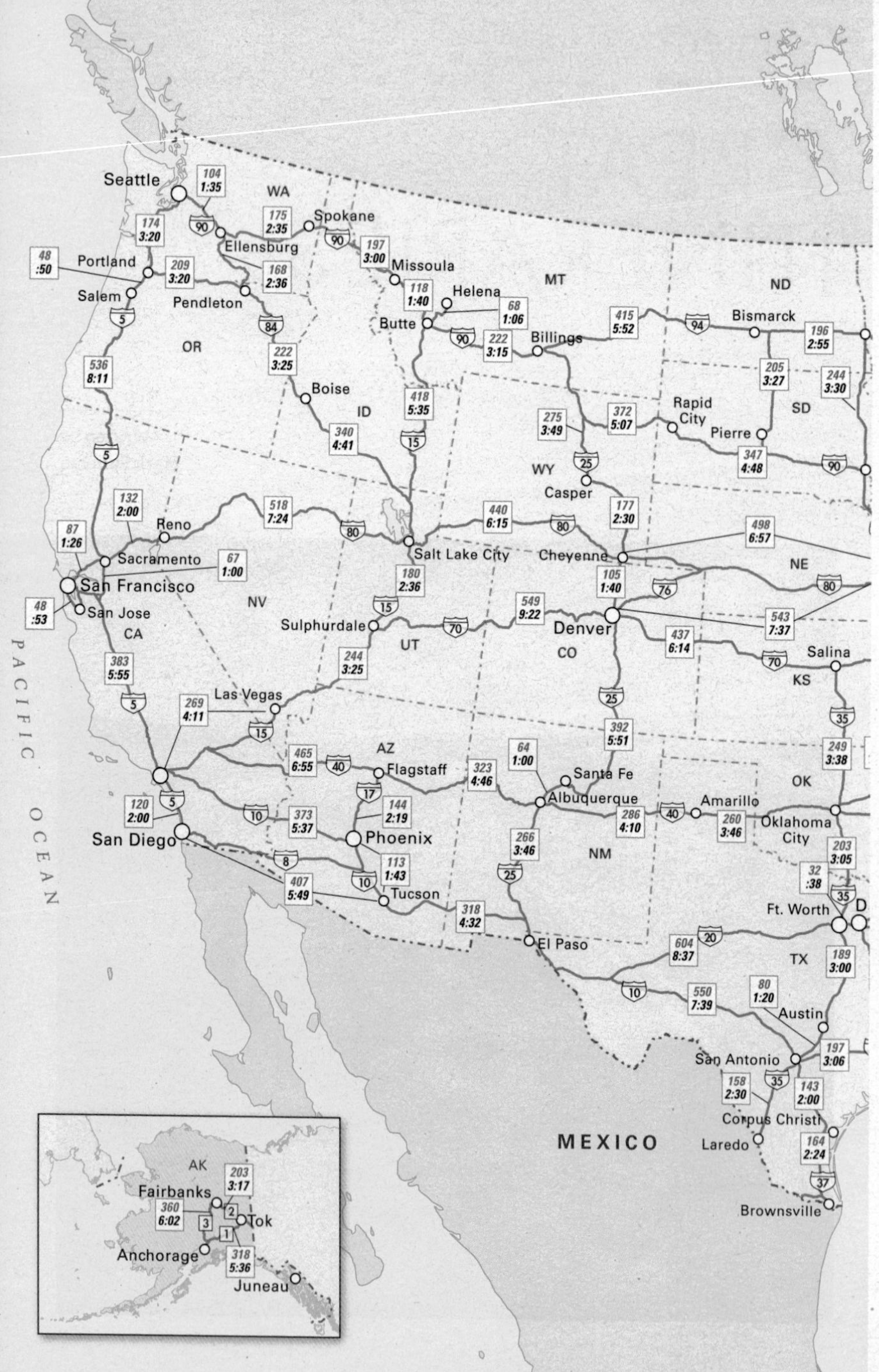

Seattle
Spokane
Ellensburg
Missoula
Portland
Salem
Pendleton
Helena
Butte
Billings
Bismarck
Boise
Rapid City
Pierre
Casper
Reno
Sacramento
San Francisco
San Jose
Salt Lake City
Cheyenne
Denver
Sulphurdale
Salina
Las Vegas
Flagstaff
Santa Fe
Albuquerque
Amarillo
Oklahoma City
San Diego
Phoenix
Tucson
El Paso
Ft. Worth
Austin
San Antonio
Corpus Christi
Laredo
Brownsville
Fairbanks
Tok
Anchorage
Juneau
WA
MT
ND
OR
ID
SD
WY
NE
NV
UT
CO
KS
CA
AZ
NM
OK
TX
AK
MEXICO
PACIFIC OCEAN

# Mileage and Driving Times

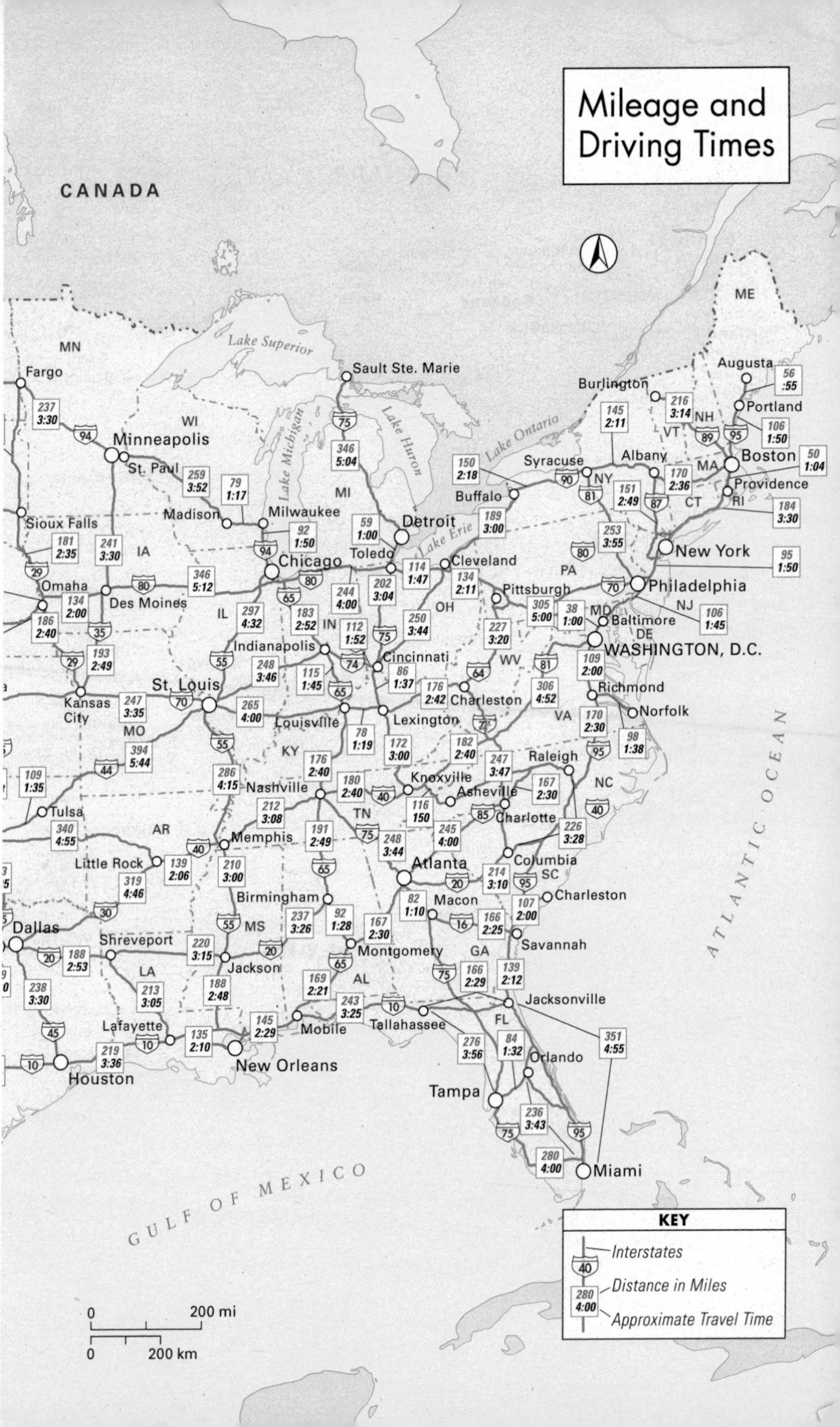

**KEY**

40 — *Interstates*

280 — *Distance in Miles*

4:00 — *Approximate Travel Time*

0 — 200 mi

0 — 200 km

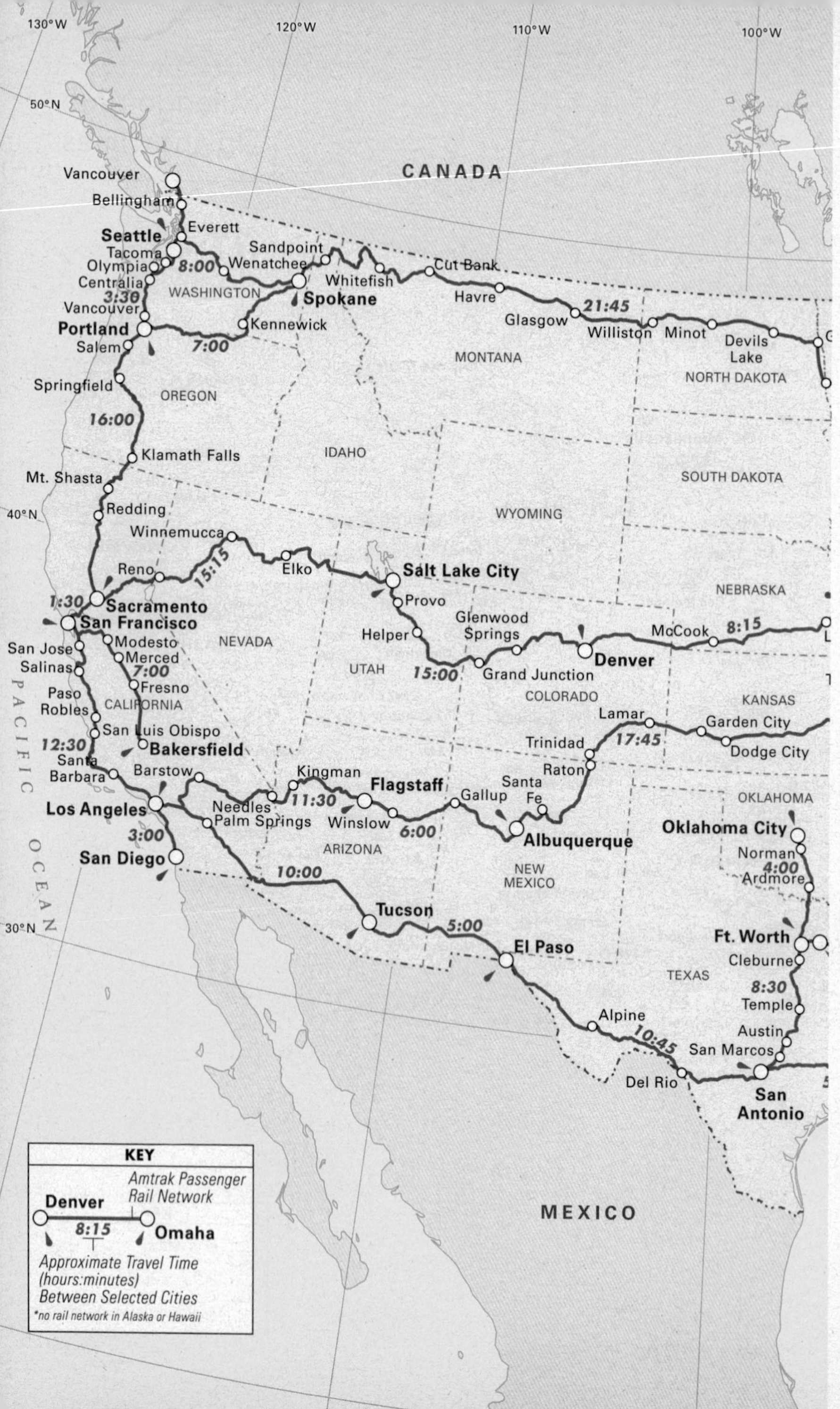

130°W
120°W
110°W
100°W
50°N
40°N
30°N
CANADA
MEXICO
PACIFIC OCEAN
WASHINGTON
OREGON
IDAHO
MONTANA
NORTH DAKOTA
SOUTH DAKOTA
WYOMING
NEBRASKA
NEVADA
UTAH
COLORADO
KANSAS
CALIFORNIA
ARIZONA
NEW MEXICO
OKLAHOMA
TEXAS
Vancouver
Bellingham
Everett
Seattle
Tacoma
Olympia
Centralia
Vancouver
Portland
Salem
Springfield
Klamath Falls
Mt. Shasta
Redding
Sacramento
San Francisco
San Jose
Salinas
Paso Robles
San Luis Obispo
Santa Barbara
Los Angeles
San Diego
Modesto
Merced
Fresno
Bakersfield
Barstow
Needles
Palm Springs
Reno
Winnemucca
Elko
Salt Lake City
Provo
Helper
Glenwood Springs
Grand Junction
Denver
McCook
Sandpoint
Wenatchee
Spokane
Whitefish
Cut Bank
Havre
Glasgow
Williston
Minot
Devils Lake
Kennewick
Kingman
Flagstaff
Winslow
Gallup
Santa Fe
Albuquerque
Lamar
Trinidad
Raton
Garden City
Dodge City
Tucson
El Paso
Alpine
Del Rio
San Antonio
San Marcos
Austin
Temple
Cleburne
Ft. Worth
Ardmore
Norman
Oklahoma City
8:00
3:30
7:00
16:00
21:45
1:30
15:15
7:00
12:30
15:00
8:15
17:45
11:30
6:00
3:00
10:00
5:00
10:45
4:00
8:30
KEY
Amtrak Passenger Rail Network
Denver
Omaha
8:15
Approximate Travel Time (hours:minutes) Between Selected Cities
*no rail network in Alaska or Hawaii

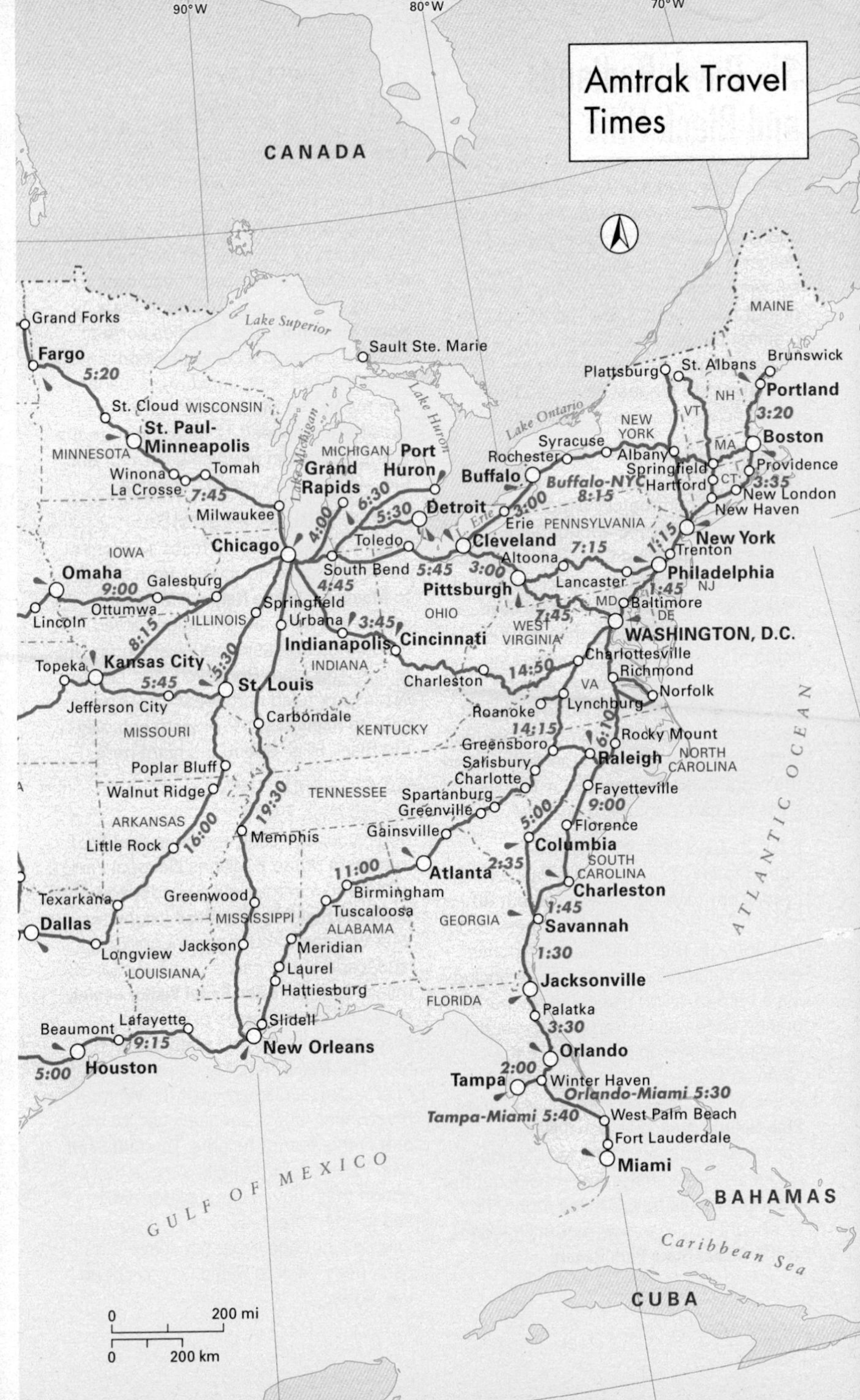

Amtrak Travel Times
CANADA
90° W
80° W
70° W
Lake Superior
Lake Michigan
Lake Huron
Lake Ontario
Lake Erie
Grand Forks
Fargo
5:20
St. Cloud
WISCONSIN
St. Paul-Minneapolis
MINNESOTA
Winona
La Crosse
Tomah
7:45
Milwaukee
MICHIGAN
Grand Rapids
Port Huron
6:30
4:00
5:30
Detroit
Sault Ste. Marie
Toledo
Chicago
IOWA
Omaha
9:00
Galesburg
Ottumwa
Lincoln
ILLINOIS
8:15
South Bend
5:45
4:45
Springfield
Urbana
3:45
Indianapolis
Cincinnati
INDIANA
OHIO
Topeka
Kansas City
5:30
5:45
St. Louis
Jefferson City
MISSOURI
Carbondale
KENTUCKY
Charleston
14:50
WEST VIRGINIA
Buffalo
Buffalo-NYC 8:15
Rochester
Syracuse
Albany
NEW YORK
3:00
Erie
PENNSYLVANIA
Cleveland
7:15
Altoona
3:00
Pittsburgh
Lancaster
Philadelphia
1:45
NJ
MD
Baltimore
DE
7:45
WASHINGTON, D.C.
Plattsburg
St. Albans
VT
NH
MAINE
Brunswick
Portland
3:20
Boston
MA
Springfield
Providence
Hartford
CT
3:35
New London
New Haven
New York
1:15
Trenton
Charlottesville
Richmond
Norfolk
VA
Lynchburg
Roanoke
14:15
6:10
Rocky Mount
Greensboro
Salisbury
Raleigh
NORTH CAROLINA
Charlotte
Fayetteville
9:00
Spartanburg
Greenville
5:00
Florence
Gainsville
Columbia
SOUTH CAROLINA
2:35
Atlanta
11:00
Charleston
1:45
Savannah
GEORGIA
1:30
Jacksonville
FLORIDA
Palatka
3:30
Orlando
2:00
Tampa
Winter Haven
Orlando-Miami 5:30
Tampa-Miami 5:40
West Palm Beach
Fort Lauderdale
Miami
Poplar Bluff
Walnut Ridge
TENNESSEE
19:30
16:00
ARKANSAS
Memphis
Little Rock
Birmingham
Tuscaloosa
ALABAMA
Texarkana
Greenwood
MISSISSIPPI
Dallas
Longview
Jackson
Meridian
Laurel
LOUISIANA
Hattiesburg
Slidell
Beaumont
Lafayette
9:15
New Orleans
Houston
5:00
GULF OF MEXICO
ATLANTIC OCEAN
BAHAMAS
Caribbean Sea
CUBA
0
200 mi
0
200 km

# Six Days: Badlands and Black Hills

The national parks of southwestern South Dakota—along with the state park and two national memorials nearby—deliver a surprising variety of sights: the swaying grasses and abundant wildlife of one of the country's few remaining intact prairies, the complex labyrinth of passages and unique geologic formations in one of the world's longest caves, and some of the richest fossil beds on Earth.

### DAY 1: RAPID CITY AND WIND CAVE

The closest commercial airport is Rapid City Regional Airport, about 70 miles northeast from Wind Cave. Arrive in the morning to pick up your rental car and make the 1½-hour drive to **Wind Cave National Park,** with more than 33,000 acres of wildlife habitat aboveground (home to bison, elk, pronghorn, and coyotes) and one of the world's longest caves below. Take an afternoon cave tour and a short drive through the park. Spend the night in **Hot Springs,** about 10 miles from the park's southern boundary.

### DAY 2: CUSTER STATE PARK

Spend today at Custer State Park, which is adjacent to Wind Cave; it's about 36 miles or a 45-minute drive northeast from Hot Springs. The 71,000- acre park has exceptional drives, lots of wildlife (including a herd of 1,400 bison), and fingerlike granite spires rising from the forest floor (they're the reason this is called the Needles region of South Dakota). While you're in the park, be sure to visit **Limber Pine Natural Area,** a National Natural Landmark containing spectacular ridges of granite. If you have time, check out the **Cathedral Spires** trail, 3 miles round-trip. Overnight in one of five mountain lodges at the **Custer State Park Resort.**

### DAY 3: JEWEL CAVE AND CRAZY HORSE

Today, venture down U.S. 16 to **Jewel Cave National Monument,** 13 miles west of the town of Custer, an underground wilderness where you can see beautiful nailhead and dogtooth spar crystals lining its more than 195 miles of passageways. After visiting Jewel Cave, head back to Custer and take U.S. 16/385 to **Crazy Horse Memorial** (about 7 miles north of Custer), home to a colossal mountain carving of the legendary Lakota leader and the Indian Museum of North America. Afterward, head 12 miles north to the former gold- and tin-mining town of **Hill City,** where you'll spend the night.

### DAY 4: MOUNT RUSHMORE

This morning, travel 12 miles or about a 30-minute drive northwest from Hill City to **Mount Rushmore National Memorial,** where you can view the huge carved renderings of Presidents Washington, Jefferson, Theodore Roosevelt, and Lincoln. Afterward, head northwest for 23 miles back to **Rapid City,** the eastern gateway to the Black Hills. Spend the night here.

### DAY 5: BADLANDS NATIONAL PARK

Begin your day early and drive east (via Interstate 90) to Badlands National Park, a 244,000-acre geologic wonderland. The **Badlands Highway Loop Road** (Highway 240) wiggles through the moonlike landscape of the park's north unit for 32 miles. Stop in at **Ben Reifel Visitor Center,** at the far eastern edge of the park, to pick up a trail map and head out on a hike. The **Notch Trail,** 1½ miles round-trip, offers spectacular views of the White River Valley, but is definitely not for anyone with a fear of heights. The **Cliff Shelf** trail, ½ mile round-trip, is a more mellow option that showcases rock formations and juniper forest, as well as occasional wildlife sightings. After you leave the park, head back to Rapid City to spend the night.

### DAY 6: BEAR BUTTE AND RAPID CITY

The airport in Rapid City is about 10 minutes southeast of town. If you have time to pass before your flight out, head about 30 minutes out of town to **Bear Butte State Park** for an epic hike. The trail to the top of the mountain is just under 2 miles in length. The top of the mountain has great views of the Black Hills to the southwest. If you have time, there's also a 2½-mile trail around Bear Butte Lake.

## One Week: Maui and the Road to Hana

Lounging beside the pool or napping on a sandy beach may fulfill your initial fantasy of a tropical Hawaiian vacation, but Maui has much more to offer: underwater encounters with rainbow-colored fish, an icy dip in a jungle waterfall, or a trek across the moonlike landscape of a dormant volcano.

### DAY 1: GET SETTLED

On your way out of Kahului Airport, stop at Costco, Target, or Walmart to pick up beach gear, sunscreen, food, and drink. Once ensconced at your hotel or condo, unwind from your long flight by exploring the grounds, dozing by the pool, or splashing in the ocean—it's why you came to Maui, isn't it?

**Logistics:** Road signs will point you to the two main resort areas: Highway 311 (Maui Veterans Highway) to 31 (Piilani) south to Kihei and Wailea, and Highway 380 (Kuihelani) to 30 (Honoapiilani) west to Lahaina and Kapalua.

### DAY 2: SURF AND SAND

Head to the nearest beach for snorkeling, swimming and sunbathing, or surfing in the gentle waves of Cove Park in Kihei or Launiupoko in West Maui. If golf's more your game, hit the tournament-quality golf links in the resort areas; cheaper rates can be found at the scenic Waiehu, Waikapu, and Maui Lani courses in Central Maui. Spend the evening (it'll be cooler) visiting Lahaina town, which is packed with shops, restaurants, and art galleries.

**Logistics:** Many hotels and condos offer free shuttle service to golfing, shopping, and dining. Driving to Lahaina from South Maui, take Highway 310 (North Kihei Road) and turn left on Highway 30 (Honoapiilani).

### DAY 3: ADVENTURE ON LAND AND SEA

Get a different view of the island—and discover what's beneath the surface—on a full- or half-day boat excursion to Molokini, a crescent-shaped islet that sits 3 miles off South Maui; or take a snorkeling, scuba diving, or dolphin- and whale-watching trip. If you prefer dry land, head to Maui Tropical Plantation in Waikapu, which offers tram tours and a country store; it's also the home base for Flyin Hawaiian Zipline and Maui Zipline's introductory course. Plan to be back early enough for a sunset luau at your resort or at Old Lahaina Luau.

**Logistics:** Boat tours leave from Maalaea Harbor in South Maui and Lahaina Harbor in West Maui. To get to the Maui Tropical Plantation from West Maui, follow Highway 30 (Honoapiilani) south to Waikapu; from South Maui, take Highway 310 (North Kihei Road) and turn right onto Highway 30.

### DAY 4: HALEAKALA AND UPCOUNTRY

Sunrise at the 10,000-foot summit of this dormant volcano is so popular that the National Park Service now requires reservations (make yours as early as possible, up to 60 days in advance of your visit). To avoid the crush, consider planning your day in reverse. Start with some great body surfing at Baldwin Beach Park on the North Shore, followed by lunch in the former plantation town of Paia, home to charming boutiques and cafés. Once

Upcountry, tour Surfing Goat Dairy, Ali'i Kula Lavender farm, or MauiWine, before heading to the Haleakala summit in the afternoon when the park is uncrowded. It's not sunrise, but the spectacular sunset vista encompasses at least three islands and the broad expanse separating Maui's two mountains.

**Logistics:** To reach Haleakala from South Maui, take Highway 311 (Maui Veterans Highway) out of Kihei to connect with Highway 36 (Hana) and then Highway 37 (Haleakala). From West Maui, follow Highway 30 (Honoapiilani) to 380 (Kuihelani), which connects with 36.

### DAY 5: ROAD TO HANA

Today's the day to tackle the 600 curves of the Road to Hana (Highway 36/360). There aren't a lot of dining options in Hana, but many hotels offer picnic baskets for the road, or fill your cooler and gas tank in Paia, the last chance for provisions. Pause to stretch your legs at the Keanae Arboretum, picturesque Keanae Landing, or any of the roadside waterfalls. Approaching Hana town, turn into Waianapanapa State Park, with its rugged lava outcroppings, black-sand beach, trails, and caves with freshwater pools. There isn't much reason to stop in Hana town, except for lunch at the food trucks if you didn't bring your own, so continue on to the Kipahulu District of Haleakala National Park, site of the Pools of Oheo (nicknamed Seven Sacred Pools) and 400-foot Waimoku Falls. (Check for updates on closures due to flash flooding and landslides.) Don't leave Kipahulu without visiting the grave site of famed aviator Charles Lindbergh, who is buried at 19th-century Palapala Hoomau Church.

**Logistics:** Follow directions to Haleakala, but stay on Highway 36/360 (Hana).

### DAY 6: BEACH DAY

A full day is needed to recover from a trek to Hana, so take it easy with a visit to the Maui Ocean Center, where you'll be mesmerized by the sharks, rays, and tuna circling the 750,000-gallon open-ocean tank. Then spend the rest of the day relaxing in the water or at the spa with lunch beside the pool.

**Logistics:** From South Maui, take Highway 31 (Piilani) to 310 (North Kihei Road), then head a short distance left on Highway 30 (Honoapiilani). From West Maui, head south on Highway 30 to Maalaea/Maui Ocean Center.

### DAY 7: CENTRAL MAUI

Squeeze in a final session at the beach or pool before checking out of your hotel and heading to Central Maui to be closer to the airport. If you like history, Hale Hoikeike at the Bailey House features the island's largest collection of Hawaiian artifacts. Just five minutes up the road is Iao Valley State Park and one of the most photographed landmarks in Hawaii: Iao Needle. Eat like a local with lunch or an early dinner at Umi, Miko's, or A Saigon Cafe in Wailuku or Da Kitchen, Ichiban, or Tin Roof in Kahului. If there's still time, visit Kanaha Beach Park by Kahului Airport to watch world-class wind- and kite surfers or shop for gifts and souvenirs at the many malls.

**Logistics:** From South Maui, take Highway 311 (Maui Veterans Highway) all the way to 32 (Kaahumanu) in Kahului, then turn left toward Wailuku; from West Maui, Highway 30 (Honoapiilani) leads right into Wailuku town. Kahului Airport is a 10-minute drive from here.

## One Week: The Underground Railroad

The first known mention of a network to help escaped slaves was in 1831, when an enslaved man named Tice Davids fled from his owner in Kentucky by swimming across the Ohio River. Unable to find him, his owner bitterly complained that Davids "must have gone off on an underground railroad."

Historians believe that abolitionists in the town of Ripley, Ohio, helped him escape. One Ohio man who had helped countless people escape to freedom said that the comment from the angry owner helped them name a movement that lasted until the Civil War: the Underground Railroad.

There were countless routes of the Underground Railroad, including some to the Northeast through New England and others south through Texas or Florida. But the northerly routes through the Midwest—through states like Ohio, Indiana, and Iowa—were some of the most important. And many stops along the way have been restored and are open to the public.

## DAYS 1 AND 2: MARYLAND

The **Harriet Tubman Byway** is a 125-mile trail running from Cambridge to Goldsboro, taking you past sites where the influential abolitionist led enslaved people to freedom. Stops along the way include hidden waterways, safe houses, churches, and other places that served as way stations along the Underground Railroad. Start your day at the **Harriet Tubman Underground Railroad Visitor Center,** which is home to permanent exhibits on Tubman, the Underground Railroad. and those who escaped slavery. Some of the major sites along the trail include the **Harriet Tubman Museum and Educational Center,** the **Tuckahoe Neck Meeting House** and the **Jacob and Hannah Leverton House.** The driving tour takes about three to four hours.

## DAYS 3 AND 4: OHIO

It's quite a long haul to the town of Ripley, Ohio (eight hours from Maryland), where Davids is believed to have escaped, but it's worth the trip, especially if you overnight halfway. You can visit the **John P. Parker House.** Parker, a former enslaved person who managed to buy his freedom from his owner, helped countless people escape from the "borderlands" in Kentucky. Parker founded an iron foundry in Ripley, and was one of the few African Americans to be granted a patent in the 19th century. Also in Ripley is the **John Rankin House,** which belonged to a prominent minister believed to be one of the most active "conductors" on the Underground Railroad. The beautifully restored house, on a bluff overlooking the Ohio River, is a National Historic Landmark. In the town of Ashtabula is the home of Colonel William Hubbard and his wife, Katharine. Near Lake Erie, it was often the last stop for enslaved people before crossing into Canada. It's now the **Hubbard House Underground Railroad Museum.**

## DAY 5: INDIANA

Across the state line in Indiana, the home of Levi and Catharine Coffin was known as the "Grand Central Station of the Underground Railroad." More than 1,000 freedom-seekers found a safe haven at this Federal-style house dating from 1839. It's now known as the **Levi Coffin House Interpretive Center.**

## DAYS 6 AND 7: ILLINOIS

To the west is Oakland, Illinois, where you'll find the **Dr. Hiram Rutherford House.** A friend of Abraham Lincoln, the famous abolitionist helped an enslaved man named Anthony Bryant escape with his wife and children. He was sued by the slave owner, who happened to be defended by Lincoln. Lincoln lost the case, later saying, "I do hate the institution of slavery, but all citizens deserve a fair case." Other landmarks in Illinois include Jacksonville's **Beecher Hall,** the first building to be built at Illinois College. The college was a center of the abolitionist movement, and many professors and students helped people who were escaping to the north. In Princeton is the **Owen Lovejoy House,** owned by a Congregationalist minister who had seen his brother, an abolitionist newspaper publisher, killed by a pro-slavery mob. Lovejoy was later elected to the U.S.

House of Representatives, where he was known for his speeches decrying slavery.

# One Week: Fly-Fishing Itineraries

Fly-fishing has been around for centuries, but America turned it into an art form. It has its own language, form of dress, and complicated rituals. These vary from region to region, so the most dedicated anglers travel to far-flung regions to try them out.

## ONE WEEK: BIG SKY COUNTRY

Home to the nation's best fly-fishing, this is a remote region, and the nearest major gateway is Montana's Missoula International Airport. When your plane touches down, Rock Creek is still about 90 minutes away. But the sight of the Rocky Mountains in the distance will keep you going.

### ROCK CREEK, MT

East of Missoula, Montana, the 52-mile-long Rock Creek isn't just one of the best trout fishing spots in the United States—it ranks among the top four or five in the world. The reason? An unbelievable variety of fish, including westslope cutthroat trout, cutbow trout, and bull trout, along with Arctic grayling and Rocky Mountain whitefish. And then, of course, there's that Rocky Mountain scenery. Most of the creek runs through Lolo National Forest, so there's plenty of easy access from the road, as well as cabins where you can bunk down for the night. Several miles are on private property at the Ranch at Rock Creek, a luxury getaway for those who don't fancy roughing it.

### HENRY'S FORK, ID

It's around five hours to Henry's Fork, one of the most hallowed fishing spots in Idaho, but the pilgrimage is worth it. The uppermost peaks of the Grand Tetons come into view as you float along this 150-mile-long tributary to the even larger Snake River. The scenery is spectacular, bordered on three sides by craggy peaks rising more than 10,000 feet. Anglers have different opinions on the matter, but the glassy waters running through Harriman State Park are often regarded as the finest stretch of the river. That's not to say it's easy—these wild rainbows are used to flies and can be extraordinarily picky. One of the most respected local outfitters is TroutHunter, located in the community of Last Chance, Idaho. You can opt to stay in the rustic lodge here, or splurge on more luxurious accommodations at Henry's Fork Lodge.

### FLAT CREEK, WY

Two hours south of Henry's Fork, Flat Creek meanders through the waving grasses of the National Elk Refuge. It feels remote and undiscovered, but the bustling tourist town of Jackson is within easy driving distance. The season here is intentionally cut short—just August to October—which means that these waters aren't overfished. That doesn't mean the fishing is easy, and even the shadow of an overanxious angler can spook the fish. Even experts go away empty-handed. But if you're lucky, you'll snag the elusive Snake River fine-spotted cutthroat trout. Jackson's Reel Deal offers day trips to this unmissable destination.

## ONE WEEK: THE NORTHEAST

This trip, which takes you through some of the best mountain scenery in the Northeast, begins in New York City. Before you know it, you're driving through hilly terrain crisscrossed by rivers and creeks. Look up: this is one of the best places to spot bald eagles.

### WILLOWEMOC CREEK, NY

Start out in the place where American fly-fishing began to flourish back in the 1870s: in the Catskill Mountains, an easy two-hour drive from New York City. This 27-mile-long tributary to the Beaverkill River begins in the southern flank of the Beaverkill Range and winds its way though pristine valleys lined with towering hemlock and spruce trees. The official season here is April to November, although some catch-and-release areas are open year-round. The best place to start out, especially for beginners, is the hamlet of Livingston Manor, home to the Catskill Fly Fishing Museum. One of the most experienced local experts is the legendary Joan Wulff, owner of Wulff School of Fly Fishing. The Willowemoc has prodigious amounts of wild brook trout, whose bellies are a vivid orangey-red when they are spawning. These beauties are often on the menu at a nearby inn called the Arnold House, where you can also bed down for the night.

#### BATTENKILL RIVER, VT

It's a 3½-hour drive to the Green Mountains of Vermont, where cold springs bubble up to create this 65-mile-long tributary to the Hudson River. The Battenkill makes southern Vermont one of the favorite fly-fishing destinations on the East Coast. Manchester is the center of the action, partly because of the presence of the outdoors company Orvis, which tests out its new fly-fishing equipment in these waters. Consequently, the wild browns and brookies found here are jokingly called the "most educated trout in all the land." Orvis runs its own one- and two-day fly-fishing schools for those who are new to the sport or want to brush up their skills. The American Museum of Fly Fish is also located in Manchester, cementing its reputation.

#### ANDROSCOGGIN RIVER, NH

It's another 3½ hours to Berlin, New Hampshire, one of the popular fly-fishing spots on the Androscoggin River. Once polluted by the paper mills set along its shores, these wide, gentle waters are now one of the premier float fishing destinations in the Northeast. The river starts at Lake Umbagog and runs for more than 125 miles, including 53 miles in New Hampshire, before emptying out into the Gulf of Maine. Rainbow, brown, and brook trout are common in the swirling eddies, but so are more unusual catches like landlocked Atlantic salmon. At the height of summer, anglers head to the warm waters for largemouth and smallmouth bass. New Hampshire has a long season compared with many nearby states, extending from January to mid-October.

## Eight Days: Blue Ridge Parkway

Moseying through the southern Appalachians, this classic parkway, with a speed limit of 45 mph tops, forces you to slow down. All the better to take in the majestic beauty of wild forests, splashing waterfalls, and misty mountains, with plenty of hiking, camping, and picnicking along the way. Started in 1935 for the express purpose of showcasing the mountains, the parkway winds 465 miles between Shenandoah National Park at Rockfish Gap, Virginia, in the north and Great Smoky Mountains National Park at Cherokee, North Carolina, in the south.

### DAYS 1 AND 2: CHARLOTTE TO GREAT SMOKY MOUNTAINS NATIONAL PARK

Fly or drive into Charlotte to kick off your Blue Ridge Parkway tour. Drive three hours to Bryson City, a walkable, outdoorsy town on the edge of Great Smoky Mountains National Park that offers a relaxing vibe along the Tuckasegee River. Check out the petite downtown, and/or fish, kayak, or paddleboard. The national park is within a hiking boot's distance, with plenty of trails to head out and explore, including the 4-mile **Deep Creek Loop,** which takes in two pretty waterfalls. **The Bistro at the Everett Hotel** is hands down the nicest place to eat in town. Stay at the **McKinley Edwards Inn,** an upscale retreat in a landmark building, or the **Folkestone Inn,** originally a 1920s mountain farmhouse.

On Day 2, be sure to spend some time in Great Smoky Mountains National Park before striking out on the parkway. If nothing else, drive to the top of **Clingmans Dome,** the park's loftiest peak at 6,643 feet. Here, hike half a mile to the observation tower and gulp in the refreshing mountain air as you take in the 360-degree views of blue-hued peaks marching off into the distance.

## DAYS 3 AND 4: ASHEVILLE, NC

Drag yourself out of bed early to arrive just after sunrise at the **Oconauftee Visitor Center** in Cherokee, near the Blue Ridge Parkway's southern terminus, where elk calmly graze in the meadows. Drive three hours to Asheville. Poke into art galleries, Appalachian craft shops, indie coffee shops, bookstores, and breweries (there are over 60 of them) in this funky, laid-back, music-and-beer-filled mountain town. The most famous site is the **Biltmore House and Estate,** the 250-room Gilded Age mansion of George Vanderbilt, which remains the nation's largest private house and is open with a variety of tours.

Spend your second day tubing down the **French Broad River.** You'll lazily drift past the muraled warehouses of Asheville's **River Arts District,** and pull off at outdoor bars along the last stretch. **Smoky Park Supper Club** offers wood-fired pork chops, trout, New York strip, and more along the river. Stay at **JuneBug Retro Resort.**

## DAY 5: BLOWING ROCK, NC

In the morning, hit the parkway for three hours, taking in the scenery on the way to Blowing Rock. Stretch your legs along the way at the 1.75-mile (round-trip) **Linville Falls Plunge Basin Trail** at milepost 316, starting at the Linville Falls Visitor Center, a gorgeous waterfall trek along Linville Gorge. Or poke into the cute mountain town of **Banner Elk,** a historic alpine burg near Grandfather Mountain, about 15 minutes off the parkway via NC 105 and NC 184. Wine-taste at Banner Elk Winery or simply browse shops and galleries in the sweet downtown. When you arrive at Blowing Rock, explore the nature-loving town's upscale shops, galleries, cafés, and the **Blowing Rock Art & History Museum,** perfect for hanging out after a day of driving—and/or hiking, fishing, and communing with nature in the surrounding wildlands. Spend the night at **Green Park Inn.**

## DAY 6: ROANOKE, VA

Four hours away is the largest city along the parkway. It has the culture, fine eats, and lodging variety that go with urban living—though the mountains always loom in the distance. Check out the neon Roanoke Star atop **Mill Mountain** (and hike the Star Trail); find treasures at **Black Dog Salvage,** home of the hit TV show *Salvage Dawgs*; and browse the historic **Roanoke City Market,** operating since 1862. **Center in the Square** is home to the city's art, science, and history museums, along with live theater, dance, and opera. Explore Park, right off the parkway, is another must-stop, with a museum, ziplines, hiking and biking trails, and more. Stay at the luxe **Hotel Roanoke,** dating from 1882.

## DAY 7: STAUNTON AND SHENANDOAH NATIONAL PARK

In the morning, make the 3½-hour drive to Shenandoah National Park. In Staunton, a quintessential small Shenandoah Valley town, take an architectural walking tour of one of six historic districts filled with a panoply of buildings by esteemed architect T. J. Collins (Beverley Street is a good place to start), visit the **Woodrow Wilson Birthplace and Library,** attend a Shakespeare play at the **Blackfriars Playhouse,** the world's only creation of Shakespeare's indoor theater, or go wine or beer tasting. In this foodie town, try the hard-to-score-a-seat **Shack** or Southern-inspired **Zynodoa.**

## DAY 8: CHARLOTTE

Take your final drive (this one is four hours) among endless blue hills of the parkway on your way back to Charlotte to end the tour. On the way back, if you have time, stop at **Natural Bridge,** a rock arch carved by Cedar Creek, located at Exit 180 off Interstate 81.

## Ten Days: Ultimate Southwest

Red rocks and geological wonders fill this superstar itinerary spanning the best of Nevada, Utah, and Arizona. You'll explore Zion's massive sandstone cliffs and narrow slot canyons, the hoodoos (odd-shape pillars of rock left by erosion) of Bryce Canyon, and the overwhelming majesty of the Grand Canyon, close to 300 river miles long, 18 miles wide, and a mile deep.

### DAY 1: LAS VEGAS, NV

Fly into Las Vegas to kick off your Southwest trip with a bang. Stroll along the **Strip,** see a spectacular live show, take a ride in a gondola at the **Venetian,** people-watch on **Fremont Street,** sit by the pool—whatever your heart desires. Stay at the **Bellagio** of *Ocean's 11* fame for the ultimate bragging rights.

### DAY 2: ROUTE 66

Hit the road early to start your drive toward the Grand Canyon. You can drive straight there, but we recommend taking a kitschy, colorful detour along America's Mother Road for a dose of nostalgia and Americana, heading from **Kingman** to **Seligman.** Dip into the **Arizona Route 66 Museum** in Kingman and grab a bite at **Mr. D'z Route 66 Diner,** a '50's-style diner where jukebox tunes play. Then move along Route 66 and visit the **Hackberry General Store,** where you can pose for pictures with vintage cars, signs, gas pumps and highway memorabilia while sipping a bottle of sarsaparilla. Next, stop in Seligman, where you simply must order a soda and pose by signs at **Delgadillo's Snow Cap Drive-In.** By evening, you'll reach **Tusayan** or nearby **Grand Canyon Village**; either are a great base for your Grand Canyon adventures over the next few days. If you've got time, hike (or take the shuttle) to **Yavapai Point,** just west of the visitor center in the South Rim Village, to catch the sunset.

### DAYS 3, 4, AND 5: GRAND CANYON NATIONAL PARK

If you stayed in Tusayan or Grand Canyon Village, you're practically at the park's South Rim entrance this morning. If you didn't make it yesterday, begin today's tour with a stop at the **Grand Canyon Visitor Center,** near **Mather Point** in the South Rim Village, for the latest maps and information. While you're there, check out the **Historic District,** with its early-19th-century train depot and other buildings, many built by the Santa Fe Railroad. Get your bearings with a drive on the 7-mile-long Hermit Road. Hike the **Rim Trail,** a nearly flat path (much of which is paved) that hugs the edge of the canyon from the village to Hermit's Rest, 2.8 miles to the west.

On your second day in the park, tackle the upper section of one of the "Corridor Trails"—**South Kaibab** or **Bright Angel**—which start at the South Rim and meet in the **Bright Angel Campground** at the bottom of the canyon (the third Corridor Trail, **North Kaibab,** connects the bottom of the canyon to the North Rim). Bright Angel, the easier of the two, is one of the most scenic paths into the canyon; the trailhead is near **Kolb Studio,** at the western end of the village. If you booked a helicopter tour, mule ride, or white-water-rafting tour in advance, this is the day to do it.

For your last morning in the park, sign up for an interpretive ranger-led program; they cover a wide variety of subjects, including geology, history, and wildlife, so pick up a list at the Grand Canyon Visitor Center.

### DAY 6: ANTELOPE CANYON AND PAGE

Drive 2½ hours north to Antelope Canyon, possibly the world's most spectacular geological slots. Located within the Navajo Nation, the canyon has long been a cherished land; the tribe runs popular 90-minute tours through its rocky twists and turns several times a day, and advance reservations are necessary. After your tour, head to the closest town, Page, to dig into brisket, ribs, and pulled pork at **Big John's Texas Barbeque.** Page isn't exactly known for its nightlife, but you'll find a good selection of beers on tap at the **State 48 Tavern.** Stay at **Lake Powell Resort,** which has a pool, hotel bar, and a view of beautiful Lake Powell, or go all out with five-star luxury in the desert at **Amangiri** in nearby Canyon Point, Utah.

### DAY 7: BRYCE CANYON NATIONAL PARK

Get an early start and drive 2½ hours to Bryce Canyon National Park, known for its many magnificent hoodoo rock formations. Start your tour at the visitor center, about 1 mile past the park entrance. Central to your tour of Bryce Canyon is the 18-mile-long main park road, where numerous scenic turnouts reveal vistas of bright red-orange rock. If you're visiting from mid-April to late October, the free Bryce Canyon Shuttle will take you to many of the park's most popular attractions. Trails worth exploring include the 1-mile **Bristlecone Loop Trail** and the 1.3-mile **Navajo Loop Trail,** both of which will get you into the heart of the park. At the end of the day, camp out at Sunset or North campground.

### DAYS 8 AND 9: ZION NATIONAL PARK

In the morning, head to Zion National Park, about an hour and 45 minutes southwest of Bryce, to explore hanging gardens, rock formations, and stellar hiking trails. Enter at the south entrance and head to the Zion Canyon Visitor Center, south of the junction of the Zion–Mount Carmel Highway and the **Zion Canyon Scenic Drive.** Then explore the scenic drive, either in your own vehicle (January through early February only) or via the park's shuttle (purchase in advance at 🌐 *recreation.gov* as they are not sold in the park). Intrepid hikers will want to tackle the **Narrows**, Zion's infamous 16-mile-long gorge cut by the Virgin River, which requires hikers to spend more than half of their time walking, wading, or swimming in the fast-flowing river. For everyone else, Zion offers plenty of other hiking options. The **Emerald Pool** trails (about 1 mile each) take you on a fairly easy hike from Zion Lodge, about 3 miles from Canyon Junction, to Lower and Upper Emerald Pool and waterfalls. Stay tonight and tomorrow in **Springdale,** the bustling town just outside the park (1.1 miles from the south entrance).

Spend the next day exploring the **Kolob Canyons,** in the northwestern corner of the park, about 40 miles from Canyon Junction. Take the Kolob Canyons Road 5 miles to its end at the Kolob Canyons Viewpoint, where you'll get fabulous views of the surrounding red rock canyons. For a spectacular 5-mile hike, drive about 2 miles back on the Kolob Canyons Road to the **Taylor Creek Trail,** which takes you past historic homesteaders' cabins and through a narrow box canyon to the **Double Arch Alcove,** a large arched grotto.

### DAY 10: LAS VEGAS AND HOOVER DAM

Come full circle by heading back to Las Vegas; it's nearly a three-hour drive. If you have time before you fly or drive out, take in another over-the-top Vegas experience or make a trip to see one more geological wonder: the Hoover Dam. The man-made marvel lies about 40 minutes outside of town.

# Twelve Days: Natural Wonders of the Ozarks

The hills of the Ozarks roll up from the beds of sparkling rivers and peak as the grand oak and hickory trees seem to sway on the ledge of limestone bluffs. The region winds its way through the southern portion of Missouri and into northern Arkansas and eastern Oklahoma, just barely touching the edge of southeastern Kansas. The air is as pure as the hearts of the people in the region, where mom-and-pop shops thrive alongside boutique hotels, chef-driven restaurants, and world-renowned art museums. A road trip through the region offers the chance to uncover the charming folklore, natural beauty, and undiscovered gems of the Ozark Mountains.

## DAY 1: LITTLE ROCK, AR

Start your journey in Little Rock, Arkansas, a city of tales and trails. The tales begin with the Little Rock Central High School on the **U.S. Civil Rights Trail,** and the trails begin with the **Big Dam Bridge** that connects 14 miles of riverside trails throughout the city. The trail connects Little Rock's bustling **River Market District** to countless breweries and restaurants and even provides pedestrian-cyclist access to the **Clinton Presidential Center.** Grab a bite at **The Fold: Botanas & Bar,** a repurposed gas station with modern Ark-Mex at its finest. Spend the night at the **Empress of Little Rock,** listed on the National Register of Historic Places for its pure representation of Victorian architecture.

## DAY 2: BUFFALO RIVER, AR

Drive two hours north to for some epic canoeing on Buffalo River. The country's first designated "National River," Buffalo runs for 135 miles through the spectacular Ozark Mountain region. It passes some of the region's most majestic waterfalls and sheer bluffs before it flows into the White River near Buffalo City. A canoe trip down the river with **Buffalo Outdoor Center,** perhaps within sight of a tremendous herd of elk, is one of the best ways to experience the Ozark Mountains.

## DAY 3: EUREKA SPRINGS, AR

Hit the road early and drive two hours to Eureka Springs. More than 60 natural springs bubble and spring from this quirky Victorian town, where a series of winding staircases guides visitors up and down the steep terrain to boutique shops, family-owned restaurants (chain stores are banned), and miles of hiking trails. An active artist enclave colors the town with an artsy vibe, but it's the underground catacombs and sinister story behind the town's largest hotel that keeps intrigue alive. Stay at the **1886 Crescent Hotel and Spa,** known as "the Grand Ol' Lady of the Ozarks" and grab coffee and cinnamon rolls from **the Eureka Springs Coffee House** in the morning.

## DAY 4: BRANSON, MO

In the morning, drive about an hour and a half to Branson, Missouri, a fun-filled destination that's like a family-friendly Las Vegas. AR 23, one of the state's most scenic drives, connects with the fastest way to get to Branson via 86 East and 65 North. Upon arrival you'll notice Branson has an authentic American small-town charm like few other towns can even imagine. Pies are sweeter in Branson, shopping is friendlier, and the entertainment is as clean as the streets of its historic downtown. **Branson Landing** is where the nightlife action happens in town, but for an authentic Branson meal, head to the **Farmhouse Restaurant** to fill up on chicken-fried steak, fried okra, and the famous blackberry cobbler. Stay at the lakefront condos at **Still Waters Resort** overlooking Branson's Table Rock Lake.

## DAYS 5 AND 6: ST. LOUIS, MO

Hit the road for a six-hour drive to St. Louis, breaking up the day with a stop in Thayer, Missouri. This small town is just 10 miles from **Grand Gulf State Park,** which is more commonly known as the "Little

Grand Canyon." On your first night in St. Louis, check into the charming **Fleur-de-Lys Mansion, Luxury Inn at the Park** and try award-winning St. Louis barbecue at **the Shaved Duck.**

On your second morning, head to the only **National Blues Museum** in the country and ride to the top of the city's famous **Gateway Arch** via tram. St. Louis is also naturally suited for adventures, with its **Citygarden,** caverns, and nature reserves.

### DAYS 7 AND 8: LAKE OF THE OZARKS, MO

Say goodbye to the city and drive three hours to **Osage Beach,** one of the quaint towns surrounding Lake of the Ozarks, where everything revolves around the water. Speedboats, pontoons, fishing boats, and Jet Skis can all be rented at an hourly rate, and even the local spas offer floating therapies. Stay at the **Inn at Harbour Ridge,** located just outside the city limits of Osage Beach on a lakefront property nearby a community dock and swimming platform.

On your second day, hit the water again or take a break from the summertime heat and join a guided tour of the 60°F **Bridal Cave** at Camdenton, Missouri, about 20 minutes away. It features mineral deposits shaped like giant columns and massive draperies. Bridal Cave has more onyx formations than any other cavern.

### DAY 9: BAXTER SPRINGS, KS

Head two hours and 40 minutes to the historic town of Baxter Springs, Kansas. It's just a few miles from the OK-KS-MO Tri-State Marker (stand in three states at one time!), where it sits along Historic Route 66 with preserved gas stations and vintage service buildings. The town's Native American and Route 66 history are preserved within the **Baxter Springs Heritage Center & Museum.** Stay the night in Rose Cottage and eat at Rita's Roost Bistro & Sweet Shop for diner-style hot dogs and burgers.

### DAY 10: TENKILLER STATE PARK, AR

Drive Historic Route 66 as you pass over the Kansas border into Oklahoma toward the **Blue Whale of Catoosa** (one of the kitschier roadside attractions along this historic route). From there you'll begin to weave your way back and forth over the Arkansas River before arriving in Tenkiller State Park. There are more than 130 miles of shoreline surrounding **Lake Tenkiller.** Along with water sports and fishing, the clear waters of the lake provide ideal conditions for scuba diving to the lake's sunken airplane fuselage, school bus, helicopter, and two boats. Boats and Jet Skis can pull right up to the floating deck at **Clearwater Café** at Pine Cove Marina on Tenkiller Lake, where steaks are cooked to order and onion rings come stacked a foot high. RV and tent campgrounds line the park grounds, but it's the state park's 38 cabins that offer the best views and plots along the lake.

### DAY 11: HOT SPRINGS NATIONAL PARK, AR

Today your drive is about three hours. Follow Interstate 40 through Oklahoma, and, just before crossing the Arkansas River, veer onto U.S. 71 South into Fort Smith, Arkansas, where you'll soon be driving out of the Ozarks and into the Ouachita National Forest. Arrive at Hot Springs, home to some of the most prized thermal waters in the country (143°F and packed full of minerals). Run the bases around one of the first MLB spring training fields in the country or soak in the gangster history at **Bathhouse Row**—once a favorite vacation spot for legendary criminals Al Capone, Lucky Luciano, and Bugsy Siegel. The **Superior Bathhouse Brewery** serves upscale pub food and craft beers brewed from the thermal waters of the national park inside a renovated bathhouse. Former speak-easy and mobster hangout, the **Ohio Club,** is still a hot spot for nightlife in Hot Springs. Stay at the chic **Hotel Hale,** which operates inside a renovated bathhouse along Bathhouse Row.

### DAY 12: LITTLE ROCK, AR

Head back to Little Rock to end your trip. During your 1½-hour drive, keep an eye out for roadside stands selling quartz crystals as you drive along Arkansas's scenic Highway 7 toward Owensville, then cross through the last stretches of the **Ouachita National Forest** before taking the scenic route into Little Rock on Kanis Road. Grab brunch at **At the Corner, a Modern Diner** or all-you-can-eat pancakes over at **Mugs Café.**

## Two Weeks: Highway 101

In the pages of Great American Road Trips, the drive from San Diego to Seattle should be at the very top. The route, which glides along the coast from Southern California's sunny beaches to Northern California's redwoods, then on to rocky Oregon shores and the rain forests of Olympic National Park, is beyond beautiful. Along the way, the West Coast's most dynamic cities, each one a worthy destination in and of itself, line up like the pearls in a 2,878-mile-long necklace. From its epic views to its incredible food, its hiking trails to its city streets, San Diego to Seattle 101 is the trip of a lifetime.

### DAY 1: SAN DIEGO

Go straight for the city's nautical heart by exploring the restored ships of the **Maritime Museum** at the waterfront in Downtown. Victorian buildings—and plenty of other tourists—surround you on a stroll through the Gaslamp Quarter. Plant yourself at a Downtown hotel and graze your way through the neighborhood's many restaurants. If you have time, visit the **San Diego Zoo,** one of the best in the country.

### DAY 2: LOS ANGELES

California-dream your way out of San Diego and along the Pacific Coast Highway (PCH). Pass through Orange County's classic beach communities before heading slightly inland to the heart of Los Angeles. Wander through massive **Griffith Park** (don't miss the historic Griffith Observatory) or stop by the **La Brea Tar Pits** for a glimpse of prehistoric Los Angeles. Some of the country's best modern art is housed at the **Los Angeles County Museum of Art** (LACMA). Nostalgic musts in Hollywood include the **Hollywood Walk of Fame** along Hollywood Boulevard and the celebrity footprints cast in concrete outside Grauman's Chinese Theatre (now known as the **TCL Chinese Theater**). Or, spend time exploring the coastal town of **Santa Monica** and its iconic pier before hitting the road to Santa Barbara.

### DAY 3: SANTA BARBARA

Navigate north up the PCH towards celebrity hangout Santa Barbara; the drive takes two hours. Don't leave without exploring the highlights of this strolling along **State Street,** through the red-tile-roofed buildings of downtown to the gorgeous Santa Barbara County Courthouse and take in the views from its tower. Before leaving town, stop at the **Mission Santa Barbara,** widely considered the finest of the 21 California missions. Outside the city you enter wine country and pass through Solvang, one of the West Coast's quirkiest towns, before returning to the coast and San Luis Obispo.

### DAY 4: BIG SUR

Get an early start and drive to Big Sur. Get a look at the iconic **McWay Falls** from Highway 1, then hit the trail at **Julia Pfeiffer Burns State Park** or the water at **Sand Dollar Beach** or **Andrew Molera State Park.** You can make camp at Julia Pfeiffer Burns State Park or stay in a hotel.

## DAYS 5 AND 6: SAN FRANCISCO

Get up bright and early to make your way to the Bay Area, past the artist colony of Carmel and the town of Monterey (the setting for John Steinbeck's 1945 novel *Cannery Row*) where you should stop for a quick lunch at the roadside favorite Sam's Chowder House in Half Moon Bay for a bowl and a beer on the patio. It's about two hours north from Monterey to San Francisco. From the **"Painted Ladies"** (Victorian homes) of the Haight and back-alleys of the largest **Chinatown** outside Asia, San Francisco is one of the country's most enchanting cities. The murals in the **Mission** neighborhood, seals at **Fisherman's Wharf,** North Beach's **Coit Tower,** and downtown museums like the **SFMoMa** are among the many must-sees, and you will easily be able to fill your two nights with activities. In **Golden Gate Park,** linger amid the flora of the Conservatory of Flowers and the San Francisco Botanical Garden at Strybing Arboretum, soak up some art at the de Young Museum, and find serene refreshment at the San Francisco Japanese Tea Garden. The Pacific surf pounds the cliffs below the Legion of Honor art museum, which has an exquisite view of the **Golden Gate Bridge**—when the fog stays away.

## DAY 7: POINT REYES NATIONAL SEASHORE

It's a short drive today over the Golden Gate Bridge and up Highway 1 to the Point Reyes National Seashore and the oyster-rich waters of Tomales Bay. The tiny, historic town of **Point Reyes Station** has a handful of pleasant shops and restaurants. It's a lovely stop before hitting the wildlands of the national seashore a few miles down the road. The Point Reyes National Seashore is an unusual mix of historical ranching and dairy lands and protected wilderness. See the wild tule elk at **Tomales Point,** whale watch from the 150-year-old **Point Reyes Lighthouse,** and get a look at the elephant seal colony at **Chimney Rock.** When you've had your fill of Point Reyes, hit the road to drive up the inland side of Tomales Bay. **The Marshall Store,** a roadside joint with barbecued oysters, Dungeness crab sandwiches, and other delights from the bay, is always worth a stop.

## DAY 8: MENDOCINO

It's a day of spectacular views and quaint coastal towns as you continue up the PCH towards Mendocino. In **Bodega Bay,** tool around town on a bike or rent a kayak for a few hours on the water. Four miles from the coast is the village of Bodega, the filming location for Alfred Hitchcock's 1963 film *The Birds*. Mendocino is a laid-back town and mecca for artists and gallery owners. Check out the **Mendocino Art Center** then browse some of the many galleries in town. If you prefer your art in liquid form, there are a number of wineries in nearby **Anderson Valley.**

## DAY 9: EUREKA

Today's route takes you away from the coast and into the weird and wonderful world of rural Northern California on the Redwood Highway (Highway 101). At the day's end, you're back at the coast in Eureka, a city which rose to prominence during the gold rush era. The entire town of Eureka has been named a historic landmark but the best-preserved blocks are located in Old Town. Explore the neighborhood on foot, and don't forget to check out the **Carson Mansion,** considered the grandest Victorian home in the United States.

## DAY 10: BROOKINGS, OR

Bouncing back and forth from coast to forest, today's drive takes you north through **Redwood National and State Parks** and over the Oregon state border. Stop in at Crescent City to check out the beautiful **Battery Point Lighthouse,** one of the oldest on the West Coast. Redwood National and State Parks is a collection of protected spaces stretching almost 50 miles from Crescent City to Orick, California. Walk among the redwoods in **Jedediah Smith Redwoods,** visit lush Fern

Canyon in **Prairie Creek Redwoods,** and watch the Roosevelt elk graze near **Gold Bluffs Beach.** The redwoods and coastal views don't stop at the Oregon border. In Brookings, take a hike along the Oregon Redwoods Trail and admire the rock formations rising out of **Lone Ranch Beach.**

### DAY 11: NEWPORT

Head north from Brookings, through the fishing town of Bandon, past the **Oregon Dunes National Recreation Area,** and on to Newport. When you reach Newport, see otters and fish endemic to this region of the Pacific at the **Oregon Coast Aquarium,** or walk along the town's historic bay front, where seafood processing has been ongoing for over 100 years. At the northern end of town, the **Yaquina Head Lighthouse** stands tall above Nye Beach's long stretch of sand.

### DAY 12: ASTORIA

Highway 101 sweeps inland today, passing through the outer edge of **Tillamook State Forest** before heading back to the coast and the site where Lewis and Clark first saw the Pacific. The day's drive ends in **Astoria,** a port town and one of the stars of 1985's *The Goonies.* Go for a stroll along **Cannon Beach,** a wide swath of golden sand punctuated by massive monoliths, including the 235-foot-tall **Haystack Rock.** Break for some cheese (and a tour) at the **Tillamook Creamery** in Tillamook. Learn about Lewis and Clark's epic adventure to discover the West in the early 19th century and peek inside their winter shelter, Fort Clatsop, at the **Lewis & Clark National Historic Park.** In Astoria, *Goonies* fans will get a kick out of the **Oregon Film Museum,** while aficionados of architecture and design will enjoy the **Flavel House Museum.**

### DAY 13: OLYMPIC NATIONAL PARK

It's your last day along the coast, so soak in the views as you cross the border into Washington State and head up to **Lake Quinault** in Olympic National Park. In the industrial harbor town of **Aberdeen,** you'll find several homages to Kurt Cobain, who grew up here in the '70s and '80s. See memorials to the man above and below the bridge in Kurt Cobain Memorial Park, and get a look at his childhood home at 1210 East First Street. Then drive to Olympic National Park. While you won't be able to see the entirety of this place that covers more than a million acres of diverse landscape, you can explore its lower reaches. On Lake Quinault you can swim, fish or boat in the lake, or hike the **Quinault Rain Forest Trail** and spend the night in **Lake Quinault Lodge.**

### DAY 14: SEATTLE

Backtrack to Aberdeen then head east through the state capital of Olympia and north on Interstate 5 to the bustling city of Seattle. Whether it's your first time in Seattle or your 100th, the city's greatest hits—including the delicate sculptures at the **Chihuly Garden & Glass Museum,** the bustling seafood market **Pike Place,** and the iconic **Space Needle**—never get old. Options a little further off the beaten track include a visit to the **Fremont Troll,** the **Science Fiction Museum and Hall of Fame,** and **Seattle Underground.**

## Two Weeks: Route 66

When singer Bobby Troupe wrote the song "Route 66" back in 1946, chances are he had no idea he'd be inspiring generations of bucket-listers to hit the road. Lyrics directing you to drive "From Chicago to L.A./ More than two thousand miles all the way" are better than any map.

Route 66 was replaced by an interstate highway in 1984, but you can still drive on sections of the original road for almost the entire journey. Along the way you pass weird tourist attractions, abandoned towns that went bust when travelers stopped coming, and some of the country's most beautiful scenery.

### DAY 1: "FROM CHICAGO ..."

Get your camera ready, because on the northwestern corner of Adams Street and Michigan Avenue in Downtown Chicago are two signs: the top one reads "Historic Route 66," and the one below simply says "Begin." You'll be itching to begin your journey, but spend the night in Chicago so you have plenty of time to visit the unmissable sights, including the **Art Institute of Chicago** and **Millennium Park,** home of the Cloud Gate, which most closely resembles an enormous silver bean.

### DAY 2: "NOW YOU GO THROUGH ST. LOUIS"

It's 4½ hours from Chicago to St. Louis, Missouri, but a great place to break up the journey is Pontiac, Illinois. Here you'll find the **Route 66 Hall of Fame and Museum,** one of many dedicated to the Mother Highway. Don't forget to head around back for the massive mural featuring a Route 66 marker—your second photo op.

Stop for lunch at Springfield's **Cozy Dog Drive-In,** which claims to have invented the corn dog, then head south past the historic **Chain of Rocks Bridge** to St. Louis. It's worth a detour here to see the **Gateway Arch**—travelers along Route 66 certainly did when this engineering marvel opened in 1965. Dinner is at a burger joint locals love—**Carl's Drive-In**—followed by a "concrete" milkshake from the walk-up window at **Ted Drewes Frozen Custard.** Spend a glamorous night at **St. Louis Union Station Hotel.**

### DAY 3: "JOPLIN, MISSOURI"

On your way out of St. Louis, stop by Route 66 State Park, where the visitor center is in a former lodging called the Bridgehead Inn. Nearby is the now closed Route 66 Bridge, which once shuttled travelers across the Meramec River. A short drive south you'll find the **Meramec Caverns,** one of the largest cave systems in the world.

Halfway to Joplin is Springfield, Missouri, known as the "Birthplace of Route 66" because the first stretch of roadway was here. (There's a sign at Springfield's Park Central Square, your third photo op.) In a nearby Victorian-era storefront is the city's oldest tavern, **Linberg's.** The dining room, with gorgeous woodwork and a pressed-tin ceiling, is a good spot for lunch.

The Mother Road used to run straight through Joplin, and locals celebrate this fact at **Route 66 Mural Park.** When you're ready for a dinner break, head to nearby Carthage for a burger at **Whisler's Drive Up.** (Just remember that it closes on the early side.) If you're looking for after-dark entertainment, you can't beat the **Route 66 Drive-In,** which opened for business in 1949.

### DAY 3: "OKLAHOMA CITY IS MIGHTY PRETTY"

Your next step along the journey is Kansas, although Route 66 barely grazes the southeast corner of the Sunflower State. Before you know it you'll be in Oklahoma, which has the longest drivable stretch of the original Route 66. A great spot to stretch your legs along the way is the enormous **Blue Whale,** a roadside in the community of Catoosa.

You'll know you've reached Tulsa when you catch sight of the **Golden Driller,** dedicated to workers in the region's oil industry. This is definitely the place for a blast-from-the-past lunch. Our favorites include **Ike's Chili** (a modest place that's been in business more than a century), **Tally's Café** (the chicken sandwich has won numerous awards), and **Waylan's Ku-Ku Burger** (the last outpost of a cuckoo clock–themed eatery that used to spread across the Midwest).

Depending on the year, Route 66 followed several different roads through Oklahoma City. The city is built on top of the oil fields, and there are even derricks on the grounds of the **Oklahoma State**

**Capitol.** Dinner should be at the glitzy **Cheever's,** recognizable from its slightly confusing neon sign reading "Flowers." For generations the historic building held a family-owned flower shop. If there's a concert at the iconic Tower Theater, that's where you want to spend the evening.

### DAY 4: "YOU SEE AMARILLO"

Heading west, you can learn all about the Mother Road at the **Oklahoma Route 66 Museum** in Clinton. You can't miss it, as it has some of the flashiest neon anywhere in these parts. (If you do, it's a half-hour drive to Elk City's **National Route 66 Museum.**) Crossing into Texas—just 179 miles of the panhandle—you'll encounter some interesting diversions, such as the **Devil's Rope Museum,** which pays homage to barbed wire. Take our word for it and order the tasty fried catfish down the road at the **Red River Steak House.**

Amarillo has one real attraction, a world-famous art installation called **Cadillac Ranch.** These 10 classic cars buried fender first in the prairie are worth a little detour. Then it's off to dinner at the **Big Texan Steak Ranch,** where anyone finishing a 72-ounce slab of beef gets a free meal. (Aren't you glad you didn't fill up back in McLean?)

### DAYS 5, 6, AND 7: "GALLUP, NEW MEXICO"

Today is one of the longest drives on this itinerary, but the desert scenery is stunning. For a late breakfast or early lunch, stop in Adrian at the **Midpoint Café,** more or less the halfway point of this journey. Crossing the border into New Mexico, Tucumcari has a string of beautiful neon signs in front of classic motor lodges. The best is the swooping bird atop the **Blue Swallow Motel.**

In the early days, Route 66 took a sharp detour north, looping around Santa Fe before heading south again. It's worth the detour to take in this smart, sophisticated city in the desert. Don't miss the **Georgia O'Keeffe Museum,** dedicated to one of the 20th century's most famous painters. It's a short stroll from leafy **Santa Fe Plaza,** where you'll find award-winning restaurants in every direction. Treat yourself at upscale **Sazón**. Stay the night at **La Fonda on the Plaza.**

Better yet, stay three nights, because there's plenty to see in and around Santa Fe. Meander along the streets around Santa Fe Plaza, ducking into any of the dozens of art galleries. Take in the 17th-century adobe abodes along De Vargas Street. Marvel at the majesty of the San Miguel Mission or the charm of Loretto Chapel. Reserve ahead for dinner at **La Plazuela in Santa Fe.**

The next morning—or afternoon, if you're so enchanted by Santa Fe that you find it difficult to leave—head south to Albuquerque for lunch at **66 Café,** a diner that started out life as a Phillips 66 gas station. You can get the lay of the land from the top of the Sandia Mountains with the help of the **Sandia Peak Tramway.** Set off into the desert at **Petroglyph National Monument,** where indigenous people carved patterns into the stone hundreds of years ago. Dine at **Mac's La Sierra Family Restaurant,** which has been serving Southwestern favorites since 1952. Overnight at the adobe-style **El Vado Motel,** a Route 66 classic dating from 1937.

The next day head west to Gallup. The most unusual attraction here is the tiny **Navajo Code Talkers Museum,** honoring Navajo speakers who created a simple but unbreakable code used for communications during World War II. The historic **El Rancho,** dating from 1937, is a popular spot for dining and dreaming.

### DAYS 8, 9, AND 10: "FLAGSTAFF, ARIZONA. DON'T FORGET WINONA"

Cross the border to Arizona, whose towns are name-checked more often than any other state in the song. On your way to Flagstaff, take a hike past perfectly preserved trees at **Petrified**

**Forest National Park,** visible on both sides of the highway.

Actually, you can forget Winona, even though the song urges you otherwise. Head straight to Flagstaff, where there's a historic downtown where you just have to take a stroll and perhaps stop for lunch at the century-old **Weatherford Hotel.** With three bars, it's a bit too noisy for an overnight stay. For that we suggest driving 30 miles west to the quieter town of Williams, where you can stay at a classic motel like the **Lodge on Route 55.** Dinner is at another longtime favorite, **Rod's Steak House.**

There's so much to see in the area that you should budget three nights in the Williams area. First and foremost is the **Grand Canyon,** an hour's drive north. Plan ahead and you can score a room at one of the lodges inside the national park. If you're a mountain biker, **Kaibab National Forest** is a must. Crumbling parts of Route 66 have been incorporated into trails like Devil Dog Loop.

### DAY 11: "KINGMAN"

Heading west, stop for a bite in Seligman at **Delgadillo's Snow Cap Drive-In.** Exit off the highway here, as there's a 90-mile segment of Old Route 66 between Seligman and Barstow that really gives you the flavor of the open road. Kingman has a strip of historic buildings along its main street, including the now-defunct Beale Hotel. Lunch family-style at **Rutherford's 66 Family Diner.** Overnight in Kingston, or make your way through the tourist trap of Oatman (where the streets are full of burros looking for a handout) and on to the Arizona-California border, where you can choose from several lodgings on the Colorado River.

### DAYS 12 AND 13: "BARSTOW, SAN BERNARDINO"

Crossing into California, Barstow is the gateway to **Joshua Tree National Park.** It's worth budgeting a day at this otherworldly landscape, especially if your jam is hiking or rock climbing. Stay in **Twentynine Palms** or one of the other communities near the entrance.

Barstow itself is home to the jam-packed Route 66 Mother Road Museum, where almost none of the "treasures" on exhibit are labeled. Stop in Barstow for some delicious Mexican food at Rosita's, or head to Amapola Rico Taco in San Bernardino. For one last taste of Route 66 kitsch, stay at the **Wigwam Motel,** where 20 concrete teepees make for surprisingly roomy accommodations.

### DAY 14: ".. TO L.A."

San Bernardino is the edge of the suburbs of L.A., so from here on out the road is extremely well traveled. Head through the center of this crowded city to **Santa Monica Pier,** where you'll find the sign marking the end of the road. It's your last photo op of the journey, and it's a beauty.

## Two Weeks: Ultimate Northeast

The northeast offers epic road-tripping on a miniature scale: a few hours behind the wheel can take you from sea level to the highest point in the northeastern United States. Along the way, duck into picture-postcard towns for clam shacks, craft beer, and maple syrup shots; collect covered-bridge and lighthouse selfies to shore up your Yankee cred. It's not all small-town life—in Portland, Providence, and Boston, soak up the history and culture that keep New England a creative hotbed.

### DAYS 1 AND 2: PHILADELPHIA

Start your whirlwind trip in the Cradle of Liberty. Devote your first morning to exploring **Independence National Historical Park.** The two most popular sights are Independence Hall (where the Constitution and Declaration of Independence were signed) and the Liberty Bell Center.

But don't neglect the Independence Visitor Center, where you must make a reservation (March through December) to tour Independence Hall. If you have extra time, visit the **Benjamin Franklin Museum** on Franklin Court. Have lunch at nearby **Reading Terminal Market.** In the afternoon, you can stay in Old Town to see more historic sights, including the Carpenter's Hall, Christ Church, the Betsy Ross House, and Elfreth's Alley, or you can delve deeper into the Constitution at the National Constitution Center or the American Revolution at the aptly named Museum of the American Revolution. At night, dinner and nightlife beckon in nearby Center City.

Devote Day 2 to Philly's art and museums. **Philadelphia Museum of Art** on Benjamin Franklin Parkway, followed by lunch in the museum's lovely dining room, will be enjoyable to almost anyone; it's the city's widest-ranging art museum. But if your interest is Impressionist, Postimpressionist, and early modern American art, the **Barnes Foundation** may be a better destination (reservations required). In the afternoon explore one of Philadelphia's distinct neighborhoods. Stroll around **Rittenhouse Square** and stop in at the Rosenbach Museum and Library, which has a diverse collection ranging from the original manuscript of James Joyce's *Ulysses* to the works of beloved children's author Maurice Sendak. There's also Society Hill, Queen Village, and South Philadelphia for the **Mummer Museum** on 9th Street and the outdoor Italian Market. Set aside time to dine in one of the city's best restaurants or take in a concert.

### DAYS 3, 4, 5: NEW YORK CITY

You could spend weeks in New York and not scratch the surface of all there is to see and do in the Big Apple, but you'll need three days minimum to see the big sights. Begin your first day at the **Empire State Building** or **Top of the Rock,** taking in the panoramic view of the city. Next head up to the **Metropolitan Museum of Art.** You could easily spend a whole day here, but you'll exhaust yourself if you do. Luckily, just behind the museum lies beautiful **Central Park,** where you can relax on a bench, rent a rowboat, or explore a meadow and watch the world go by. Exit the park's south end at 5th Avenue and work your way downtown, browsing the department stores and shops that abound. If you're there at dusk, walk instead south on 7th Avenue toward the bright lights of **Times Square** and catch a Broadway show.

On Day 2 seek out some history via a ferry trip to the **Statue of Liberty and Ellis Island.** You can beat the crowds with any early start. Allow yourself about six hours if you plan to do a thorough visit with guided tours. If not, you can be back in Manhattan by lunchtime. After lunch, stroll through the **Wall Street** area, home of the colonial-era Fraunces Tavern, mid-19th-century Trinity Church, and St. Paul's Chapel, Manhattan's oldest surviving church building. Also here is the **World Trade Center site,** complete with time line and memorial. Just north are the neo-Gothic Woolworth Building (don't miss the splendid gilded lobby) and City Hall. Hop on the N or R train to 8th Street, where you can stroll around **Washington Square Park** and **Greenwich Village.**

On your last day in town, do what many New Yorkers do on their days off—wander. Make your way to **Chinatown** for a dim sum breakfast or tapioca-filled soft drink. From here head north to **SoHo** and **Nolita** for galleries, chic boutiques, and restaurants. If you haven't eaten by now, hit a café a few blocks north in the happening **East Village,** home to yet more shops and vintage stores. From **Union Square,** walk up Broadway to the fashionable **Flatiron District** with its inimitable Flatiron Building. Take a break in **Madison Square** and soak up the surrounding skyline. Have dinner in one of the neighborhood's noted restaurants.

## DAY 6: NEW HAVEN, CT

Wake up and head to New Haven, Connecticut. The Constitution State's second-largest city is home to **Yale University,** named for British shipping merchant Elihu Yale. Take an hour-long walking tour with one of the university's guides and feast your eyes on the iconic Gothic-style structures that adorn the campus. After you've worked up an appetite, a stop for New Haven–style pizza is a must. Less than a mile from campus are two institutions known for thin-crust pies cooked in brick ovens: **Pepe's Pizzeria** and **Sally's Apizza.** For the burger enthusiast, there's **Louis' Lunch** on Crown Street. Spend the night in town.

## DAY 7: PROVIDENCE, RI

Get an early start, and head north on Interstate 95 to make your way toward Providence. Rhode Island's capital holds treasures like **Benefit Street,** with its Federal-era homes, and the **RISD Museum of Art** at the Rhode Island School of Design. Be sure to savor a knockout Italian meal on Atwells Avenue in Federal Hill—**Pane e Vino** is a popular choice. For dessert, it's hard to top the cannoli at **Scialo Bros. Bakery.** If you're visiting in early June, sample authentic eats from all over Italy, while live music fills the streets, during the Federal Hill Stroll. Spend the night in a downtown Providence hotel for easy access to sights and restaurants.

## DAYS 8 AND 9: BOSTON, MA

A short drive north on Interstate 95 will bring you to Boston, New England's cultural and commercial hub. To savor Boston's centuries-old ties to the sea, take a half-day stroll past **Faneuil Hall** and **Quincy Market** or a boat tour of the harbor. From the **Boston Common,** the 2.5-mile **Freedom Trail** links treasures of America's fight for independence, such as the **USS *Constitution*** (better known as "Old Ironsides") and **Old North Church** (of "one if by land, two if by sea" fame). Be sure to walk the gas-lighted streets of Beacon Hill, too, pausing on **Acorn Street** for an iconic photograph. Boston's North End is home to **Paul Revere's Home,** and has great Italian dining options like **Antico Forno** and cannolis from **Mike's Pastry.** At night, order chowder and Sam Adams at **Union Oyster House** or a nightcap at the Liberty Hotel's **Clink** bar.

The following day, either explore the massive **Museum of Fine Arts** and the grand boulevards and shops of **Back Bay,** perhaps heading to the **Isabella Stewart Gardner Museum** to take in some world-class art in a palatial setting. Or visit colorful **Cambridge,** home of Harvard University and the Massachusetts Institute of Technology (MIT). Lively **Harvard Square** is a perfect place to do some people-watching or catch a street performance; the **All Star Sandwich Bar** is an excellent choice for lunch.

## DAYS 10 AND 11: PORTLAND, ME

From Boston, hit the road early and drive two hours to Portland, Maine, stopping in **Portsmouth, New Hampshire,** or **Ogunquit Beach** to stretch your legs if you wish. Spend the day exploring Maine's largest city, its historic neighborhoods, shopping and eating lobster rolls in the **Old Port** (which has a great craft beer scene), or visiting one of several excellent museums. A brief side trip to Cape Elizabeth takes you to **Portland Head Light,** Maine's first lighthouse. From Portland it's easy to add on an extension to **Acadia National Park** if you have another day to spare.

## DAY 12: WHITE MOUNTAINS, NH

In the morning, pass thick forests broken by glassy lakes as you drive west to Lincoln, New Hampshire, home of the beautiful White Mountains. Spend a day exploring the **Flume Gorge** in Franconia Notch or leaf-peeping on a drive through Kancamagus Highway. Spend the night at **Omni Mount Washington Resort,** recalling the glory days of White Mountain resorts. Beloved winter activities here include snowshoeing and skiing on the grounds; you can even zipline. Afterward, defrost with a cup of steaming hot cider.

### DAYS 13 AND 14: STOWE, VT

Next, set out for the village of Stowe. Its proximity to **Mt. Mansfield** (Vermont's highest peak at 4,395 feet) has made Stowe a popular ski destination since the 1930s. If there's snow on the ground, hit the slopes, hitch a ride on a one-horse open sleigh, or simply put your feet up by the fire and enjoy a Heady Topper (an unfiltered, hoppy, American Double IPA). In warmer weather, pop into the cute shops and art galleries that line the town's main street and sample some of the finest cheddar cheese and maple syrup that Vermont has to offer. Rejuvenate at **Topnotch Resort,** which offers more than 100 different treatments. Spend your last two nights here, taking optional excursions to the **Ben & Jerry's Factory** or to nearby **Shelburne Farms, Lake Champlain,** or **Burlington** before you bid adieu to the Northeast.

## Two Weeks: The Great Lakes

If you grew up near a Great Lake you were likely drilled with the HOMES acronym in grade school to keep them straight: Huron, Ontario, Michigan, Erie, and Superior. Filled with folklore (hello, shipwrecks!) and rimmed with lighthouses, cultural landmarks, and resort towns, plus—in recent years—a thriving surfing culture and wine regions, these five freshwater lakes captivate first-time visitors. No, you cannot see across the lake and yes, these waters are deep. Ticking off five lakes in 14 days might seem ambitious, but hear us out. Using this carefully crafted route, all the Great Lakes are seamlessly woven into an easy-to-follow itinerary packed with signature regional eats, blissful hikes, and natural wonders.

### DAYS 1 AND 2: CHICAGO

Kick off your trip at the soaring heights of **Skydeck Chicago at the Willis Tower** for a grand view of the city and Lake Michigan. Then take a walking tour of downtown, visiting museums like the **Art Institute of Chicago.** Indulge in one of Chicago's three famous culinary treats—deep-dish pizza, hot dogs, or Italian beef sandwiches. After dark? Sip a cocktail at a hidden speakeasy like **the Drifter** or catch a theater show.

On your second day, catch an El train north to **Wrigley Field** for Cubs baseball; grab a dog at the seventh-inning stretch, and sing your heart out to "Take Me Out to the Ball Game." Afterward, soak up a little beer and atmosphere on the patio at one of the local sports bars. Finish up with an outdoor concert in Grant or **Millennium Park.** Make sure to get your picture taken in the mirrored center of the Bean—the sculpture that's formally known as **Cloud Gate.**

### DAY 3: INDIANA DUNES NATIONAL PARK

This is one of your easiest driving days, a quick trip of around an hour, traveling south down Interstate 94 then Interstate 90 towards Indiana. No need to set your clocks forward one hour: northwest Indiana, including **Indiana Dunes National Park,** is on Central Standard Time. Hugging 15 miles of Lake Michigan shoreline, the national park's 15,000 acres include 50 miles of trails. Into bicycling? Pack the bikes to explore the **Calumet and Porter Brickyard Bike Trails.** On the northern tip of the park, **Old Lighthouse Museum** in Michigan City (run by the local historical society) is the state's oldest remaining lighthouse.

### DAY 4: CLEVELAND

Buckle up bright and early for your nearly five-hour ride to what many call the North Coast (tacking on an hour for Eastern Standard Time), following Interstate 90 East all the way. Few people know that Cleveland has beaches and—gasp!—islands (Lake Erie Islands: hop a ferry from Sandusky, an hour west of Cleveland, to the chain of 26 islands). Stroll Lake Erie's shoreline or just chill on the sand at **Edgewater Park Beach** downtown. If you're a hard-core music fan, don't miss the **Rock & Roll Hall of Fame** in downtown Cleveland. Spend the night at **Schofield Hotel.**

## DAYS 5 AND 6: NIAGARA FALLS

You can opt to stay in Buffalo for a day, or make the drive along Interstate 190 North (hop off at Exit 21) straight to Niagara Falls. You'll need time to explore the falls, which straddles the United States and Canada, and where Lake Erie drains into Lake Ontario. Book a one-day tour with Gray Line. Two of the three falls are in the United States: **Bridal Veil Falls** and **American Falls**. The other (**Horseshoe Falls**, the largest) lies in Ontario, Canada. The Frederick Law Olmsted–designed Niagara Falls State Park—the country's oldest state park—offers a mix of overlooks (viewing sites) as well as trails to hike.

## DAY 7: DETROIT

In the morning, take the four-hour drive west to America's Motor City, spending a day exploring sights such as the **Detroit Motown Museum** and **Detroit Institute of Arts,** or picnicking on **Belle Isle** before grabbing drinks in public-art-filled alley, **the Belt.** Stay in a cool hotel like **the Siren** before heading out bright and early.

## DAY 8: TRAVERSE CITY

Next up, drive to Traverse City. If you love wine, Traverse City is your jam as it's the state's most developed (and revered) wine region with two AVAs: **Old Mission Peninsula AVA** and **Leelanau Peninsula AVA.** The town of 16,000 residents also hugs Lake Michigan along the shores of Grand Traverse Bay. Tasting rooms are akin to Napa and Sonoma with food-pairing packages, vineyards on-site, and grand tasting rooms. **Green Bird Organic Cellars** is a cute winery stop; it's on a 67-acre farm, and the owners produce both estate wines and hard ciders.

## DAYS 9 AND 10: MACKINAC ISLAND

Leaving Traverse City, travel north on Interstate 75 North to Mackinaw City, driving through the Gaylord State Forest Area. You'll hop the **Star Line Mackinac Island Ferry** ($29 round-trip) to car-free Mackinac Island. The ferry trip takes 18 minutes, and parking is available near the ferry's departure point. Even if you aren't staying at the Grand Hotel, pop over for a self-guided tour of the grand estate, one of Mackinac Island's most photographed buildings. Two lighthouses are on the island: **McGulpin Point Lighthouse** and **Old Mackinac Point Lighthouse.** A horse-drawn carriage tour is a fun way to explore the island in less than a day—and don't forget to buy some fudge as a souvenir.

## DAY 11: PICTURED ROCKS NATIONAL LAKESHORE

From Mackinaw City, drive two hours to Pictured Rocks National Lakeshore—named for the mineral stains on its cliffs—in Munising, which hugs the south shore of Lake Superior. Take a few days to explore the great outdoors of the region by kayaking through gorgeous sea cliffs, hiking, and camping.

## DAYS 12 AND 13: GREEN BAY AND DOOR COUNTY

Pack up and head out early. U.S. 41 South traces the western shoreline of Green Bay through Wisconsin until you hit the city of Green Bay, before curling northeast to Sturgeon Bay. This is the largest city in Door County, a resort community popular with Chicagoans and Milwaukeeans and on the southern portion between Green Bay and Lake Michigan. Door County is home to five state parks with easy hikes and stunning water views. Closest to Sturgeon Bay are **Whitefish Dunes State Park** (on the Lake Michigan side) and **Peninsula State Park** (on the Green Bay side).

### DAY 14: MILWAUKEE

From Sturgeon Bay it's 2½ hours to Milwaukee, where you should celebrate your road trip finish with a pint of the city's finest beer or a visit to the **Milwaukee Art Museum.** Spend the night or leave in the evening to make your way back down to Chicago to fly out. Alternatively, you could tack on a few days to your itinerary and head west to Minnesota.

## Two Weeks: Big Sky

Circling the northern reaches of the Rocky Mountains, this road trip through Montana, Idaho, and Wyoming is one of the most stunning exhibitions of nature to be found in this world, or the next. Out here, the landscape is dense with national forests and national monuments lauded for their stunning beauty and cultural histories, not to mention three separate national parks: Glacier, Yellowstone, and Grand Teton. Over 14 days, the itinerary careens over mountain passes, through emerald forests, and along the banks of sapphire lakes and rivers. While this route will knock the socks off of just about anyone, for those willing to get out in nature to hike, kayak, and horseback ride, the word "epic" doesn't even begin to describe it.

### DAY 1: BOZEMAN

Fly into Bozeman Yellowstone International Airport (BZN) and spend the day exploring bustling **Main Street** filled with cool cafés and restaurants, or get out and enjoy hiking, mountain biking, fly-fishing, hot springs, and skiing in the area. Bed down at the stylish **RSVP Hotel** or **the Lark,** a sunny downtown hotel with an outdoor wood-burning fireplace and a patio overlooking Main Street.

### DAYS 2 AND 3: GLACIER NATIONAL PARK

Head northwest out of Bozeman towards the Montana state capital **Helena,** then north via Interstate 15. By the time you hit Highway 89, the views of Flathead National Forest and the Rocky Mountains are in full bloom. It takes about five hours to reach Glacier National Park, which has more than 700 miles of hiking trails to do solo or with a Glacier Guide. Fish at the park's many lakes and rivers (no permit required) and take a drive down the famed **Going-to-the-Sun Road,** one of the country's most spectacular National Historic Landmarks. Camp out at one of the 13 campgrounds or book a few nights at the rustic **Izaak Walton Inn.**

### DAY 4: MISSOULA

Make a stop in beautiful **Whitefish** before heading south along the eastern shore of **Flathead Lake** (Highway 35) and into the city of Missoula. Explore the ghostly remains of **Garnet,** an early gold-mining town, or soak up some culture at the **Missoula Art Museum.** If you're visiting in winter, hit the slopes at the **Montana Snowbowl.** During the summer, they run zipline tours over the chairlifts.

### DAY 5: REDFISH LAKE

Today's route takes you through hundreds of miles of national forest and across the border into Idaho. Along the way, stop in Salmon, Idaho, take a rigorous hike to the **Goldbug Hot Springs** for a soak, or stop in at the **Sacajawea Interpretive, Cultural, and Education Center,** which delves into the history of the Lewis and Clark Expedition and the Agaidika Shoshone-Bannock Nation from which their indigenous guide hailed. You'll set up for the night in Stanley (stay in the suites and private cabins of **Stanley High Country Inn** with a rustic aesthetic adorned with modern touches) and then venture 20 minutes to **Redfish Lake** for an epic hiking adventure or a sunset cruise.

### DAY 6: SUN VALLEY

Take in the beauty of the Sawtooth National Forest on today's short one-hour drive from Stanley to Sun Valley and the neighboring town of Ketchum. Sun Valley is a posh, all-season outdoor getaway. At the **Resort,** ski or snowboard in winter, and golf, go for a horseback ride, or hike the trails of **Bald Mountain** in summer. Have an elegant dinner at Sun Valley's original dining room, the Ram, and stay in Hotel Ketchum. At this point you can opt for an extension to **Shoshone Falls** in southern Idaho or head straight to Jackson and the Tetons.

## DAY 7: JACKSON HOLE

Drive along the volcanic moonscape of **Craters of the Moon National Monument** and westward through southern Idaho until you hit Jackson, the southern gateway to **Grand Teton National Park.** If you need to stop and stretch your legs on the way, stop in **Idaho Falls** to stroll along the River Walk and see the eponymous waterfall. You'll find plenty of lodging options in Jackson for your first night. The charming town is dense with art galleries and boutiques. The **National Museum of Wildlife Art** has an impressive collection of artistic renderings of animals from around the world. Get your own look at those that frequent this region of Wyoming at the **National Elk Refuge** on the edge of town. If you're here in ski season, dedicate your day to **Snow King Mountain Resort, Grand Targhee Resort,** and **Jackson Hole Mountain Resort**—"the Big One."

## DAYS 8 AND 9: GRAND TETON NATIONAL PARK

In the morning, drive the 5 miles north to Grand Teton National Park, a land of rugged natural beauty. Popular sites and trails in the park include **Jenny Lake,** the **Taggart Lake Trail,** the **Mormon Row Historic District** and, of course, **Grand Teton** itself. On your first day, explore just north of Jenny Lake, pulling over to the **Leigh Lake Trailhead** for a hike. You can take the 3.8-mile loop around **String Lake,** or head north, then take the right-hand branch of the trail and follow the eastern shore of the lake (turn around at the campground on **Trapper Lake**) for a 9-mile hike. Spend your two nights at any of the excellent lodges or cabins in the park.

Your second day in the park, head back to Jenny Lake and catch a shuttle boat across to the western side, where you can take either a short hike along the **Cascade Canyon Trail** (2 miles round-trip) or hike the **Forks of Cascade Canyon,** a 9.6-mile trip that's well worth the effort. If you'd rather explore Jenny Lake from the water, rent a canoe or kayak or take a guided tour.

## DAYS 10, 11, 12: YELLOWSTONE NATIONAL PARK

Get up bright and early to drive just 7 miles north to reach Yellowstone, festooned with hot springs and geysers. Spend your first day on the park's 142-mile **Grand Loop Road.** This road forms a big figure eight as it passes nearly every major Yellowstone attraction, and offers interpretive displays, overlooks, and short trails along the way. For the most authentic Yellowstone experience, spend the night under the stars at the quiet **Slough Creek Campground** in Lamar Valley.

On your second day in the park, visit **Old Faithful** and take a short hike (about 2½ miles round-trip) around **Mystic Falls,** then head up to the Canyon Village section of the park for a look at the **Grand Canyon of Yellowstone,** with its two separate waterfalls. For a more strenuous option, hike from **Dunraven Pass** to the summit of **Mt. Washburn** for wildflowers, wildlife, and panoramic views (6.2 miles round-trip).

For your third day, explore the northern part of the park, starting with the **Mammoth Hot Springs** area, with its terraced limestone formations. From there, head past Tower-Roosevelt to the Lamar Valley in the far northeast corner of the park for gorgeous mountain views, enormous herds of bison, and your best chance to spot wolves. Then check out the **Mud Volcano** and **Sulphur Caldron** in the Hayden Valley area, just south of Canyon Village.

### DAY 13: CODY

Leave Yellowstone from the eastern entrance then drive an hour on towards Cody, a historic town with a Wild West pedigree. Named for showman Buffalo Bill Cody, the town of Cody takes great pride in its Old West history. Check out authentic cabins and artifacts from Wyoming's pioneer days at **Old Trail Town** or stop in at the **Buffalo Bill Center of the West,** a complex of five museums that includes the Buffalo Bill Museum, the Plains Indians Museum, and the Cody Firearms Museum. Stay at a former working cattle ranch, **K3 Guest Ranch Bed & Breakfast,** which offers Western-themed accommodations and an all-inclusive breakfast cooked over a campfire.

### DAY 14: BOZEMAN

Head out early and drive three hours to end your tour where you began. There is much to do in the university town of Bozeman. See an impressive collection of dinosaur fossils at the **Museum of the Rockies** or browse the shops and galleries downtown. If you're traveling in winter, hit the slopes at **Bridger Bowl Ski Area.** Grab dinner at the **Blackbird Kitchen,** a cute Italian spot with a wood-fired oven, or splurge on the last dinner of your road trip at **Open Range,** a classic Montana steak house. End your night on the town at the Bozeman institutions **Rockin' R Bar** and **the Haufbrau House.**

## Two Weeks: Southern Music and Nightlife

The music of the Southeast United States is like America's heartbeat, influencing artists in genres ranging from country to blues to jazz. It's where small-town musicians performed at humble venues like juke joints and honky-tonks before hitting it big like B.B. King, Elvis Presley, Dolly Parton, and countless others. Celebrate it all in varied terrain from cityscapes to the bayou, from the plains to the Appalachian Mountains.

### DAY 1: ATLANTA, GA

Start your epic tour of the Southeast in Georgia's capital. Spend the day outside walking trails along the **BeltLine** before stopping for lunch at **Krog Street Market,** or stay downtown to get up close to marine life at the **Georgia Aquarium** (the largest in the United States). Tour the **Martin Luther King Jr. National Historic Site,** which includes MLK's childhood home, his church, and a visitor center with exhibits on the civil rights movement. In the evening, sip brews at **SweetWater Brewing Company** or head to one of the many bars and restaurants.

### DAY 2: ATHENS, GA

Head two hours to the east to Athens, the launching pad for famed rock groups such as the B-52s and R.E.M., and the home of the University of Georgia. Visit the downtown clubs that made names for countless artists, including the **40 Watt Club** and the **Georgia Theatre.** You can also catch a performance at the historic **Morton Theatre,** a former vaudeville theater where Cab Calloway and Bessie Smith played. Spend a night at **the Graduate Hotel Athens,** located in a former iron foundry not far from campus. It has **the Foundry,** an in-house music venue, along with a spa and coffee shop.

### DAYS 3 AND 4: NASHVILLE, TN

The next day, head north to Nashville, stopping in the small town of Lynchburg, also known as the home of **Jack Daniel's Distillery.** It's here that all of the company's whiskey sold worldwide is produced. Take a tour or buy some bottles to go, waiting until you're clear to drive the rest of the way to Nashville (it's about 2½ hours total). When you get to Nashville, eat some famous "Nashville hot chicken," at **Prince's Hot Chicken,** where it was created, and then head out on the town to **Honky Tonk Highway** of Lower Broadway for live music and raucous nightlife.

The next day, start at the **Country Music Hall of Fame,** a sprawling museum that traces the genre's influences from church hymns and Appalachian "old time" music. The nearby, but attached, **Johnny Cash & Patsy Cline Museums** showcase items belonging to both artists, including the chair Cash used in his final music video and kitchen furniture from Cline's Virginia home. End your day at the **Grand Ole Opry,** a long-running radio broadcast that has made names out of countless country musicians.

## DAY 5: MUSCLE SHOALS, AL

Spend the morning of Day 5 in Nashville and then head to northwest Alabama's Muscle Shoals, a town with legendary recording studios referred to as a "small town with big sound." Visit **Fame Recording Studio** where big names like Aretha Franklin and Alicia Keys have recorded big hits. Alternatively, spend a third night in Nashville.

## DAYS 6 AND 7: MEMPHIS, TN

Bright and early, make the 2½-hour drive to Memphis, stopping at **the West Tennessee Delta Heritage Center/Tina Turner Museum** in the small town of Brownsville, which honors the local girl who became one of the world's most incredible performers. Make it to Memphis, that must-see destination for music lovers, for dinner, where you can get your fill of Memphis dry rub barbecue from the **Bar B Q Shop.** Afterward, head to **Beale Street,** the city's famous entertainment district where the music is always playing, with venues like **B.B. King's Blues Club** and **Rum Boogie Cafe. Hernando's Hideaway** is another music venue and restaurant where Elvis and his contemporaries played, now serving local beer and burgers. Stay at the grand **Peabody Hotel.**

On Day 7, visit **Graceland,** the residence of Elvis, which showcases his funky decor and impressive car collection. Then head to **Sun Studio,** offering tours of where the "Million Dollar Quartet" of Elvis, Johnny Cash, Jerry Lee Lewis, and Carl Perkins came together. Or head to the **Stax Museum of American Soul Music** to see exhibits on the recording label's iconic artists like Otis Redding and Carla Thomas.

## DAY 8: CLARKSDALE, MS

Take the one-hour drive south to Clarksdale to kick off your tour of the **Mississippi Blues Trail.** It starts when you see the giant electric guitars over the intersection of Highways 61 and 49, where it's said musician Robert Johnson sold his soul to the devil so he could play guitar. Clarksdale has iconic blues landmarks commemorating area musicians like Ike Turner, Muddy Waters, and Sam Cooke. Enter one of the juke joints (small music clubs) still in operation, like **Red's Lounge** or **Ground Zero Blues Club** (where Morgan Freeman is a co-owner)—both on the same block.

## DAY 9: JACKSON, MS

Head down to Jackson, Mississippi's state capital, for more Blues Trails stops, in addition to the **Mississippi Freedom Trail,** a collection of noteworthy sights related to the civil rights movement. There's Medgar Evers's House plus the sight of the 1963 Woolworth sit-in. You can delve deeper at **the Mississippi Civil Rights Museum** and **the Smith Robertson Museum and Cultural Center.** Explore the **Fondren District,** where you can tuck into soul food and barbecue, and eat at the newer bars and restaurants now on the scene.

## DAYS 10 AND 11: NEW ORLEANS

Three hours south of Jackson brings you to the birthplace of jazz and host of the most festive party in the South, **Mardi Gras.** (If you're really into jazz, time your visit for the Jazz Fest in October or Mardi Gras in February.) Spend your day exploring the **French Quarter,** taking a ghost tour, and seeking out live jazz musicians in front of **Jackson Square** and **Congo Square** in the Tremé (where greats like Jelly Roll Morton and Louis Armstrong once lived). Grab a po' boy or some gumbo for dinner and head to **Frenchmen Street** to legendary clubs like **Blue Nile** and **the Spotted Cat** to see today's best jazz musicians play live.

On Day 11, revive yourself with coffee and beignets at **Café du Monde** before exploring the **Bywater** and **Marigny** neighborhoods, the mansions and gardens of the **Garden District,** or galleries in the **Art District.** If you're a Mardi Gras fanatic, head to **Mardi Gras World** to see giant festive floats, and at night, descend upon **Bourbon Street** to partake in the revelry.

### DAY 12: FLORA-BAMA

It's a three-hour drive from New Orleans to the "Flora-Bama," a general name given to the towns along the Florida and Alabama state line, including Gulf Shores and Orange Beach. The **Hugh Branyon Backcountry Trail** connects these beach communities through a paved bike path where you might spot an alligator lazily sleeping on the creek bed. **Gulf State Park** also has trails and beaches. End your night at the **Flora-Bama Lounge,** a legendary dive bar on the state line. It frequently hosts country music acts, mechanical bull riding, and even church services in the maze of rooms covered with discarded bras. Sip on a Bushwhacker, a boozy slushie popular on the coast.

### DAY 13: SOUTH WALTON, FL

From Flora-Bama, it's about 2½ hours to South Walton, Florida, home to beautiful beach towns and the **30 A Songwriters Festival,** which draws more than 175 songwriters for over 225 performances at more than 25 venues on the beach. Even if you're not here for the epic festival in January, this is a good place to sink your toes into sugar-white sand year-round. Explore the town of **Seaside,** which was used as the main filming location for the movie *The Truman Show,* and the dunes of **Grayton Beach State Park** before catching live music at **Red Bar** or at **Bud and Alley's.** Spend the night at **WaterColor Inn** or rent a seaside cottage.

### DAY 14: MACON TO ATLANTA, GA

Stay another day or two at the beach or make your way back to Atlanta to come full circle on your journey. If you go back to the Peach State, stop a few hours south of Atlanta in Macon, the birthplace of Southern rock. It was here that Otis Redding, the Allman Brothers Band, and Little Richard all performed and got their start. Learn about these influential artists at the **Big House,** the **Allman Brothers Band Museum,** and the **Capricorn Museum.** Give yourself a few hours to savor the music.

## Two Weeks: Bourbon Country

Louisville, Kentucky, is, and probably always will be, the heart of bourbon country, so it's the perfect place to begin and end an eight-day, six-state whirlwind whiskey road trip to discover not just Kentucky bourbon and Tennessee whiskey, but contributions from Virginia, Ohio, Indiana, and more as whiskey distilling booms across all 50 states. It goes without saying, but we'll say it anyway: it's especially important to drink responsibly throughout this itinerary and never drink and drive.

### DAY 1: LOUISVILLE, KY

Bourbon is best in this town, where you can base yourself for excursions to a few distilleries on the Bourbon Trail. Stop in Shelbyville, about 45 minutes from Louisville, and check out the **Bulleit Distilling Co. Visitor Experience.** A half hour from Shelbyville is Versailles, where you'll want to stop to explore **Woodford Reserve Distillery** for a far more traditional approach to whiskey making. Stay at **Vu Guesthouse,** a boutique with mystique to spare.

### DAYS 2 AND 3: LEXINGTON, KY

Visit the **Old Pepper Distillery,** where James E. Pepper is once again being distilled after the lot sat abandoned for more than 50 years. Now revitalized, it's the centerpiece of the Lexington Distillery District, featuring 25 acres of shops, eateries, and plenty of spots to stop for additional sips. Don't venture off without touring the distillery's fascinating (small) history museum. With more than 400 horse farms in the city, Lexington is the "horse capital of the world," so you may want to check out a stately site like **Keeneland Race Course** to enjoy the beautiful grounds, scope out some stellar horses, or catch a Thoroughbred race. It's open daily to the public. Spend the night at **Origin Lexington.**

## DAY 4: BARDSTOWN, KY

Today's goal is only about 60 miles southwest of Lexington, but it's smack between two classic distilleries you won't want to miss. On the way, just over a half hour from Lexington, Lawrenceburg is home to **Wild Turkey Distillery,** where the world's longest-tenured master distiller continues to oversee whiskey traditions that predate Prohibition. You'll also find Matthew McConaughey's favorite bourbon, **Longbranch,** here (he created it). The tour and tasting will take one hour. Bardstown is more than a place to crash for the night. Depending on how early you get started today, you should be able to visit at least one or two of its main attractions, including the **Oscar Getz Museum of Whiskey History, Women's Civil War Museum,** and **My Old Kentucky Home** mansion. There are even a couple of distilleries in town if you're up for more tasting (you're done driving for the day, so go for it).

## DAY 5: MAMMOTH CAVE, KY

Start fairly early today and head to Mammoth Cave National Park, home of the world's longest known cave system, just over an hour from Bardstown. Arrange a spelunking or hiking tour to explore on a cave tour (**Cleveland Avenue** is one of the best) and head to lunch at the **Porky Pig Diner** before or after your adventure. You can stay nearby or head to Nashville, about a 1½-hour drive away.

## DAYS 6 AND 7: NASHVILLE, TN

You'll trip over things to do in Nashville (hello, **Grand Ole Opry** and **Honky Tonk Highway**!), but make sure one of them is a visit to **Nelson's Green Brier Distillery.** With a dramatic history including shipwreck and lost family fortune on the way to seeking the American dream, Charles Nelson went from soap maker to grocer to distiller, becoming one of the pioneers of whiskey bottling before Prohibition closed the business. Generations later, descendants rediscovered the distillery and relaunched the brand exactly 100 years after it closed. Stay on theme with dinner at **Whiskey Kitchen.** Alongside the city's largest collection of whiskeys, you'll find delish pub fare like the Fried Green Tomato BLT, Lowcountry Pulled Pork sandwich, and a city staple, Nashville Hot Fried Chicken. Slip into Nashville's new urban style with a stay at **Fieldhouse Jones** in the city's artsy East Nashville neighborhood.

## DAY 8: BLOOMINGTON, IN

It's almost a five-hour drive to Bloomington from Nashville, but make a stop about two hours in to **Abraham Lincoln Birthplace National Historic Park,** the first memorial to Lincoln, or in Borden to **Starlight Distillery** at Huber's Orchard, Winery & Vineyards, about an hour from the Abe Lincoln detour or three hours direct from Nashville. When in Bloomington, tour **Fountain Square** or **Hoosier National Forest.** In the evening, visit Bloomington's first craft distillery, **Cardinal Spirits,** for dinner, drinks, and a tour. You're halfway through your whirlwind whiskey odyssey now, so take a break to appreciate sips of Cardinal's vodka, gin, or rum—these are the specialty here. Check in to the **Showers Inn Bed & Breakfast** for a cozy stay in the center of town.

## DAYS 9 AND 10: INDIANAPOLIS AND COLUMBUS, OH

Head north to Indianapolis before venturing east along Interstate 70 East for the majority of today's shorter drive (four hours total). A stop in Indianapolis will keep the second leg just over 2½ hours. While in the capital city, stop by **Westfork Whiskey Co.** for smooth sips of distilled Indiana grains in the tasting room. Other options include checking out the **Eiteljorg Museum of Native American and Western Art, White River Gardens, Kurt Vonnegut Museum and Library,** and, of course, **Indianapolis Motor Speedway.** When you make it to Columbus, tour **Middle West Spirits,** where it's all about appreciating the good life: one cofounder describes a sip here as an "everyday special occasion." Try the ryes, including dark pumpernickel, and remember that bourbon doesn't have to be made in Kentucky—it's just a myth—so give it a go, perhaps in a cocktail at **Service Bar,** on-site. Stay at the **Blackwell Inn.**

## DAY 11: PURCELLVILLE, VA

Today's drive is the longest of the trip clocking in at just over 6½ hours, traveling west into northeast Virginia. You may be surprised to learn that Virginia is the birthplace of American whiskey, but it's true. Visit **Catoctin Creek Distilling Company** to tour the facility, try a whiskey flight, and snag a bottle of Virginia's most awarded whiskey, Roundstone Rye, to take home. A tour and tasting combo here will take about an hour. You're clearly in town for Catoctin Creek, but this is wine country, so you may want to check out one or two of the many surrounding wineries. For a less alcohol-centered activity, there aren't many spots more charming than **Blooming Hill Lavender Farm,** open to the public for strolling and shopping. **Springdale Village Inn** is the bed-and-breakfast for you in Purcellville.

## DAYS 12 AND 13: ALEXANDRIA, VA AND MAXWELTON, WV

An hour east of Purcellville, stop at **George Washington's Distillery** at Mount Vernon in Alexandria to tour a re-creation of one of the nation's earliest large-scale whiskey distilleries, and one of the most profitable ventures on Washington's estate. Sample one last taste of Virginia whiskey at **KO Distilling** in Manassas, about 45 minutes west of Alexandria. Try a flight of Bare Knuckle whiskeys, including straight bourbon, wheat, and rye, from this relative newcomer to the craft distilling scene. Have lunch in Manassas before the final 3½-hour haul to Maxwelton. At **the Bone BBQ,** you'll find pulled pork, hickory-smoked chicken, smoked turkey, brisket, and more served with sweet-potato fries and mac 'n' cheese. Finally, arrive in Maxwelton. Get a taste of Appalachian whiskey at **Smooth Ambler Spirits** in the West Virginia mountains, where they believe their clean water, crisp air, and ideal climate produce some of the country's top spirits.

## DAY 14: LOUSIVILLE, KY

Make the five-hour drive back to Louisville, which you can break up by stopping in Charleston, about 3½ hours into your drive. When you make it to Louisville, celebrate: there is a ton of whiskey and bourbon to be had here. The great news is you can walk to many of the distilleries (or their outposts) in town, so you can taste a little more enthusiastically than when you were driving. Three spots you must hit are **Old Forester Distilling Co.,** home of America's first bottled bourbon; **Angel's Envy Distillery,** finished in port wine casks; and **Rabbit Hole Distillery,** a hypermodern outfit with an art collection as covetable as its spirits. Have one last carnivorous feast at **Steak & Bourbon** where, as you'd guess, large slabs of beef and an even larger bourbon collection (about 70 varieties) are the specialties.

# Two Weeks: Great American Baseball Road Trip

If you're looking for a romanticized version of baseball history, head to Dyersville, Iowa. That's where you can tour the baseball diamond used in the movie *Field of Dreams*. (It's actually lots of fun, especially for kids.) But if you want to discover the sport's real history, take this driving tour from Boston's Fenway Park to Chicago's Wrigley Field. Besides the stadiums along the route—and there are a lot—we point you to some interesting landmarks where baseball history was made. This trip involves a minimum of 24 hours of driving, so you're talking about a trip lasting a week or two. Feel free to use it as a jumping-off point for your own baseball fantasy trip.

## DAYS 1 AND 2: BOSTON

Start at one of baseball's most beloved landmarks, Boston's **Fenway Park.** Opened in 1912, it's Major League Baseball's most venerable ballfield still in use today. You'll want to catch a game, but it's also well worth taking a tour for a chance to take in the sweeping views from the roof deck overlooking right field.

Heading out of town, consider a brief side trip to Holliston, Massachusetts, one of several towns that claims to be the inspiration of Ernest L. Thayer's immortal ode to baseball, "Casey at the Bat." There's an actual neighborhood called **Mudville,** and you can take a selfie with the "Welcome to Mudville" sign or the truly terrible statue of the fictional ballplayer.

## DAY 3: COOPERSTOWN, NY

It's a little less than four hours west to Cooperstown, New York, home to the **National Baseball Hall of Fame.** This don't-miss destination is jam-packed with memorabilia from the sport's earliest days. One of the most interesting exhibits documents the challenges black players faced before and after Jackie Robinson was recognized as the first black player in the major leagues when he joined the Brooklyn Dodgers in 1947. (It also documents how a former slave named Moses Fleetwood Walker actually broke the color line in 1884.) If you're in town in May, catch the annual Hall of Fame Classic at **Doubleday Field,** a handsome ballfield dating back to 1920.

## DAYS 4 AND 5: NEW YORK CITY

A four-hour drive south through the Hudson Valley takes you to New York City, home to two major league teams that spark a bitter rivalry between the hometown fans: the Yankees and the Mets. The Bronx Bombers play at **Yankee Stadium,** a 50,287-seat behemoth built in 2009. Although it doesn't have the history of the original stadium built in 1923—where 74,200 fans streamed through the turnstiles to see Babe Ruth play on opening day—it's still one of the most breathtaking ballparks to take in a game. Don't miss Monument Park, which displays the retired numbers of the team's greatest players.

The same year the Yankees moved to their new home, the Mets did the same. Shea Stadium was a classic, but **Citi Field** has plenty of fans who say the 41,922-seat stadium skillfully blends the old and the new. (And it has a Shake Shack in center field.) Jackie Robinson also gets a shoutout here, and the Jackie Robinson Rotunda is a must for those who love the history of the game.

At this point you have a choice: head directly west toward Pittsburgh, or continue south toward Philadelphia, Baltimore, and Washington, D.C. The latter is a slightly longer route, adding about two hours to your driving time, but takes in three more ballfields. (Tough choice, we know.)

## DAY 6: PATERSON, NJ AND WILLIAMSPORT, PA

If you decide on the westerly route, make a stop in Paterson, New Jersey. Here is a little-known landmark: **Hinchliffe Stadium,** one of the last surviving stadiums that hosted Negro League baseball in the 1930s and 1940s. The Black Yankees played here, drawing crowds from all over the region. Declared a National Historic Landmark in 2013, the art deco stadium has been sadly neglected, but there are plans to return it to its former luster.

You also should consider a stop at **Howard J. Lamade Stadium** in Williamsport, Pennsylvania. Thousands of fresh-faced baseball players return here year after year for the Little League World Series. The stadium, built in 1959, holds 40,000 fans, and even more stake out a spot on the hill rising up beyond the outfield. Williamsport is also home to another "Casey at the Bat" statue, this one a little more dignified. Spend the night here.

## DAYS 7 AND 8: PHILADELPHIA, PA

If you are headed south, your next stop is Philadelphia, home to the Phillies and **Citizen Bank Park.** On average there are more home runs here than at just about any other major league field, so you're bound to see some action. And when a Phillies player knocks one out of the park, a replica of the Liberty Bell peals. (You don't see that at every stadium.)

## DAY 9: BALTIMORE, MD

In Baltimore, **Oriole Park at Camden Yards** is one of the most beloved stadiums in the sport. Built in 1992, its style, a throwback to classic ballfields of the early 20th century, influenced architects for a generation. (When you see PNC Park in Pittsburgh, you'll likely recognize echoes of this beauty.) Nearby is the **Babe Ruth Birthplace and Museum,** which pays tribute to the man who is still regarded as one of the best players in history.

## DAYS 10 AND 11: WASHINGTON, D.C.

The Washington Nationals play at **Nationals Park,** another retro-style stadium built in 2008. It was the first stadium built with eco-friendliness in mind, so it uses less power and encourages its fans to ride their bikes to the game. The quirkiest part of a game here is seeing the Presidents Race, featuring big-headed versions George Washington, Thomas Jefferson, Abraham Lincoln, and Teddy Roosevelt sprinting through the outfield.

## DAY 12: PITTSBURGH, PA

At this point you're going to Pittsburgh, home of **PNC Park.** The city skyline provides an excellent backdrop to the games. Unlike a lot of the rowdier stadiums, the home field of the Pittsburgh Pirates is somewhere to bring the whole family. Kids are even encouraged to run the bases after games on Sunday.

Before there was PNC Park, the Pirates played at Forbes Field, where one of baseball's most fondly remembered plays took place. It was here that second baseman Bill Mazeroski hit a home run over the left-center outfield wall in Game 7 of the 1960 World Series, cementing a win over the Yankees. The stadium is long gone, but the **Forbes Field Wall** still stands on the campus of the University of Pittsburgh. Have your photo taken in front of the wall, still marked with the number 406 to show how far he sent the ball.

## DAY 13: CLEVELAND, DETROIT, OR CHICAGO

Heading west, you pass pretty close to **Progressive Field** in Cleveland (the biggest video screen in baseball) and **Comerica Park** in Detroit (with a Ferris wheel with cars shaped like baseballs); both downtown stadiums well worth a detour.

## DAY 14: CHICAGO

Power through another four to five hours to Chicago. Built in 1914 on the North Side of Chicago, **Wrigley Field** is still a classic. (Fans rank it right behind the hands-down favorite, Fenway Park.) You can feel the history—imagine Babe Ruth's famous "called shot" during the 1932 World Series. And Wrigleyville is the perfect neighborhood for a hometown team.

## Three Weeks: West Coast National Parks

From the otherworldly desertscapes, soaring redwoods, and eye-popping canyons of California to the volcanic peaks, lush rain forests, and pristine beaches of the Pacific Northwest, the West Coast contains some of the country's most celebrated national parks. You probably already have destinations like Yosemite, Crater Lake, and Mt. Rainier on your bucket list, and on this tour you'll have the opportunity to see what makes these iconic parks so special. We hope you like driving, since you'll need a minimum of three weeks to complete the journey.

### DAY 1: LOS ANGELES OR PALM SPRINGS

You have two options for a base. You could stay in the City of Angels for your epic West Coast tour, spending the first day strolling along the **Hollywood Walk of Fame** or soaking up the sun on **Santa Monica** beach. For dinner, head to the **Reel Inn,** a funky, old-school spot in Malibu that's perfect for a casual seafood feast and is perhaps most famous for its mahimahi sandwiches and pepper-seared ahi salads.

The second option is Palm Springs, a small desert city that's a popular gateway to Joshua Tree National Park. The Coachella Valley's classic desert resort community is worth at least a short stop on the way to the park to stroll among downtown's distinctive design shops, galleries, and eateries and maybe even to ride the thrilling **Palm Springs Aerial Tramway,** which carries passengers through Chino Canyon to an elevation of 8,516 feet, near the summit of Mt. San Jacinto. Here you can hop out for a view east that takes in Joshua Tree, and even set out on an alpine hike.

### DAYS 2 AND 3: JOSHUA TREE NATIONAL PARK

This 800,000-acre expanse of the Mojave and Sonoran deserts contains hundreds of the distinctive Joshua trees for which the park is named. It can be appreciated in a day, but allowing two will give you the chance to explore some of the scenery a bit farther afield, such as making the somewhat challenging 2-mile hike to **Lost Horse Mine.** Joshua Tree's Park Boulevard extends for more than 50 miles through the park, and especially if you're staying in Palm Springs one or both nights, it's worth either starting or ending on this drive via the park's southeastern entrance off Interstate 10.

Must-sees that are easy to access from the main park road include the boulder-strewn paths around **Skull Rock** and the **Jumbo Rocks Campground** and **Hidden Valley** and **Cap Rock,** which you can tour via easy loop trails dotted in places with Joshua trees. Be sure to make the 6-mile side drive to **Keys View** overlook, from which you can see the San Andreas Fault and the Salton Sea, and on clear days, the craggy mountain peaks of northern Mexico. Stay at **29 Palms Inn.**

### DAY 4: DEATH VALLEY NATIONAL PARK

Four hours away is your next stop. At 3.4 million square miles, Death Valley is the largest U.S. national park outside Alaska, and although its name hints at some of the hottest temperatures and most unforgiving terrain in the world, it's also a land of considerable diversity, with multicolored canyons, 11,000-foot peaks, undulating sand dunes, and fragrant wildflower meadows. Start the day with a drive along 9-mile **Artist's Drive,** admiring the brilliantly hued landscape, then continuing on a short distance north to the rewarding 2-mile **Golden Canyon Interpretive Trail.** Later in the day, check out **Zabriskie Point,** which takes in the park's dramatic, multihued hills, and **Dante's View,** a mile-high lookout in the Black Mountains from which you can see many of Death Valley's most remarkable features. Stay in **Inn at Furnace Creek.**

### DAYS 5 AND 6: SEQUOIA AND KINGS CANYON

Because getting here entails a long six-hour drive, and Sequoia and Kings Canyon are actually two distinct but contiguous parks, it's worth developing a strategy before deciding on your exact route. If time is limited or you're traveling by RV, plan to spend one night in **Kings Canyon's Grant Corner Village,** limiting your time in Sequoia to the park's northern reaches, and arriving via Highway 180. If you're able to stay two nights and you're driving a vehicle shorter in length than 22 feet, you could drive to Sequoia the first night via windy but scenic Highway 198 to see towering, ancient conifers—the world's largest trees—and then spend a second night in Kings Canyon appreciating sweeping alpine peaks and valleys. Stay at the grand, cedar-and-stone **Wuksachi Lodge** in Sequoia, and timber-frame **John Muir Lodge** in Kings Canyon.

### DAY 7: YOSEMITE NATIONAL PARK

Take a 3½-hou drive to Yosemite, one of the most celebrated landscapes in America. During a shorter stay, you can view the stands of imposing sequoia trees in **Mariposa Grove** in Wawona, which is the easiest area to access if coming from Fresno. And you can focus the rest of your time on the iconic sites of Yosemite Valley—admiring legendary **El Capitan** (the largest exposed-granite monolith on the planet), checking out the roaring triple cascades of 2,425-foot-tall **Yosemite Falls,** driving (or taking a free park shuttle) to the overlook atop **Glacier Point** for an astounding view of the valley, and embarking on one or two shorter or even half-day hikes, such as the 3-mile **Mist Trail** to **Vernal Fall** or the 8.5-mile **Panorama Trail** from Glacier Point, which provides you terrific views of **Half Dome.** Stay at the grand stone-and-timber **Ahwahnee.**

### DAY 8: LASSEN VOLCANIC NATIONAL PARK

Get up bright and early for a six-hour drive to Lassen, named for the now dormant plug volcano at its heart. The 165-square-mile national park is more diverse than its name suggests, offering miles of trails through dense alpine forests and wildflower meadows. The drive north along Lassen Park Highway is a gem, passing by the Devastated Area, which still shows evidence of the volcano's 1915 eruption, and leading to the gorgeous scenery around **Manzanita Lake,** where you can visit the excellent **Loomis Museum** and enjoy a stroll along the 1-mile **Lily Pond Nature Trail.** Other draws include the 3-mile round-trip **Bumpass Hell Trail,** which reveals some of the park's most exciting geothermal features, including steam vents, mud pots, and boiling lakes, and assuming you're fit for a 2,000-foot climb, undertaking the 2.5-mile hike to the 10,457-foot summit of **Lassen Peak.** Stay at the **Highlands Ranch Resort.**

### DAY 9: CRATER LAKE NATIONAL PARK

A four-hour backcountry drive through northeastern California's sparsely populated Lassen and Modoc national forests and southern Oregon's Cascade Range abounds with bewitching natural scenery. Once you've arrived, the 33-mile **Rim Drive** loop around America's clearest and deepest lake offers dazzling views at numerous vista points, especially Sun Notch, Discovery Point, and Cloudcap Overlook, which also affords views of the park's highest point, Mt. Scott, an 8,934-foot volcano. If you have a full day to visit the park, take a boat cruise to Wizard Island and hike to the top of this cinder cone, which rises 763 feet above the lake's surface, for a distinctive view of the rim and the lake. This is also a good place to hike part of the **Pacific Crest Trail,** which extends 33 miles through the park. Stay at **Crater Lake Lodge.**

### DAY 10: MT. HOOD AND PORTLAND

Take a four-hour drive north to Portland, where you can stretch your legs and grab lunch, checking into a hip hotel. Then head to Mt. Hood, Oregon's tallest peak. Hike there and return to spend the night in Portland, perhaps on the East Side, where you can peruse the bistros and bars of the **Alberta Arts District.** Alternative options include powering through another hour of driving to **Mt. St. Helens,** a powerful volcano that erupted in 1980. You can get a good view from the **Johnson Ridge Observatory.**

### DAY 11: MOUNT RAINIER NATIONAL PARK

Onward! From Mt. St. Helens it's two hours to Mt. Rainier; from Portland it's about two hours 20 minutes. Make your first stop **Henry M. Jackson Memorial Visitor Center** followed by a stroll amid the wildflower-carpeted meadows around the park's lofty Paradise section, on the mountain's southern slope. One slightly ambitious but highly rewarding hike from this area is the 5-mile round-trip **Skyline Trail,** which leads over sheer alpine ridges to an astounding overlook, **Panorama Point.** Overnight at **Paradise Inn.**

### DAY 12: NORTH CASCADES NATIONAL PARK

It's a long haul (6½ hours) to this somewhat underrated and remote park that's home to many of the last surviving glaciers in the Lower 48 as well as nearly 800 square miles of stunning wilderness and glacial lakes. Apart from remote **Stehekin,** the park's most popular draws are the 95-mile stretch of Highway 20 (aka the North Cascades Highway) that traverses the park and offers a slew of hiking trailheads—some of them through coniferous old-growth forest—and memorable vistas, the most famous of which is 5,477-foot **Washington Pass.** If you're driving through the park in just one day, stop and soak up the views of intensely turquoise-blue **Diablo Lake** from the vista point at mile marker 132, and check out **Gorge Creek Falls,** where you can admire a radiant 242-foot cataract. Stay at **Silver Bay Inn.**

### DAYS 13 AND 14: OLYMPIC NATIONAL PARK

You know the drill—wake up early for your six-hour drive to one of the most geographically diverse parks in the country. This 1,442-square-mile expanse of jagged, snowcapped mountain peaks, peaceful rain forests, rippling alpine lakes, and stunning, boulder-strewn beaches is best enjoyed over a few days, ideally overnighting in a couple of different areas. If you're short on time and have just one night, plan to stay in **Port Angeles** and drive to mile-high Hurricane Ridge for the rugged 3-mile **Hurricane Hill** loop hike. Then as you make your way around the Olympic Peninsula, spend an hour or two traipsing through **Hoh River Rain Forest**—sometimes dubbed the quietest place in the United States—and time your visit to explore the coast at **Ruby Beach** and **La Push** late in the day to enjoy the sunset. If you're able to spend a bit more time in the park, explore the shores and nearby woodlands of **Lake Quinault** and its gorgeous **Lake Quinault Lodge.**

### DAY 15: LEWIS AND CLARK NATIONAL HISTORICAL PARK

Follow U.S. 101 west from Port Angeles to kick off your five-hour drive to this Oregon park, stopping in the town of **Aberdeen** along the way. Arrive and explore this engaging historical park with units on both the Washington and Oregon sides of the mouth of the mighty Columbia River. Spend the morning in Oregon, visiting the interpretive center and re-creation of Fort Clatsop, and set out on the 1½-mile

**Netul Landing Trail.** Later in the day, cross back into Washington to explore **Cape Disappointment State Park,** with its rugged sea cliffs and beach hikes, two lighthouses that you can reach by short and easy trails, and the **Lewis & Clark Interpretive Center,** which is perched high on a bluff and presents interesting exhibits about the Corps of Discovery expedition as well as the region's natural and human history. This part of the park is beautiful at sunset. Stay at **Adrift Hotel.**

### DAY 16: OREGON DUNES NATIONAL RECREATION AREA

The five-hour journey to Oregon Dunes is a simple, straight shot down U.S. 101, also known as the Oregon Coast Highway. However, this is also one of the prettiest coastal drives in the country. Encompassing a 40-mile swath of shoreline that's home to the largest expanse of natural sand dunes in North America, this popular spot for beachcombing and dune buggy rides is a fun place to kick off your shoes and cavort in the wind and sun. Some dunes reach as high as 500 feet. At **Honeyman Memorial State Park** in Florence, you can book dune buggy tours. For a quieter ramble, pull off at the **Oregon Dunes Day Use Area,** just off U.S. 101 across from Lost Lake (near mile marker 201), and scamper among these giant mounds of sand. Stay at **River House Inn.**

### DAY 17: REDWOOD NATIONAL AND STATE PARKS

Drive three hours south along the coast to Redwood National Park and State Parks, the definitive place to walk amid towering giants, which can rise to more than 350 feet and differ from the sequoias in that they grow near the coast. Start with **Del Norte Coast Redwoods State Park,** where you can saunter along the pristine sands of **Wilson Beach** and **False Klamath Cove** and explore several large groves of redwoods. The best place to spend the bulk of your time is the **Prairie Creek Redwoods State Park** section, which is just off U.S. 101. Here you can drive 10-mile **Newton B. Drury Scenic Parkway,** admiring trees along the way, stopping at several points—notably the Big Tree Wayside—for short hikes. Stay in Crescent City, grabbing a pint of craft beer at **SeaQuake Brewing** in the evening.

### DAY 18: POINT REYES NATIONAL SEASHORE

It's five hours to this 71,000-acre national seashore set on a lush, windswept peninsula in the Pacific, just 30 miles north of San Francisco. It's a pristine patchwork of drives and hikes atop 100-foot sea cliffs, along pristine beaches, and past wildlife-rich estuaries. It's worth driving to the farthest point in the park, **Lighthouse Visitor Center,** for a trek over a dramatic headland where you can often spy gray whales just off the coast during the winter and spring migratory periods. Stay in **Olema House.**

### DAY 19: PINNACLES NATIONAL PARK

Three hours from Point Reyes, this remarkable volcanic landscape feels like two separate places, as it's accessed from either the east or west, and there's no road connecting the two entrances. From Point Reyes National Seashore, take Highway 1 through the gorgeous Marin Headlands to U.S. 101, continue south over the **Golden Gate Bridge** through San Francisco, and continue on. In the eastern section of the park, you can view the excellent exhibits at the **Bear Gulch Nature Center,** before embarking on the **Bear Gulch Trail** to the famed **Bear Gulch Caves.** On the western side, drive to the Chaparral Trailhead area for a grand view of the park's High Peak, and take the 2½-mile **Balconies Cliffs-Cave Loop.** For any of these hikes to the park's caves, make sure you pack a flashlight before setting out.

## DAY 20: CHANNEL ISLANDS NATIONAL PARK

It's four hours on Highway 101 to this nautical park that comprises five islands off the coast of **Santa Barbara, Ventura,** and **Oxnard.** The only way to visit any of them is via a boat excursion (or your own private boat). A few different companies offer a variety of cruises to the archipelago, some specializing in scuba diving, kayaking, and other activities. There are no lodging or dining options in the park, other than camping and picnicking, but there are few prettier coastal locales in California for these activities. If you have just a day, the best plan is to stop by the park visitor center in Ventura to learn about the islands, which range in size from 1-square-mile Santa Barbara to the quite extensive 96-square-mile **Santa Cruz Island**. You could then take an hour-long excursion on one of Island Packers high-speed catamarans to Santa Cruz Island from either Ventura or Oxnard. Once on the island, you can hike amid the unspoiled landscape of 2,500-foot mountains and dramatic canyons, viewing the many kinds of flora and fauna that thrive here, and learn about the indigenous Chumash communities that once lived here. Stay in **Rosewood Miramar Beach** in Santa Barbara.

## DAY 21: LOS ANGELES

And, exhale! It's an hour and 30 minutes to Los Angeles, where you're finished with your whirlwind adventure of the entire West Coast. From Ventura, U.S. 101 is the fastest and most direct way into Los Angeles, but branching off onto coastal Highway 1 in Oxnard and continuing along it through Malibu and Santa Monica offers much prettier scenery, and depending on traffic, it doesn't necessarily take much longer.

Chapter 3

# NEW ENGLAND



Written by
Andrew Collins

# WELCOME TO NEW ENGLAND

## TOP REASONS TO GO

★ **Leaf-peeping:** Ogle autumn at Moosehead Lake in Maine, the Kancamagus Highway in New Hampshire, Scenic Route 100 in Vermont, and U.S. 7 in the Berkshires.

★ **American history:** Explore fascinating colonial historic sites, such as Plimoth Patuxet Museums, Salem, Boston's Freedom Trail, and Walden Pond.

★ **Coastal charm:** Sail, bike, and beachcomb on a beautiful island, maybe Nantucket or Martha's Vineyard in Massachusetts, Mount Desert Island in Maine' or Block Island in the Ocean State.

★ **Mountain majesty:** In Vermont's Green Mountains, New Hampshire's White Mountains, and interior Maine, some of the East Coast's tallest peaks beckon hikers in summer and skiers and snowboarders in winter.

★ **Seafood:** Eat your way through the region's many hubs of artisanal food and drink, including Burlington, New Haven, Portland, and Providence.

**1 Connecticut.** Vibrant small cities, alluring coastal towns, grand old inns, and a pair of famous casinos appeal to a wide range of visitors.

**2 Maine.** Classic villages, rocky shorelines, lobster shacks, and picturesque main streets abound along the coast, while the rugged interior attracts outdoors enthusiasts.

**3 Massachusetts.** Home to New England's largest city, this diverse state also offers seaside, a thriving arts scene, and elegant country inns.

**4 New Hampshire.** Portsmouth is the star of the state's 18-mile coastline, while the Lakes Region is a popular summertime escape, and the White Mountains' dramatic vistas attract year-round visitors.

**5 Rhode Island.** The nation's smallest state has big draws: great sailing and glitzy mansions in Newport, beautiful beaches in South County and Block Island, and a hip scene in Providence.

**6 Vermont.** The peaceful Green Mountain State has farms, freshly starched towns and lively small cities, quiet country lanes, and bustling ski resorts.

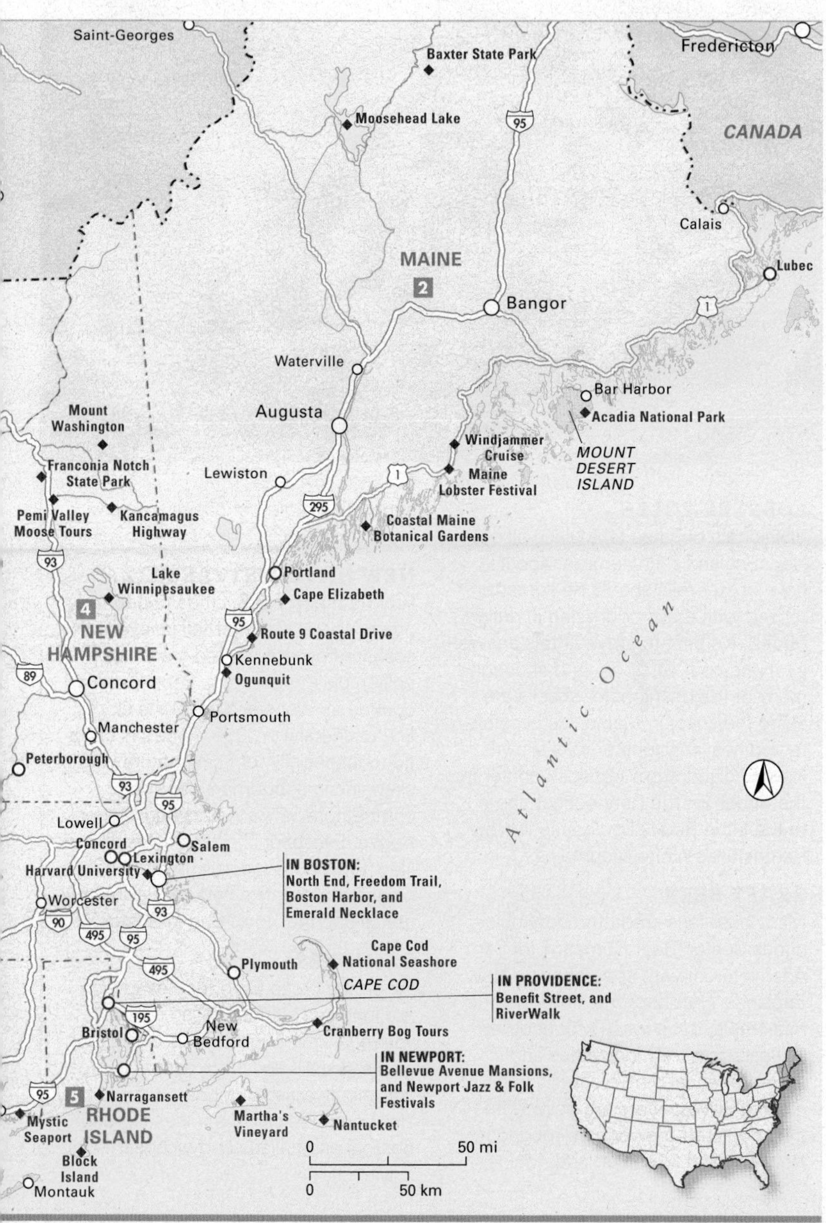

Saint-Georges
Baxter State Park
Fredericton
Moosehead Lake
95
CANADA
Calais
MAINE
2
Lubec
Bangor
1
Waterville
Bar Harbor
Augusta
Acadia National Park
Mount
Washington
Windjammer
Cruise
MOUNT
DESERT
ISLAND
Franconia Notch
State Park
Lewiston
1
Maine
Lobster Festival
295
Pemi Valley
Moose Tours
Kancamagus
Highway
Coastal Maine
Botanical Gardens
93
Lake
Winnipesaukee
Portland
Cape Elizabeth
4
NEW
HAMPSHIRE
95
Route 9 Coastal Drive
Kennebunk
Ogunquit
89
Concord
Atlantic Ocean
Manchester
Portsmouth
Peterborough
93
95
Lowell
Concord
Salem
Lexington
Harvard University
IN BOSTON:
North End, Freedom Trail,
Boston Harbor, and
Emerald Necklace
Worcester
90
93
495
95
Cape Cod
National Seashore
Plymouth
495
CAPE COD
IN PROVIDENCE:
Benefit Street, and
RiverWalk
195
Bristol
New
Bedford
Cranberry Bog Tours
IN NEWPORT:
Bellevue Avenue Mansions,
and Newport Jazz & Folk
Festivals
95
5
Narragansett
RHODE
ISLAND
Mystic
Seaport
Martha's
Vineyard
Nantucket
0
50 mi
Block
Island
Montauk
0
50 km

# WHAT TO EAT AND DRINK IN NEW ENGLAND

Lobster roll

## LOBSTER ROLLS
Passionate debates take place all over New England each summer about how lobster rolls should be served: tossed with mayo or drizzled in drawn butter? It's best to arrive at this answer by trying both versions. And although many of the best lobster shacks are along the coast in Maine, it's possible to find heavenly lobster rolls all over New England, from Abbot's Lobster in the Rough on the Connecticut shore to the Little Red Schoolhouse in New Hampshire's White Mountains.

## CRAFT BEER
Many beer fans credit the now ubiquitous Boston Beer Company (of Sam Adams fame) with spearheading New England's craft beer movement in the mid-1980s, but it wasn't for another 20 years that truly innovative and entrepreneurial brewers really began making waves. There are now more than 600 craft breweries throughout New England, with Portland, Maine, supporting more per capita than any city in America.

## NEW HAVEN–STYLE PIZZA
Among the first U.S. cities to popularize pizza, New Haven first fell in love with coal-fired-oven, blistered-crust Neapolitan pies when Frank Pepe Pizzeria opened on Wooster Street (the city's tiny Little Italy) in 1925. Pepe's is still a go-to (especially for its signature white clam version), but many fans favor competitors Sally's Apizza and Modern Apizza. Exceptional pizza thrives all over New England, especially in Little Italy neighborhoods, like Federal Hill in Providence and the North End in Boston.

## GRINDERS
When the bread used for a sandwich is a long and slender Italian roll, and you're in New England, this de rigueur staple of delis and pizza parlors is most commonly called a grinder. But you may also see them called spukies (around Boston) and Italian sandwiches (mostly in Maine).

### WHOOPIE PIES

Consisting of two soft moon-shaped cakes (they're also sometimes called moon pies) and traditionally filled with a creamy vanilla frosting, whoopie pies are said to originate in either Massachusetts, New Hampshire, Maine, or (let's not even go there) Pennsylvania, but they're a favorite sweet all around New England today. Maine probably leads the way in whoopie pie adoration, and gourmet shops there now offer up all kinds of imaginative flavors: think salted caramel or gingerbread.

### PANCAKES AND MAPLE SYRUP

The quintessential New England breakfast, fluffy pancakes topped with local maple syrup (with Vermont and New Hampshire being the region's top producers) are a year-round delight. Note that Rhode Island has its own variation, the silver-dollar-size johnnycake made with cornmeal batter, and that pumpkin pancakes are a hit in autumn.

### ARTISANAL CHEESE

From smaller dairies with cult followings—like Willow Hill and Twig Farm in Vermont, Sandwich Creamery in New Hampshire, and Appleton Creamery in Maine—to bigger national players such as Cabot Creamery, Jasper Hill, and Vermont Creamery, New England abounds with exceptional cheese makers. To sample some of the best, attend the Vermont Cheesemakers' Festival, typically held in July in Shelburne Falls.

Pancakes with maple syrup

Clam chowder

### CLAMS

These smiling bivalves are a top delicacy up and down the coast but especially in Rhode Island, home of the fictional town of Quahog on TV's *Family Guy* (in honor of the state's most popular clam variety). Quahogs (like littlenecks and cherrystones) are hard-shell clams and are popular in chowder (the Rhode Island version has a clear rather than creamy broth), pasta sauces, and eaten raw on the half shell. Soft-shell clams, known as steamers, are what you find fried (whole belly or in strips) at clam shacks all around the region.

### ICE CREAM

Long before Ben & Jerry's brought its wildly wonderful frozen treats to Vermont, New England had already been awash with ice cream stands. Favorites like Gifford's in Maine and Kimball Farm in Massachusetts have been going strong for generations, while new artisanal makers—Arethusa in Connecticut, Walpole in New Hampshire, SoCo in the Berkshires—appeal more to today's foodies.

# New England Regional Snapshot

## Know Before You Go

### SEASONS MATTER

With a climate that shifts constantly—not only throughout the year, but sometimes hour by hour—New England is a destination with strong seasonality. Rates at hotels, traffic on roads, and crowds at restaurants and attractions soar in the fall in the mountains, in summer on the beaches, and in winter in the ski towns. Prepare accordingly, and consider shoulder seasons for better deals and fewer people.

### HIT THE OPEN ROAD

Outside of Boston and the downtowns of a few other cities that can be explored easily on foot, a car is the best way to see most of New England's key sites. The region is crisscrossed by both speedy interstates and dozens upon dozens of often windy and scenic two-lane roads. Although buses and trains connect a number of communities, they aren't so useful for getting out and seeing the countryside.

## Planning Your Time

It's relatively easy to cover a lot of ground in New England. Maine is actually larger than the other five states combined, so we're talking about a relatively small region. You can drive from coastal Connecticut to coastal Maine—passing through three states along the way—in about three hours if you don't hit much traffic. It's possible to see the key sites in New England in five to seven days, but two weeks is ideal.

## Road Trips

**3 days:** Boston to Portland to Bar Harbor

**3 days:** Provincetown to Hyannis to Newport

**4 days:** White Mountains to Stowe to the Berkshires to the Litchfield Hills

## Big Events

**Boston Marathon.** Held on Patriot's Day (which is always the third Monday in April), the oldest annual marathon on the globe is a huge annual draw.

**Maine Lobster Festival.** This August gathering in Rockland draws legions of fans of what might just be New England's favorite food.

**Dartmouth Winter Carnival.** A tradition since 1911, this four-day February festival in New Hampshire is notable for snow sculpture contests and polar bear swims.

## What To ...

### READ

*Little Women* by Louisa May Alcott

*The Cider House Rules* by John Irving

*It* by Stephen King

*The Secret History* by Donna Tartt

*Infinite Jest* by David Foster Wallace

### WATCH

*Good Will Hunting* (movie filmed in Boston and Cambridge)

*Jaws* (movie filmed on Martha's Vineyard)

*Moonrise Kingdom* (movie filmed in Rhode Island)

*Stepford Wives* (two movies, both filmed in Connecticut)

### LISTEN

*The Cars* by The Cars (album)

*Anticipation* by Carly Simon (album)

*Heart Break* by New Edition

*Farmhouse* by Phish (album)

*America, The Beautiful* by the Boston Pops Orchestra (album)

### BUY

Maple syrup in Vermont and New Hampshire

Sportswear at L.L. Bean in Maine and Orvis in Vermont

Boston Red Sox gear at Fenway Park

## Contacts

### AIR

Major Airports

**Connecticut.:** BDL

**Maine:** PWM

**Massachusetts:** BOS

**New Hampshire:** MHT

**Rhode Island:** PVD

**Vermont:** BTV

### BOAT

**Bay State Cruise Company.** ☎ *877/783–3779* 🌐 *baystatecruisecompany.com.*

**Block Island Express.** ☎ *401/466–2212* 🌐 *goblockisland.com.*

**Block Island Ferry.** ☎ *866/783–7996* 🌐 *blockislandferry.com.*

**Boston Harbor Cruises.** ☎ *877/733–9425* 🌐 *bostonharborcruises.com.*

**Freedom Cruise Line.** ☎ *508/432–8999* 🌐 *freedomferry.com.*

**Hy-Line Cruises.** ☎ *800/492–8082* 🌐 *hylinecruises.com.*

**Island Queen.** ☎ *508/548–4800* 🌐 *islandqueen.com.*

**Isles of Shoals Steamship Company.** ☎ *800/441–4620* 🌐 *islesofshoals.com*

**Maine State Ferry.** 🌐 *maine.gov/mdot/ferry.*

**Steamship Authority.** ☎ *508/477–8600* 🌐 *steamshipauthority.com.*

**Vineyard Fast Ferry.** ☎ *401/295–4040* 🌐 *vineyardfastferry.com.*

### BUS

**BoltBus.** ☎ *877/265–8287* 🌐 *boltbus.com.*

**C&J Bus Lines.** ☎ *603/430–1100* 🌐 *ridecj.com.*

**Concord Coach Lines.** ☎ *800/639–3317* 🌐 *concordcoachlines.com.*

**Dartmouth Coach.** ☎ *603/448–2800* 🌐 *dartmouthcoach.com.*

**Go Bus.** 🌐 *gobuses.com.*

**Greyhound.** ☎ *800/231–2222* 🌐 *greyhound.com.*

**Megabus.** ☎ *877/462–6342* 🌐 *us.megabus.com.*

### TRAIN

**Amtrak.** ☎ *800/872–7245* 🌐 *www.amtrak.com.*

**Metro-North Railroad.** ☎ *877/690–5114* 🌐 *mta.info/mnr.*

**Shore Line East.** ☎ *877/287–4337* 🌐 *shorelineeast.com.*

### SUBWAY

**Massachusetts Bay Transportation Authority.** ☎ *617/222–3200* 🌐 *www.mbta.com.*

### VISITOR INFORMATION

🌐 *ctvisit.com*

🌐 *visitmaine.com*

🌐 *visitma.com*

🌐 *visitnh.gov*

🌐 *visitrhodeisland.com*

🌐 *vermontvacation.com*

# Connecticut

"Connecticut Yankees" or "Nutmeggers" enjoy 253 miles of shoreline that blows salty sea air over beach communities like Old Lyme and Stonington, while patchwork hills and peaked mountains fill the state's northwestern corner, and once-upon-a-time mill towns line rivers such as the Housatonic. Connecticut has seemingly endless farmland in the northeast, where cows might just outnumber people, as well as chic New York City bedroom communities such as Greenwich and New Canaan, where boutique shopping bags are the dominant species. You can travel from just about any point in Connecticut to any other in less than two hours.

## Bucket List Picks

The following boxes contain our picks for the top sights and experiences in Connecticut.

- ○ Mystic Seaport
- ○ Sheffield Island
- ○ Hartford's Nook Farm
- ○ Essex Steam Train and Riverboat
- ○ Litchfield
- ○ New Haven

# Mystic Seaport

## The Nation's Largest Maritime Museum

The largest maritime museum in the United States (and some would say the world, though the the U.K.'s National Maritime Museum in Greenwich also contends for the title), Mystic Seaport encompasses 19 acres of indoor and outdoor exhibits, and includes a re-created New England coastal village, a working shipyard, and more than 2 million artifacts that provide a fascinating look at the area's rich shipbuilding and seafaring heritage. In narrow streets and historic homes and buildings, craftspeople give demonstrations of open-hearth cooking, weaving, and other skills. The museum's more than 500 vessels include the *Charles W. Morgan*, the last remaining wooden whaling ship afloat. You can climb aboard for a look, or for sail-setting demonstrations and reenactments. Surrounding downtown Mystic has plenty of interesting boutiques and galleries.

## Don't Miss

Just up the road from the seaport, Mystic Aquarium is best known for the famous Arctic Coast exhibit, but you can also see African penguins, harbor seals, graceful sea horses, and Pacific octopuses here.

## Best Restaurants

To feast on some of the state's best lobster, mussels, crabs, or clams on the half shell, head to Abbott's Lobster in the Rough in sleepy Noank, a few miles southwest of Mystic. Most seating is outdoors or on the dock. *abbottslobster.com.*

## Getting Here and Around

Mystic is off Interstate 95 in coastal southeastern Connecticut, just east of the small cities of Groton and New London.

**Mystic Seaport.** *75 Greenmanville Ave., Mystic, CT* *860/572–0711* *mysticseaport.org* *$19.*

# Sheffield Island

## Summertime Clambakes

It doesn't get more enchanting New England than sea, sand, and a clambake feast beneath a picturesque lighthouse. Every Thursday night in summer, the Seaport ferry in south Norwalk takes passengers on a scenic boat ride to a 3-acre Sheffield Island for a tour of the 10-room, four-story 1868 lighthouse and a classic New England clambake. Collect seashells on the beach, take in the Long Island Sound views, and then head to the tented pavilion on the lighthouse lawn for a sunset dinner that includes steamed clams and mussels—for an upcharge, you can splurge for 1½-pound steamed lobster. Ferries leave from South Norwalk's SoNo District, which is adjacent to the outstanding Maritime Aquarium at Norwalk.

## Don't Miss

The city's coastal SoNo business district is a hot spot for trendy shopping, culture, and dining, most of it along North Main and Water Streets.

## Best Wildlife Cruise

The Maritime Aquarium also leads marine-mammal cruises aboard the 64-foot *Spirit of the Sound* catamaran. You can spot seals, migratory birds, and myriad marine life on these scenic narrated adventures. ⊕ *maritime-aquarium.org.*

## When to Go

The clambakes take place on Thursday evenings from June through September, but the aquarium and SoNo remain fun and lively year-round.

## Getting Here and Around

SoNo is just off Interstate 95 in the southwestern Connecticut city of Norwalk.

**Sheffield Island Cruises.** ✉ *Washington and N. Water St., Norwalk, CT* ☎ *203/838–9444* ⊕ *seaport.org* 🎫 *From $65.*

# Hartford's Nook Farm

## Mark Twain's World

Built in 1874, this grand 25-room mansion was the home of Samuel Langhorne Clemens, better known as Mark Twain, until 1891. Twain wrote his most important works during the years he lived here, including *The Adventures of Tom Sawyer, Adventures of Huckleberry Finn*, and *A Connecticut Yankee in King Arthur's Court*. The house features interior decor designed by Louis Comfort Tiffany, including elaborate stenciling and carved woodwork. Visit the Billiard Room where Twain did his writing and see the bed carved with angels where he slept. A contemporary museum on the grounds presents a Ken Burns documentary, a café, and gift shop. The Nook Farm neighborhood also contains the Connecticut Science Center, the State Capitol, and Wadsworth Atheneum Museum of Art.

## Don't Miss

Next to Twain's house at what is now the Harriet Beecher Stowe Center, the abolitionist and author (1811–96) spent her final years in this 1871 Victorian Gothic cottage. Stowe's personal writing table and effects are inside.

## Best Restaurant

First and Last Tavern is one of the state's most hallowed pizza parlors, serving superb thin-crust pies (locals love the puttanesca) since 1936. *firstandlasttavern.com.*

## Getting Here and Around

The museum and Nook Farm neighborhood are just a five-minute drive west of downtown Hartford, just off Interstate 84.

**Mark Twain House and Museum.** *351 Farmington Ave., Hartford, CT* *860/247–0998* *marktwainhouse.org* *$19.*

# Essex Steam Train and Riverboat

## Take In Connecticut's Prettiest Scenery

Offering some of the best views of the Connecticut River valley from 1920s-era coaches pulled by a vintage steam locomotive and an old-fashioned riverboat, the Essex Steam Train and Riverboat is the only steam train and riverboat connection in the country. Chug through quintessential New England landscapes, from the neatly preserved 19th-century shipbuilding town of Essex to Deep River, passing by genuinely quaint hamlets and tidal wetlands along the way. At Deep River Landing, passengers board the vintage *Becky Thatcher* riverboat for a serene cruise along the Connecticut River.

## Don't Miss

A magnificent 1876 Victorian-gingerbread "wedding cake" theater, East Haddam's Goodspeed Opera House played a vital role in the preservation and development of American musical theater and mounts performances April–early December.

## When to Go

Essex Steam Train and Riverboat runs from May through December and offers special kid-themed North Pole Express rides around the holidays, but the scenery is especially stunning in prime leaf-peeping season in late October.

## Getting Here and Around

Essex is near the coast on Route 9, just off Interstate 95. Bucolic Route 154 meanders up through the same charming towns as the steam train and riverboat. To get to Gillette Castle, take Route 148 and the historic Chester–Hadlyme Ferry.

**Essex Steam Train and Riverboat.** ✉ *1 Railroad Ave., Essex, CT* ☎ *860/767–0103* 🌐 *essexsteamtrain.com* 🎟 *From $19.*

# Litchfield

## Quintessential New England

The scenic, 300-year-old northwestern Connecticut town offers a combination of beautiful scenery (especially during leaf-peeping season), historic interest and charm, great hiking, and critically acclaimed dining. The cultural hub of the surrounding Litchfield Hills, this town's impressive Litchfield Green and white Colonial and Greek Revival homes that line the broad elm-shaded streets were once graced by the likes of Harriet Beecher Stowe, author of *Uncle Tom's Cabin*, and her brother, abolitionist preacher Henry Ward Beecher, both born and raised here, as well as many famous Americans who earned their law degrees at the Litchfield Law School, the infamous Aaron Burr among them. These days, the village center abounds with lovely but expensive boutiques and art spaces, including P. S. Gallery, Jeffrey Tillou Antiques, and Serendipity.

## Don't Miss

Make the scenic 15-mile drive south to the colonial town of Woodbury, which is said to have more antiques shops than in the rest of the Litchfield Hills combined. Five magnificent colonial churches line Main Street, which is also home to one of the state's best farm-to-table eateries, Good News Restaurant.

## When to Go

The Litchfield Hills are the most gorgeous part of Connecticut for admiring fall foliage throughout the month of October.

## Getting Here and Around

Litchfield's walkable downtown is at the junction of U.S. 202 and Route 63, about 30 miles west of Hartford. For a stunning drive, continue north on Route 63 to U.S. 7, and into the Berkshires in Massachusetts.

# New Haven

## Arts Hub

Though the city is best known as the home of Yale University, the prestigious museums and highly respected theaters downtown make New Haven one of New England's leading arts centers. Within easy walking distance of the city's stately 16-acre Yale Green and the gracious Gothic architecture of Yale's campus, you can view original works by John Constable and Thomas Gainsborough in the sleek Louis I. Kahn–designed Yale Center for British Art, admire Audubon prints and an original Gutenberg Bible at the Beinecke Rare Book and Manuscript Library, and see everything from Etruscan vases to Picassos and van Goghs.

## Don't Miss

Long famous as a city where producers premiered shows to see if they had what it takes to open on Broadway, New Haven has a world-class theater scene, and tickets to shows are quite reasonable compared to New York City. Top venues include the Shubert Performing Arts Center (which also presents music and dance), the highly regarded Long Wharf Theatre, and the Yale Repertory Theatre, where Yale Drama students including Lupita Nyong'o, Francis McDormand, Paul Newman, and Meryl Streep have taken the stage.

## Best Offbeat Attraction

One of the more peculiar stops is the Cushing Center at Yale's Whitney Medical Library, where you can examine more than 400 jars containing human brains.

## Getting Here and Around

New Haven's downtown core is easily reached from Interstates 95 and 91.

**Visit New Haven.** ✉ *28 Orange St., New Haven, CT* ☎ *203/777–8550* 🌐 *visitnewhaven.com.*

## When in Connecticut

### CONNECTICUT ART TRAIL

With locations spanning from New London to Greenwich and north to Hartford, the Connecticut Art Trail connects more than 20 world-class museums and historic sites, with a focus on Connecticut's role as the cradle of the American Impressionist movement which thrived here from shortly after the Civil War until the 1910s. A must is the Weir Farm National Historic Site in Wilton, where you can tour the farmhouse and grounds that belonged to one of the icons of American Impressionism, J. Alden Weir. Other greats like Childe Hassam, Henry Twachtman, and Willard Metcalfe spent time near the coast in the Lyme Art Colony at a rather grand boardinghouse that's now the art-filled Florence Griswold Museum. And in Greenwich, you can visit the site of the state's first American Impressionist art colony, the Bush-Holley House.

**Do This:** The nation's oldest public art museum, the stunningly renovated Wadsworth Atheneum in Hartford contains not only superb collections of American (and European) Impressionists, but also more than 50,000 works spanning 5,000 years, along with 7,000 items documenting African American history and culture in partnership with the Amistad Foundation.

### GROTON'S SUBMARINE HERITAGE

Home to the Naval Submarine Base New London (the U.S. Navy's first) and to the Electric Boat Division of General Dynamics, designer and manufacturer of nuclear submarines, Groton is often referred to as the "submarine capital of the world." Kids and adults love learning about these intriguing underwater vessels at the Submarine Force Museum, where you can tour the world's first nuclear-powered submarine, the *Nautilus*, which launched and commissioned in Groton in 1954. She is permanently berthed here at the museum, a repository of artifacts, documents, photographs, and interactive exhibits detailing the history of the U.S. Submarine Force component of the U.S. Navy.

**Do This:** Across the Thames River in the historic seafaring city of New London, visit the 100-acre campus of redbrick buildings that's home to the prestigious U.S. Coast Guard Academy. A museum explores the Coast Guard's 200 years of maritime service and includes some 200 ship models, as well as figureheads, paintings, uniforms, and cannon.

**Submarine Force Library & Museum.** ✉ *1 Crystal Lake Rd., Groton, CT* ☎ *860/694–3174* 🌐 *ussnautilus.org* 🎫 *Free.*

### NEW HAVEN PIZZA

Even more famous than Yale among foodies, New Haven's Wooster Street "Little Italy" has been drawing pizza lovers for nearly a century. The city's "apizza" style is defined by its thin, chewy, blistered crusts, which are baked in a coal-fired brick oven. For everything from the original tomato pie to white clam and other specialty pies, check out these three authentic New Haven pizzerias: Frank Pepe's Pizzeria Napoletana, which began in 1925 and is especially known for its white-clam pizza (try it with bacon for a memorable twist); Sally's Apizza, which is just two blocks away and has been Pepe's main rival since it opened in 1938; and Modern Apizza, which is a few blocks around the corner and has been going strong since 1934.

**Do This:** Pizza is but one element of New Haven's impressive culinary chops. Also visit Louis' Lunch, a vintage luncheonette that opened in 1895 and is recognized as the birthplace of the "hamburger sandwich." And check out the many superb international—especially Asian—eateries downtown.

**Wooster Square.** ✉ *Wooster and Olive Sts., New Haven, CT* ☎ *203/624–4444* 🌐 *visitnewhaven.com.*

### PHILIP JOHNSON GLASS HOUSE

For nearly 60 years, right up until his death in 2005, the seminal modernist architect Philip Johnson lived with his partner in this modest but visually mesmerizing glass-walled house that he spent three years designing in the late 1940s. Per his bequest, ownership of the house passed on to the National Trust for Historic Preservation, which gives guided tours of this fascinating structure that also include other parts of the 49-acre estate in the affluent commuter town of New Canaan.

**Do This:** There are several tour options available, including a basic one-hour house tour, but for the most immersive experience, book the Extended Tour, which lasts 2½ hours and covers areas of the estate, including his studio, painting and sculpture galleries, and strolling along a mile of pathways that traverse the property. Tours leave from the visitor center and design store in New Canaan's attractive downtown (which you may recognize from Ang Lee's 1997 movie *The Ice Storm*).

**Visitor Center.** ✉ *199 Elm St., New Canaan, CT* ☎ *203/594–9884* 🌐 *theglasshouse.org* 🎫 *From $25.*

## Cool Places to Stay

**Inn at Stonington.** The views of Stonington Harbor and Fishers Island Sound are spectacular from this waterfront inn with a 400-foot pier, and where each individually decorated room has a fireplace, and most have whirlpool baths. ✉ *60 Water St., Stonington, CT* ☎ *860/535–2000* 🌐 *innatstonington.com* $ *From $195.*

**Mayflower Inn & Spa.** Running streams, rambling stone walls, and rare-specimen trees fill this country manor–style inn's 28 manicured acres, which includes a 20,000-square-foot spa and one of the state's most refined restaurants. ✉ *118 Woodbury Rd., Washington, CT* ☎ *860/868–9466* 🌐 *aubergeresorts.com/mayflower* $ *From $705.*

**Winvian Farm.** This private 113-acre hideaway consists of 18 imaginative and luxuriously outfitted cottages, each with a distinctive, often amusing, theme: the Stone Cottage is made with massive boulders with a wavy-slate roof and an enormous fireplace; the Helicopter Cottage contains—you guessed it—a genuine 17,000-pound U.S. Coast Guard helicopter (the fuselage has been refitted with a wet bar). ✉ *155 Alain White Rd., Morris, CT* ☎ *860/567–9600* 🌐 *winvian.com* $ *From $799.*

# Maine

Counting all its nooks, crannies, and crags, Maine's coast would stretch for thousands of miles if you could pull it straight. The southern coast is the most visited section, stretching north from Kittery to just outside Portland, but don't let that stop you from heading farther "Down East" (this nautical term is Maine-speak for "up the coast"), where you'll be rewarded with the majestic mountains and rugged coastline of popular Acadia National Park. Slow down to explore the museums, galleries, and shops in the larger towns and cities, like Portland.

## Bucket List Picks

The following boxes contain our picks for the top sights and experiences in Maine.

- ○ Acadia National Park
- ○ Cape Elizabeth
- ○ Baxter State Park
- ○ Ogunquit
- ○ Maine Lobster Festival
- ○ Portland
- ○ Windjammer Cruise
- ○ Moosehead Lake
- ○ Coastal Maine Botanical Gardens
- ○ Route 9 in Kennebunkport
- ○ Lubec

# Acadia National Park

## The Highest Point on the North Atlantic Seaboard

At 1,530 feet, Cadillac Mountain dominates New England's only national park, Acadia, a rugged 49,000-acre tract of surf-pounded granite coastline and an interior graced by sculpted mountains, sheer cliffs, quiet ponds, and lush, deciduous forests. The park also has graceful stone bridges, miles of carriage roads, and a 27-mile Park Loop Road, which you can drive to Cadillac's summit. But the most memorable way to access the summit is to hike to the top via the 4-mile round-trip North Ridge Trail.

## Don't Miss

Bar Harbor is the artistic, culinary, and social center of Mount Desert Island, and the main entry point to Acadia National Park. Distinctive shops, excellent restaurants, and historic are clustered along Main, Mount Desert, and Cottage Streets; take a stroll down West Street to admire Bar Harbor's many fine old houses.

## Best Restaurant

Easily accessed by car along the Park Loop Road or one of the Acadia National Park's carriage roads, Jordan Pond House is famous for its warm popovers. 🌐 *jordanpondhouse.com.*

## When to Go

The trails and inlets of Acadia National Park, as well as the village of Bar Harbor, are at their most stunning from June through October.

## Getting Here and Around

The park and Bar Harbor are on Mount Desert Island, off Route 3, about 40 miles south of Interstate 95 in Bangor.

**Hull Cove Visitor Center.** ✉ *25 Visitor Center Rd., Bar Harbor, ME* ☎ *207/288–3338* 🌐 *nps.gov/acad* 🎫 *$30.*

# Cape Elizabeth

## Iconic Lighthouses

Venture along scenic Highway 77 through South Portland to affluent Cape Elizabeth, where a detour along two-lane Shore Road shows off the famed Portland Head Light, which you may recognize from Edward Hopper's eponymous 1927 painting. The towering, white-stone lighthouse—commissioned by George Washington in 1790—stands over the keeper's quarters, a white home with a blazing red roof. It's now a museum that anchors the walking paths, beach, and picnic areas of 90-acre Fort Williams Park. Continue south to the dramatic 1828 Cape Elizabeth Light, which Winslow Homer depicted in numerous paintings. You can get a great photo of it from the end of Two Lights Road in the surrounding state park of the same name.

## Don't Miss

At the tip of Cape Elizabeth's gorgeous Prout's Neck peninsula, the seaside Winslow Homer Studio was the great landscape painter's home between 1883 until his death in 1910. It's easy to see how this rocky, jagged peninsula might have been inspiring. The Portland Museum of Art leads 2½-hour strolls through the historic property.

## Best Lobster Rolls

Maine's best lobster rolls are dispensed from Bite Into Maine, a food truck overlooking idyllic Portland Head Light. *biteintomaine.com.*

## Getting There and Around

Cape Elizabeth is off Route 77, 5 miles southeast of Portland.

**Portland Head Light.** *1000 Shore Rd., Cape Elizabeth, ME 207/799–2661 portlandheadlight.com $2.*

# Baxter State Park

## Hike the North End of the Appalachian Trail

Baxter State Park is the jewel in the crown of northern Maine: a 210,000-acre wilderness area that surrounds Mt. Katahdin, Maine's highest mountain and the terminus of the Appalachian Trail. Every year, the 5,267-foot peak draws thousands of hikers to make the daylong summit, rewarding them with stunning views of forests, mountains, and lakes. The crowds climbing Katahdin can be formidable on clear summer days and fall weekends, so if it's solitude you crave, tackle one of the park's many other mountains.

## Don't Miss

A spectacular 92-mile corridor of lakes, ponds, streams, and rivers, the Allagash Wilderness Waterway park cuts through vast commercial forests, beginning near the northwestern corner of Baxter State Park and running north to the town of Allagash, 10 miles from the Canadian border. From May to mid-October, the Allagash is prime canoeing and camping country.

## Best Outfitter

Based in Millinocket, New England Outdoor Center offers guided hikes throughout Baxter State Park, including treks to Katahdin's summit. But these knowledgeable pros can also get you out canoeing and kayaking on the Allagash and St. John rivers, and white-water rafting on the Penobscot River. 🌐 *neoc.com*.

## Getting Here and Around

Millinocket, on Route 157 about 10 miles west of Interstate 95, is the gateway to Baxter State Park and Allagash Wilderness Waterway. It's about a 15-mile drive to get to the park.

**Reservation Office.** ☎ *207/723–5140* 🌐 *baxterstatepark.org* 🎫 *$15*.

# Ogunquit

### Quintessential Seaside Town

Named by the Abenaki tribe, Ogunquit means "beautiful place by the sea" and it delivers exactly what it says on the label. A resort village since the late 19th century, the town made a name for itself as an artists' colony. Still a center of creativity with a superb summer-stock theater, the Ogunquit Playhouse, the town has become something of a mini Provincetown, with a gay population that swells in summer. The bustling nightlife and restaurant scene revolves around downtown's charming Ogunquit Square, which is within walking distance of Ogunquit Beach.

### Don't Miss

Perkins Cover, a neck of land off Shore Road in the lower part of Ogunquit village, has a jumble of sea-weathered fish houses and buildings that were part of an art school. These have largely been transformed into inviting shops and restaurants. When you've had your fill of browsing, stroll out along Marginal Way, a mile-long, paved footpath that hugs the shore of a rocky promontory known as Israel's Head. In the other direction, it's a short stroll to the small but excellent Ogunquit Museum of American Art.

### Best Restaurant

Northern Union, known for seasonally inspired small plates and entrées like seared scallops and lobster fettuccine, has a spot-on wine pairing that you won't find elsewhere in the area. 🌐 *northern-union.me.*

### When to Go

This bustling beach town is at its prime in summer, but that's also when rates are highest.

### Getting Here and Around

Ogunquit is along both U.S. 1 and Interstate 95, about 35 miles southwest of Portland.

# Maine Lobster Festival

### The Best Lobster in the United States

This annual get-together that draws thousands of devotees of lobsters takes place in early August and is this popular coastal region's largest annual event. About 10 tons of lobsters are steamed in a huge lobster cooker—you have to see it to believe it. The festival, held in Harbor Park in Rockland, includes a parade, live entertainment, a lobster dinner, an all-you-can-eat blueberry-pancake breakfast, a "Steins and Vines" beer and wine tasting, and—of course—the crowning of the Maine Sea Goddess.

### Don't Miss

Considered the gateway to Penobscot Bay, Rockland is a lovely Mid-Coast Maine town with plenty to offer beyond its beloved lobster festival (and also the well-attended North Atlantic Blues Festival in July). One must is the renowned Farnsworth Art Museum, which is devoted to Maine-related works of the famous Wyeth family, including illustrator N. C. Wyeth and his famed son, landscape painter Andrew Wyeth.

### Best Restaurant

James Beard Award–winning chef Melissa Kelly's world-class restaurant Primo, which occupies a restored Victorian home, serves some of the finest farm-to-table fare in coastal New England. And although this is no seafood shack, there is often a butter-poached 1½-pound lobster with risotto on the menu. 🌐 *primorestaurant.com*.

### When to Go

The lobster festival takes place in early August, which is perhaps the most enchanting time to explore this stretch of Maine's Mid-Coast.

### Getting There and Around

Rockland is on U.S. 1, about midway between Brunswick and Bar Harbor.

# Portland

## New England's Best Beer City

Maine's largest city may be considered small by national standards—its population is just 66,500—but its character, spirit, and fantastic food and beverage scene make it feel much larger. It's well worth at least a day or two of exploration, even if all you do is spend the entire time eating and drinking at the many phenomenal restaurants, craft cocktail bars, and craft breweries scattered across the city. A good place to begin an ale tour is along the cobblestone streets of the historic Port District at Maine's original brewpub, Gritty McDuff's, which offers live music on weekends. Within a mile, you can then drop by some of the city's newer hot spots, such as Rising Tide, Austin Street, and up-and-coming Banded Brewing, which is known for unusual offers like the Alma sour ale.

## Don't Miss

Although it doesn't brew its own beer, Novare Res Bier Café in Old Port offers some three dozen rotating drafts. Maine craft beers occupy at least eight of the taps at any given time, and the rest span the globe.

## Best Restaurant

In between beer tastings, head to Duckfat, a jam-packed eatery in Old Port that's famous for signature Belgian fries—made with Maine potatoes cooked, yes, in duck fat—and creative sandwiches duck-confit banh mi and Oaxacan-style smoked brisket. 🌐 *duckfat.com.*

## When to Go

Craft beer is in season year-round in Portland, although the city is at its liveliest in summer and early fall.

## Getting There and Around

Portland is off Interstate 95 via Interstate 295 in southwestern Maine.

# Windjammer Cruise

### Picture-Postcard Maine

Designed primarily to carry cargo, these mostly wood-hulled beauties were built all along the East Coast in the 19th and early 20th centuries. During a windjammer excursion, which typically lasts from one to eight days, passengers can often participate in the navigation, be it hoisting a sail or playing captain at the wheel. The Camden Windjammer Festival, held Labor Day weekend, is a great time to gather and watch the region's fleet sail into the harbor, and most boats are open for tours.

### Don't Miss

More than any other town on Penobscot Bay, Camden is the picture-postcard Maine coastal village, and a wonderful place to spend time before or after a windjammer cruise. The town's compact size makes it perfect for exploring on foot: tony shops, restaurants, and galleries line downtown streets. On the north side of town are the Camden Hills; drive or hike to the summit at the state park for mesmerizing views.

### Best Adventure on Land

For a stunning walk or drive, take the two-lane paved road to Rockport. Lining the way are some of the most beautiful homes in Maine. 🌐 *camden-rockland.com.*

### When to Go

Windjammer Cruises along Maine's coast are most enjoyable from June to September, which is also a beautiful time to visit Camden and Rockport.

### Getting Here and Around

Camden and Rockport are along U.S. 1 on Maine's Mid-Coast, between Brunswick and Bar Harbor.

**Maine Windjammer Cruises.**
☎ *207/236–2938* 🌐 *mainewindjammer-cruises.com.*

# Moosehead Lake

## Maine's Most Beautiful Body of Water

The Moosehead Marine Museum runs three- and seven-hour afternoon trips on Moosehead Lake, the largest mountain lake in the Northeast, and at nearly 250 feet, one of the deepest. Cruises are given aboard the 115-foot *Katahdin*, a National Historic Site and stately steamship (converted to diesel) that has been a fixture on this lake for over a hundred years. The boat and the free shoreside museum have displays about these steamships, which transported people and cargo for a century starting in the 1830s.

## Don't Miss

Mt. Kineo State Park occupies most of a 1,200-acre peninsula that's accessible only by boat and that offers gorgeous hiking trails that summit its spectacular 700-foot cliffs. You can also play a round on the 9-hole Mt. Kineo Golf Course, one of the oldest courses in New England. The park preserves the former Mt. Kineo House resort, once a thriving upscale summer retreat.

## Best Town

Tucked at the southern end of island-dotted, mostly forest-lined Moosehead Lake, Greenville is an outdoors lover's paradise. Boating, fishing, and hiking are popular in summer, snowmobiling and ice fishing in winter. 🌐 *destinationmooseheadlake.com.*

## Getting Here and Around

The departure point for Katahdin Cruises and the best town for exploring Moosehead Lake, Greenville is on Route 6 in west-central Maine, about a three-hour drive north of Portland.

**Katahdin Cruises.** ✉ *12 Lily Bay Rd., Greenville, ME* ☎ *207/695–2716* 🌐 *katahdincruises.com.*

# Coastal Maine Botanical Gardens

### Prettiest Public Garden

Set aside at least two hours to amble among the roses, lupines, rhododendrons, and contemporary art installations at the 300-acre Coastal Maine Botanical Gardens. Highlights include the "children's garden," a wonderland of stone sculptures, rope bridges, small teahouse-like structures with grass roofs, and even a hedge maze. Pine-shaded, fern-lined trails curve down to several tranquil woodland gardens and a dock on Boothbay's scenic Back River. The on-site restaurant and café, as well as the bookshop and resource library, are also delightful.

### Don't Miss

The shoreline of the surrounding Boothbay Peninsula is a craggy stretch of inlets, where pleasure craft anchor alongside trawlers and lobster boats tied up in the snug village of Boothbay Harbor, which feels like a smaller version of Bar Harbor.

### Best Hotel

The Adirondack chairs on the immense lawn of the Topside Inn have one of the best bay views on the Maine Coast. ⊕ *topsideinn.com.*

### When to Go

The gardens are stunning when in full bloom in summer, but there's beautiful floral scenery in spring and fall colors from late September to late October.

### Getting Here and Around

Boothbay is on Route 27, 14 miles south of U.S. 1 at Wiscasset, about 30 miles east of Freeport.

**Coastal Maine Botanical Gardens.** ✉ *132 Botanical Gardens Dr., Boothbay, ME* ☎ *207/633–8000* ⊕ *mainegardens.org* 🎫 *$22.*

# Route 9 in Kennebunkport

### Maine's Great Coastal Road

Begin the stunning Route 9 coastal drive at U.S. 1 south of Kennebunk, following the road east through the famous resort community of Kennebunkport, sometimes described as the Hamptons of the Pine Tree State. A resort area since the 19th century, its most recent residents—the dynastic Bush family—have made it even more famous. Follow Route 9 east to the fishing village of Cape Porpoise, and plan on some beachcombing along breathtaking 3-mile-long Goose Rock Beach. The route continues past the charming resort villages of Camp Ellis and Ocean Park to Saco Bay, where you might stop for a picnic at Ferry Beach State Park.

### Don't Miss

Clothing boutiques, art galleries, and convivial restaurants line Kennebunkport's bustling Dock Square, spreading out along the nearby streets and alleys. Walk onto the drawbridge to admire the tidal Kennebunk River.

### Best Sailing Adventure

The 1½-hour cruises on the three-mast *Pineapple Ketch* are offered midday and again at sunset and depart from Nonantum Resort on the Kennebunk River. Typically, this 38-foot boat skirts the coast, past the mansions and the Bush compound at Walker's Point, and on to Goat Island Lighthouse and Cape Porpoise Harbor. 🌐 *pineappleketch.com*.

### When to Go

This scenic coastal town is at its prime in summer and fall, although hotels are far less expensive in winter.

### Getting Here and Around

Route 9 runs along the coast through Kennebunkport and Old Orchard Beach, connecting at both ends with U.S. 1, between Ogunquit and Portland.

# Lubec

## First Sunrise in the United States

The nation's easternmost point of land is marked by candy-stripe West Quoddy Head Light, which dates to 1806, and is just a short drive south of tiny, charming downtown Lubec. You can't climb the tower, but the former lightkeeper's house has a great museum and the mystical 2-mile path along the bluffs in the surrounding 540-acre Quoddy Head State Park yields magnificent views of Canada's Grand Manan Island. You can often see whales and seals—as well as ubiquitous bald eagles—just offshore.

## Don't Miss

Don't forget to bring your passport: this area is a perfect base for day trips to New Brunswick's Campobello Island, reached by a bridge—the only one to the island—from downtown Lubec. There you can visit Roosevelt Campobello International Park, and tour the 34-room rustic summer cottage of the family of President Franklin Delano Roosevelt.

## Best Restaurant

Perched on the water in downtown Lubec, Waterstreet Tavern and Inn turns out some of the sweetest scallops you'll ever eat. It's also a great place to grab an early evening beverage or a slice of blueberry pie with sea views. 🌐 *watersttavernandinn.com.*

## When to Go

Lubec is pretty quiet in winter, although a contingent always visits on New Year's Eve to see the first sunrise of the new year. Summer is the most pleasant time to visit, and Roosevelt Campobello International Park is closed November through mid-May.

## Getting Here and Around

Lubec is on Route 189 on the Maine coast, at the Canadian border, about 10 miles northeast of U.S. 1.

## When in Maine

### L.L. BEAN

Founded in 1912 as a mail-order merchandiser after its namesake invented a hunting boot, L.L. Bean's giant flagship store attracts more than 3 million shoppers annually and is open 24 hours a day, 365 days a year, right in the heart of Freeport's outlet shopping district. A massive 16½-foot-tall statue of its signature rubber boot greets you outside the front door and you can still find the original hunting boots, along with cotton and wool sweaters, outerwear of all kinds, and camping equipment, plus all kinds of fun gifts and goods. As you walk through the store, note the impressive display of taxidermied animals, and the giant 3,500-gallon aquarium of freshwater Maine fish.

**Do This:** After a dizzying day of shopping, enjoy some fresh air on the beautiful trails at Wolfe's Neck Woods State Park, with its fragrant pine and hemlock forests and pristine salt marsh estuaries.

**L.L.Bean Flagship Store.** ✉ *95 Main St., Freeport, ME* ☎ *877/755–2326* 🌐 *llbean.com* 🎫 *Free.*

### MAINE MARITIME MUSEUM

For an engaging look at the state's rich seafaring heritage, spend at least a half day visiting this cluster of historic buildings in Bath that once made up the Percy & Small Shipyard. Tours show how New England's massive wooden ships were built, and in the boat shop, you can still watch boatbuilders wield their tools. Inside the main museum, you can view ship models, paintings, photographs, and other artifacts, and a separate historic building houses a fascinating lobstering exhibit. There's also an excellent gift shop and bookstore, and you can grab a bite to eat in the café or bring a picnic to eat on the grounds. The town of Bath has been a shipbuilding center since 1607, and the result of its prosperity can be seen in its handsome mix of Federal, Greek Revival, and Italianate homes.

**Do This:** In summer, the museum offers a variety of nature and lighthouse cruises on the scenic Kennebec River—one takes in 10 lights. The 142-foot Grand Banks fishing schooner *Sherman Zwicker* docks here during the same period.

**Maine Maritime Museum.** ✉ *243 Washington St., Bath, ME* ☎ *207/443–1316* 🌐 *mainemaritimemuseum.org* 🎫 *$18.*

### OWLS HEAD TRANSPORTATION MUSEUM

In the rural coastal community of Owls Head, just south of bustling Rockland, you'll find one of the Northeast's most impressive collections of planes, vehicles, and other forms of transportation—even antique bicycles, nearly all of them in operational condition. These beautifully restored and maintained gems include a 1929 Rolls-Royce Tourer, a 1919 Harley-Davidson motorcycle, 1909 Bleriot monoplane, and a 1926 Ford Model T snowmobile (this is Maine, after all).

**Do This:** It's a scenic 10-minute drive from the museum to one of Maine's older lighthouses, Owls Head, which sits at the tip of a rugged, 80-foot-high headland that guards the western entrance to Penobscot Bay. The old keeper's house has been turned into the American Lighthouse Foundation Interpretive Center, and in summer you can take a tour to the top of the light.

**Owls Head Transportation Museum.** ✉ *117 Museum St., Owls Head, ME* ☎ *207/594–4418* 🌐 *owlshead.org* 🎫 *$14.*

### PENOBSCOT NARROWS BRIDGE AND OBSERVATORY

An "engineering marvel" is how experts describe the 2,120-foot-long Penobscot Narrows Bridge, which opened in 2006 and which is taller than the Statue of Liberty. It's certainly beautiful to look at—from the surrounding countryside it pops up on the horizon like the towers of a fairy-tale castle. Spanning the Penobscot River across from Bucksport, the bridge's 437-foot observation tower is the tallest in the world; an elevator shoots you to the top. In summer, the observatory often offers moonrise viewings.

**Do This:** On the mainland (west) side of the bridge, you can visit Fort Knox, the state's largest historic garrison. It was constructed between 1844 and 1869, when—despite a treaty with Britain settling boundary disputes—invasion was still a concern. The fort never saw any real action, but it was used for troop training and to keep guard during the Civil War and the Spanish-American War. Visitors can explore the many rooms and passageways, and guided tours are given during the warmer months.

**Penobscot Narrows Bridge and Observatory.** ✉ *711 Fort Knox Rd., Prospect, ME* ☎ *207/469–6553* 🌐 *maine.gov/mdot/pnbo* 🎫 *$7.*

## Cool Places to Stay

**Appalachian Mountain Club Maine Wilderness Lodges.** When you truly want to get away from it all, head to the Appalachian Mountain Club's 70,000 acres in Maine's moose-abundant 100-Mile Wilderness, where you can choose between two historic sporting-camp retreats, Gorman Chairback and Little Lyford, both of which have rustic cabins and a bathhouse with hot showers, woodstoves, and a woodsy main lodge with a fireplace, sitting area, and long tables where meals are served family-style. ✉ *Maine Highlands* ☎ *603/466–2721* 🌐 *outdoors.org/lodging-camping/maine-lodges* $ *From*Varies by cabin.

**Little River Lighthouse.** Located on an otherwise uninhabited 15-acre island at the mouth of a river less than 20 miles from the Canadian border, this is one of a handful of New England lighthouses that offers overnight stays—accommodations are in a restored 1888 keeper's house with three guest rooms and a fully equipped kitchen. ✉ *Cutler Harbor, Cutler, ME* ☎ *877/276–4682* 🌐 *www.littleriverlight.org* $ *From $150.*

**Norumbega Inn.** With its stone-castle-like facade, this oft-photographed B&B built in 1886 looks like something out of a novel by Stephen King, but its beautifully designed interior abounds with creature comforts. ✉ *63 High St., Camden, ME* ☎ *207/236–4646* 🌐 *norumbegainn.com* $ *From $299.*

**Press Hotel.** Portland's sleekest hotel is a pared-down, mid-century-modern stunner with a fun typography and printing theme alluding to the building's past, stylish furnishings handcrafted by Maine artisans, and a sophisticated gallery featuring contemporary works by Maine artists. ✉ *119 Exchange St., Portland, ME* ☎ *207/808–8800* 🌐 *www.thepresshotel.com* $ *From $169.*

**White Barn Inn.** For a romantic, indulgent overnight stay, look no further than this exclusive inn known for its attentive, old-school service and plush trappings—some quarters have fireplaces, hot tubs, and luxurious baths with steam showers, and you can pamper yourself in the elegant spa and dine in the superb restaurant housed in a pair of restored 1820s barns. ✉ *37 Beach Ave., Kennebunk, ME* ☎ *207/967–2321* 🌐 *aubergeresorts.com/whitebarninn* $ *From $391.*

# Massachusetts

Massachusetts is far more than just Boston, but the capital city is a great place to start. Sports, culture, and tourism come together here, where you can eat a Fenway frank while watching the Boston Red Sox, or follow the red line of the Freedom Trail to Paul Revere's House. Step outside the city limits to see how the American Revolution began in nearby Lexington and Concord, or head to the rolling mountains of the Berkshires. In every corner of the Bay State, you'll find exciting opportunities. But take a word of advice from us: if you're coming in the winter, dress warm.

## Bucket List Picks

The following boxes contain our picks for the top sights and experiences in Massachusetts.

- ○ The Freedom Trail
- ○ Boston Harbor
- ○ The Emerald Necklace
- ○ Harvard University
- ○ Lexington and Concord
- ○ Salem
- ○ Plymouth
- ○ Martha's Vineyard
- ○ Cape Cod National Seashore
- ○ Nantucket
- ○ Mass MoCA
- ○ Tanglewood
- ○ Cranberry Bog Tours
- ○ Boston's North End

# The Freedom Trail

## Follow the Forefathers

Walk in the footsteps of America's forefathers and pay tribute to renowned figures like Paul Revere, John Hancock, and Ben Franklin as you follow the red stripe marking the 2.5-mile Freedom Trail through Boston's most historic neighborhoods. The pedestrian trail connects 16 of the city's most historic sites related to the American Revolution, laying out Boston's colonial history on the very streets where some of the country's most important events unfolded several hundred years ago. In one day, you can visit Faneuil Hall; the site of the incendiary Boston Massacre; and the Old North Church, where lanterns hung to signal Paul Revere on his thrilling midnight ride. Faneuil Hall adjoins Quincy Market, a good spot to grab a bite to eat, with its three block-long annexes filled with international food stalls and souvenirs.

## Don't Miss

The perfect ending to a walk along the trail? A walk to the top of the Bunker Hill Monument, in Charlestown, for the incomparable vistas. The hill was the site of one of the first battles of the Revolutionary War.

## Best Bar

Sam Adams Boston Taproom has a roof-deck beer garden and serves both the classics and plenty of exclusive rotating taps, like the Mango Guava IPA and Sugar Plum Fairy Belgian Quad. 🌐 *samadamsbostontaproom.com.*

## Getting Here and Around

The trail's starting point, Boston Common, is in the center of the city, accessed by numerous bus and T lines.

**Boston Common Visitors Center.** ✉ *139 Tremont St., Boston, MA* ☎ *617/357–8300* 🌐 *thefreedomtrail.org* 🎫 *Free.*

# Boston Harbor

## America's Big Teapot

Revolutionaries famously dumped British tea into the Boston Harbor in protest during the Boston Tea Party of 1773, and today this waterfront part of town spanning the Seaport and Waterfront districts is packed with marine marvels and cultural gems. Take a walk along the Boston Harborwalk for stunning views of the water, learn about American history at the Boston Tea Party Ships & Museum, where you can catch reenactments and sip the tea that started it all, then visit the nearby New England Aquarium. Just outside, Boston Harbor Cruises offers excursions on the USS *Constitution*, tours of the harbor, brunch cruises, and sunset and fireworks adventures.

## Don't Miss

The New England Aquarium is justly renowned for its four-story, 200,000-gallon ocean-reef tank—one of world's largest.

## Best Waterfront Museum

A 15-minute walk along the waterfront, the Institute of Contemporary Art is housed in a breathtaking cantilevered edifice that juts out over the Boston waterfront. 🌐 *icaboston.org.*

## When to Go

The waterfront and harbor cruises, including whale-watching tours, are best enjoyed May through October.

## Getting Here and Around

The Boston Tea Party Ships & Museum can be accessed by South Station. The New England Aquarium is along the downtown Long Wharf waterfront, accessed by the T and just off Interstate 93.

**New England Aquarium** ✉ *1 Central Wharf, Boston, MA* ☎ *617/973–5200* 🌐 *neaq.org* 🎫 *$32.*

**Boston Tea Party Ships & Museum** ✉ *306 Congress St., Boston, MA* ☎ *617/338–1773* 🌐 *neaq.org* 🎫 *$29.95.*

# The Emerald Necklace

### The Most Beautiful Urban Trail

Designed in the late 19th century by landscape architect Frederick Law Olmsted, this delightful string of green spaces and parks runs nearly 10 miles from one end of the city to the other and includes the Boston Common and Public Garden, Back Bay Fens, the Riverway, Olmsted Park, Jamaica Pond, Arnold Arboretum, and Franklin Park. You can walk along shady paths, row a boat on Jamaica Pond, visit the zoo at Franklin Park, or just laze away an afternoon sitting under a tree. The Emerald Necklace Conservancy provides tours, maps, exhibits, and other info from its visitor center in the Back Bay Fens.

### Don't Miss

The stunning Isabella Stewart Gardner Museum—with its Gothic tapestries, Spanish leather panels, and majestic Venetian courtyard—contains such masterpieces as Titian's *Europa*, Giotto's *Presentation of Christ in the Temple*, and John Singer Sargent's *El Jaleo*.

### Best Experience

Attending a game at Fenway Park is a blast even if you're not a big sports fan. A short stroll from the Emerald Necklace, Fenway Park stands out for its towering "Green Monster" left-field wall. 🌐 *redsox.com*.

### When to Go

The gardens of the Emerald Necklace, and Arnold Arboretum in particular, burst with color from mid-April through mid-October, which also coincides with baseball season.

### Getting Here and Around

You can access the Emerald Necklace at numerous points, key ones being the Back Bay Fens, Jamaica Pond, Arnold Arboretum, and Franklin Park.

**The Emerald Necklace.** 🌐 *emerald-necklace.org*.

# Harvard University

## America's Oldest College

One of the world's most prestigious and storied educational bodies, Harvard University and its tree-studded, shady, and redbrick campus has weathered the footsteps of students since 1639, although the oldest buildings date from the 18th century and collectively chronicle American architecture from the colonial era to the present. Holden Chapel, completed in 1744, is a Georgian gem. The graceful University Hall was designed in 1815 by Charles Bulfinch. Sever Hall, completed in 1880 and designed by Henry Hobson Richardson, represents the Romanesque revival that was followed by the neoclassical Widener Library, a highlight of any campus visit.

## Don't Miss

Tides of students, tourists, political activists, and colorful street performers make up the nonstop pedestrian flow of Harvard Yard, the most celebrated of Cambridge crossroads.

## Best Museum

In 2014, the combined collections of the Busch-Reisinger, Fogg, and Arthur M. Sackler museums were united under one glorious, mostly glass roof, in the seven-level Harvard Art Museums designed by Renzo Piano. Highlights include American and European paintings and works by German expressionists. 🌐 *harvardartmuseums.org*.

## Getting Here and Around

Harvard's campus is in the heart of Cambridge, just across the Charles River from Boston easily reached by public transit or by car via Memorial Drive.

**The Smith Campus Center.** ✉ *1350 Massachusetts Ave., Cambridge, MA* ☎ *617/495–1573* 🌐 *harvard.edu* 🎫 *Free.*

# Lexington and Concord

## Revolutionary Towns

Just northwest of Boston, Lexington and nearby Concord embody both the spirit of the American Revolution as well as Early American literature. Sites of the first skirmishes of the Revolutionary War and where patriot leader Paul Revere warned that the British were coming, these two quintessential New England towns were also home to some of the country's first substantial writers, including Ralph Waldo Emerson, Nathaniel Hawthorne, Louisa May Alcott, and Henry David Thoreau.

## Don't Miss

Minute Man National Historical Park preserves the key sites of the American Revolutionary War's opening battle, on April 19, 1775. See the point where Revere's midnight ride ended with his capture by the British. *nps.gov/mima.*

## While You're Here

For devotees of Early American literature, a trip to Concord isn't complete without a pilgrimage to Henry David Thoreau's most famous residence, Walden Pond.

## When to Go

Autumn lovers, take note: Concord is a great place to start a fall foliage tour. As lovely as it is in summer, Walden Pond can get crowded and visitors are sometimes turned away.

## Getting Here and Around

Walden Pond is in Concord off Route 126 at Route 2. It's 5 miles west of Minute Man National Historical Park, which is off Interstate 95, about 20 miles northwest of Boston.

**Walden Pond State Reservation.** *915 Walden St., Concord, MA* *978/369–3254* *mass.gov/locations/walden-pond-state-reservation* *Parking: $8 Massachusetts residents, $30 out-of-state.*

# Salem

## Be Witched

Long infamous for the witchcraft hysteria that emerged from the trials of 1692, when several Salem-area girls fell ill and accused some of the towns-people of casting spells on them, this historic city just north of Boston has quite a lot going for it year-round, but especially in October when its streets, bars, restaurants, and attractions are fully festooned in Halloween decorations and patronized by costumed revelers and lovers of all things witch-kitsch. Dress the part to join in the fun and take a walking tour, join a parade, and book a tarot reading, but also be sure to visit the Salem Witch Museum, which occupies a striking Gothic Revival church overlooking Salem Common. Another must-visit is the 1668 House of the Seven Gables, immortalized in Nathaniel Hawthorne's classic novel, and home to the famous secret staircase and some of the finest Georgian furnishings in the country.

## Don't Miss

The world-class Peabody-Essex Museum celebrates superlative works from around the globe and across time.

## Best Hotel

Elegantly restored, the Hawthorne Hotel celebrates the town's most famous writer, overlooks the town common, and is an easy walk from local museums and the waterfront. The tavern on-site is an atmospheric spot for dinner and drinks. 🌐 *hawthornehotel.com.*

## Getting Here and Around

Salem's pedestrian-friendly historic core is at the junction of Routes 1A, 114, and 107, about 15 miles northeast of Boston.

**Salem Common.** ✉ *Hawthorne Blvd. at Brown St., Salem, MA* ☎ *978/741–3252* 🌐 *salem.org* 🎫 *Free.*

# Plymouth

### Land of the Pilgrims' Pride

On December 26, 1620, 102 weary men, women, and children disembarked from the *Mayflower* to found the first permanent European settlement north of Virginia (they had found their earlier landing in Provincetown to be unsuitable). Today Plymouth is characterized by narrow streets, clapboard mansions, shops, antiques stores, and a scenic waterfront. To mark Thanksgiving, the town holds activities including historic-house tours and a parade. Historic statues dot the town, including William Bradford, Pilgrim leader and governor of the colony for more than 30 years, on Water Street; a Pilgrim maiden in Brewster Gardens; and Massasoit, the Wampanoag chief who helped the Pilgrims survive, on Carver Street.

### Don't Miss

Against the backdrop of the Atlantic Ocean, Plimoth Patuxet Museums (formerly known as Plimoth Plantation) is a fascinating living museum that shares the rich, interwoven story of the Plymouth Colony and the indigenous Wampanoag homeland through engaging daily programs and interactive experiences.

### Best Tour

To get a sense of what life was like for Pilgrims on the journey to Plymouth, climb aboard this meticulous replica of the legendary *Mayflower*.

### When to Go

Note that the Plimoth Patuxet Museums complex is closed late November–mid-March.

### Getting Here and Around

The Plimoth Patuxet Museums are 3 miles south of downtown Plymouth, off Route 3A, about 40 miles southeast of Boston and 20 miles northwest of the bridge to Cape Cod.

# Martha's Vineyard

## Bike New England's Most Beautiful Island

With more than 60 miles of gently (and steeply) undulating roads, relatively little car traffic, numerous cycling trails, and captivating views in every direction, Martha's Vineyard is the ultimate New England island to tour on a bike. Far less developed than Cape Cod, Martha's Vineyard abounds with scenic and sophisticated diversions, including the charming villages of Vineyard Haven, Oak Bluffs, and Edgartown. And then there's the quiet, simpler beauty: the ancient docks and weathered fishing boats of Menemsha Harbor, and the serene landscapes—especially if you make the few-minute ferry ride to sleepy Chappaquiddick Island—of gardens at Mytoi and dunes, salt marshes, and tidal flats of Cape Poge Wildlife Refuge.

## Don't Miss

At the southwestern tip of the island, the spectacularly striated, red-clay Aquinnah Cliffs and adjoining Moshup Beach are a must-stop on your bike tour. Native American crafts and food shops line the short approach to the overlook, and you can tour the 1799 Gay Head Lighthouse.

## Best Seafood Market

At the Net Result you'll find some of the island's freshest and tastiest seafood at this casual market and seafood shack. ⊕ *mvseafood.com.*

## Getting Here and Around

Most visitors get here by ferry—car and passenger boats connect with Falmouth, Hyannis, and a few other ports. You'll find bike rental shops by the ferry landings in Vineyard Haven, Oak Bluffs, and Edgartown. You can also fly here from Hyannis and New Bedford.

**Martha's Vineyard Chamber of Commerce.** ✉ *24 Beach St., Vineyard Haven, MA* ☎ *508/693–0085* ⊕ *mvy.com.*

# Cape Cod National Seashore

## New England's Prettiest Beaches

Extending 30 miles from Chatham to Provincetown and encompassing Cape Cod's outer "hook," this 43,000-acre swatch of superb beaches, undulating dunes, marshes and wetlands, and pitch-pine and scrub-oak forest is laced with walking, biking, and horseback trails. Even when the rest of Cape Cod feels packed with summer revelers, it's possible to find solitude here. Highlights include Fort Hill, with its pastoral hills that roll gently down to Nauset Marsh and is popular with bird-watchers and nature photographers, and Marconi Station, where a lookout deck marks the spot where the first American wireless message to Europe was sent. Don't miss the boardwalk trail through a gorgeous Atlantic white cedar swamp.

## Don't Miss

You'll find some of New England's prettiest beaches at Cape Cod National Seashore, with two of the most spectacular in Provincetown: Race Point Beach and Herring Cove Beach.

## Best Dune Tour

Art's Dune Tours has been taking eager passengers into the dunes of Province Lands since 1946. Head out at sunset for a stunning ride, available with or without a clambake feast. 🌐 *artsdunetours.com.*

## When to Go

Cape Cod is warmest and most alluring—but also crowded—in summer.

## Getting Here and Around

The national seashore is located along U.S. 6 and has two visitor centers, one in Eastham and one in Provincetown.

**Cape Cod National Seashore Salt Pond Visitor Center.** ✉ *50 Nauset Rd., Eastham, MA* 🌐 *nps.gov/caco* 🎫 *$25 per vehicle.*

# Nantucket

## The Whaling Capital of the World

At the height of its prosperity in the early 19th century, Nantucket's harbor bustled with whaling ships and merchant vessels and it was known as the whaling capital of the world—no small feat for an island that is a mere 14 miles long by 3½ miles wide. The entire town of Nantucket is now an official National Historic District, encompassing more than 800 pre-1850 structures within 1 square mile. Day-trippers usually take in the architecture and historical sites, dine at one of the many delightful restaurants, and browse in pricey boutiques.

## Don't Miss

With exhibits that include a fully rigged whaleboat and a skeleton of a 46-foot sperm whale, the exceptional Whaling Museum offers a crash course in the island's colorful history.

## Hippest Hotel

A short stroll from the ferry dock and numerous restaurants, Life House Nantucket occupies a 200-year-old sea captain's house with a garden terrace and fire pit. 🌐 *lifehousehotels.com*.

## When to Go

Nantucket is a prime summer destination, but the mellow yet still mild spring and fall shoulder seasons are quite pleasant and far less expensive.

## Getting Here and Around

You can get most easily to the island by car or passenger ferry and by plane from Hyannis. Seasonal ferries also run to several other ports around the East Coast, and to Martha's Vineyard. Most attractions and businesses are in Nantucket Town, within walking distance of the ferry, and taxis and buses can get you farther afield.

**Nantucket Tourism.** ✉ *25 Federal St., Nantucket MA* ☎ *508/228–0925* 🌐 *nantucket-ma.gov.*

## Mass MoCA

### The Berkshires' Best Art

Set in the handsome 1860s redbrick buildings that once housed the Sprague Electrical Company, Massachusetts Museum of Contemporary Art (Mass MoCA) is the nation's largest center for contemporary visual and performing arts. In this 250,000-square-foot multi-building museum you can admire wall drawings of Sol LeWitt, an immersive light-based exhibit by James Turrell, and sculptures from Louise Bourgeois.

### Don't Miss

Just 6 miles west, Williamstown is famous in summer for its renowned Williamstown Theatre Festival and year-round for prestigious Williams College, home to the fantastic Williams College Museum of Art and its excellent American and 20th-century collections. Within walking distance, you can tour one of the nation's notable small art museums, the Clark Institute.

### Best Hotel

Across the street from Mass MoCA, the Porches Inn occupies a series of 1890s former workers' cottages that have been restored and connected with one long porch. 🌐 *porches.com.*

### When to Go

In October, the area is home to some of the most spectacular fall foliage in the Berkshires, but the area's art museums are open and well worth a visit any time of year.

### Getting Here and Around

Mass MoCA is in North Adams, just off Route 2, in the Berkshires—and the very northwestern corner of the state.

**Mass MoCA.** ✉ *87 Marshall St., North Adams, MA* ☎ *413/664–4111* 🌐 *mass-moca.org* 🎫 *$20.*

# Tanglewood

## Summer Symphonies

Set in the verdant landscape of the Berkshire hills, the 529-acre summer home of the Boston Symphony Orchestra since 1937, Tanglewood hosts world-famous musicians and attracts up to 350,000 music lovers every season. The 5,000-seat main shed hosts larger concerts; the more intimate Seiji Ozawa Hall seats around 1,200 and is used for chamber music and solo performances. Among the most rewarding ways to experience Tanglewood is to purchase lawn tickets, arrive early with blankets or lawn chairs, and enjoy a picnic under the stars. Except for the occasional big-name concert, lawn tickets are quite reasonable.

## Don't Miss

This sophisticated little town in the Berkshires—home to a number of posh inns and eateries—is also home to Shakespeare and Company, an acclaimed theater group that presents the works of the Bard and other writers. One of these, the Rose Footprint Theatre, reflects the dimensions of the Rose, Shakespeare's first performance space in London.

## Best Pre-Show Dinner

Make a delectable feast of Mediterranean small plates and hand-tossed pizzas at Brava, a dapper downtown Lenox bistro. 🌐 *facebook.com/bravabarlenox*.

## When to Go

Concerts at Tanglewood typically take place from late June through early September, while Shakespeare and Company performs year-round.

## Getting There and Around

Lenox is in the heart of the Berkshires, off U.S. 7 and 20.

**Tanglewood.** ✉ *297 West St., Lenox, MA* ☎ *617/266–1200* 🌐 *bso.org* 🎟 *Varies by performance.*

# Cranberry Bog Tours

### All-American Harvest

Cape Cod's famous cranberry industry took off in Harwich in 1844, when Alvin Cahoon was its principal grower. Today you'll still find working cranberry bogs throughout Harwich, including Leo and Andrea Cakouneses' farm just off U.S. 6. They operate with informative and family-friendly 90-minute tours of their farm, during which you'll learn all about the harvesting and processing of these iconic tart berries used in everything from Thanksgiving relishes to juices, cookies, and candies. You'll also see lots of cute animals who work on this farm, and you can buy cranberry products and other goods at the farmstand.

### Don't Miss

In the Upper Cape village of Cataumet, near Falmouth, family-owned Somerset Creamery has been producing rich, thick ice cream since 1937. It's the destination on Cape Cod for a refreshing scoop of Cranberry Bog ice cream, a beloved cranberry-based concoction studded with dark chocolate, craisins, and walnuts.

### Best Restaurant

Cape Sea Grill uses what's locally available as the inspiration for an ever-changing and creative menu that's complemented by a vibrant, welcoming atmosphere. There are also generous wine, martini, and drink lists. 🌐 *www.capeseagrille.com*.

### When to Go

Cranberries have a surprisingly long growing season—April to November—but come in fall to see them when they're red and ripe.

### Getting There and Around

Harwich is 84 miles southeast of Boston via MA 3.

**Cranberry Bog Tours** ✉ *1601 Factory Rd., Harwich, MA* ☎ *508/432–0790* 🌐 *cranberrybogtours.com* 🎫 *$15.*

# Boston's North End

## Food, Glorious Italian Food

You can eat your way through one of America's most colorful and prolific Little Italy neighborhoods in Boston's North End. This is the city's haven not only for Italian restaurants but also for Italian groceries, bakeries, boccie courts, churches, social clubs, and street-corner debates over home-team soccer games. July and August are highlighted by a series of street festivals, or feste, honoring various saints, and by local community events that draw people from all over the city. A statue of St. Agrippina di Mineo—which is covered with money when it's paraded through the streets—is a crowd favorite. Although gentrification has diluted the quarter's ethnic character some, linger for a moment along Salem or Hanover Street and you can still hear people speaking with Abruzzese accents.

## Don't Miss

Take a stroll down Hanover Street, the North End's main thoroughfare, and you'll find all the cannoli and cappuccinos your heart could desire. Hanover's excellent bakeries include Modern Pastry Shop, Mike's Pastry, or a block over on Salem Street, Bova's Bakery.

## While You're Here

Walk off all the calories in the Paul Revere mall on 370 Hanover Street, pausing on a bench in the greenery to admire Revere's statue.

## Getting Here and Around

The North End is easily accessible; take the Orange or Green Line to the Haymarket T stop. Like most of Boston, the neighborhood is extremely walkable.

**The North End.** ✉ *Hanover St., from Cross to Commercial Sts., Boston, MA* ☎ *888/733–2678* 🌐 *northendboston.com.*

# When in Massachusetts

## CASTLE HILL ON CRANE ESTATE

This 59-room Stuart-style mansion, built in 1927 and depicted memorably as Jack Nicholson's love nest in *The Witches of Eastwick,* is part of the Crane Estate, a glorious patch of more than 2,100 acres along the Essex and Ipswich rivers, encompassing Castle Hill, Crane Beach, and the Crane Wildlife Refuge. Although the original furnishings were sold at auction, the mansion has been elaborately furnished in period style and is open for tours. There's also fishing, kayaking, and other activities on-site as well as accommodations in the opulent and exquisite Inn at Castle Hill. The estate is a lovely base for exploring Cape Anne, a rocky and scenic peninsula just 30 miles northeast of Boston that's home to such picturesque fishing and boating towns as Essex, Rockport, Gloucester, and Manchester-by-the-Sea.

**Do This:** Shaped appropriately like a giant fried-clam box, the funky Clam Box roadside stand has been serving Ipswich's famous bivalves—along with oysters, scallops, and other delights front the sea—since 1935.

**The Crane Estate.** ✉ *290 Argilla Rd., Ipswich, MA* ☎ *978/356–4351* 🌐 *thetrustees.org* 🎫 *$20 per vehicle.*

## MONTAGUE BOOKMILL

This incredibly picturesque 1840s mill complex along the Pioneer Valley's Saw Mill River—since converted into a quintet of businesses that include a vintage music store and an outstanding arts and crafts gallery—exudes old New England. The Bookmill is a quirky, well-stocked secondhand bookshop whose comfortable chairs make it easy to curl up with a book. The good-humored staffers at the adjoining Lady Killigrew café serve craft beer, strong coffee, and delicious Brie–apple–apricot jam sandwiches. The fantastic waterfall views from the deck of Alvah Stone, which serves eclectic lunch and dinner fare, justify its slightly elevated prices.

**Do This:** A short drive south you can explore the charming downtowns of Amherst and Northampton, with their lively college campuses and fervent creative—and especially literary—vibes. Book lovers should make a point of visiting the Emily Dickinson Museum, the Federal-style home in which the legendary poet lived and wrote for decades, and the light-filled Eric Carle Museum, which celebrates and preserves not only the works of renowned children's book author Eric Carle, who penned *The Very Hungry Caterpillar,* but also original picture-book art by Maurice Sendak, Margot Zemach, William Steig, Ashley Bryan, and many others.

**Montague Bookmill.** ✉ *440 Greenfield Rd., Montague, MA* ☎ *413/367–9206* 🌐 *montaguebookmill.com* 🎫 *Free.*

## PROVINCETOWN'S COMMERCIAL STREET

Stretching 2½ miles through Provincetown, with wonderful harbor views along the way, Commercial Street is one of the liveliest and most colorful main thoroughfares on the Eastern Seaboard. Here in the heart of what could be considered America's original LGBTQ summer resort, you'll find an astounding diversity of fun stops as you make your way from the East End to the West End, passing offbeat card and gift shops, prestigious art galleries, hip home-accent galleries, sassy purveyors of club and swimwear, buzzy bars, campy cabarets, lively restaurant patios, and an impressive array of historic buildings in every many architectural styles—Greek Revival, Victorian, Second Empire, and Gothic, to name a few. In summer, Commercial Street is practically a parade of people-watching, but it's a pleasant stroll even in the peaceful off-season months.

**Do This:** Founded in 1914 to collect and exhibit the works of artists with local connections, the impressive Provincetown Art Association and Museum contains more than 3,000 works by a mix up-and-comers and established 20th-century figures like Milton Avery, Robert Motherwell, Claes Oldenburg, Man Ray, John Singer Sargent, Andy Warhol, and Agnes Weinrich. The museum store is fantastic.

**Provincetown Chamber of Commerce.** ✉ *307 Commercial St., Provincetown, MA* ☎ *508/487–3424* 🌐 *ptownchamber.com.*

## Cool Places to Stay

**Lands End Inn.** Built in 1904 on a sweeping bluff in Provincetown's historic West End, this wildly ornate and idiosyncratic former summer home is now a fascinating inn with one-of-a-kind rooms—many with unusual architectural details like domed ceilings, cozy alcoves and lofts, stained-glass windows and Tiffany lamps, and huge decks overlooking the water. ✉ *22 Commercial St., Provincetown, MA* ☎ *508/487–0706* 🌐 *landsendinn.com* [$] *From $150.*

**Liberty Hotel Boston.** This chic Luxury Collection hotel—formerly Boston's 1850s Charles Street Jail—is famous both as a place to roost in luxury and revel in its swank Liberty Affairs bar; rooms are either in the original granite building or an adjacent 16-story modern tower, and feature rich hardwood floors, herringbone-patterned walls, and artwork that focuses on the building's rich history. ✉ *215 Charles St., Boston, MA* ☎ *617/224–4000* 🌐 *libertyhotel.com* [$] *From $185.*

**Red Lion Inn.** An inn since 1773, this imposing building in the Berkshires has hosted presidents, senators, and other celebrities; these days lodging is situated between a large main building and nine annexes, so if you want to experience a historic environment filled with antiques, request a room in the main building, keeping in mind that many rooms are cozy and have thin walls, but the ambience is endearingly authentic. ✉ *30 Main St., Stockbridge, MA* ☎ *413/298–5545* 🌐 *redlioninn.com* [$] *From $182.*

**Winnetu Oceanside Resort.** A departure from most properties on Martha's Vineyard, the contemporary Winnetu—styled after the grand multistory resorts of the Gilded Age—has successfully struck a fine balance in that it both encourages families and provides a contemporary seaside-resort experience for couples, with rooms that have full kitchens and decks or patio and a huge pool. ✉ *31 Dunes Rd., Edgartown, MA* ☎ *508/335–1133* 🌐 *winnetu.com* [$] *From $325.*

# New Hampshire

New Hampshire's mountain peaks, clear air, and sparkling lakes have attracted trailblazers and artists (and untold numbers of tourists) for centuries. The state's varied geography—not to mention the range of outdoor activities its mountains, lakes, and forests support—is part of the attraction, but hospitality and friendliness are major factors, too: visitors tend to feel quickly at home in this place of beauty and history. Whether you're an outdoors enthusiast seeking adventure or just want to enjoy a good book on the porch swing of a century-old inn, you'll find plenty of opportunities to fulfill your heart's desire.

## Bucket List Picks

The following boxes contain our picks for the top sights and experiences in New Hampshire.

- ○ Lake Winnipesaukee
- ○ Franconia Notch State Park
- ○ Kancamagus Highway
- ○ Mt. Washington
- ○ Pemi Valley Moose Tours
- ○ Dartmouth
- ○ Cornish
- ○ Peterborough

# Lake Winnipesaukee

## Beauty in a High Place

With about 240 miles of shoreline dotted with inlets and coves, Lake Winnipesaukee, which means "beautiful water in a high place," is the largest lake in New Hampshire and the state's big summer destination. The lake is encircled by well-preserved colonial and 19th-century villages, but Wolfeboro with its artsy boutiques, galleries, and eateries, and summering celebrities is the original and best summer resort. The nostalgic sign on the outskirts of this quietly upscale town on New Hampshire's largest body of water welcomes you to "The Oldest Summer Resort in America," thanks to a summer house built here in 1769.

## Don't Miss

Less than 10 miles north of Lake Winnipesaukee, the peaceful village of Holderness straddles two of the state's most scenic lakes, Squam and Little Squam, both of which have been spared from excessive development but do offer some memorable inns, perfect for a tranquil getaway. Don't miss the Squam Lakes Natural Science Center's nature trails, pontoon boat cruises, and 1-acre Kirkwood Gardens.

## Best Lake Views

Looking like a fairy-tale castle, Castle in the Clouds, a grand 1914 mountaintop estate, is anchored by an elaborate mansion with 16 rooms. 🌐 *castleintheclouds.org*.

## When to Go

The entire Lakes Region is at its prime for beauty and bustle in summer.

## Getting Here and Around

Wolfeboro is at the junction of Routes 28 and 109 at the southeast end of Lake Winnipesaukee.

**Wolfeboro Area Chamber of Commerce A.** ✉ *32 Central Ave., Wolfeboro, NH* ☎ *603/569–2200* 🌐 *wolfeborochamber.com*.

# Franconia Notch State Park

### Family Fun in the White Mountains

Traversed by the Appalachian Trail, this stunning 6,692-acre state park feels as epic as a national park and offers dozens of diversions, including myriad hiking trails, summer swimming at Echo Lake Beach, and winter downhill skiing at Cannon Mountain, whose 4,080-foot summit observation deck you can explore on the Aerial Tramway. The dramatic, narrow, 800-foot-long Flume Gorge is reached from a modern visitor center via a picturesque 2-mile loop hike along wooden stairways.

### Don't Miss

Robert Frost's year-round home from 1915 to 1920 is a modest homestead on a peaceful unpaved road in Franconia. It's surrounded by well-tended gardens and offers sweeping mountain views. Out back, you can follow short trails marked with lines from his poetry. Poetry readings are scheduled some summer evenings.

### Best Restaurant

In the Dexter family for generations, Polly's Pancake Parlor has been serving up pancakes and waffles (from its own original recipe, with several batter options available, including cornmeal and gingerbread) since the 1930s. 🌐 *pollyspancakeparlor.com.*

### When to Go

There's plenty to enjoy in Franconia Notch State Park year-round, from hiking and admiring the foliage in summer and fall to great skiing in winter.

### Getting Here and Around

The park is bisected by Interstate 93, between Lincoln and Franconia.

**Cannon Mountain Aerial Tramway.**
✉ *260 Tramway Dr., Franconia, NH*
☎ *603/823–8800* 🌐 *nhstateparks.org*
🎫 *Free.*

# Kancamagus Highway

## New Hampshire's Most Scenic Road

In 1937, two local roads were connected from Lincoln to Conway to create this remarkable 34½-mile designated National Scenic Byway through a breathtaking swath of the White Mountains. This section of Route 112 known as the Kancamagus—often called simply "the Kanc"—contains no businesses or billboards and is punctuated by overlooks, picnic areas, and memorable hiking trailheads. The road's highest point, at 2,855 feet, crosses the flank of Mt. Kancamagus, near Lincoln—the most perfect place to view the fiery displays of foliage each autumn.

## Don't Miss

Connected to the Kanc via Bear Notch Road, scenic U.S. 302 winds northwest from the town of Bartlett through steep, wooded mountains on either side of spectacular Crawford Notch State Park. You can picnic and hike to Arethusa Falls, the longest drop in New England, or to the Silver and Flume cascades—they're among more than a dozen outstanding trails.

## Best Hike

There are several excellent hikes along the Kancamagus Highway, but the most rewarding trek is the easy 6-mile round-trip Lincoln Woods hike, which follows a picturesque railroad bed, crosses a dramatic suspension bridge over the Pemigewasset River, and ends at a swimming hole formed by dramatic Franconia Falls.

## Getting Here and Around

The Kancamagus Highway is the span of Route 112 between Lincoln and Conway.

**Kancamagus Highway.** ✉ *Rte. 112, Lincoln, NH* ☎ *603/536–6100* 🌐 *fs.usda.gov/whitemountain.*

# Mt. Washington

## Ascend the Northeast's Highest Peak

At 6,288 feet, Mt. Washington is a land of superlatives. It's the tallest peak in the northeastern United States, and the world's highest winds, 231 mph, were recorded here in 1934. You can take a guided van tour, a drive, or a hike to the summit—a number of challenging trails circle the mountain and access the other peaks in the adjoining Presidential Range. The drive to the top, along narrow, curving Mt. Washington Auto Road, which climbs 4,600 feet in about 7 miles, is truly memorable.

## Don't Miss

Featuring a dramatic 28-mile network of both mild and wild cross-country ski and mountain-biking trails at the foot of Mt. Washington, Great Glen Trails Outdoor Center provides access to more than 1,100 acres of backcountry. You can also book to the summit, via SnowCoach, a nine-passenger van refitted with triangular snowmobile-like treads.

## Best Train Ride

Since 1869, the Mount Washington Cog Railway has chugged its way up to the summit along a 3-mile track on the mountain's west side. Today it's a beloved attraction—a thrill in either direction. 🌐 *thecog.com*.

## When to Go

The cog railroad runs from May through December, and the auto road is open early May to late October.

## Getting Here and Around

The Mt. Washington Auto Road is off Route 16, about 12 miles north of Jackson. The cog railroad station is on the opposite (west) side of the mountain, off U.S. 302 in Bretton Woods and the historic Omni Mount Washington Resort.

# Pemi Valley Moose Tours

## Fall for New England's Largest Mammal

Among the many majestic creatures that inhabit New Hampshire's rugged forests, moose—of which there are 3,500 to 4,000—are perhaps the most beguiling and mysterious. Weighing about 1,000 pounds on average, and standing at about 6 feet at their shoulders, these powerful animals are the largest mammals in the Northeast. How to see them? You may just be lucky enough to spy one through your car window—U.S. 3 and Routes 16 and 26 in northern New Hampshire's Great North Woods are a good bet, especially at dusk in summer. But you can greatly increase your odds by taking a three-hour guided excursion with Pemi Moose Tours—moose are seen on about 97% of these trips.

## Don't Miss

The isolated and alluring Great North Woods, centered on the town of Pittsburgh, occupies the 250-square-mile northern tip of the state. The 90-mile drive up U.S. 3 from Littleton to the Canadian border is a favorite for moose and other wildlife viewing.

## Best Hotel

Old-world elegance and stunning views of the upper White Mountains define the Mountain View Grand Resort and Spa. 🌐 *mountainviewgrand.com.*

## When to Go

Moose tours are offered early May through mid-October, which is also the best time to enjoy the scenery.

## Getting Here and Around

Pemi Moose Tours operates out of Lincoln in the White Mountains, on Route 112, just off Interstate 93. The Great North Woods lies about 30 miles north via U.S. 3.

**Pemi Valley Moose Tours Office.** ✉ *136 Main St., Lincoln, NH* ☎ *603/745-2744* 🌐 *moosetoursnh.com* 🎫 *$35.*

## Dartmouth

### The Stateliest Small-Town College Campus

The poet Robert Frost spent part of a brooding freshman semester at this Ivy League school before giving up college altogether, but Dartmouth counts politician Nelson Rockefeller, actor Mindy Kaling, TV producer Shonda Rhimes, and author Theodor ("Dr.") Seuss Geisel among its many illustrious grads. The buildings clustered around the picturesque green, which is lovely for strolling, include the Baker Memorial Library, which houses such literary treasures as 17th-century editions of William Shakespeare's works and Mexican artist José Clemente Orozco's 3,000-square-foot murals.

### Don't Miss

The college's excellent Hood Museum of Art contains works by Picasso, Rothko, and Miró and is housed in a series of austere, copper-roof, redbrick buildings arranged around a courtyard, and the Hopkins Center for the Arts bears a striking resemblance to Lincoln Center—architect Wallace K. Harrison designed both structures.

### Best Restaurant

With its stone fireplace, cathedral ceiling, and rustic-elegant barnlike interior, Ariana's in the venerable Lyme Inn turns out farm-fresh modern American fare with international influences. It overlooks a colonial green, 10 miles from Hanover. 🌐 *arianasrestaurant.com.*

### Getting Here and Around

Hanover is just across the Connecticut River from Interstate 91 in Vermont and 10 miles up Route 120 from Interstate 89.

**The Dartmouth Green.** ✉ *N. Main and Wentworth Sts., Hanover, NH* ☎ *603/646–1110* 🌐 *dartmouth.edu.*

# Cornish

## The Longest Covered Bridge

The 449-foot Cornish–Windsor Bridge connects New Hampshire to Vermont across the Connecticut River. Erected in 1866, it is the longest covered wooden bridge in the United States that carries automobile traffic. The notice on the bridge reads, "Walk your horses or pay two dollar fine." Serene and picturesque Cornish has two more scenic covered bridges and is also famous for having been home of the late reclusive author J. D. Salinger as well as a number of other acclaimed writers and artists over the years, Maxfield Parrish and Augustus Saint-Gaudens among them.

## Don't Miss

The pastoral Saint-Gaudens National Historic Site celebrates the life and artistry of the leading 19th-century sculptor. In summer you can tour his house (with original furnishings), studio, and galleries, and year-round it's a pleasure to explore the 150 gorgeous acres of lawns, gardens, and woodlands dotted with casts of his works and laced with 2½ miles of hiking trails.

## Best Ice Cream

One of the Northeast's best purveyors of artisanal, small-batch ice cream, the modest parlor in Walpole Creamery always features a long list of both regular and seasonal flavors, such as Fijian ginger, fresh peach, wild blueberry, and mint–dark chocolate chip. 🌐 *walpolecreamery.com.*

## Getting Here and Around

Just off Route 12A, about 20 miles south of Hanover, the Cornish–Windsor Bridge crosses the Connecticut River, leading to Interstate 91 in Vermont.

**Greater Claremont Chamber of Commerce.** ✉ *24 Opera House Sq., Claremont, NH* ☎ *603/543–1296* 🌐 *greaterclaremontnh.org.*

## Peterborough

### Venerable Arts Hub

While summering in the town's famed MacDowell artists' colony in this longtime hub of creativity in the lush Monadnock Mountains, Thornton Wilder wrote the classic play *Our Town*, basing it on Peterborough itself. This is also where Aaron Copland and Leonard Bernstein composed some of their iconic works, and James Baldwin, Willa Cather, and Alice Walker wrote novels. The town continues to draw big crowds in summer for its Monadnock Music and Peterborough Folk Music Society concerts, and especially for performances by the Peterborough Players.

### Don't Miss

You can play instruments or try on costumes from around the world and indulge your cultural curiosity at the nonprofit Mariposa Museum, which is dedicated to hands-on exploration of international folk art.

### Best Hike

Said to be America's most climbed mountain—more than 400 people sometimes crowd its bald peak—Mt. Monadnock rises to 3,165 feet, and on clear days you can see the Boston skyline. Five trailheads branch out into more than two dozen trails of varying difficulty. 🌐 *nhstateparks.org.*

### When to Go

Performances of the Peterborough Players and Monadnock Music groups take place in summer, but hiking Monadnock is lovely through autumn.

### Getting Here and Around

Peterborough is in south-central New Hampshire, at the junction of Route 101 and U.S. 202. It's about 15 miles east of Mt. Monadnock.

**Peterborough Players.** ✉ *55 Hadley Rd., Peterborough, NH* ☎ *603/924–7585* 🌐 *peterboroughplayers.org.*

# When in New Hampshire

## CANTERBURY SHAKER VILLAGE

Established in 1792, this village 20 miles southwest of Lake Winnipesaukee flourished in the 1800s and practiced equality of the sexes and races, common ownership, celibacy, and pacifism. The last member of the religious community passed away in 1992. Shakers invented such household items as the clothespin and the flat broom and were known for the simplicity and integrity of their designs. Engaging guided tours—you can also explore on your own—pass through some of the 694-acre property's more than 25 restored buildings, many of them with original furnishings. Crafts demonstrations take place daily.

**Do This:** The on-site Creamery Café serves light lunch fare in a beautiful Shaker-design dining room and sells seasonal vegetables and maple syrup. An excellent shop sells handcrafted wares, from handcrafted round boxes to soaps and lotions to home furnishings.

**Canterbury Shaker Village.** ✉ *288 Shaker Rd., Canterbury, NH* ☎ *603/783–9511* 🌐 *shakers.org* 🎟 *$20.*

## CURRIER MUSEUM OF ART

In a historic residential neighborhood in the state's largest city, this superb museum maintains an astounding permanent collection of works by European and American masters, among them Claude Monet, Edward Hopper, Winslow Homer, John Marin, Andrew Wyeth, and Childe Hassam. It presents excellent rotating exhibits of contemporary art, too. Be sure to set aside some time to stroll a few blocks west to the Manchester's bustling dining and nightlife strip, Elm Street, which has a number of excellent cafés, cocktail bars, and craft breweries.

**Do This:** The Currier also arranges guided tours of the nearby Zimmerman House. Completed in 1950, it's New England's only Frank Lloyd Wright–designed residence open to the public. Wright called this sparse, utterly functional living space "Usonian," a term he used to describe several dozen similar homes based on his vision of distinctly American architecture.

**Currier Museum of Art.** ✉ *150 Ash St., Manchester, NH* ☎ *603/669–6144* 🌐 *currier.org* 🎟 *$15.*

## PICKITY PLACE

Set down a remote wooded lane near the Massachusetts border, this endearing 1786 cottage looks right out of a fairy tale, and indeed, it served as the model for artist Elizabeth Orton Jones for her illustrations of the popular 1948 edition of the children's tale, *Little Red Riding Hood.* These days it's the centerpiece of a hilltop estate surrounded by fragrant gardens patrolled by a friendly team of cats and consisting of a nursery, a gift shop that sells herbs and gourmet goods, and an inviting restaurant that serves delicious locally sourced prix-fixe lunches that feature produce grown on the property.

**Do This:** Walk off your meal with a ramble among the 80 contemporary sculptures set throughout the 140-acre Andres Institute of Art, which is 10 miles away in Brookfield. The hilly property that used to occupy a small ski area is laced with peaceful trails.

**Pickity Place.** ✉ *248 Nutting Hill Rd., Mason, NH* ☎ *603/878–1151* 🌐 *pickityplace.com* 🎟 *Free.*

## PORTSMOUTH

More than a quaint harbor town with a long, colorful history, Portsmouth is an upscale community with trendy farm-to-table restaurants, contemporary art galleries, and cultural venues that host nationally recognized speakers and performers. Settled in 1623 as Strawbery Banke, Portsmouth grew into a prosperous port before the Revolutionary War. Today, swank cocktail bars, jumping live music, and late-night eateries create a convivial evening buzz in downtown's Market Square.

**Do This:** Located on the site of Portsmouth's original seaport, known as Puddle Dock, Strawbery Banke is an indoor-outdoor living history museum depicting local life from the late 1600s until the 1950s. The first English settlers named the area for the wild strawberries growing along the shores of the Piscataqua River, and the name lives on in this 10-acre outdoor history museum with 37 homes and other structures dating from 1695 to 1820.

**Strawbery Banke Museum.** ✉ *14 Hancock St., Portsmouth, NH* ☎ *603/433–1100* 🌐 *strawberybanke.org* 🎫 *$20.*

### SUNAPEE

Greater Lake Sunapee's pristine 6-square-miles of water—one of the highest and cleanest in New Hampshire—is the perfect peaceful retreat for families, artists, nature lovers, and anyone seeking lakeside tranquility. On the west shore you'll find Sunapee Harbor, an old-fashioned summer resort community with a large marina, a small museum, a few restaurants and shops on the water, and a tidy village green with a gazebo. Mt. Sunapee State Park has a pretty beach and a 3,000-foot mountain with excellent skiing and hiking. The beloved League of New Hampshire Craftsmen's Fair, the oldest crafts fair in the nation, takes place in August.

**Do This:** A buffet dinner is included on the two-hour sunset cruises aboard Sunapee Cruises' MV *Kearsarge,* a vintage-style steamship. 🌐 *sunapeecruises.com.*

**Lake Sunapee Region Chamber of Commerce.** ✉ *328 Main St., New London, NH* ☎ *603/526–6575* 🌐 *lakesunapeeregion-chamber.com* 🎫 *Free.*

## Cool Places to Stay

**Pickering House Inn.** Following an extensive two-year renovation, this striking yellow 1813 Federal mansion within walking distance of Lake Winnipesaukee now ranks among New Hampshire's most luxurious small inns, with its ultracushy rooms and superb adjacent restaurant, Pavilion. ✉ *116 S. Main St., Wolfeboro, NH* ☎ *603/569–6948* 🌐 *pickeringhouse-wolfeboro.com* [$] *From $325.*

**Squam Lake Inn.** Graceful Victorian furnishings fill this peaceful farmhouse inn a short stroll from Squam Lake, the setting of *On Golden Pond,* each of its 10 rooms richly outfitted with comfortable beds, organic toiletries, and soft bathrobes; rates include a sumptuous gourmet breakfast. ✉ *28 Shepard Hill Rd., Holderness, NH* ☎ *603/968–4417* 🌐 *squamlakeinn.com* [$] *From $194.*

**Sugar Hill Inn.** Although this upscale inn surrounded by neatly manicured gardens dates to 1789, it has a decidedly current vibe, from its sumptuous rooms with such modern perks as whirlpool tubs, gas fireplaces, and Bose sound systems, to the superb prix-fixe restaurant serving contemporary American fare. ✉ *116 NH 117, Sugar Hill Rd., Sugar Hill, NH* ☎ *603/869–7543* 🌐 *sugarhillinn.com* [$] *From $215.*

**Wentworth by the Sea.** Nearly demolished in the 1980s, one of coastal New England's most elegant Victorian grand resorts—where the likes of Harry Truman and Gloria Swanson once vacationed—has been meticulously restored and now ranks among the cushiest golf, boating, and spa getaways in New Hampshire. ✉ *588 Wentworth Rd., New Castle, NH* ☎ *603/422–7322* 🌐 *wentworth.com* [$] *From $251.*

# Rhode Island

"Rhode Island: 3% Bigger at Low Tide," reads a locally made T-shirt—an exaggeration, of course: the state geologist calculates it's actually more like 0.5%. But the smallest state's size is a source of pride, given all there is to do within its 1,500 square miles. You may find it hard to choose among so many experiences: historic walks, fine dining, and the WaterFire display in Providence; apple picking and riverboat cruises in the Blackstone Valley; fishing trips and beach excursions in South County and Block Island; pedaling along Bristol's bike path; and taking sunset sails in Newport and touring the Gilded Age mansions.

## Bucket List Picks

The following boxes contain our picks for the top sights and experiences in Rhode Island.

- ○ Newport Jazz and Folk Festivals
- ○ Providence's Benefit Street
- ○ Providence's RiverWalk
- ○ Bellevue Avenue Mansions
- ○ Block Island
- ○ Bristol
- ○ Narragansett

# Newport Jazz and Folk Festivals

## New England's Hottest Concerts

Held at Fort Adams State Park, on a scenic peninsula that juts into the city's yacht-filled harbor, the Newport Jazz and Newport Folk festivals are among the country's most respected music showcases. Held the last weekend in July and launched in 1959, the Newport Folk Festival books acts spanning folk, blues, country, bluegrass, folk rock, alt-country, indie folk, and folk punk. It's where, controversially, Bob Dylan went electric in 1965, and where the likes of Johnny Cash, Arlo Guthrie, Dolly Parton, and—more recently—Moses Sumney, Portugal the Man, and Sharon Van Etten have performed. The grandfather of all jazz festivals, founded in 1954, Newport Jazz is held the first weekend in August and featured Miles Davis and Frank Sinatra back in the day and Terence Blanchard, Ravi Coltrane, and Corinne Bailey Rae more recently.

## Don't Miss

Home of the largest coastal fortification in the United States, Fort Adams State Park hosts not only music festivals but also sailing events like the Volvo Ocean Race. The views of Newport Harbor are exquisite.

## Grab a Bite

Scales & Shells turns out innovative seafood, funky Zelda's is an inviting bistro with one of the best drinks menus in town, and the Red Parrot is a favorite.

## Getting Here and Around

Fort Adams State Park is across Newport Harbor from downtown Newport, off Harrison Avenue.

**Fort Adams State Park.** ✉ *Harrison Ave., Newport, RI* ☎ *401/848–5055* 🌐 *www.discovernewport.org/events/fairs-and-festivals* 🎟 *Varies.*

# Providence's Benefit Street

## Architectural Showplace

Stretching just over a mile on Providence's East Side, this cobblestone street is a museum mile comprising some of the country's best-preserved concentrations of colonial architecture and passing through the campuses of Brown University and the Rhode Island School of Design. The city's wealthiest families lived along the "mile of history" during the 18th and early 19th centuries. For a peek inside, take a tour of the city's most famous 18th-century home, the three-story John Brown House Museum. Brown's stately College Hill campus is dominated by Gothic and Beaux Arts structures.

## Don't Miss

The gorgeous RISD Museum of Art (known as "Riz Dee") houses more than 86,000 objects ranging from ancient art to work by contemporary artists, from Cézanne and Picasso to Warhol and Hockney.

## Best Historic Site

Philadelphia architect William Strickland designed the 1838 Providence Athenaeum in which Edgar Allan Poe courted the poet Sarah Helen Whitman. An 1870s Manet print that illustrated Poe's "The Raven" hangs in the rare book room. 🌐 *providenceathenaeum.org.*

## When to Go

Benefit Street and the surrounding campuses of Brown University and RISD are especially pleasant during the temperate spring and fall months, but they're enjoyable to explore any time of year.

## Getting Here and Around

Benefit Street is just east of and a short walk across the Providence River from downtown.

**The Rhode Island Historical Society.** 🌐 *rihs.org.*

# Providence's RiverWalk

## Rhode Island's Most Dynamic Promenade

Venetian-style footbridges, seasonal gondola rides, art installations, cobblestone walkways, historic monuments, quaint shops, excellent restaurants, and an amphitheater encircling a tidal basin make this 4-acre park along the Woonasquatucket River the place to take in the views and activity in downtown Providence. In summer, RiverWalk park is a gathering place for free concerts and for WaterFire, an award-winning fire sculpture installation on downtown's three rivers featuring music and nearly 100 burning braziers that rise from the water between dusk and midnight.

## Don't Miss

Curving across the lower end of the Providence River, the sleek and contemporary Providence Pedestrian Bridge is decked with artful wooden benches and is a lovely spot for a walk or a bike ride, especially at sunset. It connects the up-and-coming Jewelry District to Wickenden Street and Fox Point, with its international restaurants and quirky cafés.

## Best Restaurant

In a city where culinary newcomers tend to garner all the attention, Hemenway's continues to stand out for serving absolutely stellar seafood. 🌐 *hemenwaysrestaurant.com.*

## When to Go

The downtown riverfront is lovely to stroll along from spring through fall, which is also when occasional WaterFire events take place about a dozen times a year.

## Getting Here and Around

The Providence riverfront is in the heart of the city's walkable downtown, just off Interstates 95 and 195.

**RiverWalk.** ✉ *Memorial Blvd., Providence, RI* ☎ *401/456–0200* 🌐 *goprovidence.com.*

# Bellevue Avenue Mansions

## USA's Most Opulent Homes

The Gilded Age mansions of Bellevue Avenue are the go-to attraction for many Newport visitors. These ornately detailed late-19th-century homes, designed with a determined one-upmanship by the very wealthy, are almost obscenely grand. Their owners—Vanderbilts, Astors, Belmonts, and other budding aristocrats who made the city their playground for a mere six–eight summer weeks each year—helped establish the best young American architects and precipitated the arrival of the New York Yacht Club, which turned Newport into a sailing capital of the world.

## Don't Miss

A visit to the 70-room "summer cottage" owned by Cornelius Vanderbilt II, the Breakers offers a peek into the private lives of the one-percenters of the Gilded Age.

## Best Stroll

See the backyards of Newport's Gilded Age mansions while strolling along the 3½-mile Cliff Walk. 🌐 *cliffwalk.com.*

## When to Go

Many of the most prominent mansions on Bellevue Avenue close from January through mid-April.

## Getting Here and Around

Most of Newport's Gilded Age mansions are on Bellevue Avenue, a short drive southeast of downtown, or a leisurely half-hour to hour-long walk.

**Newport Mansions.** ✉ *424 Bellevue Ave., Newport, RI* ☎ *401/847–1000* 🌐 *newportmansions.org* 🎟 *$26.*

# Block Island

## New England's Most Dramatic Sea Cliffs

With a rugged, windswept beauty that's reminiscent of the coast of Scotland, laid-back Block Island lies about 12 miles off the state's southern coast. The Nature Conservancy designated the island one of the "Last Great Places on Earth" (one of only 12 in the Western Hemisphere) in 1991, commending its efforts to preserve the island's precious ecosystem. You'll find the most awe-inspiring terrain atop the 200-foot cliffs traversed by the Mohegan Trail, from which you can see all the way to eastern Long Island on a clear day. A steep set of more than 100 stairs leads to a picturesque beach at the bottom. Also along the trail stands Southeast Lighthouse Museum, which is housed inside an 1875 redbrick lighthouse with gingerbread detail. Among the island's prettiest stretches of white sand, 3-mile Crescent Beach runs north from the main village, Old Harbor.

## Don't Miss

Animal lovers will want to stop at the 1661 Inn Animal Farm located on the property of Block Island Resorts to spot black swans, yaks, fainting goats, and a famed ZeDonk—zebra-donkey hybrid. 🌐 *blockislandresorts.com/exotic-farm-and-gardens*.

## When to Go

Block Island is most pleasant for a visit from late spring through early fall. Winter is chilly, but beautiful. Just keep in mind that many accommodations and restaurants close in the off-season.

## Getting Here and Around

You can reach Block Island by car ferry from Point Judith, at the south tip of Narragansett, and by seasonal passenger ferry from Newport, Fall River, New London, and Montauk. There are also daily 12-minute flights from the town of Westerly. The island is best explored by bike. 🌐 *www.blockislandferry.com*.

# Bristol

## The Nation's Oldest Fourth of July Party

America's longest-running Fourth of July celebration, which features a 2½-mile parade, has been taking place in Bristol since 1785. The town celebrates this heritage with a red-white-and-blue center stripe down Hope Street, which bisects its charming business district. Bristol sits on a 10-square-mile peninsula between Narragansett Bay and Mount Hope Bay and was once a boatbuilding center, and the southern end of the East Bay Bike Path, which crosses the access road for Colt State Park, a great spot for picnicking and kite flying.

## Don't Miss

A beautifully situated museum on Bristol Harbor that's devoted to the sport of yachting and that honors the Herreshoff Manufacturing Company—maker of yachts for eight consecutive America's Cup defenses—the Herreshoff Marine Museum has several dozen boats ranging from an 8½-foot dinghy to the *Defiant*, a 75-foot successful America's Cup defender.

## Best Restaurant

Run by the same family since 1966, Common's Lunch sits on the town green in the quaint coastal town of Little Compton, a picturesque 18-mile drive south of Bristol. 🌐 *commonslunch.com*.

## When to Go

The undeniable favorite time to experience Bristol is during the Fourth of July Parade, but the town is lovely year-round.

## Getting Here and Around

Bristol is in southeastern Rhode Island's East Bay region, midway between Providence and Newport on Route 114. It's another 18 miles south to Little Compton.

# Narragansett

## Rhode Island's Prettiest Beaches

A lively summer-long resort destination since the Victorian era, "'gansett" still has as its main landmark The Towers, the last remaining section of the 1886 Narragansett Pier Casino designed by McKim, Mead & White. The town is much quieter these days, but its historic charm, rocky coastline hikes, and pretty beaches still draw day-trippers, beach lovers, and hikers. Take a scenic drive down Route 1A to see the ocean and grand old shingle-style homes. Favorite spots for enjoying the sand include Narragansett Town Beach and Roger W. Wheeler State Beach.

## Don't Miss

A little corner of Narragansett with a lively working fishing village, Port of Galilee is where you can eat at a fish shack, go for a swim at Salty Brine State Beach, or just watch fishermen unload their catch. From the port of Galilee, it's a short drive to Point Judith Lighthouse, an 1857 tower with a beautiful ocean view.

## Best Restaurant

Aunt Carrie's has been a must for locals every summer since it opened in 1920. Try the Indian pudding, a traditional dessert made with cornmeal, molasses, and spices. 🌐 *auntcarriesri.com.*

## When to Go

Summer is the prime season to experience Narragansett's beaches. Late spring and early autumn are far less crowded.

## Getting Here and Around

Narragansett is along the coast in southern Rhode Island, just off U.S. 1 via Route 108 and Route 1A, about 15 miles west of Newport and 30 miles south of Providence.

**South County, Rhode Island.** 🌐 *southcountyri.com.*

# When in Rhode Island

## INTERNATIONAL TENNIS HALL OF FAME

Tennis fans especially—but really any lovers of history, art, and architecture—shouldn't miss visiting the birthplace of American tournament tennis. The beautifully designed museum contains interactive exhibits, a holographic theater that simulates being in a room with Roger Federer, displays of tennis attire worn by the sport's biggest stars, video highlights of great matches, and memorabilia that includes the 1874 patent from England's Queen Victoria for the game of lawn tennis. The 6-acre site just up the street from Newport's famous mansions is home to a grandstand, the shingle-style Newport Casino, which opened in 1880 and was designed by architects McKim, Mead & White, and the opulent Casino Theatre.

**Do This:** Anybody can play on the 13 grass tennis courts, one clay court, and in the indoor tennis facility—just try to book a few days in advance, especially on weekends. And in mid-July, you can attend the prestigious Hall of Fame Tennis Open, which also features a Hall of Fame induction ceremony.

**International Tennis Hall of Fame.** ✉ *194 Bellevue Ave., Newport, RI* ☎ *401/849–3990* 🌐 *tennisfame.com* 🎫 *$16.*

## OLD SLATER MILL

Concord and Lexington may legitimately lay claim to what Ralph Waldo Emerson called "the shot heard round the world" in 1776, but Pawtucket's Slater Mill provided the necessary economic shot in the arm. Built in 1793, this focal point of the Blackstone River Valley National Historical Park was the first successful water-powered spinning mill in America; it touched off the industrial revolution that helped secure America's sovereign independence in the early days of the republic. The museum complex explores this second revolution with expert interpretive guides dressed in period clothing, who demonstrate fiber-to-yarn and yarn-to-fabric processes and discuss how industrialization forever changed this nation.

**Do This:** Drive about 15 miles up the Blackstone River from Pawtucket to visit the cleverly designed Museum of Work & Culture in Woonsocket, which occupies another prominent former mill. This interactive museum examines the lives of American factory workers and owners during the Industrial Revolution, with a focus on the many French Canadian immigrants who toiled in the city's textile mills.

**Blackstone River Valley National Historical Park.** ✉ *67 Roosevelt Ave., Pawtucket, RI* ☎ *401/521–7266* 🌐 *nps.gov/blrv* 🎫 *$12.*

## PROVIDENCE'S FEDERAL HILL

Federal Hill has been the heart of the city's Italian community for generations. Around colorful DePasquale Plaza and along the main drag, Atwells Avenue, you'll find a slew of inviting, old-world Italian restaurants. Favorites include Angelo's Civita Farnese, with its flavorful eggplant Parmesan and braciola like grandma used to make, and romantic, warmly lighted Pane e Vino, which stands out for its exceptional wine list and sophisticated fare like Narragansett Creamery burrata with prosciutto di Parma, and bone-in veal chops with mushroom demi-glace.

**Do This:** After dinner, walk a few blocks south into the hip and increasingly trendy foodie neighborhood of West Broadway for dessert at Tricycle Ice Cream, whose delicious small-batch ice cream sandwiches come in imaginative flavors. Consider the toasted-coconut cookies with Thai tea ice cream, or peanut butter cookies with banana pudding ice cream.

**Federal Hill.** ✉ *Atwells and De Pasquale Aves., Providence, RI* ☎ *401/456–0200* 🌐 *goprovidence.com.*

### TOURO SYNAGOGUE

Newport is home to the nation's oldest synagogue. In 1658, more than a dozen Jewish families, whose ancestors had fled Spain and Portugal during the Inquisition, founded a congregation in Newport. A century later, Peter Harrison designed this two-story Palladian house of worship for them. The oldest surviving synagogue in the country, Touro was dedicated in 1763 and its simple exterior and elegant interior remain virtually unchanged.

**Do This:** The John L. Loeb Visitors Center has two floors of state-of-the-art exhibits on early American Jewish life and Newport's colonial history.

**Touro Synagogue.** ✉ *85 Touro St., Newport, RI* ☎ *401/847–0700* 🌐 *tourosynagogue.org* 🎫 *$12.*

### WATCH HILL LIGHTHOUSE

For generations, the seaside village of Watch Hill has attracted movers and shakers looking for a low-key getaway. Its nearly 2 miles of gorgeous beaches—including Napatree Point Conservation Area—are a great spot to see shorebirds and raptors and take in the sunset. A highlight of any visit is touring the tiny museum at the often-photographed 1808 Watch Hill Lighthouse, which contains the original Fresnel light, letters and journals from lighthouse keepers, and photos of the hurricane of 1938. Nearby on Bay Street, you can go for a ride on Flying Horse Carousel, one of the oldest in America—it dates to the 1870s.

**Do This:** Overlooking the Watch Hill Cove since it first opened as an ice cream parlor in 1916, the Olympia Tea Room is now one of South County's most sophisticated and charming bistros. Varnished wood booths and a long marble counter echo the restaurant's rich history. The kitchen focuses on local and artisanal ingredients served with simple elegance, including whole roasted flounder and braised lamb shanks. The sommelier has curated a wine list with hundreds of selections—more than 40 available by the glass.

**Watch Hill Lighthouse.** ✉ *14 Lighthouse Rd., Westerly, RI* ☎ *401/596–7761* 🌐 *watchhilllighthousekeepers.org* 🎫 *Free.*

## Cool Places to Stay

**Renaissance Providence Downtown Hotel.** This posh hotel occupies one of Providence's most mysterious addresses, a stately nine-story Neoclassical Revival building constructed as a Masonic temple between 1926 and 1928 but unoccupied for an inconceivable 75 years—the decor pays tribute to building's history photos of vintage graffiti found in the long-empty corridors during its restoration. ✉ *5 Ave. of the Arts, Providence, RI* ☎ *401/919–5000* 🌐 *marriott.com* [$] *From $152.*

**Rose Island Lighthouse.** Visible at the mouth of Narragansett Bay from the soaring Claiborne Pell bridge and reached via seasonal Jamestown Newport Ferry, this 1870 lighthouse beside colonial Fort Hamilton offers overnight accommodations in several different buildings, including the keeper's apartment, the museum, the 1912 Foghorn Building, and the dramatically high-ceilinged Fort Hamilton Barracks. ✉ *Rose Island, Newport, RI* ☎ *401/847–4242* 🌐 *roseisland.org* [$] *From $259.*

**Weekapaug Inn.** Guest rooms at this lovingly restored inn on Quonochontaug (Quonnie) Pond are furnished with luxury linens and the work of area artists, and the extensive amenities include bocce and shuffleboard, yoga and nature classes, seasonal swimming at a private beach, a lap pool, a stellar restaurant, and access access to programs and services at the nearby Ocean House, a sister property. ✉ *25 Spray Rock Rd., Westerly, RI* ☎ *401/637–7600* 🌐 *weekapauginn.com* [$] *From $370.*

# Vermont

Vermont is a land of hidden treasures and unspoiled scenery. Wander anywhere in the state—nearly 80% is forest—and you'll find pristine countryside dotted with farms and framed by mountains. Tiny towns with picturesque church steeples, village greens, and clapboard colonial-era houses are perfect for exploring. In fall the leaves have their last hurrah, painting the mountainsides in yellow, gold, red, and orange, but almost anywhere you go, no matter what time of year, the Vermont countryside will make you reach for your camera.

## Bucket List Picks

The following boxes contain our picks for the top sights and experiences in Vermont.

- ○ Stowe Mountain Resort
- ○ Burlington and Lake Champlain
- ○ Morse Farm Maple Sugarworks
- ○ Bennington
- ○ Quechee Gorge
- ○ Marsh-Billings-Rockefeller National Historical Park
- ○ Middlebury Tasting Trail
- ○ Hildene
- ○ Ben & Jerry's Factory

# Stowe Mountain Resort

## Ski Vermont's Tallest Mountain

The name of the village is Stowe, and the name of the 4,395-foot mountain is Mt. Mansfield—but to generations of skiers, it's all just plain "Stowe." The area's mystique attracts as many serious skiers as social ones. Stowe is a giant among Eastern ski mountains with intimidating expert runs, but skiers of all abilities enjoy the long, satisfying runs from the summit. Improved snowmaking capacity, new lifts, and free shuttle buses that gather skiers along Mountain Road have made it all much more convenient. Yet the traditions remain, like the Winter Carnival in January and the Sugar Slalom in April.

## Don't Miss

Stowe village is tiny but charming—just a few blocks of shops and restaurants clustered around a picture-perfect white church with a lofty steeple. Check out the superb Vermont Ski and Snowboard Museum.

## Best Après-Ski

One of the country's most celebrated bars, The Matterhorn Bar is packed on winter weekends. 🌐 *matterhornbar.com.*

## When to Go

Ski season runs from late November to early April, but events like the Vermont Renaissance Faire, Music in the Meadow, Stowe Jazz Festival, and Foliage Festival take place in summer and fall.

## Getting Here and Around

The ski area is 8 miles northwest of downtown Stowe on Route 108, and a 45-minute drive east of Burlington.

**Stowe Mountain Resort.** ✉ *5781 Mountain Rd., Stowe, VT* ☎ *802/253–3600* 🌐 *stowe.com.*

# Burlington and Lake Champlain

## New England's Largest Lake

As you drive along Main Street toward downtown Burlington, it's easy to see why this city is often called one of the most livable small cities in the United States—that's when it's not being called the "third funkiest city in the world" or "#1 Bass Fishing Capital." Stroll downtown Burlington for cool bars and galleries; just beyond, Lake Champlain shimmers beneath the towering Adirondacks on the New York shore. The revitalized Burlington waterfront teems with outdoors enthusiasts who bike or stroll along its 7½-mile recreation path, picnic on the grass, laze in the sand at North Beach, and ply the waters in sailboats and motor craft in summer. Take narrated dinner and sunset sails offered by Lake Champlain Shoreline Cruises on the 363-passenger *Ethan Allen III*.

## Don't Miss

Pedestrian-only Church Street Marketplace is Burlington's center of commerce and activity, with boutiques, cafés, restaurants, and street vendors by day, and a lively bar scene at night.

## Best Restaurant

Honey Road has garnered James Beard Award nominations for its highly creative takes on eastern Mediterranean cuisine. 🌐 *honeyroadrestaurant.com*.

## Getting Here and Around

Burlington is in northwestern Vermont just off Interstate 89, and the Lake Champlain waterfront is at the end of College Street, a short walk down the hill from downtown.

**Burlington Information Center.** ✉ *Waterfront Park, end of College St., Burlington, VT* ☎ *802/860–0606* 🌐 *helloburlingtonvt.com.*

# Morse Farm Maple Sugarworks

### Vermont's Most Celebrated Syrup

With eight generations of sugaring, the Morses may be the oldest maple family in existence, so you're sure to find an authentic experience at their farm. More than 5,000 trees produce the sap used for syrup (you can sample all the grades), candy, cream, and sugar—all sold in the gift shop. Grab a creemee (soft-serve ice cream), take a seat on a swing, and stay awhile.

### Don't Miss

Here in the nation's smallest capital city, the regal Vermont State House building features a gleaming dome topped by the goddess of agriculture and columns of Barre granite measuring 6 feet in diameter. A half-hour tour takes you through the governor's office and the house and senate chambers. Interior paintings and exhibits make much of Vermont's sterling Civil War record.

### Best Restaurant

Ask Vermont's great chefs where they go for a tremendous meal, and Hen of the Wood inevitably tops the list. The setting is riveting: a converted, utterly romantic 1835 gristmill beside a waterfall, in historic Waterbury, about 12 miles northwest of Morse Farm. 🌐 *henofthewood.com.*

### When to Go

The farm and shop are open year-round, and sell fresh seasonal veggies in summer. But for a truly authentic experience, visit during the March sugaring season.

### Getting Here and Around

The farm is just 3 miles north of downtown Montpelier, which is off Interstate 89 in central Vermont.

**Morse Farm Maple Sugarworks.** ✉ *1168 County Rd., Montpelier, VT* 🌐 *morsefarm.com* 🎟 *Free.*

# Bennington

## Home to Vermont's Highest Observation Deck

From miles away you can spy the striking Bennington Battle Monument, a stone obelisk that rises 306 feet over stately Old Bennington historic district. It commemorates General John Stark's Revolutionary War victory over the British, and the observation deck, at 200 feet up serves views as far as the Berkshires in Massachusetts to the south and the Adirondacks in New York to the west. Then make your way into Bennington's Victorian downtown, home to Vermont's oldest indie bookstore, the Bennington Bookshop. Tour the exceptional Bennington Museum, which contains the world's largest collection of works by Grandma Moses.

## Don't Miss

A short drive northwest of downtown, visit the verdant grounds of prestigious Bennington College. Walk in the footsteps of such esteemed alumni as actor Peter Dinklage and novelist Donna Tartt.

## Best Restaurant

Finish your day of exploring Bennington's old-world charms with an apple-crisp whiskey sour and blueberry-bacon grilled cheese at the Miller's Toll. 🌐 *millerstoll.space.*

## When to Go

The town is pretty year-round and especially lively when college is in session, but to visit the monument you need to come when it's open (May–October), with early October being the best time to experience the fall foliage.

## Getting Here and Around

Bennington lies at the junction of U.S. 7 and Route 9, about 25 miles south of Manchester.

**Bennington Battle Monument.**
✉ *15 Monument Cir., Bennington, VT*
🌐 *benningtonbattlemonument.com*
🎟 *$5.*

## Quechee Gorge

### Vermont's Deepest Chasm

An impressive 165-foot-deep canyon cut over thousands of years by glacial activity and the Ottauquechee River, the stunning Quechee Gorge sits just downriver from the small, historic mill town of Quechee. Most people view the gorge from U.S. 4. To escape the crowds, visit the adjacent state park, where you can hike several trails down to the river. There's camping, too—perfect for a moonlight view of this natural wonder. Just a half-mile away, hundreds of dealers sell their wares at Quechee Gorge Village antiques and crafts mall, which is set in a reconstructed barn that also houses a country store, a hip gastropub, and a toy and train museum.

### Don't Miss

Next to Quechee Gorge, Vermont Institute of Natural Science Nature Center has 17 raptor exhibits, including bald eagles, peregrine falcons, and owls. All caged birds have been found injured and are unable to survive in the wild.

### Best Shop

A restored woolen mill by a waterfall holds the region's most interesting attraction, Simon Pearce, a marvelous glassblowing factory, store, and restaurant. 🌐 *simonpearce.com.*

### When to Go

You can appreciate the gorge and Simon Pearce's mill-side setting at its most dramatic after winter snowmelt in late spring, and also in early October during prime foliage season.

### Getting Here and Around

Quechee is on U.S. 4, just a few miles west of the junction of Interstates 89 and 91, 7 miles east of Woodstock and 12 miles west of Hanover, NH.

**Quechee State Park.** ✉ *5800 Woodstock Rd., Hartford, VT* 🌐 *vtstateparks.com* 🎟 *$4.*

# Marsh-Billings-Rockefeller National Historical Park

## Vermont's Only National Park

The nation's first national park focused on conserving natural resources, this pristine 555-acre spread includes the mansion, gardens, and carriage roads of Frederick H. Billings, a financier and the president of the Northern Pacific Railway. You can learn about its history at the visitor center, tour the residential complex with a guide, and explore the 20 miles of trails and old carriage roads that climb Mt. Tom. The surrounding town of Woodstock is a Currier & Ives print come to life, with well-maintained Federal-style houses surrounding the village green.

## Don't Miss

Also founded by Frederick H. Billings, Billings Farm and Museum is one of the oldest operating dairy farms in the country. Pick up some raw-milk cheddar while you're here.

## Best Restaurant

With the table literally on the farm, Cloudland Farm delivers a unique farm-to-table experience. *cloudland-farm.com.*

## When to Go

With more limited hours in winter at Billings Farm and Museum and Woodstock looking particularly splendid when flowers are in bloom or leaves are turning, summer and fall are ideal times to visit.

## Getting Here and Around

The national historic park and Billings Farm are just a short drive northwest of Woodstock's cute downtown, which lies at the junction of U.S. 4 and Route 12, a 20-minute drive west of the junction of Interstates 89 and 91.

**Carriage Barn Visitor Center.** 54 *Elm St., Woodstock, VT 802/457–3368 nps.gov/mabi $8.*

# Middlebury Tasting Trail

## Sip Your Own Way

Among Vermont's craft beer, cider, spirits, and wine explosion, the Middlebury area stands out, with a large cluster of producers with welcoming tasting rooms. Seven, all within a 10-mile radius of downtown, are located along this artisan trail, including one of the nation's leading cideries, Woodchuck Cider House. Known for its refreshing pear, Granny Smith, and raspberry ciders, Woodchuck has a pub, gift shop, and cider house, and a self-guided tour. Other worthy stops on the trail include Lincoln Peak Vineyard and Otter Creek Brewery.

## Don't Miss

In this center of academic life that's anchored by the pretty campus of Middlebury College, you'll find a fervent arts scene that includes the outstanding Vermont Folklife Center, with its folk paintings, antiques, and photography, as well as downtown's Edgewater Gallery which features fine jewelry, ceramics, and more.

## Best Restaurant

The Bobcat Cafe and Brewery in Bristol is fun and funky. 🌐 *thebobcat-cafe.com.*

## When to Go

Late summer into the mid-October fall foliage season is an ideal time to sip crisp ales and ciders.

## Getting Here and Around

Most places on the Middlebury Tasting Trail are along a 5-mile stretch of U.S. 7, with a few on side routes. Middelbury is between Rutland and Burlington, and is 15 miles east of the Lake Champlain Bridge to New York.

**Middlebury Tasting Trail.** ✉ *U.S. 7, Middlebury, VT* ☎ *802/388–7951* 🌐 *middtastingtrail.com.*

# Hildene

### The Lincoln Family's Summer Home

On the outskirts of one of Vermont's stateliest resort towns, the summer home of Abraham Lincoln's son Robert provides fascinating insight into the lives of this fabled family. Robert Lincoln enjoyed his own illustrious career, serving as secretary of war, U.S. ambassador to Great Britain, and later president of the Pullman Palace Car Company. He built this lavish 24-room Georgian Revival mansion in 1905, and it's now the centerpiece of a beautifully preserved 412-acre estate that holds many of the family's prized possessions. Be sure to step aboard the restored 1903 Pullman car, hike the miles of trails and the wetland boardwalk, view the elaborate formal gardens, and stroll around the farm.

### Don't Miss

The home is in Manchester, a town at the base of 3,840-foot Mt. Equinox (you can drive or hike to the top) which has a beautiful village center and the American Museum of Fly Fishing.

### Best Hotel

The Equinox Resort in quaint Manchester Village has been the fancy hotel in town since the 18th century. *equinoxresort.com.*

### When to Go

Hildene is prettiest in late June when the gardens bloom with more than 1,000 peonies.

### Getting Here and Around

The estate is just off Route 7A, 2 miles south of bustling Manchester, which is in the southwest corner of the state, at the junction of U.S. 7 and Route 30.

**Hildene.** *1005 Hildene Rd., Manchester, VT 802/362–1788 hildene.org $23.*

# Ben & Jerry's Factory

## America's Most Famous Ice Cream

The closest thing you'll get to a Willy Wonka experience in New England, the 30-minute tours at the main factory of this legendary brand famous for supporting progressive social causes are unabashedly corny and only skim the surface of the behind-the-scenes goings-on, but this flaw is forgiven when the samples are dished out. To see the machines at work, visit on a weekday (but call ahead to confirm if they will indeed be in operation). Free, family-friendly outdoor movies are shown on the verdant grounds on summer Fridays.

## Don't Miss

Arguably even more fun than visiting the factory floor itself is strolling through the "Flavor Graveyard," where flavors of yore (remember Wavy Gravy and Holy Cannoli?) are given a tribute with tombstones inscribed with cheeky poetry.

## Other Great Ice Cream

Less than an hour's drive southwest of Ben & Jerry's in the charming town of Vergennes, you can sample the delicious small-batch ice cream and sorbet at lu-lu. Tantalizing flavors include raspberry buttermilk and honey-lavender. 🌐 *luluvt.com.*

## When to Go

There's really no bad time to stop by for a dish of ice cream, even in winter. But the outdoor picnic areas with Green Mountains views are best enjoyed in summer.

## Getting Here and Around

Ben & Jerry's is on Route 100, just a mile north of Interstate 89 in Waterbury, and 9 miles south of Stowe.

**Ben & Jerry's Factory.** ✉ *1281 Waterbury-Stowe Rd., Waterbury, VT* ☎ *802/882–2047* 🌐 *benjerry.com* 🎫 *$4.*

# When in Vermont

## AMERICAN PRECISION MUSEUM

A stone's throw from the famous covered bridge that crosses the Connecticut River between New Hampshire and Vermont, this stately four-story 1846 former armaments factory is packed with fascinating exhibits that shine a light on the ingenuity behind how all sorts of things are made, from sewing machines to automobiles. A curator from the Smithsonian saved the building from demolition in 1966 and turned it into this imaginative museum where docents demonstrate how many tools and machines work.

**Do This:** After visiting the museum, you can embark on one of the state's prettiest and most popular hikes, the 5.7-mile Weathersfield Trail up to the fire tower atop 3,144-foot Mt. Ascutney, from which you can take in marvelous views of the upper Connecticut River valley. Afterward, head to Harpoon Brewery beer hall, where you can sample classic New England–style IPAs and tasty barbecue on the patio, or stroll through the adjacent riverside sculpture garden.

**American Precision Museum.** ✉ *196 Main St., Windsor, VT* ☎ *802/674–5781* 🌐 *americanprecision.org* 🎫 *Free.*

## DOG MOUNTAIN

Set on an idyllic 150-acre mountaintop in Vermont's sparsely populated and picturesque Northeast Kingdom, Dog Mountain is pooch paradise, complete with swimming ponds, hiking trails, an art gallery full of dog-related artwork, and even a Dog Chapel. The sign outside says "Welcome all creeds, all breeds, no dogmas allowed." And on any given day, you will find all breeds and creeds here. Originally an art studio for the late Stephen Huneck, Dog Mountain was conceived when Huneck recovered from a near-death experience and was moved to create a place for pet-people to celebrate the spiritual bond they have with their dogs.

**Do This:** Thousands of pet owners visit Dog Mountain annually to post messages and photos in the chapel and to gain closure for lost canine companions, but Dog Mountain is also a place for pups and their people to play and run and roll in the grass.

**Dog Mountain.** ✉ *143 Parks Rd., St. Johnsbury, VT* ☎ *800/449–2580* 🌐 *dogmt.com.*

## KING ARTHUR BAKING

A mecca for fans of baking (or just eating amazing baked goods), this shop is stocked with all the ingredients and tools in the company's Baker's Catalogue, including flours, mixes, and local jams and syrups. The bakery has a viewing area where you can watch products being made, and you can learn to bake them yourself at classes conducted on-site. The store is a fine spot for a quick bite; the timber-frame café serves high-quality pizzas, sandwiches, and baked items.

**Do This:** For a more substantial meal, head to the tiny Victorian village of White River Junction, just 5 miles south, which has a terrific little clutch of noteworthy foodie endeavors. Drop by Tuckerbox café for deftly prepared Turkish food and coffees, and Elixir for gorgeous farm-to-table fare. Or for a leisurely, boozy brunch, book a table at Piecemeal Pies, which turns out delish duck-fat home fries and fried buttermilk-brined Vermont rabbit and cheddar waffles with chili-maple syrup.

**King Arthur Baking Flagship Campus.** ✉ *135 U.S. 5 S, Norwich, VT* ☎ *802/649–3361* 🌐 *kingarthurbaking.com* 🎫 *Free.*

## SHELBURNE FARMS

Founded in the 1880s as a private estate for two very rich New Yorkers, this 1,400-acre farm is much more than an exquisite landscape: it's an educational and cultural resource center with a working dairy farm, an award-winning cheese producer (the venue hosts the renowned Vermont Cheesemakers Festival each August), an organic market garden, and a bakery whose aroma of fresh bread and pastries is an olfactory treat. Children and adults alike get a kick out of hunting for eggs in the oversize coop, milking a cow, and watching the chicken parade. If you fall in love with the scenery, arrange a romantic dinner at the lakefront mansion, or spend the night.

**Do This:** While in the area, visit the Shelburne Museum. You can trace much of New England's history simply by wandering through the 45 acres and 38 buildings of this museum, which has an outstanding 150,000-object collection of art, design, and Americana consisting of antique furniture, fine and folk art, quilts, trade signs, and weather vanes; there are also more than 200 carriages and sleighs.

**Shelburne Farms.** ✉ *1611 Harbor Rd., Shelburne, VT* ☎ *802/985–8498* 🌐 *shelburnefarms.org* 🎫 *$8.*

### VERMONT COUNTRY STORE

This venerable shop in a quiet village northeast of Manchester opened in 1946 and is still run by the Orton family, though these days it has become something of an empire, with a large catalog and online business. One room is set aside for Vermont Common Crackers and bins of fudge and copious candy. In others you'll find nearly forgotten items such as Lilac Vegetol aftershave, as well as practical items like sturdy outdoor clothing. Nostalgia-evoking implements dangle from the rafters. There's a second store on Route 103 in Rockingham, just off Interstate 91.

**Do This:** The associated Mildred's Grill and Dairy Bar next door serves three country meals a day, including mac and cheese with aged Vermont cheddar and hot fudge sundaes.

**Vermont Country Store.** ✉ *657 Main St., Weston, VT* ☎ *802/824–3184* 🌐 *vermontcountrystore.com* 🎫 *Free.*

## Cool Places to Stay

**Hill Farm Inn.** Few Vermont lodgings can match the commanding views of Mt. Equinox and the surrounding hillscape from this former dairy farm built in 1830, whether you're relaxing on the large wraparound porch, around the fire pit (where you can roast s'mores), or by the outdoor hot tub. ✉ *458 Hill Farm Rd., Sunderland, VT* ☎ *802/375–2269* 🌐 *hillfarminn.com* $ *From $277.*

**Hotel Vermont.** This cool, stylish boutique hotel just steps from Waterfront Park has the sort of spacious, comfy lobby that you actually want to hang out in, ideally while sipping a craft cocktail from the adjacent Juniper restaurant. You'll also find gorgeously appointed rooms with local artwork. ✉ *41 Cherry St., Burlington, VT* ☎ *802/651–0080* 🌐 *hotelvt.com* $ *From $179.*

**Trapp Family Lodge.** Built by the Von Trapp family (of *The Sound of Music* fame), this Tyrolean-style lodge offers thrilling mountain vistas, a cozy beer hall that's perfect for après-ski relaxation, and a concert series and several festivals during the warmer months. ✉ *700 Trapp Hill Rd., Stowe, VT* ☎ *802/826–7000* 🌐 *trappfamily.com* $ *From $175.*

**Woodstock Inn & Resort.** This romantic 1890s inn, one of northern New England's most memorable accommodations, is steps from Woodstock's fine eateries and inviting shops and features plenty of great amenities on property, including an impressive full-service spa, an acclaimed golf course, and several exceptional restaurants. ✉ *14 The Green, Woodstock, VT* ☎ *802/332–6853* 🌐 *woodstockinn.com* $ *From $229.*

Chapter 4

# THE MID-ATLANTIC



Written by
Jillian Wilson

# WELCOME TO THE MID-ATLANTIC

## TOP REASONS TO GO

★ **The Big Apple:** From its 840-plus-acre Central Park to world-class museums and stunning skyline views, New York City tops many a bucket list.

★ **The Appalachian Trail:** Virginia is home to more miles of the famous trail than any other state. There are many access points throughout the state, but the most popular, and most scenic, is Shenandoah National Park.

★ **The nation's capital:** Washington, D.C., is a sight every American should see, from the National Mall and Tidal Basin to the White House and the Smithsonian's 19 galleries and museums.

★ **Coastal charm:** Dine at a Maryland crab shack, take a water taxi in Lewes, Delaware, soak up the sun on Virginia Beach, and sail in Annapolis to take in the region's waterfront beauty.

★ **American foundations:** In Philadelphia, walk in the footsteps of America's founding fathers at Independence National Historical Park, where the Declaration of Independence forged a new democracy.

1 **Delaware.** Enjoy the beautiful beaches, marvelous mansions, and craft beer scene in this small wonder.

2 **Maryland.** Eat crabs at a seafood shack on Chesapeake Bay, then drive to Baltimore to visit the Inner Harbor.

3 **New Jersey.** Spend some time at the Jersey Shore enjoying the beach and the boardwalk.

4 **New York.** From bustling Manhattan to the serene Catskills to the famous Finger Lakes, there is a lot to love.

5 **Pennsylvania.** Explore the birthplace of America at Independence Hall, then take in the impressive Valley Forge.

6 **Virginia.** Hike the mountain trails of Shenandoah National Park, enjoy the Monticello-area wineries, and stroll Virginia Beach.

7 **Washington, D.C.** The White House, the Lincoln Memorial, the Washington Monument—landmarks are found in every corner of the nation's capital.

8 **West Virginia.** Drive along the winding country roads and hear traditional mountain music.

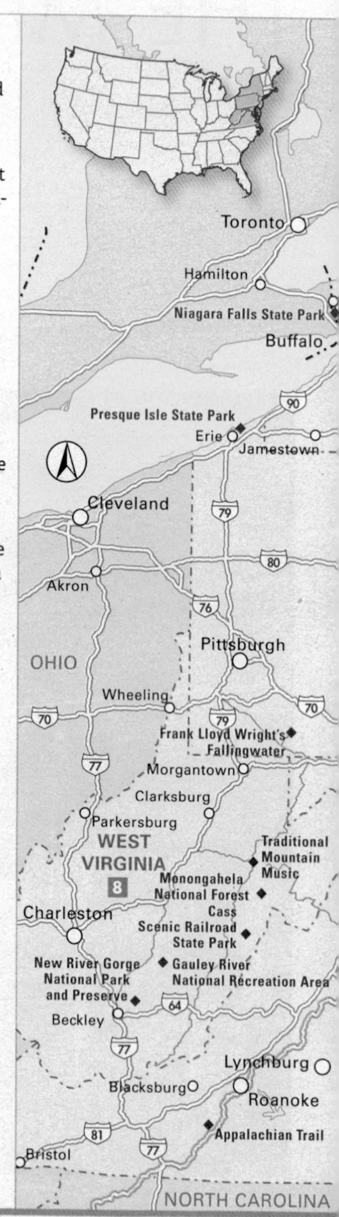

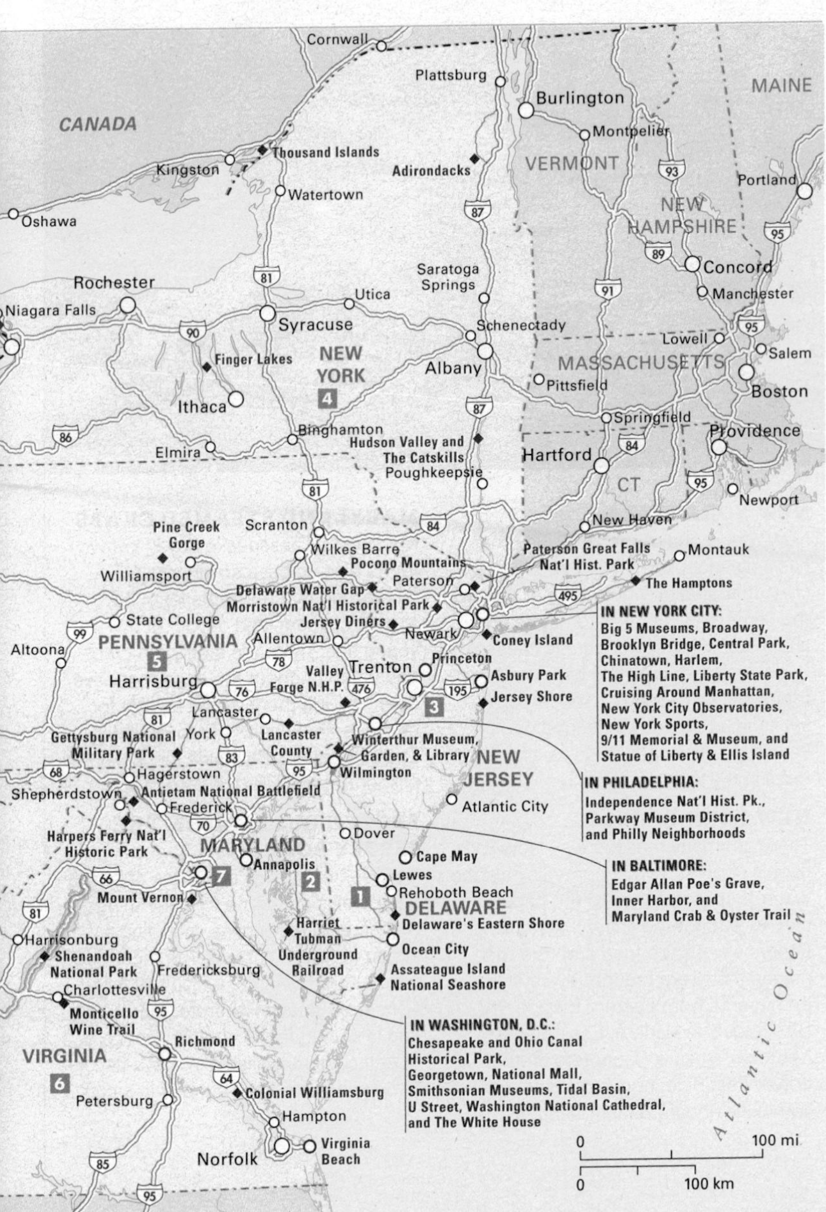
CANADA
MAINE
VERMONT
NEW HAMPSHIRE
MASSACHUSETTS
CT
NEW YORK
4
PENNSYLVANIA
5
NEW JERSEY
3
MARYLAND
2
7
DELAWARE
1
VIRGINIA
6
Atlantic Ocean
Cornwall
Plattsburg
Burlington
Montpelier
Thousand Islands
Kingston
Adirondacks
Watertown
Portland
Oshawa
Concord
Manchester
Saratoga Springs
Rochester
Utica
Niagara Falls
Syracuse
Schenectady
Lowell
Salem
Finger Lakes
Albany
Pittsfield
Boston
Ithaca
Springfield
Providence
Binghamton
Hudson Valley and The Catskills
Elmira
Poughkeepsie
Hartford
Newport
Pine Creek Gorge
Scranton
New Haven
Wilkes Barre
Paterson Great Falls Nat'l Hist. Park
Montauk
Pocono Mountains
Williamsport
Paterson
The Hamptons
Delaware Water Gap
Morristown Nat'l Historical Park
State College
Jersey Diners
Newark
Coney Island
Altoona
Allentown
Harrisburg
Princeton
Valley Forge N.H.P.
Trenton
Asbury Park
Jersey Shore
Lancaster
Lancaster County
Gettysburg National Military Park
York
Winterthur Museum, Garden, & Library
Wilmington
Hagerstown
Shepherdstown
Antietam National Battlefield
Frederick
Atlantic City
Harpers Ferry Nat'l Historic Park
Dover
Annapolis
Cape May
Lewes
Mount Vernon
Rehoboth Beach
Harriet Tubman Underground Railroad
Delaware's Eastern Shore
Harrisonburg
Ocean City
Shenandoah National Park
Fredericksburg
Assateague Island National Seashore
Charlottesville
Monticello Wine Trail
Richmond
Colonial Williamsburg
Petersburg
Hampton
Norfolk
Virginia Beach
IN NEW YORK CITY:
Big 5 Museums, Broadway, Brooklyn Bridge, Central Park, Chinatown, Harlem, The High Line, Liberty State Park, Cruising Around Manhattan, New York City Observatories, New York Sports, 9/11 Memorial & Museum, and Statue of Liberty & Ellis Island
IN PHILADELPHIA:
Independence Nat'l Hist. Pk., Parkway Museum District, and Philly Neighborhoods
IN BALTIMORE:
Edgar Allan Poe's Grave, Inner Harbor, and Maryland Crab & Oyster Trail
IN WASHINGTON, D.C.:
Chesapeake and Ohio Canal Historical Park, Georgetown, National Mall, Smithsonian Museums, Tidal Basin, U Street, Washington National Cathedral, and The White House
0
100 mi
0
100 km
87
93
95
89
91
81
90
86
84
495
99
78
76
476
195
83
68
70
66
64
85

# WHAT TO EAT AND DRINK IN THE MID-ATLANTIC

New York pizza

### NEW YORK PIZZA

New York is one of the few cities that has a distinct pizza style. Expect a thick crust that gradually gets thinner toward the center. A ladleful of tomato sauce and a sprinkling of mozzarella cheese traditionally serve as the base, and toppings like pepperoni, mushrooms, sausage, or onions are loaded on. Locals love Rubirosa in Nolita and Joe's Pizza in the West Village.

### NEW YORK BAGELS

There are many reasons why New York bagels reign supreme: some say it's the water that contributes to the bagel's chewy, but not too chewy, texture. Others say it's the tried-and-true techniques that were brought by Jewish immigrants from Eastern Europe. Try Bo's Bagels in Harlem, Ess-a-Bagel in Midtown, Russ & Daughters on the Lower East Side, or one of the city's Tompkins Square Bagels locations.

### MARYLAND STEAMED CRABS

Maryland's Chesapeake Bay is known for its blue crabs, a small, tasty crustacean that residents learn how to catch, steam, and devour at a young age. There are family-run crab houses throughout the state that have been serving them by the bushel for decades. Try Schultz's Crab House in Essex, Cantler's Riverside Inn in Annapolis, or Captain Billy's in Newburg.

### FROZEN CUSTARD ON THE JERSEY BOARDWALK

New Jersey's miles and miles of beach boardwalks are home to many things that scream Americana, including a scoop of frozen custard. The most popular is Kohr Brothers, which has locations from Beach Haven to Cape May and is known for its creamy scoops of frozen custard available in a two-flavor twist and served in a cone or in a cup.

## CLASSIC NEW YORK COCKTAILS

Perhaps the city's most famous cocktail is its namesake, the whisky- or rye-based Manhattan, which is said to have been created by a bartender at The Manhattan Club in the late 19th century. Times Square's Knickerbocker Hotel is where the gin and vermouth martini was first served. Many other cocktail bars, including Attaboy, Death & Company, and the NoMad Bar also serve exemplary versions.

## PHILLY CHEESESTEAK

People travel far and wide to try this sandwich made of chopped beef, onions, and cheese and served on a long roll. There is much debate about who created the first and where to find the best today. The ultimate cheesesteak rivalry is between Pat's King of Steaks and Geno's Steaks, located across the street from each other in the city's Italian Market.

## NEW JERSEY PORK ROLL VS. PENNSYLVANIA TAYLOR HAM

John Taylor created this pork-based meat product in 1856. In the years since, it has become a favorite on eggy breakfast sandwiches at diners throughout the area. It's been the subject of much debate between Pennsylvania (which calls it by its brand name, Taylor Ham) and New Jersey (which prefers the plain-and-simple pork roll). But wherever you are, it tastes the same.

Amish whoopie pies

Philly cheesesteak

## AMISH WHOOPIE PIES

Many believe that whoopie pies—two round cake patties sandwiched with frosting—were created by the Amish community in Lancaster County, Pennsylvania. Whether or not the Amish first created this dessert, farm stands throughout Lancaster serve them in classic flavors like chocolate, spiced pumpkin, and red velvet.

## BUFFALO WINGS

The exact origins of Buffalo wings are hotly contested, but it is largely agreed that the tangy wings were made famous by the city's Anchor Bar, which now has locations across the country. There are many places throughout the Buffalo area—including Gabriel's Gate and Duff's Famous Wings—to get an order of the saucy staple.

## PEPPERONI ROLL

For West Virginia's classic pepperoni roll, the meat is baked into a soft white-bread roll. The snack food was created as a no-refrigeration-necessary meal for coal miners throughout the region. Today, the snack is available throughout Appalachia in convenience stores and in casual restaurants.

# The Mid-Atlantic Regional Snapshot

## Know Before You Go

### PLAN A WARM-WEATHER VISIT

The Mid-Atlantic region can get extremely cold in the winter, making it not ideal for many of the area's best outdoor activities. Visit in the spring, summer, or fall to enjoy boating, beaching, hiking, and city exploring.

### HIT THE BEACH

Beach towns reign supreme throughout much of the Mid-Atlantic region. New Jersey, Delaware, Maryland, and Virginia are all loved for their seaside towns complete with oceanfront boardwalks, white-sand beaches, beachfront bars and restaurants, and summertime rentals.

### BOOK FAR AHEAD

When visiting the major cities in the Mid-Atlantic region, advance planning is required if you're looking to visit some of the more popular attractions. Be sure to make reservations if you're planning to go to a particular restaurant or on a specific tour.

## Planning Your Time

The region is vast, but easily driveable. Most of the major destinations can be reached by car within a few days. Staying in Washington, D.C., or Baltimore is ideal for exploring the areas to the north, south, east, and west.

## Road Trips

**2 Days:** Washington, D.C. to Annapolis

**3 Days:** New York City to the Finger Lakes

**4 Days:** Philadelphia to Woodstock, NY

## Big Events

**New York City Marathon.** The world's top runners, along with amateurs pushing themselves to the limit, head to New York City every fall for the iconic event that winds through the five boroughs.

**Welcome America.** Billed as the "Birthplace of America," Philadelphia hosts an annual July 4th celebration complete with a parade through the historic district, free museum events, and a huge fireworks display accompanied by live music.

**Cherry Blossom Festival.** Every spring, thousands of cherry trees around the Jefferson Memorial and throughout all of Washington, D.C., are suddenly covered with delicate white blossoms.

## What To . . .

### READ

*Such a Fun Age* by Kiley Reid

*The Great Gatsby* by F. Scott Fitzgerald

*John Henry Days* by Colson Whitehead

*Misty Of Chincoteague* by Marguerite Henry

### WATCH

*Sex and the City* (series set in New York City)

*The Wire* (series set in Baltimore)

*Night at the Museum: Battle of the Smithsonian* (film set in Washington, D.C.)

*Eternal Sunshine of the Spotless Mind* (film set in New York)

### LISTEN

*The Velvet Underground & Nico* by the Velvet Underground (album)

*Who Is Jill Scott? Words and Sounds Vol. 1* by Jill Scott (album)

*We Sing, We Dance, We Steal Things* by Jason Mraz (album)

### BUY

New York Yankees baseball cap

Coffee beans from Philadelphia's La Colombe

Virginia peanuts

West Virginia Timberwolves sweatshirt

Model plane from the National Air and Space Museum

Apple cider doughnuts from New York's Hudson Valley

Print from Pittsburgh's Andy Warhol Museum

Quilt from Pennsylvania Amish country

## Contacts

### AIR

**Major Airports**

**New York.** JFK, LGA, ALB

**New Jersey.** EWR

**Pennsylvania.** PHL, PIT

**Maryland.** BWI

**Washington, D.C.** IAD

**Virginia.** RIC, DCA

**West Virginia.** CRW

### BUS

**BoltBus.** ☎ *877/265–8287* 🌐 *www.boltbus.com.*

**Greyhound.** ☎ *800/231–2222* 🌐 *www.greyhound.com.*

**Megabus.** ☎ *877/462–6342* 🌐 *us.megabus.com.*

### METRO/SUBWAY

**Metropolitan Transit Authority.** 🌐 *new.mta.info.*

**New Jersey Transit.** ☎ *973/275–5555* 🌐 *www.njtransit.com.*

**Southeastern Pennsylvania Transportation Authority.** ☎ *215/580–7800* 🌐 *www.septa.org*

**Washington Metropolitan Area Transit Authority.** ☎ *202/637–7000* 🌐 *www.wmata.com.*

**Metro Subwaylink (Maryland).** ☎ *410/539–5000* 🌐 *www.mta.maryland.gov/schedule/metrosubway.*

**Port Authority (Pittsburgh).** ☎ *412/566–5500* 🌐 *www.portauthority.org.*

### TAXI

**Yellow Cab.** ☎ *800/609–8731* 🌐 *www.yellowcabnyctaxi.com.*

**New Jersey Taxi.** ☎ *973/509–3333* 🌐 *www.njtaxis.com.*

**P215 Get A Cab.** ☎ *215/535–6700* 🌐 *www.215getacab.com.*

**ZTrip.** ☎ *410/369–3030* 🌐 *www.ztrip.com/baltimore.*

**Yellow Cab.** ☎ *202/544–1212* 🌐 *www.dcyellowcab.com.*

**Yellow Cab of the Shenandoah.** ☎ *540/622–6060* 🌐 *www.taxicabinfrontroyalva.com.*

**West Virginia: C&H Taxi.** ☎ *304/344–4902* 🌐 *www.chtaxi.com.*

### TRAIN

**Amtrak.** ☎ *800/872–7245* 🌐 *www.amtrak.com.*

### VISITOR INFORMATION

🌐 *www.nycgo.com*

🌐 *www.discoverupstateny.com*

🌐 *www.visitnj.org*

🌐 *www.visitpa.com*

🌐 *www.visitphilly.com*

🌐 *www.washington.org*

🌐 *www.visitmaryland.org*

🌐 *www.virginia.org*

🌐 *www.wvtourism.com*

# Delaware

Delaware's founding fathers signed the U.S. Constitution before others, earning Delaware the nickname "the First State." Although rich in colonial political history, today the state is a business leader—64% of Fortune 500 companies are here. Shoppers love Delaware, too, as the state imposes no sales tax. Varied landscapes keep Delaware from feeling like America's second-smallest state. Rolling hills and hardwood forests lay north. Vast tidal marshes and dunescapes line the shore. Gleaming corporate center Wilmington is a short train ride to New York, Philadelphia, and Washington, D.C.

## Bucket List Picks

The following boxes contain our picks for the top sights and experiences in Delaware.

- ○ Delaware's Eastern Shore
- ○ Lewes
- ○ Wilmington
- ○ Winterthur Museum, Garden, and Library

# Delaware's Eastern Shore

## Miles of Mind-Blowing Beaches

The Atlantic Ocean gently laps against Delaware's eastern coast, making way for miles and miles of beautiful seashore. Full-time residents and weekenders visit the beaches in the summer months for sunbathing, swimming, boating, and shoreline biking. The different beaches that make up the area each have distinct vibes. Party animals often head to Dewey Beach, while Bethany Beach is quieter.

## Don't Miss

With its mile-long boardwalk featuring family-friendly attractions like the Funland Amusement Park, Rehoboth Beach is a beloved destination for families. It's also been a gay getaway for years, drawing members of the LGBTQ community from Baltimore and Washington, D.C. The popular Dogfish Head Brewery has a brewpub here, and there are plenty of other food and drink options facing the beach and on nearby streets.

## Best Activity

In the late 17th century, William Penn opened Cape Henlopen to residents of the area, making Cape Henlopen State Park one the country's oldest public parks. Today, the historic waterfront continues to be a popular destination for Delaware residents. It's a draw for its hiking and biking trails, swimmable shores, kayaking opportunities, and fishing and clamming areas. 🌐 *destateparks.com/beaches/capehenlopen.*

## Getting Here and Around

A car is the best way to reach Delaware's Eastern Shore. The area is almost equidistant from Philadelphia International Airport and Baltimore/Washington International Thurgood Marshall Airport.

**Visit Delaware.** 🌐 *www.visitdelaware.com/beaches.*

# Lewes

## First Town in the First State

The oldest town in Delaware is Lewes, an oceanfront community that was founded in 1631. Today, the area is visited for its historic sites, its beach access, and its small-town feel. The area is easily explored by foot. Within the half-mile historic area, visitors can find museums, restaurants, shops, and more, and not far away are plenty of waterfront areas for sunning, swimming, fishing, and boating.

## Don't Miss

The fastest, and most scenic, way to get to New Jersey from Delaware is aboard the Cape May–Lewes Ferry, which transports guests between Lewes, Delaware, and Cape May, New Jersey, located directly across the Delaware Bay. The ferry ride takes 85 minutes and passes lovely lighthouses and picturesque harbors. 🌐 *www.cmlf.com*.

## Best Activity

Make plans to visit the Zwaanendael Museum, named for the first European settlement in the area. A variety of special exhibits tell the story of the region, including the shipwrecks that dot the coast and the part it played in the War of 1812. 🌐 *history.delaware.gov/zwaanendael-museum*.

## Best Tour

Cape Water Tours offers a wide range of on-the-water tours in the Lewes area. The evening cruises are perfect for taking in the sunset, but you might also want to sail off in search of dolphins or hear about the region's spooky lighthouses. 🌐 *www.capewatertaxi.com*.

## Getting Here and Around

It's easiest to drive to Lewes, but once you're here most attractions are accessible by foot or bike.

**Lewes.** ☎ *302/245–0304* 🌐 *www.lewes.com*.

# Wilmington

## Big City with Small-Town Appeal

You know from the gleaming glass office buildings that Wilmington is a big city, but its walkable thoroughfares, charming neighborhoods, and waterfront promenade give it plenty of small-town appeal. There are plenty of places downtown for dining and drinking, with the good spirits often spilling out into the streets. Riverfront Wilmington, the delightful walkway along the Christiana River, is home to an array of attractions, including the Delaware Children's Museum, the Delaware Theatre Company, Tubman-Garrett Riverfront Park, and Frawley Stadium.

## Don't Miss

In recent years, the Delaware Art Museum has grown to encompass a large collection of American art, British Pre-Raphaelite art, and contemporary art, making it a favorite for art enthusiasts from all over. Locals love that it offers free admission on Sundays from April to December. ⊕ *delart.org.*

## Best Activity

Located just 6 miles outside Wilmington is New Castle, a small but lively town on the Delaware River. You'll find cobblestone streets and colonial buildings that have barely been touched by time, in addition to a number of great restaurants, bars, and shops. The town dates back to 1640, and its history is celebrated at the many museums throughout the area.

## Getting Here and Around

Philadelphia International Airport is the closest major airport, about a 20-mile drive down Interstate 95. With six downtown stops, the River Taxi is a great way to see the city. ⊕ *wilmwaterattractions.com/river-taxi.*

# Winterthur Museum, Garden, and Library

### Delaware's Shimmering Jewel in the Crown

One of America's richest families, the du Ponts lived on sweeping estates in the Delaware countryside that are now open to the public. Winterthur Museum, Garden, and Library is the largest and most opulent of the properties, and it draws history lovers from around the region. The mansion, which was the childhood home of Henry Francis du Pont, is surrounded by 1,000 acres of rolling hills and manicured gardens. In addition to rotating exhibitions, the home features a 90,000-object collection of American-made or American-used items from 1640 to 1860.

### Don't Miss

The nearby Hagley Museum and Library, located at the site of E. I. du Pont's gunpowder works, includes a historic home, some restored mills, and worker communities. The French-inspired Nemours Estate features a beautiful mansion surrounded by the country's largest formal French gardens, a vintage car collection within the stately garage, and hundreds of acres of woodlands and meadows.

### Getting Here and Around

The three mansions are all within driving distance, but a car is necessary to visit the destinations.

**Winterthur Museum, Garden, and Library.** ✉ *5105 Kennett Pike, Winterthur, DE* ☎ *302/888–4600* 🌐 *www.winterthur.org* 🎫 *$20.*

## When in Delaware

### DOGFISH HEAD BREWERY

Beer fans nationwide know about Dogfish Head Brewery, an award-winning craft brewery famous for its 60-minute IPA and 90-minute IPA. Since the brewery was founded, it has rapidly expanded its offerings to include tasting rooms, brewpubs, and even a hotel. The main brewery and tasting room are located in the town of Milton.

**Do This:** Pose for a picture in front of the unmissable Steampunk Treehouse, a functional sculpture made of recycled materials. The tree house weighs 8 tons and is a towering 40 feet tall.

**Dogfish Head Brewery.** ✉ *6 Cannery Village Center, Milton, DE* ☎ *382/684–1000* 🌐 *www.dogfish.com/brewery/tasting-room.*

### DOVER INTERNATIONAL SPEEDWAY

Racing fans often head to Delaware's Dover International Speedway to watch some of the sport's top names make their way around the 1-mile oval track. The racetrack hosts races throughout the year and has been a NASCAR venue since 1969. Miles the Monster is the speedway's mascot, and is a favorite with kids.

**Do This:** In addition to racing, the track hosts the massive Firefly Music Festival, which takes place each September and welcomes musicians like Post Malone, The Killers, and Mumford & Sons.

**Dover International Speedway.** ✉ *1131 N. DuPont Hwy., Dover, DE* ☎ *800/441–7223* 🌐 *www.doverspeedway.com* 🎫 *Varies with event.*

## Cool Places to Stay

**Bellmoor Inn and Spa.** Two blocks from Rehoboth Beach's top dining and shopping spots, the Bellmoor Inn and Spa pampers you with soothing spa treatments and two sparkling pools. The beach is a 10-minute walk, but those who don't feel like walking can hop aboard a beach shuttle. ✉ *6 Christian St., Rehoboth Beach, DE* ☎ *302/227–5800* 🌐 *www.thebellmoor.com* $ *From $500.*

**Dogfish Inn.** Delaware residents love their Dogfish Head Brewery, so much so that the team behind the craft brewery opened the Dogfish Inn in Lewes. The 16 rooms are minimalist but carefully crafted to emit an outdoorsy vibe. ✉ *105 Savannah Rd., Lewes, DE* ☎ *302/644–8292* 🌐 *www.dogfish.com/inn* $ *From $300.*

**Hotel DuPont.** The Italian Renaissance-inspired Hotel DuPont has graced downtown Wilmington for nearly 100 years. The 217 European-style rooms are spacious and chic, and the hotel restaurant, Le Cavalier, is beloved by locals. ✉ *42 W. 11th St., Wilmington, DE* ☎ *302/594–3100* 🌐 *www.hoteldupont.com* $ *From $315.*

**Inn at Montchanin Village and Spa.** Once a part of the du Pont family's estate at Winterthur, the Inn at Montchanin Village and Spa has been restored to honor its history and to add all modern amenities. There's an on-site spa and restaurant. ✉ *528 Montchanin Rd., Montchanin, DE* ☎ *302/888–2133* 🌐 *montchanin.com/about.html* $ *From: $165.*

**Massey's Landing.** For beachgoers and boating enthusiasts, Massey's Landing is the ideal place to spend a few days. The waterfront campground has safari-style tents and beachfront cottages for overnight stays. ✉ *20628 Long Beach Dr., Millsboro, DE* ☎ *302/947–2600* 🌐 *www.masseyslanding.com* $ *From $180.*

# Maryland

Maryland's mythic hero is the waterman, who prowls the Chesapeake in his skipjack, dredging oysters. Today the waterman is a symbol of contemporary Maryland: not in the manner in which he works, but in the variety of his catch. Maryland has always been a land of diversity, and from its rich Civil War history to the contemporary appeal of Baltimore's Inner Harbor, Maryland casts a wide net.

## Bucket List Picks

The following boxes contain our picks for the top sights and experiences in Maryland.

- ○ Maryland Crab and Oyster Trail
- ○ Annapolis
- ○ Harriet Tubman Underground Railroad
- ○ Baltimore's Inner Harbor
- ○ Edgar Allan Poe's Grave
- ○ Chesapeake & Ohio Canal National Historical Park
- ○ Antietam National Battlefield
- ○ Assateague Island National Seashore
- ○ Ocean City

# Maryland Crab and Oyster Trail

## The Mid-Atlantic's Biggest Seafood Festival

Thousands of seafood lovers head to the state every year to get their hands on some Chesapeake blue crabs at one of the state's famous crab shacks. Also a draw are the freshly caught oysters that are shucked throughout seafront restaurants. The official Maryland Crab and Oyster Trail starts on the Eastern Shore, heads to the Annapolis area, and then fans out across the rest of state.

## Don't Miss

Ask any local and they will have their favorite crab shack or oyster spot. If you don't get a personal recommendation, head to standbys like The Crab Claw in St. Michael's, Nick's Fish House in Baltimore, or Woody's Crab House in North East.

## Best Activity

Marylanders love to celebrate the state's maritime history and the season's bounty at the seafood held annually all across the state, including the Crisfield Crab and Clam Bake, the Tilghman Island Seafood Festival, and the Saint Mary's County Crab Festival.

## When to Go

Blue crab season runs from spring to late fall. Many of the best seafood restaurants are outdoor establishments, making Maryland the ideal summertime destination.

## Getting Here and Around

Baltimore/Washington International Thurgood Marshall Airport is the place to fly to, and a car is pretty much required to get to the stops on the trail.

**Maryland Crab and Oyster Trail.** ☎ *877/209–5883* 🌐 *www.visitmaryland.org/article/maryland-crab-oyster-trail.*

# Annapolis

## America's Sailing Capital

The grandeur and pageantry of the United States Naval Academy draw visitors to the state capital of Annapolis, but there are also the cobblestone streets dating back four centuries and a lovely location on Chesapeake Bay. A slice of Americana, the must-visit Annapolis Historic District has stately homes dating back to the colonial era. Annapolis is renowned as one of the country's sailing capitals, so you can take in an exciting race, rent a sailboat, or hop aboard a leisurely cruise around the port.

## Don't Miss

Watch the boats come and go at Ego Alley, where boaters are known to show off their yachts and sailing vessels to those strolling the downtown area.

## Best Tour

Learn about the ghostly side of the city's history on a tour of the downtown district. Annapolis Tours and Crawls runs 90-minute walks to haunted locations around the city, and guides share lots of creepy tales. 🌐 *www.toursandcrawls.com/tours/ghost-tours.*

## Best Activity

Spend a day on the shores of Sandy Point State Park, a beachfront public park located on the Chesapeake Bay. It's a family-friendly spot for swimming, sunbathing, crabbing, and picnicking, and is home to two short walking trails, too.

## Getting Here and Around

On Chesapeake Bay, Annapolis is 45 minutes south of Baltimore and just under an hour east of Washington, D.C.

**Sandy Point State Park.** 🌐 *dnr.maryland.gov/publiclands/pages/southern/sandypoint.aspx.*

# Harriet Tubman Underground Railroad

### The Long Road to Freedom

This 125-mile trail, running from Cambridge to Goldsboro, takes you past sites where the influential abolitionist led enslaved people to freedom. Stops along the way include hidden waterways, safe houses, churches, and other places that served as way stations.

### Don't Miss

Start your day at the Harriet Tubman Underground Railroad Visitor Center, which is home to permanent exhibits on Tubman, the Underground Railroad, and those who escaped slavery. 🌐 *www.nps.gov/hatu/planyourvisit/index.htm.*

### Best Activities

Some of the major sites along the trail include the Harriet Tubman Museum and Educational Center, the Tuckahoe Neck Meeting House, and the Jacob and Hannah Leverton House.

### Did You Know?

Harriet Tubman was often referred to by the name "Moses" after the prophet Moses who led his people to freedom.

### Before You Go

For a more enriching experience and better understanding of the challenges faced on the road to freedom, watch Amazon's drama series *The Underground Railroad* by award-winning director Barry Jenkins.

### Getting Here and Around

Since the trail spans more than 120 miles, it's best accessed by car. The tour runs through much of Maryland, making it accessible from many points throughout the state. The driving tour takes about three to four hours.

**Harriet Tubman Underground Railroad.** 🌐 *www.visitmaryland.org/scenic-byways/harriet-tubman-underground-railroad.*

# Baltimore's Inner Harbor

## One of the Country's Best Urban Waterfronts

One of Baltimore's most-visited destinations is the Inner Harbor, a waterfront neighborhood that just as popular with locals as it is with out-of-towners. The area was once known for its steel mills and shipyards, and today you can learn about its seafaring past while you board some of the centuries-old vessels, including a three-masted beauty called the USS *Constellation.* There are also world-class museums, waterfront restaurants, and spectacular views.

## Don't Miss

A can't-miss attraction at the Inner Harbor, the sprawling National Aquarium is home to more than 750 species of underwater creatures. The permanent exhibits range from a thriving coral reef, a 225,000-gallon tank called Shark Alley, and six gregarious bottlenose dolphins at Dolphin Discovery. ⊕ *aqua.org.*

## Best Restaurant

The Rusty Scupper is an Inner Harbor institution that has been serving fresh seafood alongside views of the water for decades. ⊕ *www.rusty-scupper.com.*

## Best After-Dark Activity

The city's best night on the town just might be at Power Plant Live!, a neighborhood on the Inner Harbor that promises rowdy bars, cool nightclubs, fun restaurants, and more. ⊕ *www.powerplantlive.com*

## Getting Here and Around

Once you're in downtown Baltimore, most of the attractions of the Inner Harbor are reachable by foot.

**Baltimore Information.** ☎ *877/225–8466* ⊕ *baltimore.org* 🎟 *Free.*

# Edgar Allan Poe's Grave

### Baltimore's Spookiest Unsolved Mystery

One of the spookiest spots in America is the grave of poet Edgar Allan Poe, the poet whose life—and afterlife—are shrouded with mystery. For 75 years, a mysterious stranger dressed in a dark coat and hat pulled low over his face appeared at the graveside at Westminster Hall and Burial Grounds every January 19, raising a glass of cognac in his honor and leaving behind three roses. It's still a chilling place to visit. There are plenty of other Poe spots in Baltimore, where he lived and died.

### Don't Miss

Start your tour at the Edgar Allan Poe House and Museum, his home during the 1830s, where you'll see artifacts like his chair and desk and a collection of works that he wrote in Baltimore. *$10.*

### Literary Stop

At the Enoch Pratt Free Library, a collection of first-edition books and manuscripts draw Poe fans from all over. *www.prattlibrary.org* *Free.*

### Best Tour

A stop at Westminster Hall and Burial Grounds, where Poe's grave is located, is a must. *www.westminsterhall.org* *$5.*

### Ghostly Stop

The Horse You Came In On Saloon in Fell's Point is believed to be the place where Poe had his final drink. Some say his spirit can be seen wandering the historic bar. *www.thehorsebaltimore.com.*

### Getting Here and Around

The attractions linked to Edgar Allan Poe are scattered throughout the city. Some are within walking distance from one another while others require short drives or cab rides.

## Chesapeake & Ohio Canal National Historical Park

### A Mule Boat Ride Back in Time

A waterway that allowed for coal to be transported from western Maryland to Washington, D.C., the Chesapeake & Ohio Canal was operational for nearly 100 years. Canal boats full of coal were pulled by mules, who navigated a tow path on the shore. At night they'd actually sleep in a stable aboard the boats. Today you can follow these same paths for nearly the entire length of the 184-mile canal. A scenic place to start is the Great Falls Tavern Visitor Center, northwest of Washington, D.C.

### Don't Miss

The Billy Goat Trail is a popular hiking and biking spot along the C&O Canal. Its actually three different trails that offer challenging hiking and even some rock climbing. The trails are accessible at the towpath entrance at Great Falls Tavern.

### Good to Know

There are visitor centers located along the route, including in popular spots like Cumberland and Williamsport. The visitor centers are a great place to pick up brochures and maps, learn helpful information about the route, and start a hike. *www.canaltrust.org/plan/highlights-and-amenities/co-canal-visitor-centers.*

### Getting Here and Around

There are many entrances to the C&O Canal, but the one at the Great Falls Tavern Visitor Center in Potomac is among the most accessible.

**Great Falls Tavern Visitor Center.** *11710 Macarthur Blvd., Potomac, MD* *301/767–3714* *www.nps.gov/choh* *Free.*

# Antietam National Battlefield

### A Somber Reminder of "America's Bloodiest Day"

Antietam National Battlefield was the scene of one of the worst clashes during the Civil War. During the battle on September 17, 1862, more than 23,000 soldiers were killed or injured and led to President Abraham Lincoln's issuing of the Emancipation Proclamation. Today, Antietam is a national park that draws visitors from around the country and around the world. It's a chance to learn about the history of the battle, see some of the original cannons and other military equipment, and duck into a church, field hospital, and other historic buildings.

### Don't Miss

Following the battle, a mill property owned by Joshua Newcomer, now known as the Newcomer House, was used to care for those who were injured. It is now home to the Heart of the Civil War Heritage Area Exhibit. *www.heartofthecivilwar.org/newcomer-house.*

### Best Hikes

There are a range of self-guided hiking tours of the key battlefields. Most are easy to moderate and range from a quick stroll around a scenic loop to a longer hike taking you 2 miles. The short Tidball Trail brings you to one of the best overlooks of the battlefield, while the Snavely Ford Trail follows the banks of Antietam Creek.

### Getting Here and Around

The battlefield is best reached by car; parking is available in lots surrounding the national park.

**Antietam National Battlefield.** *5831 Dunker Church Rd., Sharpsburg, MD* *301/432–5124* *www.nps.gov/anti* *$10.*

# Assateague Island National Seashore

### Wild Horses Running Along the Beach

Assateague Island National Seashore draws animal lovers from all over who want to catch a glimpse of the wild horses that make their home on this barrier island surrounded by Chincoteague Bay to the west and the Atlantic Ocean to the east. The horses—originally brought here by farmers during the 17th century—roam freely, but spend any amount of time here and they are sure to gallop by. Many visitors also enjoy hiking or camping on the sandy shores, while others find the open water ideal for kayaking, fishing, crabbing, and swimming.

### Don't Miss

The wild horses are a must-see for anyone visiting the island. Rangers at the visitor center will be able to tell you the best places to spot them. Remember not to feed or touch the animals.

### Best Tour

Park rangers lead tours of the island during the spring and summer. Book one at the Assateague Island Visitor Center.

### Best Activity

The vast majority of people drive to Assateague, but cycling is a great way to spend a day at the seashore. Bikes are available for rent at Assateague Outfitters. 🌐 *www.assateagueoutfitters.com.*

### Getting Here and Around

The fairly remote area is best accessed by car. Baltimore/Washington International Thurgood Marshall Airport is the closest aiport at about 130 miles away.

**Assateague Island Visitor Center.** ✉ *7206 National Seashore La., Berlin, MD* ☎ *410/641–1441* 🌐 *www.nps.gov/asis* 🎫 *$25 per car.*

# Ocean City

## Maryland's Seaside Party Town

Stretching some 10 miles along a narrow barrier island off Maryland's Atlantic coast, action-packed Ocean City draws millions from neighboring states (New Jersey, Pennsylvania, Virginia, and Delaware) and the District of Columbia virtually year-round to its broad beaches and the innumerable activities and amenities that cling to them, as well as to the quiet bay side between the island and the mainland. "O.C." is a premier Mid-Atlantic leisure-travel destination, at once big and small, sprawling and congested, old and new, historic and hip, noisy and quiet, sophisticated and tacky, expensive and not, and everything in between. The oceanfront boardwalk is a big draw, with arcades and amusement parks, making this a hit with families.

## Don't Miss

Make plans to stroll at least part of the 3-mile-long boardwalk, a favorite activity in Ocean City. Kids love the towering Ferris wheel and the carousel dating back to 1902. For food, stop for fresh fish at Harrison's Harbor Watch or Bull on the Beef for a classic pit beef sandwich.

## Best Tour

Ocean City Food Tours has seafood-focused tours that show you how to crack open a hard-shelled crab. 🌐 *ocfoodietour.com.*

## Getting Here and Around

Traffic can be heavy, so many people choose to explore Ocean City by bike. For travel along the boardwalk, the Boardwalk Tram is an affordable and quick way to get from place to place.

## When in Maryland

### CHAPS PIT BEEF

In 1987, the first Chaps Pit Beef opened, serving its now-famous sandwich. The original location is still open today on Pulaski Highway and is frequented by those looking for Baltimore's signature sandwich. The menu is mostly Baltimore-style barbecue, with many meaty options beyond the pit beef sandwich.

**Do This:** Stop by for lunch or dinner and order the signature dish at Chaps Pit Beef.

**Chaps Pit Beef.** ✉ *5801 Pulaski Hwy., Baltimore, MD* ☎ *410/483–2379* 🌐 *chapspitbeef.com.*

### FREDERICK

Frederick is the kind of place where you can visit a historic site in the morning, an interesting museum in the afternoon, then join the locals at a hip martini bar. The Monocacy National Battlefield is nearby, as is Flying Dog Brewery, Maryland's largest craft brewery.

**Do This:** Pedego Electric Bikes lead guided bike tours of Frederick that bring you past historic sites and beautiful parks. Guides share information on history, fun facts, and tidbits about the town's development, too. 🌐 *www.pedegoelectricbikes.com/dealers/frederick.*

### ORIOLES PARK AT CAMDEN YARDS

With a name that calls to mind Maryland's brilliantly colored state bird, the Baltimore Orioles are the city's hometown baseball team. They play at the eye-catching Orioles Park at Camden Yards in downtown Baltimore, known as one of the most beautiful stadiums in baseball.

**Do This:** If you're a big-time baseball fan, head to the nearby Babe Ruth Birthplace and Museum. 🌐 *baberuthmuseum.org.*

**Camden Yards.** ✉ *333 W. Camden St., Baltimore, MD* ☎ *888/248–2473* 🌐 *www.mlb.com/orioles.*

### ST. MICHAELS

Waterfront St. Michaels is named for an Episcopal church established in the town in 1677. The Chesapeake Bay town is a favorite with boating enthusiasts and seafood fans, as well as architecture buffs who come to see its streets lined with late-18th- and early-19th-century structures. Enjoy Maryland crabs at The Crab Claw and take in views of the Inn at Perry Cabin, a hotel made famous by the film *Wedding Crashers.*

**Do This:** Learn about the area's vast maritime history at the Chesapeake Bay Maritime Museum, which is also home to a working shipyard where shipwrights can be seen working on oceangoing vessels.

**Chesapeake Bay Maritime Museum.** ✉ *St. Michaels, MD* 🌐 *cbmm.org.*

## Cool Places to Stay

**The Inn at Perry Cabin.** Most famously known as the setting for the film *Wedding Crashers,* the Inn at Perry Cabin has a waterfront setting on Maryland's Eastern Shore. Relaxing and serene, the hotel grounds have restaurants, bars, a pool, and plenty of space for outdoor lounging. ✉ *308 Watkins La., St. Michaels, MD* ☎ *888/805–8885* 🌐 *innatperrycabin.com* $ *From $800.*

**Sagamore Pendry Hotel.** Located in Baltimore's trendy Fells Point neighborhood, the luxurious Sagamore Pendry Hotel combines a historic vibe and a waterfront setting. The pool offers prime harbor views, as do many of the plush guest rooms and suites. ✉ *1715 Thames St., Baltimore, MD* ☎ *443/552–1400* 🌐 *www.pendry.com/baltimore* $ *From $480.*

# New Jersey

The "Garden State" has the third-largest state park system in the country and is almost entirely bordered by water—the Atlantic Ocean (and the famous Jersey Shore) to the east, the Delaware River to the west, and the Delaware Bay to the south. Along the Hudson River run the famous Palisades, with its heart-stopping views of the Manhattan skyline. But it also has its own unique culture marked by diners and shore life that are epic in their own right.



## Bucket List Picks

The following boxes contain our picks for the top sights and experiences in New Jersey.

- ○ Liberty State Park
- ○ Asbury Park
- ○ Jersey Shore
- ○ Jersey Diners
- ○ Cape May
- ○ Morristown National Historical Park
- ○ Princeton
- ○ Paterson Great Falls National Historical Park
- ○ Delaware Water Gap

# Liberty State Park

## Epic Views of the Manhattan Skyline

The 1,212-acre Liberty State Park has one of the most spectacular views anywhere. Located along the mouth of the Hudson River in Jersey City, it offers unobstructed views of the Manhattan skyline, the Statue of Liberty, and Ellis Island. The waterfront walking paths through the park through the picnic areas, playgrounds, and moving memorials.

## Don't Miss

One of the most moving memorials to the September 11, 2001, attacks on the World Trade Center is the Empty Sky Memorial at Liberty State Park. It features two stainless-steel walls printed with the names of the 749 New Jersey residents who lost their lives that day. It sits on the waterfront facing Manhattan.

## If You Have Kids

On the western edge of the park is Liberty Science Center, which has plenty of hands-on exhibits that will keep kids occupied for hours. 🌐 *lsc.org.*

## Best Tour

To get to Ellis Island or the Statue of Liberty, take a ferry operated by Statue Cruises. They depart from Jersey City's Liberty State Park. ☎ *877/523–9849* 🌐 *www.statuecruises.com/cruises/new-jersey-reserve* 🎫 *From $19.*

## Getting Here and Around

Newark Liberty International Airport is a little over 10 miles away.

**Liberty State Park.** ✉ *200 Morris Pesin Dr., Jersey City, NJ* ☎ *201/915–3403* 🌐 *www.nj.gov/dep/parksandforests/parks/liberty.html* 🎫 *Free.*

# Asbury Park

## New Jersey's Coolest Beach Town

It's easy to see why Asbury Park is considered one of the Jersey Shore's coolest beach towns. The Stone Pony music venue made Asbury a household name decades ago when musicians like Bruce Springsteen, The Ramones, and Blondie graced its stage, but Asbury Park is still known for its exciting arts, culture, and dining scenes. The Asbury Park Boardwalk is a prime spot for people-watching. The downtown streets are filled with favorites like the Asbury Hotel—check out the rooftop bar—the Asbury Brewing Company, and the Asbury Festhalle and Biergarten.

## Don't Miss

Take advantage of the varied offerings at the majestic landmark known as the Asbury Park Convention Hall—part music venue, part dining and drinking destination. Within Convention Hall, the Asbury Oyster Bar is particularly popular for its namesake bivalve. 🌐 *apboardwalk.com/portfolio/convention-hall.*

## Walking Tour

Asbury is known for its outdoor murals, the brainchild of a local gallery owner. Both local and national artists were commissioned to create murals along the boardwalk and throughout downtown. 🌐 *woodenwallsproject.com*

## When to Go

Visit Asbury Park in the summer when there are plenty of outdoor dining and drinking destinations.

## Getting Here and Around

Asbury Park is about 45 miles from Newark Liberty International Airport and about 57 miles from Manhattan. The town is accessible by New Jersey Transit trains as well.

**Asbury Park.** 🌐 *www.visitnj.org/city/asbury-park.*

# Jersey Shore

### Where Life's a Beach

The coastal region of New Jersey, fondly known as the Jersey Shore, extends for 141 miles from Perth Amboy in the north to Cape May in the south. Any New Jersey resident will have an opinion about the best beach town, which they have likely been visiting for decades. Many weekenders love Sandy Hook National Seashore, a 6-mile-long stretch of sand accessible by car, bus, and even ferry. Ocean City is a family-friendly destination because of its popular boardwalk. Other popular towns include Seaside Heights, which was made famous by MTV's *Jersey Shore*, Long Beach Island, and Wildwood.

### Don't Miss

Island Beach State Park is one of the largest undeveloped barrier islands in the country. Visitors love the relaxed atmosphere and the opportunity for swimming, kayaking, or fishing at different parts of the 10-mile-long island. 🌐 *www.state.nj.us/dep/parksandforests/parks/island.html.*

### Best Tour

Hop aboard Salt Marsh Safari's 40-foot pontoon boats and tour the salt marshes along the coast. Tours depart from Stone Harbor and last for two hours. ☎ *609/884–3100* 🌐 *www.skimmer.com* 🎫 *From $30.*

### When to Go

Summer is by far the best time to visit the Jersey Shore. While the beaches are crowded and traffic can be bumper-to-bumper, you can't beat the summertime swimming, surfing, and other outdoor activities.

### Getting Here and Around

The Jersey Shore is best reached by car, but many beach towns like Manasquan, Long Branch, and Brigantine are accessible via New Jersey Transit trains and buses. Seastreak ferries take you from Manhattan to Sandy Hook. 🌐 *seastreak.com.*

# Jersey Diners

## Diner Capital of the World

New Jersey is fondly known as the "diner capital of the world" with an estimated 500 diners populating the state. Each of the diners has its own personality and go-to menu items, but all share the same approachable vibes. Many are retro-themed, remaining almost untouched since the 1950s, and some are open 24 hours a day. The menus at the state's diners are uniformly long, with classic American options for everyone, including grilled cheese, milkshakes, burgers, pancakes, pies, deli sandwiches, omelets, and much more.

## Don't Miss

Clinton Station Diner, a 24-hour operation in Clinton, New Jersey, stands out with its partially converted dining car. The menu features classics like salads, fries, deli sandwiches, Reubens, breakfast combos and more, in addition to a full bar, but what it's really known for are its burger-eating challenges, which result in free meals for victors.

## Good to Know

East Newark's Tops Diner has received numerous accolades for its excellent food and fun vibes, so it's no wonder it's been called one of the best diners in the country. Tops has been serving classic American fare since 1942 with options like egg platters, breakfast sandwiches, and pancakes.

## When to Go

Most diners are open from early morning to late night — if not 24 hours a day. It's a rite of passage to order something delicious and greasy late into the night.

## Getting Here and Around

There are diners in every county and most towns throughout the state.

# Cape May

## America's Original Seaside Getaway

The southernmost point in New Jersey is Cape May, a seaside town with a year-round population just shy of 4,000 people. At the height of summer, that number jumps to 40,000 or even 50,000 people. Known for its picturesque beaches, Victorian mansions, quaint B&Bs, and historic hotels, Cape May is a popular destination from late spring to early fall. Beyond the downtown area, Cape May Lighthouse and the adjacent Cape May Point State Park are big draws.

## Don't Miss

With plenty of room for the animals to roam, the Cape May County Park and Zoo is rated among the best in the country. More than 500 animals, including lions, cheetahs, and snow leopards live on 85 beautiful acres of parkland. ☎ *609/465–5271* 🌐 *www.capemaycountynj.gov/1008/Park-Zoo.*

## Best Tour

Cape May Whale Watcher offers an array of tours, including an excellent whale and dolphin watch. If you don't spot one, you'll receive a free pass for a future date. ☎ *609/884–5445* 🌐 *capemaywhalewatcher.com* 🎫 *From $50.*

## When to Go

Cape May is definitely a summer destination, although some prefer spring and fall.

## Getting Here and Around

Best reached by car, Cape May is the last exit on the Garden State Parkway. For a more special trip, the Cape May–Lewes ferry takes you on an 80-minute float across the Delaware Bay from Lewes, Delaware.

**New Jersey Shore Region.** 🌐 *www.visitnj.org/regions/shore.*

# Morristown National Historical Park

## In George Washington's Footsteps

George Washington and his Continental Army spent two bitterly cold winters in New Jersey. Morristown National Historical Park memorializes their struggle at several different sites, including two Continental Army encampments and a fortified hilltop nicknamed Fort Nonsense. The Ford Mansion, home to Theodosia Ford and her children, became headquarters for Washington and a close group of advisors, including Alexander Hamilton.

## Don't Miss

Be sure to visit the soldier huts at Jockey Hollow. The rebuilt structures resemble the wood structures where the soldiers lived during the cold winters in Morristown.

## Best Tour

Grab a map and head off on a self-guided tour of the 27 miles of trails throughout the park. Trails are marked by their difficulty level.

## When to Go

To best enjoy the park's hiking trails, the fall, spring, and summer are the best times to visit.

## Getting Here and Around

Since the main sites are spread around the Morristown area, it's best to have a car when visiting Morristown National Historical Park. The attraction is off of Interstate 287 in Morristown, New Jersey.

**Morristown National Historical Park.** ✉ *30 Washington Pl., Morristown, NJ* ☎ *973/539–2016* 🌐 *www.nps.gov/morr/index.htm* 🎫 *Free.*

# Princeton

### Ivy League Attractions

Princeton may be best known for its resident Ivy League university, and its Gothic Revival architecture in buildings like Blair Hall, Holder Hall, and Cleveland Tower make it well worth exploring. But the town itself is also a gem, and Nassau Street and the surrounding thoroughfares are popular among locals and visitors for their variety of shops, restaurants, and taverns. Residents take pride in Princeton Battlefield State Park, a 681-acre historic park where, on January 3, 1777, General George Washington and his troops defeated a group of British foot soldiers. Today, the expansive park is home to the Clark House Museum.

### Don't Miss

The 5-acre Morven Museum and Garden was built by Richard Stockton, a signer of the Declaration of Independence, in the 1750s. Many New Jersey governors lived at the property before it was opened to the public. 🌐 *www.morven.org.*

### Best Tour

The impressive Princeton University Art Museum is home to more than 97,000 works of art. Self-guided tours of the museum are available, but guided tours at 2 on Saturdays and Sundays include an interesting commentary on the collection. 🌐 *artmuseum.princeton.edu.*

### When to Go

The many public parks throughout Princeton make warm weather the best time to go. Visit in spring to see the trees and flowers in bloom or in summer to enjoy hikes through the countryside.

### Getting Here and Around

Princeton is located halfway between New York City and Philadelphia. It's about 40 miles from Newark Liberty International Airport and is accessible by NJ Transit and Amtrak.

# Paterson Great Falls National Historical Park

### New Jersey's Niagara

A 77-foot-high waterfall is the centerpiece of Paterson Great Falls National Historical Park. During the Industrial Revolution, Paterson was the country's first planned industrial community, and hydro power from the falls was used to power the town. Visit for sweeping waterfall views, set out on one of the many walking trails through the park.

### Don't Miss

Walk along the Great Falls footbridge for uninterrupted aerial views for the waterfall.

### Best Tour

There are several ranger-led tour options if you book in advance, and a kids junior ranger program. You can also download a free self-guided walking tour app. ⊕ *www.nps.gov/pagr*

### When to Go

The park is open year-round. Spring, summer, and fall are the best times to visit this park since the footbridge closes when the weather gets icy.

### Getting Here and Around

A few minutes off I–80, the state park is less than a 30-minute drive from Newark Liberty International Airport. Parking is available at Overlook Park and along Maple Street.

**Paterson Great Falls National Historical Park.** ✉ *72 McBride Ave., Paterson, NJ* ☎ *973/523–0370* ⊕ *www.nps.gov/pagr/index.htm* 🎫 *Free.*

# Delaware Water Gap

### New Jersey's High Point

Located on the New Jersey and Pennsylvania border, the Delaware Water Gap is a picturesque point where the Delaware River meets the Appalachian Mountain Range. There are miles of hiking trails of varying skill levels that bring explorers past waterfalls, to mountaintop overlooks, and along riverfront walks. There are also historic sites, including Millbrook Village.

### Don't Miss

1,803 feet above sea level is High Point State Park, the highest point in New Jersey. The park offers hiking trails, swimming areas, and the state's first natural area: the 850-acre Dryden Kuser Natural Area. *www.state.nj.us/dep/parksandforests/parks/highpoint.html.*

### When to Go

The Delaware Water Gap is an all-year place to visit. In cold weather, locals love it for snowshoeing and other winter sports. In the warmer months, it's ideal for swimming and boating.

### Getting Here and Around

The Delaware Water Gap is a huge area, so it has many access points. A car is pretty much required to explore it.

**Kittatinny Point Visitor Center.** *1 I–80, Columbia, NJ* *570/426–2452* *www.nps.gov/dewa/index.htm* *Free.*

# When in New Jersey

## GROUNDS FOR SCULPTURE

There are nearly 300 outdoor sculptures—some towering more than 30 feet—on display across 42 acres of land. The landscape itself is reason enough to visit, and walking paths take you past ponds and meadows. Inside the museum, six galleries welcome a rotating lineup of up-and-coming artists.

**Do This:** Plan to have lunch at one of the facility's on-site restaurants. Visit Rat's Restaurant, named for *The Wind in the Willows* character, to be transported to the French town of Giverny. For a more casual meal, the Van Gogh Cafe sells picnic lunches that come complete with a bottle of wine.

**Grounds for Sculpture.** ✉ *80 Sculptors Way, Hamilton Township, NJ* ☏ *609/586–0616* 🌐 *www.groundsforsculpture.org* 🎟 *$12.*

## HOLLAND RIDGE FARMS

Immigrating from Holland, Casey Jansen founded a wholesale tulip company. Years later, he and his family opened Holland Ridge Farms, a pick-your-own flower farm spanning 153 acres in Cream Ridge, New Jersey. People from throughout the region visit in the summer to ride tractors, pet farm animals, and enjoy lunches.

**Do This:** The tens of thousands of flowers make for an ideal backdrop for family photos. Bring your camera—or your own photographer—for an unforgettable shot.

**Holland Ridge Farms.** ✉ *86 Rues Rd., Cream Ridge, NJ* 🌐 *www.hollandridgefarms.com* 🎟 *$12.*

## LUCY THE ELEPHANT

The country's oldest roadside attraction is the six-story-tall Lucy the Elephant, a wood and tin elephant located by the beach in Margate, New Jersey. The giant structure was created by James V. Lafferty in 1881 as a way to draw tourists to the beachfront community. More than 130 years later, the towering elephant is still a draw for visitors of all ages.

**Do This:** The only way to explore the inside of the towering elephant is on a 25-minute guided tour. From the howdah (the bedlike structure at the top of the elephant's back), you can take in great views of Margate.

**Lucy the Elephant.** ✉ *9200 Atlantic Ave., Margate City, NJ* ☏ *609/823–6473* 🌐 *lucytheelephant.org* 🎟 *$8.*

## NEW JERSEY PINELANDS NATIONAL RESERVE

The country's first national reserve, the New Jersey Pinelands includes about 1.1 million acres in seven counties in the southern part of New Jersey. It's home to a wide array of wildlife and plants. The sheer size can be overwhelming, but the Candace McKee Ashmun Pinelands Education Exhibit in the Richard J. Sullivan Center for Environmental Policy and Education is a good place to start to learn about the region.

**Do This:** The 19th village of Allaire, once a bustling community that was home to 400 people, has been preserved to show off a way of life that no longer exists. You can explore 13 of the original buildings, including a bakery, a boardinghouse, and a blast furnace where iron was once smelted. 🌐 *allairevillage.org.*

**New Jersey Pinelands National Reserve.** ✉ *15 Springfield Rd., New Lisbon, NJ* ☏ *609/894–7300* 🌐 *www.nj.gov/pinelands/index.shtml* 🎟 *Free.*

## STERLING HILL MINING MUSEUM

New Jersey may not be famous for its mining, but the history of Sterling Hill Mine might just make up for that. Without taking a stance on mining, the museum discusses the history of the industry, its effects on the community, and its long-term consequences. Located at the site of the former zinc mine, the museum includes a 1,300-foot tunnel through the actual mine. It's accessible via two-hour-long guided tours.

**Do This:** Inside the mine, keep an eye out for the Rainbow Tunnel, a colorful exhibition that highlights the fluorescent zinc ore.

**Sterling Hill Mining Museum.** ✉ *30 Plant St., Ogdensburg, NJ* ☎ *973/209–7212* 🌐 *www.sterlinghillminingmuseum.org* 🎟 *$13.*

### THOMAS EDISON NATIONAL HISTORICAL PARK

Thomas Edison called West Orange, New Jersey, home for close to 50 years, and the site of his former home and laboratory are now known as Thomas Edison National Historical Park. The laboratory is where Edison invented devices like the phonograph and the motion picture camera. There are more than 300,000 items in the museum's collection, making this one of the National Park Service's most expansive museums. The house explores the Edison family's daily life.

**Do This:** Embark on the self-guided tour of the home, which shares stories about Edison and his family.

**Thomas Edison National Historical Park.** ✉ *211 Main St., West Orange, NJ* ☎ *973/736–0550* 🌐 *www.nps.gov/edis/index.htm* 🎟 *$15.*

## Cool Places to Stay

**Asbury Hotel.** Located in the heart of Asbury Park, this lively, colorful hotel has an interesting history, delicious food, and a laid-back vibe. The guest rooms are comfortable, sleek, and minimalist. The rooftop bar, called Salvation, is a draw because of its ocean views, delicious cocktails, and DJs spinning the hottest tunes. ✉ *210 5th Ave., Asbury Park, NJ* ☎ *732/774–7100* 🌐 *www.theasburyhotel.com* $ *From $170.*

**Congress Hall.** When driving through Cape May, it's impossible to miss towering Congress Hall, America's oldest seaside resort and one of the most charming places to stay in New Jersey. While there is a ton to do in Cape May, guests never have to leave hotel grounds because of the four restaurants and swimming pool. ✉ *200 Congress Pl., Cape May, NJ* ☎ *609/884–8421* 🌐 *www.caperesorts.com/congress-hall* $ *From $179.*

**Lambertville House Hotel.** This historic hotel first opened its doors in 1812, and since then has hosted notables like President Andrew Johnson and General Ulysses S. Grant. The rooms are all classically decorated to match the hotel's history and offer modern amenities like gas fireplaces and whirlpool tubs. ✉ *32 Bridge St., Lambertville, NJ* ☎ *609/397–0200* 🌐 *lambertvillehouse.com* 🎟 *From $210.*

**The MC Hotel.** In the community of Montclair, this lodging reflects the area's diverse and exciting arts scene. The hotel has a sleek rooftop bar and lounge with stunning views of the city skyline, an indoor-outdoor Mediterranean restaurant, and art created by up-and-coming artists. ✉ *690 Bloomfield Ave., Montclair, NJ* ☎ *844/624–6835* 🌐 *themchotel.com* $ *From $184.*

# New York

Say the words "New York" and icons like Times Square and the Statue of Liberty may be the first things that pop to mind. But the state is also very much a destination for appreciating the outdoors, in every season. Across New York, from Niagara Falls to the tip of Long Island, there are breathtaking hiking trails, lakes and rivers for fishing and boating, mountains for skiing, and lovely ocean beaches for relaxing.

## Bucket List Picks

The following boxes contain our picks for the top sights and experiences in New York.

- ○ Central Park
- ○ Ellis Island and the Statue of Liberty
- ○ Niagara Falls State Park
- ○ Broadway
- ○ Brooklyn Bridge
- ○ Coney Island
- ○ Hudson Valley and the Catskills
- ○ Big Five Museums
- ○ The Hamptons
- ○ The Adirondacks
- ○ Chinatown
- ○ Thousand Islands
- ○ 9/11 Memorial and Museum
- ○ The High Line and Hudson Yards
- ○ The Finger Lakes
- ○ Observatories
- ○ Cruising Around Manhattan
- ○ New York Sports
- ○ Harlem

# Central Park

### New York's Big Backyard

Upwards of 40 million people visit New York City's iconic Central Park every year, but with its 843 acres of wide-open spaces, you can usually find a spot all to yourself. Designed by Frederick Law Olmsted and Calvert Vaux in 1858, Central Park was created to give city dwellers lots of fresh air. The park is now home to major attractions including the Central Park Zoo, with more than 130 species of animals; Sheep Meadow and its sunbathers; and Conservatory Water and its regatta of model boats. Wollman Rink is a wintertime destination for ice-skaters, while the open-air Delacorte Theater is the summertime home to Shakespeare in the Park.

### Don't Miss

Paddleboats are available for rent at the Loeb Boathouse on Central Park Lake, one of the park's largest bodies of water. Visit the restaurant at the boathouse for a post-paddle treat.

### Best Tour

The sheer size of Central Park can make it overwhelming. Guides for Central Park Bike Tours take you to the best spots and point out filming locations for New York City–based shows like *Sex and the City* and *Friends.* 🌐 *www.centralpark.com/tours/bike.*

### Good to Know

The park starts at 59th Street in Midtown Manhattan and continues up for more than 50 blocks to 110th Street in South Harlem. In other words, the park is huge, measuring 3 miles long.

### Getting Here and Around

Central Park is located in the heart of Manhattan, making it easily accessible. Penn Station is less than 2 miles away.

**Central Park.** 🌐 *www.centralparknyc.org* 🎫 *Free.*

# Ellis Island and the Statue of Liberty

## America's Great Gateway

In the late 19th century and early 20th century, more than 12 million immigrants came to America by way of Ellis Island, which is located at the mouth of the Hudson River. You're likely to have at least one ancestor who passed through the grand doorways of this French Renaissance–style structure, and that's why a visit here is so moving. On nearby island Liberty Island stands the Statue of Liberty, a symbol of hope for anyone whose first sight of America was from New York Harbor.

## Don't Miss

On Ellis Island, visit the National Museum of Immigration, located within the ornate main building. Many people visit the museum to scour the easily searchable historic records for family members' names. Others visit to learn about the important role that Ellis Island played through artifacts and heirlooms.

## Good to Know

A short ferry ride away from Ellis Island is the Statue of Liberty, a towering structure that was a gift from the French. The Statue of Liberty Museum, which opened in 2019, explores the history of the statue and exhibits artifacts like the original torch. It also offers prime views of Lady Liberty.

## When to Go

Both attractions are open all year, but visiting in the warmer months is ideal to enjoy the ferry ride.

## Getting Here and Around

Both Ellis Island and the Statue of Liberty are only reachable by ferries from Battery Park in Manhattan and Liberty State Park in Jersey City. Ferry tickets grant you access to both destinations.

**Ellis Island.** 🌐 *www.statueofliberty.org* 🎫 *$24 for ferry ride.*

# Niagara Falls State Park

## Three Spectacular Waterfalls

There isn't just one spectacular waterfall in Niagara Falls State Park. In the country's oldest state park are three separate sights: Horseshoe Falls (this is the U-shaped one that most people think of when they hear "Niagara Falls"), American Falls, and Bridal Veil Falls. At its highest points, the falls tumble 176 feet. Beyond the falls, the state park features includes several islands: Goat Island—with great views and several attractions of its own—Luna Island, and Three Sisters Islands.

## Don't Miss

Catch a glimpse of the falls from above at Niagara Falls Observation Tower, which has the only panoramic view of all three waterfalls. It sits between American Falls and Bridal Veil Falls. ⊕ *www.niagarafallsstatepark.com/attractions-and-tours/observation-tower.*

## Best Tour

On the *Maid of the Mist* boat tour, visitors get to view Horseshoe Falls from below on a 20-minute boat tour. The boat gets so close that guests get waterproof ponchos to protect them from the mist. ⊕ *www.maidofthemist.com.*

## When to Go

Niagara Falls is most enjoyable in warmer weather when there is no snow or ice to worry about.

## Getting Here and Around

Buffalo–Niagara International Airport is about 30 miles away.

**Niagara Falls Visitor Center.** ✉ *332 Prospect St., Niagara Falls, NY* ☎ *716/278–1794* ⊕ *www.niagarafallsstatepark.com* 🎫 *Free.*

## Broadway

### They Say the Neon Lights Are Bright

Only a handful of theaters actually face the avenue that gave New York City's theater district its name. Most of the 40 or so theaters are on side streets, from the Nederlander way down on 41st to the Vivian Beaumont up on 65th. The oldest ones, like the New Amsterdam, are Beaux Arts gems from the days of the Zeigfeld Follies. If you can't see a show at the Shubert or the Booth, at least stroll by to see a couple of architectural masterpieces. Nearby, Shubert Alley is filled with starry-eyed theater fans waiting to enjoy a post-performance slice of cheesecake at Junior's.

### Don't Miss

New Yorkers hate Times Square, and will do anything they can to avoid it, but it's a must for first-timers. The billboards are dazzling, and the illuminated red stairs above the TKTS booth are a great place to see the ball that drops every New Year's Eve.

### Good to Know

While shows often sell out months in advance, the TKTS booth in Times Square sells heavily discounted same-day Broadway tickets. 🌐 *www.tdf.org.*

### When to Go

The busiest seasons are around the holidays and in the summer months. You're more likely to get tickets in January or February.

### Getting Here and Around

Broadway is located in the middle of Manhattan, making it accessible from all over. Both of the city's major train stations, New York Penn Station and Grand Central Station, deposit you blocks from the district.

**Theaters and tickets.** ✉ *On and around Times Square, Manhattan, NY* 🌐 *www.broadway.com.*

# Brooklyn Bridge

### The City's Most Gorgeous Gateway

Perhaps more than any other activity, New Yorkers send their out-of-town visitors for a stroll across the Brooklyn Bridge. The wide walking and biking paths are a big draw for those who want to take in panoramic views of the Manhattan skyline—and, of course, pose for pictures. The bridge opened in 1883 after more than 10 years of construction, and the engineering marvel is still the most beautiful of the city's gateways. On the Brooklyn side, Brooklyn Bridge Park is well worth the walk.

### Don't Miss

Go for a walk through DUMBO, a Brooklyn neighborhood whose name is short for Down Under the Manhattan Bridge Overpass. It's full of converted warehouses, cobblestone streets, and prime Manhattan views, and is known for its excellent independently owned eateries.

### Best Activity

Dating back to 1922, Jane's Carousel is a wooden merry-go-round that was moved to Brooklyn Bridge Park from Youngstown, Ohio. The painstakingly detailed carousel is enclosed in a glass pavilion, making it an all-year attraction. 🌐 *www.janescarousel.com.*

### When to Go

The bridge is busiest in the summer months, so if you're looking to avoid crowds, visit before Memorial Day or after Labor Day.

### Getting Here and Around

The Brooklyn Bridge and the DUMBO neighborhood are easily accessible via the subway.

**Brooklyn Bridge Park.** 🌐 *www.brooklynbridgepark.org.*

# Coney Island

## By the Beautiful Sea

More than a century ago, Coney Island ranked among the country's preeminent seaside resorts, and even though its heyday has passed, an aura of faded glory endures. Decades-old concessions line the boardwalk, and plenty of outsize characters keep Coney Island weird, especially during the annual Mermaid Parade. Minor-league baseball team the Brooklyn Cyclones plays at Coney Island's MCU Park, and the New York Aquarium sits right near the boardwalk.

## Don't Miss

Luna Park is home to the Cyclone, a wooden roller coaster that has been in operation since 1927. It's the second steepest in the world and always has a line of excited thrill-seekers waiting in line.

## Good to Know

The first Nathan's Hot Dogs opened here in 1916. The hot dogs are still a staple here, and a world-famous hot dog–eating contest takes place every year on July 4th.

## When to Go

Coney Island is open from Easter to Halloween. The summer months are ideal if you're looking to swim or sunbathe, but come in spring or fall if you're looking to avoid the crowds. The Mermaid Parade takes place on the Saturday closest to summer solstice, usually late June.

## Getting Here and Around

Located at the bottom of Brooklyn, Coney Island is easily accessible by car. From Manhattan, it's about an hour away by subway.

**Luna Park.** 🌐 *lunaparknyc.com.*

# Hudson Valley and the Catskills

## Marvelous Mountain Getaways

Known for their hiking trails, gushing waterfalls, and forest-topped mountains, the Hudson Valley and the adjacent Catskills have been an escape for New Yorkers for decades. These all-year destinations are popular for their resorts like Hunter and Windham mountains in the winter, colorful foliage in and around Catskill Park in autumn, and shopping in quaint villages like Woodstock and Hudson all year. N.Y.C. expats have opened chic bars, restaurants, and hotels throughout the area, and upscale crowds that once went to the Hamptons head to the DeBruce in Livingston Manor or Kenoza Hall in nearby Kenoza Lake.

## Don't Miss

Near the town of Hudson, Olana State Historic Site is the former estate of Frederic Edwin Church, a renowned painter. His lofty estate is now a state park and museum. The 250 acres of grounds are open for tours. 🌐 *www.olana.org*.

## Best Activity

A wide range of galleries and museums beckon, especially a rainy afternoon. Visitors love Dia: Beacon, Opus 40 in Saugerties, and Hudson Valley MOCA in Peekskill.

## When to Go

The Hudson Valley and the Catskills are year-round destinations.

## Getting Here and Around

Albany International and Stewart International are the closest airports, but a car is necessary to get around.

**The Catskills.** 🌐 *www.visitthecatskills.com*.

# Big Five Museums

## The Best of the Best

It's no secret that New York City has some of the best museums in the world. There are upwards of 100 museums in New York City, ranging from massive institutions (the Whitney Museum of Art) to smaller, topic-specific attractions (the Museum of Sex). While most of the city's museums are well worth a visit, the five that are most deserving are fondly known as the Big Five: the Metropolitan Museum of Art, American Museum of Natural History, the Museum of Modern Art, the Solomon R. Guggenheim Museum, and Intrepid Sea, Air, and Space Museum.

## Don't Miss

The Metropolitan Museum of Art has been a destination for art fans for generations. The Met is the largest art museum in the country and features everything from a complete Egyptian temple to a Frank Lloyd Wright house. 🌐 *www.metmuseum.org*.

## Best for Kids

The Hayden Planetarium at the American Museum of Natural History takes you to infinity and beyond. 🌐 *www.amnh.org/exhibitions/permanent/hayden-planetarium*.

## Good to Know

To ensure access on the day you'd like to visit, advance tickets are a good idea.

## Getting Here and Around

The Big Five are easily accessible by subway.

**The Metropolitan Museum of Art.** 🌐 *www.metmuseum.org*
**The American Museum of Natural History.** 🌐 *www.amnh.org*
**The Museum of Modern Art.** 🌐 *www.moma.org*
**The Solomon R. Guggenheim Museum.** 🌐 *www.guggenheim.org*
**The Intrepid Sea, Air & Space Museum.** 🌐 *www.intrepidmuseum.org*

# The Hamptons

## Glittering Summer Playground

On the eastern end of Long Island, the Hamptons are the summertime destination for New Yorkers who have plenty of money (or want to give the impression that they do). If the gossip columns report on a lavish fundraiser or a celebrity behaving badly, it's likely to be in the Hamptons. Towns like Sag Harbor, Southampton, and Montauk sit along miles of sandy beaches and have a wide assortment of high-end bars, restaurants, and boutiques. Come for the quintessential summer activities: swimming, boating, and lounging in the sun (usually behind a privacy fence).

## Don't Miss

At the easternmost point on Long Island, Montauk Lighthouse is the ideal place for sweeping ocean views. Dating back to the late 18th century, the lighthouse has beautiful grounds and an on-site museum. 🌐 *montauk-lighthouse.com*.

## Best Beach

Southampton's Coopers Beach is often rated one of the best beaches in the country—and for good reason. Open to the public (unlike a number of beaches in the area), it's beloved for its white sand, picturesque dunes, and many beachfront mansions in the distance.

## When to Go

The Hamptons are hopping in the summer. If you're weary of crowds, visit before Memorial Day or after Labor Day.

## Getting Here and Around

The Hampton Jitney arrives from New York City, making stops in towns like East Hampton, Southampton, and Montauk. A car is the easiest way to get around, but Uber is always available.

## The Adirondacks

### A Breath of Fresh Air

More than 6 million acres make up northern New York's Adirondacks, an area known for its brilliant blue lakes, towering evergreen forests, and picturesque villages. The vast expanse is made up of 12 smaller regions, with the most well-known being Lake Placid, Lake George, Lake Champlain, and Saranac Lake. Visit for skiing, snowshoeing, and sledding in the winter and for boating, swimming, and hiking in the summer.

### Don't Miss

Known by some as the "Grand Canyon of the Adirondacks," Ausable Chasm is an outdoor adventure park offering activities ranging from hiking to river rafting to rock climbing. The sandstone gorge is a lovely place for picnics. 🌐 *www.ausablechasm.com.*

### Best Activity

Thousands and thousands of people head to Gore Mountain every year for its winter sports, especially skiing and snowboarding. In the warmer months, the attraction offers hiking and biking. 🌐 *goremountain.com.*

### When to Go

It's a year-round destination, and it's one part of the state that's hopping all winter.

### Getting Here and Around

Amtrak's Adirondack service offers a scenic ride from New York's Penn Station. Plattsburgh International Airport serves the region.

**The Adirondacks.** 🌐 *www.iloveny.com/places-to-go/adirondacks.*

# Chinatown

## The Best of Chinese Culture

Manhattan's Chinatown, a bustling area filled with restaurants, grocery stores, and specialty stores, is regularly regarded as one of the best in the country. Although Chinese is the dominant culture here, it's not hard to find other Asian fare, such as Thai and Malaysian. Want to learn more about the neighborhood? Head to the Museum of Chinese in America. Nom Wah Tea Parlor, the Hong Kong Supermarket, and the Original Chinatown Ice Cream Factory are delicious diversions.

## Don't Miss

There are also Chinatowns in the Sunset Park neighborhood of Brooklyn and the Flushing neighborhood of Queens. They are less flashy, but New Yorkers swear the food is more authentic.

## Best Restaurant

New Yorkers love Joe's Shanghai and Nom Wah Tea Parlor and will regularly wait in line for their delicious (and inexpensive) pork buns, dumplings, and dim sum, but you can't go wrong with any restaurant that's filled with locals.

## Beyond Chintatown

While Midtown's Koreatown is barely a block long, it's home to dozens and dozens of excellent Korean restaurants. Little Manila in Queens is a great place to eat a Filipino meal. Bordering Manhattan's Chinatown is Little Italy, a go-to place for traditional red-sauce dishes.

## Getting Here and Around

The subway runs to nearly all the neighborhoods mentioned here.

**Chinatown.** 🌐 *www.iloveny.com/listing/chinatown/1664.*

# Thousand Islands

## Castles and Cruises

Located along the St. Lawrence River is Thousand Islands, an archipelago that consists of more than 1,864 individual islands. Some are home to cottages and castles, while others are uninhabited areas ideal for outdoor exploration. If you get tired of exploring communities like Alexandria Bay, Sackets Harbor, and Cape Vincent, head across the border to find other quaint villages in Canada. Visit the area for boating, fishing, swimming, and quaint-town exploration.

## Don't Miss

Castles built by wealthy industrialists dot the islands near Alexandria Bay. The 120-room Boldt Castle was begun in 1900, left unfinished for more than 70 years, then finished in spectacular fashion. Modest in comparison is the 28-room Singer Castle.

## Best Tour

Clayton Island Tours is the best way to see the Thousand Islands. Head to Rock Island Lighthouse aboard a glass-bottomed boat, or take a sunset cruise on the St. Lawrence River. 🌐 *claytonislandtours.com/boat-tours.*

## When to Go

Because everything is focused on the weather, summer is the best time to visit the Thousands Islands.

## Getting Here and Around

Watertown International Airport is about 30 miles from most Thousand Islands destinations.

**Thousand Islands.** 🌐 *visit1000islands.com.*

# 9/11 Memorial and Museum

## New York's Most Moving Memorial

It's impossible not to be moved by Memorial Plaza, the centerpiece of the 9/11 Memorial and Museum. A pair of 30-foot-tall waterfalls occupy the giant, square footprints where the Twin Towers once stood. Edging the pools are bronze panels inscribed with the names of the nearly 3,000 people who were killed in the 1993 and 2001 terrorist attacks. In the museum, interactive exhibitions tell the story of the attacks and honor the lives lost.

## Don't Miss

Built on the site of One World Trade Center is the Freedom Tower, rising to 1,776 feet tall. After a truly thrilling elevator ride to the top, see the city from above the clouds at One World Observatory. *www.oneworldobservatory.com*

## Best Tour

Embark on a self-guided tour of the 110,000-square-foot 9/11 Memorial and Museum. The permanent collection consists of 70,000 items that were either found at the site or donated by survivors, their friends and family, or first responders.

## Getting Here and Around

New Jersey's PATH trains travel directly to the World Trade Center station. The subway gets you here, as well.

**9/11 Memorial and Museum.** *180 Greenwich St., New York, NY* *312/212–8000* *911tributemuseum.org* *$25.*

## The High Line and Hudson Yards

### New York's "Park in the Sky"

The High Line almost didn't happen. The 1½-mile-long "park in the sky," once an elevated train line, was originally scheduled for demolition. It was residents who demanded it be transformed into a public space complete with swaths of greenery, meandering pathways, and areas for lounging about on the grass or under the trees. It was so popular that it was extended to Hudson Yards, an upscale shopping arcade built on top of what used to be the rail yards outside Penn Station. Its most notable structure is the Vessel, a beehivelike set of staircases that affords great views.

### Don't Miss

At the southern end of the High Line is the Whitney Museum of Art, which occupies a sleek building facing the Hudson River. Its collections of modern masterpieces make it well worth a visit before or after your High Line journey. 🌐 *whitney.org.*

### When to Go

Summer can be hot and too busy. Fall is a great time to stroll along the High Line and Hudson Yards.

### Best Break

Directly below the High Line between 15th and 16th Streets, Chelsea Market is a great stop when you're looking to fuel up during your exploration of the area. There are numerous eateries, but the Mexican street food at Los Tacos No. 1 is unbeatable.

### Getting Here and Around

Penn Station is about 1 mile away, making it easy to get to on foot, by cab, or on the subway. The 34 Street–Hudson Yards station is the closest subway stop.

**The High Line.** ✉ *New York, NY* ☎ *212/500–6035* 🌐 *www.thehighline.org* 🎟 *Free.*

# The Finger Lakes

## The Northeast's Largest Wine-Making Region

More than 550 million years ago, huge sheets of ice carved out the V-shaped valleys that make up New York's Finger Lakes region. Today these long, narrow lakes are known for their on-the-water activities, quaint towns, and more than 100 wineries. There's also a thriving restaurant scene and an ever-growing number of craft beer breweries. In between, set aside some time for hiking, biking, swimming, and sailing.

## Don't Miss

At the northern end of the region's largest body of water—lovely Seneca Lake—sits the town of Geneva, a historic hamlet that attracts many visitors each year. Downtown Geneva is home to boutiques, breweries, eateries, and views of the water from Seneca Lake State Park. Nearby are sprawling wineries, including the must-visit Belhurt Castle and Winery. 🌐 *www.belhurst.com.*

## Best Tour

As the vineyards are not always close together, see the area on a guided tour. Crush Beer and Wine Tours offers a wide variety of excursions, taking in the Canandaigua Lake Wine Trail, the Keuka Wine Trail, and the Seneca Lake Wine Trail. 🌐 *crushbeerwinetours.com.*

## When to Go

This is definitely a warm-weather destination.

## Getting Here and Around

Greater Rochester International Airport is the closest airport to the Finger Lakes.

**The Finger Lakes.** 🌐 *www.fingerlakes.org.*

# Observatories

### Views for Days

It's no secret that Manhattan has one of the world's most impressive skylines. The builders of the city's iconic skyscrapers didn't forget to add observation decks where you can take in the view, often while eating dinner or enjoying an expertly mixed cocktail. We all know there's one at the top of the Empire State Building (spoiler: it's the final scene of *Sleepless in Seattle* and countless other movies), but wouldn't you rather gaze out at this marvelous building from the Top of the Rock Observation Tower in Rockefeller Center?

### Don't Miss

The Empire State Building Observatory is one of the most popular spots to take in the skyline. The main deck observatory is on the 86th floor, offering 360-degree views of the city and way beyond. 🌐 *www.esbnyc.com.*

### Best Tour

The self-guided tour of One World Observatory, located at the top of the Freedom Tower, is amazing. The best part (if you don't have a fear of heights) is the glass floor where you look straight down. 🌐 *www.oneworldobservatory.com.*

### Good to Know

Manhattan has plenty of rooftop bars, but one of our favorites in the Cantor Roof Garden Bar at the Met. 🌐 *www.metmuseum.org.*

### Getting Here and Around

Most of the best observatories are located within bustling parts of Manhattan, which means they are easy to access by subway, in a cab, or on foot.

# Cruising Around Manhattan

## The Best Views of New York's Skyline

One of the best ways to take in the New York City skyline is from one of the boats that circle the island. Some, like Circle Line Cruises, are intended to give you the best possible views. Others, like the Staten Island Ferry, just happen to pass by jaw-dropping sights.

## Don't Miss

The New York City Ferry System has six routes that shuttle between Manhattan, Brooklyn, Queens, the Bronx, and Governor's Island. They are intended for commuters, so they are the same price as the subway. The views are sublime. 🌐 *www.ferry.nyc.*

## Best Tour

Circle Line Cruises offers an array of tours, including a "Best of New York" tour that takes you past the Statue of Liberty and other monumental attractions. A sunset cruise shows off the Williamsburg Bridge and the Empire State Building. 🌐 *www.circleline.com.*

## When to Go

New York City gets cold and windy in the winter, especially on the water. Boat tours are best saved for spring and summer.

## Getting Here and Around

Piers along the East River and the Hudson River are where most boats and ferries depart.

# New York Sports

### Cheer on the Yankees (or the Mets)

There's nothing like sitting in the stands and cheering on the Yankees—that is, unless you're a fan of the Mets. Or the Nets. Or the Knicks. New York City is filled with sports fans. The main venues are spread around the city: the Bronx is home to Yankee Stadium, while Queens is home to the Mets at Citi Field. Madison Square Garden, New York City's top entertainment venue, hosts hockey's Rangers and basketball's Knicks.

### Don't Miss

Yankee Stadium is the best place to watch America's favorite pastime while chowing down on a ballpark hot dog. The stadium was completely rebuilt in 2009 but still reflects the ballpark's original 1923 design. Within the stadium is the New York Yankees Museum, home to a variety of artifacts. 🌐 *www.mlb.com/yankees/ballpark*.

### Good to Know

Fans purchase season tickets year after year, so plan ahead to score decent seats.

### Getting Here and Around

Since New York sports are such a draw, reaching any one of the stadiums or arenas is easy. The subway leaves you, at most, a few blocks from most sporting centers.

# Harlem

## Music, Culture, and Food

One of Upper Manhattan's most famous neighborhoods, Harlem has long been known as a haven for black culture: jazz, poetry, art, and more. During the Great Migration, millions of African Americans from the South moved here in search of a better life. Today, the area continues to be a draw, with attractions like the Langston Hughes House, El Museo del Barrio, and soul food standouts like Sylvia's.

## Don't Miss

The historic Apollo Theater was a haven for black performers starting in 1934, when musicians like Louis Armstrong, Duke Ellington, Ella Fitzgerald, and Sam Cooke graced the stage. The 1,500-seat theater still welcomes performers throughout the year. It's a tough crowd, so success here means you're going places. 🌐 *www.apollotheater.org.*

## Best Tour

Sample some of Harlem's delicious dishes with Taste Harlem's food tours. You'll head to six locations to sample African, Caribbean, and soul food. 🌐 *www.tasteharlem.com.*

## Good to Know

For a Prohibition-era experience, visit Bill's Place, a speakeasy-style jazz club where Bill Saxton, a saxophone player, plays for audiences on the same stage that welcomed jazz greats like Billie Holiday. 🌐 *www.billsplaceharlem.com.*

## Getting Here and Around

The Harlem–125th station is a Metro North commuter rail stop in Harlem. The 125th Street subway station also drops you here.

## When in New York

### THE CLOISTERS AND FORT TRYON PARK

Located in Fort Tyron Park in Upper Manhattan's Washington Heights neighborhood, this unforgettable museum is made up of four authentic cloisters brought over brick by brick from France and Spain. There's also a French Romanesque chapel, a 12th-century chapter house, and a Romanesque apse. One room is devoted to the 15th- and 16th-century Unicorn Tapestries, which date to 1500—a must-see masterpiece of medieval mythology. Surrounding the interior spaces are acres and acres of lush gardens that add even more beauty to this unique spot.

**Do This:** Listen to one of the audio tours as you stroll the grounds. You'll hear interviews with curators, conservators, and educators about the art and architecture of medieval Europe.

**The Cloisters.** ✉ *99 Margaret Corbin Dr., New York, NY* ☎ *212/923–3700* 🌐 *www.metmuseum.org/visit/plan-your-visit/met-cloisters* 🎫 *$25.*

### HOME OF FRANKLIN D. ROOSEVELT NATIONAL HISTORIC SITE

In Hyde Park is Springwood, the stately home of the Roosevelt family. Franklin Delano Roosevelt—the country's longest-serving president—returned here often even when his governmental duties were wearing on him. When he was gravely ill during his fourth term, it functioned as a remote White House. This site is also where you'll find the Franklin D. Roosevelt Presidential Library and Museum.

**Do This:** The comparatively modest Eleanor Roosevelt National Historic Site preserves a house called Val-Kill where the First Lady spent time away from her official duties at nearby Springwood. She gathered around her an always-changing group of intellectuals and activists, many of them women. 🌐 *www.nps.gov/elro.*

**Home of Franklin D. Roosevelt National Historic Site.** ✉ *4097 Albany Post Rd., Hyde Park, NY* ☎ *845/229–5320* 🌐 *www.nps.gov/hofr* 🎫 *$20.*

### HOWE CAVERNS

A true natural wonder, Howe Caverns takes you 16 stories belowground into another world. Following an elevator ride straight down, the 90-minute tours are both on foot and in a boat that floats along the cave's mirrorlike large lake. Geologists estimate that Howe Caverns are millions of years old, and they are continuously changing. The stalactite and stalagmite formations grow by about an inch every 100 years.

**Do This:** For more adventurous types, Howe Caverns offers two-hour spelunking adventures. All caving supplies are provided, and you'll crawl through tight spaces and explore areas of the caverns most people never see.

**Howe Caverns.** ✉ *255 Discovery Dr., Howes Cave, NY* ☎ *518/296–8900* 🌐 *howecaverns.com* 🎫 *$25.*

### MORRIS-JUMEL MANSION

The historic Morris-Jumel Mansion dates back to 1765, when it was a summer home on 135 acres of land belonging to British colonel Roger Morris and his family. Located in what is now Washington Heights, the home was built on one of New York City's highest points, where there were views of New York Harbor, New Jersey, and even Connecticut. Today, the home is open for tours throughout the year.

**Do This:** Right outside the front door is the untouched-by-history Sylvan Terrace, a one-block-long stretch of late-19th-century homes lining a cobblestone street.

**Morris-Jumel Mansion.** ✉ *65 Jumel Terr., New York, NY* ☎ *212/923–8008* 🌐 *www.morrisjumel.org* 🎫 *$10.*

## ROOSEVELT ISLAND

Located in the middle of New York's East River is 2-mile-long Roosevelt Island, a historic spot that was once home to psychiatric hospitals and prisons. Today it's a largely residential retreat with pretty parks, waterfront walks, and sweeping views of Manhattan. Accessible via the super-scenic Roosevelt Island Tramway, the island is a great place to visit for outdoor spaces like Franklin D. Roosevelt Four Freedoms Park and Roosevelt Island Lighthouse.

**Do This:** Visit Roosevelt Island Lighthouse, by the same architect who designed St. Patrick's Cathedral and Grace Church. The tower was built with stone mined by inmates from the island's penitentiary. Views from here are jaw-dropping.

**Roosevelt Island.** 🌐 *www.nycgo.com/boroughs-neighborhoods/manhattan/roosevelt-island.*

## SMORGASBURG

Called the "Woodstock of Eating," the country's largest weekly open-air food festival is a favorite among both locals and visitors. Food trucks and vendors line up at different parks throughout New York City; depending on the day of the week, the food-fueled event can be found in Williamsburg, Prospect Park, or the World Trade Center. The event regularly sees crowds of 20,000 to 30,000 enjoying everything from loaded lobster rolls to sweet waffles topped with ice cream.

**Do This:** Vendors change frequently, but don't pass up organic ice cream from Blue Marble, a slice of cake from Gooey & Co., or a maple-bacon cupcake from Butter & Scotch.

**Smorgasburg Festival.** 🌐 *www.smorgasburg.com.*

## STORM KING ART CENTER

This Hudson Valley standout has dozens of large-scale sculptures tumbling across its 500 acres of grounds. The works on view include masterpieces by Alexander Calder, Sarah Sze, and Isamu Noguchi. Take the free shuttle, or walk through the grounds and find the perfect spot for a picnic lunch.

**Do This:** There are four main areas to explore: Museum Hill, North Woods, Meadows, and South Fields. Each has its own unique landscape, so be sure to visit them all.

**Storm King Art Center.** ✉ *1 Museum Rd., New Windsor, NY* ☎ *845/534–3115* 🌐 *stormking.org* 🎫 *$20 per car.*

## STRAND BOOK STORE

"Eighteen miles of books" is the slogan of Manhattan's massive Strand Book Store, and once you step inside you might think they are lowballing that figure. A few blocks south of Union Square, the Strand is known for a few things: its large collection of rare and collectible books, its readings with interesting authors, and its incredibly knowledgeable—and occasionally prickly—staff.

**Do This:** If you're looking for souvenirs, the shop has extremely literate T-shirts and totes.

**Strand Book Store.** ✉ *828 Broadway, New York, NY* ☎ *212/473–1452* 🌐 *www.strandbooks.com.*

## WILLIAMSBURG

This quintessentially cool neighborhood is a destination for those in search of trendy restaurants, bars, and boutiques. Located directly across the East River from Manhattan's equally trendy Lower East Side, Williamsburg is home to renowned restaurants like Lilia, St. Anselm, and Sunday in Brooklyn, shops like Catbird and Awoke Vintage, and bars like Radegast Hall and Biergarten.

**Do This:** Brooklyn Brewery is headquartered in Williamsburg in a giant factory space near the waterfront. Visit for a wide selection of beers, special drafts, and tasty food. 🌐 *brooklynbrewery.com.*

**Williamsburg.** 🌐 *www.nycgo.com/articles/what-to-do-williamsburg-brooklyn.*

## Cool Places to Stay

**Belhurst Castle and Winery.** Resembling one of the grand "cottages" once built as country retreats for famous families like the Astors and Vanderbilts, Belhurst Castle is stunningly beautiful. Overlooking Seneca Lake, it's one of the most lavish places to stay in the Finger Lakes. ✉ *4069 W. Lake Rd., Geneva, NY* ☎ *315/781–0201* 🌐 *www.belhurst.com* [$] *From $270.*

**The Box House Hotel.** With a hip vibe, Brooklyn's Box House Hotel is filled with original artworks and one-of-a-kind furnishings. Loftlike spaces can accommodate up to six people. The 10,000-square-foot rooftop space has a retractable cover and unobstructed views of Manhattan, Brooklyn, and Long Island City. ✉ *77 Box St., Brooklyn, NY* ☎ *718/383–3800* 🌐 *theboxhousehotel.com* [$] *From $330.*

**Camp Orenda.** If you like the idea of camping more than the reality, then head to this upscale retreat in Adirondack State Park. The tents are actually canvas-walled cabins furnished with all the usual creature comforts. Bathrooms and showers are communal. ✉ *90 Armstrong Rd., Johnsburg, NY* ☎ *518/251–5001* 🌐 *camporenda.com* [$] *From $250.*

**The Inns of Aurora.** This cluster of historic homes overlooks Cayuga Lake in New York's Finger Lakes region. It's hard to pick a favorite, so let us recommend two: the 1903 Rowland House has a wraparound porch, a Grecian temple in the garden, and a private boathouse, and the 1909 Wallcourt Hall started out as Miss Goldsmith's School for Girls and maintains a quirky style. ✉ *391 Main St., Aurora, NY* ☎ *315/364–8888* 🌐 *innsofaurora.com* *From $400.*

**Mohonk Mountain House.** Its jumble of towers, turrets, and chimneys make Mohonk Mountain House a delight. It looks like a cliff-side castle with its large stone facade and towering structures. The rate includes meals, activities, guided hikes, and amenities like an indoor pool. ✉ *1000 Mountain Rest Rd., New Paltz, NY* 🌐 *www.mohonk.com* [$] *From $551.*

**The Plaza.** The Plaza is definitely ready for its closeup, having added its unmistakable allure to films like *Home Alone 2, North by Northwest, The Great Gatsby,* and more. Located along the southern edge of Central Park, the French Renaissance–style masterpiece opened in 1907 as a lavish getaway for well-to-do travelers. ✉ *768 5th Ave., New York, NY* ☎ *212/759–3000* 🌐 *www.theplazany.com* [$] *From $750.*

**Scribner's Catskill Lodge.** Tucked within the Catskill Mountains, Scribner's Catskill Lodge has a cachet that draws in-the-know weekenders from Manhattan and Brooklyn. There are sleek, modern rooms with balcony views of the valley below, an on-site restaurant, and indoor and outdoor spaces for hanging out with fellow guests. ✉ *13 Scribner Hollow Rd., Hunter, NY* ☎ *518/628–5130* 🌐 *www.scribnerslodge.com* [$] *From $300.*

# Pennsylvania

From the dramatic hills of Pittsburgh across rolling farmland and majestic forest to the narrow streets of colonial Philadelphia, Pennsylvania provides a wide range of experiences. The state reflects a rich history—from halcyon days as the seat of the American Revolution and a fledgling nation's first capital through its role as a leader in the country's transformation into an industrial powerhouse—and its role today as a leader in the health-care and pharmaceutical industries, a center for the arts, and a burgeoning tourist destination.

## Bucket List Picks

The following boxes contain our picks for the top sights and experiences in Pennsylvania.

- ○ Independence National Historical Park
- ○ Philadelphia's Neighborhoods
- ○ Parkway Museum District
- ○ Gettysburg National Military Park
- ○ Pine Creek Gorge
- ○ Lancaster County
- ○ Presque Isle State Park
- ○ Valley Forge National Historical Park
- ○ The Pocono Mountains
- ○ Frank Lloyd Wright's Fallingwater

# Independence National Historical Park

## The Cradle of America

Much of America's earliest history can be traced back to Independence National Historical Park, a three-block-long park that is home to Independence Hall and the Liberty Bell. They may not have the instant name recognition, but attractions like the Second Bank of the United States, Congress Hall, and the National Constitution Center are all well worth a visit. It's a bit of a theme park—throughout the area are actors dressed in 18th-century garb, horse-drawn carriages, and cobblestone streets—but the pull of history is undeniable. All the sites are within walking distance of one another.

## Don't Miss

Independence National Historical Park can be overwhelming. Visit Independence Visitors Center to pick up detailed maps and to hear about any special events going on that day.

## Best Tour

You have to join a guided tour to see Independence Hall. Tours are first come, first served and depart every 15 minutes. A highlight is the Assembly Room, where the signing of the Declaration of Independence and the U.S. Constitution took place.

## When to Go

This part of town is busy in summer and whenever the kids are out of school. Visit in the fall for smaller crowds and shorter lines.

## Getting Here and Around

Philadelphia International Airport is about a 20-minute drive from Independence National Historical Park.

**Independence National Historical Park.** ☎ *215/965–2305* 🌐 *www.nps.gov/inde/index.htm* 🎫 *Varies.*

## Philadelphia's Neighborhoods

### A Taste of Philly

Ask any local and they'll quickly tell you their favorite neighborhood in Philadelphia. The heart of the city is Rittenhouse Square, an upscale neighborhood known for its brownstones, brand-name shopping, cool bars, and award-winning restaurants. Next to Rittenhouse Square, Midtown Village is home to the city's Gayborhood, an area with bustling bars and rainbow-painted crosswalks, in addition to some of the city's most popular restaurants. Old City is loved for its history—Independence National Historical Park is the big draw—along with its boutiques, galleries, and monthly First Friday open houses.

### Don't Miss

Fishtown is loved for its one-of-a-kind bars and restaurants. Breweries like Evil Genius Brewing, Tired Hands Brewing Company, and Philadelphia Brewing Company all have Fishtown outposts, while bars like Martha, Johnny Brenda's, and Frankford Hall pour a curated selection of brews.

### Eat This

West Philadelphia is known for its African fare, and dishes from Ethiopia or Senegal aren't hard to find. Visit Kilimandjaro on Chestnut Street for roasted meats, Bintou on Elmwood Avenue for spiced lamb, or Wazobia on North 11th Street for fried guinea fowl.

### Best Tour

There's a reason Philadelphia is known as the "City of Murals." Mural Arts enriches neighborhoods with colorful murals on otherwise drab walls. Tours might cover a particular neighborhood, or a theme like Black History Month. 🌐 *www.muralarts.org*.

### Getting Here and Around

Philadelphia International Airport is about a 20-minute drive from most parts of the city.

# Parkway Museums District

### Mile of Masterpieces

Some of the country's leading museums line Philadelphia's Benjamin Franklin Parkway, which runs from City Hall to the Philadelphia Museum of Art. The roughly mile-long stretch is lined with flags from all of the countries in the world, picturesque parks, and educational institutions. Put these on your must-see list: the Barnes Foundation, the Franklin Institute, the Academy of Natural Sciences at Drexel University, and the Rodin Museum.

### Don't Miss

Pretend that you're Rocky Balboa and run up the famous steps of the Philadelphia Museum of Art. There's a sculpture of the world's most famous fictional boxer in front of the museum.

### Best Tour

Explore the outdoor art installations along Benjamin Franklin Parkway on the Association for Public Art's free self-guided tours. The 1.3-mile trek features major works like Robert Indiana's *Love* sculpture, Rodin's *The Thinker*, and Alexander Stirling Calder's Swann Memorial Fountain. 🌐 *www.associationforpublicart.org/tours/along-the-benjamin-franklin-parkway.*

### When to Go

There are exciting exhibitions throughout the year, but spring, summer, and fall are best for walking from location to location.

### Getting Here and Around

The Parkway Museums District is located in the center of the city, making it easily accessible from Amtrak 30th Street Station and less than a 20-minute drive from Philadelphia International Airport. All major attractions are a short walk apart.

**Parkway Museums District.** ✉ *Benjamin Franklin Pkwy., Philadelphia, PA* 🌐 *www.parkwaymuseumsdistrict-philadelphia.org.*

# Gettysburg National Military Park

## Site of the Country's Biggest Battle

History buffs should allow about two days to explore the vast Gettysburg National Military Park, downtown Gettysburg, and the surrounding attractions. The sprawling park honors the place where the 1863 Battle of Gettysburg was fought by more than 165,000 Union and Confederate soldiers, making it the largest battle ever fought in North America. Today, the national park includes the battlefield and other important sites like the 17-acre Gettysburg National Cemetery.

## Don't Miss

Beginning your day at the Gettysburg National Military Park Museum and Visitor Center is a good way to get your bearings. The Morgan Freeman–narrated short film *A New Birth of Freedom* gives you the history of the Battle of Gettysburg and its important role in history.

## Best Tour

Gettysburg Battlefield Bus Tours offers a number of guided tours led by guides who know an incredible amount about the area. 🌐 *www.gettysburgbattlefieldtours.com.*

## When to Go

Snow and ice can make it hard to get around the sprawling park, and certain areas are known to close for weather. Spring, summer, and fall are the best times to visit.

## Getting Here and Around

Gettysburg is best reached by car. Parking is available in municipal lots throughout the town. The closest airport is Harrisburg International Airport, about 40 miles away.

**Gettysburg.** ✉ *1195 Baltimore Pike, Gettysburg, PA* ☎ *717/334–1124* 🌐 *www.nps.gov/gett/index.htm* 🎫 *Free.*

# Pine Creek Gorge

## Pennsylvania's Vast Natural Wonder

The stunningly beautiful Pine Creek Gorge is often referred to as the Grand Canyon of Pennsylvania because it is nearly a mile wide and descends nearly 1,500 feet. The views along the Gorge are breathtaking: overlooks at Colton Point State Park and Leonard Harrison State Park are two of the best places to take in the majesty of the place. The natural wonder runs for more than 45 miles along Pine Creek, a scenic river that is perfect for kayaking, canoeing, and white-water rafting.

## Don't Miss

The 62-mile Pine Creek Rail Trail, a former section of the New York Central Railroad, is beloved by walkers, runners, hikers, cyclists, and cross-country skiers. The trail meanders through the bottom of Pine Creek Gorge and winds past small towns and quiet green spaces.

## Best Tour

For an on-the-water tour of the Grand Canyon of Pennsylvania, seek out Pine Creek Outfitters' guided rafting or kayaking tours. Guides share information on the history of the region and wildlife that calls it home. 🌐 *www.pinecrk.com/guided/guided.html.*

## When to Go

The ideal time to visit Pine Creek Gorge is April to October. Come October, it's a great location to take in the autumn colors.

## Getting Here and Around

There are multiple entry points to Pine Creek Gorge, and all of them are most easily reached by car. Park at Leonard Harrison State Park or Colton Point State Park.

**Pennsylvania Grand Canyon.** ✉ *4797 Rte. 660, Wellsboro, PA* ☎ *570/724–3061* 🌐 *pacanyon.com/index.html* 🎟 *Free.*

# Lancaster County

### America's Oldest Amish Settlement

You'd never know from the buggies traversing the quiet country lanes that Lancaster County is less than two hours away from the bustling streets of Philadelphia. Lancaster is synonymous with Amish Country, and the Amish population is crucial to the area's economy and culture. Downtown Lancaster has become a cultural hub in recent years, with plenty of interesting restaurants, craft breweries, and art galleries, while northeastern Lancaster County is known for its antiques and is home to more than 1,000 quaint shops. To learn more about Pennsylvania Dutch history, visit the 300-year-old Amish Farm and House.

### Don't Miss

Established in 1832, the Strasburg Railroad, America's oldest continuously operating railroad, offers 45-minute train rides through the farmland of Lancaster County. ⊕ *www.strasburgrailroad.com.*

### Eat This

Keep an eye out for farmers' markets and roadside stands that sell Pennsylvania Dutch classics like shoofly pie and whoopie pies, along with sweet butters, jams, and jellies. Try Bird-in-Hand Farmers' Market (in the town of the same name) and Busy Bee's Farm Market in Ronks.

### Getting Here and Around

Lancaster Airport is about 6 miles away from downtown Lancaster. A car is ideal if you want to reach some of the out-of-the-way parts of Lancaster County.

**Lancaster County.** ☎ *717/299–8000* ⊕ *www.co.lancaster.pa.us.*

# Presque Isle State Park

## Pennsylvania's Only "Seashore"

Located on Lake Erie, Presque Isle State Park is a picturesque 3,200-acre peninsula that is home to a sandy coastline, more than a dozen beaches, and prime waterfront views. Visitors head to Presque Isle—the name translates as "almost an island" in French—for on-the-water or in-the-water activities like swimming, fishing, and boating, in addition to land-based activities like hiking, cycling, and cross-country skiing.

## Don't Miss

Located at the entrance to Presque Isle State Park is Tom Ridge Environmental Center Foundation, dedicated to Presque Isle's history, wildlife, and outdoor attractions. The best view of the state park is from the 75-foot-tall observation deck. ⊕ *www.trecf.org.*

## Best Tour

Presque Isle Boat Tours offers 90-minute narrated floats on Lake Erie. Guides point out sights like Presque Isle Lighthouse. ⊕ *piboattours.com.*

## When to Go

Presque Isle State Park is open year-round. Winter is best for cross-country skiing and ice-skating, while summer is ideal for boating and swimming.

## Getting Here and Around

Presque Isle State Park is 4 miles from downtown Erie, making it easily accessible from the city. The entrance to the park is less than 4 miles from Erie International Airport.

**Erie County.** ✉ *301 Peninsula Dr., Erie, PA* ☎ *814/833–7424* ⊕ *www.pagreatlakes.com/erie-county* 🎟 *Free.*

# Valley Forge National Historical Park

## In Washington's Footsteps: America's Coldest Winter

Valley Forge National Historical Park tells the story of the harsh winter endured by General George Washington and the Continental Army in 1777 and 1778. Located in King of Prussia—about 45 minutes outside Philadelphia—the vast national park covers 3,500 acres of rolling hills, open fields, and tree-covered valleys.

## Don't Miss

See the Isaac Potts House, which is the historic home that Washington made his headquarters. The home was built in 1768, and much of the original structure remains. 🌐 *www.nps.gov/vafo/learn/historyculture/washingtons_headquarters.htm.*

## Best Tour

The nine-stop encampment tour brings you to Artillery Park, National Memorial Arch, Muhlenberg's Brigade, and other sites. The attractions are spaced out, so the tour is best covered by car. 🌐 *www.nps.gov/vafo/planyourvisit/encampmenttours.htm.*

## When to Go

The huge park is beautiful all year, though a trip during winter gives an appreciation for the harsh conditions the soliders faced here. The 20-plus miles of walking and biking trails are always accessible.

**Valley Forge National Historical Park.** ✉ *1400 N. Outer Line Dr., King of Prussia, PA* ☎ *610/783–1000* 🌐 *www.nps.gov/vafo/index.htm* 🎟 *Free.*

# Pocono Mountains

## Pennsylvania's Relaxing Retreat

The Pocono Mountains—more casually known as the Poconos—are a series of thickly forested peaks running along the Delaware Water Gap. Quaint towns are sprinkled around four mostly rural counties: Carbon, Monroe, Pike, and Wayne. Dozens and dozens of resorts provide a wide range of outdoor pursuits. Visit for skiing and snowboarding in the winter or swimming, boating, and other activities in summer.

## Don't Miss

Small towns like Honesdale, Stroudsburg, Jim Thorpe, and Milford are known for their varied arts scenes and eclectic dining offerings.

## Best Family-Friendly Experience

Great Wolf Lodge offers plenty of activities for families. There's a huge indoor water park with waterslides, a wave pool, a lazy river, and pools for splashing and lounging. There are some tasty on-site dining options. 🌐 *www.greatwolf.com.*

## Best Tour

Leaving from Jim Thorpe, the Lehigh Gorge Scenic Railway is a 16-mile ride along the Lehigh River and through breathtaking Lehigh Gorge State Park. 🌐 *www.lgsry.com.*

## Getting Here and Around

The Poconos is a vast area that requires a car to get around. The closest large airport is Wilkes-Barre Scranton International Airport.

**Pocono Mountains.** 🌐 *www.pocono-mountains.com.*

# Frank Lloyd Wright's Fallingwater

## Architectural Masterpiece

About an hour and a half southeast of Pittsburgh is Frank Lloyd Wright's undisputed masterwork—a stone, concrete, and glass house dramatically cantilevered over a waterfall. Instantly recognizable to architecture fans, Fallingwater was designed in 1935 for Edgar J. Kaufmann, who owned the largest department store in Pittsburgh. Using native sandstone, Wright's design incorporated much of what was already on the site, including rocks, trees, and a rushing creek. While a number of Wright-designed properties are open for tours, Fallingwater is the only one that became a public space with its original furniture and artwork.

## Don't Miss

Self-guided tours of the grounds are a great way to take in the natural beauty of Pennsylvania's Laurel Highlands.

## Good to Know

The surrounding 5,000 acres of land is known as Bear Run Nature Reserve. It's a serene place for outdoor walks and hikes.

## When to Visit

While Fallingwater is beautiful all year round, in June and July rhododendrons cover the grounds.

## Getting Here and Around

Fallingwater is about 65 miles from Pittsburgh. It's best accessed by car.

**Fallingwater.** ✉ *1491 Mill Run Rd., Mill Run, PA* ☎ *724/329–8501* 🌐 *fallingwater.org* 🎫 *$18.*

# When in Pennsylvania

## ANDY WARHOL MUSEUM

The country's largest single-artist museum features an enormous collection of Warhol's works—including paintings, prints, sculptures, and videos—ranging from his early days as a student to the height of his career. The most famous items in the collection include Warhol's 1960s pop art paintings of celebrities like Marilyn Monroe and Elizabeth Taylor and his iconic series called Campbell's Soup Cans. Nearly half a million objects make up the museum's collection of items he saved over the course of 40 years.

**Do This:** The Warhol Store is a fan favorite for its quirky items related to Warhol.

**Andy Warhol Museum.** ✉ *117 Sandusky St.,Pittsburgh, PA* ☎ *412/237–8300* 🌐 *www.warhol.org* 🎫 *$20.*

## BUSHKILL FALLS

The most impressive of this park's eight waterfalls—and the one for which it's named—is more than 100 feet tall. Wooden boardwalks and bridges along the walking trails take you past the other seven waterfalls. Exhibits explore the history of the falls, the wildlife that lived nearby, and the Native Americans that once called the area home.

**Do This:** Two-person paddleboats are available for exploring Twin Lakes. They cost $6 per person, which includes a life jacket.

**Bushkill Falls.** ✉ *138 Bushkill Falls Trail, Bushkill, PA* ☎ *888/287–4545* 🌐 *www.visitbushkillfalls.com* 🎫 *$15.*

## MCGILLIN'S OLDE ALE HOUSE

On Philadelphia's Drury Street you'll find McGillin's Olde Ale House, the oldest continuously operating pub in the city. Irish immigrants Catherine and William McGillin opened the bar in 1860, living one floor above with their 13 children. Today, McGillin's is known for its quirks, including signs from now-shuttered Philadelphia establishments, old liquor licenses, and kitschy figurines. The bar focuses on southeastern Pennsylvania draft beers, including its namesakes McGillin's Real Ale, McGillin's Genuine Lager, and McGillin's 1860 IPA.

**Do This:** Around the holidays, the pub is transformed into a winter wonderland.

**McGillin's Olde Ale House.** ✉ *1310 Drury St., Philadelphia, PA* ☎ *215/735–5562* 🌐 *mcgillins.com.*

## MT. WASHINGTON LOOKOUT

For the best views of Pittsburgh, visit Mt. Washington Overlook. Don't let the name fool you, though: Mt. Washington is basically a large hill, rising only about 450 feet. Stroll to Point of View Park to photograph the stunning city skyline and to view a bronze sculpture of George Washington and Guyasuta, a Seneca leader, during a meeting in the 18th century.

**Do This:** The Duquesne Incline, a cable car, takes guests up the side of Mt. Washington to the Observation Deck. The 100-plus-year-old tracks were once used as a coal hoist. 🌐 *www.duquesnein-cline.org/index.html.*

**Mt. Washington Overlook.** ✉ *136–160 Grandview Ave., Pittsburgh, PA* ☎ *877/568–3744* 🌐 *www.visitpa.com/region/pittsburgh-its-countryside/mount-washington-overlook* 🎫 *Free.*

## THE MÜTTER MUSEUM

You haven't really experienced "weird" until you've visited Philadelphia's Mütter Museum, a collection of medical oddities. The items in the collection date back to the 7th century BCE and include an impressive array of medical devices, wax models, skeletons, and more. In the main room upstairs are more than 139 human skulls in a towering display case, part of the famous Hyrtl Skull Collection. The museum is one of only two places in the world that displays pieces of Albert Einstein's brain.

**Do This:** One of the museum's most famous permanent exhibits is The Soap Lady, whose body is encased in adipocere, a fatty substance that preserves the body. Her body was exhumed from a Philadelphia-area cemetery in 1875 and now lies in a glass case.

**College of Physicians of Philadelphia.** ✉ *19 S. 22nd St., Philadelphia, PA* ☎ *215/560–8564* 🌐 *muttermuseum.org* 🎟 *$20.*

### PHILADELPHIA'S MAGIC GARDENS

Artist Isaiah Zagar has been creating mosaics throughout Philadelphia's South Street area for decades. When some works he created on vacant lots were almost destroyed, the community opened a museum dedicated to his work. Magic Gardens showcases Zagar's immersive murals, made up of found objects like mirrors, glass bottles, and bicycle tires. There's a two-level outdoor sculpture garden and two indoor galleries.

**Do This:** While the sculpture garden is covered top to bottom with tiles, the areas outside the museum are great spots for a photo op.

**Magic Gardens.** ✉ *1020 South St., Philadelphia, PA* ☎ *215/733–0390* 🌐 *www.phillymagicgardens.org* 🎟 *$15.*

### PITTSBURGH'S STRIP DISTRICT

The coolest neighborhood in Pittsburgh, the Strip District has to be on your to-do list. Running alongside the Allegheny River, it's beloved for its independent-minded coffee shops, restaurants, art galleries, and other destinations. The historic area was once an industrial hub, and its mills, factories, and warehouses now hold wineries, distilleries, food halls, and even an opera house.

**Do This:** Have a sandwich at the Strip District's famous Primanti Brothers. There are locations throughout Pennsylvania, but the original is located on 18th Street within the Strip. It's known for sandwiches piled high with meat, coleslaw, and French fries. 🌐 *primantibros.com.*

**Strip District.** ✉ *Smallman St., Pittsburgh, PA* ☎ *412/281–7711* 🌐 *www.visitpittsburgh.com/neighborhoods/strip-district.*

## Cool Places to Stay

**Four Seasons Hotel Philadelphia.** At the top of Philadelphia's highest skyscraper is the luxurious Four Seasons Hotel Philadelphia, which complements its gorgeous guest rooms with multiple bars and restaurants and a world-class spa. On the 59th floor, you can dine at Jean-Georges Philadelphia. ✉ *1 N. 19th St., Philadelphia, PA* ☎ *800/819–5053* 🌐 *www.fourseasons.com/philadelphia* $ *From $700.*

**The Inn at Jim Thorpe.** In the heart of a National Register Historic District, the Inn at Jim Thorpe has charm to spare. Its cast-iron balcony has a wonderful view of the nearby brick storefronts, and many guests while away the hours here. ✉ *24 Broadway, Jim Thorpe, PA* ☎ *800/329–2599* 🌐 *innjt.com* $ *From $200.*

**Polymath Park.** This architectural gem, designed by Frank Lloyd Wright, is available for overnight stays. The grounds span 125 miles in the Laurel Highlands. ✉ *187 Evergreen La., Acme, PA* ☎ *877/833–7829* 🌐 *www.franklloydwrightovernight.net* $ *From $380.*

**Skytop Lodge.** One of the most popular lodgings in the Pocono Mountains, Skytop Lodge has a bevy of outdoor activities, including kayaking, fishing, golfing, and hiking. In addition to rooms in the handsome main building, there are cottages throughout the property and an inn on the golf course. ✉ *1 Skytop Lodge Rd., Skytop, PA* ☎ *855/345–7759* 🌐 *www.skytop.com* $ *From $179.*

# Virginia

A wonderland for history buffs, Virginia has an incredible past that's still on display. It's possible to visit the Virginia of George Washington or Thomas Jefferson (their historic homes are here), skip through colonial times in Williamsburg, or absorb the power of the Civil War in Manassas. But don't miss the appeal of modern Virginia, from its wineries to its beaches.

## Bucket List Picks

The following boxes contain our picks for the top sights and experiences in Virginia.

- ○ Shenandoah National Park
- ○ Colonial Williamsburg
- ○ Monticello Wine Trail
- ○ Richmond
- ○ Virginia Beach
- ○ Appalachian Trail
- ○ Mount Vernon

# Shenandoah National Park

## Virginia's Ribbon of Green

Though Shenandoah National Park is only a narrow ribbon on the map, stretching for 70 miles through the Blue Ridge Mountains, it's one of Virginia's most epic attractions. The 200,000-acre nature preserve is bisected by the 105-mile Skyline Drive, one of the country's most beautiful road trips. Bears, deer, and other woodland creatures are known to cross Skyline Drive, so slow down and enjoy the views. Hikers can find beautiful terrain just yards from the drive on some of the park's 500 miles of trails.

## Don't Miss

To see a different side of Shenandoah, make your way to Big Meadows to explore a high-altitude meadow that is beloved for its excellent stargazing. Big Meadows Campground is one of the most popular in the park.

## Good to Know

The three main visitor centers—Mobile Visitor Center, Harry F. Byrd Sr. Visitor Center, and Dickey Ridge Visitor Center—are great places to start your exploration.

## Getting Here and Around

Shenandoah is about 90 minutes from both Washington, D.C., and Richmond, Virginia.

**Shenandoah National Park Headquarters.** ✉ *3655 U.S. 211, Luray, VA* ☎ *540/999–3500* 🌐 *www.nps.gov/shen/index.htm* 🎫 *$30 per car.*

## Colonial Williamsburg

### A Walk Through History

A history lesson come to life, Colonial Williamsburg is the largest living-history museum in the country. The destination is a family-friendly locale with beautifully restored 18th-century buildings—a courthouse, carpenter's workshop, blacksmith shop, and more—that are a delight to explore. Actors play the parts of townspeople, and they're happy to talk about life in colonial days.

### Don't Miss

On the grounds of Colonial Williamsburg, the DeWitt Wallace Decorative Arts Museum houses finely made household items from the colonial period, including one of the largest collections of British ceramics outside England. Also worth a visit is the Abby Aldrich Rockefeller Folk Art Museum. *www.colonialwilliamsburg.org/locations/dewitt-wallace-decorative-arts-museum.*

### Good to Know

History is constantly being uncovered at Colonial Williamsburg, where archaeologists still conduct field research at designated areas. Guests can visit the archaeology dig sites to learn about the recent findings, and maybe even witness an exciting discovery.

### Getting Here and Around

Colonial Williamsburg is located off Route 60 in Virginia, making it easy to reach by car.

**Colonial Williamsburg Visitors Center.** *101 Visitor Center Dr., Williamsburg, VA* *855/771–3290* *www.colonialwilliamsburg.org* *$36.*

# Monticello Wine Trail

### Birthplace of American Vintages

Wine making has been a strong tradition throughout Virginia since colonial times, and this wine trail, inspired by Thomas Jefferson's vision of grape growing at his Monticello home, connects the best vineyards in the region. The Monticello Wine Trail extends throughout the Blue Ridge Mountains and includes dozens of wineries producing excellent reds, whites, and rosés. Many offer vineyard walks, cellar tours, and tastings throughout the year. Some have on-site eateries with delicious dishes chosen to show off the latest vintages. Break up the adventure with a stop at the place that started it all, Monticello, just outside Charlottesville.

### Don't Miss

Family-owned Veritas Vineyard and Winery is beloved for its delicious wines made on the premises. It makes a wide range of wines, including all of the staples: effervescent sparklers, dry reds, and fruity rosés. The vineyard has some of the most beautiful views of the mountains. 🌐 *veritaswines.com.*

### When to Go

Visit in the spring, summer, or fall to enjoy a glass of wine outdoors while taking in the expansive views of the Blue Ridge Mountains. You'll also see grapes still on the vine.

### Getting Here and Around

The wineries are spread out, but all are within about 30 miles of Charlottesville.

**Monticello Wine Trail.** 🌐 *monticellowinetrail.com.*

# Richmond

## Virginia's Capital of Cool

Richmond's cool factor has increased exponentially in recent years. Neighborhoods throughout the city are now home to renowned restaurants, quaint bakeries, and one-of-a-kind shops, many of which are outposts of famous establishments in New York or Washington, D.C. In fast-growing Scott's Addition, you'll find more than a dozen breweries, cideries, and distilleries, many of which are housed within converted warehouses. Favorites include the Veil Brewing Company, Blue Bee Cider, and Reservoir Distillery. For food, try Boulevard Burger and Brew, Fat Dragon Chinese Kitchen and Bar, or Supper.

## Don't Miss

Stroll down colorful Cary Street in Richmond's Carytown neighborhood. The thoroughfare is home to a mix of locally owned shops, restaurants, and ice-cream parlors. The historic Byrd Theatre is a favorite among locals for lavish interior.

## While You're Here

The James River Park Pipeline Walkway is a spectacular bridge that gives you views of the James River's Bailey's Island and Devil's Kitchen Island, both of which are heaven for bird-watchers. Below are the rushing waters of the Pipeline Rapids.

## When to Go

While Richmond's weather is fairly mild all year, colder months can be dismal and gray. Summer is hot and humid, so try to visit in spring or fall.

## Getting Here and Around

Richmond International Airport is a short drive away. For those arriving by train, Richmond's Main Street Station welcomes multiple Amtrak trains each day.

# Virginia Beach

## More Than Fun in the Sun

While the sun and sand is definitely the main draw in Virginia Beach, the 3-mile-long boardwalk, which runs for almost 40 blocks, is where everyone ends up sooner or later. There's an old-fashioned fishing pier, a waterfront park, and lots of family-friendly fun. You can also commune with nature on a bike trail.

## Don't Miss

Virginia Beach's First Landing State Park—Virginia's most popular state park—is where colonists first touched dry land in the early 17th century. Native American canoes were already navigating these waters long before that. Today there are 20 miles of hiking trails and a mile and a half of beachfront access. 🌐 *www.dcr.virginia.gov/state-parks/first-landing.*

## Best Tour

A must for nature loves, Rudee Tours offers whale-watch excursions and dolphin-watching trips. 🌐 *www.rudeetours.com.*

## When to Go

Summer is prime time for visiting Virginia Beach, but it can get noisy and crowded. Make reservations well before the summer season.

## Getting Here and Around

Norfolk International Airport is a 25-minute drive from Virginia Beach. Once you're in Virginia Beach, much of the area is accessible by foot or by bike.

**Virginia Beach.** 🌐 *www.visitvirginiabeach.com.*

# Appalachian Trail

## 500 Miles of Forests and Farmland

The Appalachian Trail runs from Georgia to Maine, but almost a quarter of the world-famous hiking trail can be found in Virginia. There are 555 miles waiting to be explored, and sections are appropriate for everyone from first-timers to seasoned experts. It's a combination of forests and farmland, and can be accessed at many points throughout the state. More than 100 miles of the trail run through breathtaking Shenandoah National Park, and the fairly level terrain makes it a popular starting place for newer hikers.

## Don't Miss

Near the border of West Virginia is an entrance to the Appalachian Trail that is ideal for those who are looking for a challenging hike. Along this 54-mile route, hikers pass through Sky Meadows State Park.

## Best Tour

The Appalachian Tour Conservancy has a great list of hiking routes that can be completed in a day. In Virginia, popular short hikes include the 4-mile-long Apple Orchard Falls Trail from Bedford to Lynchburg, the 2.6-mile Chestnut Knob Trail in Tazewell and Wytheville, and the 4-mile hike to the summit of Mary's Rock near Luray.

## Getting Here and Around

The Virginia portion of the Appalachian Trail can be accessed at many points, including Shenandoah National Park and George Washington and Jefferson National Forests.

**Appalachian Trail.** 🌐 *appalachiantrail.org/explore/explore-by-state/virginia.*

# Mount Vernon

### George Washington's Riverfront Home

Set on a hillside overlooking the Potomac River, George Washington's estate is one of the most visited sites in Northern Virginia. You can stroll around the estate's 500 acres and three gardens, visiting the kitchen, carriage house, slave quarters, and—down the hill toward the boat landing—the tomb of George and Martha Washington. There's also a 4-acre farm with a reconstruction of George Washington's 16-sided barn as its centerpiece. Two on-site museums contain hundreds of artifacts.

### Don't Miss

Some of the most memorable experiences at Mount Vernon, particularly for kids, are in the Museum and Education Center. Interactive displays, movies with special effects straight out of Hollywood, life-size models, and Revolutionary artifacts illustrate Washington's life and contributions.

### When to Visit

Mount Vernon is open throughout the year, but you'll want to visit in warmer months when you can stroll around the grounds.

### Getting Here and Around

Mount Vernon is a 30-minute drive from Washington, D.C. It's also possible to visit by taking a 20-minute bus ride from the Huntington Station of Metrorail.

**Mount Vernon.** ✉ *3200 Mount Vernon Memorial Hwy., Mount Vernon, VA* ☎ *703/780–2000* 🌐 *www.mountvernon.org* 🎟 *$26.*

# When in Virginia

### ARLINGTON NATIONAL CEMETERY

One of the most serene spots near the nation's capital, this 639-acre military cemetery draws tourists from all over the world. The welcome center at Memorial Drive is a great first stop for those who are seeking out the graves of the monumental figures buried here, including Supreme Court justices (Thurgood Marshall), presidents (John F. Kennedy), and civil rights heroes (Medgar Evers). Located on a hill overlooking the Potomac River, the Tomb of the Unknowns honors the fallen soldiers who remained unidentified.

**Do This:** The changing of the guard ceremony at the Tomb of the Unknowns is a moving, must-see Army tradition that takes place at different times throughout the day depending on the season.

**Arlington National Cemetery.** ✉ *Memorial Ave., Arlington, VA* ☎ *877/907–8585* 🌐 *www.arlingtoncemetery.mil* 🎫 *Free.*

### NATURAL BRIDGE

This stunning limestone arch has been gradually carved out by Cedar Creek, which flows past more than 200 feet below. It was a sacred site for the Monacan Native American tribe, who called it the "Bridge of God." The arch is part of the larger Natural Bridge State Park, which has miles of hiking trails.

**Do This:** Start your day at the Natural Bridge State Park Visitor Center, where you can learn about the area's history.

**Natural Bridge State Park.** ✉ *6477 S. Lee Hwy., Natural Bridge, VA* ☎ *540/291–1326* 🌐 *www.dcr.virginia.gov/state-parks/natural-bridge* 🎫 *Free.*

### OLD TOWN ALEXANDRIA

One of the quaintest communities in northern Virginia is Old Town Alexandria, not far from Washington, D.C. Facing the Potomac River, the historic area has cobblestone streets lined with handsome brick buildings that hold exquisite restaurants, interesting bars, and unique shops. On the waterfront is the Torpedo Factory, a former munitions factory that is now filled with studios for artists.

**Do This:** Stroll along King Street, peeking down narrow alleys and into pretty gardens along the way. Grab a coffee from renowned Misha's Coffeehouse to fuel your walk along the downtown street.

**Old Town Alexandria.** 🌐 *www.visitalexandriava.com/old-town-alexandria.*

# Cool Places to Stay

**The Cavalier Virginia Beach.** This beachfront hotel opened during the Roaring Twenties and has hosted presidents, movie stars, and famous writers during its 100-year history. Because of its hilltop location, most of the gorgeous guest rooms have views of the ocean. ✉ *4200 Atlantic Ave., Virginia Beach, VA* ☎ *757/425–8555* 🌐 *www.marriott.com/hotels/travel/orfak-the-cavalier-virginia-beach-autograph-collection* [$] *From $300.*

**Lewis Mountain Cabins.** In Shenandoah National Park, the rustic Lewis Mountain Cabins have fans who return year after year. They aren't luxurious, but they couldn't be more homey. Cabins have one or two bedrooms and outdoor spaces ranging from breezy porches to covered picnic areas. ✉ *Skyline Dr., Elkton, VA* ☎ *877/847–1919* 🌐 *www.goshenandoah.com/lodging/lewis-mountain-cabins* [$] *From $100.*

# Washington, D.C.

With its neoclassical government buildings and broad avenues, Washington, D.C., looks its part as America's capital. Majestic monuments and memorials pay tribute to notable leaders and great achievements, and merit a visit. But D.C. also lives firmly in the present, and not just politically; new restaurants and bars continually emerge, upping the hipness factor in neighborhoods from Capitol Hill to U Street.

## Bucket List Picks

The following boxes contain our picks for the top sights and experiences in Washington, D.C.

- O The National Mall
- O The Tidal Basin
- O The White House
- O Georgetown
- O Washington National Cathedral
- O Smithsonian Museums
- O U Street

# The National Mall

## America's Front Yard

Fondly known as "America's front yard," Washington, D.C.'s National Mall is a must-visit destination in the nation's capital. It's like a huge compass in the center of the city. If you stand at the Washington Monument, the White House is to the north, the Capitol to the east, the Lincoln Memorial (and the Vietnam Veterans Memorial) to the west, and the Jefferson Memorial to the south.

## Don't Miss

Across the street from the National Mall, the Martin Luther King, Jr. Memorial commemorates the life and legacy of the country's best known civil rights leader. His likeness seems to materialize out of a massive slab of granite. *www.nps.gov/mlkm/index.htm.*

## Best Tour

Want the inside scoop on Washington? Free Tours by Foot offers little-known facts about the attractions surrounding the National Mall. Reservations are required. *freetoursbyfoot.com/national-mall-tour.*

## Getting Here and Around

The National Mall is located in the heart of Washington, making it easy to access by foot, by bike, or by public transportation. Metrorail's Smithsonian Station stop deposits you in the center of the National Mall.

**The National Mall.** *900 Ohio Dr. SW, Washington, DC* *202/426–6841* *www.nps.gov/nama/index.htm* *Free.*

# The Tidal Basin

## Cherry Blossom Central

Steps from the National Mall, the Tidal Basin is a man-made reservoir in West Potomac Park. Home to some of the most picturesque views in Washington, the Tidal Basin is a must-do for visitors. The 107-acre basin is ringed by cherry trees, a gift from Japan in 1912. During the annual Cherry Blossom Festival—or often just before or just after—the area is awash with pink and white blossoms.

## Don't Miss

On the western shores of the Tidal Basin is the Franklin Delano Roosevelt Memorial, honoring the 26th president. The South Dakota granite walls have 21 of his quotations, including: "The only thing we have to fear is fear itself." 🌐 *www.nps.gov/frde.*

## When to Go

To see the cherry blossoms in all their glory, visit in early April. To enjoy the views with the sun reflecting off the water or to rent a paddleboat, visit in the summer.

## Getting Here and Around

The Tidal Basin is close to many of D.C.'s other must-see attractions, including the National Mall. The Smithsonian Metro station is about a 15-minute walk from the area.

**The Tidal Basin.** 🌐 *www.nps.gov/articles/dctidalbasin.htm.*

# The White House

### The Executive Mansion

Designed in 1792 by Irish architect James Hoban, the country's most famous residence was known officially as the Executive Mansion until 1902, when President Theodore Roosevelt renamed it the White House. It was opened in 1800, but was partly destroyed in 1814 when British forces set fire to many government buildings throughout the city. Hoban himself led the restoration efforts. Today, millions of people pose in front of the fence surrounding the White House catching a glimpse of its north or south portico.

### Don't Miss

The best vantage points can be found at Lafayette Square and the Ellipse.

### Best Tour

Tours of the White House are hard to come by, as they must be requested through a member of Congress.

As an easy alternative, explore the surrounding area on one of DC By Foot's self-guided tours. You'll see the General Andrew Jackson statue in Lafayette Square and St. John's Episcopal Church, better known as the "Church of the Presidents." 🌐 *freetoursbyfoot.com/self-guided-tour-of-white-house-lafayette-park.*

### When to Go

In the winter, the White House is decorated with festive lights for the holiday season.

### Getting Here and Around

The McPherson Square Metro stop is closest to the White House.

**The White House.** ✉ *1600 Pennsylvania Ave., NW Washington, DC* ☎ *202/456–1111* 🌐 *www.whitehouse.gov* 🎫 *Free.*

# Georgetown

### Urban Splendor

There's much more to this neighborhood than its namesake university. Located on the Potomac River, quaint Georgetown radiates outward from the busy intersection of Wisconsin Avenue and M Street. On the surrounding blocks are cobblestone streets, elegant homes, and upscale boutiques. Follow the towpath along the Chesapeake and Ohio Canal, or even take a ride in one of its low-slung canal boats, for a completely different vantage point.

### Don't Miss

Often called the "Secret Garden," the 27-acre Dumbarton Oaks sits on the highest hill above Georgetown. Locals love the meandering trails through manicured gardens and classical fountains. The on-site museum is a treasure trove of Byzantine art. 🌐 *www.doaks.org.*

### Best Restaurant

The 10-acre Georgetown Waterfront Park has plenty of interesting eateries, including the very popular Farmers Fishers Bakers. There are sweeping views of the Potomac River and the John F. Kennedy Center for the Performing Arts. 🌐 *www.farmersfishersbakers.com.*

### Getting Here and Around

Georgetown is one of the few downtown neighborhoods that isn't served by Metrorail. It's a 20-minute walk from the Foggy Bottom/GWU station.

**Georgetown.** 🌐 *www.georgetowndc.com.*

# Washington National Cathedral

### America's Westminster Abbey

It's official name is the Cathedral Church of St. Peter and St. Paul, but the world knows it as Washington National Cathedral. Like its 14th-century Gothic counterparts, the stunning cathedral has a nave, flying buttresses, transepts, and vaults that were built stone by stone. In the years since it opened, the cathedral has hosted major events, including the state funerals for Presidents George H. W. Bush and Ronald Reagan. Presidential prayer services were held here for Joe Biden, Donald Trump, and Barack Obama.

### Don't Miss

The 50-plus-acre Washington National Cathedral Gardens, also known as Cathedral Close, are well worth a visit. The expanse is meticulously maintained and features a wide range of colorful flowers and plants.

### Good to Know

The Gothic-style cathedral took 83 years to complete and is one of the largest in the world. Gaze upward and you'll see 112 gargoyles (they channel rainwater away from the building) and 1,130 other grotesques. One is shaped like Darth Vader.

### Getting Here and Around

The cathedral is located in the Cathedral Heights section of Washington. It's easily accessible by car from anywhere in the city.

**The Cathedral Church of St. Peter and St. Paul.** ✉ *3101 Washington Ave. NW, Washington, DC* ☎ *202/537–6200* 🌐 *cathedral.org* 🎫 *Free.*

# Smithsonian Museums

## World-Class Art

The Smithsonian Institution, known around the world simply as the Smithsonian, has 19 galleries and museums, along with the National Zoological Park, in Washington, D.C. Many of them—including the National Gallery, the National Museum of Natural History, and the National Museum of American Art—are among the finest in the world. The Hirschhorn Museum and Sculpture Garden is a modernist masterpiece, and the National Museum of the American Indian is among the country's best newer museums. The National Air and Space Museum is a fan favorite, with items like the 1903 Wright Flyer and Neil Armstrong's Apollo 11 spacesuit.

## Don't Miss

The National Museum of African American History and Culture is the newest of the Smithsonian museums, and also one of the best. The collection features thousands and thousands of important items, including Harriet Tubman's shawl, Nat Turner's Bible, and a sign from President Barack Obama's 2008 campaign headquarters. 🌐 *nmaahc.si.edu.*

## Best Activity

Away from most of the other museums is the National Portrait Gallery, which has paintings of every president since George Washington. It's also the permanent home of Kehinde Wiley's portrait of President Obama and Amy Sherald's portrait of the former First Lady Michelle Obama. 🌐 *www.npg.si.edu.*

## Getting Here and Around

The museums are spread out throughout Washington, D.C., with the bulk of the Smithsonian attractions located at the National Mall. All are easily accessible by car and public transit.

**Smithsonian Museums.** 🌐 *si.edu/museums* 🎫 *Free.*

# U Street

## Washington's Cultural Corridor

In the early part of the 20th century, U Street was a hub for African American culture. The area became known as "Black Broadway" because of its theaters and music venues that welcomed some of the biggest names in jazz, including Duke Ellington, Louis Armstrong, Cab Calloway, and Sarah Vaughn. Today this diverse neighborhood has experienced a lively resurgence of arts and culture—and the crowds are back. Ethiopian food, offbeat boutiques, and live music are the draw.

## Don't Miss

Ben's Chili Bowl has been a U Street staple since 1958, and among its many fans is President Barack Obama. Its tasty half-smoke—a sausage topped with spicy chili, mustard, and onions—is the reason to visit. 🌐 *benschilibowl.com.*

## Best Tour

The U Street area has tons of brightly colored murals celebrating the area's history and culture. MuralsDC Project has a self-guided walking tour. 🌐 *muralsdcproject.com/u-street-corridor-walking-tour.*

## Getting Here and Around

The U Street area is walkable and easily accessible from all parts of Washington, D.C. The U Street/African-American Civil War Memorial/Cardozo Metro station puts you in the middle of the action.

**U Street.** 🌐 *washington.org/dc-neighborhoods/u-street.*

# When in Washington, D.C.

## ADAMS MORGAN

Named for two elementary schools that were desegregated in the 1950s—Adams had been for white students, while nearby Morgan had been for black students—this vibrant neighborhood is a multicultural celebration. Bars, coffee shops, and restaurants line 18th Street and spill out onto many of the adjacent blocks, making this a good place to start your explorations. Be sure to visit Tryst for coffee, Tail Up Goat for Mediterranean fare, and Roofers Union for rooftop cocktails.

**Do This:** One of the spots that helped establish this as a foodie destination is Perry's, a Japanese restaurant with a wonderful rooftop dining area. 🌐 *www.perrysam.com.*

**Adams Morgan.** ✉ *18th St. NW, Washington, DC* ☎ *202/997–0783* 🌐 *admodc.org/history-of-adams-morgan.*

## BLUES ALLEY

For the past five decades, Blues Alley in the upscale Georgetown neighborhood has been hosting up-and-coming and big-name jazz and blues musicians. Over the years, the venue has welcomed storied performers including Ella Fitzgerald, Tony Bennett, and Stan Getz. Wynton Marsalis, Pat Martino, and others have recorded live albums here.

**Do This:** The club is also a popular bar and restaurant, so come before a show and enjoy delicious Southern fare.

**Blues Alley.** ✉ *1073 Wisconsin Ave. NW, Washington DC* ☎ *202/337–4141* 🌐 *bluesalley.com/index.cfm* 🎟 *Varies.*

## DISTRICT WHARF

Southwest D.C., the smallest of the city's quadrants, has recently become a destination of its own thanks to the District Wharf, the mile-long walk next to the Potomac River. It's an exciting place for locals and visitors to try out kayaking and stand-up paddleboarding, take a boat tour of the waterfront, or just sit back and enjoy the view of the city's many monuments. There are plenty of green spaces for picnic lunches.

**Do This:** The Municipal Fish Market, America's oldest continuously operating seafood market, offers the freshest catch of the day. It's anchored the eclectic neighborhood since 1805.

**District Wharf.** ✉ *Wharf St. SW, Washington, DC* ☎ *202/789–7000* 🌐 *www.wharfdc.com.*

## EASTERN MARKET

The indoor-outdoor Eastern Market is a popular destination in the tree-lined neighborhood of Capitol Hill. The handsome brick market has been providing the community with fresh meat, fish, cheese, and produce for more than 100 years. Vendors sell homemade pasta, delicious dairy products, and fresh-cut flowers. Drop by on Sunday, when the covered walkway and adjacent lot are filled with arts and crafts vendors.

**Do This:** Fuel up at the Market Lunch, a restaurant that has called Eastern Market home since 1978. It promises "great food, no frills," and it delivers with North Carolina barbecue and Chesapeake Bay crab cakes. 🌐 *www.marketlunchdc.com.*

**Eastern Market.** ✉ *225 7th St. SE, Washington, DC* ☎ *202/215–6993* 🌐 *easternmarket.net* 🎟 *Free.*

## FREDERICK DOUGLASS NATIONAL HISTORIC SITE

Abolitionist, orator, and statesman Frederick Douglass lived in the nation's capital for 17 years. Today, his handsome Anacostia home has been painstakingly restored to reflect its appearance in 1895. You can explore the rooms where he wrote the final edition of his autobiography, *The Life and Times of Frederick Douglass.*

**Do This:** At the visitor center, don't pass up a chance to watch the 19-minute film called *Fighter for Freedom: The Frederick Douglass Story.*

**Frederick Douglass National Historic Site.** ✉ *1411 W St. SE, Washington, DC* ☎ *202/426–5961* 🌐 *www.nps.gov/frdo/index.htm* 🎫 *Free.*

## LIBRARY OF CONGRESS

Books worms, look no further! The Library of Congress is the largest library in the world, with over 170 million books, recordings, photographs, newspapers, maps, and manuscripts. Each day they receive around 15,000 items and add more than 10,000 items to its collections. The Library even houses materials in approximately 470 languages. The catch? All books can only be used on the premises and cannot be checked out. But don't let that deter you from a visit; the impressive architecture of the building and the expansive collection of artwork is enough to make it worth a visit.

**Do This:** Check out the copper-domed Thomas Jefferson Building, the oldest of the three buildings that make up the library. The dome, topped with the gilt "Flame of Knowledge," is ornate and decorative, with busts of Dante, Goethe, and Nathaniel Hawthorne perched above its entryway.

**The Library of Congress.** ✉ *101 Independence Ave SE, Washington, DC* ☎ *202/707–5000* 🌐 *www.loc.gov* 🎫 *Free.*

# Cool Places to Stay

**The Line Hotel.** A true institution in the vibrant Adams Morgan neighborhood, the Line Hotel is part luxury lodging, part hip bar and restaurant. Located in a former church, the space has soaring ceilings, huge Palladian windows, and rooftop spaces with eye-popping views. ✉ *1770 Euclid St. NW, Washington, DC* ☎ *202/588–0525* 🌐 *www.thelinehotel.com/dc* [$] *From $149.*

**The Mansion on O Street.** Each of the more than 100 rooms within the Mansion on O Street is individually decorated to provide a one-of-a-kind experience. The hotel is a favorite among celebrities and political figures because of the hotel's code of silence: information on guests is never shared. ✉ *2020 O St. NW, Washington, DC* ☎ *202/496–2000* 🌐 *omansion.com* [$] *From $375.*

**Swann House.** With a classic bed-and-breakfast vibe, Swann House is an oasis within the bustling city. Housed in an 1883 Dupont Circle mansion, the building maintains many of its original features, from glittery chandeliers to finely carved fireplaces. Rooms tucked away in the turret have the most charm. ✉ *1808 New Hampshire Ave. NW, Washington, DC* ☎ *202/265–4414* 🌐 *www.swannhouse.com* [$] *From $361.*

**The Watergate Hotel.** The Watergate—the name might sound familiar because it lent its name to a scandal that brought down a president—blends a midcentury modern aesthetic with luxurious touches that are very 21st century. Room 214, used during the infamous break-in, has tongue-in-cheek touches like binoculars and a reel-to-reel tape recorder. The views of the Potomac River are stunning. ✉ *2650 Virginia Ave. NW, Washington, DC* ☎ *844/617–1972* 🌐 *www.thewatergatehotel.com* [$] *From $300.*

# West Virginia

With more than 226,500 acres of state parks, forests, and recreation areas, and more than a million acres of federal lands, West Virginia offers a quick escape from the urban centers of Baltimore, Philadelphia, Pittsburgh, and Washington, D.C. Historic towns, ski resorts, caverns, and unparalleled natural scenery draw visitors to the Mountain State.

## Bucket List Picks

The following boxes contain our picks for the top sights and experiences in West Virginia.

- ○ Gauley River National Recreation Area
- ○ New River Gorge National Park and Preserve
- ○ Traditional Mountain Music
- ○ Harpers Ferry National Historical Park
- ○ Cass Scenic Railroad State Park
- ○ Monongahela National Forest

# Gauley River National Recreation Area

### America's Best Rapids

For many white-water rafting fans, there's nothing better than an exciting and exhilarating ride down the 25-mile-long Gauley River. The free-flowing river's rocky sections make for a challenging trip, as do its stretches of Class V-plus rapids. It's one of the wildest trips on the East Coast. Some gentler sections are perfect for kids. As you're traveling through spectacular gorges, keep an eye out for songbirds like the cerulean warbler.

### Don't Miss

Ace Adventure Resort has two options for rafters: the Fall Upper Gauley (for more experienced rafters) and the Fall Lower Gauley (open to those of all levels, including those who have never tried white-water rafting before). 🌐 *aceraft.com/white-water-rafting/gauley-river-rafting.*

### When to Go

White-water rafting is a summertime activity, but hiking and other activities are pleasant in spring and fall.

### Getting Here and Around

Roanoke–Blacksburg Regional Airport in Virginia is about 2½ hours away.

**Gauley River National Recreation Area.** ✉ *104 Main St., Glen Jean, WV* ☎ *304/465–0508* 🌐 *www.nps.gov/gari/index.htm* 🎫 *Free.*

## New River Gorge National Park and Preserve

### America's Newest National Park

One of the country's newest national parks, West Virginia's New River Gorge runs through a particularly gorgeous stretch of the Appalachian Mountains. The park includes 70,000 acres of land along the New River, which, contrary to its name, is one of the country's oldest rivers. To take in it all, be sure to visit Grandview Visitor Center, situated 1,400 feet above the river. Already one of the most popular climbing areas in the country, New River Gorge has sheer sandstone cliffs that provide a challenge for even pro climbers.

### Don't Miss

Marvel at the New River Gorge Bridge, which towers 876 feet above the river. The graceful structure is the longest steel span in the western hemisphere. It's among the most photographed sights in all of West Virginia. Daredevil BASE jumpers leap from the structure every October to celebrate Bridge Day.

### Best Tour

The 17-stop African American Heritage Auto Tour is a self-guided tour of the New River Gorge area. Learn about the African American people who worked in the mines, on the railroads, and who lived in the communities.

### Best Activity

Adventures on the Gorge is one of the best outfitters offering rafting trips through the national park. ⊕ *www.adventuresonthegorge.com.*

### Getting Here and Around

Raleigh County Memorial Airport in Beaver is the closest airport to the national park. A car is necessary for touring this area.

**Grandview Visitor Center.** ✉ *Grandview Rd., Beaver, WV* ⊕ *www.nps.gov/neri/index.htm* 🎟 *Free.*

## Traditional Mountain Music

### County Roads, Take You Home

The music of West Virginia is a major part of the state's culture and history. Known as Appalachian music, the genre combines elements of bluegrass, folk, and country. You can enjoy it at outdoor festivals, music halls, backyard barbecues, and lots of other places. Performers traditionally play stringed instruments like the banjo, fiddle, and guitar while vocalists sing about the things that make the region special.

### Don't Miss

Along Route 219 are plenty of destinations that make up the Traditional Mountain Music Trail. The first stop on the trail is Davis & Elkins College, home to summertime's Augusta Heritage Festival and many concerts throughout the year. Additional stops include Big Timber Brewing Company, the Purple Fiddle, and Carnegie Hall in Lewisburg.

### Good to Know

Some of the biggest annual events celebrating traditional mountain music include the five-day Appalachian String Band Festival and the West Virginia State Folk Festival.

### Getting Here and Around

Music venues can be found all over the state, making a car pretty much necessary.

**Mountain Music Trail.** 🌐 *wvtourism.com/heart-of-mountain-music.*

# Harpers Ferry National Historical Park

### A Page from the History Books

Located at the confluence of the Potomac and Shenandoah rivers, Harpers Ferry is West Virginia's easternmost point. It comes up in history books surprisingly often, most notably in 1859 when abolitionist John Brown led a failed revolt that he hoped would bring an end to slavery. There's plenty here to keep you occupied today, including Civil War battlefields, museums, and hiking trails. Start at the Harpers Ferry Visitor Center, which provides guests with with maps, trail information, and helpful history.

### Don't Miss

The downtown area, known as Lower Town, is the most popular destination for visitors. Look for beautifully restored businesses from the period, including Mrs. Stipes' Boarding House and Frankel's Clothing Store.

### Best Tour

The Harpers Ferry area has 22 miles of hiking trails through historic sites. Take a self-guided walking tour of the Chesapeake and Ohio Canal National Historical Park, which goes through the town.

### When to Go

Summer can be hot in Harpers Ferry, making fall and spring ideal times to visit. In fall, the foliage is a true must-see.

### Getting Here and Around

Harpers Ferry is a little over an hour away from both Washington, D.C., and Baltimore.

**Harpers Ferry Visitor Center.** ✉ *171 Shoreline Dr., Harpers Ferry, WV* ☎ *305/535–6029* 🌐 *www.nps.gov/hafe/index.htm* 🎫 *$20 per car.*

# Cass Scenic Railroad State Park

## Train Ride Through Spectacular Scenery

History comes alive at Cass Scenic Railroad State Park, home to a working steam locomotive steam that can take you on an 11-mile trip to Bald Knob, a breathtaking mountain peak. The railroad was built in 1901 to transport lumber from the nearby forests to the mill in the town of Cass. Many of the open-sided passenger cars in use today are converted logging cars.

## Don't Miss

The train is the draw at Cass Scenic Railroad State Park, but be sure to visit the community of Cass, a company town built for workers at nearby Cheat Mountain. There's a soda fountain, a sit-down restaurant, a gift shop, and a museum dedicated to railroading history.

## Good to Know

To get the full experience, stay overnight in one of the Cass Company Houses, which used to house workers. Set behind picket fences, they have lots of character. 🌐 *wvstateparks.com/places-to-stay/cabins/cass-scenic-railroad-cabins.*

## When to Go

Visit in the fall for views of the colorful foliage on the mountain range.

## Getting Here and Around

The state park is just a short drive over the border from Virginia. Roanoke is 130 miles away, while Charlottesville is 125 miles away.

**Cass Depot.** ✉ *242 Main St., Cass, WV* ☎ *833/987–2757* 🌐 *wvstateparks.com/park/cass-scenic-railroad-state-park* 🎫 *$55.*

# Monongahela National Forest

## West Virginia's Mountain Paradise

The views of the Allegheny Mountains from the 919,000-acre Monongahela National Forest are breathtaking. The sheer size of the park is hard to comprehend at first, because it spans 10 counties. This is one of the most biologically diverse areas of the country, which you'll notice as you pass through stands of white and chestnut oak, maple, sycamore, birch, and mountain ash trees. The area is beloved for its hiking (there are literally hundreds of miles of trails), mountain biking, and boating.

## Don't Miss

The Seneca Rocks are one of the most popular attractions at Monongahela National Forest. Gaze up at the breath-taking rock formations, or grab some gear and climb them.

## Best Tour

Embark on a self-guided tour of the Cranberry Mountain Nature Center to learn about the plants and animals that call the national forest home. There's an easy-to-conquer nature trail that surrounds the nature center, too.

## Good to Know

The winding Highland Scenic Highway takes you past four beautiful overlooks with views as far as the eye can see.

## Getting Here and Around

Monongahela National Forest is remote, which is why many people love it, and getting here is a bit of a trek. A car is a necessity.

**Monongahela National Forest.** ✉ *200 Sycamore St., Elkins, WV* ☎ *304/363–1800* 🌐 *www.fs.usda.gov/mnf* 🎫 *Free.*

# When in West Virginia

## ABOLITIONIST ALE WORKS

Inspired by the abolitionists and insurrectionists who are major figures in West Virginia's history, Abolitionist Ale Works doesn't make beer like anyone else. Located in the historic community of Charles Town, West Virginia, the brewery is known for its one-of-a-kind drafts like its Notorious FIG Stout, Elderberry Saison, and Labor Haze IPA.

**Do This:** While you're downtown, look for the green cupola that marks the Jefferson County Courthouse. It's the spot where abolitionist John Brown was tried for treason for inciting a slave rebellion in 1859. 🌐 *discoveritallwv.com/attractions/charles-town.*

**Abolitionist Ale Works.** ✉ *129 W. Washington St., Charles Town, WV* ☎ *681/252–1548* 🌐 *www.abolitionistaleworks.com/index.asp.*

## HILLBILLY HOT DOGS

Hillbilly Hot Dogs lives up to its name: the restaurant occupies a converted bus and is surrounded by items that are normally found in junkyards. There are more than a dozen West Virginia–style sausages on the menu, but start off with the namesake hot dog, which comes loaded with chili sauce, mustard, and onions. This is a popular spot for road-trippers, so expect a lunchtime rush, particularly on weekends.

**Do This:** Here's your photo op! The Homewrecker comes in two unbelievable sizes—15 inches and 30 inches—and is loaded with jalapeño slices, sautéed peppers and onions, chili sauce, slaw, and shredded cheese.

**Hillbilly Hot Dogs.** ✉ *6951 Ohio River Rd., Lesage, WV* ☎ *304/762–2458* 🌐 *www.hillbillyhotdogs.com.*

## SHEPHERDSTOWN

Along the Potomac River you'll find Shepherdstown, a community that played a crucial role in our nation's history. The town was established in 1762, making it one of the oldest in West Virginia. Many of the buildings here were built before the Revolutionary War (at the Sheetz House, the family made muskets for George Washington's troops), and Civil War–era history can be found at nearly every corner (the Chapline-Shenton House was used as a hospital for Confederate soldiers during the Battle of Antietam). Union troops soon occupied the town to preserve the Baltimore and Ohio Railroad route.

**Do This:** Explore by bike or boat at Shepherdstown Pedal and Paddle. There's no better way to travel to nearby Antietam Battlefield. www.thepedalpaddle.com. The town is also said to be one of America's most haunted, and Shepherdstown Mystery Walks leads you on 90-minute walking tours that include lots of ghostly stories. 🌐 *shepherdstownmysterywalks.com.*

## THE WASHINGTON HERITAGE TRAIL

The 136-mile George Washington Heritage Trail winds through three West Virginia counties: Morgan, Berkeley, and Jefferson. There are more than 40 stops along the way—including Berkeley Springs, a colonial-era spa town our first president helped to found.

**Do This:** According to historians, Washington bathed in a tublike rock formation during his teen years when he'd visit Berkeley Springs as a surveyor's assistant. You can see the spot in in Berkeley Springs State Park.

**The Washington Heritage Trail.** 🌐 *washingtonheritagetrail.com.*

### WEST VIRGINIA CAPITOL COMPLEX

Sitting next to the Kanawha River is Charlestown's opulent West Virginia Capitol Complex, an 18-acre area that is home to the gold-domed capitol building and the stately governor's mansion. Both are open for tours and surrounded by monuments, historical markers, and the beloved West Virginia State Museum.

**Do This:** Mere steps from the capitol building, the dazzling West Virginia State Museum has a theatrical take on the state's history. Step through the door of a log cabin, duck your head as you enter a coal mine, and walk along a street lined with storefronts. 🌐 *www.wvculture.org/museum/State-Museum-Index.html.*

**West Virginia Capitol Complex.** ✉ *Kanawah Blvd. E, Charleston, WV* ☎ *304/558–4839* 🌐 *www.wvculture.org/agency/capitol.html* 🎟 *Free.*

### WEST VIRGINIA PENITENTIARY

The Gothic-style West Virginia Penitentiary is an eerie-looking place, crowned with turrets and battlements. It held some of the state's most hardened criminals between 1876 and 1995, but now it's a destination for brave souls. The 90-minute guided tours take you through a cell block nicknamed "the Alamo" that was reserved for the most dangerous prisoners.

**Do This:** Three-hour-long Twilight Tours are creepy, but by far the creepiest are the six-hour "Ghost Hunts" where you roam the empty corridors on your own.

**West Virginia Penitentiary.** ✉ *818 Jefferson Ave., Moundsville, WV* ☎ *304/845–6200* 🌐 *wvpentours.com* 🎟 *$14.*

## Cool Places to Stay

**Ace Adventure Resort.** If you want to get your adrenaline pumping, head to this resort a few miles from New River Gorge. Ziplining and white-water rafting are both available right on the property, and the 1,500 acres out plenty of other activities at your doorstep. The cabins are rustic but have tons of amenities. ✉ *1 Concho Rd., Oak Hill, WV* ☎ *800/787–3982* 🌐 *aceraft.com* 💲 *From $250.*

**Blackwater Falls State Park Lodge.** Dozens of fully furnished cabins are available for overnight stays within Blackwater Falls State Park. The comfortable cabins have plenty of privacy, but are close to great outdoor adventures. You can also stay in the main lodge, which has the usual creature comforts plus a pool. ✉ *1584 Blackwater Lodge Rd., Davis, WV* ☎ *304/259–5216* 🌐 *wvstateparks.com/places-to-stay/lodges/blackwater-falls-state-park-lodges* 💲 *From $179.*

**Capon Springs and Farms.** Year after year, folks head back to the gracious Capon Springs and Farms, an all-inclusive resort on 4,700 acres in the mountains of West Virginia. Rates include three meals per day and access to the resort's many amenities, including hiking trails and a fishing pond. Spring water fills the swimming pool and the soaking baths in the spa. There's a plantation-style main house and 14 other individually decorated cottages. ✉ *3818 Capon Springs Rd., High View, WV* ☎ *304/874–3695* 🌐 *www.caponsprings.net* 💲 *From $150.*

**The Greenbrier.** West Virginia's most famous hotel is The Greenbrier, a sprawling resort that has hosted presidents, diplomats, and celebrities of all stripes. On 11,000 acres, the luxurious lodging has more than a dozen restaurants, four golf courses, a casino, and spa. Beneath the Greenbrier is a bunker that was intended for use by Congress during the Cold War. ✉ *101 W. Main St., White Sulphur Springs, WV* ☎ *855/453–4858* 🌐 *www.greenbrier.com* 💲 *From $400.*

Chapter 5

# THE SOUTHEAST

Written by
Cameron Roberts

# WELCOME TO THE SOUTHEAST

## TOP REASONS TO GO

★ **Listen to the music:** The blues, country, and rock clubs of Memphis, New Orleans, Nashville, and the Mississippi Delta are reason enough to visit the region.

★ **Trace the Civil Rights Movement:** From Alabama to Atlanta, see how brave African American activists fought hard to change America for the better.

★ **Hit the beaches:** The southeastern coast stretches from North Carolina's Outer Banks to the Florida Keys, and is home to some of the best beaches in the country.

★ **Explore charming cities:** The South has a unique and often complicated past that's well preserved in the historical squares, buildings, homes, and museums in cities like New Orleans, Savannah, and Charleston.

★ **Get a taste of the South:** Whether you dive into a Lowcountry boil, find the best fried chicken in Atlanta, or stop at roadside stands for casual delicacies like boiled peanuts, eating is a main activity in the South.

1 **Alabama.** Civil rights history and a new wave of hip culture in Montgomery and Birmingham attract many visitors.

2 **Florida.** White sand beaches, theme parks, and unique wetlands make the largest state in the Southeast popular.

3 **Georgia.** Savannah and Atlanta paint a pretty picture of history, culture, and the arts.

4 **Kentucky.** Bourbon, horses, and music are draws to a hilly state so pretty it more than earns its Bluegrass name.

5 **Louisiana.** New Orleans is the star, but Cajun Country and wetlands make it varied.

6 **Mississippi.** Home to the rich blues history of the Delta region, the literary grace of Oxford, and a coastline of beaches.

7 **North Carolina.** Go from majestic mountains to lovely beaches in a matter of hours.

8 **South Carolina.** Historic Charleston and the Lowcountry are big draws.

9 **Tennessee.** From the bright lights of Nashville to the trails of the Great Smokies, this state has it all.

Cincinnati
WEST VIRGINIA
WASHINGTON, D.C.
Louisville Museum Row
Kentucky Derby
Kentucky Bourbon Trail
Charleston
Charlottesville
Louisville
University of Kentucky Basketball
Lexington's Distillery District
Richmond
Evansville
Lexington
Red River Gorge
Beckley
VIRGINIA
Owensboro
KENTUCKY
Roanoke
Mammoth Cave
Bluegrass Country
Norfolk
Bowling Green
IN NASHVILLE:
Country Music Hall of Fame,
Grand Ole Opry, and
Honky Tonk Highway
Bristol
Danville
Kitty Hawk
Great Smoky Mountains N.P.
Appalachian Trail
Durham
Nashville
Greensboro
Raleigh
Outer Banks
Knoxville
Dollywood
The Triangle
Blue Ridge Parkway
NORTH CAROLINA
Murfreesboro
Gatlinburg
Cades Cove
Asheville
TENNESSEE
Charlotte
Small Carolina Mountain Towns
Chattanooga
Jocassee Gorges
Huntsville
Greenville
Wilmington
Blue Ridge and the Chattahoochee Forest
Anderson
Florence
Muscle Shoals
Wilmington Beaches
Columbia
Congaree National Park
Myrtle Beach
Gadsden
Athens
Atlanta
SOUTH CAROLINA
Aiken
Birmingham
IN ATLANTA:
Atlanta's BeltLine,
Georgia Aquarium, and
MLK Jr. National Historical Park
Augusta
Summerville's Sweet Tea Trail
Tuscaloosa
Lowcountry
Charleston
Roll Tide
Charleston Beaches
ALABAMA
Beaufort
Gullah Geechee Cultural Heritage Corridor
Columbus
Dublin
Hilton Head
Selma
Montgomery
Savannah
Tybee Island
GEORGIA
Douglas
Brunswick
Jekyll Island
Okefenokee Swamp
Valdosta
Cumberland Island
Amelia Island
Atlantic Ocean
Mobile
The Emerald Coast
Tallahassee
Jacksonville
Pensacola
St. Augustine
Gulf Shores & Dauphin Island
Apalachicola
Gainesville
Daytona Beach
Ocala
Ocala National Forest
Crystal River
Titusville
IN OCEAN SPRINGS:
Biloxi & the Gulf Coast Scenic Byway,
and Mississippi Blues Trail
Orlando
The Space Coast
Orlando Theme Parks
Kissimmee
Tampa
Vero Beach
St. Petersburg
FLORIDA
Fort Pierce
Gulf of Mexico
Sarasota
Siesta Key
West Palm Beach
Fort Myers
Sanibel Island
Fort Lauderdale
Naples
Miami
Wynwood and Little Havana
Miami Beach
Coral Gables
The Everglades
Nassau
0 100 mi
0 100 km
Key West
The Florida Keys
BAHAMAS

# WHAT TO EAT AND DRINK IN THE SOUTHEAST

Shrimp and grits

## SHRIMP AND GRITS

An iconic dish that several states claim (and compete over), shrimp is paired with flavored, usually cheesy grits, often topped with green onions and cooked with bacon. It's on menus everywhere in the Southeast—coastal Carolinas and New Orleans being hot spots. Fresh shrimp is plentiful throughout the region, with Gulf Coast and Atlantic varieties each having their own unique texture and flavor profile.

## BARBECUE

You could craft an itinerary based on barbecue alone in the Southeast, where cooking styles vary from state to state. There's a whole world of sauce to explore: vinegar-based concoctions in the Carolinas, hundreds of ketchup- and mustard-based variations, plus the mayonnaise-heavy Alabama sauce and dry rubs in Memphis. Slow-cooked pulled pork is on any worthwhile menu, but chicken, brisket, and ribs are finger-licking good, too.

## BOURBON

The best bourbon—sweet and strong brown liquor, barrel-aged and made from corn mash—has been produced in the American South since the 18th century. True enthusiasts should visit the distilleries of Kentucky, where 95% of the world's bourbon is made, including big names like Jim Beam, Evan Williams, and Maker's Mark.

## FRIED CHICKEN

You haven't had fried chicken until you've tasted it crisped to perfection in the Southeast. You'll see it on menus everywhere, but you're missing out if you don't order it from a gas station or hole-in-the-wall counter shop at least once on your trip (trust us). Nashville hot chicken—with a spicy sauce and coating—is the dish to order in its namesake city.

## CATFISH

These large, endearingly ugly bottom-feeders are abundant in all types of waterways in the Southeast. The best catfish fillets are thin, lightly fried, and stuffed into a po' boy, roll, or served on a plate with slaw and other Southern sides. Seek out fried catfish in the no-frills roadside stops of rural Mississippi and Louisiana.

### LOWCOUNTRY BOIL

This celebratory dining experience abounds in the backyards and casual restaurants of the South Carolina coast, where shrimp and other fresh crustaceans, sausage, corn, and potatoes are boiled in a large pot with plenty of spices, then poured over a newspaper or checkered cloth–covered table. Louisiana's traditional crawfish boil is similar.

### CUBANO

Aside from freshly caught seafood, the biggest influence on South Florida food is its Cuban population, with *ropa vieja, arroz con pollo, croquetas,* and more found in the Miami area, Tampa, and other Florida cities. The Cubano (Cuban sandwich)—pressed bread with pickles, cheese, roast pork, and a slice of ham—is a must-try.

### BRUNSWICK STEW

There's a debate over Brunswick stew's origin—Georgia, Virginia, and North Carolina all claim it—and each state's iteration has its slight differences (Kentucky's burgoo is also similar).

Key lime pie

Barbecue

Regardless of its origin, the stew of slow-simmered pulled pork, tomato, beans, and corn is simply delicious anywhere in the South.

### PIE

You can't get more Southern than a slice of pie perfected with generations of family recipes. The delectable desserts vary from state to state, such as key lime pie, pecan pie, sweet potato pie, Kentucky Derby pie (chocolate and pecan or walnut), Mississippi mud pie (chocolate and whipped topping), and peach cobbler. Should we go on?

### CRAFT BEER

Like barbecue, the craft breweries of the Southeast could fill a whole itinerary. SweetWater in Atlanta and New Belgium in Asheville were early adopters to the trend and now distribute nationally.

### SAZERAC

One of the world's original cocktails is a source of pride in New Orleans. A proper one is made from rye whiskey, sugar, Peychaud's bitters, and an absinthe rinse; served chilled in a rocks glass with a lemon twist. Drink one in New Orleans's French Quarter, where it was invented by the Creole apothecarist Antoine Peychaud in the 1800s.

# The Southeast Regional Snapshot

## Know Before You Go

### PLAN AROUND HURRICANE SEASON

From June to November much of the Southeast braces for monster storms. The biggest storms are likely in August and September, but you should check 🌐 *nhc.gov* before and during trips that fall in this time.

### COLLEGE FOOTBALL IS KING

In the South, football isn't just a sport, it's a way of life. Teams from the SEC and ACC compete from late August to January and will occupy the region every Saturday. Join in a tailgate or watch the game at a bar, and you'll really get to know the locals. Tickets are easy to buy.

### SOME GAS STATIONS ARE FOOD MECCAS

Southerners know the best meals in town aren't always served on white tablecloths. Often, they come golden-fried or hot out of the oven, tucked in a red-and-white-checked paper sleeve from behind the counter at an Exxon station. If you just stop to pump gas, you're likely missing out on some great fried chicken, Cajun meats, and Delta hot tamales.

## Planning Your Time

The Southeast is a huge region, comprised of nine states. When road-tripping, some long, rural drives are inevitable. Both Nashville and Atlanta make good central bases. The Gulf Coast (New Orleans to Destin) and the Atlantic Coast (the Outer Banks to Jacksonville) are each fine itineraries for a week or so. Some places in Florida (like Miami and Disney) deserve a trip of their own.

## Road Trips

**2 weeks:** Southern Music and Nightlife (Athens to Nashville to Memphis to New Orleans to Clarksdale)

**1 week:** Bourbon Country (Louisville to Nashville)

**1 week:** Civil Rights Trail (Jackson to Atlanta)

**3 Days:** Mississippi Blues Trail (Gulfport to Memphis)

**1 Day:** Alligator Alley (Naples to Miami)

## Big Events

**Mardi Gras.** On Fat Tuesday, many New Orleanians don costumes, face paint, and masks, and then take to the streets for the last hurrah before Lent.

**Kentucky Derby.** Clutching mint juleps, dolled-up spectators stand on their seats and roar during the "greatest two minutes in sports," rain or shine, at this great horse race.

**Art Basel.** The biggest event on any Miami social calendar, this annual art show draws artists from all over the world and is followed by fabulous parties and city-wide events.

## What To ...

### READ

*The Yellow House* by Sarah Broom

*Salvage the Bones* by Jesmyn Ward

*Swamplandia!* by Karen Russell

*The Sound and the Fury* by William Faulkner

*Bastard Out of Carolina* by Dorothy Allison

*Garden & Gun* (magazine)

### WATCH

*Selma* (movie set in Alabama)

*Walk the Line* (movie set in Tennessee)

*Secret Life of Bees* (movie set in South Carolina)

*Atlanta* (television series set in Georgia)

*Moonlight* (movie set in Florida)

### LISTEN TO

*The Bitter Southerner* (podcast)

"Another Sunday in the South" by Miranda Lambert

"New Orleans Bump" by Jelly Roll Morton

"Tennessee Homesick Blues" by Dolly Parton (song)

"Sweet Home Alabama" by Lynyrd Skynyrd (song)

### BUY

Bourbon from Kentucky

Cafe du Monde coffee from New Orleans

Disney gear from Florida

Sweetgrass baskets from South Carolina

## Contacts

### AIR

**Alabama.** BHM

**Florida.** MIA, EYW, FLL, JAX

**Georgia.** ATL

**Kentucky.** CVG, LEX, SDF

**Louisiana.** MSY

**Mississippi.** JAN, GPT

**North Carolina.** RDU, CLT

**South Carolina.** CHS

**Tennessee.** BNA, MEM

### BUS

**Greyhound.** ☎ *800/231–2222* 🌐 *www.greyhound.com*

**MARTA (Atlanta).** ☎ *404/848–5000* 🌐 *www.itsmarta.com*

**Miami-Dade County Metrobus.** ☎ *305/468–5900* 🌐 *www.miamidade.gov*

**New Orleans Regional Transit Authority.** ☎ *504/248–3900* 🌐 *www.norta.com*

**WeGo Public Transit (Nashville).** ☎ *615/862–5950* 🌐 *www.nashvillemta.org*

### BOAT

**North Carolina Ferry System (OBX).** ☎ *800/293–3779* 🌐 *www.ncdot.gov*

**Fort Lauderdale Water Taxi** ☎ *954/467–6677* 🌐 *watertaxi.com*

### METRO/SUBWAY

**MARTA (Atlanta).** ☎ *404/848–5000* 🌐 *www.itsmarta.com*

**Music City Star Train (Nashville).** ☎ *615/862–8833* 🌐 *www.rtarelaxandride.com*

### TRAIN

**Amtrak.** ☎ *800/872–7245* 🌐 *www.amtrak.com*

**Brightline (South Florida).** ☎ *844/920–2392* 🌐 *www.gobrightline.com*

**Tri Rail (South Florida Regional Transit).** ☎ *800/874–7245* 🌐 *www.tri-rail.com*

### VISITOR INFO

🌐 *alabama.travel*

🌐 *www.visitflorida.com*

🌐 *www.exploregeorgia.org*

🌐 *www.kentuckytourism.com*

🌐 *www.louisianatravel.com*

🌐 *visitmississippi.org*

🌐 *www.visitnc.com*

🌐 *discoversouthcarolina.com*

🌐 *www.tnvacation.com*

# Alabama

A blend of thought-provoking history, modern cities, and natural beauty make this state "Sweet Home Alabama." Elaborate homes dot Huntsville, where the Saturn rocket was designed, and Montgomery's modern state government buildings stand near major sights on the Civil Rights Trail. Birmingham, a major medical research center, has 99 historic neighborhoods.

## Bucket List Picks

The following boxes contain our picks for the top sights and experiences in Alabama.

- ○ Gulf Shores and Dauphin Island
- ○ Montgomery
- ○ Birmingham
- ○ Muscle Shoals
- ○ Selma
- ○ U.S. Space & Rocket Center
- ○ Roll Tide

## Gulf Shores and Dauphin Island

### Land of Sunsets

Thirty-two miles of white-sand beaches lie just south of Mobile, across the bay, at Gulf Shores, where 6,500 acres of reserves and state parks protect much of the area. It's where locals in the know kick back and relax as they watch the sun dip into the Gulf. On the shore of Mobile Bay in Fairhope and Point Clear, incredible sunsets are not-to-be-missed events, especially over fresh seafood at waterfront restaurants. At the picturesque western peninsula past Gulf Shores, tour Fort Morgan, the star-shaped, haunted grounds of an early-1800s fort used through several wars.

### Don't Miss

Dauphin Island is known as the sunset capital of the state, since the Gulf beach receives more than its fair share of unobstructed, colorful evening shows. From Fort Morgan, visitors can take the car ferry to the barrier island, which is surrounded by Mobile Bay, Mississippi Sound, and Gulf waters. It has quieter beaches than Gulf Shores and great bird-watching.

### When to Go

The National Shrimp Festival—with musical entertainment, an outdoor village, and plenty of shrimp—is held at the beach over four days in early October, when the weather is nice and some of the heat of summer has burned off.

### Best Detour

To the east of Gulf Shores, Perdido Key State Park (right over the state line into Florida) is one of the prettiest protected beaches around.

### Getting Here and Around

Gulf Shores is 53 miles from Mobile and 34 miles from Pensacola, Florida. The Mobile Bay Ferry travels between Fort Morgan at Gulf Shores, and Fort Gaines at Dauphin Island (a scenic 40 minutes) for $16 per vehicle.

# Montgomery

### Birthplace of the Civil Rights Movement

Few places in the United States have done a better job of laying out the stakes of the civil rights movement than Montgomery, the city where the movement was born and one that is still reckoning with its role in the slave trade and era of slavery that followed. The Legacy Museum and the National Memorial for Peace and Justice, the must-see attractions here, have been driving forces in Montgomery's growth as a tourist destination.

### Don't Miss

The Legacy Museum explores the Atlantic slave trade and enduring damage wrought by slavery, with exhibits focusing on lynching, racial segregation ("Jim Crow") laws, and mass incarceration. The National Memorial for Peace and Justice documents and memorializes the thousands of lynchings that occurred since the Civil War through 1950. Each county where the Equal Justice Initiative has documented a lynching gets a steel plaque, where names and dates are recorded.

### Good to Know

The Legacy Museum and the National Memorial for Peace and Justice are three-quarters of a mile apart. A shuttle runs between them every 10 minutes.

### Getting Here and Around

Atlanta is 160 miles northeast of Montgomery, a 2½-hour drive via Interstate 85 south. American and Delta also fly into Montgomery Regional Airport (MGM). Downtown is walkable, though it's nice to have a car or rideshare for further exploration.

**The Legacy Museum.** ✉ *115 Coosa St., Montgomery, AL.* **The National Memorial for Peace and Justice.** ✉ *417 Caroline St., Montgomery, AL* 🌐 *museumandmemorial.eji.org.*

## Birmingham

### Hip Southern City

While Montgomery is slowly creeping up on it, Birmingham is still Alabama's hippest city. Downtown is home to historic buildings (some turned coworking spaces and hotels), fine dining, museums, a half-dozen breweries, and one of the coolest and weirdest little bars in the country, The Atomic Lounge. In Avondale, converted warehouses have become coffee shops, music venues, and breweries like Cahaba Brewing Company. You'll also find great food in Avondale, from taco trucks to barbecue. Historians consider Birmingham the cradle of the civil rights movement.

### Don't Miss

A good night out in Birmingham starts with dinner at SAW's Soul Food, beers next door at Avondale Brewing Company, and a finale at Atomic Lounge for craft cocktails, costumes, and guaranteed fun. Order the Sex Panther if you want your drink to come with a temporary tattoo.

### Best Museum

The excellent Birmingham Civil Rights Institute traces African Americans' struggle for equality back to the 1800s. The Movement Gallery focuses on dramatic episodes of the 1955–63 civil rights movement. Located in the Civil Rights District, the museum can be part of a larger tour including Kelly Ingram Park, where large civil rights demonstrations were staged, and the 16th Street Baptist Church, the site of the 1960s bombing that killed four young girls. 🌐 *www.bcri.org.*

### Getting Here and Around

Downtown and Avondale are within walking distance to attractions, but it's best to have a car or rideshare to explore. Fly into Birmingham's airport (BHM) or drive; Montgomery is about 87 miles away.

# Muscle Shoals

## Low-Key Music Capital

Real fans of rock and R&B know that Alabama has made (and continues to make) an indelible impact on American music. Called the small town with big sound, Muscle Shoals (plus neighboring Sheffield, Tuscumbia, and Florence) has drawn many major international artists to create excellent music over the decades, especially from the 1950s to '70s. W. C. Handy, known as the "Father of the Blues," was the first artist to come out of the region, and you can still visit the one-room cabin where he grew up. Muscle Shoals is still home to many recording studios, including FAME, which hosted acts like Etta James and Aretha Franklin, in addition to contemporary artists like Alicia Keys and Demi Lovato. After exploring, enjoy casual small restaurants and hip, divey bars, or visit the Alabama Music Hall of Fame, which highlights the state's notable musicians.

## Don't Miss

Muscle Shoals Sound Studios is more than just a humble building on the highway. The music studio was created in 1969, when local musicians broke off from FAME to draw big national performers like the Swampers. In 2009, The Black Keys recorded the first album here in 30 years, *Brothers*. The studio and museum are now run by the Muscle Shoals Music Foundation. 🌐 *www.muscleshoalssoundstudio.org.*

## Before You Go

Watch the documentary *Muscle Shoals*, which features interviews with artists like Bono, Jimmy Cliff, Keith Richards, and Alicia Keys, who speak in awe of the area, their experience cutting records there, and what they call the "Muscle Shoals sound."

## Getting Here and Around

This area along the Tennessee River is 80 miles from Huntsville and a two-hour drive to Birmingham.

## Selma

### Walk the Road of Civil Rights Heroes

The Selma to Montgomery March of 1965 marked a pivotal moment in U.S. history, leading in just a few months to the passage of the federal Voting Rights Act (which was partially invalidated by a 2013 U.S. Supreme Court decision). To understand the protest, you must visit the small Alabama city, and travel its 54-mile National Historic Trail spanning from Selma to Montgomery along U.S. 80. Before you begin, tour the Old Depot Museum's Civil Rights room to see scrawled hospital records preserving names of the injured brought in after the bridge attack. You can also visit the National Voting Rights Museum, which showcases official state police photos taken on Bloody Sunday.

### Don't Miss

Walking across Selma's Edmund Pettus Bridge to honor those who marched in support of the Voting Rights Act is a must.

### Then and Now

When John Lewis and the Rev. Hosea Williams of the Southern Christian Leadership Conference led 500 marchers across the Edmund Pettus Bridge on Sunday, March 7, 1965, they were met by a crowd of police. The brutality of the attack shocked the nation. Two weeks later, when the march was finally allowed to proceed, Lewis joined Martin Luther King Jr. and other clergies, leading the way across the bridge and to Montgomery. As of January 2021, a name change for the bridge is in the works (Pettus was a Confederate general and KKK member), with many calling for the name John Lewis Bridge.

### Getting Here and Around

Selma is a good day trip from Montgomery, which is 54 miles away. It's just under two hours to Birmingham from Selma.

# U.S. Space & Rocket Center

## Huntsville, Rocket City

In the early 1950s, the Redstone rocket was developed in Huntsville, launching America's space program. Space, technology, and defense industries remain key economic sectors here. Today, you can experience missions to the moon and beyond at the U.S. Space & Rocket Center, which has a collection of rockets, space memorabilia, and simulators that mimic rocket launches and gravity forces. Go for a guided Sea TREK in the Underwater Astronaut Trainer or act like a military jet pilot at Aviation Challenge. The center runs a bus tour of NASA labs and shuttle test sites.

## Don't Miss

Train like an astronaut at the U.S. Space & Rocket Center's Space Camp and Space Academy. There's a weeklong camp for kids, but adults and families can join the fun, too. 🌐 *www.spacecamp.com.*

## While You're Here

If you're interested in the cosmos, visit Von Braun Astronomical Society. The planetarium might take you back to grade-school field trips, but learning about stars never gets old. Clear night skies over the city's plateaus come to life during astronomy programs presented by society members and guest speakers. The facility, located on a mountain in Monte Sano State Park, includes two telescope-equipped observatories, an astronomical library, and a solar telescope. 🌐 *www.vbas.org.*

## Getting Here and Around

Huntsville is 100 miles north of Birmingham, and about 100 miles southwest of Chattanooga, Tennessee. Both cities have airports; you could also reach Huntsville from Nashville International Airport, about a two-hour drive.

# Roll Tide

### Kings of College Football

Even rivals can't deny the dominance of University of Alabama Crimson Tide, one of the country's winningest teams in college football. In Tuscaloosa, home of the storied team, you'll find that football is more than just a sport, and tailgating during home games is a Saturday ritual, the epitome of game day in the South. The town is also home to some of the most fanatic fans in the land, and visiting Bryant-Denny Stadium and the bars and streets of this college town—where you'll hear raucous shouts of "Roll Tide!"—is quite a spectacle.

### Don't Miss

Tailgating, that all-American pastime of parking among fans and sitting on the back of a pickup truck with a cool beer, is the best way to soak up the atmosphere of Bama's team spirit, even if you don't set foot in the stadium.

### When to Go

Home games against the Crimson Tide's biggest rivals are the most energized (sometimes belligerent) events to attend; throughout the Southeast fans hold fierce loyalties to their teams. Come for the annual Iron Bowl (against the Auburn Tigers), or for games against the Louisiana State Tigers—ticket prices often go up to the hundreds for these hot events.

### Good to Know

In the stadium, see if you can spot the elephant mascot, Big Al, and the team's retro jerseys and helmets.

### Getting Here and Around

Tuscaloosa is a 50-minute drive southwest of Birmingham on Interstate 20, but you can also fly into Tuscaloosa National Airport (TCL).

**The University of Alabama, Bryant-Denny Stadium.** ✉ *920 Paul W. Bryant Dr., Tuscaloosa, AL* 🌐 *www.rolltide.com.*

# When in Alabama

### F. SCOTT AND ZELDA FITZGERALD HOUSE

Literary fans will be jazzed to see the world's only dedicated museum to Scott and Zelda Fitzgerald in Zelda's hometown of Montgomery, where she was born in 1900. The power couple came back to Montgomery to live for about six months from 1931 to 1932 in this house, when Scott was writing *Tender Is the Night,* and Zelda began work on her only published novel, *Save Me the Waltz.*

**Do This:** Plan an hour to explore the museum, and check out Zelda's paintings, Scott's books, various possessions, and their clothing.

**The Scott and Zelda Fitzgerald Museum.** ✉ *919 Felder Ave. No. 919, Montgomery, AL* ☎ *334/264–4222* 🌐 *www.thefitzgeraldmuseum.org.*

### MOBILE MARDI GRAS

Mobile, Alabama, and not New Orleans, has the oldest Mardi Gras celebration in the United States. The carnival festivities started in 1703 when Mobile, then Fort Condé, was the capital of the French colonial empire. The town has been awash in colorful parades and masquerade balls in the weeks leading up to Fat Tuesday ever since. In the heart of busy downtown is Bienville Square, a park with an ornate cast-iron fountain and shaded by centuries-old live oaks. One of the city's main thoroughfares, Dauphin Street, has thriving restaurants, bars, and shops.

**Do This:** Catch beads and—the best prize of all—Moon Pies from the costumed revelers who parade down Dauphin Street. Head to Moe's Original BBQ for a post-parade drink.

### TALLADEGA SUPERSPEEDWAY

Nascar's longest track makes for some serious speeds over 200 mph. The track can also be dangerous, and there have been a few major accidents and deaths, leading some to claim that "Dega" is cursed. Several NASCAR events take place here in a normal year (tickets start around $65). The land around Talladega is pretty and wooded; RV camping is very popular at campgrounds near the speedway, but there are more scenic spots further into the Talladega National Forest. Nearby Cheaha State Park and Cheaha Mountain are especially nice to explore.

**Do This:** Race day or not, you can get close to the cars at the on-site International Motorsports Hall of Fame. A self-guided tour takes about an hour, and showcases three exhibit rooms, the history of NASCAR, and the careers of its legends. There are many cars on display as well as race memorabilia, and guides here often offer an informative tour of the track as well.

**International Motorsports Hall of Fame.** ✉ *3366 Speedway Blvd., Lincoln, AL* 🌐 *www.motorsportshalloffame.com* 🎟 *$12.*

# Cool Place to Stay

**Grand Hotel in Point Clear.** Laze in the sun or get active at one of the Gulf Coast's greatest treasures, circa 1847. The Grand's 550 acres feature contemporary suites, seven restaurants, a 20,000-square-foot, European-style spa, two golf courses, and 10 tennis courts. The pool area has a water park, fountains, geysers, and waterfalls. You can rent sailboats or kayaks at the man-made beach. ✉ *One Grand Blvd., Point Clear, AL* ☎ *251/928–9201* 🌐 *www.marriott.com* [$] *From $385.*

# Florida

Talk about a vacation powerhouse. From Miami's world-famous beach to family-friendly theme parks to the quiet expanse of the Everglades, the Sunshine State has more than its fair share of bucket list–worthy stops. Whether you visit the powdery white beaches of the Panhandle or vibrant coral reefs of the Florida Keys, the ocean is always calling—for sailing, fishing, diving, swimming, and other water sports. Stray off the path a few miles, and you might glimpse a bit of the Florida of old, including cigar makers and mermaids.

## Bucket List Picks

The following boxes contain our picks for the top sights and experiences in Florida.

- ○ Orlando Theme Parks
- ○ The Everglades
- ○ The Florida Keys
- ○ Miami Beach
- ○ Siesta Key
- ○ St. Augustine
- ○ Sanibel Island
- ○ The Emerald Coast
- ○ Crystal River
- ○ Amelia Island
- ○ The Space Coast
- ○ Wynwood, Miami
- ○ Little Havana
- ○ Ocala National Forest
- ○ Fort Lauderdale

# Orlando Theme Parks

## Where the Magic Happens

Walt Disney World and Universal Studios are both bucket list destinations in their own right. The beloved characters of Magic Kingdom, the countries of EPCOT, and the live animals of Animal Kingdom make Disney World a favorite. Universal Studios and Islands of Adventure have loud, fast, high-energy attractions, including the incredible Wizarding World of Harry Potter where muggles can explore a full-scale version of Diagon Alley before boarding a magical train at Platform 9¾.

## Don't Miss

A magical evening in Orlando should include Butterbeer at the Leaky Cauldron in Universal Studios, or fireworks at the Magic Kingdom after dinner in Cinderella's Castle.

## Best Ride

Space Mountain is one of the world's most imaginative roller coasters, takes you on a trip into the depths of outer space—in the dark.

## When to Go

Visit in the fall for the EPCOT Food and Wine Festival.

## Getting Here and Around

Orlando International Airport is about a 20-minute drive to Universal Studios and a 25-minute drive to Magic Kingdom. The parks themselves are about 10 miles apart, but it's best to have two to three days to explore each park.

**Walt Disney World, Magic Kingdom.** ✉ *1180 Seven Seas Dr., Lake Buena Vista, FL* 🌐 *www.disneyworld.disney.go.com* 🎟 *From 109.* **Universal Studios.** ✉ *6000 Universal Blvd., Orlando, FL* 🌐 *www.universalorlando.com* 🎟 *From $109.*

# The Everglades

## America's River of Grass

More than 1.5 million acres of South Florida's 4.3 million acres of subtropical, watery wilderness were given national park status and protection in 1947 with the creation of Everglades National Park. It's one of the country's largest national parks and is recognized by the world community as a Wetland of International Importance, an International Biosphere Reserve, and a World Heritage site.

## Don't Miss

The self-guided Anhinga Trail is the place to spot alligators and swamp wildlife.

## Best Tour

Coopertown is the oldest airboat operator in the Everglades and one of the only airboat operators allowed in national park boundaries. The nearly 75-year-old business offers 35- to 40-minute tours. 🌐 *coopertownairboats.com.*

## When to Go

Winter is the best, and busiest, time to visit the Everglades. Temperatures and mosquito activity are more tolerable, while low water levels concentrate the resident wildlife, and migratory birds settle in for the season.

## Getting Here and Around

Miami International Airport (MIA) is 34 miles from Homestead and 47 miles from the eastern access to Everglades National Park. Southwest Florida International Airport (RSW), in Fort Myers, a little over an hour's drive from Everglades City, is the closest major airport to the Everglades' western entrance.

**The Everglades.** ✉ *40001 State Hwy. 9336, Homestead, FL* 🌐 *www.nps.gov/ever* 🎫 *$30.*

# The Florida Keys

### Most Laid-Back Vacation

The southernmost string of islands in the contiguous United States, where "no shoes, no shirt, no problem" is a way of life, the Keys are like no other place in America. Take an epic road trip from the tippity top (Key Largo) to the tippity bottom (Key West) along Florida Keys Scenic Highway and appreciate the Keys' overflowing bursts of bougainvillea, shimmering waters, and mangrove-lined islands. Whether you snorkel at John Pennekamp Coral Reef State Park in Key Largo or bar crawl in Key West, you're in for major R&R.

### Don't Miss

Key West is the most popular of the Keys. Snap a selfie at the "Southernmost Point of the Continental U.S." buoy before catching sunset on Mallory Square.

### Best Tour

Amusing anecdotes spice up the guided tours of Ernest Hemingway's home. While living here between 1931 and 1942, the author wrote about 70% of his life's work, including classics like *For Whom the Bell Tolls.* 🌐 *www.hemingwayhome.com.*

### Best Key Lime Pie

The signature citrus dessert is on just about every menu in the archipelago, but the best is at Blue Heaven in Key West.

### Good to Know

The Keys provide plenty of boating and snorkeling opportunities, but there are few beaches. The exception is Bahia Honda State Park in Big Pine Key, which has three superb beaches.

### Getting Here and Around

Head south out of Miami towards Highway 1, the only road to the Keys and one that's prone to standstill traffic. It's 60 miles to Key Largo from MIA.

# Miami Beach

## Party in the Magic City

The hub of Miami Beach is South Beach and its energetic Ocean Drive, lined with neon-lit hotel lounges and sidewalk cafés, bronzed cyclists zooming past palm trees, and visitors flocking to see the action. Daylight should be spent on the beach itself, whether Jet Skiing, snapping a picture with the colorful lifeguard towers, or lounging at renowned resorts like Soho Beach House. At dusk, Miami Beach is a hotbed of nightlife with bars and lounges.

## Don't Miss

Drag brunch at the Palace is a great way to embrace the glitz of Ocean Drive. If you're looking for a quieter spot, head inland to Sweet Liberty.

## Best Tour

Take an Art Deco Tour to spot the beach's iconic pastel 1930s–50s architecture, the biggest collection in the world. Snap a pic of the iconic Breakwater or the Colony Hotel on Ocean Drive. 🌐 *www.mdpl.org/tours.*

## Best Nightlife

There's nightlife for every mood and budget in Miami Beach, whether you want to sip craft cocktails by a pool lined in twinkle lights (Broken Shaker) or party 'til dawn at a packed club (LIV).

## When to Go

Winter is high season in Miami Beach, with Art Basel in January and South Beach Food and Wine Festival in February. Low season is summer, when you can get great deals at "Miami Spice" restaurants and Miami Spa Month.

## Getting Here and Around

Cross over Biscayne Bay via 395, 195 to get to Miami Beach from mainland Miami (which is technically a separate city), about a 25-minute drive from Miami International Airport (MIA).

# Siesta Key

## America's Whitest Quartz Sand

Across the water from Sarasota lie the barrier islands of Siesta Key and Lido Key, with myriad beaches, shops, hotels, and some of the whitest sand you've ever seen. Siesta Key beach has fine, powdery quartz sand that squeaks under your feet, very much like the sand along the state's northwestern coast, because it comes from tiny particles that form the rocks of the Appalachian Mountains. With 40 acres of nature trails, Siesta Key is exceptionally wide and long, providing ample space for all types of activities well worth an afternoon or two of your time.

## Don't Miss

Siesta Key really comes to life around sunset on Sundays, with the weekly, festival-like gathering for the Siesta Key Drum Circle. Music, dancing, and oddball entertainment attract a lively crowd of festive spectators and beachgoers; bring a blanket or beach chair and get there early to snag a good spot in the parking lot. 🌐 *www.scgov.net.*

## Best Water Sports

Siesta Sports Rentals rent kayaks, stand-up paddleboards, bikes, beach chairs, scooters, and beach wheelchairs and strollers. Guided kayaking trips are also available. 🌐 *www.siestasportsrentals.com.*

## Best Hotel

Nearby Turtle Beach Resort & Inn is reminiscent of a quieter time; many of the cottages at the warm, affordable, pet-friendly resort date to the 1940s. 🌐 *www.turtlebeachresort.com* [$] *From $475.*

## Getting Here and Around

Many of the large U.S. carriers fly to Sarasota–Bradenton International Airport (SRQ) which is about 11 miles from Siesta Key.

# St. Augustine

## USA's "Oldest" City

Along the banks of the shining Matanzas River in the northeastern corner of Florida lies St. Augustine, the nation's "oldest" city. It shows its age with charm, its history revealed in the narrow cobblestone streets, the horse-drawn carriages festooned with flowers, and the coquina bastions of the Spanish fort that guard the bay like sentinels. Officially invaded in 1565 by Spanish explorers, St. Augustine is the site of the fabled Fountain of Youth, but travelers find additional treasures in the Historic District. Terra-cotta roofs and narrow balconies overhang a wonderful hodgepodge of shops and eateries that can be happily explored for weeks before venturing to the idyllic beaches of Anastasia State Park.

## Don't Miss

Castillo de San Marco is the focal point of St. Augustine. This massive and commanding fort was completed by the Spanish in 1695, and it looks every day of its three-plus centuries.

## Best Tour

Old Town Trolley Tours is the best way to soak up the sights and sounds of the historic district; they offer a few good tour options, including the entertainingly spooky Ghosts & Gravestones Tour. *trolleytours.com/staugustine* *$25.*

## While You're Here

Saint Augustine Distillery is easily the best spirit maker in Florida, and a fun, popular place to take a tour—and get a taste of Florida-made bourbon and cane vodka. *www.staugustinedistillery.com.*

## Getting Here and Around

Jacksonville International Airport (JAX) is the region's air hub (55 miles north of St. Augustine).

# Sanibel Island

## America's Best Shelling Beach

Sanibel Island is so famous for being the world's best shelling ground that there's a term for the stance shell seekers take here when bending over to pick up shells: the telltale "Sanibel stoop." Why's the shelling so great here? It's a function of the unusual east–west orientation of the island's south end. Just as the tide is going out and after storms, the pickings can be superb, and you can carry out bags of conchs, whelks, cockles, and other bivalves and gastropods. (Remember, it's unlawful to pick up live shells.) Away from the beach, flowery vegetation decorates small shopping complexes, pleasant resorts and condo complexes, mom-and-pop motels, and casual restaurants.

## Don't Miss

Shelling is great anywhere along Sanibel's Gulf front. Remote Bowman's Beach (off Sanibel-Captiva Road at Bowman's Beach Road) offers the best shell selection.

## Best Museum

Make Bailey-Matthews National Shelling Museum your first stop and you'll soon be giving your own talks on the beach. ⊕ *www.shellmuseum.org.*

## While You're Here

More than half of Sanibel is occupied by J. N. "Ding" Darling National Wildlife Refuge, a subtly beautiful 6,300 acres of wetlands and jungly mangrove forests named after a conservation-minded Pulitzer prize–winning political cartoonist. ⊕ *www.fws.gov/dingdarling* *$10.*

## Getting Here and Around

Southwest Florida International Airport, in Fort Myers, is the closest to Sanibel (28 miles); it's about 150 miles from the Miami area.

# The Emerald Coast

### Florida's Best-Kept Secret

Beaches along the Gulf Coast from Destin to Panama City have the whitest powdery sand and sparkliest emerald waters in all of Florida. Many of the smaller beaches along the stretch, namely the 16 small towns (including Seaside, WaterColor, and Grayton Beach) strung together along Scenic Highway 30A in South Walton, don't see the same influx of tourists as the rest of the Sunshine State, giving much of the Panhandle the quieter feel of a true local treasure. These towns offer a unique mix of Southern charm, unspoiled nature, and small communities where you can walk or bike everywhere.

### Don't Miss

At Grayton Beach State Park, you can climb sandy trails or paddleboard on lakes that show how Florida was before it was ever developed. Or take a day trip to Seaside, the all-American small town planned to be picture-perfect—so perfect it was the setting for the film *The Truman Show.*

### Best Activity

In WaterColor, try stand-up paddleboarding at the Boathouse—you'll paddle past lily pads and pine trees before you see something very rare: coastal dune lakes. They're only found in a few other places in the world, including New Zealand.

### Good to Know

These beaches don't have your typical sand—it's pure Appalachian quartz that was dropped off by a glacier a few thousand years back, and it's so powder-soft it squeaks.

### Getting Here and Around

Destin–Fort Walton Beach Airport (VPS) serves Florida's Gulf Coast, about 15 miles from Destin. From there it's an easy drive to 30A beach towns like Seaside.

# Crystal River

### Manatee Capital of the World

Situated along Florida's peaceful Nature Coast, Crystal River National Wildlife Refuge is a refuge for the manatee, and its natural-spring area is a low-key getaway spot in one of the most pristine and beautiful areas in the state. It's also one of the few places on the planet where you can legally swim with manatees (while abiding by the manatee sanctuary's strict interaction guidelines). Kings Bay, around which hundreds of manatees congregate in winter, feeds crystal clear water into the river at 72°F year-round.

### Don't Miss

Book a tour at Crystal River National Wildlife Preserve from November to March for the best chance to see manatees. Several companies, such as Crystal Lodge Dive Center, offer swimming tours. Or, book a 2½-hour tour in a crystal clear, glasslike kayak. 🌐 *www.fareharbor.com/getupandgokayaking-crystalsprings.*

### Best Spring

Three Sisters' Springs is the best place to swim and kayak through refreshing natural spring water in Crystal River.

### Good to Know

Sometimes called "sea cows," manatees are aquatic relatives of elephants. They can weigh more than 1,500 pounds and live 50-plus years but move very slowly, making them subject to frequent boat accidents. While they were once endangered, there are now more than 6,000 in Florida's coastal waters. Do your part to ensure their safety by respecting them. Never touch or chase a manatee, and abide by all interaction rules.

### Getting Here and Around

The closest and biggest airport near Crystal River is Tampa International Airport (75 miles).

# Amelia Island

## Florida Beach With a Southern Accent

At the northeasternmost reach of Florida, Amelia Island has beautiful beaches with enormous sand dunes along its eastern flank, a state park with a Civil War fort, sophisticated restaurants, interesting shops, and accommodations that range from bed-and-breakfasts to luxury resorts. The town of Fernandina Beach is on the island's northern end; a century ago casinos and brothels thrived here, but those are gone. Today there's little reminder of the town's wild days, though one event comes close: the Isle of Eight Flags Shrimp Festival, held during the first weekend of May.

## Don't Miss

Fernandina Historic District is home to Florida's oldest lighthouse, oldest bar, oldest hotel, and more than 50 blocks of buildings on the National Register of Historic Places.

## Best Activity

Horseback riding on the beach at Amelia Island State Park is a can't-miss activity. Arrange a ride with Kelly Seahorse Ranch concession within the park. Rides leave the ranch and follow along miles of untouched Atlantic shore. *www.kellyranchinc.net* *$100 per person, per hour.*

## Good to Know

Amelia Island gets its nickname, Isle of the Eight Flags, because it is the only place in the United States where eight different flags have flown: French, Spanish, British, Patriots, Green Cross, Mexican Revolutionary, the Confederacy, and finally the United States.

## Getting Here and Around

Airlines fly nonstop to Jacksonville from major U.S. cities. From Jacksonville, the drive to Amelia Island is about 30 to 45 minutes.

# The Space Coast

## Countdown to Liftoff

America's space program—past, present, and future—is the star of a visit to Florida's Space Coast from Titusville to Melbourne. The region is humming again, and rockets are flying again, thanks to a revitalization of the nation's space program by companies such as SpaceX and Blue Origin. In Cape Canaveral, rockets launch, and in Titusville, you can see the space shuttle *Atlantis* up close. The Kennedy Space Center Visitor Complex is a must-see for anyone interested in America's space program, and Merritt Island National Wildlife refuge has arguably Florida's best bird-watching. The area is also home to a popular cruise ship port, Port Canaveral, and the laid-back town of Cocoa Beach, where surfing champion Kelly Slater caught his first wave.

## Don't Miss

Within Canaveral National Seashore, Playalinda Beach—the longest stretch of undeveloped coast on Florida's Atlantic seaboard—provides one of the best views for rocket launches.

## Best Activity

No trip to Florida would be complete without a visit to the Kennedy Space Center's Space Shuttle Atlantis exhibit, where a full day can be spent experiencing the life and history of the American space shuttle program. *www.kennedyspacecenter.com* *$57.*

## While You're Here

The Exploration Tower at Port Canaveral is equal parts museum and scenic overlook, and the seventh-floor observation deck offers views of the ocean and space center.

## Getting Here and Around

The region's location just 50 miles east of Orlando makes it a popular destination for side trips from Walt Disney World and beach getaways pre- or post-cruise.

# Wynwood, Miami

## America's Coolest Street Art

Miami Beach may win the popularity contest, but Wynwood is undoubetdly the Magic City's coolest neighborhood—one that's become an international hot spot for street artists. With an impressive mix of colorful murals, one-of-a-kind shops and art galleries, public art displays, see-and-be-seen bars, breweries, slick restaurants, and plenty of eye-popping graffiti, it's the grungy artistic side of Miami you don't see on the beach (the Brooklyn of Miami, you might say).

## Don't Miss

Check out the Wynwood Walls, a cutting-edge enclave of modern urban murals, reflecting diversity in graffiti and street art. More than 50 well-known and lesser-known artists including Shepard Fairey have transformed 80,000 square feet of warehouse walls into an outdoor museum of sorts.

## Best Nightlife

The neighborhood is known for its nightlife scene, whether you prefer a come-as-you-are bar (Gramps) to a festive brewery (Veza Sur) to a sports bar (Grails) or the many late-night clubs in between.

## When to Go

Any time is a good time to visit Wynwood, but come in February for its contemporary art fair, Art Wynwood. ⊕ *www.artwynwood.com.*

## Getting Here and Around

Wynwood is located north of Downtown Miami, between Interstate 95 and Northeast 1st Avenue from 29th to 22nd Streets (it's a 30-minute drive from Miami Beach). Parking is a pain, so it's best to take a rideshare and explore the district on foot.

**Wynwood Walls.** ✉ *2520 NW 2nd Ave., Miami, FL* ⊕ *www.miamiandbeaches.com/neighborhoods/wynwood.*

# Little Havana

## Heart of Cuban Culture

First settled en masse by Cubans in the early 1960s, after Cuba's Communist revolution, Little Havana is the core of Miami's Hispanic community. Lined with cigar factories, cafés selling guava pastries and rose-petal flan, botanicas brimming with candles, and Cuban clothes and crafts stores, the area's sights and sounds transport you to Old Havana, an authentic slice of the vibrant culture in the United States. Giant hand-painted roosters span the neighborhood, an artistic nod to real-life counterparts that roam the streets.

## Don't Miss

Your "Welcome to Little Havana" photo op shines on 27th Avenue and 8th Street. Afterward, watch a slice of Old Havana unfold in Domino Park, where the community gathers to play.

## Best Restaurant

You can't leave without ordering a heaping platter of *lechón asado* (roasted pork loin) or *ropa vieja* (shredded beef) at cheap, no-frills institution, Versailles. For something more atmospheric, head to Cafe La Trova.

## Best Nightlife

Salsa dance with a Cuba libre in hand at Ball & Chain, a legendary bar circa 1935 that nods to Old Havana. Afterward, order ice cream next door at Azucar Ice Cream Company, known for its guava-flavored Abuela Maria.

## Getting Here and Around

Located in mainland Miami, Little Havana's semiofficial boundaries are 27th Avenue to 4th Avenue on the west, Miami River to the north, and Southwest 13th Street to the south. You'll need to drive (or Uber/Lyft) into Little Havana, since public transportation here is limited; but once on Calle Ocho, it's best to experience the neighborhood on foot.

**Little Havana.** ✉ *S.W. 8th St., Miami, FL.*

# Ocala National Forest

## Dive Into Florida's Natural Springs

Florida at its most natural, this breathtaking 383,000-acre national forest off Route 40 has lakes, springs, rivers, hiking trails, campgrounds, and historic sites. It also has the largest off-highway vehicle trail system in the Southeast and three major recreational areas: Alexander Springs, Salt Springs, and Juniper Springs. Alexander Springs, with its crystal clear water reflecting the bright Florida sky, sandy bottom, and consistent temperature around 70°F, is great for swimming. At Juniper Springs, you'll find a stone waterwheel house, a campground, a natural-spring swimming pool, and hiking trails. Canoe rentals operate inside the national forest. The draw to Salt Springs is a natural saltwater spring where Atlantic blue crabs come to spawn each summer.

## Don't Miss

The Black Bear Scenic Byway is a picturesque drive from Silver Springs to the Atlantic Coast at Ormond Beach—and through the heart of Ocala National Forest.

## Best Stop

Silver Springs, a park at the Forest's western edge, has the world's largest collection of artesian springs, the last uninhabited spring run in Florida. Visitors can canoe, kayak, ride in a glass-bottom boat, hike, camp, and picnic. The park, inhabited by hundreds of rhesus monkeys, was the setting for many *Tarzan* movies. *silversprings.com.*

## Getting Here and Around

Ocala National Forest is an hour south of Gainesville, and a little over an hour north of Orlando.

**Ocala National Forest.** *17147 E. State Rd. 40, Silver Springs, FL www.fs.usda.gov/ocala.*

# Fort Lauderdale

### The Venice of America

More than 165 miles of canals and waterways earned Fort Lauderdale the nickname "the Venice of America," but it's also been dubbed the Yachting Capital of the World. Take to the waterways to appreciate this coastal beauty, one of the best places to boat right up to a restaurant in South Florida. Explore expansive beaches, showstopping resort hotels, an exploding food scene, and a burgeoning cultural scene.

### Don't Miss

What Lincoln Road is to South Beach, Las Olas Boulevard is to Fort Lauderdale. The street is home to the city's best shops and restaurants.

### Best Tour

At once a sightseeing tour and a mode of transportation, the water taxi is a smart way to experience most of Fort Lauderdale and Hollywood's waterways. There are 15 scheduled stops and on-demand whistle stops, and the system has three connected routes: the Fort Lauderdale, the Margaritaville Express, and the New River Route. It's possible to cruise all day while taking in the sights. 🌐 *watertaxi.com* 🎫 *$28.*

### Best Restaurant

Boat right up to Casa Sensei, a waterfront restaurant along the Himmarshee Canal. 🌐 *casasensei.com.*

### When to Go

Time your visit for the Fort Lauderdale International Boat Show in October, when the Yachting Capital of the World displays more than 1,000 types of boats and superyachts. (🌐 *www.flibs.com*).

### Getting Here and Around

Fly into Miami (MIA) or Fort Lauderdale (FLL). While you can use the water taxi to get around, you can also order Uber/Lyft.

## When in Florida

### THE DALÍ MUSEUM

Inside and out, the waterfront Dalí Museum is almost as remarkable as the Spanish surrealist's work. The state-of-the-art building has a surreal geodesic-like glass structure called the Dalí Enigma, as well as an outdoor labyrinth and a DNA-inspired spiral staircase leading up to the collection. The mind-expanding paintings in this downtown headliner include *Eggs on a Plate Without a Plate, The Hallucinogenic Toreador,* and more than 90 other oils. You'll also discover more than 2,000 additional works including watercolors, drawings, sculptures, photographs, and objets d'art. The museum also hosts temporary collections from the likes of Pablo Picasso and Andy Warhol. Free hour-long tours are led by well-informed docents.

**Do This:** The Tampa–St. Pete's region has its share of boutique districts, spotted with shops and sidewalk cafés; Tampa's Hyde Park Village and downtown St. Petersburg's Beach Drive are among the top picks if you're looking to check out some upscale shops and dine alfresco while getting the most of the area's pleasant climate.

**The Dalí Museum.** ✉ *1 Dali Blvd., St. Petersburg, FL* ☎ *727/823–3767* 🌐 *www.thedali.org* 🎟 *$25.*

### FLORA-BAMA MULLET TOSS

You may exclaim, "now I've seen everything" after witnessing this event at the world-famous Flora-Bama Lounge in Perdido Key, which sits atop a beautiful beach on the state line between—you guessed it—Florida and Alabama. The beach lounge is home to the annual "Mullet Toss," in which lively locals compete to see who can throw a fish farthest across the state line drawn in the sand (and drink the most beer).

**Do This:** Drive, boat, or paddleboard in to the Flora-Bama Yacht Club, a waterfront open-air eatery that serves fresh Gulf seafood. Stay for the live music on the beach, or head over to the Flora-Bama bar if you're in the mood for a wild night out. 🌐 *www.florabamayachtclub.com.*

**Flora-Bama Mullet Toss Event.** ✉ *17401 Perdido Key Dr., Perdido Key, FL* ☎ *850/492–0611* 🌐 *www.florabama.com/mullet-toss* 🎟 *$15.*

### MANSIONS OF PALM BEACH

Long reigning as the place where the crème de la crème go to shake off winter's chill, Palm Beach continues to be a seasonal hotbed of platinum-grade consumption. It's been the winter address for heirs of the iconic Rockefeller, Vanderbilt, Colgate, Post, Kellogg, and Kennedy families. Strict laws govern everything from building to landscaping, and not so much as a pool awning gets added without a town council nod.

**Do This:** Whether you aspire to be a former president or a rock legend (Kennedy, John Lennon, Rod Stewart, Jimmy Buffett—all onetime or current Palm Beach residents), no trip to the island is complete without gawking at the megamansions lining its perfectly manicured streets. Start at Casa de Leoni on 450 Worth Avenue before heading to Il Palmetto on 1500 South Ocean Boulevard.

### WEEKI WACHEE MERMAID SHOW

At Weeki Wachee Springs, the spring flows at the remarkable rate of 170 million gallons a day with a constant temperature of 74°F. The spring has long been famous for something only Florida would think up: live "mermaids," clearly not the work of Mother Nature, as they wear bright costumes and put on an Esther Williams–like underwater choreography show that's been virtually unchanged since the park opened in 1947. The park is considered a classic piece of Florida history and culture. In summer, Buccaneer Bay water park opens for swimming, beaching, and riding its thrilling slides and flumes.

**Do This:** Take a snorkel tour of the river, paddle a canoe, or board a wilderness boat ride for an up-close look at raccoons, otters, egrets, and other semitropical Florida wetlands wildlife.

**Weeki Wachee Springs.** ✉ *6131 Commercial Way, Spring Hill, FL* ☎ *352/597–8484* 🌐 *www.weekiwachee.com* 🎟 *$13.*

## Cool Places to Stay

**Castle Hotel.** An I-Drive landmark for more than 20 years, Marriott's Autograph Collection took over in recent years and transformed it from kitschy to classy: from a pink and purple cartoon castle to a sophisticated refuge of white and silver, filled with art. The rooftop terrace offers views of Universal—and Hogwarts Castle—along with the nightly fireworks. The courtyard's round, heated swimming pool offers a serene escape from International Drive's frenzy. ✉ *8629 International Dr., Orlando, FL* ☎ *407/345–1511* 🌐 *www.marriott.com.* [$] *From $100.*

**Faena Hotel.** This towering beachfront property on Miami Beach is a stunning reinvention of the art deco 1948 Saxony Hotel with dramatic common areas and prolific art installations. Gawk at the details throughout the "Cathedral" lobby, which glitters with gold-leafed columns, or scope out nirvana at the 22,000-square-foot, high-design Tierra Santa Spa, which is rooted in South America's rich indigeneous culture. Enjoy some burlesque in the 220-seat dinner theater and later retreat to your glamorous room, decked out in art deco–style interiors. ✉ *3201 Collins Ave. Miami Beach, FL* 🌐 *www.faena.com/miami-beach* [$] *From $600.*

**Grayton Beach Camping.** One of the most scenic spots along the Gulf Coast, this 2,220-acre park has salt marshes, rolling dunes covered with sea oats, crystal-white sand, and contrasting blue-green waters. There's swimming, fishing, and snorkeling here, as well as hiking on many trails around the marsh and woods, and an elevated boardwalk that winds over the dunes to the beach. Thirty fully equipped cabins and a campground provide overnight options; cabins sleep up to six, and the beach is a leisurely five-minute walk away via a private boardwalk. ✉ *8300 Main Park Rd., Santa Rosa Beach, FL* 🌐 *floridastateparks.reserveamerica.com.* [$] *From $110.*

**Jules' Undersea Lodge.** Dive 30 feet below the surface to sleep with the fishes at the only undersea hotel in the United States, located in Florida's snorkeling and diving capital, Key Largo. Aquatic life swims past a glass dome over the bedroom, but there are still some comforts of land, including a microwave, TV, and refrigerator. ✉ *51 Shoreland Dr., Key Largo, FL* ☎ *305/451–2353* 🌐 *jul.com* [$] *From $675.*

**Life House Little Havana.** Inspired by the Cuban heritage of Little Havana, these tropical, retro digs make you feel like you've discovered a truly local Miami—one that's heating up. Stay in seriously cool adult bunk beds complete with their own wooden staircase, get cozy at the rooftop bar and community living room, grab vegan food at Parcela restaurant, and lie in hammocks in the lush courtyard. ✉ *528 S.W. 9th Ave., Miami, FL* ☎ *866/466–7534* 🌐 *www.lifehousehotels.com* [$] *From $200.*

# Georgia

Georgia encompasses two Souths—the Old South of Savannah with its elegant homes, planned squares, and Spanish moss–draped live oaks, and the New South of Atlanta, a bustling high-rise metropolis with enough to keep visitors busy for weeks. For white-columned mansions and visions of the past, look no further than central Georgia. There's coastline here, too, with lush barrier islands stretching all the way to Florida.

## Bucket List Picks

The following boxes contain our picks for the top sights and experiences in Georgia.

- ○ Atlanta's BeltLine
- ○ Athens
- ○ Jekyll Island
- ○ Tybee Island
- ○ Cumberland Island
- ○ Savannah
- ○ Okefenokee Swamp
- ○ Martin Luther King, Jr. National Historical Park
- ○ Blue Ridge and the Chattahoochee Forest
- ○ Georgia Aquarium

# Atlanta's BeltLine

## The Great Connector

A 33-mile railway turned greenway, the BeltLine is an outdoor oasis of trails and parks that encircles Atlanta's urban metropolis, connecting more than 40 neighborhoods (and continuously expanding). During the warmer months, you can expect to find a consistent stream of people biking, jogging, or walking as they make their way around Old Fourth Ward, West End, and Virginia-Highland. On any given day, you can take a yoga class or attend a festival in one of the green spaces that run along the loop.

## Don't Miss

The Eastside Trail section of the BeltLine links to great dining and hangout options, like Krog Street Market, Rathbun's, and Ladybird Grove & Mess Hall.

## Good to Know

While exploring the Eastside Trail, you can stop into the Atlanta BeltLine Center (between Historic Fourth Ward Park and Krog Street Tunnel) for an air-conditioned break and to learn more about the greenspace and the neighborhoods it connects.

## While You're Here

Piedmont Park runs just off the northeast section of the BeltLine and is the perfect place to escape the frenetic energy of the city for a picnic with smashing views of the Midtown skyline.

## Getting Here and Around

Walkable stretches of the BeltLine can be found on the east (Old Fourth Ward and Virginia Highland) and west (West End) sides of the city, but there are ambitious plans to expand. To bike the trail, rent from Atlanta Bicycle Barn or pick up a bike from any of the Relay Bike Share stations near the BeltLine.

**Atlanta BeltLine Center.** ✉ *112 Krog St. NE No. 14, Atlanta, GA* 🌐 *beltline.org.*

# Athens

## Rock Powerhouse

An artistic jewel of the American South, Athens is known as a breeding ground for famed rock groups such as the B-52s and R.E.M. It's no wonder creative types from all over the country flock to its trendy streets in hopes of becoming, or catching a glimpse of, the next big act to take the world by storm. At the center of this musical whirlwind is the University of Georgia (UGA), giving the quaint but compact city a distinct flavor that falls somewhere between a misty Southern enclave, a rollicking college town, and a smoky, jazz club–studded alleyway. Of course, it all goes "to the Dawgs" if the home team is playing on home turf, with students taking over the bars, but even then, Athens remains a blend of Mayberry and MTV. The effect is as irresistible as it is authentic.

## Don't Miss

You must make a pilgrimage to 40 Watt Club, a famed indie-rock club known for helping to launch the careers of R.E.M., the B-52s, and other local bands that grew out of the college scene. Nirvana, the Flaming Lips, and Sonic Youth all played here back in the day. Today, you'll see a mix of local and national acts gracing the stage—from country to punk to pop. 🌐 *www.40watt.com.*

## While You're Here

Find funky dive bars like Sister Louisa's Church throughout town, try craft beers at Creature Comfort Brewery, and eat killer cuisine at Five & Ten and Seabear Oyster Bar.

## Getting Here and Around

Athens is about 70 miles east of Atlanta on Interstate 20. The downtown and campus area are very walkable.

# Jekyll Island

## Relax Like a Rockefeller

From the Gilded Age to the Great Depression, the Vanderbilts and Rockefellers, Morgans and Astors, Macys, Pulitzers, and Goodyears all shuttered their 5th Avenue castles and retreated to elegant cottages on the wild coastal island of Jekyll Island. It's been said that when the island's distinguished winter residents were all "in," a sixth of the world's wealth was represented. Jekyll Island is still a 7½-mile playground, but it's no longer restricted to the rich and famous. A water park, picnic grounds, and facilities for golf, tennis, fishing, biking, and jogging are all open to the public. One side of the island is lined by nearly 10 miles of hard-packed Atlantic beaches; the other by the intracoastal waterway and picturesque salt marshes. Deer and wild turkey inhabit interior forests of pine, magnolia, and moss-veiled live oaks. Egrets, pelicans, herons, and sandpipers skim the gentle surf.

## Don't Miss

Jekyll Island's clean, mostly uncommercialized public beaches are free and open year-round.

## A Closer Look

Head to Jekyll Island Club Resort for a glimpse of the island's glorious heyday. The sprawling 1887 resort was once described as "the richest, the most exclusive, the most inaccessible club in the world," and its old-world charm persists. 🌐 *www.jekyllclub.com.*

## Getting Here and Around

Many choose to fly into Jacksonville International Airport (JAX) to reach Jekyll Island (65 miles south); Savannah/Hilton Head International Airport (SAV) is 90 miles north, and Atlanta is about a five-hour drive. By car, travel through Brunswick and take the Jekyll Island Causeway ($6 per car per day).

# Tybee Island

## Frolic With Dolphins

This barrier island east of Savannah, formerly known as Savannah Beach, has been a destination since the 1920s, when a train connected downtown to the beach pavilion where jazz bands played. These days the island is a mix of kitschy shops and interesting restaurants, making a wonderfully quirky beach town. Whether you're looking to work on your tan, spend a day on a fishing charter, or paddle around in a kayak, this is a must-see during the summer months. Best of all, Tybee Island's myriad water activities, including stand-up paddleboarding and cruises, can help you catch a glimpse of the island's dolphins.

## Don't Miss

Kayaking off Tybee Island via Captain Mike's or Captain Derek's outposts is an unforgettable experience, and you just might get close to schools of dolphins. For those really wanting to ditch the world, the paddle from Tybee Island to the uninhabited barrier island of Little Tybee is the perfect remedy. The only beings you'll see are egrets, ibis, osprey, Atlantic bottlenose dolphins, and maybe a manatee or two along the way.

## Need a Break?

For lunch on Tybee, It's hard to beat the huge patio overlooking bird-filled marshlands at the casual Crab Shack, with a diverse menu featuring seafood platters, barbecue, and sandwiches.

## Getting Here and Around

Tybee is a short (15- to 20-minute drive) from Savannah and its airport (SAV).

# Cumberland Island

### Vacation Like a Carnegie

This 18-mile spit of land off the coast of St. Marys is a national treasure, with nearly unspoiled sanctuary of marshes, dunes, beaches, forests, lakes, and ponds. Although it has a long history of human habitation, it remains much as nature created it: a dense, lacework canopy of live oak shades, sand roads, and foot trails through a thick undergrowth of palmetto. Wild horses roam freely on the pristine beaches, and waterways are home to gators, sea turtles, otters, and more than 300 species of birds. During the 1880s, the family of Thomas Carnegie (brother of Andrew) built several lavish homes here.

### Don't Miss

The 36,347-acre Cumberland Island National Seashore has pristine forests and marshes marbled with wooded nature trails, 18 miles of beaches, and opportunities for fishing, bird-watching, and viewing the ruins of Thomas Carnegie's great estate, Dungeness.

### Where to Stay

Hike in to one of the island's pretty campsites, or book a night at the famed Greyfield Inn, the 1900 Carnegie home turned resort, sitting on 1,000 private acres on the island's south side.

### Good to Know

Bear in mind that since there are no facilities, you must bring everything you need, including your own food, drinks, and sunscreen.

### Getting Here and Around

The only way to access the island is by private boat or via the *Cumberland Queen II* ferry from St. Marys (45 minutes). The passenger ferry allows no cars, so prepare to explore the island on foot. St. Marys is about two hours south of Savannah by car.

# Savannah

## Historic Squares and Southern Charm

Dripping with Southern charm, Savannah beckons with stately architecture, rich history, and a culinary scene that spans classic down-home cooking to James Beard Award nominees. This is the place to appreciate art in lauded museums, people-watch in flower-filled squares, and imagine the past as you walk under canopies of live oaks draped in Spanish moss in Forsyth Park.

## Don't Miss

As America's first planned city, Savannah is perhaps most recognized for its 22 squares, the diverse group of parks that dot the Historic District. Telfair (home to the Owens-Thomas House), Franklin (site of the historic First African Baptist Church), and Monterey (full of history and pretty views), are just some of the best squares to visit.

## Good to Know

Purchase a Telfair Museums ticket ($20) for access to modern art, beautiful antiquities, and a traditional 19th-century Savannah mansion, the Owens-Thomas House.

## While You're Here

Check out hot restaurants like The Grey or Husk, and head to the rooftop bar at Peregrin on Perry Street, where gorgeous views include the Cathedral Basilica of St. John the Baptist.

## Best Museum

SCAD Museum of Art, an architectural marvel that rose from the ruins of the oldest surviving railroad building in the United States, covers fashion and African American arts and culture. 🌐 *www.scadmoa.org.*

## Getting Here and Around

Savannah/Hilton Head International Airport (SAV) is about a 20-minute drive from downtown. Savannah is 100 miles from Charleston.

# Okefenokee Swamp

### Land of the Trembling Earth

Larger than all of Georgia's barrier islands combined, the Okefenokee National Wildlife Refuge covers 700 square miles of southeastern Georgia and northeastern Florida, and is the largest intact freshwater wetlands in the contiguous United States. The term "swamp" hardly does the Okefenokee justice; the refuge contains numerous and varied landscapes, including aquatic prairies, towering virgin cypress, sandy pine islands, and lush subtropical hammocks. Alligators, otters, bobcats, white-tailed deer, turtles, bald eagles, red-tailed hawks, herons, cranes, and black bears all make their home here.

### Don't Miss

At Okefenokee's southwestern entrance, Stephen C. Foster State Park is an 80-acre island park offering trips to the headwaters of the Suwannee River, Billy's Island. The park is home to hundreds of species of birds and a large cypress-and-black-gum forest, a majestic backdrop for one of the thickest growths of vegetation in the southeastern United States.

### Best Tour

Many choose to visit on a day trip, but real adventurers can go deeper, securing a permit for multiday itineraries along the nearly 120 miles of boat trails. Book a guided overnight canoe trip with Okefenokee Adventures for a memorable experience. 🌐 *www.okefenokeeadventures.com.*

### Getting Here and Around

Located about two hours south of Savannah, there are three main entrances to Okefenokee: the main entrance is outside of Folkston, GA; western entrance (Stephen C. Foster Park) just east of Fargo, GA; and the northern entrance (Okefenokee Swamp Park) is outside the town of Waycross.

## Martin Luther King, Jr. National Historical Park

### Walk in MLK's Footsteps

Dr. Martin Luther King Jr. grew up in a home off of Auburn Avenue. His former home is now a National Historic Site that's part of 35 acres dedicated to the civil rights leader. A very short walk from Dr. King's childhood home are blocks full of significant monuments and museums related to Dr. King, including the King Center and Ebenezer Baptist Church. At the King Center, you'll see the crypt of Dr. King and Coretta Scott King, and the Eternal Flame. Nearby is the International Civil Rights Walk of Fame.

### Don't Miss

Ebenezer Baptist Church, the district's Gothic revival–style church, came to be known as the spiritual center of the civil rights movement. Members of the King family preached at the church for three generations. Sitting in the sanctuary on a quiet day when light is shining through the stained-glass windows can be a powerful experience.

### Planning Your Time

Set aside at least an hour or two to walk around Auburn Avenue and its many surrounding monuments, historical buildings, and the World Peace Rose Garden.

### Good to Know

A limited number of visitors are allowed to tour MLK's Birth Home each day, and must be arranged once on-site. Arrive early to sign up.

### Getting Here and Around

King Memorial Transit station is the Marta stop here, and there is an even more convenient Atlanta Streetcar (tram) stop across from the Ebenezer Baptist Church.

**Martin Luther King, Jr. National Historical Park.** ✉ *450 Auburn Ave. NE Atlanta, GA* 🌐 *www.nps.gov/malu.*

# Blue Ridge and the Chattahoochee Forest

## A Breath of Fresh Mountain Air

North Georgia, home to the 750,000-acre Chattahoochee National Forest, is known for its abundant natural wonders and its cool mountain air. Blue Ridge is one of the most pleasant small mountain towns here. After you've eaten breakfast or lunch and shopped for antiques, gifts, or crafts at Blue Ridge's many small shops, you can explore the scenic surroundings; Fannin County (of which Blue Ridge is the county seat) is known as the "Trout Capital of Georgia," and the beautiful Toccoa River is a popular destination for fly-fishing, hiking, canoeing, and more. Just 15 miles southwest of Blue Ridge is the scenic town of Ellijay. Billed as "Georgia's Apple Capital," Ellijay is popular for its orchards and antiques shops.

## Don't Miss

Brasstown Bald, about 50 miles east of Blue Ridge, is the highest peak in Georgia and home to fun, rigorous hikes; south of Blue Ridge is Springer Mountain, the southern endpoint of the Appalachian Trail.

## Best Tour

Ride the rails on Blue Ridge Scenic Railway's four-hour, 26-mile round-trip excursion along the Toccoa River. The trip includes a stop in McCaysville, smack on the Georgia–Tennessee state line. 🌐 *www.brscenic.com.*

## When to Go

Visit in fall, when roadside stands brimming with ripe apples dot the landscape. The annual Georgia Apple Festival takes place on the second and third weekends of October.

## Getting Here and Around

It's an easy drive from Atlanta to the Georgia foothills, about a 1½-hour trip to the town of Blue Ridge.

# Georgia Aquarium

## America's Largest Aquarium

With more than 10 million gallons of water, Atlanta's wildly popular Georgia Aquarium is the nation's largest. The 604,000-square-foot building, an architectural marvel resembling the bow of a ship, has tanks of various sizes filled with more than 80,000 animals, representing 500 species. You'll spot beluga whales, dolphins, stingrays, and more floating past. But not everything has gills: there are also penguins, sea lions, sea otters, river otters, sea turtles, and giant octopuses. Admission includes entry to all public exhibits, shows, and galleries.

## Don't Miss

The aquarium's 6.3-million-gallon Ocean Voyager Gallery is the world's largest indoor marine exhibit, with 4,574 square feet of viewing windows that bring you face to face with whale sharks, the largest fish in the world.

## Best Tour

The aquarium offers 45-minute behind-the-scenes tours every half hour and daily dolphin shows; but to go further, swim with sea creatures on a diving adventure through the Ocean Voyager exhibit—or even cage dive with sharks ($240–$280).

## While You're Here

It's easy to combine a trip to the aquarium with a visit to several notable sites within walking distance: the National Center for Civil and Human Rights, Centennial Olympic Park, and the World of Coca-Cola Museum.

## Getting Here and Around

There are two Marta stations near the aquarium, at Civic Center and Peachtree Center.

**Georgia Aquarium.** ✉ *225 Baker St. NW, Atlanta, GA* 🌐 *www.georgiaaquarium.org* 🎫 *$35.95.*

## When in Georgia

### ATLANTA UNITED FC SOCCER CLUB

Atlanta United home games at Mercedes-Benz Stadium (shared with the Atlanta Falcons) have broken attendance records in recent years, carrying with them a welcome air of excitement about soccer that feels international. The team has one of the largest fan bases in all of U.S. soccer, and won the MLS Cup in 2018, and the U.S. Open and Campeones Cups in 2019.

**Do This:** The Brewhouse Cafe, Eldertree Public House, and Midway are some of Atlanta's best soccer pubs.

**Mercedes-Benz Stadium.** ✉ *409 Nelson St. SW, Atlanta, GA* ☎ *470/341–1500* 🌐 *www.atlutd.com.*

### ETOWAH INDIAN MOUNDS

Dating back to AD 1000, this prominent site of Mississippian culture is the place to see and learn about the way of life of the Southeast's early peoples. Aside from the six mounds here (large earthen hills with flat tops, used by the Etowah people as foundations to important buildings, the largest being the temple mound), there is a plaza, a river trail, and a museum with artifacts and art on display.

**Do This:** Walk the 1.1 mile interpretive trail (marked with educational and historic signposts) along the Etowah River.

**Etowah Indian Mounds.** ✉ *Cartersville, GA* ☎ *770/387–3747* 🌐 *www.gastateparks.org/EtowahIndianMounds* 🎫 *$6.*

### MARY MAC'S TEA ROOM

Local celebrities and ordinary folks have lined up for the country-fried steak and fried chicken here since 1945. In the Southern tradition, the servers will call you "honey" and pat your arm to assure you that everything's all right. It's a great way to experience Southern food and hospitality all at once.

**Do This:** There's no better place in Atlanta to try Southern favorites like fried chicken, collard greens, fried okra, mac and cheese, and sweet tea.

**Mary Mac's Tea Room.** ✉ *224 Ponce de Leon Ave. Atlanta, GA* ☎ *404/876–1800* 🌐 *www.marymacs.com*

### PROVIDENCE CANYON

Dubbed Georgia's "Little Grand Canyon" for its stunning red rocks, Providence Canyon is within driving distance from many Southern cities and well worth a day of hiking. The 1,000-acre park has 16 canyons layered in red rock of at least 43 shades, from deep ruby to peach. Ten miles of hiking loops in the park allow access to the canyons, many of which you can walk through. The formations were created not by natural forces but poor farming practices in the 1800s which destroyed and eroded the land, and these staggering canyons are also a sobering reminder of the toll human interference can take on our environment.

**Do This:** Hike the Canyon Loop Trail, blazed with white markers and a 2.5-mile loop starting at the visitor center. The easy hike allows access to Canyons 1 through 9, which are marked with signposts. Note that the climb up the canyons is steep and rough.

**Providence Canyon.** ✉ *Lumpkin, GA* ☎ *229/838–6202* 🌐 *www.gastateparks.org/ProvidenceCanyon* 🎫 *Parking $5.*

### TALLULAH GORGE STATE PARK

The 1,000-foot-deep Tallulah Gorge is one of the most impressive in the country. In the late 1800s this area was one of the most visited destinations in the Southeast, drawing tourists who came to see the roaring falls on the Tallulah River. Then, in 1912, to provide electric power, the "Niagara of the South" was dammed, and the falls and tourism dried up. Today the State of Georgia has designated more than 20 miles of the state park as walking and mountain-biking trails. There are also a 16,000-square-foot interpretive center, a 63-acre lake with a beach, a picnic shelter, and 50 tent and RV sites.

**Do This:** Take to the 80-foot-high suspension bridge (part of the Hurricane Falls Loop Trail) and imagine the tightrope walkers that twice braved such heights at the gorge.

**Tallulah Gorge.** ✉ *Tallulah Falls, GA* ☎ *706/754–7981* 🌐 *www.gastateparks.org/TallulahGorge* 🎫 *Parking $5.*

## Cool Places to Stay

**Amethyst Garden Inn.** With plenty of historical appeal of its own, this tall, purple Victorian is within walking distance to Savannah's Historic District and Forsyth Park. The inn stands out for its bright jewel tones and ornate decor in its interior, where you'll be graciously served decadent Southern breakfasts with fluffy biscuits and cheesy grits. Alongside the antiques, canopy beds, and crystal chandeliers, modern comforts include high-quality linens, private bathrooms, and a pool. ✉ *402 E. Gaston St., Savannah, GA* ☎ *912/234–7716* 🌐 *www.amethystgardensavannah.com* $ *From $325.*

**Candlelight Forest.** On a dreamy 250-acre property in the forests of northwest Georgia (near Cloudland Canyons State Park and Lookout Mountain), your pick of unique accommodations include a mountain craftsmen home, two sophisticated tree houses, and a lodge reminiscent of a European fairy tale. Lawn games, outdoor movies, fire pits, and hammocks help visitors enjoy nights here; days are for hiking and visiting with the property's pygmy goats. When you tire of the rustic setting and activities—and visiting nearby waterfalls and lakes—the city of Chattanooga, Tennessee, is a 25-minute drive. ✉ *9862 Hwy. 193 Chickamauga, GA* 🌐 *www.candlelightforest.com* $ *From $196.*

**Graduate Athens.** Centered around a former ironworks facility, this hip boutique hotel offers fresh, modern rooms, a full-service spa, a coffee shop, and a restaurant and livé-music venue—aptly named the Foundry. The property underwent a complete renovation in 2015, so the atmosphere is historic but modern and playful. With the inn's great amenities and villagelike setting, there's little need to leave the property, but if you do, you'll find the Classic Center Theater, the university campus, and historic downtown within easy walking distance. ✉ *295 Dougherty St., Athens, GA* ☎ *706/549–7020* 🌐 *www.graduatehotels.com/athens* $ *From $197.*

**Hotel Clermont.** There's no better stay within walking distance of Ponce City Market and the BeltLine, and for a cool factor combined with modern conveniences and vintage touches, there may be no better stay in Atlanta. Lush foliage and wicker and rattan seating welcome you in the lobby, as does an ice-cold PBR in honor of legendary stripper Blondie, whom you may be lucky enough to catch at the downstairs lounge. The building itself dates to 1924, but with spacious rooms, foolproof complimentary Wi-Fi, and freshly made kombucha in the café, the experience is far from old-school. ✉ *789 Ponce De Leon Ave. NE, Atlanta, GA* ☎ *470/485–0485* 🌐 *www.hotelclermont.com* $ *From $336.*

# Kentucky

From bourbon distilleries and horse races to Mammoth Cave—the longest cave system in the world—there's plenty to check off your to-do list in the "Bluegrass State." If you happen to be in the horse-farm region around Lexington early in spring, notice the sea of tiny buds in the fields of Kentucky: bluegrass does indeed have a bluish-purple color. This lush carpet of bluegrass grows in limestone-based soil, rich in calcium and phosphates, making it ideal feed for the Thoroughbred racehorses that are raised in the region.

## Bucket List Picks

The following boxes contain our picks for the top sights and experiences in Kentucky.

- ○ Kentucky Bourbon Trail
- ○ Lexington Horse Country
- ○ Kentucky Derby
- ○ University of Kentucky Basketball
- ○ Louisville's Museum Row
- ○ Mammoth Cave
- ○ Lexington's Distillery District
- ○ Bluegrass Country
- ○ Red River Gorge

## Kentucky Bourbon Trail

### Top-Shelf Tour

Kentucky, where bourbon was first commercially produced in 1783, still makes close to 95% of the world's bourbon (and more than 2 million barrels a year!), making it the definitive home of the spirit. Visit the country's top distilleries around Louisville and Lexington, a picturesque area full of rolling hills of the lush bluish grass that earns the state its nickname. There's a storied history to whiskey here (you'll get a mouthful of it while touring), but the bourbon country of today is a decade or two into a great resurgence, with an entire map of distilleries that have detailed tours and tastings.

### Don't Miss

Big-name distilleries include Maker's Mark, Jim Beam, and Evan Williams, but just as worthy are exciting newcomers like Church & Key, on gorgeous historical grounds, and black-owned distillery Fresh Bourbon Distilling.

### Best Tour

A great introduction to the history, traditions, and continual refinement of Kentucky bourbon making is Buffalo Trace, located in the state capital of Frankfort. Some of the country's finest brands—from Pappy Van Winkle to W. L. Weller—pour from the charred oak barrels here. 🌐 *www.buffalotracedistillery.com.*

### Best Restaurant

Wallace Station is the spot for lunch while visiting nearby distilleries like Woodford Reserve and Wild Turkey; its large Kentucky-style sandwiches help soak up the tastings.

### Getting Here and Around

Lexington and Louisville are good bases. Distilleries are between 20 and 60 miles from Lexington, and about an hour from Louisville.

# Lexington Horse Country

## Winner's Circle

The hundreds of horse farms in the Lexington area (often referred to as the horse capital of the world) are often family-owned operations passed on for generations, and are largely responsible for the Derby and champion winners you see hit the tracks today. Touring a horse farm adds history and context to the racing industry, and is also a way for visitors to walk the picturesque grounds and interact with the animals themselves. Heritage Farm, in Goshen, is home to an amazing restaurant and a variety of activities; Spendthrift Farm is responsible for some big recent winners; and Claiborne Farm is the former pasture of Secretariat.

## Don't Miss

Keeneland, while less well-known than Churchill Downs, is at the heart of horse racing. Some of the best Thoroughbred racing in the world takes place here. You can tour the grounds, where the movie *Secretariat* was filmed, year-round. 🌐 *www.keeneland.com*.

## Best Horse Farm

At Mill Ridge Nursery Farm near Keeneland, there's a special dedication to the women behind horse racing, starting with Alice Chandler, the farm's founder, and a key figure in Kentucky racing history. The farm has sired a Kentucky Derby and seven Breeders' Cup winners; most importantly, you get to pet foals. 🌐 *www.millridge.com*.

## Getting Here and Around

Base yourself in Lexington for an easy drive to the horse farms in the surrounding countryside. Lexington's Blue Grass Airport (LEX) is conveniently located across the highway (1½ miles) from Keeneland. Louisville is a 1½-hour drive.

# Kentucky Derby

### One for the Books

It's been called "the greatest two minutes in sports" for a reason. The stakes are high as Thoroughbreds race to win the first leg of the Triple Crown and their jockeys a big purse prize. Big hats and bow ties fill the stands of Churchill Downs while many a mint julep is sipped tracking and betting on greats like Authentic and American Pharoah. Of course, there's more to Churchill Downs than Derby Day (though that is certainly its crowning event). On other race days during the season, you'll encounter fewer people, and there are choice activities from sun up (for morning racehorse workouts) to sundown (at Downs After Dark, an event combining racing under the lights with live, local art).

### Don't Miss

The Kentucky Derby Museum is both an on-site museum dedicated to the track and the Derby (check out the jockey jerseys), and the host of events, tours, and visitor packages.

### Good to Know

While there's no strict dress code for general admission, dressing to impress—in your biggest hat or loudest bow tie—is the name of the game, whether you're in the stands or a private suite.

### When to Go

The Kentucky Derby takes place on the first Saturday of May; book far in advance.

### Getting Here and Around

Louisville International Airport (SDF) is a convenient 4 miles from Churchill Downs.

**Churchill Downs.** ✉ *700 Central Ave., Louisville, KY* 🌐 *www.churchilldowns.com.*

# University of Kentucky Basketball

### Go Wild for the Wildcats

Claiming the title of best team in NCAA Division I history (in overall wins and most NCAA tournaments won), the Wildcats are kind of a big deal in Lexington. Even if you're not a die-hard fan, attending a UK game can be a chance to see the best of the best shoot hoops. Current NBAers like Demarcus Cousins, Devin Booker, and Anthony Davis are among alumni. Across from campus on Maxwell Street, Shop Local Kentucky is the place for fun, unofficial Cats and Kentucky gear.

### Don't Miss

Aside from attending a game at Rupp Arena (where you can spend the night at the Hyatt Regency next door), visitors can buy gear, tour the pretty campus, and get fanatic at a local bar.

### Best UK Bar

Winchell's, a tried-and-true sports bar (with at least two dozen flat screens), also serves surprisingly good renditions of casual Kentucky specials like beer cheese, hot browns, and Kentucky Derby pie. It's worth a visit just for the hearty grub, but game days are especially fun. 🌐 *www.winchellsrestaurant.com.*

### Good to Know

Single-game tickets are officially available through Ticketmaster, though season-ticket holders use sites like Stubhub to resell. Even when capacity is limited, it's possible to find a ticket. Price varies greatly (sometimes starting around $25) depending on the quality of the seat and the specific game.

### Getting Here and Around

Lexington's Blue Grass Airport (LEX) is 6 miles from the university. It's a little over an hour drive from Lexington to Louisville.

**Rupp Arena.** ✉ *430 W. Vine St., Lexington, KY* 🌐 *www.ukathletics.com.*

# Louisville's Museum Row

## Heavy Hitters

Downtown Louisville's Museum Row has a little bit of everything the small city is known for—its famous figures and moments in history, arts and science, plus good food and bourbon. Great stops include the Louisville Slugger Museum, the interactive Kentucky Science Center, Frazier History Museum, Muhammad Ali Center, and Center for the Arts, which houses small- and large-scale plays and musicals. Evan Williams, Angel's Envy, and Old Forester Distillery are also along Main Street.

## Don't Miss

The Louisville Slugger Museum is a home run of a museum, where a seven-story baseball bat leans against the building housing the museum and bat factory. (An appropriately sized baseball is embedded in one window of the plate-glass factory next door, too.) Autographed bats of virtually every baseball great are on display. *www.sluggermuseum.com* *From $7.*

## Need a Break?

When you've worked up an appetite after exploring, stop in to Royals Hot Chicken, Decca, or Biscuit Belly (for brunch).

## Getting Here and Around

Downtown and the East Market District (also called Nulu) are very walkable parts of Louisville; in general, Louisville is quite small and manageable. Rideshares are available everywhere, and the airport (SDF) is about a 10-minute drive from downtown.

**Museum Row.** *W. Main St., Louisville KY* *www.museumrowonmain.com.*

# Mammoth Cave

### Spelunk Your Heart Out

Spanning a distance of more than 400 miles, Mammoth Cave is the world's longest cave system, with its own unique ecosystem and miles of underground world that still have yet to be mapped or fully explored. The best place to experience a little stretch of this massive system is Mammoth Cave National Park. The National Park Service offers a range of themed tours throughout the year to different sections of the cave, ranging from an easy quarter-mile to a physically demanding six-hour exploration. In the aboveground sections of the park, there are also campgrounds and hiking, biking, and kayaking trails (the Green River runs through here).

### Don't Miss

It's tradition to go for lunch at the Porky Pig Diner before or after spelunking.

### Best Tour

Ranger-led Cleveland Avenue Tour is the choice for active visitors who are interested in a fairly deep dive and care as much about the fascinating geology as the cave's history. The Accessible Tour allows guests to visit part of Cleveland Avenue without stairs (enter via elevator). *$22.*

### Good to Know

Certain tours aren't for those with limited mobility, or who are claustrophobic. It can also be chilly inside the caves (around 55°F).

### Getting Here and Around

Mammoth Cave National Park is in Kentucky "Cave Country," 89 miles southeast of Louisville International Airport and close to the city of Bowling Green, Kentucky (45 minutes).

**Mammoth Cave.** *www.nps.gov/maca* *Free park entry; cave tours from $8.*

## Lexington Distillery District

### Whiskey Wonderland

Lexington's trendy Distillery District is where history meets hipsterdom. The 25-acre drinking and entertainment area is on the grounds of one of Lexington's oldest distilleries, James E. Pepper, which opened its doors during the American Revolution. After sitting in ruins for 50 years, the historic distillery underwent massive renovation and began making whiskey again in 2017, and is largely responsible for the revitalization of the Distillery District. Today's revamped James E. Pepper and the rest of the historic grounds welcome some of the most fun dining and entertainment options in Lexington.

### Don't Miss

The historic roots and architecture of the place, along Town Branch creek, add a scenic, cool vibe to the area, with Middle Fork, formerly a popular food truck, all the rage for dining, and Ethereal Brewing the favorite spot for craft beer. There's often live music outdoors here, as well as fire pits and games like bocce.

### Best Distillery Tour

A tour of James E. Pepper Distillery focuses both on the history of the legendary spot (Colonel Pepper is the most famous and colorful figure here) and the art of making whiskey—both the traditions and the new distillers' modern touches. Oh, and the whiskey is also very good. 🌐 *www.jamesepepper.com* 🎫 *$20.*

### Getting Here and Around

Lexington's Blue Grass Airport (LEX) is about a 10-minute drive (5 miles) from the Distillery District, or a short cab drive from downtown. It's a little over an hour's drive from Louisville to Lexington.

**Lexington Distillery District.** ✉ *1228 Manchester St. No. 100, Lexington, KY* 🌐 *www.lexingtondistillerydistrict.com.*

# Bluegrass Country

### Storm a Barn

Bluegrass country's happenin' string music takes its name from the Bluegrass State (after one of its early founders, Kentucky native Bill Monroe, formed a band with the "Bluegrass Boys"). Both the history of bluegrass music, and its current musical iterations, can be enjoyed in Kentucky, with festivals, museums, and active music venues around the state. The Bluegrass Hall of Fame ($12), in Owensburg, Kentucky, is a good place to start, and they also have a calendar of live music.

### Don't Miss

The Kentucky Opry, in Benton, is an excellent place to see a show, as is inside the barn at the Renfro Valley Entertainment Center.

### Best Venue

The Renfro Valley Entertainment Center, off of Interstate 75 in Mount Vernon, is surrounded by beautiful countryside and includes an amphitheater, shops, campground, and a music venue inside a historical barn. Gospel shows are noteworthy. 🌐 *www.renfrovalley.com.*

### When to Go

The Jerusalem Ridge Bluegrass Celebration is a four-day festival held in September at the childhood farm of Bill Monroe, the father of bluegrass, near Rosine, Kentucky. 🌐 *www.jerusalemridgefestival.com.*

### Getting Here and Around

Good nightclubs and large concert venues abound in Lexington and Louisville, but rural venues also have authentic bluegrass, gospel music, and festivals. You'll have to travel to these small towns to discover them: many are south of Louisville and Lexington, and others (like the Kentucky Opry) are east along the Country Music Highway.

# Red River Gorge

### World-Class Rock Climbing

Kentucky is gorge-ous (sorry, we had to) and this park proves it. A canyon system on the Red River, the gorge is perhaps best known as a world-class rock-climbing and hiking destination. Unique geological features such as natural stone arches, hidden caves, exposed rock faces, and giant sandstone cliffs ensure that every hike in the gorge's forested trail network is beautiful, or as some like to say, a Jurassic wilderness experience.

### Don't Miss

For the best day hike, take the Bison Way Trail to the Sheltowee Trace National Recreation Trail, the backbone of the forest's trail system. Then, go up Indian Staircase, offering a panoramic view of the gorge.

### Where to Stay

Sleep among woodland creatures at tree houses nestled high into the forest or built into the cliffs. They vary in size and degree of luxury, from glamping in solar-powered domes to staying in large homes with hot tubs and Wi-Fi. All are unique, well designed, and a very adventurous way to experience the area. $ *From $199.*

### Good to Know

Humans have used the land here for 12,000 years, and it is still important to Native American communities today. Follow all rules and regulations when climbing and hiking, both for your safety and out of respect for the land.

### Getting Here and Around

Red River Gorge is an hour's drive east of Lexington. While you come here for the natural wonders, there are a few good restaurants, campgrounds and cabins, and a skylift nearby at Natural Bridge State Resort Park.

**Red River Gorge Geological Area.** ✉ *Stanton, KY* 🌐 *www.redrivergorge.com.*

## When in Kentucky

### COCAINE BEAR

The legend of "Pablo Escobear" is full of bizarre details: it all starts in the 1980s, when a drug-smuggling Lexingtonian and party-boy lawyer named Andrew Thornton fell to his death after getting tangled in his parachute, abandoning his small plane in the woods—and the pounds and pounds of cocaine that were on board for delivery. Months later, a black bear was found dead in the forest near the crash, having tragically overdosed on about $15 million worth of cocaine dropped by Thornton. After undergoing a long journey, changing hands from many improbable owners, the (alleged) original taxidermied cocaine bear is on display at the Kentucky for Kentucky store in Lexington.

**Do This:** The Kentucky for Kentucky store is a legendary place to visit for Kentucky clothing and memorabilia—and to hear more about the cocaine bear, and other colorful stories about the Bluegrass State.

**Kentucky for Kentucky.** ✉ *720 Bryan Ave., Lexington, KY* ☎ *859/303–6359* 🌐 *www.kyforky.com.*

### COUNTRY MUSIC HIGHWAY

U.S. 23 is a great way to explore eastern Kentucky or as part of a musical road trip of the greater South. Loretta Lynn, Chris Stapleton, Billy Ray Cyrus, and Rick Skaggs are just some of the legends to emerge from these scenic hills and hollers. You can visit state parks, art centers, country music birthplaces, several museums along the way—and the feuding grounds of the Hatfields and McCoys.

**Do This:** Make a detour in Staffordsville, Kentucky, at the U.S. 23 Country Music Highway Museum, and then continue on through the town of Paintsville to visit the historic coal company store of Webb's Grocery and the birthplace of Loretta Lynn.

**Country Music Highway.** ✉ *U.S. 23 in East Kentucky* 🌐 *www.countrymusichighway.com.*

### HARLAND SANDERS CAFE AND MUSEUM

The historic home of Kentucky Fried Chicken is in Corbin, Kentucky, and it's worth a visit if you're heading to Lexington or Louisville from the south. In the 1930s, Sanders began his humble restaurant here as a way to satisfy diners travelling Route 25. By the 1950s, when Interstate 75 was built and left the road and town in the dust, Sanders had begun selling franchises. This location (where he developed his secret recipe) is now a museum and restaurant.

**Do This:** Driving through this area of Kentucky is picturesque, especially during fall when the leaves change and the backdrop of the bluffs looks especially dramatic. Head to the nearby Cumberland Falls for more scenery.

**Corbin Tourism.** ✉ *688 Hwy. 25, Corbin, KY* ☎ *606/528–2163* 🌐 *www.corbinkytourism.com.*

## Cool Place to Stay

**The Brown.** Opened in 1923, this grand but intimate hotel has a gilded second-floor lobby that gleams with marble and polished wood. Rooms are furnished with fine reproductions and luxurious bedding. A special Louisville dish, the hot brown, was invented here—you can order the turkey, bacon, and cheese sandwich–casserole hybrid from room service. It's worth a stop at the bar—for an incredible bourbon selection—even if you don't make this downtown landmark your stay. ✉ *335 W. Broadway, Louisville, KY* ☎ *888/888–5252* 🌐 *www.brownhotel.com* $ *From $177.*

# Louisiana

The good times are always rolling in Louisiana, a mix of swampland and vibrant towns as well as a melting pot of French, Creole, African, and American cultures. Its largest city, New Orleans, bursts with the jovial sounds of jazz, beckoning travelers to its French Quarter and festive Mardi Gras celebrations, with a colorful parades, loud music, and larger-than-life floats. Don't dare leave without tasting a beignet, po'boy, and gumbo.

## Bucket List Picks

The following boxes contain our picks for the top sights and experiences in Louisiana.

○ The French Quarter

○ Louisiana Swamps

○ Cajun Country

○ Lake Pontchartrain

○ Bywater and Marigny

○ Mardi Gras

○ The Tremé

○ The Whitney Plantation and Museum

○ Haunted New Orleans

# The French Quarter

### Historic Heart and Soul

New Orleans's oldest neighborhood is visually stunning, with Creole cottages, Spanish colonial architecture, and cobblestoned streets steeped in legends of brothels and pirates, ghosts and fires, and more packed with activity than anywhere else in the city. You must take a romp down rowdy Bourbon Street at least once; stroll the French Market; window-shop the galleries and antiques stores on Royal Street; get your fortune told at Jackson Square overlooking iconic St. Louis Cathedral; and eat a po' boy or two. When in need of respite, tuck into one of the Quarter's best courtyards at Sylvain or Café Amelie.

### Don't Miss

It's practically a rite of passage to order beignets and café au lait from Café Du Monde, New Orleans's mainstay coffee stand since 1862. It's cash only. 🌐 *shop.cafedumonde.com*.

### Best Bar

Lafitte's Blacksmith Shop, a ramshackle one-story building often called the oldest standing building in New Orleans, was once the workshop of infamous pirate Jean Lafitte. The front room is packed with tourists and rowdy locals drinking Abita beer and the shop's frozen "Purple Drink," a sugary, boozy specialty. The back room is a piano bar where revelers sing along to Billy Joel. 🌐 *www.lafittesblacksmithshop.com*.

### Getting Here and Around

It's fairly unpleasant to drive around the Quarter because of congestion, which is why you'll see streets filled with pedestrians and pedicabs. Parking can be expensive ($20 in most garages) and hard to find on the street. The St. Charles Avenue, Canal Street, and Rampart streetcar lines all go to the Quarter, and it's easy to walk around once you're here.

# Louisiana Swamps

## Bewitching Bayous

Southeastern Louisiana's swamps and wetlands are known for their eerie beauty—with jutting cypress knees, swinging Spanish moss, and picturesque palmetto palms—and carry whole ecosystems in their submerged fields and forests. These are the places to spot alligators, especially on a sunny day with a boating guide who's expert at drawing them out with treats. For a relatively quick trip to scenic swamplands, where you'll spot alligators and other fauna from a walking trail and boardwalk, head to Jean Lafitte National Park and Preserve about 20 miles outside New Orleans. Also close to New Orleans, you can board an airboat to explore the Manchac or Honey Island Swamp.

## Don't Miss

Atchafalaya Basin, an 800,000-plus-acre swamp wilderness just northeast of Lafayette, is the largest wetland and swamp in the country—larger than the Florida Everglades—and home to bald eagles, alligators, black bears, and the tens of millions of pounds of crawfish that the country eats every year. Canoe, rent a boat, or walk the trails.

## Best Tour

You'll find boat rentals on the edge of the Atchafalaya Basin along Henderson Levee Road. McGee's Louisiana Swamp & Airboat Tours offers speedy airboat rides ($50), and slower-paced swamp boat rides, including a sunset weekend tour. More adventurous visitors can rent canoes from McGee's to peacefully explore the swamplands on their own. 🌐 *www.mcgeesswamp-tours.com*.

## Getting Here and Around

The Atchafalaya National Wildlife Refuge lies between Baton Rouge and Lafayette, Louisiana. The area welcome center is in the town of Breaux Bridge, just west of Lafayette.

# Cajun Country

## Culture and Crawfish Capital

When Acadians (French-Canadian colonists) arrived along the bayous of Louisiana in the 18th century, they brought a way of life revolving around food, family, and music. After centuries of calling this area home, meeting with influences of African, Spanish, Italian, Creole, and Native American peoples, the Acadian corner of the world continues to flourish. Visit Lafayette and surrounding towns like Breaux Bridge, St. Martinville, Abbeville, and New Iberia, trying foods like boudin sausage, cracklins, and crawfish; "cutting a rug" at Cajun dance halls and music festivals; and touring cultural centers like LARC's Acadian Village.

## Don't Miss

The crawfish capital of the world is Breaux Bridge, a small town full of personality, where there's a legendary crawfish festival every spring. There are also many antiques shops, nearby bayous, and great Cajun food. On Saturday, Zydeco Breakfast at Buck and Johnny's is the can't-miss event.

## While You're Here

It's essential to stop for boudin—a speciality sausage stuffed with rice and seasoning—at one of the humble stands around Interstate 10 and its backroads, such as Poche's or Billy's.

## When to Go

Festivals like Cajun Mardi Gras, Festival International de Louisiane, and Black Pot Festival bring Cajun Country to life in spring.

## Getting Here and Around

Lafayette is the biggest city in Cajun Country, 135 miles west of New Orleans. From Lafayette, you can easily explore the Atchafalaya National Wildlife Refuge and the towns of Breaux Bridge, St. Martinville, Abbeville, and New Iberia.

# Lake Pontchartrain

### Water, Water Everywhere

Head any direction from New Orleans, and you'll hit water soon enough. For a particularly epic drive and day trip from the city, head north across the Lake Pontchartrain Causeway, the longest continuing bridge over water in the world. The flat, four-lane bridge, spanning 23.8 dizzying miles with views of nothing but blue sky and lake, is nothing short of an end-of-the-earth drive (and long enough to need its own police force). On the north shore of the lake, you'll find small communities like Mandeville and Abita Springs that make for a pleasant visit.

### Don't Miss

After crossing, head southwest to Grand Isle, a coastal town with a popular fishing beach, and see the land simply melt away as you approach the Gulf. Aside from the simple raised road, everything from telephone poles to houses on stilts is surrounded by water.

### Good to Know

As you approach any fishing beach in Louisiana, look out for roadside stands selling the freshest shrimp, crabs, and fish to take home or enjoy boiled.

### Best Stop

At the end of your drive, stop at the beaches of Grand Isle State Park. Fish, camp, bird-watch, climb the observation tower, or take a walk along the interpretive nature trail. Fun fact: Grand Isle is the only inhabited barrier island in Louisiana, and the resort town is also the setting of Kate Chopin's novel *The Awakening*.

### Getting Here and Around

From New Orleans, follow Interstate 10 West towards Mandeville to cross Lake Pontchartrain (about a 45-minute drive). To reach Grand Isle, head west towards LA 308 to eventually reach the slow road of LA 1 (a two-hour drive).

# Bywater and Marigny

## Epic NOLA Nightlife

The New Orleans neighborhoods of the Bywater and Faubourg Marigny are a mix of colorful shotgun houses, tropical plants and community gardens, small businesses, and muraled industrial spaces. They're at the core of the Crescent City's most innovative and creative activity, where newly arrived artists and entrepreneurs add to their historic legacy. Frenchmen Street is the place for packed-in live music, but elsewhere at night in the Bywater and Marigny, locals sip cocktails in the secret gardens of Bacchanal or N7, dance the night away at bars on St. Claude Avenue, or enter the magical, interactive world of the Music Box Village.

## Don't Miss

Frenchmen Street in the Marigny, lined with popular cafés, clubs, and live-music joints like the Spotted Cat Music Club and Blue Nile, is the ultimate night out for music lovers.

## Best Restaurant

Saint-Germain, located in an unassuming section of St. Claude Avenue in the Bywater has two equally enjoyable personalities. In the small dining room, the chef serves incredible prix-fixe multicourse dinners, and some of the most inventive cuisine in the city. Alternatively, at the narrow bar and in the garden out back, you can sip glasses of natural wine while enjoying a smaller bistro menu of crudité and fried-chicken sandwiches.

## Getting Here and Around

The Marigny is the smaller of the two neighborhoods and sits between the French Quarter and Bywater (also known as the Upper Ninth Ward) along the Mississippi River. There is a bus, and a short streetcar line (Rampart Street) that runs from the French Quarter to St. Claude in the Bywater.

# Mardi Gras

### The Main Event

Mardi Gras means so much more to New Orleans than beads, booze, and Bourbon Street; it's a historic and cultural event at the core of the city's identity. New Orleanians celebrate Fat Tuesday, traditionally one last day of indulging in rich foods before the start of Lent, with epic parades, balls, house floats, and concerts, with revelers lining the streets and balconies day and night. Carnival season begins long before Fat Tuesday (Krewe du Vieux and Chewbacchus are the parades to catch in earlier weeks) and appeals to costume-clad partygoers, music and art lovers, foodies, families, and more, from all over the world.

### Don't Miss

During parades along St. Charles Avenue, the area near the Interstate 10 underpass, in the Lower Garden District/CBD, is the place to catch extended performances by marching bands.

### Best Stop

The Backstreet Cultural Museum is the Mardi Gras meeting place for tribes of Mardi Gras Indians, African American krewes clad in elaborate, painstakingly hand-sewn bead and feather getups. The museum also holds a rich collection of costumes and musical artifacts year-round. 🌐 *www.backstreetmuseum.org*.

### When to Go

Major parades take place from the Thursday before Fat Tuesday through Mardi Gras evening. The best places to catch one are along St. Charles Avenue in the Garden District and CBD, and along Canal Street in the French Quarter/CBD (many parades end here).

### Getting Here and Around

Parade routes block traffic for much of Mardi Gras week, one of the reasons so many New Orleanians have the day(s) off. Be prepared to walk, or plan far ahead for parking in the Garden District and Uptown.

# The Tremé

## Birthplace of Jazz

The jubilant sounds of trumpets, trombones, and cornets fill the air every night of the year in the New Orleans neighborhood where jazz was born. Just above the French Quarter, the Tremé is the place it all began, home of legends including Louis Armstrong, Jelly Roll Morton, and Trombone Shorty. Congo Square, a small cobblestone square off Rampart Street, was historically the Sunday meeting place (and the only meeting place allowed) for enslaved people to sing, dance, and celebrate African music and culture. A tradition born of oppression eventually formed the roots of contemporary jazz, and today musicians still gather here for percussion jams. Elsewhere in the city, Frenchmen Street, Preservation Hall, New Orleans Jazz Museum, and the Musical Legends Park are good places to explore the sounds of the city.

## Don't Miss

Catch live music in Congo Square in Louis Armstrong Park or in the excellent small music clubs like Kermit's Tremé Mother-in-Law Lounge or Treme Hideaway.

## Good to Know

The WWOZ livewire (🌐 *www.wwoz.org*, and on 90.7 FM) runs through a daily list of live music throughout New Orleans.

## When to Go

Events like Jazz Fest (late April–early May) and French Quarter Festival (typically the third week of April) are the way to pack an entire weekend (or two) with the best local music acts.

## Getting Here and Around

You can walk to Congo Square and Frenchman Street from the French Quarter or take a cab or rideshare. Once there, plan to walk the few blocks picking clubs to enter at your leisure.

## The Whitney Plantation and Museum

### A Sobering Memorial

Between New Orleans and Baton Rouge, many antebellum plantations along the Mississippi are open to visitors, filled with period antiques, evoking tales of Yankee gunboats and the ghosts of former residents. But the Whitney is the only antebellum mansion in this scenic stretch (and the only museum in all of Louisiana) that's exclusively dedicated to the history of slavery and the memory of those it harmed. The museum, opened by a retired lawyer in 2014, is on the grounds of a former indigo and sugarcane plantation dating back to 1752. Scenes from the movies *Django Unchained* and *12 Years a Slave* were filmed here.

### Don't Miss

Seek out the original cabins and the commemorative "Children of Whitney" statues by Woodrow Nash.

### Good to Know

To visit the Whitney, you must book a guided tour ahead of time ($25 per adult, and a little over an hour) but this experience is well worth it. An incredibly somber and emotional tour contains recorded personal accounts from formerly enslaved workers, and walks through the well-maintained grounds, including historical structures and former dwellings of enslaved peoples, museum exhibits, artifacts, and memorials.

### Getting Here and Around

The museum, located on the west bank of the Mississippi River, is an hour's drive between New Orleans and Baton Rouge. Avoid taking a rideshare since return service will be all but nonexistent. To get there, take Interstate 10 to Exit 194 and plan to spend the better part of a day taking it all in.

**The Whitney Plantation and Museum.** ✉ *5099 Hwy. 18, Wallace, LA* 🌐 *www.whitneyplantation.org* 🎫 *$25.*

# Haunted New Orleans

## Spirits of the Dead

To truly know New Orleans is to understand its strong ties to the spiritual realm, to voodoo practices, legendary ghost stories, and eerily beautiful cemeteries where more than a few things have been said to go bump in the night. Ghost tours typically take visitors through the famous aboveground graves of St. Louis Cemetery No. 1, the oldest and most famous of New Orleans's cities of the dead. Tours will also walk the grounds and weave in the legends of the city's most haunted sites, like Storyville, the former red-light district, and the LaLaurie Mansion, former home of the cruel and torturing slave owner dramatized in *American Horror Story.*

## Don't Miss

The superstitious should not skip Marie Laveau's House of voodoo, a place to learn about voodoo priestess Marie Laveau, who ruled over all things occult in the 19th century. She lived blocks from Congo Square, where she would lead chants, sell talismans, and gather useful information. Visit Laveau's grave in St. Louis Cemetery No. 1. 🌐 *www.voodooneworleans.com.*

## Best Tour

To experience it all with a dose of extra drama, spend a couple of hours with Ghost City Tours or French Quarter Phantoms, and book a haunted hotel for extra frights. Stays at the Cornstalk Hotel, Bourbon Orleans, and Le Pavillion all come with ghost stories old and new.

## Getting Here and Around

Most haunted history and ghost tours meet in the French Quarter near the St. Louis Cathedral and Jackson Square. While St. Louis Cemetery No. 1 is the most famous, you can easily hop a street car to arrive at No. 2 (300 North Claiborne Avenue) and No. 3 (3421 Esplanade Avenue).

# When in Louisiana

## ABITA MYSTERY HOUSE

Artist John Preble's strange vision—sort of a Louisiana version of the Watts Towers of Los Angeles—is an obsessive collection of found objects (combs, old musical instruments, paint-by-number art, and taxidermy experiments gone horribly awry) set in a series of ramshackle buildings, including one covered in mosaic tiles. The museum is truly odd and entertaining.

**Do This:** Make a day out of a visit to this quaint town. Alongwith the Abita Brewery, there are small shops and restaurants. On the Tammany Trace, you can bike or walk along scenic stretches of the North Shore.

**Abita Mystery House.** ✉ *22275 Hwy. 36, Abita Springs, LA* ☎ *985/892–2624* 🌐 *www.ucmmuseum.com.*

## AVERY ISLAND

While Avery Island is best known as the headquarters of Tabasco hot sauce—it has been privately owned by the creators, the Avery-McIlhenny family, for almost 200 years—it's also home to a wildlife refuge for snowy egrets and more than 50 archaeological sites. A unique ecological treasure, the island is actually a solid salt dome that rises above its flat coastal marsh surroundings and covers more than 2,000 acres. Most geologists credit its creation to salt deposits left over from an ancient seabed. After a fun tour of the Tabasco factory, take time to appreciate the island's flora and fauna.

**Do This:** Avery Island is about 45 minutes southeast of Lafayette, so it makes a good day trip when exploring Cajun Country. New Iberia, the closest town, has lodging and restaurants. While you're on the island, marvel at the natural wonderland of Bird City—a sanctuary created for the snowy egret—and walk through the island's beautiful botanical gardens with a serene Buddhist temple and live oaks draped in Spanish moss.

**Avery Island.** ✉ *Hwy. 329, Avery Island, LA* 🌐 *www.tabasco.com/visit-avery-island.*

## MANCHAC MANSION

There's nothing quite as eerie as a house rising up in the middle of a swamp. This site, the ruins of a submerged house surrounded by water and cypress forest, make Manchac Swamp a particularly intriguing—and haunting—place to paddle. Canoe in Trails Adventures leads excellent guided tours of the swamp, though you can also rent your own to paddle the area and continue up through Lake Maurepas. The swamp is northwest of New Orleans via Interstate 10 West and Interstate 55.

**Do This:** Local boaters know it's essential to stop at Middendorf's nearby for lunch—after a paddle or for a picnic po' boy to go. The restaurant is famous for its paper-thin fried catfish.

**Canoe & Trail Adventures.** ✉ *Manchac Swamp, Ponchatoula, LA* ☎ *504/233–0686 (Canoe and Trail Adventures)* 🌐 *www.canoeandtrail.com.*

## MUSEUM OF DEATH

The oddity of this French Quarter museum is in the name. With serial-killer artwork and exhibits on all things death related, from the Manson family to ancient funeral traditions, this museum can be graphic and is certainly not for everyone, including young audiences. That said, it's a fascinating place to explore something which is, well, an essential part of life.

**Do This:** Combine a trip to this museum with other small, funky ones nearby, including the New Orleans Pharmacy Museum and the Historic Voodoo Museum.

**Museum of Death.** ✉ *227 Dauphine St., New Orleans, LA* ☎ *504/593–3968* 🌐 *www.museumofdeath.net.*

## Cool Places to Stay

**The Chloe.** A hip local restaurant group recently took over this historic mansion on Saint Charles Avenue, painting it a moody blue-green, and adding an art deco pool area, excellent restaurant, and impeccable interior decor. The house was originally designed by architect Thomas Sully, responsible for many of the area's most impressive mansions, and there are unique architectural features honored throughout the public spaces in rooms, in tucked away dining areas, and in seemingly hidden passages and entryways. Rooms have touches of luxury with local boutique bath products. ✉ *4125 St. Charles Ave., New Orleans, LA* ☎ *504/541–5500* 🌐 *www.thechloenola.com* [$] *From $489.*

**Country Charm Bed and Breakfast.** Stay along the water at a funky fishing cabin here, and you'll get the best of the natural world of Cajun Country—with nearby culture and fun in Lafayette and in the small town of Breaux Bridge. Even if fishing is not your thing, the outdoor area overlooking the lake is appealing. The suites, decorated with antiques, and the hospitality and friendly touches provided by hosts are all you would want and expect from a place touting "country charm." ✉ *1144 Lawless Tauzin Rd., Breaux Bridge, LA* ☎ *337/332–3616* 🌐 *www.countrycharmbb.com* [$] *From $170.*

**Hotel Peter and Paul.** A longtime resident of the Marigny neighborhood teamed with a boutique-hotel group to renovate this former church and rectory, creating this one-of-a-kind hotel, supremely rooted in place. The unique architectural touches, careful color schemes (a different one on every floor), and sparse but dramatic oversized European antiques are just some of the features that make it so aesthetically pleasing. Food and drink is brought to you by the team behind Bacchanal. ✉ *2317 Burgundy St., New Orleans, LA* 🌐 *www.hotelpeterandpaul.com* [$] *From $289.*

**St. Francisville Inn.** Full of luxurious touches and ornate detail, this Victorian inn ticks the box for southern charm. The surrounding town of St. Francisville, with antiques shops, restaurants, and hikes at nearby Tunica Falls, is just two hours from New Orleans and makes for a great side trip. There are 11 well-appointed rooms with marble bathrooms, a pool and lounge area, great restaurant, and front-porch rocking chairs overlooking lush gardens. ✉ *5720 Commerce St., St. Francisville, LA* ☎ *225/635–6502* 🌐 *www.stfrancisvilleinn.com* [$] *From $314.*

# Mississippi

Today's Mississippi is a multifaceted landscape of rich history, legendary musical heritage, mouthwatering culinary delights, and adventurous outdoor recreation. From the natural splendor of the mighty Mississippi River to the sandy beaches of the Gulf Coast, Mississippi celebrates diversity and creativity through her people, geography, sights, and sounds. Journey along miles of hiking and biking trails or relish authentic sounds of blues, country, or rock 'n' roll in the birthplace of it all.

## Bucket List Picks

The following boxes contain our picks for the top sights and experiences in Mississippi.

- ○ Mississippi Blues Trail
- ○ Oxford
- ○ Jackson
- ○ Natchez Trace Parkway
- ○ Clarksdale
- ○ Biloxi and the Gulf Coast Scenic Byway
- ○ Ocean Springs
- ○ Tupelo

# Mississippi Blues Trail

## Soul of the South

Travel the Mississippi Delta and you'll discover the roots of American music. Stops are mapped out on the Blues Trail's website, and each includes a signpost detailing its historical significance. Landmarks include juke joints and restaurants, record shops and hotels, eclectic museums, and birthplaces of greats like Muddy Waters, B. B. King, and Sam Cooke. The Trail runs the length of the state from New Orleans to Memphis, with most concentrated stops in the northwest–Mississippi Delta region.

## Don't Miss

B. B. King's birthplace is in the small town of Berclair, and Clarksdale is generally considered the best town for juke joints.

## Best Road Snack

The Mississippi hot tamale is slightly smaller and spicier than its Latin American counterpart. These treats are a specialty throughout the Mississippi Delta region, and road-trippers should look for the small stands along country roads throughout their trip. Scott's Hot Tamales serves some of the best. 🌐 *www.scottshottamales.com.*

## When to Go

The Mississippi Delta is quite warm in early fall, with great blue skies and heat shimmering off the fields. If you're lucky, you'll spot the cotton bolls opening up before harvest.

## Getting Here and Around

The Blues Trail encompasses the whole state, but most stops are within the Delta region: the fertile valley between the Yazoo and Mississippi rivers, with Memphis, Tennessee, to the north, and Jackson, Mississippi, to the south. From Memphis International Airport, it's about a 1½-hour drive (70 miles) to Clarksdale, Mississippi.

# Oxford

## Home of Southern Gothic Literature

The main event in the land of William Faukner is to visit the famed Southern writer's home and haunts. Among its other celebrated former residents are Larry Brown, Barry Hannah, and John Grisham. Barry Hannah and Faulkner are at rest in St. Peter's Cemetery, and the second floor of the University of Mississippi library holds special collections of works by Oxford's best-known authors; the University ("Ole Miss") also throws a spectacular football game. Wandering the campus and frequenting local watering holes in town, visitors can rub elbows with Oxford's current literati.

## Don't Miss

Rowan Oak, Faulkner's historic home, offers tours for $5. A pleasant walk through Bailey's Woods, between Rowan Oak and the University of Mississippi Museum, provides real-life illustrations to familiar Faulkner scenes. 🌐 *www.rowanoak.com.*

## Best Bookstore

A literary stroll through Oxford should end at Square Books, a renowned bookstore in Town Square. There are signed books from local and visiting authors, an expansive Faulkner collection, and an impressive selection of wider Southern and literary fiction. 🌐 *www.squarebooks.com.*

## When to Go

Balmy Mississippi fall, during Ole Miss football season, is a good time to visit Oxford. The Oxford Conference of the Book typically takes place in March.

## Getting Here and Around

The university-owned Oxford-University Airport is for public use, but it's rare to find a flight into Oxford. The best way to get here is to fly into Memphis International Airport and drive 1½ hours south.

# Jackson

## Capitol of Blues and Freedom

Civil rights history, blues music production, and food and booze (both historic and up-and-coming) are what make Mississippi's state capitol worth visiting. The Mississippi Freedom Trail passes through here, with several landmarks and museums commemorating the city's civil rights leaders—and the sobering acts of violence, and centuries of racism, that spurred the movement. There's also the Mississippi Museum of Natural Science, and several stops on the Mississippi Blues Trail. Soul food, barbecue, "fish houses," and a smattering of newer bars and restaurants, all make up Jackson's best libations.

## Don't Miss

The Mississippi Freedom Trail marks historical spots including Medgar Evers's House, where the activist was murdered in 1963, and sight of the 1963 Woolworth sit-in. Two noteworthy museums go deeper into history and its figures: the Mississippi Civil Rights Museum and the Smith Robertson Museum and Cultural Center. 🌐 *civilrightstrail.com/destination/jackson.*

## Best Neighborhood

Jackson's Fondren District—home to artists, shops, and cafés, and a cocktail bar at Brent's Drugs—is a great neighborhood for walking and soaking up the sights and sounds of the city.

## While You're Here

During college football season, score tickets to see Jackson State's Marching Band, the Sonic Boom of the South, who made a virtual cameo performance in the 2021 presidential inauguration.

## Getting Here and Around

The Jackson–Medgar Wiley Evers International Airport (JAN) is about 6 miles from downtown. Jackson is a two-hour drive from Memphis, and three hours from New Orleans.

## Natchez Trace Parkway

### Drive Through History

Natchez Trace Parkway is a slow and scenic road following what was once the Natchez Trail, a 440-mile American Indian footpath running from Natchez, Mississippi, to Nashville, Tennessee. Make a drive of it, stopping at a beautiful cypress swamp near Canton, plus two waterfalls (Jackson Falls and Fall Hollow Waterfall) as well as a natural spring (Rock Spring) and parts of the original path. There's also a visitor center at the trail's northern point in Tupelo, and a few landmarks highlighting the former "stands" (inns) of European and American traders, plus points of local American Indian history.

### Don't Miss

In Port Gibson, southwest of Jackson, visitors can walk part of the original, much-eroded "Sunken Trace," canopied by ancient forest.

### Best Stop

The southernmost destination on the trail is the town of Natchez. Its small but impactful Natchez Museum of African American Culture, with free guided tours, is a worthwhile way to spend a couple of hours. Some Mississippi River cruises dock here.

### Good to Know

Bear in mind that the trace speed limit is slow, and this scenic parkway is not the fastest way to reach anywhere. In Tupelo, pick up a map and talk to a ranger about what sections you'd like to see.

### Getting Here and Around

Within Mississippi, the trace extends north to south, from Tupelo to Natchez. Memphis and Jackson both make good bases for a short road trip along the trace.

**Natchez Trace Parkway.** 🌐 *www.nps.gov/natr.*

# Clarksdale

### Land of the Delta Blues

At an intersection of Highways 61 and 49, marked today by a blue pole affixed with electric guitars called the "Crossroads," musician Robert Johnson sold his soul to the devil so he could play guitar. It's no surprise then, that this Mississippi Delta town is home to several iconic blues landmarks commemorating area musicians like Ike Turner, Muddy Waters, and Sam Cooke. Today's Clarksdale is a mix of commemorative Blues Trail plaques, small museums, sleepy streets, "eat places" (casual traditional Delta restaurants), and a few still-active music joints.

### Don't Miss

The best way to feel the blues is to enter one of the town's historic juke joints (small music clubs that still in operation), like Ground Zero Blues Club (where Morgan Freeman is a co-owner) and Red's Lounge at 398 Sunflower Avenue—both on the same block.

### Best Museum

The Delta Blues Museum provides a deep understanding of the blues and is home to some impressive pieces of music history, including the remnants of the cabin where Muddy Waters lived when he was a sharecropper at Stovall Farms. 🌐 *www.deltabluesmuseum.org* 🎫 *$12.*

### When to Go

Each April the Juke Joint Festival draws talented area musicians for a few days of live music, food, and lots of good company. 🌐 *www.jukejointfestival.com.*

### Getting Here and Around

From Memphis International Airport, it's about a 1½-hour drive (70 miles southwest) to Clarksdale.

# Biloxi and the Gulf Coast Scenic Byway

## The Great Coastal Road Trip

The stretch of U.S. Route 90 that runs along Mississippi's Gulf Coast is a popular trip from New Orleans; locals know that one of the true treats is a stop at Duong Phong on the way out of town, the James Beard Award winner famous for banh mi and Vietnamese pastries. Pass Christian, Waveland, and Bay St. Louis are popular beach towns here, with free beaches, Gulf-side restaurants and funky small shops; Biloxi, the last and largest town along the way, is full of casinos and resorts. The annual Frida Fest, in the eclectic little town of Bay St. Louis, brings lovers of the Mexican artists together in July, for fun activities and art.

## Don't Miss

In Waveland, camp out in Buccaneer State Park surrounded by mossy oak and marsh, hike the 1.8-mile Pirate's Alley Nature Trail, then hit the water before driving to the next beach town.

## Best Detour

Travelling along Interstate 10 from New Orleans, visitors will see signs for the John C. Stennis Space Center, one of 10 NASA field sites in the country and the largest rocket-engine testing center. Nearby, the Infinity Science Center is the official museum, with indoor and outdoor exhibits dedicated to space learning and NASA history.

## Order This

Royal reds, a large and sweet species of shrimp (it's been compared to lobster) and unique delicacy to the area, appear on Mississippi Gulf menus beginning in late summer.

## Getting Here and Around

It takes an hour or so to reach Biloxi from New Orleans International Airport (MSY) but you can also fly into Biloxi (Gulfport-Biloxi International Airport).

# Ocean Springs

### Small Town Funk

For a small town, Oceans Springs holds an incredibly concentrated amount of funk and personality, attracting artists and musicians, as well as the entrance and visitor center for the Gulf Islands National Seashore. The area's best-known artist is Walter Anderson, who has a museum here, a gallery, and several public murals. Pottery, crafts, and art inspired by the strange, sometimes haunting Gulf Shore landscape, are on display in shops throughout the town. There's also the Shed, a funky barbecue joint with live music and sprawling porches.

### Don't Miss

Aunt Jenny's Catfish Restaurant isn't just the Ocean Springs spot for fried catfish fillets—it's full of colorful local history as well. After their meal, guests can request a tour (peppered with local lore) of the Julep Room Lounge, an underground music club where Elvis used to hang. 🌐 *auntjennyscatfish.com*.

### Best Museum

Walter Anderson Museum of Art showcases the best of prolific painter and craftsman Walter Anderson. The New Orleans–born artist made a home in Ocean Springs, and his best works are ethereal landscapes and other media reflecting a spiritual and imaginative relationship with his Gulf Shores surroundings. The museum exhibits other local and up-and-coming artists as well. 🌐 *www.walterandersonmuseum.org*.

### Getting Here and Around

Ocean Springs is located between Interstate 10 (connects to New Orleans) and U.S. Route 90, about 22 miles east (30 minutes) of Gulfport–Biloxi International Airport, and 100 miles (1½ hours) from New Orleans International Airport (MSY).

# Tupelo

### Birthplace of Elvis

This north Mississippi town's claim to fame is being the humble hometown of the King of Rock and Roll. There are plenty of Elvis-related activities: tours, landmarks, and a summer festival dedicated to the King and Elvis-inspired art. But there are some other small-town wonders to enjoy: cute and quaint barbecue and burger shops, a summer concert series, and even a meadery. The Natchez Trace Parkway begins in Tupelo, and visitors can dive into the history of the trace and its inhabitants at the visitor center.

### Don't Miss

Elvis Presley's two-room home on the outskirts of town is now a museum. *elvispresleybirthplace.com* *$19.*

### Best Tour

Elvis' Tupelo Self-Guided Bicycle Tour is the ultimate way to tour the King's hometown. Rent a bike at Trails and Treads before accessing the free bicycle tour map (*www.tupelo.net/elvis-tupelo-self-guided-bicycle-tour*) to explore 13 stops where the King grew into a legend. Aside from his house, there's Tupelo Hardware, where Elvis's mother bought him his first guitar, and a stop at Tupelo's oldest restaurant, Johnnie's Drive-in, where guests can sit at the same booth as Presley.

### Best Restaurant

Clay's House of Pig serves mouthwatering barbecue in a decidedly rustic location: the inside of a bait-and-tackle shop.

### Getting Here and Around

Contour Airlines (*www.contourairlines.com*) flies to Tupelo Regional Airport from Nashville. The closest major airport is Memphis International Airport (MEM), a little over a 1½-hour drive.

# When in Mississippi

## BIRTHPLACE OF KERMIT THE FROG

A shack along the river seems fitting for the birthplace of America's favorite amphibian, celebrated in this small museum in Jim Henson's hometown. Explore Henson's childhood and inspiration at this small creek-side museum. It's hokey, but hey, it's not easy being green.

**Do This:** Before or after exploring, get a drive-through catfish sandwich at Gino's Hamburgers and Catfish in nearby Greenville, Mississippi. The sandwich is cheap, messy, and everything you want from a Mississippi road stop.

**Birthplace of Kermit the Frog.** ✉ *415 S. Deer Creek Dr. E, Leland, MS* ☎ *662/686–7383* 🌐 *www.birthplaceofthefrog.com* 🎫 *Free.*

## MCCARTY'S POTTERY

This shop is an unlikely hidden gem in a small Delta town, Merigold. (The town itself is a similarly unknown detour worthwhile for its charm.) The couple ceramicists opened their kiln in the 1950s, and have since been showcased in museums and lauded with awards. Today the shop sells all sorts of fine goods made from Mississippi clay, from whimsical animal figurines to fine serving dishes, and everything in between. Surrounded by slightly wild and equally whimsical gardens, this road stop is unassuming, but loaded with character and history.

**Do This:** This pot shop serves lunch! Call ahead to reserve a spot—and check the daily menu—at the Gallery Restaurant, a unique and affordable multicourse dining opportunity.

**McCarty's Pottery.** ✉ *101 St. Mary St., Merigold, MS* ☎ *662/748–2293* 🌐 *www.mccartyspottery.com.*

## MISSISSIPPI PETRIFIED FOREST

This seemingly unexpected roadside attraction 26 miles northwest of Jackson makes for a peaceful stop on a road trip through Mississippi. Beginning in the gift shop, visitors make their way along a walking path through the only preserved petrified forest in this part of the country. Pamphlets and markers tell the ancient history of the trees. The visit ends in a small museum of natural artifacts.

**Do This:** Have lunch at the Flora Butcher on the nearby town of Flora's quaint main street. The old-school butcher shop sells quality cuts of local meat.

**Mississippi Petrified Forest.** ✉ *124 Forest Park Rd., Flora, MS* 🌐 *www.mspetrified-forest.com* 🎫 *$7.*

# Cool Places to Stay

**Shack Up Inn.** Rough around the edges and steeped in history, with plenty of music along the way, it doesn't get more Delta than lodging in these old sharecropper cabins (with an on-site juke joint). This is rustic Americana at its best ("the Ritz we ain't," the Shack Up Inn boasts), with plenty of front-porch rocking chairs. ✉ *001 Commissary Cir. Rd., Clarksdale, MS* 🌐 *www.shackupinn.com* $ *From $100.*

**Travelers Hotel Clarksdale.** For decades, the Delta region has been a meeting place of creative minds, and this hip spot follows suit. The 20-room hotel is run by a cooperative of artists, and you're sure to meet some interesting people here. In the open-air lobby, surrounded by local art, you'll find craft beer on tap and locally roasted coffee; throughout, there's loads of natural light, historic industrial features, and handmade furniture in each room. ✉ *212 3rd St., Clarksdale, MS* ☎ *662/483–0693* 🌐 *www.stayattravelers.com* $ *From $144.*

# North Carolina

From the Outer Banks' secluded barrier islands to the Smoky Mountains' majestic peaks, North Carolina is an outdoor enthusiast's dream. There are scenic drives along the Blue Ridge Parkway, quaint mountain towns, and numerous opportunities for hiking, biking, and fishing. Urban adventures include hip Asheville, host to America's largest privately owned home, Biltmore Estate, and university-centric cities like Raleigh, Durham, and Chapel Hill.

## Bucket List Picks

The following boxes contain our picks for the top sights and experiences in North Carolina.

- O Great Smoky Mountains National Park
- O The Outer Banks
- O Asheville
- O Blue Ridge Parkway
- O Appalachian Trail
- O The Triangle
- O Small Carolina Mountain Towns
- O Wilmington Beaches

# Great Smoky Mountains National Park

## USA's Most Popular Park

Great Smoky may be the most visited national park in the United States, but that doesn't mean there's no peace or wonder to be found. The park straddles the state line between North Carolina and Tennessee, and the Carolina side is far less visited than Gatlinburg and Pigeon Forge in Tennessee. The area provides boundless opportunities for off-the-beaten-path outdoor adventures such as hiking and fishing, and you will almost always spot elk in the evening and early morning, as well as wild turkeys, deer, and perhaps bears.

## Don't Miss

Camping in Great Smoky is like having a backstage pass to the park's majesty; there are developed sites at Cataloochee, Balsam Mountain, and Smokemont. Secure a backcountry permit to plan an epic overnight hiking trip. 🌐 *smokiespermits.nps.gov.*

## Best Stop

One of the most memorable and eerie sites in Great Smoky is the Cataloochee Valley, a community that was abandoned when taken over by the NPS in 1934. You can visit many of the original buildings that were left behind.

## While You're Here

The Mountain Farm Museum next to the Oconaluftee Visitor Center is perhaps the best re-creation anywhere of an Appalachian mountain farmstead.

## Getting Here and Around

The most popular park entrance on the North Carolina side is Oconaluftee in Cherokee. Asheville, about a 1½-hour drive from the Oconaluftee entrance, is a good base.

**Oconaluftee Visitor's Center.** ✉ *1194 Newfound Gap Rd., Cherokee, NC* 🌐 *www.nps.gov/grsm.*

# The Outer Banks

## The Country's Wildest Beaches

Home to mysterious shipwrecks, the Lost Colony of Roanoke, and the Wright Brothers' first flight, this scenic string of barrier islands and their small towns (from Corolla south through Ocracoke) has no shortage of fascinating history. The wild horses of Corolla, however, take the cake. These feral mustangs, allegedly stranded here in the 1500s by Spanish explorers, now roam free (and are protected) on the OBX's northern beaches. Pair the ethereal sight with historic lighthouses you can climb plus beautiful beaches with white sand and pristine water, and you can see why the Outer Banks continue to draw seasoned vacationers to its shores.

## Don't Miss

Within Cape Hatteras National Seashore, a 60-mile geographical treasure great for shelling, surfing, birding, fishing, camping, and lighthouse exploring, the undeveloped Coquina Beach and Ocracoke Island beaches are some of the Outer Banks' loveliest shorelines.

## Best Tour

Race along 20 miles of beach with Wild Horse Adventure Tours' entertaining, informative guides in an open-air Hummer along Corolla's uninhabited beaches for some great photo ops of the wild horses. *wildhorsetour.com* *From $160.*

## Getting Here and Around

The closest large, commercial airports are Norfolk International Airport (ORF) in Virginia, a two-hour drive, and Raleigh-Durham International Airport (RDU), a four-hour drive. North Carolina Highway 12 is the only road connecting the Outer Banks. Ferry travel is also prevalent; Ocracoke Island, in the south, can be reached only by boat or ferry.

# Asheville

## Hippest Mountain Town

A scenic mountain town that seems always to be growing, Asheville has a few personalities, but that's half the fun. It has an outdoorsy side, which beckons you to trek trails along the Blue Ridge Parkway and Catawba River; a tourist-driven downtown, with lots of shops, excellent restaurants, and breweries within walking distance of one another (craft brews from DSSOLVR are a must). West Asheville is edgier and artsy, with some of the town's best dining and small shops (try Sunny Point Café for brunch).

## Don't Miss

The River Arts District is home to standout studios and galleries, plus breweries and bars along the river, but 12 Bones Barbecue is reason enough to visit the area.

## While You're Here

Tour the largest private home in America, the Biltmore Estate, to find the opulent yin to the laid-back yang of the town.

## Good to Know

The North Asheville Tailgate Market, open Saturday in spring and summer on the UNC-A campus, is Asheville's best seasonal farmers' market.

## Best Activity

Tubing down the French Broad River in summer via French Broad Outfitters is a must. Once aboard your inner tube, you'll lazily drift past the muraled warehouses of Asheville's River Arts District, and—perhaps the best part—pull off at outdoor bars along the last stretch. 🌐 *www.frenchbroadoutfitters.com.*

## Getting Here and Around

Asheville Airport (AVL) is about 15 miles from downtown. Downtown Asheville is easily walkable, and there's a bus system (ART), but you'll want a car if you plan to explore the surrounding mountains.

# Blue Ridge Parkway

### Land of the Sky

Driving the Blue Ridge Parkway's winding roads, past mountain peaks as far as the eye can see, is an epic journey. Stopping to hike or swim in a waterfall along the way takes the trip to the next level. The parkway's 252 miles within North Carolina wind down the High Country through Asheville, ending near the entrance of Great Smoky Mountains National Park. Highlights include Mt. Mitchell (the highest mountain peak east of the Rockies), Grandfather Mountain, and Mt. Pisgah. Nearly all the towns and cities along the route offer accommodations, dining, and sightseeing. In particular, Boone, Blowing Rock, Burnsville, Asheville, Waynesville, Brevard, and Cherokee are all near popular entrances to the parkway.

### Don't Miss

Linville Falls, one of North Carolina's most photographed waterfalls, is an easy ½-mile hike from the Linville Falls Visitor Center at milepost 316.4. The trail winds through evergreens and rhododendrons to overlooks with views of tumbling cascades.

### Best Stay

If you love the parkway, stay at Pisgah Inn. At mile marker 408 in Canton, this tranquil motel on top of Mt. Pisgah lands guests along the parkway, with hiking trails of its own—and an observation deck. The restaurant has great views and serves memorable mountain trout and fried chicken. There is also a large national park campground nearby. ⊕ *www.pisgahinn.com*.

### Getting Here and Around

You can access the parkway from Highway 70 east of Asheville, and south of town from Highway 191, near Interstate 26 and Biltmore Park (about a 15-minute drive from Asheville Regional Airport).

# Appalachian Trail

## Highest Point of America's Ultimate Hike

The famous 2,000-mile-plus hiking trail from Maine to Georgia has beautiful elevated stretches in North Carolina—the most mountainous section of the whole trail. The Appalachian Trail (or A.T. if you want to sound like a local) runs through Great Smoky Mountains National Park, along the Carolina-Tennessee border and past the popular Clingman's Dome. The trail also runs through the historic town of Hot Springs: stand on Main Street and you're technically on the trail. This former railroad town is a stopover for many hikers, so there are adventure outfitters, campgrounds, and several restaurants with good local craft beer.

## Don't Miss

Climbing the steep stairs of the observation tower at Clingman's Dome, at the highest point of the entire A.T., is an essential experience for panoramic views of the Great Smokies.

## Best Day Hike

Max Patch, a trail near Hot Springs, will get you "I hiked the A.T." bragging rights. West of Asheville, it takes a winding drive to get to—but the views at the top of this bald are worth it. There's a 1.5-mile loop to the top, and a longer, strenuous hike (9.7 miles) from Lemon Gap to Max Patch.

## Après Climb

The old resort at Hot Springs is still active, and you can book a soak in the private spring-fed tubs to soothe your muscles after your climb.

## Getting Here and Around

Hot Springs is about 45 minutes northwest of Asheville. In Great Smoky, many hikers start in the southwest of the park and take the A.T. up to Clingman's Dome; there is also parking at the base of the observation tower.

## The Triangle

### Food and Culture Capital

The Triangle area—Raleigh, Durham, Chapel Hill, and surrounding towns—is the most concentrated area of culture in North Carolina, competing with places like Atlanta for international, on-trend food and drink as well as art and nightlife. Raleigh is biggest, Durham is hippest, and Chapel Hill has the "college town" feel. Visit the latter for a nostalgic night out on Franklin Street or downtown Durham for intimate shows at Pinhook and Motorco, tapas at Mateo, or the craft beer at Ponysaurus Brewing Company. If the outdoors appeals, you'll be pleased to know many parts of the Triangle are tucked into the woods, such as Raleigh's Capital Greenway and Duke Forest Trail.

### Don't Miss

North Carolina Museum of Art (NCMA) on Raleigh's west side is a heavy hitter in Southern art with more than 5,000 years of artistic heritage, including one of the nation's largest collections of Jewish ceremonial art. The museum hosts touring exhibitions of works by such artists as Caravaggio and Rodin. The 164-acre park features nine monumental works of art, which visitors can view on foot or by bike. 🌐 *ncartmuseum.org*.

### While You're Here

While the NCMA is epic, Duke University's smaller Nasher Museum of Art also deserves a visit. It's incredibly well curated and manageable for an afternoon of Southern contemporary art—the photography is always fantastic—and there's a lovely little café.

### Getting Here and Around

Raleigh-Durham International Airport (RDU) serves the Triangle area and is a major hub. Interstates 40, 85, and 77, as well as several state highways, offer easy access to most of the region's destinations. Uber and Lyft are available everywhere.

# Small Carolina Mountain Towns

## Outdoor Adventures and Rustic Retreats

Folks head to the Carolina mountains for hiking and river rafting—the area's best activities. Even a short drive out of Asheville, northwest towards the Pisgah National Forest, south toward Great Smoky Mountains National Park, or northeast into High Country, promises jaw-dropping views from lookout points, seasonal roadside stands, and quaint mountain towns. Main streets of towns like Marshall have small breweries, vintage and ceramics shops, and restaurants that serve mountain cooking. South of Asheville, the towns of Hendersonville and Brevard (home of Oskar Blues Brewery and nearby trips to Sliding Rock, a natural slide that the adventurous zoom down in summer) are worth visiting.

## Don't Miss

Banner Elk, surrounded by the lofty peaks of Grandfather, Hanging Rock, Beech, and Sugar Mountains, is the place for good dining. Experience the town's Wooly Worm Festival in October, when actual woolly worms race to predict the winter weather forecast for North Carolina's High Country.

## Best Activity

White-water rafting at Blue Heron is a must. About 30 minutes northwest of Asheville, the French Broad River winds through mountains and becomes white water, with some Class II, III, and IV rapids that are safe for families, with a professional raft guide, but splashy and exciting enough for everyone. 🌐 *www.blueheronwhitewater.com.*

## Getting Here and Around

U.S. 221 (northeast) from Asheville leads to High Country towns of Banner Elk, Boone, and Blowing Rock. U.S. 25-70 (northwest) is the road to rafting outfitters, and towns of Marshall and Hot Springs.

# Wilmington Beaches

## North Carolina's Best Surf

The North Carolina coast doesn't lack beaches, but the ones around Wilmington are a little more activity-packed. The closest beach is at Wrightsville, which is its own laid-back surfing town very popular with locals, with a long boardwalk and the best waves in the area. Keep going south and there's an array of seaside restaurants at Carolina Beach, a large aquarium, historic fort, and a ferry at Kure Beach. In the other direction, north of Wrightsville, Figure 8 Island, Topsail Beach, up to Emerald Isle, are mostly quiet beach towns, with limited development, that make for great summer vacation spots.

## Don't Miss

Take the Southport–Fort Fisher Ferry from Kure Beach and Fort Fisher via U.S. Route 421 out of Wilmington. This state-operated year-round car ferry provides a 35-minute Cape Fear River ride between Old Federal Point at the tip of the spit and the mainland. Bald Head Island Lighthouse on Bald Head Island is seen en route, as well as the Oak Island Lighthouse and the ruins of Price's Creek Lighthouse—in fact, this is the only point in the United States where you can see three lighthouses at the same time. It's best to arrive early (30 minutes before departure), as it's first come, first served.

## Best Restaurant

You must have dinner at Pinpoint Restaurant when in Wilmington.

## While You're Here

Battleship North Carolina is permanently docked at the Cape Fear River; you can tour the ship itself, or take a river tour with Wilmington Water Tours.

## Getting Here and Around

Wilmington is about a two-hour drive south of Raleigh on Interstate 40.The beach is 10 minutes from downtown Wilmington.

## When in North Carolina

### GREAT DISMAL SWAMP

The forbidding name for this massive swamp—a uniquely large and wild ecosystem between northeastern North Carolina and Virginia—was possibly assigned to the area by William Byrd on one of his early-18th-century surveying expeditions. George Washington once hoped to drain it. Today the swamp is a 106,000-acre refuge and harbors bobcats, black bears, and more than 220 varieties of birds. Lake Drummond, a remarkably shallow lake that covers 3,000 acres and is only 6 feet deep, is surrounded by skinny cypress trees that lend the scene a primeval quality.

**Do This:** One hundred miles of hiking and biking trails, including a wheelchair-accessible boardwalk, cover the Dismal Swamp State Park; trails around Washington Ditch (Lake Drummond) and Jericho Lane are particularly nice (you'll cross into Virginia for most trails). There's also a self-guided auto tour, beginning at the Railroad Ditch entrance.

**Dismal Swamp State Park.** ✉ *2294 U.S. 17 N, South Mills, NC* ☎ *252/771-6593* [$] $5 per vehicle.

### SAXAPAHAW

Tiny Saxapahaw, a former cotton-mill town reinvented as an artsy farming community, makes for a good day trip from the Triangle area. The 25-minute drive takes you through acres of farmland; you can even get an overnight farm-stay experience at Terrastay Farms. Both the Saxapahaw General Store and the Eddy Pub next door are great for a meal. The deck at the Eddy overlooks Haw River, where you'll watch the herons soar, and (hopefully) spot some otters at play.

**Do This:** Explore the trails of the Saxapahaw Island Park, or rent a canoe or kayak and head out for a paddle on the river at Haw River Canoe & Kayak Co.

**Saxapahaw Island Park.** ✉ *5550 Church Rd., Graham, NC.*

## Cool Places to Stay

**Atlantis Lodge.** This 60s-style surf lodge, oceanfront on North Carolina's chill Crystal Coast, welcomes couples, families, and pets with style. It's all you'd want from a casual beach resort, and more: it has great outdoor hangout areas, bikes and ocean kayaks to rent, a saltwater swimming pool, a game room, and an on-site dog park. ✉ *123 Salter Path Rd., Atlantic Beach, NC* ☎ *252/726–5168* 🌐 *www.atlantislodge.com* [$] *From $314.*

**Cataloochee Campground.** Camping in Great Smoky is a good way to get close to all the park's hiking, fishing, and best activities while avoiding the crowds. Cataloochee is secluded, with epic scenery and a nice climate when the campground is open from April through October. Hiking trails and fishing streams can be reached from the site. There are bathrooms (but no showers) and drinking water, plus a nearby horse camp for overnight riding trips. ✉ *Great Smoky Mountains National Park, near Waynesville/Cataloochee entrance* 🌐 *www.recreation.gov/camping/campgrounds/233284* [$] *From $25.*

**The Durham.** Located in the heart of Durham, this boutique hotel with mid-century modern decor emphasizes everything local, from its overall design to the in-room snacks. The rooms are bright, service is friendly, and the hotel restaurant and bar are run by one of the best chefs in the state. The rooftop bar offers sweeping views of the city and is a favorite nightspot. ✉ *315 E. Chapel Hill St., Durham, NC* ☎ *919/768–8830* 🌐 *www.thedurham.com* [$] *From $189.*

# South Carolina

South Carolina's crown jewel is the port city of Charleston, one of the South's best-preserved cities, with beautifully restored homes and churches, cobblestone streets, hidden gardens, and a thriving culinary scene. But the state's coastal lowlands pack a punch too, featuring pretty landscapes of coastal forests and marshes, undisturbed beaches, and quaint fishing villages.

## Bucket List Picks

The following boxes contain our picks for the top sights and experiences in South Carolina.

- ○ The Lowcountry
- ○ Jocassee Gorges
- ○ Hilton Head
- ○ Charleston Beaches
- ○ Gullah Geechee Cultural Heritage Corridor
- ○ Summerville's Sweet Tea Trail
- ○ Charleston
- ○ Congaree National Park
- ○ Myrtle Beach

# The Lowcountry

## Coastal Carolina Culture

The "Lowcountry" refers to the marshy territory and sea islands along the Atlantic Coast, just south of Charleston—but it's more than just a geographic region, it's an experience. Visitors to Beaufort, Hilton Head, St. Helena, and other waterside communities are drawn to the scenic landscape, rich history, and even richer food and culture. Enjoying Frogmore Stew (or Lowcountry Boil)—seasoned shrimp and accoutrements—in a casual outdoor setting is just about as Lowcountry as it gets. Water is everywhere here, and you'll spend time admiring the marshy coastal views and balmy terrain, palmettos, or live oaks draped in Spanish moss.

## Don't Miss

Charleston City Market supports the 300-plus year tradition of weaving marsh grass into baskets, and there are some 50 Gullah resident artists selling their wares here.

## Best Day Trip

Near Beaufort, charming Old Town Bluffton has historic homes and churches on oak-lined streets dripping with Spanish moss, intermingled with new businesses like the Salt Marsh Brewing Company. The Bluffton Oyster Company (63 Wharf Street) is the place to buy fresh raw local shrimp, fish, and oysters.

## When to Go

Summer is fun for annual festivals like June's Blessing of the Fleet and Seafood Festival; May through mid-June is the big Spoleto Festival of art, music, and performance. Bivalve lovers should mark calendars for January's Lowcountry Oyster Festival and August's Seafood Beer and Wine Festival.

## Getting Here and Around

Charleston and Hilton Head make the best bases for exploring Lowcountry (Beaufort, Jasper, Colleton, and Hampton counties).

## Jocassee Gorges

### Land of Waterfalls

The Upstate of South Carolina is a land of waterfalls and wide vistas, cool pine forests, and fast rapids. Camping, hiking, white-water rafting, and kayaking are supreme in the Jocassee Gorges Wilderness Area, 50,000 acres of forest that take you past many gorges, waterfalls, and fantastic views. There's a vast network of trails here, but you can always start with a drive to get your bearings; pick up a guide at the visitor center to follow along for the best sights. Sassafras Mountain, the highest point in South Carolina, is reachable by car or hike, and the views of four states are rewarding. A few good hikes lead to waterfalls, or you can book a Waterfalls Tour with outfitters like Jocassee Lake Tours.

### Don't Miss

While it's a steep, slow drive up, Jumping Off Rock Overlook provides the best vista in the entire park.

### Best Stop

Spend time at Devils Fork State Park on Lake Jocassee, on the south end of the wilderness area, to get the most out of the water activities and natural beauty here. Lower Whitewater Falls plunges more than 200 feet over huge boulders to splash into the lake waters. You can view the falls from an overlook or from a boat on the lake. The park has accommodations, including both luxurious villas and camping facilities; hiking; boating; and fishing. 🌐 *www.southcarolinaparks.com/devils-fork.*

### When to Go

In spring, spot rare types of wildflowers in bloom from the easy Oconee Bells Nature Trail in Devil's Fork.

### Getting Here and Around

It's about a 50-minute drive from Greenville (home to the closest airport) to the Jocassee Gorge Visitor Center, and only 10 minutes further to Devils Fork and Lake Jocassee.

# Hilton Head

## America's Best Seaside Golf

Hilton Head Island is known far and wide as a vacation destination that prides itself on its top-notch golf courses and tennis programs, world-class resorts, and beautiful beaches. But the island is also part of the storied American South, steeped in a rich, colorful history. The former plantation land was bought and developed in the 1950s, and contemporary Hilton Head was planned with environmental preservation in mind. Visitors today will see an island that values its history as well as its natural beauty. The full Hilton Head experience can involve a few nights at a stylish resort, where you'll hit the links, book a spa day, relax at a beach club, or bike through tree-covered trails.

## Don't Miss

Climb Hilton Head's landmark candy-cane-stripe lighthouse to enjoy a view of Calibogue Sound.

## Best Greens

On the south end of the island, Sea Pines Resort is home to three of the most celebrated golf courses in Hilton Head: Harbour Town, Heron Point, and Atlantic Dunes. There's more than golf here, though: aside from the beach club and high-end resort amenities, the grounds at Sea Pines is home to a 605-acre public wilderness tract, the Sea Pines Nature Preserve. Here, go on a moonlight hayride or boat tour. 🌐 *seapines.com*.

## Getting Here and Around

The South Carolina coast is quite compact; Charleston is only two hours north of Hilton Head, and Savannah—the island shares its international airport (SAV)—is less than an hour away. There's also a smaller airport on Hilton Head. With resort shuttles, a trolley, and bike trails, the island is easy to explore without a car.

# Charleston Beaches

### "The Edge of America"

Many visitors think of Charleston only as its downtown peninsula, but the city actually occupies several islands across the Lowcountry's Atlantic coast. Exploring these beaches is half the fun in Charleston. Folly Beach is the Lowcountry's most iconic summer playground, a good place to start for a chill, local's experience—and to hunt for shark's teeth. The beach at Sullivan's Island is pristine, with 200 acres of walkable maritime forest adding to its beauty. Islands like Kiawah and Seabrook tend to be a mix of natural preserves and sophisticated beach clubs; riding horses on the beach at Seabrook is a great activity.

### Don't Miss

Charlestonians have been eating oysters since pre-Columbian times and the love of the bivalve has only gotten stronger since then; for a real deal oyster experience, head to Bowens Island, where the view over the tidal marshes is only matched by the taste of freshly shucked oysters.

### Best Beach

Kiawah Beachwalker Park, about 28 miles southwest of Charleston, is one of the Southeast's largest barrier islands. With 10 miles of wide, immaculate ocean beaches, it's often ranked among the country's best. You can walk for miles, shelling and beachcombing to your heart's content.

### Getting Here and Around

Charleston is the obvious base for exploring the sea islands; aside from Sullivan's Island to the north, most are just south of the city. You'll need a car to reach the beaches. Once you choose a destination, biking and walking (or kayaking) are the best modes of transport.

# Gullah Geechee Cultural Heritage Corridor

## Cradle of South Carolina Culture

Learning about the heritage of the Gullah Geechee people, descendants of Western and Central Africans brought to the South Carolina coast as slaves, is essential to understanding the area. Now an official National Heritage Area aimed to protect and promote the natural environment, history, and culture of the people, the Gullah Geechee Cultural Heritage Corridor is full of events, special programs, and heritage sites including the Sweetgrass Cultural Arts Pavilion in Mt. Pleasant, McLeod Plantation in James Island, the Gullah Museum and the Rice Museum in Georgetown, Caw Caw Interpretive Center in Ravinel, and Gullah Museum in Hilton Head.

## Don't Miss

About 9 miles southeast of Beaufort, St. Helena Island is a stronghold of the Gullah culture. Several African American–owned businesses in its tight-knit community of Frogmore make this a worthy day trip or stop en route to Fripp and Hunting Islands.

## While You're Here

Gullah cuisine is the bedrock of Charleston's culinary prowess, so it's impossible to truly say you've eaten in the Lowcountry without trying Bertha's, a James Beard American Classic.

## Best Tour

Enter the world of the Gullah Geechee (learning about the Gullah Geechee language and culture, and taking a fascinating dive into Charleston history) with Gullah Geechee Tours, the engaging and authentic tour from Gullah Geechee guides. 🌐 *www.gullahgeecheetours.com* 🎫 *$40.*

## Getting Here and Around

The Charleston area and Lowcountry Sea Islands are home to these cultural sites. Charleston, Savannah, or Hilton Head are good bases.

# Summerville's Sweet Tea Trail

## Birthplace of Sweet Tea

In the 1700s, Puritans and colonists sought respite from the heavy Charleston heat and found Summerville, a blooming paradise with a breeze. The "Official Birthplace of Sweet Tea" also prides itself on its flowers, and seeing the azaleas in bloom in spring is a joy. There's also a historic downtown full of antiques stores and small businesses. Tour many grand plantations that are preserved here, as Summerville became an icon of wealth (thanks, of course, to the profits of slavery). On the way to Middleton Place, Drayton Hall, and Magnolia Plantation from Charleston, stop at Timbo's, the famous roadside Airstream trailer for boiled peanuts.

## Don't Miss

Summerville's Sweet Tea Trail is the best way to get a little taste of the town; stop by the visitor center or download a guide online before setting out on a tour of the town's best sites, shops, and restaurants, including the Guinness Record–breaking "World's Largest Sweet Tea."

## While You're Here

You'll spend much time enjoying Summerville's contemporary charm, but touring the ruins of Colonial Dorchester State Historic Site, a 1697 settlement, is a fascinating step back in Charleston history. Well-preserved remains include a bell tower, tabby fort made of oyster shells, and shipping wharf. 🌐 *www.southcarolinaparks.com/colonial-dorchester.*

## When to Go

Visit in spring or early summer, when the flowers are in bloom, or in September for the Sweet Tea Festival.

## Getting Here and Around

Summerville is 25 miles inland from Charleston, and is best combined with a trip to the Holy City and its coast.

# Charleston

## USA's Best-Preserved City

It's obvious why filmmakers look to Charleston as a backdrop for historic movies. Dozens of church steeples punctuate the low skyline, and horse-drawn carriages pass centuries-old mansions, their stately salons offering a crystal-laden and parquet-floored version of Southern comfort. Outside, magnolia-filled gardens overflow with carefully tended heirloom plants—in fact, you can take a trip outside the city to Middleton Place, the oldest landscaped garden in the country. The city may resemble a 19th-century etching come to life—but look closer and you'll see that block after block of old structures have been restored, making this one of the South's best-preserved cities.

## Don't Miss

Get a great city introduction with a Bulldog Tours' history, food, or ghost tour. You'll learn about some of Charleston's layers, its Revolutionary War history, and get the lay of the land, including East Bay Street's famous Rainbow Row, 13 pastel row houses built between 1748 and 1845.

## Best Museum

Charleston Museum was America's first museum, founded in 1773, with exhibits and artifacts on display from the Revolutionary War, as well as galleries of natural history and African American stories. Check out historic houses that are part of the museum, and on the way, stroll some of downtown's hidden alleyways.

## Getting Here and Around

While you might want a car to explore Charleston's beaches, it's best to park downtown and explore on foot, via the free DASH trolley, or by renting a bike from Holy Spokes, the Charleston bike-share system.

## Congaree National Park

### Redwoods of the East

This nearly 27,000-acre park (the only national park in South Carolina) contains many old-growth bottomland hardwoods, the oldest and largest trees east of the Mississippi River. The water and trees are beautifully eerie. Self-guided canoe trails and 22 miles of hiking trails line the park, which is full of wildlife, including otters, deer, and woodpeckers, as well as the occasional wild boar. There's also a 2.5-mile boardwalk through the swamp. Aside from the ancient trees, there's an abundance of human history to the park, dating as far back as prehistoric people. Notably, the dense swamp served as an important landscape for African Americans escaping slavery.

### Don't Miss

Oakridge Trail (7 miles) is great for spotting wildlife, and Simis and Bates Ferry Trails trace some of the park's human history.

### Best Tour

Big Trees Hike, a three hour event covering 5 miles of swampland, takes you to the largest trees in the swamp, and is typically led by the park's founder, John Cely, or other experts.

### When to Go

Visit Congaree from mid-May to June for Firefly Festival, when synchronous fireflies (and many human visitors from all over) grace the park for a sparkling evening show.

### Getting Here and Around

Congaree is only 18 miles from the fun and sophisticated college town of Columbia, South Carolina, which is also home to the closest regional airport. The big hub of Charlotte Douglas International Airport (CLT) is 110 miles north.

**Congaree National Park.** ✉ *100 National Park Rd., Hopkins, SC* 🌐 *www.nps.gov/cong* 🎫 *Free.*

# Myrtle Beach

## Playground for Grown-Ups

It's no big city, but Myrtle Beach has bright lights aplenty. The Grand Strand boasts 60 miles of beaches, but just as many people visit for the golf and go-karts. Behind the glitz, there's deep culture and wild nature to explore. This is where shag dancing began, and you can still cut a rug with the old-timers at the clubs along Main Street in North Myrtle Beach. Several piers offer productive fishing, and Huntington Beach State Park is home to dozens of alligators that lie around lazily in the sun. Myrtle Beach is a beachside Gatlinburg, or Las Vegas sans the sin. The best approach? Relax and embrace this vacation-oriented stretch of coast in all its gaudy glory.

## Don't Miss

The massive SkyWheel along Myrtle Beach's main strip forms a landmark you can see from a mile away—but the view is even better from 200 feet up.

## Best Night Out

When the sun goes down, head to Main Street in North Myrtle Beach for a night of shag dancing and club hopping that's distinctly South Carolina. Fat Harold's Beach Club is home base, where the decor and dance floor feel like stepping back in time to a simpler age. Hop across the street to Duck's Beach Club, where live cover bands keep feet moving, before dropping into OD Arcade & Lounge for more shag dancing or a game of pool.

## When to Go

You'll find significantly reduced hotel prices, restaurant wait times, golf green fees, and beach crowds between October and March.

## Getting Here and Around

Myrtle Beach has its own international airport (MYR) right on the edge of downtown. Uber/Lyft, taxis, and a Coastal RTA bus system are available within Myrtle Beach.

# When in South Carolina

### THE BONEYARD AT BOTANY BAY

Spanish moss drapes from live oak limbs over the road as you pass centuries-old plantations on your way to sleepy Edisto Beach, South Carolina. Thousands of acres of unspoiled land, the ruins of two plantations, trails, maritime forests, and ponds surround the beach at Botany Bay Plantation Wildlife Management Area, a state park on Edisto Island. Fallen, sun-bleached trees frame ocean views on this picturesque beach, giving it its "Boneyard" name. The plantation area, including the beach, is closed Tuesdays for organized hunts; other days the beach is open sunrise to sunset. Keep in mind that because of hurricane erosion, the beach is impassable during high tide. Call ahead or check tide schedules online when planning your visit.

**Do This:** Park at the beach access and hike the half-mile Pockoy Island trail, a short and scenic way through dense wetlands to reach miles of beach. Later, continue on for a drive to view the Sea Cloud Plantation ruins.

**Botany Bay.** ✉ *Botany Bay Rd., Edisto Island, SC* 🌐 *www.edistobeach.com/botany-bay.*

### WORLD GRITS FESTIVAL

Each year the town of St. George's, outside Charleston, celebrates corn grits, a Lowcountry staple, in a pleasantly funky and fun small-town-Southern way. The festival began in 1985 when the community "discovered" (through some purchase orders) that they actually ate the most grits per capita of anywhere else in the world. The normally quiet town draws throngs of visitors for three days in April for a down-home celebration that features plenty of grits dishes, fundraising for their community, and fun activities like a grits-eating contest, rolling in the grits, a 5K, and a corn toss.

**Do This:** If you dare, sign up for the rolling-in-the-grits contest. Contestants enter a large inflatable pool filled with—you guessed it—grits, and have 10 seconds to roll in the sloppy mixture before (hopefully) successfully exiting in the pool.

**World Grits Festival.** ✉ *110 S. Parler Ave., St. George, SC* ☎ *843/563–7943* 🌐 *www.worldgritsfestival.com.*

# Cool Places to Stay

**Edisto Treehouses.** A 13-mile canoe trip on the Edisto River (about an hour inland of Charleston) ends with a stay at your own private (and rustic) oasis nestled among the trees. Small lounging decks among the branches come complete with grills; there are also screened-in sleeping lofts, hammocks, and a small outfitted kitchen. Visitors paddle in, stay the night, and continue on a leisurely 10 miles down river to the outpost in the morning. ✉ *1 Livery La., St. George, SC* ☎ *843/563–5051* 🌐 *www.canoesc.com* [$] *From $190.*

**Zero George.** The impressively restored circa-1804 buildings offer the historic charm visitors seek from Charleston, while the guest rooms and common spaces are fresh, elegant, and comfortable, pleasing the pickiest of modern travelers. Rooms have a varied decor inspired by different elements of Charleston's past—tailored British trade, airy French Romantic, and nautical Yachting Design—and feature natural linens and fabrics, marble bathrooms, and custom furniture. ✉ *0 George St., Charleston, SC* ☎ *843/817–7900* 🌐 *www.zerogeorge.com* [$] *From $224.*

# Tennessee

Tennessee's music, scenic beauty, and history are top reasons the state continues to attract, entertain, and charm the masses. Several genres of American music have their roots and branches here: bluegrass and Appalachian music in the eastern parts of the state; country, Americana, and pop in Nashville; and blues, soul, and rock 'n' roll in Memphis. Nashville's reputation as the "Music City," draws visitors to the Grand Ole Opry, Honky Tonk Row, and Country Music Hall of Fame & Museum.

## Bucket List Picks

The following boxes contain our picks for the top sights and experiences in Tennessee.

- ○ Dollywood
- ○ Graceland
- ○ Cades Cove
- ○ Grand Ole Opry
- ○ Country Music Hall of Fame
- ○ Memphis's Beale Street
- ○ Gatlinburg
- ○ Nashville's Honky Tonk Highway

# Dollywood

## The Queen of Country's Theme Park

It's worth a trip to Dolly Parton's theme park just to honor this queen of country music—but Dollywood is also just a whole lot of fun. There's plenty of corny American fair attractions and actual thrills; Lightning Rod, the world's fastest wooden roller coaster, is pretty terrifying. You can also ride a steam locomotive, catch a live show at the Back Porch Theater, visit old buildings, and ride the Smoky Mountain River Rampage—or head for the newest thrill ride, the Family FireChaser Express dual-launch coaster, which is a huge dollop of frosting on a tasty array of attractions, live shows, dining, shopping, and crafts displays.

## Don't Miss

At the entrance to the park, find a replica of the humble cabin where Dolly was raised (two rooms with no running water, indoor plumbing, or electricity) in nearby Sevierville. This re-creation allows visitors to walk inside and explore her roots.

## Where to Stay

Cabins at Oak Haven Resort provide a peaceful landing pad for Dollywood festivities, about a 20-minute drive from the park. Cabins each have pool tables, foosball tables, hot tubs, and an arcade game, and there are some shared amenities on the property—including a series of walking trails, with great views of the Smokies. ⊕ *www.oakhavenresort.com.*

## Getting Here and Around

Knoxville's McGhee Tyson Airport (TYS) is 37 miles away and the closest airport to Dollywood, but Tri-Cities Airport (TRI, near Johnson City) and Asheville Regional Airport (AVL) are each about a two-hour-drive.

**Dollywood.** ✉ *2700 Dollywood Parks Blvd., Pigeon Forge, TN* ⊕ *www.dollywood.com* 🎫 *From $69.*

# Graceland

### The King's Castle

Even non-Elvis fanatics will appreciate the kitschy excess and ridiculous glamour of the King of Rock 'n' Roll's estate (purchased for $100,000 in 1957, when Presley was 22). While touring, keep an eye out for decor details, particularly the carefully chosen wallpaper and upholstery. A recent over-the-top expansion packed in even more Elvis style, but his automobile museum is still a favorite feature, as are his famous pink Cadillac and "Jungle Room," with its green shag carpet and waterfall.

### Don't Miss

Elvis is buried outside the mansion, and tours conclude with many fans leaving tokens at his grave site.

### When to Go

The most popular (and busiest) time to visit Graceland is in August for "Elvis Week," when fans flock to Memphis to honor the King's life.

### While You're Here

Take a drive 10 minutes north to Soulsville Stax Museum of Soul Music. Look for the marquee reading "Soulsville U.S.A.," and listen for the sounds of soul icons like Otis Redding, Isaac Hayes, and Aretha Franklin as you approach the former home of Stax Records, rebuilt to look as it did during the label's heyday in the 1960s and early '70s. Inside, it's wall-to-wall music along with a history of Stax, from its beginnings as a home base for local musicians to an international sensation. Nearby, the Four Way is Memphis's oldest Soul food restaurant.

### Getting Here and Around

Graceland is only 3 miles from Memphis International Airport (MEM), and 15 minutes from downtown Memphis.

**Graceland.** ✉ *Elvis Presley Blvd., Memphis, TN* 🌐 *www.graceland.com* 🎫 *From $26.*

# Cades Cove

### Crown Jewel of the Smokies

A 6,800-acre valley surrounded by high mountains, Cades Cove has more historic buildings than any other area in Great Smoky Mountains National Park. Driving, hiking, or biking the 11-mile Cades Cove Loop Road, you can spot three old churches (Methodist, Primitive Baptist, and Missionary Baptist), a working gristmill (Cable Mill), a number of log cabins and houses in a variety of styles, and many outbuildings. The Cherokee, who hunted in Cades Cove for hundreds of years, called this valley *Tsiyahi* (place of otters), but today you're more likely to spot bears, deer, and wild turkeys.

### Don't Miss

The 11-mile Cades Cove Loop is the most popular route in the park and arguably the most scenic part of the entire Smokies. A highlight of the loop road is the Cable Mill area, with a visitor center, working water-powered gristmill, and a restored farmstead. On select days, the route is open for bicyclists only.

### Good to Know

You can rent bikes at the Cades Cove Campground Store—also one of the only places to shop for provisions within the park.

### Planning Your Time

The Loop Road gets 2 million visitors per year; at peak times traffic in and out of here can be extremely slow. Allow at least two to three hours just to drive the loop.

### Getting Here and Around

The closest park entrance to Cades Cove is in Townsend, Tennessee, about 25 miles southwest of Pigeon Forge.

**Great Smoky Mountains National Park.** ✉ *Cades Cove Loop Rd., Townsend, TN* 🌐 *www.nps.gov/grsm* 🎫 *Free.*

# Grand Ole Opry

### Country's Center Stage

The legendary country music stage and its enormously popular radio show, performed live in the Grand Ole Opry House, is an essential piece of American music history. The Opry has been broadcasting country music since 1925, making it the longest running radio broadcast in America's history, and has packed in the crowds for live music just as long. You can see superstars, legends, and up-and-coming stars on this stage and at its sister property, the historic Ryman Auditorium. The Opry seats about 4,400 people and is broadcasted live on WSM AM 650 on Tuesday, Friday, and Saturday nights, when you can join the audience. There's no better place to understand country music's past, present, and future.

### Don't Miss

Ryman Auditorium, the Opry's former home, opened for its first concert in 1892. You can tour both properties and catch country shows here as well.

### Best Shop

Head to Tubbs Record Shop for contemporary country music, Nashville classics, and a large selection of vinyl of all sorts. The shop, across from the Ryman Auditorium near the Country Music Hall of Fame, has been open since 1947. 🌐 *www.ernesttubb.com.*

### Good to Know

It's best to buy show tickets ($25–$57) well in advance.

### Getting Here and Around

The Opry is 8 miles from Nashville International Airport (BNA), and about 12 miles from downtown Nashville.

**Grand Ole Opry.** ✉ *2804 Opryland Dr., Nashville, TN* 🌐 *www.opry.com.*

# Country Music Hall of Fame

## Seeing Stars

Often called "the Smithsonian of Country Music," the Country Music Hall of Fame and Museum is Nashville's tribute to the genre's finest artists and tunes. It's an impressive full city block long, filled with plaques and exhibits highlighting performers from the old-time favorites to the latest generation of stars, a theater, and a two-story wall with gold and platinum country records. Tours of the historic RCA Studio B recording studio are also run by the museum. The extensive collection of memorabilia and rotating exhibits make this an essential stop for any music fan or history buff.

## Don't Miss

Elvis Presley's solid-gold 1960 Cadillac limo is a must-see. Circa, the museum store, is the place for Nashville-made goods and official musician merchandise.

## While You're Here

Stop at the nearby Johnny Cash Museum between Broadway and the Country Music Hall of Fame and Museum. Performance costumes, handwritten lyrics, and a wall of gold and platinum records are among the items in this museum.

## When to Go

The Country Music Association (CMA) Music Festival is typically held over four days in June; it's a festive time for country music fans to flock to Nashville.

## Getting Here and Around

The Hall of Fame is in downtown Nashville, off Broadway, and near many other attractions and hotels. Nashville's airport is about a 15-minute drive.

**Country Music Hall of Fame.** ✉ 222 *Rep. John Lewis Way S, Nashville, TN* 🌐 *www.countrymusichalloffame.org* 🎫 *From $23.*

# Memphis's Beale Street

### Barbecue and Bright Lights

Music lovers flock to Memphis for its past musical legends and their historic sights, and the still-happening beats of blues, soul, and rock at the clubs on Beale Street. At night, visitors can eat Memphis barbecue, stroll the lively blocks (adorned with historical markers commemorating music events) and pop in and out of clubs like Rum Boogie Cafe and Tin Roof, or buy tickets to a show at the New Daisy Theater. During the day, visits to Sun Studio, and to the Lorraine Motel—the location of MLK's tragic killing—now home to the National Civil Rights Museum, are essential pieces of Memphis, music, and greater American history.

### Don't Miss

Some good contemporary nightlife and live music can be found off the main stretch as well: Wild Bill's Juke Joint, in the Vollintine Evergreen District, is a local gem.

### Best Barbecue

Memphis is famous for its dry-rubbed ribs, and if you're looking for somewhere right off Beale Street, the basement dining room at Charlie Vergos' Rendezvous is an institution. It's worthwhile, though, to head further uptown (a seven-minute drive from Beale Street) to the nondescript strip mall location of Cozy Corner, where the ribs are excellent, but smoked cornish game hen is a specialty. 🌐 *www.cozycornerbbq.com.*

### Getting Here and Around

Memphis International Airport (MEM) is 11 miles from Beale Street and downtown Memphis.

# Gatlinburg

## Gateway to the Great Smokies

As a gateway to the Great Smoky Mountains National Park, Gatlinburg hosts thousands of guests a night, who come to witness the wondrous mountains that attracted visitors a century ago and to take advantage of outdoor sports and recreation, including Tennessee's only ski resort. Dollywood might be the town's official theme park, but downtown Gatlinburg is just as entertaining, with many fun and cheesy attractions, go-karts, miniature golf, and an aerial tram.

## Don't Miss

One of the longest aerial tramways in the country is at Ober Gatlinburg, and riding up the mountain provides great views of downtown Gatlinburg and surroundings.

## Best Tour

You don't have to whisper anymore to find moonshine in Gatlinburg—you can visit the state's first legal moonshine distillery, Ole Smoky Distillery. Take a tour to see the process in action, then sample magical mountain elixirs made with 200-year-old recipes and local corn. You can buy seasonal and special flavors—such as Apple Pie and Lemon Drop—that aren't available in package stores. 🌐 *olesmoky.com.*

## When to Go

Summer is busy in Gatlinburg, so late spring or fall can be nice for avoiding crowds. Some flock to Ober Gatlinburg for skiing (and other snow activities, like tubing) during winter, but you can ride the aerial tram up the mountain other times of year.

## Getting Here and Around

Gatlinburg is the main entrance to Great Smoky Mountains National Park. Knoxville airport is about a one-hour drive to Gatlinburg; both Tri-Cities Airport (near Kingsport and Johnson City) and Asheville Regional Airport are about two hours away.

# Nashville's Honky Tonk Highway

## Country on Broadway

The crown jewel of Nashville entertainment and a place that really embodies the city's soul is lower Broadway, located right in the middle of downtown. This stretch of road is called the Honky Tonk Highway, where live country and rock music pour out of nearly every window while beer flows out of every tap. Surrounding Broadway is a growing fine-arts scene with multiple galleries and plenty of restaurants cooking up Southern food (including the city's must-try Nashville hot chicken). Just a few blocks away are world-class museums and the symphony.

## Don't Miss

Robert's Western World is one of the best honky-tonks in town.

## Best Nashville Hot Chicken

Prince's was the first, but Nashville chain Hattie B's does hot chicken especially well. Rumor goes that the Nashville specialty—a cayenne-spiced and battered fried chicken—first came to be when a woman served the dish to her cheating husband as a punishment. It backfired. At Hattie's, enjoy hot chicken of varying heat levels, wash it down with a sweet tea or craft brew, and complement your meal with a delicious Southern-inspired side or two. 🌐 *www.hattieb.com.*

## Getting Here and Around

Downtown Nashville is located in the center of the circle that comprises the city. Take a cab or rideshare to go out on lower Broadway—or book the Sprocket Rocket Party Bike, for a pedaled party. 🌐 *www.sprockettours.com.*

# When in Tennessee

### CHATTANOOGA

The outdoorsy coolness of this hip little mountain city have some calling Chattanooga the new Asheville. There's plenty of hiking and biking in the area, or just take in the scenic views while in town, where the Tennessee River flows, and you can paddleboard or kayak. The Northshore neighborhood runs along the river, with parks and lots of food options (try Aretha Frankenstein's for breakfast). Hunter Museum of Art, in the Bluff View neighborhood, also overlooking the river, is large and modern and definitely worth a couple of hours.

**Do This:** Craft beer and cocktails at small Chattanooga bars and eateries are especially good; there are several local breweries, and the Chattanooga Experimental Whiskey Distillery downtown and elsewhere.

### ELKMONT FIREFLIES

What began as a logging town in the early 20th century became a lively summer colony for families, and eventually—after the NPS took it over to create Great Smoky Mountains National Park—a ghost town. These days Elkmont is primarily a campground, but its true appeal is that it provides the ideal setting for synchronous fireflies to light up the wilderness in the summer, one of the few places this happens in the United States. From the campground, follow the Elkmont Nature Trail and then to the Old Elkmont Cemetery to add a touch of spookiness—and historical relevance—to the eerily beautiful area.

**Do This:** June is when the synchronous fireflies (hundreds of lightning bugs blinking in patterned responses) light up the Elkmont area in a truly magical show.

**Elkmont Historic District.** ✉ *504 Little River Rd., Gatlinburg, TN.*

### THE LOST SEA AT CRAIGHEAD CAVERNS

Craighead Caverns is home to the second-largest underground lake in the world (and the largest in the United States), earning it the nickname "the Lost Sea." The very extensive cave system is located between Sweetwater and Madisonville, Tennessee. Former cave visitors include the Pleistocene jaguar, which left tracks in the cave about 20,000 years ago. The cave system was also extensively used by the Cherokee tribe.

**Do This:** You can take a "boat adventure" through the lake, which will start with a guided walking tour of the caverns, followed by a boat tour of the Lost Sea itself.

**Craighead Caverns.** ✉ *140 Lost Sea Rd., Sweetwater, TN* ☎ *423/337–6616* 🌐 *thelostsea.com* 🎫 *$23.95.*

### RUBY FALLS

More than 80 years ago, Leo Lambert and a small crew spent 17 hours inside this cavern before discovering what is now the world's tallest and deepest underground waterfall (145 feet) open to the public. After your visit underground, head up the 70-foot-high Lookout Mountain tower for a spectacular panorama of the Tennessee River Valley, using either your own peepers or one of the coin-operated telescopes.

**Do This:** Friday (and select Saturday) evenings from February through November, visitors can book a guided night tour of the falls, lit only by handheld lanterns.

**Ruby Falls.** ✉ *1720 South Scenic Hwy., Chattanooga, TN* ☎ *423/821–2544* 🌐 *www.rubyfalls.com* 🎫 *From $12.95.*

# Cool Places to Stay

**Blackberry Farm.** If you're looking for luxury in the Great Smokies, this lauded farm and restaurant is the place to be.

The setting is everything you can expect from the Tennessee mountains, but the amenities are what make it really decadent. Blackberry is particularly known for its excellent culinary endeavours, showcasing local ingredients, and even has its own brewery. There's also fly-fishing, horseback riding, cooking classes, and a wellness center and pool. ✉ *1471 W. Millers Cove Rd., Walland, TN* 🌐 *www.blackberryfarm.com* [$] *From $800.*

**Dive Motel & Swim Club.** Blending the laid-back vibe of a retro motor lodge with a hip pool and bar scene, this 23-room motel, from the design masterminds behind the Urban Cowboy brand in Nashville and New York, reopened under a new name in 2019. The mood is light and bright, with—unique to each room—yellow and pink shag bedspreads, nature-inspired cabin decor, vivid patterned wallpaper, and hand-painted wall murals. Flip the "party switch" in each room and a disco ball spins in tune with the music. Checkerboard flooring, an A-frame ceiling, a Malm-style fireplace, and vinyl booths are in the bar. ✉ *1414 Dickerson Pike, Nashville, TN* ☎ *615/650–9103* 🌐 *www.thedivemotel.com* [$] *From $229.*

**LeConte Lodge.** Set at 6,360 feet near the summit of Mt. LeConte in Great Smoky Mountains National Park, this hike-in lodge is remote, rustic, and remarkable (but not luxurious). Small, rough-hewn wood cabins and three group-sleeping cabins have bunk beds, propane heaters, and kerosene lamps, and there are privies with flush toilets, but no showers. The appeal of LeConte Lodge is in the mountaintop setting, where you can take in views from your deck rocking chair and stargaze at night. There is no road access to the lodge; the only way in is by hiking trail. The lodge books up quickly, using a lottery system (for the season ahead) typically beginning October 1. Breakfast and dinner are included in rates. ✉ *Great Smoky Mountains National Park, TN* ☎ *865/429–5704* 🌐 *www.lecontelodge.com* [$] *From $159.*

**Oliver Hotel.** This boutique historic hotel makes a good base for exploring Knoxville and the Great Smokies, adding a mix of city sophistication to your outdoor adventures. Rooms are well designed with a mod feel. Oliver Royale is a nice choice for dinner (and has a great bourbon list), and the hotel's other on-site restaurant, Tupelo Honey Cafe, began in Asheville as a favorite for Southern brunch. Tucked behind the hotel lobby is Knoxville's only speakeasy. ✉ *407 Union Ave., Knoxville, TN* ☎ *865/521–0050* 🌐 *www.theoliverhotel.com* [$] *From $225.*

**The Peabody Memphis.** Even if you're not staying here, it's worth a stop to see this 12-story downtown landmark, built in 1925. The lobby has the original stained-glass skylights and the travertine-marble fountain that is home to the hotel's resident ducks. (The ducks parade to the fountain at 11 am, and they depart the fountain at 5 pm.) The rooms are decorated in a variety of period styles. ✉ *118 S. 2nd St., Memphis, TN* ☎ *901/529–4000* 🌐 *www.peabodymemphis.com* [$] *From $219.*

**Union Station Hotel.** Set in a restored neo-Romanesque train station, Union Station is breathtaking with its 65-foot-high ceiling of 100-year-old Tiffany stained glass. Reflecting the city's style, each room displays a blend of curated artwork, cowhide headboards, or leather furnishings along with essential guest comforts like Wi-Fi and in-room coffee. Combining luxury of the past with nods to the present by way of local art, the hotel is a reminder to embrace the romance of slow travel. ✉ *1001 Broadway, Nashville, TN* ☎ *615/726–1001* 🌐 *www.unionstationhotelnashville.com* [$] *From $259.*

Chapter 6

# THE GREAT PLAINS

Written by
Carson Walker

# WELCOME TO THE GREAT PLAINS

## TOP REASONS TO GO

★ **From the mountains:** South Dakota's Badlands National Park exudes the same awe-inspiring beauty of the Grand Canyon, but its rugged lunar landscape is more accessible.

★ **To the prairies:** Stay in a covered wagon at the Little House on the Prairie of South Dakota, or get lost on a bucket-list worthy trip in the Flint Hills of Kansas.

★ **And the cities, too:** Spend a day in St. Louis riding to the top of the Gateway Arch or in Kansas City's 18th and Vine district enjoying lip-smacking barbecue, visiting museums, and taking in a blues concert.

★ **Active adventures:** The best way to experience the Plains is the great outdoors, whether you're on the water in the Ozarks or hiking Ouachita National Forest.

★ **American history:** Landmark moments in U.S. history are commemorated at sights including Kansas's Brown v. Board of Education National Historic Site and the Oklahoma City Memorial in OKC.

1 **Arkansas.** Hot Springs, the Ozark Mountains, and Ouachita National Forest make the "Natural State" an outdoor paradise.

2 **Iowa.** Spend a day at the Iowa State Fair and take a selfie in front of the American Gothic house in Eldon.

3 **Kansas.** Stand in the geographic center of the United States and get out on the prairie.

4 **Missouri.** Ride to the top of the Gateway Arch, then head west for Kansas City barbecue.

5 **Nebraska.** Cheer at a College World Series game, watch prairie chickens dance, and gaze at the unique geological site of Chimney Rock.

6 **North Dakota.** Extending westward from the broad, flat Red River Valley, the prairies and plateaus here make it worth a trip to the north.

7 **Oklahoma.** Drive part of Route 66, be wowed by bison, and take in the vast Wichita Mountains Wildlife Refuge.

8 **South Dakota.** From Falls Park to the Black Hills and Badlands, there's more natural beauty than you can pack into one trip.

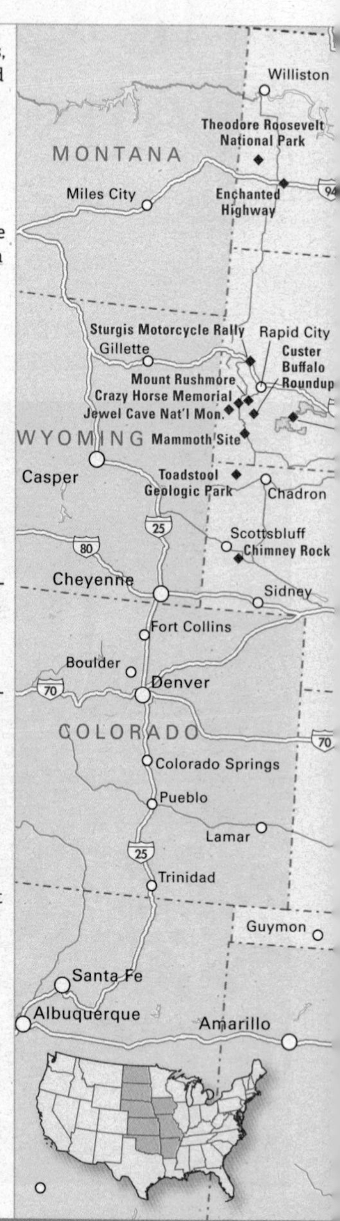

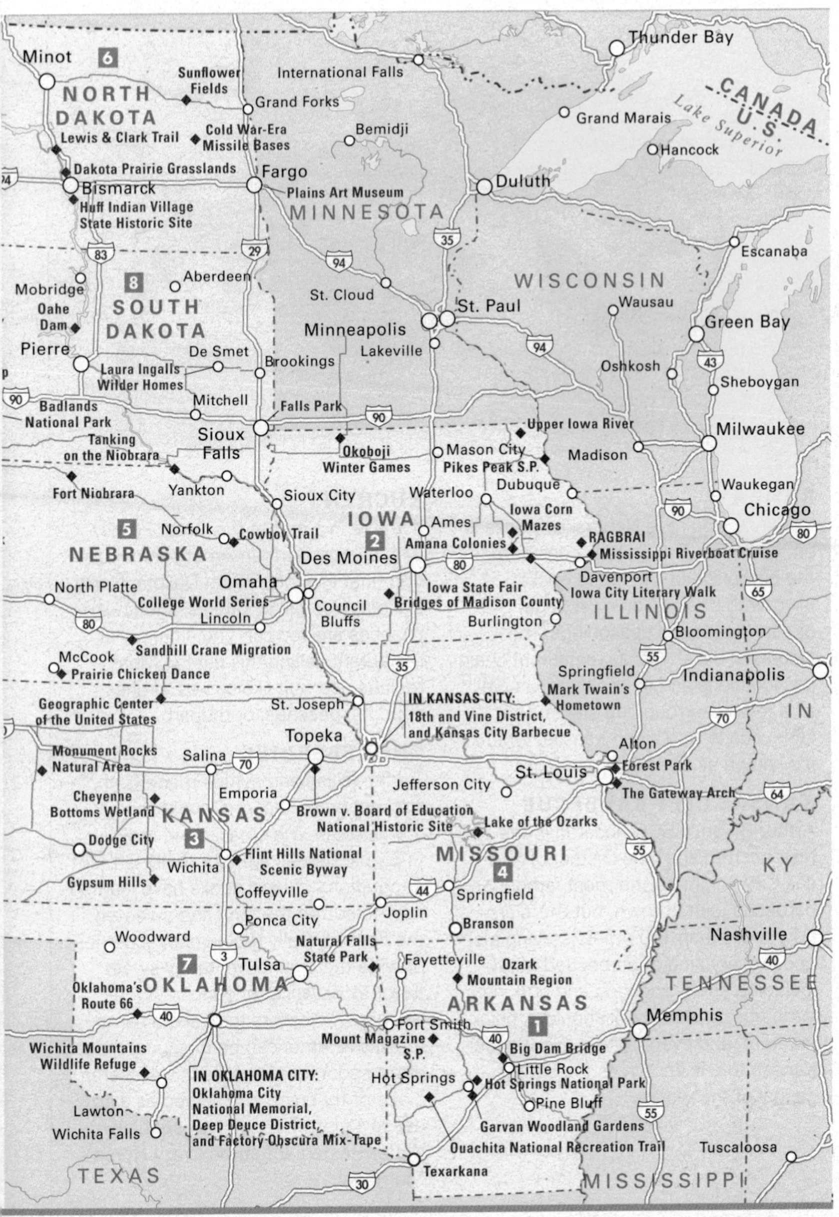
Minot
6
NORTH DAKOTA
Sunflower Fields
International Falls
Thunder Bay
CANADA
U.S.
Lake Superior
Grand Forks
Grand Marais
Lewis & Clark Trail
Cold War-Era Missile Bases
Bemidji
Hancock
Dakota Prairie Grasslands
Fargo
Bismarck
Duluth
Plains Art Museum
Huff Indian Village State Historic Site
MINNESOTA
Escanaba
Aberdeen
Mobridge
8
SOUTH DAKOTA
St. Cloud
WISCONSIN
Oahe Dam
St. Paul
Wausau
Minneapolis
Green Bay
Pierre
De Smet
Lakeville
Laura Ingalls Wilder Homes
Brookings
Oshkosh
Sheboygan
Badlands National Park
Mitchell
Falls Park
Upper Iowa River
Milwaukee
Tanking on the Niobrara
Sioux Falls
Okoboji Winter Games
Mason City
Pikes Peak S.P.
Madison
Fort Niobrara
Yankton
Sioux City
Waterloo
Dubuque
Waukegan
Iowa Corn Mazes
Chicago
5
Norfolk
Cowboy Trail
IOWA
Ames
2
Amana Colonies
RAGBRAI
Mississippi Riverboat Cruise
NEBRASKA
Des Moines
Davenport
North Platte
Omaha
Iowa State Fair
Iowa City Literary Walk
College World Series
Council Bluffs
Bridges of Madison County
ILLINOIS
Lincoln
Burlington
Bloomington
Sandhill Crane Migration
McCook
Prairie Chicken Dance
Springfield
Indianapolis
Mark Twain's Hometown
Geographic Center of the United States
St. Joseph
IN KANSAS CITY:
18th and Vine District, and Kansas City Barbecue
IN
Topeka
Alton
Monument Rocks Natural Area
Salina
Forest Park
St. Louis
Jefferson City
The Gateway Arch
Cheyenne Bottoms Wetland
Emporia
KANSAS
Brown v. Board of Education National Historic Site
Lake of the Ozarks
Dodge City
3
Flint Hills National Scenic Byway
MISSOURI
4
Wichita
KY
Gypsum Hills
Coffeyville
Springfield
Joplin
Ponca City
Branson
Woodward
Natural Falls State Park
Nashville
7
Tulsa
Fayetteville
Ozark Mountain Region
Oklahoma's Route 66
OKLAHOMA
ARKANSAS
TENNESSEE
Fort Smith
1
Memphis
Mount Magazine S.P.
Big Dam Bridge
Wichita Mountains Wildlife Refuge
Little Rock
IN OKLAHOMA CITY:
Oklahoma City National Memorial, Deep Deuce District, and Factory Obscura Mix-Tape
Hot Springs
Hot Springs National Park
Pine Bluff
Lawton
Wichita Falls
Garvan Woodland Gardens
Ouachita National Recreation Trail
Tuscaloosa
TEXAS
Texarkana
MISSISSIPPI

# WHAT TO EAT AND DRINK IN THE GREAT PLAINS

Runza

### RUNZA

You know you're in Nebraska if runza is on the menu. The state is considered the birthplace of the bread pocket filled with beef, onions, cabbage, or sauerkraut and seasonings. The Nebraska-based Runza restaurant chain has locations across the state, as well as a few in surrounding states. The sandwich is also big in Kansas, where it's known as bierock.

### KANSAS CITY BARBECUE

Arthur Bryant's BBQ, located in the historic 18th and Vine District of Kansas City, might be the most famous barbecue joint in town, but there are now more than 100 others serving just about every kind of barbecued meat, including short- and long-end pork ribs, lamb ribs, brisket, pork shoulder, chicken, ham, and even mutton. No wonder Kansas City is known as the barbecue capital of the world.

### KUCHEN

If you're in a part of the Great Plains with a large German-American population (that includes South Dakota, North Dakota, Nebraska, Kansas, and Iowa), chances are you can find a bakery or restaurant selling this pastry. Most recipes use fruit like apples, prunes, apricots, peaches, or rhubarb.

### CHOKEBERRIES

Try the jellies and syrups made from chokecherries that grow wild across the Dakotas. The small, deep-red-to-purple berries are tart, really tart, so generations of local cooks have learned how to soften the tang and sweeten the flavor. Locally grown chokecherries provide the distinctive, tangy-sweet flavor to *wojapi* (pronounced "woe-jaw-pea"), which is the Lakota name for Native American berry sauce, most often spooned atop a freshly prepared piece of fry bread and served as a dessert treat. Try it at the Laughing Water Restaurant at the Crazy Horse Memorial.

## CHISLIC

These bite-sized cubes of meat served with toothpicks are the pride of South Dakota. The legislature named it the "official state nosh," although it's also served as a main dish. The traditional meat is mutton or lamb, but beef, venison, and occasionally some other red meat are used in chislic. The South Dakota Chislic Festival is held the last Saturday of July in the farming town of Freeman.

## BISON BURGER

More and more Great Plains restaurants are serving this healthier alternative to beef burgers. Bison has less fat, so it's a bit drier. It also has more of an earthy flavor because the animals munch on grass. Don't worry about what name to use—"buffalo burger" in cafés or "bison" at an upscale evening place—the terms are interchangeable. To ship a box of the lean, flavorful delicacy home, visit the Wild Idea Buffalo shop in Rapid City.

## ARKANSAS POSSUM PIE

We know what you're thinking, and no, the recipe doesn't call for roadkill. Served in restaurants across the state, the dessert is supposedly called possum pie because it looks vanilla on the outside but is chocolate on the inside.

Bison burger

Chislic

## IOWA CHOP

Although it originated in Iowa, where hogs are said to outnumber people by roughly eight to one, this type of pork chop is popular around the Great Plains. The Iowa chop is a bone-in, center-cut loin chop that ranges from 1¼ to 1½ inches thick. The two most common ways of serving it are grilling and sautéing.

## TANKA BARS

Made in the region from a finely tuned recipe, Tanka is an energy bar that will really start your engine. Its principal ingredients include bison and berries.

## MAID-RITE SANDWICH

Iowa butcher Fred Angell came up with the idea for this sandwich in the 1920s. Also known as a loose-meat sandwich, it's not pressed like a hamburger. It's more similar to a sloppy joe, but without the tomato-based sauce. Angell started the Maid-Rite restaurant chain that still operates today across parts of the Great Plains.

## LEFSE

A Norwegian specialty, lefse is served at many holiday gatherings in North Dakota, as well as in other parts of the Great Plains. The traditional flatbread is cooked on a large griddle with potatoes, flour, butter, and milk or cream.

# The Great Plains Regional Snapshot

## Know Before You Go

### A CAR IS THE WAY TO GO

Subway service is available just about everywhere in the Great Plains, if you are referring to the sandwich shop. Public transportation isn't extensive, so your best bet is to drive your own vehicle across the wide-open spaces. Base yourself in one city and use it as a hub for exploring the region, or rent a car at one airport, head out on your journey, and return it at another. The drop-off fees usually aren't too bad.

### BYPASS THE INTERSTATES

The Great Plains sometimes get a bad rap for being flyover country where there's nothing interesting to see. But take the roads less traveled and you'll find interesting small towns, oddball roadside attractions, and mom-and-pop eateries. You'll also find some of the friendliest people you'll ever meet.

### SAMPLE A VARIETY OF FOODS

You'll never have trouble finding a steak house in the Great Plains, but this is also a prime spot for sampling buffalo and other locally raised meats. The farm-to-table movement has found its way here, so there is an emphasis on regional foods. Don't pass by the cafés that line the main streets of most towns, as they serve simple, delicious food.

## Planning Your Time

Be careful about trying to cover too much ground in too little time. The eight states in the Great Plains are huge, and you don't want to spend all of your time getting from one place to another. Consider the hub-and-spoke approach, staying in one location for a few days and setting off on day trips in different directions.

## Road Trips

**3 days:** Route 66 from St. Louis, Missouri, to Oklahoma City

**3 days:** Lincoln, Nebraska, to Davenport, Iowa

**5 days:** Rapid City, South Dakota, to Badlands National Park to Spearfish, South Dakota, to Hot Springs, South Dakota

## Big Events

**Iowa State Fair.** From butter sculptures to tractor-pulling contests, this is a mid-August slice of Americana in Des Moines.

**Oklahoma State Fair.** Drawing close to a million people, it's held every September in Oklahoma City.

**Sturgis Motorcycle Rally.** Held over 10 days in the beginning of August, this South Dakota tradition can draw half a million or more bikers.

## What To ...

### READ

*Bury My Heart at Wounded Knee* by Dee Brown

*The Grapes of Wrath* by John Steinbeck

*Little House on the Prairie* by Laura Ingalls Wilder

### WATCH

*Field of Dreams* (movie shot in Iowa)

*Dances With Wolves* (movie shot in South Dakota)

*Nebraska* (movie shot in Nebraska)

*Ozark* (show set in Missouri)

*Mud* (movie set in Arkansas)

*Deadwood* (show set in South Dakota)

*The Bridges of Madison County* (movie shot in Iowa)

### LISTEN

*Plains Folk* (NPR podcast)

"Arkansas" by Chris Stapleton (single)

"Kansas City Lights" by Steve Wariner (single)

"Route 66" by Nat King Cole, the Rolling Stones, or Depeche Mode (single)

"We're an American Band" by Grand Funk Railroad (single and album)

### BUY

Mineral water in Arkansas

Patrick Mahomes jerseys in Kansas City

Sunflower seeds in North Dakota

Tanka Bar bison jerky in South Dakota

## Contacts

### AIR

Major Airports:

**Arkansas:** XNA, FSM, LIT, TXK

**Iowa:** CID, DSM, DBQ, SUX, ALO

**Kansas:** GCK, MHK, ICT

**Missouri:** COU, JLN, MCI, SGF, STL

**Nebraska:** GRI, LNK, OMA

**North Dakota:** BIS, FAR, GFK, MOT, XWA

**Oklahoma:** LAW, OKC, TUL

**South Dakota:** ABR, RAP, FSD

### BUS

**Jefferson Lines.** ☎ *585/800-8898* 🌐 *www.jeffersonlines.com*

**Greyhound.** ☎ *800/231-2222* 🌐 *www.greyhound.com*

### TRAIN

**Amtrak.** ☎ *800/872-7245* 🌐 *www.amtrak.com*

### TAXI

**Kansas City Taxi.** ☎ *816/471-5000*

**10/10 Taxi.** ☎ *913/647-0010* 🌐 *www.1010taxi.com*

**City Taxi.** ☎ *402/933-8700* 🌐 *www.citytaxiinc.com*

**County Cab.** ☎ *314/991-5300* 🌐 *www.countycab.com*

### VISITOR INFORMATION

🌐 *arkansas.com*

🌐 *traveliowa.com*

🌐 *travelks.com*

🌐 *visitmo.com*

🌐 *visitnebraska.com*

🌐 *ndtourism.com*

🌐 *travelok.com*

🌐 *travelsouthdakota.com*

# Arkansas

Arkansas, "The Natural State," rolls out a welcome mat of lush terrain. The Ozark and Ouachita mountain ranges cradle northern and western regions, draping 10 scenic byways in a tapestry of brilliant fall color. Overall, more 600,000 acres of lakes and 9,700 miles of streams and rivers make the state a prime playground for outdoor enthusiasts who enjoy fishing, float trips and water sports, hunting, and camping. Seven national park sites plus 2.5 million acres of national forests and 52 state parks preserve and interpret Arkansas's diverse heritage, traditions, and natural resources.

## Bucket List Picks

The following boxes contain our picks for the top sights and experiences in Arkansas.

- ○ Hot Springs National Park
- ○ Big Dam Bridge
- ○ Ouachita National Recreation Trail
- ○ Ozark Mountain Region
- ○ Mount Magazine State Park
- ○ Garvan Woodland Gardens
- ○ Texarkana

# Hot Springs National Park

## An Epic Soak

You haven't really lived life to the fullest until you've soaked in Hot Springs' thermal water, melting your muscle aches away with soothing steam. The water here has been reputed to have medicinal properties for thousands of years, when indigenous peoples came to the springs. Congress created what is now Hot Springs National Park in 1832, setting aside land for the first time as a recreation area. Nine historic bathhouses dating from the early 20th century recall the days when high-society types—and, during Prohibition, gangsters and other shady figures—strolled down these streets.

## Don't Miss

There are two places in the park where you can watch the water bubbling out of the rock. (You can even reach out and touch it—it comes out of the ground at a steamy 147°F but quickly cools.) The Display Spring behind the Maurice Bathhouse flows into a shallow pool, a great place to relax and listen to the trickling water. Hot Water Cascade, at Arlington Lawn, is the largest visible spring in the park. It flows right beneath the Grand Promenade.

## Places to Soak

There aren't any places to soak within the national park, but there are two bathhouses in town that pipe in thermal springs water: the stately Buckstaff Bathhouse (🌐 *www.buckstaffbaths.com*) and the domed Quapaw Bathhouse (🌐 *www.quapawbaths.com*).

## Getting Here and Around

Hot Springs is an hour's drive southwest of Little Rock, Arkansas.

**Hot Springs National Park.** ✉ *369 Central Ave., Hot Springs, AR* ☎ *501/620–6715* 🌐 *www.nps.gov/hosp* 🎫 *Free to park, spa treatments vary.*

# Big Dam Bridge

## A Cyclist's Paradise

One of the best-loved sights of Little Rock, the capital city of Arkansas, Big Dam Bridge is the longest pedestrian- and bicycle-only bridge in North America at 4,226 feet. (No cars to share the road with here!) The bridge's name refers to its nearly mile-long span across the top of the Murray Lock and Dam. Besides providing great views of the Arkansas River below, it connects to 14 miles of trails on the Little Rock and North Little Rock sides of the river and gives riders easy access to the Clinton Presidential Center, the River Market, and other sights.

## Don't Miss

There are three trails, all of them loops, that you shouldn't overlook. The Garrison Loop and its sister trail, the Roland Loop, both start at Big Dam Bridge and head west before diverging near the eastern shore of Lake Maumelle. The Garrison Loop leads you deeper into the foothills of the Ouachita Mountains, passing several creeks as they join to form the Little Maumelle River. The Ross Hollow Loop takes you by the area's top wineries, which are located a few feet from the route. Stop and enjoy a glass as you take in the views of Lake Maumelle.

## When to Go

The Big Dam Bridge 100, Arkansas's largest cycling tour, takes place annually in late September. Participants can choose between courses from 15 to 105 miles. ⊕ *www.thebigdambridge100.com.*

## Getting Here and Around

Big Dam Bridge is in the northwestern part of Little Rock, off Interstate 430.

**Big Dam Bridge.** ✉ *7600 Rebsamen Park Rd., Little Rock, AR* ☎ *501/340–6800* ⊕ *www.littlerock.com/little-rock-destinations/big-dam-bridge* 🎫 *Free.*

# Ouachita National Recreation Trail

## Back-Country Hiking Challenge

The oldest national forest in the United States, Ouachita National Forest covers 1.8 million acres in central Arkansas and southeastern Oklahoma, and it has some serious treks. The best way to experience this swath of wilderness is the Ouachita National Recreation Trail, which runs for 192 miles across the entire length of the park with entrances in Perryville, Arkansas, to the east and Talihina, Oklahoma, to the west. The unpaved trail is a popular byway for mountain bikers, hikers, and backpackers. There are huge elevation changes—from 600 to 2,600 feet—as the trail passes through forested mountains, across sweeping valleys, and near crystal clear streams. Parts of the trail are definitely challenging, even for experts, but there's no need to hike the entire distance. Numerous access points provide opportunities for hikers of all skill levels.

## Don't Miss

Horsethief Springs Trail, closest to the Talihina, Oklahoma entrance, is a beautiful 11-mile loop hike using the Ouachita National Recreation Trail. It begins at Cedar Lake and snakes its way through several different species of trees, crossing several small streams before connecting with the Ouachita National Recreation Trail. The trail then loops back down the northern face of Winding Stair Mountain to Cedar Lake.

## Getting Here and Around

Start in the eastern boundary south of Perryville, Arkansas, on Highway 9, an hour northwest of Little Rock. Alternatively, start at the west entrance at Talimena State Park on Highway 271 near Talihina, Oklahoma, about a three-hour drive from Oklahoma City.

**Ouachita National Recreation Trail.** ✉ *100 Reserve St., Hot Springs, AR* 🌐 *www.fs.usda.gov* 🎫 *Free.*

# Ozark Mountain Region

## Ride the National River

Outdoor enthusiasts flock to the Ozark Mountain region, which covers much of northern Arkansas, for its river and lake adventures, hiking and biking trails, and quaint mountain towns filled with the sounds of folk music. There are several areas to base yourself to experience the spectacular region, including Buffalo River, Norfolk Lake, White River, and Bull Shoals Lake. Our pick? Buffalo River. The country's first designated "National River" runs for 135 miles through these parts, passing majestic waterfalls and sheer bluffs before it flows into the White River near Buffalo City. A canoe trip down the river, perhaps within sight of a tremendous herd of elk, is one of the best ways to experience the Ozark Mountains.

## Don't Miss

Kayak, canoe, or float down the great Buffalo River with the help of NPS-authorized concessionaire Buffalo River Outfitters, who rent equipment and arrange one- or multi-day trips. You can book luxury cabins through them, too. *www.buffaloriveroutfitters.com* *From $55.*

## Best Detour

About an hour northwest of Buffalo River, in Eureka Springs, is one of the most visited attractions in the Ozarks: the Christ of the Ozarks. Even nonbelievers will appreciate the sheer size of the seven-story statue, which vaguely resembles the similarly shaped Christ the Redeemer statue that rises above Rio de Janeiro, Brazil. It weighs more than 2 million pounds. *935 Passion Play Rd., Eureka Springs, AR* *www.christoftheozarks.org* *Free.*

## Getting Here and Around

The Ozark Mountain Region of Arkansas covers much of the northwest part of the state north of Interstate 40.

# Mount Magazine State Park

### Arkansas's Highest Point

Rock climbing doesn't get much better in "the Natural State" than at Mt. Magazine, home to Arkansas's highest point at 2,753 feet. The mountain's south bluff has a 1,500-foot-wide section with more than 100 routes reaching up to 80 feet high, a perfect playground for bouldering, sport climbing, and rappelling. Extreme-sports enthusiasts also love the chance to hang glide, ride ATVs, and mountain bike and hike on rugged trails, though all activities provide plenty of enchanting views of Petit Jean River Valley and Blue Mountain Lake. On a clear day, you can see about one-fourth of the state from the peak.

### Don't Miss

Snap a photo next to the signpost at Signal Hill, which marks the state's highest point. Or, take an epic hike to spot Mount Magazine Falls, a waterfall on the difficult North Rim Trail.

### By Car

If you prefer driving through the park instead of hiking, you can still access fantastic views. Take the Cameron Bluff Overlook Drive and park along the route to see the Ozark Plateau and the Arkansas River.

### Where to Stay

There are more than 15 places to camp within the state park, but for a more comfortable experience a stay at the Lodge at Mount Magazine.

### Getting Here and Around

Mount Magazine State Park is 16 miles south of Paris, Arkansas, on Scenic Highway 309. It's about a two-hour drive from Little Rock via Interstate 40 East or AR 10 East. The park is open year-round from 8 am to 5 pm.

**Mount Magazine State Park.** ✉ *16878 AR 309, Paris, AR* 🌐 *www.arkansasstateparks.com.*

# Garvan Woodland Gardens

## Not Your Average Flower Patch

Covering 210 acres in the Ouachita Mountains of southwest Arkansas, Garvan Woodland Gardens is not just a beautiful garden. Sure, there are nearly 5 miles of wooded shoreline along Lake Hamilton. And yes, you can't imagine the profusion of color in the spring, when 160 different types of azaleas line the trails, nor the dozens of species of native plants on display from spring to fall at the Perry Wildflower Overlook, where a flagstone terrace has views of the lake and Mt. Riante beyond. It's more than that. The gardens feature some surreal architecture that brings the outdoors inside, including a "floating" tree house and a light-filled timber chapel that have captured many an Instagrammer's eye.

## Don't Miss

Get your cameras out for Bob and Sunny Evans Tree House, a showstopping spectacle of angles that brings you level with the forest canopy of the garden.

## Good to Know

The Evans Children's Adventure Garden has 1½ acres of interactive activities with a waterfall and cave, an iron bridge that resembles woven tree branches, and rocks weighing more than 3,200 tons.

## When to Go

Spring is obviously the best time for blooms, but winter has the annual Holiday Light display featuring 5 million twinkling lights.

## Getting Here and Around

Garvan Woodland Gardens is located just south of Hot Springs, Arkansas, about an hour from Little Rock.

**Garvan Woodland Gardens.** ✉ *550 Arkridge Rd., Hot Springs National Park, AR* 🌐 *www.garvangardens.org* 🎟 *$15.*

# Texarkana

## The Two-State Selfie

Cross two states off your list for the price of one in Texarkana—sister cities in Texas and Arkansas. The 1930s-era U.S. Post Office and Courthouse here is the only federal building located in two states. Because of that unique geographic position, it's possible to straddle the state line while you take a pic to send to the folks back home. That reportedly makes it the second-most-photographed courthouse in the United States, right after the U.S. Supreme Court building in Washington, D.C. It's a handsome Greek Revival–style building, one that is big enough to have required a dozen buildings to be razed to make way for its construction.

## Don't Miss

The Arkansas Municipal Auditorium in Texarkana is rich in history. Elvis, Louis Armstrong, and other big names played here. It was a favorite stop along the Louisiana Hayride Circuit, which had heavy influence on modern-day country music and rock and roll. During World War II the auditorium became an important stage for up-and-coming vocalists, musicians, and variety shows.

## Getting Here and Around

Texarkana (its name a combination of Texas, Arkansas, and Louisiana) is a two-hour drive southwest of Little Rock, a 2½-hour drive northeast of Dallas, or a quick one-hour drive north of Shreveport.

**Texarkana.** ✉ *500 State Line Ave., Texarkana, AR* ☎ *903/792–3794* 🌐 *www.arkansas.com/texarkana* 🎟 *Free.*

# When in Arkansas

## CRATER OF DIAMONDS STATE PARK

Park visitors have uncovered—and taken home—more than 33,000 diamonds since the Crater of Diamonds became a state park in 1972. It's one of the only places on earth where the public can search for real diamonds, so people from all over the world make the trek to Murfreesboro, Arkansas. Visitors can bring their own mining tools or rent them from the park to search the 37-acre volcanic crater for a variety of rocks, minerals, and gemstones. Notable diamonds found at the crater include the 40-carat Uncle Sam, the largest diamond ever unearthed in the United States, the 16-carat Amarillo Starlight, the 15-carat Star of Arkansas, and the nearly 9-carat Esperanza.

**Do This:** Before heading out to the crater, spend some time in the visitor center to learn about diamonds and why so many of them are found on this site. You can also view a selection of real, uncut diamonds.

**Crater of Diamonds State Park.** ✉ *209 State Park Rd., Murfreesboro, AR* ☎ *870/285-3113* 🌐 *www.arkansasstateparks.com/parks/crater-diamonds-state-park* 🎫 *$10.*

## FAYETTEVILLE

This city in Northwest Arkansas is the home of the Razorbacks (aka University of Arkansas), so the college town is full of youthful energy. Thanks to its location on the outskirts of the Boston Mountains, it's also a popular spot for cyclists. While you're here, check out the Clinton House Museum, where Bill and Hillary Clinton made their first home.

**Do This:** Beer lovers, this one is for you. The Fayetteville Ale Trail, Arkansas' first craft-beer tasting experience features about 17 local breweries exclusively. The trail is self-guided, so you can go at your own pace and take the time to sample all the beer you want. (Guided tours are also available for those wanting some direction.) Breweries on the trail include Apple Blossom Breweing Co., Eureka Springs Brewery, Ozark Beer Co., and more. Pick up a passport at participating locations and collect stamps at each brewery location.

**Fayetteville Ale Trail.** ☎ *479/521-5776* 🌐 *fayettevillealetrail.com*

## GANGSTER MUSEUM OF AMERICA

This popular museum gives an entertaining account of how some of the country's most notorious criminals vacationed in the quaint small town of Hot Springs in the mountains of central Arkansas. It takes you back to the early 20th century when mineral water from the nearby thermal springs was not the only elixir that attracted visitors from all over the world. It was also a bootlegger's paradise during Prohibition, so the alcohol flowed, freely, at least behind closed doors.

**Do This:** There are a couple of exhibits here you shouldn't pass up. The Casino Gallery, the museum's most popular attraction, explains how the tiny town of Hot Springs ran the largest illegal gambling operation in the country between 1927 and 1967. The illegal activity here even extended to the country's favorite pastime. The Baseball Gallery documents the game's longtime connection to organized crime.

**Gangster Museum of America.** ✉ *510 Central Ave., Hot Springs, AR* ☎ *501/318-1717* 🌐 *www.thegangstermuseum.com* 🎫 *$15.*

## PRESIDENT WILLIAM JEFFERSON CLINTON'S BIRTHPLACE HOME

President Bill Clinton often talked about "believing in a place called Hope." He was referring to the Arkansas town where he lived for the first four years of his life with his mother, Virginia, and maternal grandparents, Edith Grisham and James Eldridge Cassidy. His childhood home at 117 South Hervey Street is now maintained by the National Park Service. "In this house, I learned to walk and talk. I learned to pray. I learned to read and I learned to count by number cards my grandparents tacked on the kitchen window," Clinton said in his dedication speech at the house in 1999.

**Do This:** Make sure to explore the second floor of the 1917 American Foursquare house, where the flooring and the beadboard in the hallway and nursery are among the original touches. Clinton's bedroom includes a desk and twin bed with a Hopalong Cassidy bedspread from that era.

**President William Jefferson Clinton's Birthplace Home.** ✉ *117 S. Hervey St., Hope, AR* ☎ *870/777–4455* 🌐 *www.nps.gov/wicl* 🎫 *Free.*

## Cool Places to Stay

**Beckham Creek Cave Lodge.** No caveman ever had it this good. This luxury escape is in a natural cavern that overlooks a valley in the Ozark Mountains. It has four bedrooms, four bathrooms, a large living room with a waterfall, and a fire pit. The upper floor has a round bed surrounded by hanging stalactites. ✉ *Beckham Creek Cave, Parthenon, AR* ☎ *870/365–9785* 🌐 *www.beckhamcave.com* $ *From $1,400.*

**1886 Crescent Hotel & Spa.** Famous for being one of the most haunted hotels in the country, the 1886 Crescent Hotel & Spa attracts many people interested in paranormal activity. Psychics have called it a "portal to the other side," noting the startling number of ghostly sightings in the rooms and hallways. There are also nightly tours guaranteed to scare you. ✉ *75 Prospect Ave., Eureka Springs, AR* ☎ *855/725–5720* 🌐 *www.crescent-hotel.com* $ *From $99.*

**Gables Inn Bed & Breakfast.** If you want to soak in the waters at Hot Springs, but would prefer a little privacy, this luxurious B&B is definitely the right place for you. Some rooms have heart-shaped tubs big enough for two. From here you can walk to most of the town's historic attractions, including Bathhouse Row. ✉ *318 Quapaw Ave., Hot Springs, AR* ☎ *501/623–7576* 🌐 *www.gablesn.com* $ *From $129.*

**Turpentine Creek Wildlife Refuge.** This wildlife refuge is a sanctuary for nearly 100 animals, including tigers, lions, leopards, cougars, bobcats, bears, ligers, servals, a coatimundi, and a macaw. You can join the herd (at a safe distance) by staying in the cabins, tree houses, and tent spaces. ✉ *239 Turpentine Creek La., Eureka Springs, AR* ☎ *79/253–5841* 🌐 *www.turpentinecreek.org* $ *From $125.*

**Wake Zone Luxury Houseboat Rentals.** If you love Lake Ouachita so much you don't want to leave, you don't have to. Three houseboats, *Shirley Ann, Suzanne,* and *Wendy Ann,* are calling your name. This family-owned and-operated outfit prides itself on keeping its fleet small so it can pamper its guests. ✉ *1649 N. Crystal Springs Rd., Royal, AR* ☎ *501/991–3600* 🌐 *www.houseboatingarkansas.com* $ *From $720.*

# Iowa

If you think Iowa is all corn and no substance, think again. The state, which takes its name from a Native American word meaning "beautiful land," does indeed have among the most fertile, wisely managed, and lucrative soil on the planet. In fact, Iowa's 100,000 family farms produce more pork, beef, and grain than any other state in the union. But it also has cultural riches, such as the Iowa State Fair and Iowa Literary Walk, that are not to be missed.

## Bucket List Picks

The following boxes contain our picks for the top sights and experiences in Iowa.

- ○ Bike RAGBRAI
- ○ Okoboji Winter Games
- ○ Mississippi Riverboat Cruise
- ○ Iowa Corn Mazes
- ○ Iowa State Fair
- ○ The Upper Iowa River
- ○ Pikes Peak State Park
- ○ Amana Colonies
- ○ Iowa City Literary Walk
- ○ Bridges of Madison County

# Bike RAGBRAI

## World's Oldest, Largest, and Longest Bike Touring Event

Traveling through small towns, around rolling hills, and past seemingly endless fields of corn, the Des Moines Register's Annual Great Bike Ride Across Iowa will make you appreciate the camaraderie of the sport as you join thousands of cyclists for a challenging seven-day event. Held every July, RAGBRAI started in 1973 when a couple of newspaper columnists got together for a casual ride across Iowa. Over the years it's grown into the world's oldest, longest, and largest recreational bicycle touring event. Averaging a heart-pumping 67 miles a day, the event begins somewhere along the western border on the Missouri River and ends in the east at the Mississippi River.

## Don't Miss

It may add a few miles to the route, but make sure to dip your tire in the Missouri River at the start and the Mississippi River at the end, a tradition for diehards.

## Good to Know

The route changes every year and is announced in late January. Sign up early, because RAGBRAI is limited to approximately 8,500 weeklong riders. And if a week seems like too much, don't worry. There are also spots for 1,500 daily riders.

## Getting Here and Around

The starting point changes each year, but it's always in the western part of the state. If you're flying in, you'll likely head to the international airport in Des Moines. There's also a regional airport in the western part of the state in Sioux Falls.

**RAGBRAI.** 🌐 *www.ragbrai.com* 🎫 *$175 per week.*

# Okoboji Winter Games

## Oddball Olympics

You don't have to be Lindsey Vonn to participate in the University of Okoboji Winter Games, a variety of eccentric but always fun competitions held each January in the lakeside town since the 1980s. Among the tongue-in-cheek outdoor activities are a chilling polar plunge, a keg toss, broomball, snowball fights, and human dogsled races in which teams of four people pull one rider on an inner tube along a 20-yard-long track. There are also ice auger races in which participants compete to be the first to drill a hole through the ice. Head indoors and there's axe throwing, a chili cook-off, pickleball, and even a stein-holding contest. As you can imagine, it's great fun for both participants and spectators, who come from all over to take part and sometimes win prizes.

## Don't Miss

The polar plunge is the signature, bucket-list activity of the games, when the brave line up in their swimsuits in the snow and jump (extra points for creativity) into the icy cold water of Arnolds Park. The $20 participation fee goes toward the park and local firefighters.

## While You're Here

Whether you participate in the games or not, make like a Midwesterner and ride downhill on an inner tube. The favorite local spot for this wintertime activity is Horseshoe Bend Tubing Hill, open every weekend in winter.

## Getting Here and Around

Okoboji is located in northwest Iowa near the Minnesota border. The closest large airport is in Sioux Falls, South Dakota, about 100 miles west.

**University of Okoboji.** ✉ *565 S. Hwy. 71, Arnolds Park, IA* 🌐 *www.uofowintergames.com* 🎫 *From $10.*

# Mississippi Riverboat Cruise

## Mark Twain for a Day

If you've never ridden on an old-fashioned riverboat, a trip on the *Twilight* is a great introduction to this traditional mode of travel. Standing on the deck as it chugs along, it's a great way to take in the majesty of the mighty Mississippi River, the second-longest river in the United States.

A trip of epic proportions, a two-day cruise departs and returns through the Port of LeClaire, Iowa. It includes a night of lodging at the riverfront Grand Harbor Resort in historic Dubuque, Iowa. A continental breakfast will be ready when you board, and lunch and dinner will be served as you pass picturesque river towns like Port Byron, Illinois, Princeton, Iowa, and Cordova, Illinois. There's also plenty of time to enjoy a glass of iced tea or lemonade and watch the world float by.

## Don't Miss

Before or after your cruise, take in the thousands of one-of-a-kind objects at Antique Archaeology, where they filmed the series *American Pickers* on the History Channel. The Buffalo Bill Museum is a tribute to the man behind the famous "Buffalo Bill's Wild West" extravaganzas, and also includes a lot of history about the Mississippi River, the Civil War, Native Americans, and lots more.

## Getting Here and Around

LeClaire is 15 miles northeast of Davenport, Iowa. It's also a few miles from the Quad Cities.

**Mississippi Riverboat Cruise.** ✉ *197 Front St., Le Claire, IA* ☎ *800/331–1467* 🌐 *www.riverboattwilight.com* 🎫 *From $409.*

# Iowa Corn Mazes

### Get Wonderfully Lost

Iowa's known as the "tall corn state," so if you're here during autumn harvest, it's the perfect place to wind your way through mazes that can go on for miles through fields of towering stalks. One of the best farms to test out your internal compass is Bloomsbury Farm near Atkins, which has been in the same family for five generations. Each autumn, there's a 10-acre corn maze with more than 2 miles of twisting and turning pathways that take about an hour to unravel. The farm also hosts numerous other activities throughout the year, such as butterfly releases in the spring and sunflower picking in late August, and pumpkin patches in the fall. Another fantastic location for corn mazes and pumpkin patches is Harvestville Farm near Donnellson.

### Don't Miss

Visit during Halloween for Bloomsbury's "Scream Acres" when the farm has a spooky haunted cornfield and barn crawling with zombies. Just don't watch or read *Children of the Corn* first. 🌐 *www.screamacrespark.com.*

### While You're Here

The Farm and Gift Market offers treats produced on Bloomsbury Farm, including fudge, kettle corn, and hand-dipped caramel apples.

### Good to Know

To find more reputable mazes as well as numerous other agritourism offerings like pumpkin patches and orchards, check out Iowa State University's helpful search tool. 🌐 *www.visitiowafarms.org/find-farm.*

### Getting Here and Around

Bloomsbury Farm is a 20-mile drive northwest of Cedar Rapids, Iowa, and a two-hour drive from Des Moines.

# Iowa State Fair

## Stick It to Your Diet

The Iowa State Fair is the biggest annual event in the state and one of the oldest and largest agricultural and industrial expositions in the United States. The annual event held over 11 days each August attracts more than a million people. Besides serious exhibits, it's famous for serving more than 60 foods on a stick. There are the traditional favorites, like deep-fried desserts, corn dogs, and caramel apples, and more unusual options, including key lime pie, caprese salad, and peanut butter and jelly sandwiches. There are always great concerts in the grandstand, as well as tons of free entertainment.

## Don't Miss

Tipping the scales at around 600 pounds, the crowd-pleasing Butter Cow on display each year at the Iowa State Fair has enough rich, creamy butter to slather on more than 19,000 slices of toast. Inside a 40°F cooler, layers of pure butter are applied to a steel mesh frame until the shape of a cow emerges. It measures about 5½ feet high and 8 feet long.

## Good to Know

Every four years, during presidential elections, the fair attracts politicians looking to sway the country's earliest voters. Regardless of your party affiliation, it's a great way to meet your favorite candidates.

## Getting Here and Around

The Iowa State Fairgrounds is 5 miles east of downtown Des Moines, which is located in central Iowa.

**Iowa State Fair.** ✉ *3000 E. Grand Ave., Des Moines, IA* ☎ *515/262–3111* 🌐 *www.iowastatefair.org* 🎫 *$14.*

# The Upper Iowa River

### The Midwest's Most Scenic River

Steep, rocky cliffs are not something that comes to mind when you think of Iowa's vast plains. But the Upper Iowa River in the northeast corner of the state has spectacular scenery that make it one of the most loved rivers of the Midwest. Extending for 150 miles, the Upper Iowa was one of the first in the nation to be named a National Wild and Scenic River in the 1960s. Thanks largely to the conservation groups that care for it, the river has maintained its pristine beauty, passing by dramatic vertical limestone palisades and forested bluffs. It's not uncommon to see deer stopping for a drink or wild turkeys hurrying along the shore. The current is fairly gentle, so you'll share the waterway with anglers, bird-watchers, and other outdoors enthusiasts. The best way to experience it is from a canoe.

### Don't Miss

On your canoe trip, look for the Bluffton Palisades, limestone cliffs that soar hundreds of feet above the water.

### While You're Here

There are 13 waterfalls within walking distance of the Upper Iowa River, and many springs that can be accessed off the route, including Odessa and Malanaphy Springs.

### Getting Here and Around

The Chester, Iowa, access point is 65 miles northeast of Mason City, Iowa.

**The Upper Iowa River.** 🌐 *www.upperiowariver.org/recreation/paddling.*

# Pikes Peak State Park

## Epic Climb, Epic Views

With 11 miles of trails leading through valleys and along scenic bluffs, Pikes Peak State Park is a must-see for hikers. Pikes Peak is one of Iowa's favorite nature preserves, and is known for its spectacular views of the Mississippi River, including a 500-foot-tall bluff where the Mississippi and Wisconsin rivers meet. Take the 4-mile trail to Point Ann and you'll be rewarded with views of the town of McGregor and the Mississippi. Watch for fossil remains along the way, including brachiopods, gastropods, and cephalopods.

## Don't Miss

Hike the half-mile boardwalk to Bridal Veil Falls and explore Bear Mound, an effigy built by Native Americans.

## Good to Know

Mountain bikes are allowed on the Pikes Peak trail from Homestead Park to the McGregor parking lots. There are also several campsites in the park if you love it so much you want to spend the night.

## While You're Here

The Effigy Mounds National Monument, 7 miles north of the park, preserves more than 200 mounds built by Native Americans. Hike around the 2-mile Fire Point Trail, where you can spot more than 20 mounds.

## Getting Here and Around

Pikes Peak State Park is 56 miles north of Dubuque, Iowa. Take Highway 3 west of Dubuque and then head north on Highway 53. The park is just south of the town of McGregor.

**Pikes Peak State Park.** ✉ *32264 Pikes Peak Rd., McGregor, IA* ☎ *563/873–2341* 🌐 *www.iowadnr.gov/Places-to-Go/State-Parks/Iowa-State-Parks/Pikes-Peak-State-Park* 🎫 *Free.*

# Amana Colonies

### Best of the Wurst

Indulge in über German foods like Wiener schnitzel and brats while learning about a unique culture in the United States at the Amana Colonies in east-central Iowa. These seven villages were built by Germans who fled their homeland in the mid-1800s to establish a communal society based on their religion. Though they eventually retired their communal living, the traditional culture remains. The National Historic Landmark draws visitors far and wide for food, wine, and beers as well as quality handcrafted products, art, and quaint shops that line the streets. Notice the clapboard homes, lantern-lit walkways, and traditional outfits that evoke the ways of the past.

### Don't Miss

The Wurst Festival is held every year on the Saturday before Father's Day. Wurst (the German word for sausage) purveyors from around the region gather to celebrate their craft and compete for awards. Besides the classic bratwurst, there are local beers, live music, and a Dachshund Derby that picks the fastest wiener dog in Iowa.

### Best Restaurants

The Ox Yoke Inn serves American fare, but also German favorites like sauerbraten, Wiener schnitzel, and brats, while beer and pub grub are the features at the Millstream Brau Haus.

### Getting Here and Around

To get to the town of Amana from Iowa City, drive 24 miles northwest on Interstate 80, Highway 6, and Highway 151.

**Amana Colonies Visitors Center.** ✉ *622 46th Ave., Amana, IA* 🌐 *www.amanacolonies.com* 🎟 *Free.*

# Iowa City Literary Walk

## Trace the Great American Novel

The world-famous University of Iowa Writers' Workshop has drawn thousands of talented writers over the past few decades, so it's no wonder that Iowa City was designated a UNESCO City of Literature. One of the best ways to appreciate its connection to the written word is to stroll the Iowa Literary Walk, a Hollywood Walk of Fame of sorts for authors. Blocks of downtown celebrate the works of 49 writers who have ties to Iowa, from acclaimed poets and playwrights to accomplished novelists and journalists. The walk consists of a series of bronze relief panels by artist Gregg LeFevre set into the sidewalk.

## Don't Miss

Big-name authors including Kurt Vonnegut, Flannery O'Connor, and Rita Dove, who were all part of Iowa's creative writing program, are represented on the walk; the plaque of Tennessee Williams, who lived in Iowa as a student, reads: "We're all of us sentenced to solitary confinement inside our own skins, for life!"

## While You're Here

The University of Iowa campus sits next to downtown. Take a stroll around campus and stop at the Iowa Old Capitol Building, which has a museum on the first floor that has exhibits about the history of the state.

## Good to Know

Pick up a Literary Walk booklet for a small fee at Prairie Lights Bookstore (⊠ *15 South Dubuque Street*) or Iowa Book & Supply (⊠ *8 South Clinton Street*).

## Getting Here and Around

Located in Iowa City, the Walk's bronze panels are along both sides of Iowa Avenue between Clinton Street and Gilbert Street.

# Bridges of Madison County

### A Drive Fit for the Big Screen

If you've seen the 1995 film *Bridges of Madison County* starring Meryl Streep and Clint Eastwood or read the best-selling book it was based on by James Waller, these wooden structures have already made it to your bucket list. Driving the Covered Bridges Scenic Byway is a great way to see them. The roughly 82-mile route includes many of the bridges that still dot the Iowa landscape. Five of the six wooden structures are originals built between 1870 and 1884. Other highlights along the way include a cidery, three wineries, and the Bare Bison Ranch.

### Don't Miss

At 122 feet long, the Holliwell Covered Bridge is the longest of the bridges. The Roseman Covered Bridge is supposedly haunted by the ghost of an escapee from the county jail. The Cedar Covered Bridge was originally built in 1883 but has been twice destroyed by fire.

### Good to Know

The map of the Covered Bridges Scenic Byway on the Travel Iowa website is extremely handy, so you'll probably want to print it out before your trip. 🌐 *www.traveliowa.com.*

### While You're Here

Save time to explore the Iowa Quilt Museum in the town of Winterset. This is where Liz Porter and Marianne Fons's television show *Love of Quilting* was created. If you want to bring home your own hand-stitched work of art, there are plenty of craft shops nearby.

### Getting Here and Around

Winterset, the county seat of Madison County, is 37 miles southwest of Des Moines. Take Interstate 80 west to De Soto, Iowa, then head south on Highway 169.

# When in Iowa

### AMERICAN GOTHIC HOUSE

Artist Grant Wood had arrived in Eldon, Iowa, for an art exhibition in 1930 when he spotted a little white house with a single peaked window on the second floor. He quickly sketched the unusual structure, and it eventually became the backdrop for his famous work, *American Gothic.* The house, owned by the State of Iowa, is now a museum. Wood's two models were his sister, Nan Wood Graham, and his dentist, Dr. B. H. McKeeby, though they never posed in front of the house.

**Do This:** Obviously, you have to pose for a self-portrait in front of the house.

**American Gothic House.** ✉ *300 American Gothic St., Eldon, IA* ☎ *641/652–3352* 🌐 *www.americangothichouse.org* 🎟 *Free.*

### DO THE WAVE WITH THE HAWKEYES

Fans do "the wave" at University of Iowa football games, an event that's quickly become known as one of the best traditions in college football. The wave started with a simple idea from a fan. In 2017, at the end of the first quarter of the Hawkeyes season opener, more than 70,000 football fans in Kinnick Stadium were asked to turn toward the east and wave. Patients and their families gathered on the top floor of the nearby University of Iowa Stead Family Children's Hospital waved back. Ever since, those in the stadium and in the hospital have looked forward to it each week during home games.

**Do This:** Support the University of Iowa Stead Family Children's Hospital by buying an official Iowa Wave shirt.

**Kinnick Stadium.** ✉ *University of Iowa, 886 Stadium Dr., Iowa City, IA* ☎ *319/335–9323* 🌐 *www.hawkeyesports.com* 🎟 *Varies.*

### GROTTO OF REDEMPTION

Covering an entire city block, the Shrine of the Grotto of the Redemption in West Bend, Iowa, is considered the largest grotto in the world. It's made of nine separate grottos that display scenes from the life of Christ. Paul Dobberstein began work in 1912, and it wasn't finished for 42 years. He used countless precious and semiprecious stones in the process: malachite, azurite, agate, quartz, topaz, and many others.

**Do This:** Visit the Christmas Chapel, located in Saints Peter and Paul Church next to the Grotto. Built in 1929, it contains rocks from every country and major river in the world. It is known for a 300-pound amethyst on the manger.

**The Shrine of the Grotto of the Redemption.** ✉ *208 1st Ave. NW, West Bend, IA* ☎ *515/887–2371* 🌐 *www.westbendgrotto.com* 🎟 *Free.*

# Cool Places to Stay

**Courtyard Waterloo Cedar Falls.** Built in a renovated John Deere tractor factory, the Courtyard Waterloo Cedar Falls preserves many of the original architectural details. The original warehouse floors were raised, so guests can take in the views through the massive windows that once illuminated the manufacturing operation. ✉ *250 Westfield Ave., Waterloo, IA* ☎ *319/233–5531* 🌐 *www.marriott.com* $ *From $117.*

**Field of Dreams House.** Kevin Costner won't get you coffee in the morning, but you can still enjoy a night in the three-bedroom farmhouse where the movie *Field of Dreams* was filmed near Dyersville, Iowa. You also have exclusive access to the adjacent baseball field that was used in the movie. ✉ *28995 Lansing Rd., Dyersville, IA* ☎ *888/875–8404* 🌐 *www.fieldofdreamsmoviesite.com/home-rental* $ *From $2,000.*

# Kansas

If you are a traveler who appreciates wide-open spaces, Native American history, or Wild West heritage, you will find much to enjoy in Kansas. The state was home to legendary lawmen like Wyatt Earp and James Butler "Wild Bill" Hickok, who policed once-rowdy railroad and cattle towns like Abilene, Dodge City, and Ellsworth. Perhaps Kansas's greatest claim to fame, however, is serving as home to Dorothy and Toto in *The Wizard of Oz*. Dorothy and Toto, of course, are fictional, but their story's symbolism can be found in each of the small towns, ranches, farms, and cities that makes up this "land of aaahhs."

## Bucket List Picks

The following boxes contain our picks for the top sights and experiences in Kansas.

- O Geographic Center of the United States
- O Dodge City
- O Cheyenne Bottoms Wetland
- O Flint Hills National Scenic Byway
- O Gypsum Hills
- O Monument Rocks Natural Area
- O Brown v. Board of Education National Historic Site

## Geographic Center of the United States

### The Heart of It All

A selfie taken here tells the world that you've been at the center of America. About 2 miles northwest of Lebanon, Kansas, is a stone pedestal topped with a flagpole that marks the geographic center of the 48 contiguous U.S. states, according to the U.S. Geological Survey. (The actual center is a half-mile walk to the center of the nearby field, but for most people this is close enough.)

### Don't Miss

If it's open, duck into the tiny U.S. Center Chapel under the trees. If it looks oddly familiar, you probably remember it from a 2021 Superbowl ad featuring Bruce Springsteen.

### Good to Know

What's there to do in the very middle of the United States? Well, not much. The marker is at the end of a paved road with not much but rolling plains around it, but it's a good place to stretch your legs if you're traveling through Kansas on either Highway 36 or 281.

### Getting Here and Around

Near the Nebraska border, Lebanon is 253 miles northwest of Kansas City. From Lebanon, take U.S. Highway 281 north 1 mile and turn west 1 mile on Route 191 to the marker at the end of the paved road.

**Geographic Center.** ✉ *KS 191, Lebanon, KS* 🌐 *www.kansastravel.org/geographicalcenter.htm* 🎫 *Free.*

# Dodge City

### The Wild, Wild West

Few towns evoke the Wild West like Dodge City, Kansas. Stroll along the wooden sidewalks and peer through the windows of the saloonlike businesses that line the dusty street. A must-see is the Boot Hill Museum, which offers a glimpse of life in the late 1800s. Learn about the town's unique characters like Wyatt Earp, Doc Holliday, and Bat Masterson. During summer, you can experience Dodge City's history through historical reenactments, including the famous gunfight at the O.K. Corral. You've seen shootouts in the movies, but the one in front of the Long Branch Saloon makes it seem like you're living a piece of American history.

### Don't Miss

The Dodge City Trail of Fame commemorates the many famous and infamous people who walked these streets. Some of the markers are dedicated to notable movie and television stars who have portrayed some of the famous figures. A walking tour guide is available at the Dodge City Visitor Information Center.

### When to Go

Time your trip to coincide with the Dodge City Roundup Rodeo, held several times throughout the year. They feature cowboys and cowgirls riding bulls, busting broncos, and roping calves. The rodeo season culminates at Dodge City Days, one of the largest annual festivals in Kansas. It celebrates the town's rich history and Western heritage.

### Getting Here and Around

Dodge City is 154 miles west of Wichita in southwest Kansas. When you arrive, stop at the Dodge City Visitor Information Center for a complete list of events. 🌐 *www.visitdodgecity.org.*

# Cheyenne Bottoms Wetland

## The Plains' Best Bird-Watching

The largest inland marsh in the United States, Cheyenne Bottoms has 64 square miles of wetlands that draw an impressive array of birds throughout the year. Ornithologists have spotted at least 330 species at Cheyenne Bottoms, more than at any other place in the state. In the winter, rough-legged hawks and bald eagles are among the 148 species that spend the colder months here, joining the 63 species that make their home here year-round. In the spring, more than half a million ducks and geese and thousands of other birds like sandhill and whooping cranes pass through the region during their annual migrations. In early summer, thousands of shorebirds visit the marsh. And each autumn, 250,000 or more birds stop on their journey south.

## Don't Miss

No matter the season, the best place to spot the birds is the viewing platform not far from the entrance.

## Good to Know

The Kansas Wetlands Education Center has plenty of information about birds, as well as the snakes, turtles, salamanders, and other creatures that are native to the surrounding area. The center also offers suggested driving tours and guided van tours of the wetlands. *wetlandscenter.fhsu.edu.*

## Getting Here and Around

Cheyenne Bottoms is 119 miles northwest of Wichita, Kansas, and 11 miles northeast of Great Bend, Kansas. The Kansas Wetlands Education Center is on the southern end of the wetlands.

**Cheyenne Bottoms Wetland.** *592 NE K-156 Hwy., Great Bend, KS* *877/243–9268* *www.kansastravel.org/cheyennebottoms.htm* *Free.*

# Flint Hills National Scenic Byway

## The Last of America's Tallgrass Prairie

Tallgrass prairie once covered 170 million acres of North America, but less than 4% remains intact. Most of it is in the Flint Hills. If you want to see what much of North America looked like before farming changed the landscape, this 47-mile drive is one of the few places left to experience it. The Flint Hills National Scenic Byway offers incredible views of the native grasses and flowers of the tallgrass prairie. Start at the visitor center and then spend some time exploring the 11,000-acre preserve, where you might encounter a herd of bison.

## Don't Miss

One must-see stop along the way is the Tallgrass Prairie National Preserve, managed by the National Park Service. Established in 1996, it protects a nationally significant remnant of the once vast tallgrass prairie ecosystem. 🌐 *www.nps.gov/tapr.*

## Good to Know

Much of the Flint Hills is unchanged since Native Americans were the original residents thousands of years ago. Early settlers passed by on the famous Santa Fe Trail through here, some stopping to settle the nearby towns of Council Grove, Cottonwood Falls, and Strong City.

## Getting Here and Around

The 47-mile byway on Highway 177 starts in Council Grove, Kansas, which is 77 miles southwest of Topeka and 98 miles northeast of Wichita. It ends in Cassoday.

**Flint Hills National Scenic Byway.** ☎ *620/767–5882* 🌐 *www.naturalkansas.org/flint.htm* 🎫 *Free.*

# Gypsum Hills

## Seeing Red

The Gypsum Hills belong on every nature lover's bucket list. The soil contains large amounts of iron oxide—better known as rust—causing these hills to have an unforgettable reddish tint. Also called Medicine Hills, this is a region of mesas, canyons, and buttes, much of it covered in wildflowers for much of the year. That natural beauty draws artists, photographers, and outdoors lovers of all types who want to experience the unique landscape. It's a place for history lovers as well, since the area has been home to Native Americans for centuries.

## Don't Miss

The 66-square-mile Z Bar Ranch, owned by media mogul Ted Turner, has rolling hills, sprawling canyons, and rocky outcroppings. Its wildlife includes bison, whitetail deer, antelope, coyotes, bobcats, badgers, and black-tailed prairie dogs, along with birds like turkeys, pheasants, and quail.

## When to Go

The annual Peace Treaty Festival in Medicine Lodge, Kansas, is held during the last full weekend of September. It celebrates the Native American heritage of the area. The Kansas Championship Ranch Rodeo coincides with the festival.

## Getting Here and Around

The Gypsum Hills are in south-central Kansas near the Oklahoma border. The state has designated a 42-mile scenic byway along U.S. Highway 160 between Coldwater and Medicine Lodge, which is 86 miles southwest of Wichita. You can see the Gypsum Hills along the route, but there are few places to pull over to take photographs.

**Gypsum Hills.** ✉ *Hwy. 160, Medicine Lodge, KS* 🌐 *www.visitgyphills.com* 🎫 *Free.*

# Monument Rocks Natural Area

## Castles in the Sand

Like stone fortresses rising out of the prairie, the Monument Rocks Natural Area features 50-foot-tall outcroppings of chalk and sedimentary deposits that have eroded over time to form pinnacles, spires, and buttes. The National Park Service designated the formation as the first National Natural Landmark in Kansas in 1968. In 2006, it was named one of the eight wonders of the state. Because this was part of the Kansas Sea during the Cretaceous period, the area is a rich source of fossils of marine animals.

## Don't Miss

Get up early to see the monuments at sunrise, or stick around until sunset. The sun sits low in the sky and provides dramatic shadows.

## How to Visit

Monument Rocks Natural Area sits on private property, but the owners allow anyone to visit for free. They ask that you follow the rules: no climbing, fossil hunting, motorized vehicles, or overnight stays. One more thing: no taunting the cattle that roam in the area. The site is open sunrise to sunset.

## Getting Here and Around

Monument Rocks Natural Area is on unpaved roads off Highway 83, 20 miles south of Oakley and 268 miles northwest of Wichita.

**Oakley Area Tourism.** ✉ *3083 U.S. 83, Oakley, KS* ☎ *785/671–1000* 🌐 *www.visitoakleyks.com/monument-rocks* 🎫 *Free.*

## Brown v. Board of Education National Historic Site

### Civil Rights Milestone

The simplicity of this historic site in Topeka, Kansas, belies its place in U.S. history. Congress established it in 1992 to commemorate the 1954 landmark decision of the U.S. Supreme Court that ended racial segregation in public schools. The national historic site consists of Monroe Elementary School, one of four elementary schools in the city that were designated for black children. The parents of one of those pupils, Linda Brown, filed a lawsuit so that she could attend an all-white school in her neighborhood. In that case, Brown v. Board of Education, the justices unanimously declared that "separate educational facilities are inherently unequal." They ruled that segregated schools violated the 14th Amendment to the U.S. Constitution that guarantees all citizens "equal protection of the laws."

### Don't Miss

Several galleries provide a stark look at segregation in America. The Road to Brown v. Board of Education gallery covers the barriers black Americans faced while trying to receive an education. The Legacy gallery tells the story of the civil rights movement after the ruling, including its ongoing impact. The kindergarten looks like it did in 1954, showing what it was like to attend the segregated school.

### Getting Here and Around

The site is located in downtown Topeka.

**Brown v. Board of Education National Historic Site.** ✉ *1515 SE Monroe St., Topeka, KS* ☎ *785/354–4273* 🌐 *www.nps.gov/brvb* 🎫 *Free.*

## When in Kansas

### THE CITY OF OZ (WAMEGO)

If you're a fan of *The Wizard of Oz,* you'll go over the rainbow at the Oz-themed town of Wamego, Kansas. In addition to the delightful Oz Museum, nearby businesses celebrate the Oz connection, such as Toto's Tacoz and Oz Winery, where you can sample of wines like Ruby Slippers and Yellow Brick Road. Check out the Columbian Theatre, a 19th-century opera house that has six massive oil paintings from the 1893 Chicago World's Fair that provided Baum with the inspiration for the Emerald City.

**Do This:** Follow the yellow brick road to the Oz Museum, home to more than 2,000 artifacts from L. Frank Baum's 1900 book *The Wonderful Wizard of Oz* and its 13 sequels, as well as the many film and television versions. Among the items on display: colorful posters from the various film productions, hand-painted character masks, miniatures of the flying monkeys that were used in the movie, and a reproduction of the Haunted Forest sign that warns Dorothy and her companions to "turn back."

**Oz Museum.** ✉ *511 Lincoln Ave., Wamego, KS* ☎ *866/458–8686* 🌐 *www.ozmuseum.com* 🎫 *$9.*

### EQUALITY HOUSE

The rainbow-colored Equality House in Topeka, Kansas, is the home base for the group Planting Peace. The group says the house stands as a visual reminder of its commitment to equality for everyone. It also serves as a contrast to its neighbor across the street, Westboro Baptist Church, whose members are known for protesting soldier funerals and fighting against marriage equality.

**Do This:** The group encourages visitors to take photos, show their pride, and "take some veggies or pull some weeds in our community garden."

**Equality House.** ✉ *1200 S.W. Orleans St., Topeka, KS* 🌐 *www.plantingpeace.org/campaign/equality-house* 🎫 *Free.*

### KEEPER OF THE PLAINS

The 44-foot-tall Keeper of the Plains, donated by Native American artist Blackbear Bosin, stands at the confluence of the Big and Little Arkansas rivers. Since the sculpture's installation in 1974, it has become a symbol for the city of Wichita and a tribute to the Native American tribes that continue to gather at the sacred site. You can access the display by way of two bow-and-arrow-inspired cable-stay bridges that span the two rivers.

**Do This:** Come back at night to see the fire drums on the boulders at the base of the statue illuminate the night.

**Keeper of the Plains.** ✉ *650 N. Seneca St., Wichita, KS* ☎ *316/350–3340* 🌐 *www.wichita.gov/Arts/Pages/Keeper.aspx* 🎫 *Free.*

## Cool Places to Stay

**Hotel at Old Town.** The century-old Hotel at Old Town was originally a warehouse for the Keen Kutter brand of tools. In 1999, Wichita hotelier Jack DeBoer reopened it as a luxury hotel after an extensive search for Keen Kutter items to use in the decor. ✉ *830 E. First St., Wichita, KS* ☎ *316/267–4800* 🌐 *www.hotelatoldtown.com* 💲 *From $105.*

**The Woodward Inn.** No need to go to Europe to experience a chateau, because the Woodward in Topeka is a castlelike inn built in the early 1920s. The lofty library resembles King Henry VIII library at Hampton Hall, and is built with imported timbers and stones from England. ✉ *1272 S.W. Fillmore St., Topeka, KS* ☎ *785/354–7111* 🌐 *www.thewoodward.com/woodward.html* 💲 *From $105.*

# Missouri

Missouri sits where the Midwest meets the South, and the state's central location—along with its great rivers—has made it an important hub for explorers and pioneers over the centuries. The Missouri River carried Lewis and Clark north as they began their great expedition; soon after, its banks saw the rise of the 19th-century wagon trains heading west. Once frequented by steamboats, both the Missouri and the Mississippi are now home to riverboat gambling, a controversial part of the state's tourism industry. Elsewhere in Missouri, a wealth of lakes, rivers, and caves provides plenty of opportunities for outdoor recreation.

## Bucket List Picks

The following boxes contain our picks for the top sights and experiences in Missouri.

- ○ The Gateway Arch
- ○ Branson
- ○ Lake of the Ozarks
- ○ Kansas City Barbecue
- ○ Forest Park
- ○ Mark Twain's Hometown
- ○ Kansas City's 18th and Vine District

# The Gateway Arch

### Fulfill Manifest Destiny

The 630-foot-tall Gateway Arch broke several records the day it opened in 1965. The St. Louis landmark instantly became the world's biggest arch, easily beating the 219-foot-tall Monumento a la Revolución in Mexico City. It's the tallest monument in the Western Hemisphere, and the tallest building in Missouri. Once you reach the top via the four-minute tram ride, you're treated to views that stretch up to 30 miles to the east and west.

The Gateway Arch was built to celebrate Thomas Jefferson and his idea of Manifest Destiny, since St. Louis was a major point of departure for settlers headed west. Since the arch's 50th anniversary its story has broadened to include the Native Americans who were displaced by westward expansion.

### Don't Miss

Though the ride to the top of the arch is the star of the show, spend some time in the museum at its base. It does a great job covering the history of Native Americans, explorers, pioneers and others who passed this way.

### Tours

A limited number of visitors are allowed to ascend the arch each day, so buy Tram Ride to the Top tickets early. Tours run 45 to 60 minutes.

### Good to Know

There are 1,076 steps to the top of the arch, but visitors aren't allowed to take them.

### Getting Here and Around

Gateway Arch National Park is located in downtown St. Louis. If you're driving, park in one of the downtown garages and walk to the Arch complex.

**The Gateway Arch.** ✉ *11 N. 4th St., St. Louis, MO* 🌐 *www.gatewayarch.com* 🎟 *$12.*

# Branson

## The Family-Friendly Vegas

Known for big-time entertainment for all ages, this southern Missouri city is the place to see live shows and music under bright lights, ride roller coasters, and stroll a landing lined with neon lights and spurting fountains. It's no wonder the town has been compared to Las Vegas—but one where no gambling is allowed and you can take the whole family. Fan of music shows? Branson bills itself as the "Live Music Capital of the World," and offers live shows in genres from country to bluegrass to good old-fashioned rock and roll. Are you a roller-coaster fanatic? Silver Dollar City has two unique thrill rides. Time Traveler reaches speeds of up to 50 miles per hour while you make a 10-story vertical drop. Fire-In-The-Hole is an enclosed roller coaster that includes high-speed drops and surprises around every corner.

## Don't Miss

Don't leave without seeing a live show on 76 Country Boulevard or Shepard of the Hills Expressway, the town's busiest stretches. The number of theaters is truly impressive.

## While You're Here

Take our word for it: the Titanic Museum is tons of fun. This massive re-creation of the ocean liner (the front half of it, anyway) that sank on its maiden voyage lets you wander the hallways, parlors, cabins, and grand staircase.

## Getting Here and Around

Branson is in southern Missouri, just north of the Arkansas border. If you're driving, it's 210 miles southeast of Kansas City, Missouri, and 170 miles northwest of Little Rock, Arkansas.

# Lake of the Ozarks

### The Magic Dragon Lake

Central Missouri's Lake of the Ozarks, called the Magic Dragon for its twisting reptilian shape, is one of the top waterfront vacation destinations in the Midwest, drawing more than 5 million annual visitors. If you've seen the hit show *Ozark* you know the lake is a wonderland for swimming, boating, fishing, socializing, and relaxing (minus the dramatic storyline). Most of the shoreline is privately owned, so there are plenty of vacation homes for rent that give you spectacular views.

### Don't Miss

The big idea is to get on the water. Try out a pontoon boat, which is easiest for beginners, through the numerous companies in the Lake of the Ozarks region that rent watercraft.

### While You're Here

Take a break from the summertime heat and join a guided tour of the 60°F Bridal Cave at Camdenton, Missouri. It features mineral deposits shaped like giant columns and massive draperies. Bridal Cave has more onyx formations than any other cavern.

### When to Go

Try to avoid busy Memorial Day, Independence Day, and Labor Day weekends. Late August is a great time to visit because the summer crowds have died down a bit but it's still sunny and warm.

### Getting Here and Around

Lake of the Ozarks sits halfway between Springfield and Jefferson City, Missouri. It's 173 miles southeast of Kansas City and 180 miles southwest of St. Louis.

**Lake of the Ozarks.** ✉ *985 KK Dr., Osage Beach, MO* ☎ *800/386–5253* 🌐 *www.funlake.com* 🎫 *Free.*

# Kansas City Barbecue

### Try Lip-Smacking KC 'Cue

Kansas City barbecue isn't just sauce and ribs, it's the city's identity, a way of life, and a source of delicious, delicious pride. No trip to the city would be complete without sampling the world-famous 'cue (some say it's the best in the country) marked by slowly smoked meat like chicken, pork, and beef smothered in a sweet, thick, molasses-based sauce. Create a full expedition to find the smokiest, most mouthwatering, wonderfully messy barbecue joints in town, from Arthur Bryant's in the 18th and Vine district to Joe's spots across town.

### Don't Miss

Order the fan-favorite Z-Man sandwich (smoked brisket topped with cheese and onion rings) from the original Joe's Kansas City Bar-B-Que, based out of a gas station on 47th and Mission. You'll want to grab some extra napkins, but it's oh-so-worth it. 🌐 *www.joeskc.com.*

### Best Barbecue

Perhaps the most famous place to try KC barbecue is Arthur Bryant's (aka the King of Ribs) at 18th and Brooklyn. It's said the original KC barbecue recipe was created here, and it's gained the presidential seal of approval from Truman, Carter, and Obama. 🌐 *www.arthurbryantsbbq.com.*

### Good to Know

You don't have to travel to Kansas City to try its famous barbecue. Some of the most famous barbecuers, including Arthur Bryant's, sell and ship their famous barbecue all around the USA on the website Goldbelly. 🌐 *www.goldbelly.com.*

### Getting Here and Around

More than 100 barbecue restaurants are mapped all over Kansas City on the KC BBQ Experience app. Download it to put together an epic barbecue trail and check in to your favorite spots along the way. 🌐 *www.visitkc.com/bbq/app.*

# Forest Park

## America's Best City Park

One of the nation's greatest urban parks, the 1876 Forest Park in St. Louis lets you get back to nature without ever leaving the city. This 1,300-acre park is so vast it has entire ecosystems, and includes forests, lakes, and streams. It attracts 13 million people a year, more than Busch Stadium and the Gateway Arch combined. The park is home to the Missouri History Museum, St. Louis Science Center, St. Louis Zoo, St. Louis Art Museum, and the Municipal Theatre Association of St. Louis. It's hosted everything from the 1904 Louisiana Purchase Exposition and the 1904 Summer Olympics to today's Great Forest Park Balloon Race, Shakespeare Festival of St. Louis, and Forest Park Cross Country Festival.

## Don't Miss

A variety of hyacinth, daffodils, alliums, magnolias, tulips, and gladiolus bloom throughout the spring and summer.

## Best Activities

The grounds include a city zoo, an art museum, an outdoor ice-skating rink, an outdoor theater, science museum, and ample picnic space.

## Where to Stay

The Cheshire is a romantic Tudor-style getaway within walking distance of Forest Park and the St. Louis Zoo and is a five-minute drive via Interstate 40 from downtown.

## Getting Here and Around

Forest Park is located about 5 miles west of downtown St. Louis, not far from Washington University.

**Forest Park.** ✉ *5595 Grand Dr. in Forest Park, St. Louis, MO* ☎ *314/367–7275* 🌐 *www.forestparkforever.org/visit* 🎫 *Free.*

# Mark Twain's Hometown

## Huckleberry Finn for a Day

It's not hard to imagine Tom Sawyer, Huckleberry Finn, and Becky Thatcher getting into mischief in the streets of Hannibal, Missouri. This picturesque town, the childhood home of author Mark Twain, is fun to explore. A self-guided tour through the historic district is a good introduction to Twain—whose real name was Samuel Clemens—along with the friends, family members, and various townspeople that he eventually used as models for the characters in his stories. The Mark Twain Boyhood Home & Museum explores seven buildings related to Twain's life and work.

## Don't Miss

Stop at Twain's boyhood home at 208 Hill Street, where many of his real-life experiences between 1844 and 1853 influenced his creation of Tom Sawyer and other characters. Twain's friend Laura Hawkins lived at 211 Hill Street. He immortalized her in his books as Becky Thatcher, and the two close friends stayed in touch through the years.

## While You're Here

The Museum Gallery includes the Norman Rockwell Room, with 15 original paintings that the renowned artist created for special editions of *Tom Sawyer* and *Huckleberry Finn*. They are among his most whimsical works.

## Good to Know

Twain's father, John Clemens, practiced law at 205 Hill Street. Warner Brothers Studios later bought the office building and donated it to the city because of the help the town provided while they were producing a film version of *Tom Sawyer.*

## Getting Here and Around

Hannibal, Missouri, lies along the Mississippi River in eastern Missouri, 114 miles northwest of St. Louis.

# Kansas City's 18th and Vine District

## Jazz, Baseball, and Barbecue

Just east of downtown Kansas City, this historic neighborhood at the intersection of 18th and Vine is known for its great barbecue and even better jazz. Its entertainment venues include the Kansas City Juke House, which features live blues, and the Blue Room, which highlights the countless musicians who crafted the Kansas City sound. No visit is complete with a visit to the American Jazz Museum. In addition, 18th and Vine is the heart of the city's black community, and has 35 buildings that are listed on the National Register of Historic Places. The Black Archives of Mid-America documents life in the region.

## Don't Miss

The highlight of a visit to 18th and Vine is a stop at Negro Leagues Baseball Museum, an excellent museum that chronicles often-overlooked histories of the black players who were prevented from playing in the major leagues. ✉ *1616 E. 18th St.* 🌐 *nlbm.com*.

## Best Restaurant

Arthur Bryant's BBQ is considered one of the best around. Bryant created a sauce that was a favorite of several presidents, including Harry Truman, Jimmy Carter, Bill Clinton, and Barack Obama.

## When to Go

Time your trip for the beginning of the month and you'll be able to visit the art galleries and other businesses that stay open for First Fridays.

## Getting Here and Around

The 18th and Vine neighborhood is just east of downtown Kansas City.

**18th and Vine District.** ✉ *E. 18th St. and Vine St., Kansas City, MO* ☎ *816/691–3800* 🌐 *www.18vinekc.com* 🎫 *Free.*

## When in Missouri

### GLORE PSYCHIATRIC MUSEUM

George Glore, who worked at the Missouri Department of Mental Health, started this collection of odd objects at an abandoned ward of the St. Joseph State Hospital in 1966. The museum includes historical psychiatric treatment devices (think surgical tools and other items) and artwork made by the patients of the hospital (pottery, paintings, and drawings that helped them express their pain, joy, and hopes).

**Do This:** Check out the other museums in St. Joseph, including the Black Archives Museum, the Doll Museum, the Native American Galleries, and the Wyeth-Tootle Mansion.

**Glore Psychiatric Museum.** ✉ *3408 Frederick Ave., St. Joseph, MO* ☎ *816/364–1209* 🌐 *www.gloremuseum.org* 🎫 *$7.*

### HA HA TONKA CASTLE RUINS

Kansas City businessman Robert McClure Snyder Sr. bought this property and started building a castle in 1905. He was killed a year later in an auto accident, but his sons finished the project in the 1920s. The family used it as a weekend home for a while, and it was later converted into a hotel. A fire destroyed it in 1942. Missouri bought the castle and grounds in 1978 and created a state park. The castle walls aren't stable, so you have to keep your distance.

**Do This:** After gazing the castle, spend some time in the park itself. Ha Ha Tonka State Park features sinkholes, caverns, sheer bluffs, and a huge natural bridge. A series of trails and boardwalks makes it easy to experience.

**Ha Ha Tonka Castle Ruins.** ✉ *1491 State Rd. D, Camdenton, MO* ☎ *573/346–2986* 🌐 *www.mostateparks.com/park/ha-ha-tonka-state-park* 🎫 *Free.*

## Cool Places to Stay

**Big Cedar Lodge.** This remote and rustic getaway in Missouri's Ozark Mountains overlooks Table Rock Lake. Johnny Morris, founder of Bass Pro Shops, created Big Cedar Lodge as a luxe lodging for families and friends to connect in the great outdoors. It has inviting accommodations, great restaurants, two marinas, five golf courses, and a spa. ✉ *190 Top of the Rock Rd., Ridgedale, MO* ☎ *800/225–6343* 🌐 *www.bigcedar.com* [$] *From: $279.*

**Fontaine Hotel.** This luxury hotel in Kansas City's upscale shopping district is the perfect place to get away from it all. It's near Arrowhead Stadium and Kauffman Stadium, so sports fans will be happy. ✉ *901 W. 48th Pl., Kansas City, MO* ☎ *816/753–8800* 🌐 *www.thefontainehotel.com* [$] *From: $224.*

**Hotel Vandivort.** Inspired by Springfield's rich cultural history, the Hotel Vandivort bills itself as the city's first boutique hotel. It's an active cultural hub for both locals and travelers. It's absolutely gorgeous, with a nicely restored brick face in front and a cool modernist addition in the back. ✉ *305 E. Walnut, Springfield, MO* ☎ *417/832–1515* 🌐 *www.hotelvandivort.com* [$] *From: $143.*

**Munger Moss Motel.** Step back in time to when Route 66 was a major cross-country highway with a stay at the Munger Moss Motel in Lebanon, Missouri. Built in 1946, it's one of the few remaining mom-and-pop motels along the historic highway. The same couple has owned and operated it since 1971. ✉ *1336 E. Rt. 66, Lebanon, MO* ☎ *417/532–3111* 🌐 *www.mungermoss.com* [$] *From: $65.*

# Nebraska

The Cornhusker State offers everything from city sophistication to country charm. There are places so rugged and wild they still conjure images of the Old West frontier, and there are cosmopolitan cities with fabulous shopping and superb restaurants. The terrain varies from the rolling hill country along the Missouri River, where foliage is lush and varied, to the grasslands of the Sandhills, to the Panhandle's rough breaks with their bluffs and buttes.

## Bucket List Picks

The following boxes contain our picks for the top sights and experiences in Nebraska.

- O Tanking on the Niobrara
- O College World Series
- O Sandhill Crane Migration
- O The Cowboy Trail
- O The Prairie Chicken Dance
- O Fort Niobrara National Wildlife Refuge
- O Toadstool Geologic Park
- O Chimney Rock

# Tanking on the Niobrara

## Float Downstream the Nebraska Way

Nebraska has more miles of river than any other state, so it's no wonder locals have created the ultimate outdoor activity for taking full advantage of that fact. It's called "tanking," and it's a wonderfully memorable way to spend a day on the water. Tanking involves gathering friends and family members for a float in a 6- to 8-foot round metal tank usually used for watering livestock. No paddling. Just meandering. One of the prettiest places to tank is Nebraska's Sandhills, home to the Niobrara National Scenic River.

## Don't Miss

Several outfitters can provide you with a tank on the Niobara River, including family-owned Little Outlaw in Valentine. Their four-hour trip lets you float leisurely down the river with the chance to see Nebraska's highest waterfall, the Smith Falls. 🌐 *outlawcanoe.com* 🎫 *$250.*

## Good to Know

A tank usually holds four to six people, along with coolers, boom boxes, and anything else you need for a float down a river. A trip typically lasts from two to six hours. There aren't usually many rules; when you want to cool off, just jump in the water and hop back in the tank.

## Other Places to Tank

Niobara isn't the only place you can tank. You can also book a tanking excursion on the upper Cedar River with Get Tanked, or the Elkhorn River with Tank Down the Elkhorn (this is especially convenient for those based in nearby Omaha).

## Getting Here and Around

Valentine, near the Nebraska–South Dakota border, is where you'll access the river on many tanking trips down the Niobrara. It's five hours east of Omaha on the eastern end of the state, so expect a lot of driving.

# College World Series

### Home Run in Omaha

Omaha has hosted the Men's College World Series since 1967. If you're even a casual fan of baseball, this event, held every June, is worth adding to your bucket list. It's the culmination of the National Collegiate Athletic Association Division I Baseball Championship, so the eight teams competing are the best of the best. You can see several games of America's great pastime played at the modern TD Ameritrade Park Omaha, consistently ranked as one of the finest facilities in the nation.

### Don't Miss

You're in the middle of Omaha, so there's plenty of great shopping, dining, and entertainment options nearby. Head to sights like the Heartland of America Park, the Old Market, and the Henry Doorly Zoo.

### Where to Stay

True to its name, Hotel Deco maintains the art deco style that has made it a downtown Omaha landmark since it opened in 1930. Among the amenities is the Monarch Steakhouse, which features a methodically developed in-house dry-aging program, contemporary cocktail menu, and extensive wine list. ✉ *1504 Harney St., Omaha, NE* 🌐 *www.hoteldecoomaha.com.*

### Getting Here and Around

Omaha airport, Eppley Airfield, is only 2 miles from the stadium and to downtown.

**TD Ameritrade Park Omaha.** ✉ *1200 Mike Fahey St., Omaha, NE* ☎ *402/554-4422* 🌐 *www.cwsomaha.com* 🎟 *Varies.*

# Sandhill Crane Migration

### World-Famous Flock

Every spring and fall, roughly 600,000 sandhill cranes—about 80% of those on the entire planet—take a break in their annual migration along an 80-mile-long section of the Platte River in central Nebraska. In the spring, they nibble on grain from nearby fields on their way to their summer nesting grounds to the north, and swing through the region again in the fall on their way south to their winter habitat. When they spread their 6-foot-wide wings and take flight, it's a sight to behold. Though Kearney, Nebraska, is billed as the "Sandhill Crane Capital of the World," trips to see Nebraska's sandhill crane migration are available throughout the region.

### Don't Miss

Learn more about efforts to protect the Platte River ecosystems for sandhill cranes and other wildlife by taking a guided tour of the Iain Nicolson Audubon Center at Rowe Sanctuary. It's located 20 miles east of Kearney and sits in the middle of a favorite spot for migrating sandhill cranes.

### Good to Know

Only watch the birds from designated viewing areas. Dress warmly, pay close attention to the weather, and bring binoculars or a camera with a long lens to get a close-up view.

### Getting Here and Around

Kearney, Nebraska, in the center of the crane-watching area, is 180 miles west of Omaha.

**Sandhill Crane Migration.** *www.visitnebraska.com/sandhill-crane-migration* *Free.*

# The Cowboy Trail

## America's Longest Rails-to-Trails Project

At 321 miles, the Cowboy Trail in Nebraska is the longest rails-to-trails project ever completed in the United States. About two-thirds of the distance—the 195 miles between Norfolk and Valentine—have a crushed limestone surface that's perfect for cycling. There are stops every 10 to 15 miles at 15 communities along the route, so you're never far from food and lodging. You'll cross some wooden bridges, but nature is on full display along the route. A 100-foot-wide right-of-way allows native plants to thrive and attracts songbirds, pheasants, and quail. Bald eagles can be seen in the Elkhorn River Valley and turkey vultures soar on thermals above the Niobrara River.

## Don't Miss

Late-night television star Johnny Carson grew up in Norfolk, so if you're interested in the history of television, head to the Elkhorn Valley Museum. A special gallery holds his Emmy Awards, a replica of his famous stage, and artifacts that he personally chose to display. His boyhood home is a mecca for fans.

## Getting Here and Around

Norfolk is in northeast Nebraska and Valentine is in the north-central part of the state near the South Dakota border. Omaha, Nebraska, and Sioux City, Iowa, are the closest airports.

**The Cowboy Trail.** ✉ *2201 S. 13th St., Norfolk, NE* ☎ *402/471–5443* 🌐 *www.visitnebraska.com/norfolk/cowboy-trail* 🎟 *Free.*

# The Prairie Chicken Dance

## Nature's Wildest Show

You've likely done the chicken dance at weddings. But Nebraska's greater prairie chickens truly do strut their stuff in the wild. During most of the year, these birds lead relatively quiet lives. But every spring during mating season, they let it all hang out. There's a lot of emphatic stomping, jumping, and letting out its earsplitting cry. It's nature's most entertaining display.

## Don't Miss

To see this spectacular frenzy of fowls, take a chicken dance tour with McCook, a joint effort between local and state agencies, that includes a mandatory orientation by a biologist the evening before that spells out the rules (wear dark clothing, remain silent, no phones). The next morning you and your fellow bird-watchers will gather for the early-morning viewing, which is from a distance so as not to disrupt the mating dance. Afterward, you'll be served a hot breakfast.

## While You're Here

Spend the rest of the day in and around McCook on a self-guided walking tour of the 10-block McCook's Heritage Square, including the Frank Lloyd Wright–designed Sutton House and the Museum of the High Plains. Prefer more time in nature? Head north 20 miles to Red Willow Reservoir State Recreation Area on High Butler Lake for hiking, biking, and fishing.

## Getting Here and Around

The tour leaves from McCook in southwest Nebraska, 284 miles southwest of Omaha and 262 miles northeast of Denver.

**Prairie Chicken Dance Tours.** 🌐 *www.prairiechickendancetours.com* 🎫 *$100.*

# Fort Niobrara National Wildlife Refuge

### The Great Plains in Miniature

If you could condense the entire Great Plains into one small nature preserve, it would look like the breathtaking Fort Niobrara National Wildlife Refuge. This 30-square-mile park, on the grounds of a former fort near the town of Valentine, was established in 1912 to protect native birds but soon after expanded to include large herds of elk and bison. You'll see countless deer munching on the native grasses, and a town of prairie dogs sticking their heads out of their burrows. Bald and golden eagles can be spotted during winter along the Niobrara River. You might also spot wild turkeys among the birch, burr oak, and ponderosa pine on the rolling sandhills.

Besides being rich in plant and animal life, the refuge also played a role in America's westward expansion. Fort Niobrara Military Reservation was established in 1879 to help manage relations between the Sioux people and the settlers arriving from the East. It also tried to control cattle rustlers and horse thieves. The only remnants from the fort are an old red barn and some foundations.

### Don't Miss

The self-guided driving tour is only 3½ miles long, but it takes you to a scenic overlook just off Highway 12 with views of the Nebraska Sandhills and the Niobrara River. The tour starts near the visitor center.

### Getting Here and Around

Fort Niobrara National Wildlife Refuge is 4 miles east of Valentine along the Niobrara River.

**Fort Niobrara National Wildlife Refuge.** ✉ *39983 Refuge Rd., Valentine, NE* ☎ *402/376–3789* 🌐 *www.fws.gov/refuge/Fort_Niobrara* 🎟 *Free.*

## Toadstool Geologic Park

### A Trip to the Moon

Part of Oglala National Grassland in far northwestern Nebraska, Toadstool Geologic Park's unusual name comes from unique geological formations that resemble toadstools. Many visitors are struck by the area's rocky expanse, which resembles the surface of the moon. The area is also known for its treasure trove of fossils, including the ancestors of modern dogs, horses, and even rhinoceros. In one interesting discovery, you can clearly see where two hungry entolodents (fearsome piglike creatures) were hunting for a meal along a small stream.

### Don't Miss

Set aside some time to see one of the most significant paleo-archaeological discoveries in North America in the Hudson-Meng Education and Research Center: the fossilized remains of an extinct type of bison that died here en masse. From the Toadstool Campground, take the Bison Trail for about 3 miles each way.

### Fossil Hunting

Before heading out on a hike thorugh Toadstool Geologic Park, check out the interpretive kiosk for information about the surrounding grasslands and the creatures that lived here. You'll find it's easier to spot the fossils.

### Getting Here and Around

Begin at the intersection of Highway 20 and Highway 2 near Crawford. Take Highway 2 north for 4 miles to Toadstool Road. Follow Toadstool Road for 11 miles to Road 902 and continue on Road 902 for 1½ miles to Toadstool Campground.

**Toadstool Geologic Park.** ✉ *1811 Meng Dr., Crawford, NE* ☎ *308/665–3900* 🌐 *www.fs.usda.gov* 🎫 *$3 a day.*

# Chimney Rock

## In the Footsteps of the Pioneers

When pioneers were headed west, they navigated with landmarks. One of the most recognizable was Chimney Rock, rising 480 feet above the North Platte River Valley near Bayard in southwest Nebraska. The natural formation, the result of centuries of erosion, has a wide base and a narrow spire that make it visible for miles. It's one of the most famous stops along the Mormon Trail.

The National Park Service believes the name Chimney Rock likely came from the first fur traders in the region. After examining more than 300 journal accounts of settlers moving west, historian Merrill Mattes concluded it was by far the most mentioned landmark. He said that although no special events took place there, it was a focal point for most travelers.

## Don't Miss

To hike to the base, take Chimney Rock Trail. It's an easy 1-mile out-and-back trail that offers scenic views.

## Getting Here and Around

Chimney Rock National Historic Site is 4 miles south of Bayard on Highway 26 and Road 75. The visitor center is 1½ miles south of Highway 92 on Chimney Rock Road. It houses interesting exhibits concerning life on the trails.

**Chimney Rock.** ✉ *Bayard, NE* ☎ *308/586–2581* 🌐 *www.nps.gov/nr/travel/scotts_bluff/chimney_rock.html* 🎟 *Free.*

# When in Nebraska

## CARHENGE

England has Stonehenge, but Alliance, Nebraska, has Carhenge. Designed and built by Jim Reinders as a memorial to his father, the quirky attraction consists of 38 vintage cars arranged in the same formation as the mystical Stonehenge. It's open year-round, there's no admission, and there's a gift shop where you can pick up kitschy items.

**Do This:** After taking in Carhenge, drop by the Knight Museum and Sandhills Center to learn about Native Americans who made their home here for centuries, as well as the settlers who eventually came this way.

**Carhenge.** ✉ *2151 CR 59, Alliance, NE* ☎ *308/762–3569* 🌐 *www.carhenge.com* 🎟 *Free.*

## CHEER ON THE CORNHUSKERS

Every home football game for the University of Nebraska Cornhuskers has been a sellout since 1962, back when John F. Kennedy was president, the Cuban Missile Crisis brought the country to the brink of war, and astronaut John Glenn became the first American to circle the planet. Without a professional team and no other big college teams within easy driving distance, Nebraskans generally support Big Red Football with a passion that's found in few other places.

Memorial Stadium, known as the Sea of Red, is a century old, so it's full of history. But it's also been modernized to accommodate more people on game day than Nebraska's third-largest city. Unless your college loyalties prevent it, consider joining the crowd for a game and be part of history. And wear red.

**Do This:** Before (and after) the game, grab a meal and browse among the restored warehouses in Lincoln's Historic Haymarket District, named after the square where hay and other items were bought and sold since 1867. And check out the brick mural of the first train that arrived in Lincoln on July 4, 1870.

**One Memorial Stadium.** ✉ *800 Stadium Dr., Lincoln, NE* ☎ *402/472–4224* 🌐 *www.huskers.com/sports/football* 🎟 *Varies.*

## NEBRASKA STAR PARTY

With plenty of wide-open spaces and unobscured by light pollution from big cities, the annual Nebraska Star Party is an excellent way to explore the heavens. The views from Merritt Reservoir's Snake Campground, near the north-central town of Valentine, are outstanding. The Beginner's Field School demonstrates how to explore the sky with or without a telescope. There are a lot of special programs for kids, like pop-bottle rocketry.

**Do This:** Explore the surrounding sandhills during the day. The remote region offers plenty of recreational opportunities, including short day trips to interesting historical sites. The spring-fed water and sandy beaches of Merritt Reservoir offer swimming, boating, and fishing.

**Merritt Reservoir Snake Campground.** ✉ *NE 97, Valentine, NE* ☎ *402/333–5460* 🌐 *www.nebraskastarparty.org* 🎟 *$50.*

## ROBBER'S CAVE TOUR

Lincoln, Nebraska's oldest tourist attraction, Robber's Cave has been a source of entertainment and folklore in Nebraska for more than 150 years. It was listed on the National Register of Historic Places in 2020. A small pocket of sandstone bluff was enlarged and used to store lager for Lincoln's first brewery. It both legally and illegally became a popular place for social gatherings through much of the 20th century. Thousands of etchings now cover the 5,600 square feet of tunnels. Legend has it that outlaw Jesse James hid out here, as did some of the enslaved people escaping along the Underground Railroad.

**Do This:** Joel Green, author of the book *Robber's Cave: Truths, Legends and Recollections,* leads private tours of the cave. Tours lasting 45 to 60 minutes include entertaining anecdotes he has collected from past guests.

**Robber's Cave Tour.** ✉ *925 Robbers Cave Rd., Lincoln, NE* ☎ *402/975–0598* 🌐 *www.robberscavetours.com* 🎫 *$14.*

### WORLD'S LARGEST BALL OF STAMPS

Boys Town founder Father Edward J. Flanagan saw stamp collecting as a wholesome, educational hobby for the youngsters in his care, so he launched the Boys Town Stamp Collecting Club. The youngsters started collecting and trading stamps in the 1930s. There were a lot of extra stamps in their collections, so in 1953 they started what would soon become the World's Largest Ball of Stamps. Measuring 32 inches in diameter and weighing 600 pounds, the ball was recognized as a record-setter in 1955.

**Do This:** Spend some time in the Leon Myers Stamp Center, a museum in the Boys Town Visitors Center. The center promotes stamp collecting and has exhibits on a variety of topics, including stamps designed by kids.

**Boys Town Visitors Center.** ✉ *14100 Crawford St., Boys Town, NE* ☎ *800/217–3700* 🌐 *www.boystown.org/village/Pages/worlds-largest-stamp-ball.aspx* 🎫 *Free.*

## Cool Places to Stay

**Comstock Lodge.** A visit to the 10-room Comstock Lodge puts you in the heart of Nebraska's Sandhills. Bison and elk roam the 3,000-acre property, and the grass-fed meat is available for purchase. ✉ *81785 Rd. 457, Sargent, NE* ☎ *308/527–4199* 🌐 *www.comstock-lodge.com* 💲 *From: $135.*

**Lied Lodge.** Located on Arbor Day Farm, this lodging's 140 nature-inspired rooms were built by the Arbor Day Foundation to serve as a space for like-minded individuals to discuss trees, conservation, and environmental stewardship. ✉ *2700 Sylvan Rd., Nebraska City, NE* ☎ *800/546–5433* 🌐 *www.liedlodge.org* 💲 *From: $169.*

**River Inn Resort.** A floating bed-and-breakfast on the Missouri River at Brownville, Nebraska, River Resort has a tranquil, romantic atmosphere. Activities include hiking, biking, and exploring local museums. A dinner cruise aboard the *Spirit of Brownsville* sets sail Fridays, Saturdays, and Sundays beginning Memorial Day weekend. ✉ *72898 648 A Ave., Brownville, NE* ☎ *402/825–6441* 🌐 *www.river-inn-resort.com* 💲 *From: $120.*

**Rowses 1+1 Ranch.** This working cattle ranch in central Nebraska offers "the opportunity to not play cowboy, but to be one." Guests will learn how to ride, rope, brand, and sort cattle. And you do it all mounted on a trained quarter horse that's yours for the duration of your stay. ✉ *46849 833rd Rd., Burwell, NE* ☎ *308/346–5530* 🌐 *www.1plus1ranch.com* 💲 *From: $300 per person, 3-night minimum.*

# North Dakota

North Dakota is a massive expanse of rolling prairies under intense blue skies, much of it unchanged since the expeditions led by Lewis and Clark in 1804 and 1806. This rectangular state straddles the Canadian border between Minnesota and Montana. The eastern edge, marked by the Red River, is rich soil on land so flat you can see the horizon as an uninterrupted straight line. One of its greatest treasures is Theodore Roosevelt National Park, a remarkable area that's been described both as "the Grand Canyon in miniature" and "hell with the fires put out."

## Bucket List Picks

The following boxes contain our picks for the top sights and experiences in North Dakota.

- ○ Theodore Roosevelt National Park
- ○ Dakota Prairie Grasslands
- ○ Huff Indian Village State Historic Site
- ○ North Dakota's Sunflower Fields
- ○ The Lewis and Clark Trail
- ○ The Enchanted Highway
- ○ Plains Art Museum
- ○ Cold War–Era Missile Bases

# Theodore Roosevelt National Park

## Search for Bison Like Teddy

Intent on hunting bison, Theodore Roosevelt first came to the badlands of North Dakota in 1883. It turned out that the bison that had roamed across the plains had been almost entirely wiped out by that point, but he fell in love with this spectacular region. After becoming president in 1901, he created the U.S. Forest Service as a way to protect wildlife and public lands. He also established 150 national forests, 51 federal bird reserves, four national game preserves, five national parks, and 18 national monuments.

Much of the allure of the 110-square-mile Theodore Roosevelt National Park is its lack of people. It's perfect for anyone who loves birding and wildlife viewing, hiking and backpacking, stargazing and scenic drives.

## Don't Miss

The hiking trails offer a close-up view of the unique geology of mixed prairie and rugged ravines, buttes, and tablelands.

## Getting Here and Around

The South Unit of Theodore Roosevelt National Park abuts the western end of the small town of Medora, 30 miles west of Dickinson on Interstate 94. The less-traveled North Unit is 60 miles southeast of Williston on Highway 85. Medora has numerous activities that complement a visit to the park as well as plenty of food and lodging options. Dickinson to the east and Williston to the north also cater to park visitors.

**Theodore Roosevelt National Park.** ✉ *315 Second Ave., Medora, ND* ☎ *701/623–4466* 🌐 *www.nps.gov/thro* 🎫 *$30 per vehicle.*

# Dakota Prairie Grasslands

## Solitude in a Sea of Grass

Truly a place to get away from it all, the Dakota Prairie Grasslands unlike anywhere else on earth. Little Missouri National Grassland, home to Theodore Roosevelt National Park, is the largest grassland in the United States. If you drive or hike through the park, you'll notice how the prairie gradually mixes with the badlands. The highest point in North Dakota, White Butte, is located in the southeastern corner of Little Missouri.

To the south, Cedar River National Grassland and Grand River National Grassland feature plains that stretch for miles and gently rolling hills. Parts of Cedar River and Grand River are within the boundaries of the Standing Rock Indian Reservation. Another part of the Grand River is within the Cheyenne River Indian Reservation. Both reservations are open to the public but may impose travel restrictions. In the east, home to the tallgrass prairie region, is Sheyenne, closest to the capital of Bismarck and to Fargo.

## Don't Miss

All Dakota Prairie Grasslands parks offer unbeatable hiking, but Sheyenne National Grassland has a great 17-mile water trail for canoeing and kayaking.

## Getting Here and Around

The four Dakota Prairie Grasslands are not contiguous, so be prepared to drive between them. Sheyenne National Grassland is in southeast North Dakota, about an hour southwest of Fargo. The other three grasslands—Cedar River, Little Missouri, and Grand River—are at least a four-hour drive west.

**Grand River and Cedar River.** ✉ *Off U.S. 12, Lemmon, SD* **Sheyenne.** ✉ *Rte. 27, Lisbon, ND* 🌐 *www.fs.usda.gov/main/dpg* 🎫 *Free.*

# Huff Indian Village State Historic Site

## In the Footsteps of America's First Peoples

It's one thing to read about the earliest residents of the region, but it's quite another to walk through the remains of a historic Native American settlement like the Huff Indian Village. This state historical site was home to the Mandan tribe more than 500 years ago. It was a large, complex community where an estimated 1,000 people lived. Their food came from bison hunting and farming corn, beans, and squash that they stored for their own use and also traded to nomadic people.

There are interpretive signs around the site that make it easy to do the walking tour at your own pace. You'll see rows of depressions that mark the location of more than 100 lodges that run parallel to the river bank. A large fortification ditch surrounds the entire 12-acre area.

## Don't Miss

If possible, time your visit to coincide with the annual United Tribes Technical College International Powwow, which is held the second week of September in nearby Bismarck. Drawing more than 10,000 participants and spectators from around the world, it includes dancers and singers who compete for prizes.

## Getting Here and Around

Huff is 24 miles south of Bismarck on Highway 1806. To get to the Huff Indian Village Historic Site, drive another half mile south.

**Huff Indian Village State Historic Site.** ✉ *Roughrider Tr., Huff, ND* ☎ *701/328–2666* 🌐 *www.history.nd.gov/historicsites/huff/index.html* 🎟 *Free.*

# North Dakota's Sunflower Fields

### America's Happiest Harvest

Fields of sunny yellow as far as the eye can see blanket central and northern North Dakota each August, when sunflowers reach their peak bloom. Although Kansas is officially known as the Sunflower State, North Dakota actually leads the nation in sunflower production, providing close to 40% of the nation's total crop. They're the most striking of North Dakota's many brightly colored crops, which also include the bluish-purple of flax or the brilliant green of soybeans, and have been known to cause happiness.

### Don't Miss

The fields are generally located off the highways of Lakota, Bismarck, Mapleton, and Mott, though their location changes each year.

### Good to Know

View the sunflower fields from the road rather than entering them; almost all are on private land. Definitely don't pick any.

### While You're Here

After you snap a pic of the sunflowers, stop by a small-town eatery. You'll find great-tasting food at very reasonable prices, and perhaps even a slice of North Dakota sunflower pie.

### When to Go

Peak bloom lasts from August to early September.

### Getting Here and Around

The exact location of the fields changes each year, but you can generally find them just off state or county highways in cities including Bismarck, Mott, and Lakota. Follow the sunflower map from the North Dakota Tourism board at 🌐 *www.ndtourism.com/best-places/let-amazing-sunflower-put-smile-your-face* to track optimal viewing locations.

# The Lewis and Clark Trail

## The Path of Sacajawea

North Dakota's Fort Mandan was an important stop along the journey west for the Lewis and Clark expedition, which had been dispatched by President Thomas Jefferson to survey the lands that became part of the United States after the Louisiana Purchase of 1803. It's where the expedition spent the brutal winter of 1804 and 1805. It's also where they established friendships with Sacajawea, the Shoshone woman who traveled with the expedition and helped introduce them to Native American people they met along their way to the Pacific Ocean; her French-Canadian fur trapper husband Toussaint Charbonneau, who served as translator for a time; and Sheheke-Shote, the chief of the Mandan people.

Near the present-day community of Washburn, the North Dakota Lewis and Clark Interpretive Center includes a fully furnished, full-size replica of Fort Mandan.

## Don't Miss

The 23-mile-long Sacajawea Scenic Byway, on Highway 200A from Washburn to Stanton, offers great views of the Missouri River Valley and interesting Lewis and Clark destinations, including the Knife River Indian Villages National Historic Site, Cross Ranch State Park, and Fort Clark State Historic Site.

## Getting Here and Around

Washburn is 42 miles north of Bismarck. Take Interstate 94 to the west end of Bismarck then River Road to Highway 1804 and then to Highway 83, with views of the Missouri River.

**The Lewis and Clark Trail.** ✉ *2576 8th St. SW, Washburn, ND* ☎ *701/462–8535* 🌐 *www.parkrec.nd.gov/lewis-clark-interpretive-center* 🎫 *Free.*

# The Enchanted Highway

### Magic on the Prairie

Near the towns of Regent and Gladstone, North Dakota, is one for the road-trippers: a 32-mile stretch of roadway north of town is lined with huge, 70-foot metal sculptures by sculptor Gary Greff. Massive pheasants dash across the plain, huge grasshoppers nibble on leaves, and trout leap from imaginary streams. It's truly a magical place, especially at sunset when it seems the shadows dance across the wide-open sky.

### Don't Miss

The best sculptures to seek out are "Deer Crossing" and "Geese in Flight" near Gladstone on Interstate 94, but you can easily see all of them on the quick drive. Kids especially love snapping photos of the "Tin Family" of larger-than-life farmers near Regent.

### While You're Here

If you want to take some of this enchantment home, the gift shop in Regent has miniatures of each statue. The Enchanted Castle offers hot meals and a comfy place to lay your head.

### Getting Here and Around

To reach the Enchanted Highway, take Exit 72 off Interstate 94 near Gladstone and drive 32 miles south to the town of Regent. All except "Geese in Flight" have parking areas and information kiosks.

**The Enchanted Highway.** ✉ *I–94, Exit 72, Regent ND* ☎ *701/563–6400* 🌐 *www.ndtourism.com/regent/attractions/enchanted-highway* 🎫 *Free.*

# Plains Art Museum

## Anything but Plain

Located in a 19th-century farm equipment warehouse in downtown Fargo, the Plains Art Museum has wooden floors and high ceilings with exposed wooden beams that make it the perfect spot for showing off the work of some of the best artists in the Great Plains. The museum's permanent collection contains approximately 4,000 works, many of them by noted Native American artists. There's about a dozen large-scale special exhibitions each year, along with many smaller ones that feature the art of the 20th and 21st centuries.

## Don't Miss

The only permanent work is a 13-by-24-foot oil painting on canvas in the lobby called *The North Dakota Mural* by the late James Rosenquist, who grew up in the state. He drew on his childhood memories of the Great Plains to illustrate its wide-open spaces, vistas, and skies.

## While You're Here

If you have time, sign up for a fascinating class at the museum's Katherine Kilbourne Burgum Center for Creativity. You might be throwing clay for a pot or creating your own beer stein.

## Getting Here and Around

The Plains Art Museum is located in downtown Fargo. There are a lot of great restaurants and lodging options nearby.

**Plains Art Museum.** ✉ *704 First Ave. N, Fargo, ND* ☎ *701/551–6100* 🌐 *www.plainsart.org* 🎫 *Free.*

# Cold War–Era Missile Bases

## Explore Top Secret Bunkers

North Dakota's remote regions were the perfect location for several Cold War–era military installations. Today you can tour the buildings where the crews lived and worked, learn about their day-to-day life in such a strategic location, and gain an understanding of how the bases operated. Near Cooperstown, the Ronald Reagan Minuteman Missile State Historic Site consists of two attractions: the Oscar-Zero Missile Alert Facility and the November-33 Launch Facility. They are the last remnants of intercontinental ballistic missile launch sites that were spread over a 6,500-square-mile area around northeastern North Dakota's Grand Forks Air Force Base.

## Don't Miss

At Ronald Reagan Minuteman Missile State Historic Site, ride the elevator down 50 feet to the launch control center with its red chairs and vintage computer stations. It will look familiar to fans of *War Games* or other movies with nuclear launch code scenes.

## While You're Here

Near Cavalier, the Remote Sprint Launch Site No. 3 was part of a complex designed to shoot down incoming nuclear weapons. Tours include a look at the operations bunker, the 16-silo missile field, and an actual missile.

## Getting Here and Around

The Ronald Reagan Minuteman Missile State Historic Site is 6 miles north of Cooperstown. From there, the Remote Sprint Launch Site No. 3 is 106 miles north.

**Ronald Reagan Minuteman Missile State Historic Site.** ✉ *555 113th Ave. NE, Cooperstown, ND* 🎫 *$10.*

**Remote Sprint Launch Site No. 3.** ✉ *12329 State Hwy. 5, Cavalier, ND* 🎫 *$12.*

## When in North Dakota

### BADLANDS DINOSAUR MUSEUM

North Dakota is known for dinosaur fossils, and many of them are on display at Dickinson's Badlands Dinosaur Museum. It has more fossils on display than anywhere else in the state, including full skeletons of Stegosaurus, Allosaurus, Triceratops, Edmontosaurus, Albertosaurus, and Thescelosaurus.

**Do This:** Take advantage of the hands-on exhibit that allows visitors to create mountains, coastlines, and volcanoes with an augmented reality sandbox. You can also look at bugs and minerals with a digital microscope.

**Dickinson's Badlands Dinosaur Museum.** ✉ *188 Museum Dr. E, Dickinson, ND* ☎ *701/456–6225* 🌐 *www.dickinsonmuseumcenter.com* 🎫 *$6.*

### THE WOOD CHIPPER FROM FARGO

One of the most gruesome scenes in movie history has become a must-see tourist attraction. The wood chipper used in the 1996 movie *Fargo,* written, produced, and directed by brothers Joel and Ethan Coen, is on display at the Fargo-Moorhead Visitors Center. Fans don't seem to mind that Fargo wasn't actually filmed in North Dakota's largest city.

**Do This:** Don a trapper hat with ear flaps—the folks here are happy to loan you one—and shoot your own remake of the famous scene for the folks back home.

**I-94 Visitors Center.** ✉ *2001 44th St. S, Fargo, ND* ☎ *701/282–3653* 🌐 *www.fargomoorhead.org/what-to-do/the-wood-chipper-in-fargo* 🎫 *Free.*

## Cool Places to Stay

**Coteau des Prairie Lodge.** Owned and operated by a farming family, this lodge made of logs and steel sits atop a ridge of the Coteau des Prairies Plateau, a vast expanse that stretches into South Dakota, Minnesota, and Iowa. There are homemade meals, outdoor expeditions, and plenty of wide-open spaces. ✉ *9953 141st Ave. SE, Havana, ND* ☎ *701/680–1175* 🌐 *www.cdplodge.com* [$] *From $140.*

**Enchanted Castle Hotel.** This medieval-themed hotel, restaurant, and tavern offers a unique lodging and dining experience in Regent. The steak house—named Excalibur, of course—has fun decor that includes suits of armor. It's the perfect place to stay after exploring the Enchanted Highway. ✉ *607 Main St., Regent, ND* ☎ *701/563–4858* 🌐 *www.enchantedcastlend.com* [$] *From $99.*

**Hotel Donaldson.** The handsome brick Hotel Donaldson—better known to locals as HoDo—doesn't ofer cookie-cutter rooms. Accommodations here are one-of-a-kind creations inspired by the works of artists. The rooftop hot tub makes it a special stay. ✉ *101 N. Broadway, Fargo, ND* ☎ *701/478–1000* 🌐 *www.hoteldonaldson.com* [$] *From $184.*

**Pipestem Creek Bed and Birding.** This working family farm near Carrington is a great place to stay. It's located in the prairie potholes region, the most important duck-breeding area in the nation, so it's a prime spot for bird-watchers. Numerous gardens along Pipestem Creek are beautiful places for walks. This is a great place to stay if you're taking in the sunflower bloom. ✉ *7060 Hwy. 9, Carrington, ND* ☎ *701/652–2623* 🌐 *www.pipestemcreek.com* [$] *From $100.*

# Oklahoma

The Sooner State is the geographical and cultural crossroads of America, where the green mountains of the East dissolve into the golden prairies of the West (and of course, where the wind blows sweeping down the plains). A dozen ecosystems blanket the state, which cradles 200 man-made lakes, more than 1 million surface-acres of water, and 2,000 more miles of shoreline than the Atlantic and Gulf coasts combined.

## Bucket List Picks

The following boxes contain our picks for the top sights and experiences in Oklahoma.

- ○ Oklahoma City National Memorial
- ○ Natural Falls State Park
- ○ Deep Deuce District
- ○ Oklahoma's Route 66
- ○ Wichita Mountains Wildlife Refuge
- ○ Factory Obscura Mix-Tape

# Oklahoma City National Memorial

### Moment of Remembrance

No trip to the state of Oklahoma would be complete without a stop at the Oklahoma City National Memorial and Museum, dedicated to "those who were killed, those who survived, and those changed forever" in the April 19, 1993, bombing at the Alfred P. Murrah Federal Building. The Outdoor Symbolic Memorial includes the land where the building once stood and the surrounding area that was devastated by the attack. The Field of Empty Chairs, which represents and memorializes all 168 people killed in the bombing, fills the foreground. The Reflecting Pool and memorial museum are beyond.

The interactive museum is located in the west end of the former Journal Record Building, which was built in 1923 and withstood the bombing. The museum takes you on self-guided tours through the events of the day and the world's immediate outpouring of support. The museum uses hundreds of hours of video footage to show the day's toll.

### Don't Miss

The Survivor Tree, an American elm tree just yards away from the site of the explosion survived the bomb's blast and stands tall as a symbol of hope and perseverance; its seedlings are available for purchase.

### Good to Know

If you're a runner, consider taking part in the annual Oklahoma City Memorial Marathon, which supports the memorial and museum.

### Getting Here and Around

The museum and memorial are located in downtown Oklahoma City; the memorial is open to the public 24 hours a day.

**Oklahoma City National Memorial.** ✉ *620 N. Harvey Ave., Oklahoma City, OK* 🌐 *www.memorialmuseum.com* 🎟 *Memorial, free; museum, $15.*

# Natural Falls State Park

### Where the Red Fern Grows

A dazzling 77-foot waterfall cascades through rock formations and into a beautiful pool at Natural Falls State Park. It may look familiar, because scenes for the 1974 classic film *Where the Red Fern Grows* were filmed at this park in the Ozark Mountains near the border of Arkansas. An observation platform with a picnic pavilion overlooks the falls. There's also a deck at the base of the falls, so it's possible to see the falls from above and below.

### Don't Miss

There are more than 4 miles of hiking trails fanning out through the park. You'll see a variety of plants, including ferns, liverworts, mosses, flowering dogwood, sassafras, coral berry, spicebush, redbud, and pawpaw, as well as numerous tree types such as maples, chinquapin, and white oaks.

### Spend the Night

Book at least one night in one of the park's five yurts. You won't be exactly roughing it, as there's air-conditioning, microwaves, mini-refrigerators, and other amenities. Shower and restroom facilities are a short walk away.

### Getting Here and Around

Natural Falls State Park is a 90-minute drive east of Tulsa.

**Natural Falls State Park.** ✉ *Hwy. 412 W, West Siloam Springs, OK* ☎ *918/422–5802* 🌐 *www.travelok.com/state-parks/natural-falls-state-park* 🎫 *$10.*

# Deep Deuce District

## Black History in Oklahoma City

In Oklahoma City, the Deep Deuce district was the heart of Black culture in the 1920s and 1930s. It was the hub for local blues and jazz musicians, including legends like Charlie Christian and Jimmy Rushing, who hailed from the district. Rushing, a renowned pianist, was a member of a jazz group called the Oklahoma City Blue Devils. He was inducted into the Rock and Roll Hall of Fame in 1990 for his contributions to the music scene. Count Basie, Ma Rainey, Bessie Smith, and Mamie Smith were among the performers who played here.

Deep Deuce has a long history focusing on social justice. It was home to author Ralph Ellison, whose award-winning novel *Invisible Man* focused on issues faced by Black Americans in the middle of the 20th century. The neighborhood was also where Oklahoma students organized sit-ins at segregated lunch counters in 1957.

## Don't Miss

Calvary Baptist Church was built in the early 1920s and was the social and religious center of Oklahoma City's Black population. Martin Luther King Jr. preached there in 1953 and spoke at a freedom rally in 1960.

## Best Bar

Soak up the live music and order a drink at Deep Deuce Bar and Grill. *www.deepdeucebarandgrillokc.com.*

## Getting Here and Around

The district is located in downtown Oklahoma City between Main Street and Northeast 4th Street and from Broadway to Interstate 235. The neighborhood is very walkable, with a variety of cafés, restaurants, and art galleries.

**Deep Deuce District.** *211 N. Robinson, Suite 225, Oklahoma City, OK* *405/235–3500* *deepdeucedistrict.com* *Free.*

# Oklahoma's Route 66

## Follow the Mother Road

Few other roadways conjure up images of America's past like Route 66, one of the first highways in the United States. It stretched nearly 2,500 miles from Chicago, Illinois, to Santa Monica, California, and was open between 1926 and 1985. Route 66 was the stuff of legend, with a song and a TV show named after it. It also figured prominently in John Steinbeck's novel *The Grapes of Wrath* about the westward migration during the Dust Bowl. Almost 400 miles of the road ran through the center of Oklahoma, cutting through both Oklahoma City and Tulsa and following small towns that once drew road-trippers with neon signs, diners, and motels. Today you can trace its history with top attractions including Oklahoma Route 66 Museum in Clinton and the National Route 66 & Transportation Museum in Elk City.

## Don't Miss

The Oklahoma Route 66 Museum in Clinton re-creates the heyday of the Mother Road, down to a 1957 Chevy and the counter from a diner. For some visitors, it's a trip down memory lane to a time when big band music dominated the airwaves. For younger generations, it's a great place to experience part of U.S. history that runs far deeper than a stretch of pavement.

## Good to Know

Show off to friends with a Route 66 Passport that you can get stamped at 28 spots along the way, including the famous Blue Whale in Catoosa, Oklahoma. ⊕ *www.travelok.com*.

## Getting Here and Around

Clinton, where the Oklahoma Route 66 Museum is located, is about 90 miles west of Oklahoma City, which is served by major air carriers.

**Route 66.** ⊕ *www.okhistory.org/sites/route66*.

# Wichita Mountains Wildlife Refuge

## Home on the Range

One of the oldest wildlife refuges in the United States, Wichita Mountains was established in 1901. The 92-square-mile refuge gives you a rare opportunity to experience a mixed-grass prairie that's largely been untouched—mostly because the rocky soils made it difficult to plow. Besides protecting animals in danger of becoming extinct, the refuge's purpose was to rebuild the populations of those that had already been wiped out from the area. Wildlife reintroduced over the years include American bison, Rocky Mountain elks, wild turkeys, prairie dogs, river otters, and burrowing owls. White-tailed deer and Texas longhorn cattle also graze the grasslands. Today, more than 240 species of birds, 64 reptiles and amphibians, 50 mammals, and 36 fish can be found on the refuge.

## Don't Miss

There are 15 miles of designated hiking trails that wind through scrub oak forests, across rocky mountains, and over grass-covered prairies.

## Take a Class

Wichita Mountains Wildlife Refuge has one of the largest environmental programs in the country. There are also programs on the region's Native American heritage.

## Getting Here and Around

The wildlife refuge is located 4 miles north of Cache, Oklahoma. It's a two-hour drive southwest of Oklahoma City.

**Wichita Mountains Visitor Center.** ✉ *20539 State Hwy. 115, Cache, OK* ☎ *580/429–2197* 🌐 *www.fws.gov/refuge/Wichita_Mountains* 🎫 *Free.*

# Factory Obscura Mix-Tape

## Sensory Overload

At Factory Obscura Mix-Tape, a massive boom box where you can push the buttons on the tape player is just part of this 6,000-square-foot facility filled with audiovisual fun. The immersive art experience at Factory Obscura Mix-Tape is intended to recall the days when creative types used cassette tapes to record the soundtracks to their lives. Now, instead of just sounds, it's a whole sensory overload. Mix-Tape is located in the Factory Obscura art collective just north of downtown Oklahoma City. The team of around 30 artists from a wide variety of backgrounds is constantly changing the experience, so locals often come back again and again.

## Don't Miss

Available for free at the box office are scavenger hunts for kids to help them look for clues as they explore the Mix-Tape exhibits.

## Other Great Museums

OKC museums are better than OK. The 99s Museum of Women Pilots has one of the largest collections of memorabilia about Amelia Earhart, one of the original 99s, who was the first woman to fly solo across the Atlantic Ocean. Also in Oklahoma City, the National Cowboy and Western Heritage Museum has a spectacular permanent exhibits with more than 28,000 pieces of Western and Native American art and artifacts.

## Getting Here and Around

If you're based in Oklahoma City driving to the museums is easily done, and you could pick two to explore in a day. Mix-Tape is located downtown.

**Factory Obscura Mix-Tape.** ✉ *25 N.W. 9th St., Oklahoma City, OK* ☎ *405/642–1920* 🌐 *www.factoryobscura.com/mixtape* 🎫 *$17.*

# When in Oklahoma

## CENTER OF THE UNIVERSE

It sounds like some kind of cosmic black hole, but the Center of the Universe in Tulsa is actually an acoustic anomaly. If you stand in the center of a eight-foot-wide circle and make a noise, the echoes come back even louder. If you whisper to someone directly across the circle, they can clearly hear you. The mind-bending part of it is that no one outside the circle can hear you at all. The Center of the Universe can be accessed from a brick path from the Boston Avenue pedestrian overpass.

**Do This:** While you're in Tulsa, check out the 76-foot-tall Golden Driller statue. It was created for the 1953 International Petroleum Exposition, a fair exhibiting the latest innovations in oil technology.

**The Center of the Universe.** ✉ *20 E. Archer St., Tulsa, OK* ☎ *800/558–3311* 🌐 *www.travelok.com/listings/view.profile/id.19397* 🎫 *Free.*

## HONEY SPRINGS BATTLEFIELD HISTORIC SITE

The Battle of Honey Springs was the last and largest engagement of the Civil War in the Great Plains, a decisive victory for Union troops in the effort to control what was then called Indian Territory. It took place on a rainy Friday, July 17, 1863. About 9,000 men took part, including Native American troops on both sides. Also on the scene was the First Kansas Colored Volunteers, the first African American regiment in the Union Army.

**Do This:** A reenactment of the Battle of Honey Springs allows you to experience military drills, demonstrations, and living history programs. Vendors that sell books, clothing, and reproductions of 19th-century military equipment.

**Honey Springs Battlefield Historic Site.** ✉ *1863 Honey Springs Battlefield Rd., Checotah, OK* 🌐 *www.okhistory.org/sites/honeysprings* 🎫 *Free.*

## ROGERS MEMORIAL MUSEUM

The Oklahoma community of Claremont, located just northeast of Tulsa, is best known as the hometown of Will Rogers, a homespun cowboy philosopher from the early 1900s. A century ago, he was considered to be one of the leading entertainers of the era. Rogers was a member of the Cherokee Nation, a vaudeville performer, a newspaper columnist, and a social commentator whose quotes are still widely repeated today. ("Even if you're on the right track," he once said, "you'll get run over if you just sit there.")

**Do This:** Take in the Rogers Memorial Museum and Birthplace Ranch in Oologah, Oklahoma. The museum houses the world's largest collection of Will Rogers memorabilia and his entire collection of writings.

**Rogers Memorial Museum.** ✉ *1720 W. Will Rogers Blvd., Claremore, OK* ☎ *918/341–0719* 🌐 *www.willrogers.com* 🎫 *$7.*

## SKYDANCE BRIDGE

It's a practical way for pedestrians to cross over busy Interstate 40 between downtown Oklahoma City and the Oklahoma River, but SkyDance Bridge is also much more. Inspired by Oklahoma's state bird, the scissor-tailed flycatcher, the 2012 structure is also a work of art. The bridge is 380 feet long, 197 feet tall, and is made of 412 tons of steel. It's illuminated nightly by lights that change color for holidays and other events.

**Do This:** Walk across the bridge both during the day when the panels glisten in the sun and at night when the bridge is illuminated in vivid colors.

**SkyDance Bridge.** ✉ *Near Robinson Ave. S, Oklahoma City, OK* ☎ *405/297–8912* 🌐 *www.okc.*

*gov/departments/public-works/resident-community-resources/skydance-bridge.*

### THE TOY AND ACTION FIGURE MUSEUM

In Paul's Valley, an hour south of Oklahoma City, this is the first museum in the world devoted to the art and sculpting of action figures. The museum displays more than 13,000 classic dolls dating back to the 1950s. The museum is also home to the Oklahoma Cartoonists Collection that features published comic artists and writers from Oklahoma, including Chester Gould of *Dick Tracy* and Jack and Carole Bender of *Alley Oop*.

**Do This:** Check out the tribute to World War II veterans. The exhibit is filled with 12-inch G.I. Joes in lifelike representations of various military campaigns.

**The Toy and Action Figure Museum.** ✉ *111 S. Chickasaw St., Pauls Valley, OK* ☎ *405/238–6300* 🌐 *www.toyandactionfiguremuseum.com* 🎟 *$7.*

### THE UNDERGROUND

Oklahoma City's vast Underground is a series of tunnels and walkways that connect more than 30 buildings spread among 20 square blocks. There are even restaurants and shops down there. The first tunnel dates back to the 1930s, but the system formally opened in 1974 as the Conncourse, named for banker Jack Conn, who came up with the idea. It includes about a mile of tunnels that are lit in neon colors and lined artworks.

**Do This:** Check out all the "secret" entrances, many of them through parking garages and other buildings. The Sheraton Oklahoma City Downtown is one of the most popular entrances.

**Sheraton Oklahoma City Downtown Hotel.** ✉ *1 N. Broadway Ave., Oklahoma City, OK* ☎ *405/235–3500* 🌐 *www.downtownokc.com/underground* 🎟 *Free.*

## Cool Places to Stay

**Island Guest Ranch.** First established in 1889, this working cattle ranch consists of several thousand acres of native grassland in northwest Oklahoma. You stay in rustic cabins or a bunkhouse near the lodge where meals are served. Activities include hiking, horseback riding, skeet shooting, and learning how to swing a rope. ✉ *267043 E. County Rd. 55, Ames, OK* ☎ *800/928–4574* 🌐 *www.islandguestranch.com* [$] *From $400.*

**Lake Murray Floating Cabins.** It's easier to enjoy the panoramic views of Lake Murray if you're actually on the water. These houseboats have knotty pine interiors, vaulted ceilings, circular stairways to the sleeping loft, and catwalks that stretch across the living room to the balcony. ✉ *3323 Lodge Rd., Ardmore, OK* ☎ *580/223–0088* 🌐 *www.lake-murray.org/floating-cabins* [$] *From $190.*

**The Mayo Hotel.** In downtown Tulsa, the Mayo Hotel was instantly regarded as a place for high society when it opened in 1925. It stood vacant for more than 25 years until a $42 million renovation brought back its luster, keeping the original historic charm but adding the latest technology and amenities. ✉ *115 W. 5th St., Tulsa, OK* ☎ *918/582–6296* 🌐 *www.themayohotel.com* [$] *From $129.*

**Quartz Mountain State Park Lodge.** After a day of boating, mountain biking, or rock climbing, relax in this handsome lodge on the shores of Lake Altus-Lugert. Done up in Native American, Western, and Southwestern decor, each room features four pieces of original art. ✉ *43393 Scissortail Rd., Lone Wolf, OK* ☎ *580/563–2238* 🌐 *www.travelok.com/state-parks/quartz-mountain-state-park* [$] *From $149.*

# South Dakota

Marked by windswept prairies, rugged badlands, and an emerald oasis known as the Black Hills, South Dakota is a state of rugged beauty. The chiseled spires, ragged ridges, and steep-sided canyons of Badlands National Park are awe-inspiring, while the Black Hills, with its imposing peaks and the famed Mount Rushmore monument, attracts sizable crowds in summer. At Custer State Park, don't miss the epic buffalo roundup.

## Bucket List Picks

The following boxes contain our picks for the top sights and experiences in South Dakota.

- O Badlands National Park
- O Custer Buffalo Roundup
- O Mount Rushmore
- O Crazy Horse Memorial
- O Falls Park
- O Boat Ride on Oahe Dam
- O Jewel Cave National Monument
- O Sturgis Motorcycle Rally
- O The Mammoth Site
- O Laura Ingalls Wilder Homes

# Badlands National Park

### Baddest of Them All

Until the moon opens up to tourism, a hike through the stunning landscape of Badlands National Park is about as close as you can get to taking "one small step for man, one giant leap for mankind." Because of the park's open hike policy, visitors are free to roam the entire 381 square miles of protected mixed-grass prairie. It's a great way to examine the rugged terrain that holds some of the best fossil beds anywhere in the world. Besides remnants of South Dakota's prehistoric past, the park's current residents include bighorn sheep, bison, prairie dogs, and black-footed ferrets.

### Don't Miss

Badlands Loop Road has several stops along the way to take in the scenery and watch the wildlife without ever leaving your car. The best overlook is Pinnacles Overlook; with the highest elevation in the park's North Unit, it has the greatest sweeping views, and you can see the Black Hills on the horizon if conditions are clear.

### Some Restrictions Apply

The South Unit of the park lies on the Pine Ridge Indian Reservation, so check ahead to make sure access hasn't been restricted.

### Getting Here and Around

From Rapid City, drive 75 miles east on Interstate 90. Exit 110 connects to Wall (and famous Wall Drug) to the north and the Pinnacles Entrance and Badlands Loop Road to the south. Exit 131 leads to the Northeast Entrance and the Ben Reifel Visitor Center, which is a great place to get your bearings.

**The Ben Reifel Visitor Center.** ✉ *25216 Ben Reifel Rd., Interior, SD* ☎ *605/433–5361* 🌐 *www.nps.gov/badl* 🎫 *$30 per vehicle.*

# Custer Buffalo Roundup

## Thundering Footsteps

As recently as the 1500s, as many as 60 million bison roamed North America. By the early 1900s, their numbers had dwindled to just a few thousand. Thanks to preservation efforts, there are now herds of hundreds of thousands of these majestic animals. One of the largest herds roams the Black Hills of Custer State Park in southwest South Dakota.

Every September, park rangers and volunteers gather the herd of roughly 1,300 head in a roundup that's part tourist attraction, part park management. You can't get as close as Kevin Costner did in the hunting scene of *Dances With Wolves*, but you'll see and feel the thundering bison as they're corralled. Some are rounded up and sold, but most are released back into Custer State Park, where you can enjoy their rugged beauty throughout the year.

## Don't Miss

When you're visiting Custer State Park, Sylvan Lake and Needles Highway offer amazing views of the Black Hills.

## Good to Know

Get there early to secure a good spot. The roundup starts in mid-morning, and visitors have to remain in the viewing areas until all bison are corralled, which usually happens around noon. Breakfast and lunch are covered.

## Getting Here and Around

To get to the north parking lot, head 31 miles south of Rapid City on Highways 79 and 36, then south on Wildlife Loop Road. To get to the south parking lot, head east on Wildlife Loop Road near Bluebell Campground.

**Custer State Park.** ✉ *13329 U.S. 16A, Custer, SD* ☎ *605/255–4515* 🌐 *gfp.sd.gov/buffalo-roundup* 🎫 *$20 per vehicle.*

## Mount Rushmore

### Check Out Washington's Profile

Sculptor Gutzon Borglum carved the likenesses of George Washington, Thomas Jefferson, Abraham Lincoln, and Theodore Roosevelt "to communicate the founding, expansion, preservation, and unification of the United States." Even if you've visited Mount Rushmore National Memorial before, it's worth checking out again because the visitor center and other facilities have been expanded to accommodate the 3 million people who visit each year. Other recent additions include more educational programs on Native American people who have lived in the Black Hills for centuries.

### Don't Miss

Want to get the perfect picture? The half-mile-long Presidential Trail is a great way to get closer to the sculpture and maybe even see some of the wildlife that roams the Black Hills. To get a photo of George Washington's profile, take a right on Highway 244 when you leave the main parking lot and drive around to the back of the memorial.

### When to Go

Mount Rushmore is open year-round, but try to visit in May, September, or October when the crowds aren't as bad. Most other places in the Black Hills are open, so it's a great time to explore without the summertime rush.

### Getting Here and Around

Mount Rushmore National Memorial is 24 miles south of Rapid City on U.S. Highway 16. After visiting the memorial, check out the shops, restaurants, and other attractions in nearby Keystone.

**Mount Rushmore National Memorial.** ✉ *13000 Hwy. 244, Keystone, SD* ☎ *605/574–2523* 🌐 *www.nps.gov/moru* 🎟 *Free.*

# Crazy Horse Memorial

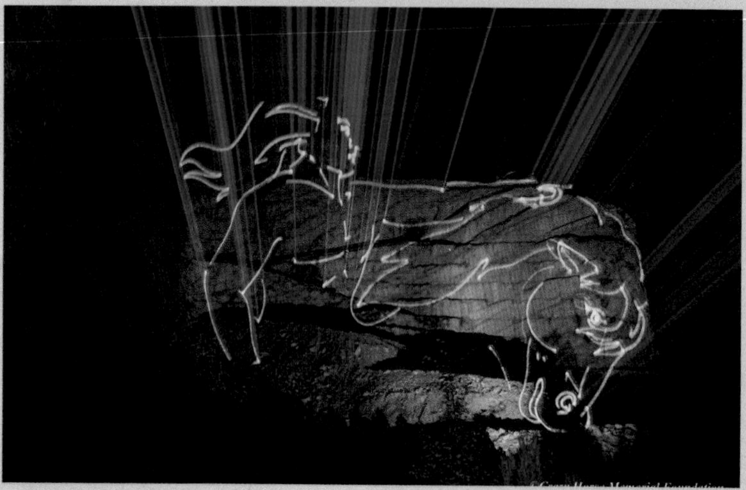

## Generations in the Making

Henry Standing Bear, chief of the Lakota people, had long sought to have a memorial honoring Native Americans in the Black Hills. "My fellow chiefs and I would like the white man to know that the red man has great heroes also," he said. Standing Bear tapped sculptor Korczak Ziolkowski to take on the project of carving a monument to Crazy Horse, a Lakota warrior who was killed while being held by U.S. troops in 1877. It's taking several generations, but Standing Bear is achieving his goal. Still in progress, the Crazy Horse Memorial is considered the world's largest mountain carving. It will depict Crazy Horse on horseback and gesturing toward his people's land.

## Don't Miss

Though the mountain carving is the main attraction, the site is home to museums featuring Native American art and artifacts from more than 300 tribes across North America.

## When to Visit

If you visit during peak season between Memorial Day and Labor Day, the "Legends of Light" laser-light show starts around sunset every evening.

## Get Up Close

If you'd like to add a bucket list hike to your visit, consider taking part in the spring or fall Volksmarch, a 6-mile trek to the top of the monument. You stand on Crazy Horse's outstretched arm and gaze at his nine-story-tall face.

## Getting Here and Around

From Rapid City, head south on U.S. Highway 16 for 37 miles. From Custer, go north 4 miles on Highway 16.

**Crazy Horse Memorial.** ✉ *12151 Ave. of the Chiefs, Crazy Horse, SD* ☎ *605/673–4681* 🌐 *www.crazyhorsememorial.org* 🎫 *$10 to $35 per vehicle.*

# Falls Park

## Sioux Beautiful

The churning waters of Falls Park—the namesake of Sioux Falls—have been attracting people for hundreds of years. Especially in years with heavy rainfall, the Big Sioux River rushes over the pink quartzite rocks and offers spectacular views from the walking trails that surround it. A five-story observation tower gives a bird's-eye view of the entire park and downtown skyline beyond. Other park attractions also include remnants of the Queen Bee Mill and the old Sioux Falls Light and Power Company Building, now home to Falls Overlook Cafe.

## Don't Miss

Falls Park lies along a 29-mile paved bicycle path following the Big Sioux River. There are dozens of great spots for photos, including a picturesque old iron bridge. The north end of the path is a perfect place to watch takeoffs and landings at the Sioux Falls Regional Airport. If the South Dakota Air National Guard's F-16s are flying, you'll be treated to a mini airshow.

## When to Visit

From November to January, Falls Park is decorated with more than 355,000 lights, including some that illuminate the water and ice on the falls.

## Getting Here and Around

The 123-acre city park is located just north of downtown Sioux Falls.

**Falls Park.** ✉ *131 E. Falls Park Dr., Sioux Falls, SD* ☎ *605/367–8222* 🌐 *www.experiencesiouxfalls.com/falls-park* 🎟 *Free.*

# Boat Ride on Oahe Dam

### Crossing the "Big Water"

Look at any map of the United States and in the middle of the Dakotas you'll notice a wider-than-usual strip of blue that extends from South Dakota's capital of Pierre to North Dakota's capital of Bismarck. That's Lake Oahe, created when engineers dammed the Missouri River in 1962. Oahe Dam, 6 miles north of Pierre, is one of the largest earth-rolled dams in the world. It was dedicated by President John F. Kennedy, who said the Oahe Dam would produce enough electricity "to light the entire city of Edinburgh, Scotland." On its 50th anniversary, experts hailed it as an "engineering marvel." Driving across it, or boating on the reservoir, is still a thrill today.

### Don't Miss

The dam created the fourth-largest artificial reservoir in the United States. The lake is an impressive 231 miles long, so boating and fishing are popular activities. Along the shore are birds ranging from sharp-tailed grouse to Canadian geese. A good entry point for boats is is Fort Yates Bay.

### While You're Here

LaFramboise Island Nature Area, located downstream in Pierre, is covered in trees and meadows. Explorers Lewis and Clark recorded the beautiful island in their journals when they passed through in 1804.

### Getting Here and Around

From Fort Pierre on the west side of the Missouri River, drive north on Highway 1806 to Highway 204, which crosses over Oahe Dam. After a stop at the visitor center, drive north on Highway 1804, which runs along the east side of Lake Oah.

**South Dakota Missouri River Tourism.** ✉ *20207 SD Hwy. 1804, Pierre, SD* 🌐 *www.sdmissouririver.com/follow-the-river/the-four-lakes-and-dams/lake-oahe* 🎫 *Free.*

# Jewel Cave National Monument

### Dazzling Depths

Even though its more than 200 miles of surveyed passages make this cave the world's third largest (Kentucky's Mammoth Cave is the longest), Jewel Cave isn't renowned for its size. Rather, it's the rare crystalline formations that abound in the cave's vast passages. Wander the dark passageways and you'll be rewarded with the sight of tiny crystal Christmas trees, hydromagnesite balloons that would pop if you touched them, and delicate calcite deposits dubbed "cave popcorn."

### Don't Miss

Year-round, you can take ranger-led tours for a fee, from a simple half-hour walk to a lantern-light tour. Surface trails and facilities are free.

### Best Tour

For those who are comfortable getting active on a moderately strenuous tour, book the Scenic Tour. The ½-mile tour led by NPS rangers involves climbing more than 700 stairs, but the paved trail leads the way to stunning chambers filled with calcite crystals and vibrant speleothems. $12. Travelers with small children or who have limited mobility can book the Discovery Talk, an accessible tour that dives into the cave's history. $4.

### While You're Here

About 30 minutes away is Wind Cave National Park. Wind Cave ranks as the sixth-longest cave in the world, but experts believe 95% of it has yet to be mapped.

### Getting Here and Around

Jewel Cave National Monument is about 13 miles west of Custer in South Dakota's Black Hills, so it can easily be combined with a day or weekend trip to the Custer Buffalo Roundup.

**Jewel Cave National Monument.** *11149 U.S. 16 Custer, SD* *605/673–2288* *www.nps.gov/jeca* Free entry; cave tours from $4.

# Sturgis Motorcycle Rally

## Hog Heaven

The largest motorcycle rally in the world is America's crowning event for all bike enthusiasts. Motorcycle racers started what is now known as the Sturgis Motorcycle Rally in the 1930s; today it's a 10-day-long marathon each August featuring live music, plenty of food and drink, people-watching and, of course, motorcycles of all shapes and sizes. As many as 750,000 people from around the world have packed Sturgis and the Black Hills region for the annual event's races, rides, and sharing a whole lot of love for their Harleys.

## Don't Miss

Motorcyle rides and races aren't the only reason to head to the rally. Performances from big-name artists like ZZ Top and Kid Rock cater to the biker crowd.

## Good to Know

Downtown is completely blocked off during the rally, so make sure you walk from one end of Main Street to the other to take it all in. Duck down the side streets as well.

## Getting Here and Around

Sturgis is 29 miles northwest of Rapid City on Interstate 90. Be ready to find lodging miles away from Sturgis because of the overwhelming demand for hotel rooms.

**Harley Davidson Rally Point.** ✉ *1040 Harley-Davidson Way, Sturgis, SD* ☎ *605/347–4422* 🌐 *www.sturgismcrallyinc.com* 🎫 *Free.*

# The Mammoth Site

## Dig Up Ice Age Fossils

The fossils of more than 60 mammoths, as well as 87 other animals from the Ice Age, have been recovered from a sinkhole at the Mammoth Site in southwestern South Dakota. The vast facility is the largest mammoth research facility in the world. In 1974, a worker clearing land for a housing project discovered the site when his blade struck what turned out to be a tusk. The museum displays full-sized replicas of mammoths, as well as the fossilized remains in the earth where they were discovered. There's a hands-on learning area for children and windows into the laboratory where scientists are still hard at work.

## Don't Miss

See a working paleontological site, the Bonebed. There's even an excavation each summer, the Ice Age Explorers Program, where you can train with professionals, excavate and screen-wash sediments, and tour the lab.

## While You're Here

If you're staying in Hot Springs, check out Evans Plunge Mineral Springs, the Pioneer Museum, and Wind Cave National Park.

## Good to Know

Don't touch the bones; they are dry and fragile.

## Getting Here and Around

From Rapid City, drive 57 miles south on Highway 79 to Hot Springs.

**The Mammoth Site.** ✉ *1800 U.S. 18 Bypass, Hot Springs, SD* ☎ *605/745–6017* 🌐 *www.mammothsite.org* 🎟 *$12.*

# Laura Ingalls Wilder Homes

### Little Houses on the Prairie

If you read the *Little House on the Prairie* books when you were a child, this tour will deliver a major dose of nostalgia, bringing to real life some of the places Laura Ingalls Wilder wrote about during her time in De Smet, South Dakota. A tour with Discover Laura includes the Ingalls home built by Charles "Pa" Ingalls in 1889, the First School of De Smet where Wilder and her sister, Carrie, attended, and a replica of Brewster School where Wilder taught when she was 15.

### Don't Miss

Lake Thompson, 10 miles southeast of De Smet, is designated a National Natural Landmark. Laura Ingalls Wilder mentioned the lake in her books, including *By the Shores of Silver Lake* and *The Long Winter.*

### While You're Here

If you have the time, visit the De Smet Cemetery, where members of the Ingalls family are buried, the Charles Ingalls homestead south of town, and the five original cottonwood trees he planted for his wife, Caroline, and his four daughters.

### Where to Stay

Covered wagons are available for rent at the Charles Ingalls Homestead near De Smet, taking the prairie experience to a whole new level. The wagons are pretty basic, but they're still a lot nicer than what carried his family across the prairie. They have electricity, fans, screened windows, and picnic tables. ☎ *605/854–3984* 🌐 *www.ingallshomestead.com/camping* $ *From $60.*

### Getting Here and Around

From Sioux Falls, De Smet is 99 miles northwest. Take Interstate 90 north to Brookings, then head west on Highway 14.

**Laura Ingalls Wilder Homes.** ✉ *105 Olivet Ave., De Smet, SD* ☎ *605/854–3383* 🌐 *www.discoverlaura.org* 🎟 *$14.*

## When in South Dakota

### BEAR BUTTE STATE PARK

The huge eruption of igneous rock rising above the plains in Bear Butte State Park is known as Mato Paha, or "Bear Mountain," in the Lakota language. Several indigenous tribes consider the mountain sacred and regularly hold religious ceremonies here. The trail to the top of the mountain, just under 2 miles in length, is a great way to see up close the colorful pieces of prayer cloth and small bundles of tobacco hanging from the trees. They represent the prayers offered by Native people during their worship and shouldn't be disturbed.

**Do This:** The top of the mountain has great views of the Black Hills to the southwest. If you have time, there's also a 2½-mile trail around Bear Butte Lake.

**Bear Butte State Park.** ✉ *20250 Hwy. 79, Sturgis, SD* ☎ *605/347–5240* 🌐 *gfp.sd.gov/parks/detail/bear-butte-state-park* 🎫 *$8 per vehicle.*

### CORN PALACE

Built in 1892, the ornate Corn Palace was intended to show the world that South Dakota, then just three years old, had a thriving agriculture industry. More than a century later, farming is still a big part of the economy. So is tourism, which the World's Only Corn Palace helped build. Roughly 500,000 people visit this landmark each year. The exterior of the building is redecorated each year with colorful murals made with actual kernels of corn and other grains.

**Do This:** The annual Corn Palace Festival is held in late August each year.

**Corn Palace.** ✉ *604 N. Main St., Mitchell, SD* ☎ *605/995–8430* 🌐 *www.cornpalace.com* 🎫 *Free.*

### DEADWOOD

Thanks to restoration efforts, Deadwood looks a lot like it did nearly 150 years ago after gold was discovered in the Black Hills. Today it's gambling that brings people to this Old West town, so you'll find casinos, restaurants, hotels, concert halls, and even full-service spas.

**Do This:** Visit Wild Bill Hickok's grave at Mount Moriah Cemetery. Soon after coming to town to seek his fortune in the gold rush, he was gunned down playing poker while holding a hand of aces and eights. Since then that's been known as the Dead Man's Hand. Another real-life character from Deadwood's past, Calamity Jane, is buried next to Hickock.

**Deadwood.** ✉ *501 Main St., Deadwood, SD* ☎ *605/578–1876* 🌐 *www.deadwood.com.*

### HOLIDAYS AT THE SOUTH DAKOTA STATE CAPITOL

The South Dakota State Capitol in Pierre is worth a visit any time of year because of its soaring rotunda, ornate woodwork, and gleaming marble floors. (The bathroom stalls, with swinging wooden doors like in an Old West saloon, are also worth a peek). The building gets into the holiday spirit between Thanksgiving and Christmas every year when around 100 trees grace the halls and rotunda. They are decorated by volunteers from various South Dakota organizations.

**Do This:** The well-regarded Cultural Heritage Center tells the fascinating history of South Dakota.

**The South Dakota State Capitol.** ✉ *500 E. Capitol Ave., Pierre, SD* 🎫 *Free.*

### PETRIFIED WOOD PARK

In the early 1930s, amateur geologist Ole S. Quammen oversaw construction of this display of petrified wood that takes up an entire block in the town of Lemmon. Besides petrified dinosaur and mammoth bones that were gathered from surrounding archaeological sites, Petrified Wood Park includes a castle and 20-foot-tall towers.

**Do This:** Make the trek during the holidays when the petrified trees are decorated with lights.

**Petrified Wood Park.** ✉ *500 Main Ave., Lemmon, SD* ☎ *605/374–3964* 🌐 *www.lemmonsd.com/new-page-2* 🎟 *Free.*

### WALL DRUG

Hand-painted billboards offering free ice water brought weary travelers to Wall Drug during the Great Depression. Now 2 million people stop every year at this funky tourist attraction whose walls are adorned with kitschy signs and oddball items. There's also a serious side to Wall Drug, which has an art gallery with more than 300 original oil paintings of the Old West. Located near Badlands National Park, it's an easy, fun stop.

**Do This:** Plan your visit to coincide with a meal. The restaurant is known for its doughnuts and coffee, but it also serves a variety of main dishes, including hot beef sandwiches and buffalo burgers. Top off your meal at the soda fountain, something that's been part of Wall Drug since the early days.

**Wall Drug.** ✉ *510 Main St., Wall, SD* ☎ *605/279–2175* 🌐 *www.walldrug.com* 🎟 *Free.*

### WOUNDED KNEE MASSACRE MONUMENT

Some monuments are spectacular. Some, like the one that marks the site of the 1890 Wounded Knee massacre, are moving because of their simplicity. On December 29, 1890, near Wounded Knee Creek in southwest South Dakota, the U.S. Army's 7th Cavalry killed as many as 300 Lakota men, women, and children. It was the last major confrontation between American soldiers and Northern Plains Indians.

**Do This:** The simple memorial, a National Historic Landmark, includes the mass grave where the victims were buried and a memorial listing many of their names. Wounded Knee is on the Pine Ridge Reservation, and the Oglala Sioux Tribe will occasionally limit travel. Call ahead before you visit.

**Wounded Knee Massacre Monument.** ✉ *Wounded Knee, SD* ☎ *605/279–2573* 🎟 *Free.*

## Cool Places to Stay

**Blue Bell Lodge.** In Custer State Park, the log cabins at Blue Bell Lodge have stone fireplaces and hand-hewn timbers that lend them plenty of rustic charm. In the evenings there are hayrides and chuckwagon dinners. ✉ *25453 Hwy. 87, Custer, SD* ☎ *605/255–4531* 🌐 *www.custerresorts.com/lodges-and-cabins/blue-bell-lodge* [$] *From $190.*

**Franklin Hotel.** Teddy Roosevelt, Babe Ruth, and John Wayne are among the guests who have stayed at this historic hotel in the town of Deadwood. Take in the view of Main Street from the open patio on the ornate roof of the Victorian-era front porch. ✉ *700 Main St., Deadwood, SD* ☎ *605/578–3670* 🌐 *www.silveradofranklin.com/lodging* [$] *From $89.*

**Under Canvas Mount Rushmore.** Camping under ponderosa pine and common juniper trees in the Black Hills would be a great experience, but add in spectacular views of Mount Rushmore and it becomes a bucket-list experience. Between early May and late September, Under Canvas Mount Rushmore offers upscale glamping accommodations that are hard to beat. There's a nature walk, fire pit, and plenty of s'mores. ✉ *24342 Presidio Ranch Rd., Keystone, SD* ☎ *888/496–1148* 🌐 *www.undercanvas.com/camps/mount-rushmore* [$] *From $384.*

Chapter 7

# THE WEST COAST AND THE PACIFIC



Written by
Andrew Collins

# WELCOME TO THE WEST COAST AND THE PACIFIC

## TOP REASONS TO GO

★ **Dramatic landscapes:** From Denali to Yosemite, see the West's iconic national parks, including desertscapes, towering snowcapped peaks, stunning coastline, active volcanoes, and the world's biggest trees.

★ **Wineries:** Sip your way through California, Oregon, and Washington's best vineyards and sample craft beer along the way.

★ **Wild things:** Spot grizzlies in Alaska, sea turtles in Hawaii, condors in California, and bald eagles, migrating whales, and seals up and down the Pacific Coast.

★ **Glaciers:** Get an up-close view of these fleeting ice formations, from trekking on Mendenhall glacier in Juneau to cruising past them in Kenai Fjords and Glacier Bay, to hiking beneath them in North Cascades National Park.

★ **Cool cities:** Los Angeles, Seattle, San Francisco, and Portland beckon with their trendy restaurants, bars, and cultural treasures, but you're never too far from wide open spaces.

**1 Alaska.** By far the largest state in the Union, the Last Frontier is a land of riveting contrasts, from the temperate rain forests and bays of the southeast to hulking snowcapped mountains and tundra to the north.

**2 California.** The nation's third-largest state is a land of incredible geographical diversity, from high peaks and boulder-strewn deserts in the interior to stunning beaches and temperate forests on the coast.

**3 Hawaii.** This tropical archipelago delights visitors with its sugary-sand beaches, lush canyons, and rain forests, thrilling volcanic peaks, and beautiful islands each with a big personality.

**4 Oregon.** With a magnificent coast of headlands and sea stacks, lush valleys from Portland to the south, and soaring volcanic peaks, the views in Oregon change from point to point but are always stunning.

**5 Washington.** The Evergreen State comprises pristine coastal and Puget Sound waterways, the snowcapped Cascade Range, and winery-studded arid valleys and hills to the east.

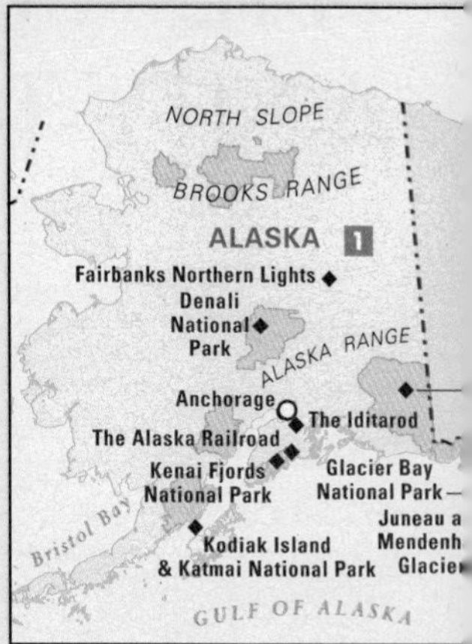


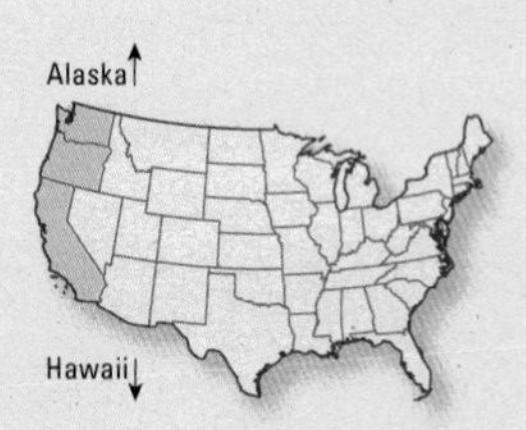


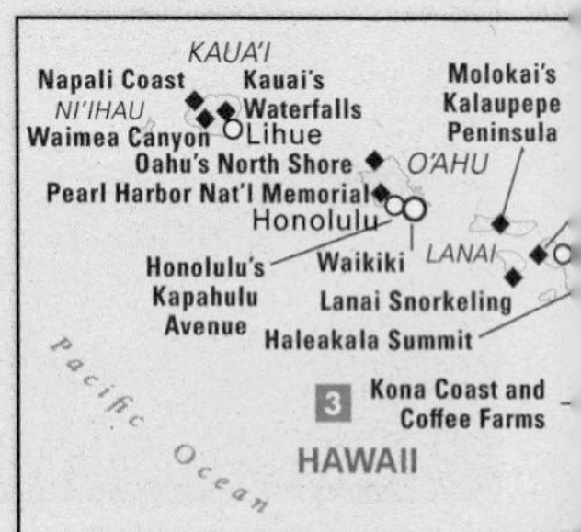

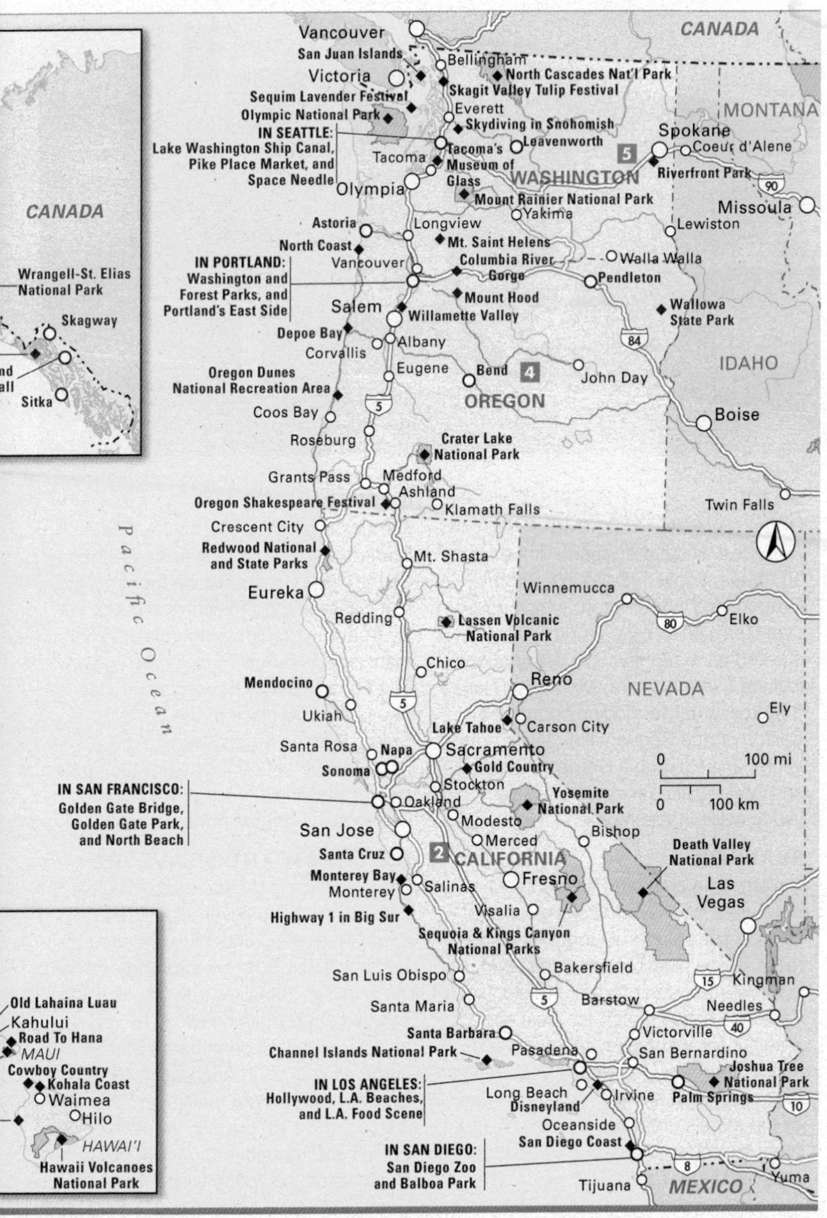
CANADA
Vancouver
San Juan Islands
Bellingham
Victoria
North Cascades Nat'l Park
Skagit Valley Tulip Festival
Sequim Lavender Festival
Olympic National Park
Everett
MONTANA
IN SEATTLE:
Lake Washington Ship Canal,
Pike Place Market, and
Space Needle
Skydiving in Snohomish
Spokane
Leavenworth
Coeur d'Alene
Tacoma
Tacoma's Museum of Glass
5
WASHINGTON
Riverfront Park
90
Olympia
Mount Rainier National Park
Missoula
Yakima
CANADA
Astoria
Longview
Lewiston
North Coast
Mt. Saint Helens
IN PORTLAND:
Washington and
Forest Parks, and
Portland's East Side
Vancouver
Columbia River Gorge
Walla Walla
Wrangell-St. Elias
National Park
Pendleton
Mount Hood
Salem
Wallowa
State Park
Skagway
Willamette Valley
Depoe Bay
84
Albany
Corvallis
Oregon Dunes
National Recreation Area
Eugene
Bend
4
John Day
IDAHO
Sitka
OREGON
5
Coos Bay
Boise
Roseburg
Crater Lake
National Park
Grants Pass
Medford
Ashland
Oregon Shakespeare Festival
Klamath Falls
Twin Falls
Crescent City
Redwood National
and State Parks
Mt. Shasta
Pacific Ocean
Eureka
Winnemucca
Redding
Lassen Volcanic
National Park
80
Elko
Chico
Mendocino
Reno
NEVADA
5
Ukiah
Lake Tahoe
Carson City
Ely
Santa Rosa
Napa
Sacramento
Sonoma
Gold Country
0 100 mi
0 100 km
IN SAN FRANCISCO:
Golden Gate Bridge,
Golden Gate Park,
and North Beach
Stockton
Oakland
Yosemite
National Park
Modesto
San Jose
Bishop
Merced
Death Valley
National Park
Santa Cruz
2
CALIFORNIA
Monterey Bay
Salinas
Fresno
Las Vegas
Monterey
Highway 1 in Big Sur
Visalia
Sequoia & Kings Canyon
National Parks
Bakersfield
San Luis Obispo
15
Kingman
Old Lahaina Luau
Kahului
Road To Hana
MAUI
Cowboy Country
Kohala Coast
Waimea
Hilo
HAWAI'I
Hawaii Volcanoes
National Park
Santa Maria
5
Barstow
Needles
40
Santa Barbara
Victorville
Channel Islands National Park
Pasadena
San Bernardino
Joshua Tree
National Park
IN LOS ANGELES:
Hollywood, L.A. Beaches,
and L.A. Food Scene
Long Beach
Disneyland
Irvine
Palm Springs
10
Oceanside
San Diego Coast
IN SAN DIEGO:
San Diego Zoo
and Balboa Park
8
Yuma
Tijuana
MEXICO

# WHAT TO EAT AND DRINK ON THE WEST COAST AND THE PACIFIC

Napa Valley wine

### WINE

Of the more than 250 official AVAs, or American Viticultural Areas, in the United States, about 175 are in California, Oregon, and Washington, which collectively form one of the world's most celebrated wine regions. Top destinations include Santa Barbara, Monterey, Napa, Sonoma, and Mendocino counties in California; the Rogue Valley, Willamette Valley, and Columbia Gorge in Oregon; and Walla Walla, Yakima Valley, and Woodinville in Washington.

### SEAFOOD

Halibut, king crab, and salmon are must-eats in Alaska. Washington and Oregon specialize in Dungeness crab, razor clams, albacore, mussels, and oysters. As you venture south along the California coast, watch for local spot prawns, rockfish, spiny lobsters, and squid on menus. And in Hawaii, cubed, raw, marinated ahi is the basis for one of the state's great delicacies, poke, but menus also feature plenty of mahimahi, ono, and blue marlin.

### COFFEE

Famous chains like Starbucks, Peets, Stumptown, and Blue Bottle launched on the West Coast, but it's the smaller cult classics that thrill connoisseurs; try Coava in Portland, Sightglass in San Francisco, and Bird Rock in San Diego. The Kona Coast of Hawaii Island stands out as the one place in the United States famous for *growing* coffee. Roughly 600 coffee farms dot the west side of the island, each producing flavorful beans grown in the rich soil.

### ICE CREAM AND SHAVE ICE

The West has gained a reputation for high-quality, often inventive ingredients—from pear-and-blue cheese at Portland's Salt & Straw to orange-cardamom at San Francisco's Bi-Rite. Other beloved shops include Molly Moon in Seattle, Sweet Rose in Santa Monica, and Wild Scoops in Anchorage. When in the Aloha State, you really want to try a dish of shave ice drizzled in Technicolor syrups and topped with mochi balls, azuki beans, and condensed milk.

## TACOS

The Mexican influence on California accounts for the tremendous popularity of this delicious street food. For modern gourmet fare, try Guerrilla Tacos in Los Angeles; for beer-battered fish tacos, head to Oscar's Mexican Seafood in San Diego; to experience what makes just about every Golden State "best taco" list, check out Nuestro Mexico in Bakersfield.

## CHEESE

An abundance of fertile farmland has given rise to a thriving cheese-making industry here, with Tillamook in Oregon among the most famous. You'll also find artisan outfits producing everything from creamy chèvres to aged and earthy sheep cheeses at farmers' markets and gourmet grocers. Look for brands like Beecher's from Seattle and Rogue Creamery in southern Oregon.

## CRAFT BEER

Portland, San Diego, and Seattle are renowned hubs of innovative craft brewing, as are smaller metropolises like Bend and Yakima (the latter grows about 75% of the nation's hops)—crisp, hoppy IPAs are a regional favorite, as are sour beers that utilize West Coast's bounty of fresh fruit. Heady Scotch ales and aromatic sips brewed with spruce tips are popular in Alaska, while Hawaii incorporates local ingredients like lemongrass, tangerines, and passion fruit.

Hawaiian shave ice

Baja fish tacos

## ASIAN FOOD

Many residents of these five states have strong ties to different parts of Asia and it's apparent in the food. Vibrant international districts thrive in Honolulu, Portland, Seattle, San Francisco, and Los Angeles. Quite a few regional Hawaiian dishes derive from a mix of Asian and European cultures, including the noodle dish saimin, the burger–fried egg dish loco moco, and the Spam-a-licious snack musubi.

## BAKED GOODS

The history of sourdough is tied to both the Alaska and California gold rushes, when French bakers opened to feed the miners. Modern artisan bakeries excel with more interesting creations, from rich kouign-amann pastries to moist and robust potato bread. Portland and L.A. are famous for doughnuts, while Hawaii is known for malasadas: deep-fried Portuguese doughnuts filled with sweet creams.

## WILD GAME

Many animals found in the wild appear on menus in this part of the world. Reindeer are often served in Anchorage at sausage stands and food trucks, while wild boar appears on many menus in Hawaii.

# The West Coast and the Pacific Regional Snapshot

## Know Before You Go

### PACK LAYERS

It's possible to experience extreme changes in temperatures, in part because of the West's varied terrain—the elevation gain in both Death Valley National Park and on Hawaii's Big Island is well over 10,000 feet, and driving just a 50 miles from the coast to inland valleys in California, Oregon, and Washington can result in huge temperature swings.

### PRICES CAN BE STEEP

Everything from gas to hotels to food can cost more in this part of the country. Many foods and other products must be shipped to Hawaii and Alaska. And cities like Seattle and San Francisco have high hotel prices, as do resorts all around Hawaii and in certain places that have very popular high seasons (many national parks in summer, Palm Springs and desert areas in winter).

### TAKE A SCENIC DRIVE

The entire Pacific region is ideal for road-tripping, given the incredible coastal and mountain scenery. That said, quite a few cities in these parts have excellent public transit systems, including Portland, Seattle, and San Francisco.

## Planning Your Time

Distances in these states are considerable. California stretches almost 800 miles north to south. Alaska is the largest state in the union (and is nearly four times larger than California). And Oregon and Washington are quite large as well. Hawaii is the only small Western state, but it takes five to six hours to fly from the mainland West Coast, and once there, flying is the only practical way to get among the different islands. To fully explore all five states, you'd need at least a month.

## Road Trips

**3 Days:** San Francisco to Los Angeles via Highway 1

**3 Days:** Homer to Anchorage to Denali NP to Fairbanks

**4 Days:** Seattle to Olympic Peninsula to Mount Rainier NP to Portland

## Big Events

**Portland Rose Festival.** Begun in 1907, this hugely attended celebration in late May and early June consists of parades, a carnival, fireworks, and dragon-boat races.

**The Iditarod.** Although spectators are few on most of this 938-mile sled-dog race, the opening day in Anchorage the first Saturday each March brings big crowds to Alaska's largest city.

**Merrie Monarch Festival.** This long-running weeklong cultural celebration and hula competition in Hilo is held Easter Week features dancing, music, and arts and crafts fairs.

**San Francisco Pride.** Held in late June since 1970, this is one of the largest LGBTQ Pride parades and festivals in the world.

## What To . . .

### READ

*Grapes of Wrath* by John Steinbeck

*Esperanza Rising* by Pam Muñoz Ryan

*Into the Wild* by Jon Krakauer

*Joy Luck Club* by Amy Tan

*Shark Dialogues* by Kiana Davenport

*Snow Falling on Cedars* by David Guterson

*Wild* by Cheryl Strayed

### WATCH

*Goonies* (movie filmed on Oregon Coast)

*The Descendants* (movie filmed in Hawaii)

*Milk* (movie filmed in San Francisco)

*Inherent Vice* (movie filmed in Los Angeles)

*Jurassic Park* (movie filmed in Hawaii)

*Portlandia* (TV show filmed in Portland)

*Twin Peaks* (movie and TV show filmed in Washington)

### LISTEN TO

*Electric Ladyland* by Jimi Henrix (album)

*Nevermind* by Nirvana (album)

*Alone In Iz World* by Israel Kamakawiwo'ole (album)

*Woodstock* by Portugal. The Man (album)

*Pet Sounds* by the Beach Boys (album)

*DAMN.* by Kendrick Lamar (album)

### BUY

Native crafts in Alaska and Hawaii

Smoked salmon in Alaska, Washington, and Oregon

Coffee in Hawaii

Books from Powell's in Portland, and Elliott Bay Book Company in Seattle

## Contacts

### AIR

**Alaska.** ANC, FAI, JNU

**California.** BUR, FAT, LAX, LGB, OAK, ONT, PSP, SAN, SBA, SFO, SJC, SMF, SNA

**Hawaii.** HNL, ITO, KOA, LIH, LNY, MKK, OGG

**Oregon.** EUG, MFR, PDX, RDM

**Washington.** BLI, GEG, PAE, PSC, SEA

### BOAT

**Alaska Marine Highway.** ☎ *907/465–3941* 🌐 *dot.state.ak.us/amhs.*

**Expeditions Lanai Ferry.** ☎ *800/695–2624* 🌐 *go-lanai.com.*

**Inter-Island Ferry Authority.** ☎ *907/225–4848* 🌐 *interislandferry.com.*

**San Francisco Bay Ferry.** ☎ *877/643–3779* 🌐 *sanfranciscobayferry.com.*

**Washington State Ferries.** ☎ *888/808–7977* 🌐 *wsdot.wa.gov/ferries.*

### METRO/LIGHT-RAIL

**Bay Area Rapid Transit (San Francisco).** ☎ *510/464–6000* 🌐 *bart.gov.*

**Los Angeles County Metropolitan Transportation Authority.** ☎ *323/466–3876* 🌐 *metro.net.*

**TriMet Portland.** ☎ *503/238–7433* 🌐 *trimet.org.*

**San Diego Metropolitan Transit System.** ☎ *619/233–3004* 🌐 *sdmts.com.*

**Sound Transit Seattle.** ☎ *206/398–5000* 🌐 *soundtransit.org.*

### TRAIN

**Alaska Railroad.** ☎ *907/265–2494* 🌐 *alaskarailroad.com.*

**Amtrak.** ☎ *800/872–7245* 🌐 *amtrak.com.*

**White Pass & Yukon Route.** ☎ *800/343–7373* 🌐 *wpyr.com.*

### VISITOR INFORMATION

🌐 *travelalaska.com*

🌐 *gohawaii.org*

🌐 *visitcalifornia.com*

🌐 *experiencewa.com*

🌐 *traveloregon.com*

# Alaska

Alaska is America's last frontier, with landscapes that stretch out seemingly to infinity. From the lush rain forests of Southeast to the vast, flat tundra in the north, you can stare in awe at the same things that take an Alaskan's breath away: calving glaciers, volcanic valleys, jagged sea cliffs, the northern lights, and more. Here you can kayak to icebergs, fly over the highest peak in North America, stay out all night celebrating the midnight sun, and spot wildlife from eagles to whales. For lovers of nature, few places exhilarate like Alaska.

## Bucket List Picks

The following boxes contain our picks for the top sights and experiences in Alaska.

- ○ Juneau and Mendenhall Glacier
- ○ Fairbanks Northern Lights
- ○ The Iditarod
- ○ Glacier Bay National Park
- ○ Denali National Park
- ○ Sitka
- ○ Anchorage
- ○ Wrangell–St. Elias National Park
- ○ The Alaska Railroad
- ○ Kodiak Island and Katmai National Park
- ○ Kenai Fjords National Park
- ○ Skagway

# Juneau and Mendenhall Glacier

### Trek the Drive-Up Glacier

Glaciers are abundant in southeast Alaska, but only a very few are as accessible as Juneau's so-called drive-up glacier, Mendenhall, which spans 12 miles and is fed by the massive Juneau Icefield. You can view the glacier from the Mendenhall Visitor Center, which has interactive exhibits, but the most unforgettable way to experience it is by trekking across the glacier's striking blue surface. You can do this by helicopter tour—these trips offer astounding views of the icefield before landing on the ice for your walk.

### Don't Miss

Book a guided glacier hike—these roughly 4-mile adventures typically include the chance to venture inside an electric-blue ice cave directly beneath the glacier.

### While You're Here

Get a bird's-eye view of Juneau's historic downtown and beautiful Gastineau Channel by riding in the Roberts Tramway some 1,800 feet up the side of Mt. Roberts.

### Best Restaurant

Alaskan king crab—a not-to-be-missed Alaskan delicacy—is the specialty of popular Tracy's King Crab Shack. The wait is entirely worth it. 🌐 *kingcrabshack.com.*

### When to Go

Although it's possible to access the glacier year-round, the best time weather-wise for visiting is May through October.

### Getting Here and Around

Mendenhall Glacier is a 12-mile drive from downtown Juneau, the only U.S. state capital that can't be reached by road: your options are ferry, cruise ship, or flight.

**Mendenhall Glacier.** ✉ *Glacier Spur Rd., Juneau, AK* 🌐 *fs.usda.gov* 🎫 *$5.*

# Fairbanks Northern Lights

## Phenomenal Skies

At 65 degrees north latitude, Fairbanks is renowned for the aurora borealis (northern lights), the midnight sun, and the most epic sunsets and sunrises. Roughly 245 nights a year, from late August to mid-April, you might experience nature's best light show. It often begins simply, as a pale yellow-green luminous band, but some evenings it can explode and fill the sky with curtains of celestial light that ripple wildly above the northern landscape. Visiting in early summer? You're still in for a show: Fairbanks experiences midnight sunshine for 70 straight days.

## Don't Miss

The best spot for sky gazing is Chena Hot Springs Resort. Located 60 miles northeast of Fairbanks, it experiences nearly 24 hours of darkness in mid-winter, making it ideal for viewing the aurora. The naturally occurring hot springs are also a welcome relief from air temperatures that reach -50°F. 🌐 *chenahotsprings.com.*

## While You're Here

Fairbanks is home to a pair of museum gems: Morris Thompson Cultural and Visitors Center and the University of Alaska Museum of the North.

## When to Go

Visit Fairbanks late summer through late spring for the best chance to view the northern lights, and from late May to late July to experience midnight sun.

## Getting Here and Around

Fairbanks is at the junction of the Parks, Steese, and Richardson highways, and also has one of the state's largest airports; in summer, you can ride on the Alaska Railroad. A car is ideal for exploring the city and getting to Chena Hot Springs.

# The Iditarod

### The Last Great Race

Alaska's most iconic and famous annual race, the Iditarod Trail Sled Dog Race, pulls in spectators (and mushers) from around the world to brave the Alaska winter to witness or to participate as racers and volunteers in a massive feat of endurance. The race, run in March, covers 1,049 snowy, backcountry miles from the official start in Willow, 90 miles north of Anchorage, to Nome, and usually takes from 8 to 15 days. Many visitors watch the dog teams take off from the ceremonial start in Anchorage, and then travel to Nome to celebrate as teams cross the finish line.

### Don't Miss

In the weeks leading up to the Iditarod, mushers open their kennels for tours. Visitors can learn about managing a team of dogs and hop on the runners of a sled to try dogsledding. Dogsled rides take place year-round; in summer rides on wheels are available.

### Best Nome Coffee Break

Bering Tea, a little coffee shop in a repurposed old A-frame house, is the perfect spot for a breakfast sandwich or midday coffee before watching Iditarod competitors complete their journey. 🌐 *beringteacoffee.com*.

### When to Go

The Iditarod kicks off in Anchorage each year with a ceremonial start the first Saturday in March.

### Getting Here and Around

To watch the ceremonial start of the race, head to 4th Avenue in downtown Anchorage. Not nearly as many spectators make it to Nome for the finish, but there are always a few thousand die-hard fans. Nome is on the remote Seward Peninsula just 160 miles from Siberia, and the only practical way to get here is by plane.

# Glacier Bay National Park

### America's Most Breathtaking Glaciers

Tidewater glaciers in 5,200-square-mile Glacier Bay National Park calve icebergs into the sea with loud blasts. Humpback whales breach, spout, and slap their tails against the water. Coastal brown bears feed on sedge, salmon, and berries, and otters and harbor seals inhabit the rocky shorelines. Bald eagles soar overhead, and mountains in the Fairweather Range come in and out of view. This magical place rewards those who get out on the water—whether it be in a cruise, a day boat, or a kayak.

### Don't Miss

Kayak rentals can be arranged through Glacier Bay Sea Kayaks. One of the best opportunities to spot wildlife is a guided one-day paddle around Bartlett Cove, which includes a nature walk.

### Best Hotel

Glacier Bay Lodge is the only accommodation within the national park. The modern yet rustic lodge with a large porch overlooking the bay blends well into the thick rain forest surrounding it. 🌐 *visitglacierbay.com.*

### When to Go

The park and its waters are most accessible and enjoyable to visit from mid-May through mid-September. The lodge and other concessionaires are closed the rest of the year.

### Getting Here and Around

The best way to see the park's most famous glaciers—such as Johns Hopkins and Margerie glaciers—is on a cruise ship. Many major cruise lines that visit Alaska include the park on their itineraries. But you can also plan a DIY adventure by flying or taking the ferry to Gustavus.

**Glacier Bay National Park.** ✉ *Gustavus, AK* 🌐 *nps.gov/glba* 🎟 *Free.*

# Denali National Park

## Home of the Great One

America's third-largest national park is also Alaska's most visited attraction, and for good reason. The 6-million-acre wilderness offers spectacular mountain views, amazing wildlife (including the "Big Five" of Alaskan animals: the moose, grizzly bear, wolf, Dall sheep, and caribou), and unforgettable landscapes. The keystone is Mt. Denali itself (aka the Great One), whose peak measures in at 20,310 feet. It's often hidden behind clouds—your odds of viewing it increase the farther you travel along the 92-mile park road. Flightseeing tours are offered from Healy; they get you up close to Denali, and many even include a glacier walk.

## Don't Miss

Famous for its views of Denali, the Eielson Visitor Center is at Mile 66 of the park road. Park rangers lead presentations and hikes from here.

## Best Restaurant

Led by a two-time James Beard Award–nominated chef, 229 Parks Restaurant and Tavern is one of the region's—and the state's—most vaunted dining experiences. *229parks.com.*

## When to Go

Denali is best visited mid-May through mid-September; many services are limited and businesses are closed the rest of the year.

## Getting Here and Around

The park headquarters is just off Highway 3, the main road between Anchorage and Fairbanks. In summer, you can drive a private car the first 15 miles of the park road; beyond that, park transportation is by bus only.

**Denali Visitor Center.** *Mile 1.5 Denali Park Rd., Denali Park, AK nps.gov/dena $15.*

# Sitka

## Cultural Crossroads

Friendly Sitka stands out for its remarkable blend of Alaska Native, Russian, and American history and its dramatic and beautiful open-ocean setting. This is one of the best Inside Passage towns to explore on foot, with St. Michael's Cathedral, Sheldon Jackson Museum, Castle Hill, Sitka National Historical Park, and the Alaska Raptor Center topping the must-see list. It was home to Tlingit people for centuries prior to the 18th-century arrival of the Russians. By 1821 the Tlingits reached an accord with the Russians, and the town prospered as a center of shipbuilding and commerce, becoming known as the Paris of the Pacific.

## Don't Miss

A 20-minute walk from downtown, the Alaska Raptor Center rehabilitates from 100 to 200 birds each year. Guests can observe injured eagles relearning survival skills, including flying and catching salmon.

## Best History Lesson

The 113-acre Sitka National Historical Park houses a small museum with fascinating historical exhibits and photos of Tlingit Native culture. Afterward, examine totem poles in the forest. 🌐 *nps.gov/sitk.*

## When to Go

May through September is the best time to visit Sitka, when days are longest.

## Getting Here and Around

Sitka is a common stop on cruise routes for smaller ships and a regular ferry stop along the Alaska Marine Highway System. Alaska Airlines also operates flights from Seattle and other Alaskan cities to Sitka. The best way to see the town's sights is on foot.

**Visit Sitka.** ✉ *104 Lake St., Sitka, AK* 🌐 *visitsitka.org.*

# Anchorage

## The Last Frontier's Big City

By far Alaska's largest and most sophisticated city, Anchorage is situated in a truly spectacular location, with permanently snow-covered peaks and volcanoes of the Alaska Range to the west of the city and part of the craggy Chugach Range within the eastern edge of the municipality. The Talkeetna and Kenai ranges are visible to the north and south. Two arms of Cook Inlet embrace the town's borders, and on clear days Denali looms on the horizon. Besides its natural beauty and opportunities for outdoor recreation, the city has an ever-growing range of restaurants, shops, a great brewpub and food scene in Midtown, plus great exhibits on Native Alaskan culture.

## Don't Miss

It's a short drive from downtown to Alaska's most popularly hiked peak, Flattop Mountain, a manageable 3-mile round-trip trek where you'll be treated to astounding views of the Anchorage Bowl and Cook inlet. Another option, Tony Knowles Coastal Trail, is a popular choice for a stroll.

## Best Cultural Experience

Anchorage Museum is an essential stop for understanding the fascinating history of the North, and especially its indigenous culture. The star of the museum is the Smithsonian Arctic Studies Center.

## While You're Here

Alaska Native Heritage Center, a living history museum, stands out for its spacious Gathering Place, where you can see interpretive displays, artifacts, demonstrations, Native dances, storytelling, and films. 🌐 *alaskanative.net*.

## Getting Here and Around

Alaska's biggest city is home to the state's largest airport, with flights from all over. The city itself is quite spread out and best explored by car.

# Wrangell—St. Elias National Park

### Mountains, Volcanoes, and Glaciers, Oh My

In a land of many grand and spectacularly beautiful mountains, those in the 13.2-million-acre Wrangell–St. Elias National Park and Preserve (America's largest national park) are perhaps the most spectacular of them all, with 18,009-foot Mt. St. Elias leading the way. This extraordinarily compact cluster of immense peaks also includes volcanoes, such as Mt. Wrangell, one of the largest active volcanoes in the world. The park is a largely undeveloped wilderness that's acclaimed for mountain-biking and primitive-hiking terrain, plus glacier spotting and fantastic rafting.

### Don't Miss

Explore the massive glaciers that stand at the foot of Kennicott—Root Glacier and Kennicott Glacier—or take a multiday, guided rafting tour along the Nizina.

### Best Tour Operator

St. Elias Alpine Guides, based in McCarthy, gives introductory mountaineering lessons, leads excursions ranging from half-day hikes to monthlong backpacking trips, and is the only authorized concessionaire that conducts guided tours of historic Kennicott buildings. 🌐 *steliasguides.com.*

### While You're Here

The abandoned Kennecott Mine is one of the national park's most interesting attractions. The abandoned structures are as impressive as the mountains they stand against.

### Getting Here and Around

The park is accessible from Alaska's highway system via either the unpaved Nabesna Road or the better-known McCarthy Road.

**Wrangell--St. Elias National Park.** ✉ *Mile 106.8 Richardson Hwy., Copper Center, AK* 🌐 *nps.gov/wrst* 🎟 *Free.*

# The Alaska Railroad

### Take the Scenic Route

Mountains, glaciers, lakes, and streams fill the ever-changing panorama of your 360-degree dome windows on the historic Alaska Railroad, one of the most comfortable and picturesque ways to travel among Alaska's top sites. The railroad runs 470 miles between Seward and Fairbanks with stops in Anchorage, Denali, Talkeetna, and several other interesting towns along the way, and the best way to soak it all in is in a dome car. Popular routes include the Denali Star between Fairbanks and Anchorage with a stop in Denali National Park; the Coastal Classic between Anchorage and Seward; and the Glacier Discovery running round-trip from Anchorage to Whittier and Grandview. The trip from Anchorage to Seward is the most scenic.

### Don't Miss

Girdwood is the best railroad town on the route. Originally called Glacier City, it got its start as a gold-mining town, but today its main attraction is the Alyeska Ski Resort, the largest ski area in Alaska. 🌐 *visitgirdwood.com.*

### Before You Depart

Less than a mile from the Alaska Railroad station in Portage, drive the 2-mile loop through the 144-acre Alaska Wildlife Conservation Center, hopping out for a look at bison, moose, and more.

### When to Go

Although limited service along part of the route is available in winter, the main season is mid-May to September.

### Getting Here and Around

The railroad stops at a number of key towns. If you're picking it up in Girdwood, it's an easy 45-minute drive on Highway 1 from Anchorage.

**Alaska Railroad.** ☎ *800/544–0552* 🌐 *alaskarailroad.com.*

# Kodiak Island and Katmai National Park

## Grizzly Bears in the Wild

Some 30,000 grizzly bears inhabit the wilds of Alaska, and two of the best places to see them are on 3,588-square-mile Kodiak Island and—on the mainland 30 miles across Shelikof Strait—Katmai National Park. Visitors to Kodiak Island typically view bears by flying out to a remote lodge that also likely offers fishing, kayaking, and other activities, or by visiting Kodiak National Wildlife Refuge—home to some of the biggest bears in the world—with a tour operator. Accessible only by plane, Katmai, known as the Valley of Ten Thousand Smokes, features a dynamic combination of volcanic activity and coastal brown bears. Float trips, hiking, and kayaking are popular activities, all with a high chance of spotting bears.

## Don't Miss

At popular Brook Falls in Katmai National Park, viewing platforms overlook a 6-foot-high cascade where salmon leap to try to make it upstream to spawn while bears stand on the edge of the falls to catch them.

## Best Lodge

The secluded Brooks Lodge is a prime location for brown bear viewing in Katmai. 🌐 *katmailand.com/brooks-lodge.*

## When to Go

Summer, especially July at Brooks Falls, is prime bear-viewing season in this part of the world.

## Getting Here and Around

Access to Kodiak Island is via the Alaska Marine Highway ferry (which makes several stops a week) or by plane. Visitors to Katmai National Park typically arrive by floatplane.

**Discover Kodiak.** ✉ *100 E. Marine Way, Kodiak, AK* ☎ *907/486–4782* 🌐 *kodiak.org.*

**Katmai National Park.** ☎ *907/246–3305* 🌐 *nps.gov/katm.*

# Kenai Fjords National Park

## Alaska's Most Spectacular Waters

A coastal parkland incised with sheer, dark, slate cliffs rising from the sea, ribboned with white waterfalls, and tufted with deep-green spruce, Kenai Fjords National Park presents a rare opportunity for up-close paddling around blue tidewater glaciers. Many outfitters offer tours of these pristine waters, and the best ones include a boat cruise around Resurrection Bay, followed by two or three hours of sea kayaking. You'll typically see frolicking sea otters, crowds of Steller sea lions lazing on the rocky shore, a porpoise or two, bald eagles, and tens of thousands of seabirds. Humpback whales and orcas are sighted occasionally.

## Don't Miss

Exit Glacier is the most accessible of the more than 40 glaciers located with the national park's 1,100-square-mile Harding Icefield.

## While You're Here

One of the best places to see the region's marine wildlife is Seward's Alaska SeaLife Center, which rehabilitates animals. You'll see fish, seabirds, and marine mammals, including harbor seals and a 2,000-pound sea lion. 🌐 *alaskasealife.org.*

## When to Go

Kenai Fjords is best explored from May through September; in winter, the road to Exit Glacier isn't plowed, and rough seas make it impractical for boating and sea kayaking.

## Getting Here and Around

Kenai Fjords National Park and Seward lie at the end of Highway 9, a 2½-hour drive south of Anchorage.

**Kenai Fjords National Park.** ✉ *1212 4th Ave., Seward, AK* 🌐 *nps.gov/kefj* 🎫 *Free.*

# Skagway

## Most Storied Gold Rush Town

Located at the northern terminus of the Inside Passage, Skagway is an amazingly preserved artifact from North America's biggest, most famous gold rush. Much of downtown forms part of the Klondike Gold Rush National Historical Park, which commemorates the frenzied stampede of 1897 that extended 430 miles north to Dawson City in Canada's Yukon. It's a must-see for anyone planning on taking a White Pass train ride, driving the nearby Klondike Highway, or hiking the Chilkoot Trail, the 33-mile route of the 1897–98 prospectors from Skagway into Canada that takes four to five days to complete but is a favorite among experienced backpackers.

## Don't Miss

Travel the gold-rush route aboard the historic White Pass & Yukon Route (WP & YR) narrow-gauge railroad. The diesel locomotives tow vintage-style viewing cars up steep inclines, hugging the walls of precipitous cliffs with views of craggy peaks, forests, and plummeting waterfalls.

## Best Restaurant

Known to attract repeat customers from as far away as Juneau, Thai restaurant Starfire earns kudos for its authentic, robustly seasoned Thai cuisine, prepared with herbs grown on-site. 🌐 *starfirealaska.com*.

## When to Go

The White Pass & Yukon Route runs only mid-May to late September, which is when Skagway is nicest.

## Getting Here and Around

Most visitors arrive on cruise ships or by plane from Juneau or Anchorage. But Skagway also offers one of the few opportunities in southeast Alaska to arrive by car, by taking the Klondike Highway south from Canadian Yukon's Whitehorse.

## When in Alaska

### GATES OF THE ARCTIC NATIONAL PARK

Entirely north of the Arctic Circle, in the center of the Brooks Range, this 8.2-million-acre park is the size of four Yellowstones and is the northernmost national park in the country. To the north lies a sampling of the Arctic foothills, with colorful tilted sediments and pale green tundra while mountains and tundra cup lovely, albeit buggy, lakes. The communities of Bettles and Anaktuvuk Pass are access points for Gates of the Arctic, which has no developed trails, campgrounds, or other visitor facilities (though there is a wilderness lodge on private land within the park). You can fly into Bettles commercially and charter an air taxi into the park or hike directly out of Anaktuvuk Pass.

**Do This:** Many visitors who make it this far north combine their visit to Gates of the Arctic with 1.14-million-acre Kobuk Valley National Park, which is home to three sets of sand dunes, remnants of retreating glaciers from the Pleistocene epoch. Like most other remote Alaska parks, Kobuk Valley National Park is undeveloped wilderness with no visitor facilities. In nearby Kotzebue, the National Park Service has a visitor center where staff can provide tips for travel into the park.

**Gates of the Arctic National Park.** *nps.gov/gaar.*

### GOLD DREDGE 8

From the comfort of a narrow- gauge railroad, take a two-hour tour of this impressive seasonal mining operation in Fox, about 10 miles north of Fairbanks. Miners demonstrate classic and modern techniques, after which visitors get to try their luck panning for gold. Many historic elements from the old El Dorado Gold Mine have been transported here, so a tour provides a fairly complete look at how Fairbanks got rich.

**Do This:** Beer lovers should definitely make the short drive to Silver Gulch for North America's northernmost brewery, Silver Gulch Brewing and Bottling Co. Check out the rotating specialty brews served at the restaurant, alongside hearty brick-oven pizzas, reindeer sausage, and beer-cheese soup. Relax in the beer garden if it's a nice day.

**Gold Dredge 8.** *1803 Old Steese Hwy. N, Fairbanks, AK 907/479–6673 golddredge8.com $43.*

### HOMER

Homer lies at the southwestern end of the Kenai Peninsula at the base of a narrow spit that juts 4 miles into beautiful Kachemak Bay and offers some of the best fishing in the state. Glaciers and snowcapped mountains form a dramatic backdrop across the water. A commercial-fishing-boat harbor at the end of Homer Spit has restaurants, hotels, sea-kayaking outfitters, art galleries, and numerous outfitters and fishing-gear rental shops. On charter-fishing excursions, which can last from a half to several days, halibut, salmon, rockfish, and lingcod are the prize catches. You can also fish for trout, salmon, steelhead, and others in the area's prolific freshwater rivers.

**Do This:** Homer's outstanding Islands and Ocean Visitors Center provides a wonderful introduction to the Alaska Maritime National Wildlife Refuge, which covers some 3½ million acres spread across some 2,500 Alaskan islands.

**Homer.** *homeralaska.org.*

### TALKEETNA

Said to be the inspiration for TV's *Northern Exposure,* Talkeetna lies at the end of a spur road near Mile 99 of the Parks Highway and is a must-visit if you're driving between Anchorage and Denali or Fairbanks. Talkeetna has a pebbly shore along the Susitna with fantastic views of Denali on a clear day. Be sure to visit the West Rib Pub and Grill, on Main Street in the back of Nagley's Store. You're likely to hear tales of the former mayor of Talkeetna, Stubbs, an affable orange cat who served as the town's leader for 19 years before he died in 2017. Grab a seat out back and wash down the delicious chili, burgers, and fries with a local microbrew.

**Do This:** Adventures in the sky is the name of the game at K2 Aviation, which has a long and esteemed history of Alaska flights. Among your options: get a bird's-eye view of Denali Park's famous peaks, land on one of its many surrounding glaciers, or land at Kahiltna Base Camp and actually attempt to climb the Great One.

**Talkeetna.** 🌐 *talkeetnachamber.org.*

### UNALASKA AND THE ALEUTIAN ISLANDS

Inhabited by Aleut people and their ancestors for thousands of years, the city of Unalaska overlooks Dutch Harbor and is by far the most popular destination in the Aleutian Islands, a chain of 14 major volcanic islands that extends southwest from the Alaska mainland for about 1,200 miles (the westernmost island, Attu Island, is closer to Japan than Anchorage). Dutch Harbor, best known from the Discovery Channel's hit show *Deadliest Catch,* is one of the busiest fishing ports in the world, processing a billion—yes, billion—pounds of fish and crab each year.

**Do This:** The Aleutian World War II National Historic Area and Visitor Center preserves bits of history from Alaska's little-known role in WWII. The Aleutian Islands saw heavy fighting through much of the war; at its peak, more than 60,000 servicemen were stationed here in the farthest and most brutal reaches of the United States.

**Unalaska.** 🌐 *unalaska.org.*

## Cool Places to Stay

**Alyeska Resort.** Most rooms in this elegant resort 40 miles southeast of Anchorage have stunning views of the Chugach Mountains and the lush forests surrounding this large and luxurious hotel at the base of Alyeska Ski Resort—even if you're not here to ski, take the aerial tram to the ski area to enjoy the sweeping vistas and dine at the excellent restaurant. ✉ *1000 Arlberg Ave., Girdwood, AK* ☎ *907/754–2111* 🌐 *alyeskaresort.com.* [$] *From $209.*

**Camp Denali and North Face Lodge.** The legendary, family-owned and-operated Camp Denali and North Face Lodge both offer stunning views of Denali and active learning experiences deep within Denali National Park, at Mile 89 on the park road. ✉ *Denali National Park, AK* ☎ *907/683–2290* 🌐 *campdenali.com* [$] *From $655.*

**Ma Johnson's Hotel.** A town with about 40 year-round residents, so far away from urban comforts, seems an unlikely place to secure an attractive room and a five-star meal, but this fun little 1920s hotel in offbeat ghost town of McCarthy is the perfect lodging for visits to surrounding Wrangell–St. Elias National Park. ✉ *100 Kennicott Ave., Chitina, AK* 🌐 *majohnsonshotel.com* [$] *From $261.*

**Pearson's Pond Luxury Inn.** On a small pond near Mendenhall Glacier, this large, jaw-droppingly landscaped home may be Alaska's finest B&B, with private balconies overlooking the lush forested surroundings, close proximity to hiking trails, and kayaks and bicycles for guest use. ✉ *9633 Kelly Ct., Juneau, AK* ☎ *907/789–3772* 🌐 *pearsonspond.com.* [$] *From $399.*

# California

California's endless wonders, from Yosemite National Park to Disneyland, are both natural and man-made. Soul-satisfying wilderness often lies close to urbane civilization. With the iconic Big Sur coast, dramatic Mojave Desert, and majestic Sierra Nevada mountains, sunny California indulges those in search of great surfing, hiking, and more. Superb food, winery visits, and spas make it easy to live the California dream.

## Bucket List Picks

The following boxes contain our picks for the top sights and experiences in California.

- ○ Redwood National and State Parks
- ○ Golden Gate Bridge
- ○ Palm Springs
- ○ Yosemite National Park
- ○ Highway 1 in Big Sur
- ○ Channel Islands National Park
- ○ Monterey Bay
- ○ Joshua Tree National Park
- ○ Disneyland
- ○ Death Valley National Park
- ○ Balboa Park and the San Diego Zoo
- ○ Lassen Volcanic National Park
- ○ Hollywood
- ○ Lake Tahoe
- ○ Golden Gate Park
- ○ Los Angeles Beaches
- ○ Sequoia and Kings Canyon National Parks
- ○ San Diego Coast
- ○ Santa Cruz
- ○ Gold Country
- ○ Mendocino
- ○ Napa and Sonoma
- ○ Santa Barbara
- ○ Los Angeles Food Scene
- ○ San Francisco's North Beach

# Redwood National and State Parks

### World's Tallest Trees

Home to the tallest trees in the world, this 172-square-mile tract of old-growth forest and spectacular Northern California coastline is a land of wonders—and not just the redwoods. You can see herds of mighty Roosevelt elk in the park's prairies, and massive Pacific gray whales off the coast during their spring and fall migrations. You can drive the 8-mile-long, narrow, and mostly unpaved Coastal Drive loop, as well as the 10-mile Newton B. Drury Scenic Parkway, a scenic two-lane ribbon of pavement through soaring redwoods, with access to numerous trails through the woods. For a simple jaunt, you can hike the Lady Bird Johnson Grove Nature Loop Trail.

### Don't Miss

Visiting Fern Canyon's lush, otherworldly surroundings—which appeared in *Jurassic Park 2*—is like visiting another world. Allow an hour to explore the ¼-mile vertical garden.

### Best Restaurant

Set in a two-story house on a quiet country road near the park, the charming Larrupin' Cafe has a romantic garden setting and candlelight. *larrupin.com.*

### When to Go

This is a great park to explore year-round, but from October through April, it can be very rainy.

### Getting Here and Around

Redwood stretches for about 50 miles up the coast, along U.S. 101, starting around 40 miles north of Eureka and extending to Crescent City, nearly to the Oregon border.

**Redwood National and State Parks.** *1111 2nd St., Crescent City, CA 707/464–6101 nps.gov/redw Free, but $5 day-use fee in adjoining state parks.*

# Golden Gate Bridge

## San Fran's Iconic Drive

With its simple but powerful art deco design, the 1.7-mile suspension span that connects San Francisco and Marin County ranks among the world's most recognizable man-made structures. Drive or bike across to fulfill all your wildest California dreams, setting aside time to explore the many cool sites on both sides. That includes the 1,400-acre Presidio park and the wild hills of the Marin Headlands, which include several viewing areas that afford phenomenal skyline vistas.

## Don't Miss

Rent a bike and pedal across the bridge; good bets for picking up wheels include Golden Gate Bridge Bike Rentals and ebike service Bay Wheels.

## While You're Here

Whether you drive or bike across the bridge, continue into Sausalito, with its bougainvillea-covered hillsides and yacht harbor, and then take a half-hour ferry ride back to San Francisco.

## Best Side Trip

A hilly 10-mile bike ride from Sausalito leads to Muir Woods National Monument, a 560-acre patch of old-growth redwoods. 🌐 *nps.gov/muwo*.

## Good to Know

San Francisco's notoriously fickle weather can be especially—shall we say—exciting around the Golden Gate Bridge. Winds and fog are common, the latter especially on summer mornings. Pack extra layers.

## Getting Here and Around

The U.S. 101 freeway crosses the Golden Gate Bridge, connecting San Francisco with Marin County.

**Golden Gate Bridge.** ✉ *Lincoln Blvd. near Doyle Dr. and Fort Point, Presidio, San Francisco, CA* 🌐 *goldengatebridge.org*.

# Palm Springs

### Swankiest Desert Town

Sun-kissed and surrounded by dazzling mountain vistas, Palm Springs has been a playground for celebrities, artists, designers, the LGBTQ community, and fans of poolside relaxation for decades. Today, this oasis of about 50,000 is embracing its glory days. Owners of resorts, bed-and-breakfasts, and galleries have renovated the city's wealth of gorgeous mid-century modern buildings. Buzzy and festive Palm Canyon Drive is packed with alfresco restaurants, retro-chic design shops, and sceney bars. And just outside downtown, you'll find resorts and boutique hotels that host lively pool parties and house swish dining establishments.

### Don't Miss

A trip on the Palm Springs Aerial Tramway provides a 360-degree view of the desert through the picture windows of rotating cars. The 2½-mile ascent through Chino Canyon, the steepest vertical cable ride in the United States, brings you to an elevation of 8,516 feet. Here you'll find an observation deck, restaurants, and a cocktail lounge.

### Best Restaurant

The gorgeous interior design and eclectic Pacific Coast dishes made from scratch lure foodies to the Uptown Design District's EIGHT-4NINE. Choose a table on the outdoor patio to soak up the mountain views. 🌐 *eight4nine.com*.

### When to Go

High season in Palm springs is late fall to early spring, which is when a number of big arts festivals and LGBTQ celebrations take place.

### Getting Here and Around

Palm Springs is 100 miles east of L.A. via Interstate 10 and is also a gateway to Joshua Tree National Park.

# Yosemite National Park

## California's Most Celebrated National Park

One of America's earliest-established and most storied national parks, Yosemite is renowned for countless iconic natural features, from the soaring granite monoliths of Half Dome and El Capitan to the shimmering cascades of Yosemite Falls and Bridalveil Fall to towering sequoias. In fact, by merely standing in Yosemite Valley and turning in a circle, you can see more natural wonders in a minute than you could in a full day pretty much anywhere else. Historic buildings include the Ahwahnee Hotel, the Mountain Room restaurant, the Ansel Adams Gallery, and the Yosemite Conservation Heritage Center.

## Don't Miss

Made up of three powerful cascades, Yosemite Falls is the highest combined waterfall in North America and the fifth highest in the world. The water from the top descends a total of 2,425 feet, and when the falls run hard, you can hear them thunder across the valley. A ¼-mile trail leads from the parking lot to the base of the falls, but for a more exciting but strenuous adventure, hike the 7.2-mile Upper Yosemite Fall Trail, a 2,700-foot climb to the top of the falls.

## While You're Here

When it's open (from around late May through October), you can drive stunning Tioga Road (Highway 120) across the park to the eastern Sierras.

## Getting Here and Around

The heart of the park, Yosemite Valley, is 80 miles northeast of Merced via Highway 140, and about 200 miles east of San Francisco.

**Valley Visitor Center.** ✉ *9035 Village Dr., Yosemite Valley, CA* ☎ *209/372–0200* 🌐 *nps.gov/yose* 🎟 *$35 per vehicle.*

# Highway 1 in Big Sur

### Ultimate California Road Trip

One of the country's most spectacular drives, Highway 1 snakes down the coast south from Monterey over historic bridges, atop sheer sea cliffs, beside scenic state parks, and through fabled Big Sur, which instead of a conventional town is a loose string of coast-hugging properties, including some gorgeous boutique resorts. Numerous pullouts along the way offer tremendous views and photo ops. On some of the beaches huge elephant seals lounge nonchalantly, seemingly oblivious to the attention of rubberneckers.

### Don't Miss

Get a look at Big Sur's iconic McWay Falls from Highway 1, then hit the trail at Julia Pfeiffer Burns State Park or the water at Sand Dollar Beach or Andrew Molera State Park.

### While You're Here

One of the most fantastic residences in the country, 115-room Hearst Castle sits in solitary splendor, crowning 127 acres of gardens and buildings high on a bluff 3 miles from Highway 1 as it curves south from Big Sur.

### Best Restaurant

Cliff-top gem Nepenthe may just have the best coastal view of any restaurant between San Francisco and Los Angeles. 🌐 *nepenthebigsur.com.*

### When to Go

Driving through Big Sur is an amazing experience year-round, but winter can bring rain, and also road closures that result from washouts and mudslides.

### Getting Here and Around

Scenic Highway 1 meanders along much of the state's coastline. The Big Sur stretch is especially dramatic if you drive it north to south, starting on the Monterey Peninsula and continuing about 100 miles to Cambria.

# Channel Islands National Park

## Galapagos of North America

Every day, tens of thousands of people gaze out at this mountainous archipelago about 11 miles off the coast from Ventura and Santa Barbara, but relatively few ever set foot on one of these eight uninhabited islands, five of which are part of the national park. For nature lovers, however, the trip here—it takes less than an hour via a high-speed cruise from the visitor center in Ventura—is an epic experience, and you may see dolphins, whales, sea lions, and myriad sea birds along the way. Activities on the islands themselves include hiking, primitive camping, and exploring some of the world's largest and deepest sea caves.

## Don't Miss

On Santa Cruz Island, you can hike amid the unspoiled landscape of 2,500-foot mountains and dramatic canyons.

## Best Island Tour

Santa Barbara Adventure Company runs kayaking and snorkeling trips at Channel Islands National Park. It's a memorable way to explore the famous sea caves around the Scorpion Anchorage on Santa Cruz Island. 🌐 *sbadventureco.com.*

## Getting Here and Around

Visiting the nautical park off the coast of Santa Barbara, Ventura, and Oxnard takes a little extra effort, as the only way to visit any of them is via a boat excursion. The park's main visitor center in Ventura Harbor is just 3 miles off U.S. 101.

**Channel Islands National Park Visitor Center.** ✉ *1901 Spinnaker Dr., Ventura, CA* ☎ *805/658–5730* 🌐 *nps.gov/chis* 🎟 *Free.*

# Monterey Bay

## Seaside Sanctuary

Monterey Bay life centers on the ocean. The bay itself is protected by the Monterey Bay National Marine Sanctuary, the nation's largest undersea canyon—bigger and deeper than the Grand Canyon. On-the-water activities abound, from whale-watching and kayaking to sailing and surfing. Bay cruises from Monterey and Moss Landing almost always encounter other enchanting sea creatures, among them sea otters, sea lions, and porpoises. Quaint, walkable towns and villages such as Carmel-by-the-Sea and Carmel Valley Village lure with smart restaurants and galleries, while sunny Aptos, Capitola, Soquel, and Santa Cruz, with miles of sand and surf, attract beach lovers.

## Don't Miss

The sea even takes center stage indoors at the world-famous Monterey Bay Aquarium, the best on the West Coast. The surrounding Cannery Row waterfront, immortalized in John Steinbeck's writing, is a fun place to explore afterward.

## While You're Here

Primordial nature resides in quiet harmony with palatial estates along 17-Mile Drive, which winds through an 8,400-acre microcosm of the peninsula's Pebble Beach coastal landscape.

## Most Charming Town

Even when its population quadruples with tourists on weekends and in summer, Carmel-by-the-Sea retains its identity as a quaint village. Charming, upscale bistros, winery tastings rooms, and art galleries line the main commercial lane, Ocean Avenue. 🌐 *carmelcalifornia.com.*

## Getting Here and Around

Scenic Highway 1 runs along the Monterey Peninsula en route between Santa Cruz and Big Sur.

# Joshua Tree National Park

## Magical Seuss Trees

Named for the distinctive yucca trees that line that fill this massive desert park, Joshua Tree teems with fascinating landscapes and life-forms. It's a world-class destination for rock climbing, a mesmerizing landscape for spring wildflower viewing, and a magical destination for stargazing—Los Angeles is just two hours away, but in this park, especially the northern half, light pollution is minimal.

## Don't Miss

Park Boulevard curves for nearly 40 miles through the park, offering countless photo ops and opportunities for easy hikes—highlights include Hidden Valley, the Barker Dam Nature Walk, Skull Rock, and the Key View overlook.

## Best Park Tour

On the NPS's engaging 90-minute Keys Ranch Tour, a guide takes you through the former home of a family that successfully homesteaded here deep in the heart of what is now Joshua Tree for 60 years. In addition to the 150-acre ranch, a workshop, store, and schoolhouse are still standing, and the grounds are strewn with vehicles and mining equipment.

## When to Go

You can enjoy this 1,238-square-mile park any time of year, but the summer months—though less crowded—can be extremely hot, with average highs well over 100°F.

## Getting Here and Around

Joshua Tree is in southeastern California, less than an hour east of Palm Springs, with entrances off of Interstate 10 and Highway 62.

**Oasis Visitor Center.** ✉ *74485 National Park Dr., Twentynine Palms, CA* 🌐 *nps.gov/jotr* 🎫 *$30 per vehicle.*

# Disneyland

### The Original Disney Park

While Florida's Disney World may be larger, Disneyland in Anaheim, California, is the original Disney park. Opened in 1955 and the only one of the Disney parks to have been overseen by Walt himself, Disneyland has a genuine historic feel, and occupies a unique place in the Disney legend. Expertly run, perfectly maintained, with polite and helpful staff ("cast members" in the Disney lexicon), the park has plenty of signature draws, such as the Indiana Jones Adventure ride and Storybook Land, and the newer Avengers Campus.

### Don't Miss

The park consists of several themed neighborhoods, some of the favorites being Main Street U.S.A., which was inspired by Walt's hometown of Marceline, Missouri; and Adventureland, a tiny tropical paradise modeled after the lands of Africa, Polynesia, and Arabia.

### While You're Here

The sprawling Disney California Adventure, adjacent to Disneyland, pays tribute to the Golden State with seven theme areas that re-create vintage architectural styles and embrace several hit films, such as *Cars*, *Toy Story*, and *Guardians of the Galaxy*, via engaging attractions.

### Best Resort for Families

Disney's Grand Californian Hotel and Spa is the most opulent of Disneyland's three hotels. The Craftsman-style Grand Californian offers views of and easy access to Disney California Adventure and Downtown Disney.

### Getting Here and Around

Disneyland is 30 miles southeast of Los Angeles via Interstate 5.

**Disneyland.** ✉ *Disneyland Dr., Anaheim, CA* ☎ *714/781–4636* 🌐 *disneyland.disney.go.com* 🎫 *From $104.*

# Death Valley National Park

## Land of Extremes

America's driest and hottest spot has a name that captures the harshness of parts of its landscape, but Death Valley is a surprisingly varied and dynamic park. It's home both to the lowest point in North America but also riotously colorful explosions of greenery and wildflowers in the spring, bizarre boulders that appear to move on their own (scientists are baffled), fascinating ghost towns, and incredible geological features, from sweeping sand dunes to mountain peaks that soar over 11,000 feet.

## Don't Miss

At 282 feet below sea level, Badwater is the lowest spot of land in North America—and also one of the hottest. A wooden platform overlooks a sodium chloride pool, a reminder that the valley floor used to contain a lake, and a trail continues beyond that.

## Best Overlook

From Dante's View, a 5,450-foot lookout in the Black Mountains, you can see across most of 160-mile-long Death Valley in the dry desert air.

## When to Go

Other than to satisfy your curiosity about how extreme heat feels, Death Valley is best avoided during the fiery months of May through September. Spring and October are still quite warm but enjoy cool nights, and winter sees lovely, temperate days. Make sure to pack plenty of water and know your limits.

## Getting Here and Around

Death Valley is in eastern California (a small part of it crosses into Nevada) and is about 100 miles north of Interstate 40. From Las Vegas, NV, it's about a two-hour drive.

**Furnace Creek Visitor Center.** ✉ *Off Hwy. 190, Furnace Creek, CA* 🌐 *nps.gov/deva* 🎟 *$30 per vehicle.*

# Balboa Park and San Diego Zoo

## Smithsonian of the West

The 1,200-acre Balboa Park is filled with superb museums and cultural institutions. Often referred to as the "Smithsonian of the West" for its concentration of museums, the park also contains a series of botanical gardens, performance spaces, and outdoor playrooms. Enchanting buildings and fountains dating from San Diego's 1915 Panama–California International Exposition are strung along the park's main east–west thoroughfare, El Prado.

## Don't Miss

San Diego's most famous attraction, the 100-acre San Diego Zoo lies at the heart of beautiful Balboa Park. Nearly 4,000 animals of some 800 diverse species roam in hospitable, expertly crafted habitats that replicate natural environments as closely as possible.

The Skyfari Aerial Tram, which soars 170 feet above the ground, gives a good overview of the zoo's layout and, on clear days, a panorama of the park, downtown San Diego, the bay, and the ocean.

## While You're Here

The Old Globe complex, comprising the Sheryl and Harvey White Theatre, the Lowell Davies Festival Theatre, and the Old Globe Theatre, offers some of the finest theatrical productions in Southern California. 🌐 *theoldglobe.org.*

## Getting Here and Around

Balboa Park is in the center of San Diego, just off Interstate 5 and directly north of downtown.

**San Diego Zoo.** ✉ *2920 Zoo Dr., San Diego, CA* ☎ *619/231–1515* 🌐 *sandiegozoo.org* 🎟 *$62.*

# Lassen Volcanic National Park

## Geothermal Wonders

Boiling springs, steam vents, and mud pots are among the belching and steaming geothermal features that dot the eerie landscapes of this 165-square-mile Northern California park. The most famous feature of the tract of peaceful forests and alpine meadows is its dormant plug dome, Lassen Peak. The volcano erupted dramatically in 1914 with a mudflower that destroyed vegetation for miles, and all sorts of evidence is still visible today, including fumaroles, boiling lakes, and bubbling hot springs.

## Don't Miss

Lassen Peak may be the most popular hike, but don't skip Bumpass Hell Trail, a 3-mile round-trip hike with hot springs, mud pots, and steam vents plus a trailhead along the main park road.

## While You're Here

An hour west of the park in Redding, Turtle Bay Exploration Park offers walking trails, an aquarium, an arboretum and botanical gardens, and the stunning Santiago Calatrava–designed Sundial Bridge, a metal and translucent glass pedestrian walkway spanning a broad bend in the Sacramento River.

## When to Go

Summer is prime time for visiting this high-elevation park, but the quieter spring and fall shoulder seasons are still beautiful. In winter, the park is open, but most services as well as much of the park road are closed.

## Getting Here and Around

Lassen Volcanic Park's two most prominent entrances are off Highway 44 about 50 miles east of Interstate 5 in Redding, and Highway 36, about 50 miles east of Red Bluff.

**Kohm Yah-mah-nee Visitor Center.** ✉ *21820 Lassen National Park Hwy., Mineral, CA* 🌐 *nps.gov/lavo* 🎫 *$30.*

# Hollywood

## Heart of American Film

The Tinseltown mythology of Los Angeles was born in Hollywood, still one of the city's largest and most vibrant neighborhoods and the best place to discover the film industry's fascinating heritage, including the Hollywood Walk of Fame, Grauman's (now TCL) Chinese Theater, and the Hollywood Museum. Although just over the hills in the San Fernando Valley, Universal Studios Hollywood has a great amusement park and Warner Bros. has some fun backlots, the venerable Paramount lot offers arguably the best glimpse of Hollywood's Golden Age, with authentic studio tours that provide an engaging look at the industry's long history. Many memorable movies and TV shows were shot here, from *Sunset Boulevard* and *Titanic* to TV's *Star Trek* and *I Love Lucy*.

## Don't Miss

With letters 45 feet tall, the city's trademark Hollywood Sign can be spotted from miles away. The icon, which originally read "Hollywoodland," was erected in the Hollywood Hills in 1923. For a great view, visit Griffith Park, where several trails from the observatory parking lot lead to close-up vantage points.

## Best Celebrity Spotting

A-listers are known to frequent Runyon Canyon, the city's most famous trail, but the 160-acre park in the middle of Hollywood is also a good place to hike, run, see the Hollywood Sign, and photograph the skyline. 🌐 *laparks.org*.

## Getting Here and Around

The heart of Hollywood is just off the U.S. 101 freeway, a short drive northwest of downtown; about 8 miles farther northwest, you'll reach the studios in the valley.

# Lake Tahoe

## Jewel of the Sierras

Whether you swim, sail, or simply rest on its shores, you'll be wowed by the overwhelming beauty of Lake Tahoe, the largest alpine lake in North America. Famous for its cobalt-blue water and surrounding snowcapped peaks that draw skiers, Lake Tahoe straddles the state line between California and Nevada. The border gives this popular Sierra Nevada resort region a split personality: some visitors are intent on low-key sightseeing and outdoor fun, while the rest head to the casinos on the Nevada side. To get a feel for the lake's wealth of offerings, drive the 72-mile road that follows the shore through wooded flatlands and past beaches, climbing to vistas on the rugged southwest side of the lake.

## Don't Miss

With a beach, marina, lodgings, and myriad activities, Zephyr Cove is a prime spot to book a cruise around the lake. One of the most interesting options is the Thunderbird Lodge Cruise & Tour.

## Best Views

Whether you ski or not, you'll appreciate the impressive view of Lake Tahoe from the Heavenly Gondola. The eight-passenger cars travel from Heavenly Village 2.4 miles up the mountain. 🌐 *theshopsatheavenly.com.*

## When to Go

Famous for skiing in winter and all kinds of other outdoor fun the rest of the year, Tahoe is always in season, but snowy weather can bring road closures, so check conditions.

## Getting Here and Around

Interstate 80 crosses just north of Lake Tahoe en route between San Francisco and Reno.

**Tahoe North.** 🌐 *gotahoenorth.com.*
**Tahoe South.** 🌐 *tahoesouth.com.*

# Golden Gate Park

## Glorious Urban Green Space

Jogging, cycling, skating, picnicking, going to a museum, checking out a concert, dozing in the sunshine—Golden Gate Park is the perfect playground for fast-paced types, laid-back dawdlers, and everyone in between. San Francisco's most alluring green space has enough world-class diversions to keep you busy for a few days. A must on sunny days is the 55-acre San Francisco Botanical Garden at Strybing Arboretum, with its very own 4-acre redwood grove. The Conservatory of Flowers is a must for horticulture lovers—don't miss the Aquatic Plants section, where lily pads float and carnivorous plants dine on bugs to the sounds of rushing water. About the park's de Young Museum, opinions vary greatly, but many adore the striking copper facade of this impressive repository of American, African, and Oceanic art, and there's no denying the impressive view from its 144-foot tower.

## Don't Miss

With its native plant–covered living roof, retractable ceiling, three-story rain forest, gigantic planetarium, living coral reef, and frolicking penguins, the Renzo Piano–designed California Academy of Sciences is another of the park's treasures.

## Best Restaurant

A short walk north of Golden Gate Park, perennially crowded Burma Superstar earns kudos for its flavorful, well-prepared Burmese food, including the extraordinary signature tea leaf salad. 🌐 *burmasuperstar.com.*

## Getting Here and Around

Golden Gate Park extends for 3 miles from Haight-Ashbury to the Pacific Ocean and is bisected by Highway 1.

**Golden Gate Park.** ✉ *Stanyan and Fell Sts., San Francisco, CA* 🌐 *goldengate-park.com.*

# Los Angeles Beaches

## West Coast Best Coast

When you're in the City of Angels, you must save a day or two to soak up the sunshine of L.A.'s legendary beach culture, from bohemian Venice Beach to ultrarich and ultracasual Malibu. Santa Monica is popular, and adjacent Santa Monica State Beach is wide and sandy. For a memorable view, climb up the stairway over PCH to Palisades Park, at the top of the bluffs. Then stroll a few blocks to downtown's pedestrian-only Third Street Promenade, with its outdoor cafés, street vendors, movie theaters, and a rich nightlife.

## Don't Miss

Be sure to check out Santa Monica Pier, which has appeared in countless movies and is famous for its 1922 Looff Carousel.

## Best People-Watching

At Venice Beach Boardwalk, the surf and sand are fine, but the main attraction is eyeing the colorful collection of passersby, especially on weekends. You can rent a bike or in-line skates and hit the Strand bike path, then pull up a seat at a sidewalk café and watch the action unfold. 🌐 *visitveniceca.com*.

## While You're Here

It's a quick hop to the Getty Center, which resembles a pristine fortified city of its own. The amazing Richard Meier design, uncommon gardens, and fascinating European art collections will keep you busy for hours. Nearby in Malibu, Getty Villa is the center's much older progenitor.

## Getting Here and Around

Santa Monica and Venice are reached via Interstate 10 and Venice Boulevard. The Getty Center is in Brentwood, on L.A.'s west side, just off Interstate 405; parking costs $20, but you can also get here via No. 734 and 234 buses.

# Sequoia and Kings Canyon National Parks

### Towering Giants and Scenic Drives

You'll feel small—in a good way—walking among some of the world's largest living things in Sequoia's Giant Forest and Kings Canyon's Grant Grove. In these adjoining national parks, including the state's oldest (Sequoia was established in 1890), you can also explore the gleaming limestone formations of Crystal Cave and drive some of the most spectacular scenic roads in the West, including the 30-mile Kings Canyon Scenic Byway, which offers views into a gaping chasm that's deeper than even the Grand Canyon.

### Don't Miss

One of California's most scenic drives, 46-mile Generals Highway connects Sequoia and Kings Canyon and is named after the landmark Grant and Sherman trees that leave so many visitors awestruck. The road passes the turnoff to Crystal Cave, the Giant Forest Museum, Lodgepole Village, and several other key attractions.

### Best Hike

At 14,494 feet, Mt. Whitney is the highest point in the contiguous United States and the crown jewel of Sequoia National Park's wild eastern side. The most popular route to the summit, the 20-mile round-trip Mt. Whitney Trail can be conquered by very fit and experienced hikers in a single day from May through October, but you must obtain a permit by lottery. 🌐 *recreation.gov.*

### Getting Here and Around

These adjoining parks are about 90 miles east of Fresno via Highways 198 (to enter from the south) and 180 (entering from the north).

**Sequoia and Kings Canyon National Parks.** ✉ *47050 Generals Hwy., Three Rivers, CA* 🌐 *nps.gov/seki* 🎫 *$35 per vehicle.*

# San Diego Coast

## Quintessential California Beaches

Friendly, laid-back, and blessed with year-round pleasant weather, San Diego is the ultimate West Coast beach destination, with a string of shoreline neighborhoods and villages that go north from downtown and its sheltered bay through lively surfing havens and along the base of dramatic sea cliffs. There's Mission Beach, near SeaWorld San Diego, with its bustling boardwalk that's frequented by walkers, cyclists, and people-watchers, and that's famous for myriad water sports. Farther north, you'll encounter the tony enclave of La Jolla, whose famously scenic cove is marked by towering palms that line a lovely promenade, and La Jolla Shores, which is known for its calm waves and sea caves and underwater canyons. Perhaps most spectacular of all, Torrey Pines State Beach offers a long, narrow stretch of pristine beach framed by picturesque sea cliffs.

## Don't Miss

The 166-acre Cabrillo National Monument sits atop rugged cliffs and shores with outstanding overlooks of both the ocean and downtown San Diego. Highlights of the preserve include the moderately difficult Bayside Trail, the Old Point Loma Lighthouse, and the tide pools.

## Best Quick Bite

A fun stop for a meal or picnic supplies, Liberty Public Market was a former naval training center and is now home to more than 30 vendors offering up a rich assortment of tasting fare, from fish tacos to pad Thai to lavender lattes and Parisian macarons. 🌐 *libertypublicmarket.com.*

## Getting Here and Around

The city's beachfront parallels Interstate 5, running north from downtown San Diego.

**San Diego Coast.** 🌐 *sandiego.org.*

# Santa Cruz

## Surf City USA

In this lively and laid-back beach town known for its free-spirited surfing culture and liberal student vibe, visitors of all ages love to explore the small city's iconic old-fashioned beachfront, which includes a colorful municipal pier that juts out into a beautiful bay and—most famously—the old-fashioned Beach Boardwalk. Its Looff carousel and classic wooden Giant Dipper roller coaster, both dating from the early 1900s, are surrounded by high-tech thrill rides and easygoing kiddie rides with ocean views. You have to pay to play, but you can wander the entire boardwalk for free while sampling carnival fare such as corn dogs and garlic fries. And it's just a short walk to downtown's bounty of fun and friendly restaurants, cafés, and bars.

## Don't Miss

The Santa Cruz Surfing Museum, inside the picturesque Mark Abbott Memorial Lighthouse, chronicles surfing history in one of America's most famous towns for this sport. It overlooks one of California's premier surfing locales, Steamer Lane.

## Best Surfing Lessons

Learn the region's most celebrated water sport with a private or group lesson from the acclaimed Surf School Santa Cruz, whose staff teaches adults and kids of all ages everything they need to ride the waves, including paddling and proper techniques. 🌐 *surfschoolsantacruz.com.*

## Getting Here and Around

Santa Cruz is along scenic Highway 1 on the north side of Monterey Bay and is just a 90-minute drive south of San Francisco.

**Santa Cruz Beach Boardwalk.** ✉ *400 Beach St., Santa Cruz, CA* 🌐 *beachboardwalk.com* 🎟 *Boardwalk free, unlimited rides $40.*

# Gold Country

### Hit the Mother Lode

When James W. Marshall burst into John Sutter's Mill on January 24, 1848, carrying flecks of gold in his hat, the millwright unleashed the glittering California gold rush with these immortal words: "Boys, I believe I've found a gold mine!" California's coastal communities soon emptied as prospectors flocked to the hills. Today you can relive the era by journeying down the serpentine Gold Country Highway, a two-lane route appropriately numbered 49, to find rip-roaring mining camps, significant strike sites like Empire Mine State Historic Park in Grass Valley, and fascinating Mother Lode towns that now buzz with indie shops, coffeehouses, and wine bars, among them Nevada City, Placerville, and Murphys.

### Don't Miss

Sprawling over three floors, the California State Railroad Museum in Old Sacramento celebrates the history of trains from their 19th-century English origins and the building of America's transcontinental railroad (Sacramento was its western terminus) to the pre–jet age glory days of rail travel and the high-speed trains in today's Europe and Asia.

### Best Gold Rush Town

Once known as the Queen City of the Northern Mines, Nevada City is the most appealing of the northern Mother Lode towns. The iron-shutter brick buildings that line downtown streets contain antiques shops, galleries, a winery, and more.

### Getting Here and Around

Highway 49 stretches for about 180 miles through the heart of the Gold Country, from Nevada City and Interstate 80 down through Placerville and Sonora.

# Mendocino

## Hollywood by the Sea

A flourishing logging town in the late 19th century, Mendocino seduces 21st-century travelers with windswept cliffs, phenomenal Pacific Ocean views, and boomtown-era New England–style architecture. Following the timber industry's mid-20th-century decline, artists and craftspeople began flocking here, and so did Hollywood: Elia Kazan chose Mendocino as a backdrop for his 1955 film adaptation of John Steinbeck's *East of Eden*, starring James Dean, and the town stood in for fictional Cabot Cove, Maine, in the long-running TV series *Murder, She Wrote*. Today, the small downtown area consists almost entirely of distinctive places to eat and shop.

## Don't Miss

Something beautiful is always abloom in the marvelous Mendocino Coast Botanical Gardens. Along 3½ miles of trails, including pathways with ocean views and overlooks for whale-watching, lie a profusion of flowers.

## Best Restaurant

Plank flooring, wood-top tables, and a gas fireplace with brick hearth lend rustic warmth to delightful Trillium Cafe, a block from the town's dramatic headlands. The menu, which emphasizes local produce and seafood, changes seasonally, and there's an exceptional list of Mendocino County wines. 🌐 *trilliummendocino.com.*

## Getting Here and Around

Every road to Mendocino is windy, narrow, and stunning, whether you get here via beautiful ocean-hugging Highway 1 by driving north from coastal Sonoma County or south from California's redwood forests. Or it's every bit as beautiful driving here through the acclaimed wine country of Anderson Valley, taking Highway 128 from northern Sonoma County.

# Napa and Sonoma

### USA's Premier Wine Regions

California has several incredible wine-making regions, all of them quite picturesque, but Napa and Sonoma stand out for their sheer variety of eye-popping landscapes. In Sonoma, walk beneath old-growth redwoods in the Russian River, stroll atop windswept cliffs along the coast, and taste wine with views of sunny, undulating vineyards at more than 400 wineries in the gorgeous inland valley. In Napa, too, it's easy to join in at famous wineries and rising newcomers off country roads, or at trendy in-town tasting rooms.

### Don't Miss

Wineries range from traditional grand estates with old-world vibes like St. Francis and Francis Ford Coppola Winery in Sonoma and Opus One in Napa to quirkier cult producers that can feel more personal, such as Scribe and Zialena in Sonoma and Harlan Estate in Napa.

### Best Towns

Yountville, Healdsburg, and St. Helena have small-town charm as well as luxurious inns, hotels, and spas. In Sonoma County, Guerneville is one of the region's most inviting towns.

### Best Foodie Hub

The oft-photographed center of Sonoma's ritziest town, the tree-shaded Healdsburg Plaza is lined on four sides with tony bistros, tasting rooms, and gourmet food shops. 🌐 *healdsburg.com*.

### Getting Here and Around

Most travelers to the Wine Country start their trip in San Francisco, about 50 miles away. Getting here takes less than an hour in normal traffic. In Napa Valley, base yourself in Napa, Yountville, or St. Helena. In Sonoma County, you can visit numerous tasting rooms on foot from Sonoma or Healdsburg.

# Santa Barbara

## Queen of the Missions

Santa Barbara has long been an oasis for Los Angelenos seeking respite from big-city life. The attractions begin at the ocean and end in the foothills of the Santa Ynez Mountains. Perhaps the biggest hit is Old Mission Santa Barbara, widely referred to as the queen of the 21 missions that were established throughout the state during the late-18th-century Spanish colonial period. But Santa Barbara's downtown, too, is a stunner, considered one of the most architecturally striking on the West Coast. (After a 1925 earthquake demolished many buildings, the city seized a golden opportunity to assume a Spanish Mediterranean style.) Walk along the main drag, State Street, and also along the side streets a couple of blocks in either direction, and you'll discover beautiful buildings, inviting shops, and restaurants.

## Don't Miss

Old Mission Santa Barbara is one of the most beautiful and frequently photographed buildings in coastal California.

## Coolest Neighborhood

A formerly industrial neighborhood near the waterfront and train station, the Funk Zone has evolved into a hip hangout filled with wine-tasting rooms, arts-and-crafts studios, murals, breweries, distilleries, restaurants, and small shops. 🌐 *funkzone.net*.

## Getting Here and Around

Santa Barbara is on the central coast, about a 90-minute drive up U.S. 101 from Los Angeles, and the mission is just north of downtown, in the city's striking foothills.

**Old Santa Barbara Mission.** ✉ *2201 Laguna St., Santa Barbara, CA* 🌐 *santabarbaramission.org* 🎫 *$15.*

# Los Angeles Food Scene

### Taste the World in Downtown L.A.

With edgy and innovative chefs, access to a bounty of fresh ingredients, and breezy restaurant patios and terraces for miles, Los Angeles has become one of the nation's most deliciously exciting food cities. The best way to experience L.A.'s vast culinary riches is to tour its most dynamic international neighborhoods. Three of the biggies are in the heart of historic downtown: Chinatown, Little Tokyo, and El Pueblo de Los Ángeles. Fanning out a bit, you can discover the amazing eats and 24/7 energy of Koreatown, and smaller but no less vibrant districts like block-long Little Ethiopia, the El Salvador Community Corridor along Vermont Street, Filipinotown, Little Armenia, Thai Town, and several others.

### Don't Miss

At Grand Central Market, handmade white-corn tamales, warm olive bread, dried figs, and Mexican fruit drinks are just the beginning. This mouthwatering gathering place is the city's largest and most active food market, the home to various artisanal vendors representing a veritable United Nations of international cultures. 🌐 *grandcentralmarket.com*. If you have time, also visit the Original Farmers' Market near Los Angeles County Museum of Art.

### While You're Here

Walk it all off at one of the architectural wonders of Los Angeles, downtown's Walt Disney Concert Hall. It's part of a complex that includes a public park, gardens, shops, and two outdoor amphitheaters.

### Getting Here and Around

The city's most historic food enclaves are downtown, at the junction of the 110 and 101 freeways. It's one of the most walkable areas of L.A., and it's served by the subway, too.

## San Francisco's North Beach

### Most Charming 'Hood

One of the older and most storied neighborhoods in a city with plenty of them, North Beach evokes everything from the Barbary Coast days to the no-less-rowdy beatnik era, which centered on the still vibrant City Lights Bookstore, a great place to take in the city's rich literary history. A few blocks away, grassy Washington Square is surrounded by pizzerias and gelato shops and is still the social heart of both surrounding Little Italy and an easy jumping-off point for visiting nearby Chinatown (the country's oldest)—a lively 17-block-quadrant always teeming with both locals and visitors—or venturing a few blocks south (and uphill) to the San Francisco Cable Car Museum.

### Don't Miss

Among San Francisco's most distinctive skyline sights, 210-foot Coit Tower in nearby Telegraph Hill offers some of the best views in the city. You can ride the elevator to the top—the only thing you have to pay for here—to enjoy panoramas of the Bay and Golden Gate bridges as well as Alcatraz Island. Surrounding Telegraph Hill is a warren of quirky, photogenic streets, secret gardens, and cypress trees full of wild parrots.

### Best Bakery

At Liguria Bakery, the Soracco family has been baking focaccia in North Beach since 1911, and many consider their fresh-from-the-oven bread—which you can order studded with olives, topped with cheese and jalapeños, or pizza style—the city's best. Arrive before noon: when the focaccia is gone, the bakery closes.

### Getting Here and Around

North Beach is a mile north of downtown's central Union Square and is easily reached by bus or on foot.

**North Beach.** 🌐 *sftravel.com.*

## When in California

### ALCATRAZ ISLAND

Thousands of visitors to San Francisco come daily to walk in the footsteps of Alcatraz's notorious criminals. The stories of life and death on "the Rock" may sometimes be exaggerated, but it's almost impossible to resist the chance to wander the cell block that tamed the country's toughest gangsters and saw daring escape attempts of tremendous desperation. Fewer than 2,000 inmates ever did time on the Rock, and though they weren't the worst criminals, they were definitely some of the worst prisoners. The boat ride to the island is brief (15 minutes), but affords beautiful views of the city, Marin County, and the East Bay.

**Do This:** The audio tour, highly recommended, includes observations by guards and prisoners about life in one of America's most notorious penal colonies. After you're back on the mainland, visit the jewel of the Embarcadero, erected in 1896, the Ferry Building and its street-level marketplace.

**Alcatraz Island.** ✉ *Pier 33, Embarcadero, San Francisco, CA* ☎ *415/981–7625* 🌐 *nps.gov/alca* 🎫 *From $40.*

### ANZA-BORREGO DESERT STATE PARK

One of the few parks in the country where you can follow a trail and pitch a tent wherever you like, Anza-Borrego Desert State Park comprises 1,000 square miles of spectacular desert and mountain wilderness. State Highway 78, which runs north and south through the park, has been designated the Juan Bautista de Anza National Historic Trail, marking portions of the route of the Anza Colonizing Expedition of 1775–76 that went from northern Mexico to the San Francisco Bay area.

**Do This:** There are 110 miles of hiking and riding trails that allow you to explore canyons, capture scenic vistas, tiptoe through fields of wildflowers in spring, and possibly see wildlife—the park is home to rare Peninsular bighorn sheep, mountain lions, coyotes, black-tailed jackrabbit, and roadrunners.

**Anza-Borrego Desert State Park.** ✉ *200 Palm Canyon Dr., Borrego Springs, CA* 🌐 *parks.ca.gov* 🎫 *$10 per vehicle.*

### BERKELEY'S GOURMET GHETTO

The success of Alice Waters's Chez Panisse defined California's international reputation as a hub of contemporary, seasonal cuisine and attracted countless food-related enterprises to a stretch of Shattuck Avenue now known as the Gourmet Ghetto. Foodies will do well here poking around the shops, grabbing a quick bite, or indulging in a feast. A jazz combo entertains the line that usually snakes down the block outside Cheese Board Pizza (1512 Shattuck); it's that good. High ceilings and red-leather booths add to the friendly, retro atmosphere of Saul's deli (1475 Shattuck), a Berkeley institution that is well known for its homemade celery tonic sodas and enormous sandwiches made with Acme bread. César (1515 Shattuck) wine bar provides afternoon tapas and late-night drinks, while the Epicurious Garden (1509–1513 Shattuck) food stands sell everything from sushi to gelato. A small terraced garden winds up to the Imperial Tea Court, a Zen-like teahouse rife with imports and tea ware.

**Do This:** Alice Waters's legendary eatery, Chez Panisse is known for its locally sourced ingredients, formal prix-fixe menus, and personal service, while its upstairs café offers simpler fare in a more casual setting. Both menus change daily and legions of loyal fans insist that Chez Panisse lives up to its reputation.

**Gourmet Ghetto.** ✉ *Shattuck Ave. between Delaware and Rose Sts., North Berkeley, CA* 🌐 *gourmetghetto.org.*

## CATALINA ISLAND

One of the only inhabited islands off America's West Coast, this 76-square-mile expanse of virtually unspoiled mountains, canyons, coves, and beaches gives visitors a glimpse of what undeveloped Southern California once looked like. A one-hour high-speed ferry from San Pedro, Long Beach, and Dana Point gets you to this rugged place popular for diving, kayaking, hiking, and biking. The main town, Avalon, is a charming, old-fashioned beach community, where yachts and pleasure boats bob in the crescent bay. Wander beyond the main drag and find brightly painted little bungalows fronting the sidewalks; golf carts are the preferred mode of transport. The nonprofit Catalina Island Conservancy owns nearly 90% of the island and helps preserve the area's natural flora and fauna, including the bald eagle and the Catalina Island fox.

**Do This:** Avalon's circular white Casino structure is one of the finest examples of art deco architecture anywhere. Its Spanish-inspired floors and murals gleam with brilliant blue and green Catalina tiles. First-run movies are screened nightly at the Avalon Theatre, noteworthy for its classic 1929 theater pipe organ and art deco wall murals. The Santa Catalina Island Company leads three tours of this historic building.

**Catalina Island.** 🌐 *visitcatalinaisland.com.*

## CAVES OF PINNACLES NATIONAL PARK

The many draws of this national park 50 miles east of Monterey at Pinnacles include 30 miles of hiking trails, hundreds of rock-climbing routes, myriad wildlife species—including once-extinct California condors—and most famous of all, distinctive caves set amid the parks craggy peaks and rocky spires. The caves found at Pinnacles are talus caves, meaning they were formed when huge boulders toppled into narrow canyons.

**Do This:** The two main cave areas are the Balconies Cave on the west side of the park, and the Bear Gulch Cave on the east side. Both are popular with hikers—flashlights or headlamps are required. The Bear Gulch Cave is home to a large colony of Townsend's big-eared bats, which rest there in winter and raise their young in the late spring and summer.

**Pinnacles National Park.** ✉ *5000 Hwy. 146, Paicines, CA* ☎ *831/389–4486* 🌐 *nps.gov/pinn* 🎫 *$30 per vehicle.*

## GRIFFITH PARK AND OBSERVATORY

Most visitors barely skim the surface of this gorgeous spot in L.A.'s Santa Monica Mountains, but those in the know will tell you there's more to the Griffith Observatory than its sweeping views and stunning Greek Revival architecture. To start, this free-to-the-public mountaintop observatory is home to the Samuel Oschin Planetarium, a state-of-the-art theater with an aluminum dome and a Zeiss star projector that plays a number of ticketed shows. Those spectacular shows are complemented by a couple of space-related exhibits, and several telescopes (naturally), as well as theater programs and events at the Leonard Nimoy Event Horizon Theater. For a fantastic view, come and watch the dazzling sunset.

**Do This:** One of the country's largest municipal parks, 4,310-acre Griffith Park is a must for nature lovers, the perfect spot for respite from the hustle and bustle of the surrounding urban areas. Bronson Canyon (where the Batcave from the 1960s *Batman* TV series is located) and Crystal Springs are favorite picnic spots. Here, in addition to Griffith Observatory, you'll find the Los Angeles Zoo, the Greek Theater, two golf courses, hiking and bridle trails, a swimming pool, a merry-go-round, and an outdoor train museum.

**Griffith Park.** ✉ *2800 E. Observatory Rd., Los Angeles, CA* ☎ *213/473–0800* 🌐 *griffithobservatory.org* 🎫 *Free.*

## HUNTINGTON LIBRARY

If you have time for just one stop in Pasadena, be sure to see this sprawling estate built for railroad tycoon Henry E. Huntington in the early 1900s. The library contains more than 700,000 books and 4 million manuscripts, but be sure to spend time in the Botanical Gardens, which include one of the world's largest groups of mature cacti and other succulents. The Shakespeare Garden, meanwhile, blooms with plants mentioned in Shakespeare's works; the Japanese Garden features an authentic ceremonial teahouse built in Kyoto in the 1960s; and the Chinese Garden, which is among the largest outside of China, sinews around waveless pools.

**Do This:** As seen in the New Year's Day Tournament of Roses Parade, the Norton Simon Museum has one of the finest collections of Western and Asian art on the West Coast. Head down to the bottom floor to see temporary exhibits and phenomenal Southeast Asian and Indian sculptures and artifacts, and don't miss a living-artwork outdoors: the garden, conceived by noted Southern California landscape designer Nancy Goslee Power. The tranquil pond was inspired by Monet's gardens at Giverny.

**Huntington Library.** ✉ *1151 Oxford Rd., San Marino, CA* ☎ *626/405–2100* 🌐 *huntington.org* 🎫 *From $25.*

## POINT REYES NATIONAL SEASHORE

One of the Bay Area's most spectacular treasures and the only national seashore on the West Coast, this 71,000-acre national seashore encompasses hiking trails, secluded beaches, dramatic cliffs, and rugged grasslands as well as Point Reyes itself, a triangular peninsula that juts into the Pacific. The infamous San Andreas Fault runs along the park's eastern edge and up the center of Tomales Bay; take the short Earthquake Trail from the visitor center to see the impact near the epicenter of the 1906 earthquake that devastated San Francisco. In late winter and spring, take the short walk at Chimney Rock, just before the park's oft-photographed lighthouse, to the Elephant Seal Overlook. Even from the cliff, the male seals look enormous as they spar, growling and bloodied, for resident females.

**Do This:** The small gateway town of Point Reyes Station has several noteworthy galleries and boutiques, plus some excellent places to eat. Among these, don't miss Cowgirl Creamery, which occupies a former hay barn. In addition to more than 200 fine cheeses—local, regional, and international—you'll find delicious deli items, gourmet goodies, and wines to pack for a perfect seashore picnic.

**Point Reyes National Seashore.** ☎ *415/464–5100* 🌐 *nps.gov/pore.*

## SAN FRANCISCO'S CASTRO DISTRICT

The social, political, and cultural center of San Francisco's thriving LGBTQ community, the Castro stands at the western end of Market Street. This neighborhood is one of the city's liveliest and most welcoming, especially on weekends. Streets teem with folks out shopping, pushing political causes, heading to art films, and lingering in bars and cafés. An 18-foot-long rainbow flag flies above Harvey Milk Plaza, named for late activist and openly gay member of the San Francisco Board of Supervisors who was tragically assassinated, along with Mayor George Moscone, in 1977. It's well worth venturing a few blocks southeast to laze on the lawn at Dolores Park, a two-square-block microcosm of life in the adjacent—and famously eclectic—Mission District.

**Do This:** A classic way to join in a beloved Castro tradition: grab some popcorn and catch a flick at the 1,500-seat art deco Castro Theatre. Built in 1922, it's the grandest of San Francisco's few remaining movie palaces. The neon marquee, which stands at the top of the Castro strip, is the neighborhood's great landmark.

**Castro District.** ✉ *Castro and Market Sts., San Francisco, CA* 🌐 *castromerchants.com.*

### SHOW TAPINGS IN LOS ANGELES

If you really want to see how the sausage is made in Hollywood, there's no better way than witnessing a live show taping. Dozens of sitcoms, talk shows, and game shows film every day in Los Angeles, and you can get tickets to be an audience member. The official Visit California Tourism Board has a helpful guide with multiple sites for where you can buy tickets. Just remember, go early, plan ahead, and try to keep quiet on the set.

**Do This:** Talk shows like Jimmy Kimmel Live! and the Late Late Show with James Corden are top experiences for those who want to be part of a live audience and see the stars in person. See how you can score tickets at 🌐 *www.discoverlosangeles.com*

### WINCHESTER MYSTERY HOUSE

Even setting aside claims of its being haunted and its having a bizarre layout that includes stairs and doorways that lead to nowhere, this leviathan 160-room room mansion with 52 skylights, 17 chimneys, and 6 kitchens ranks among one of the most strangely captivating homes in the country. Built over several decades by the widow of Winchester firearms magnate William Winchester, the palatial Queen Anne–style estate on the west side of San Jose is one of the Bay Area's most curious attractions.

**Do This:** On self-guided audio tours, you can explore this fascinating home as well as the impressive gardens. Afterward, stop for a tour of another amazing—if less idiosyncratic—654-acre estate, Filoli house and garden, midway between San Jose and San Francisco.

**Winchester Mystery House.** ✉ *525 S. Winchester Blvd., San Jose, CA* ☎ *408/247–2000* 🌐 *winchestermysteryhouse.com* 🎟 *From $10.*

## Cool Places to Stay

**The Ahwahnee.** One of the most famous historic lodges in the U.S. national park system, this landmark hotel is constructed of sugar-pine logs and features Native American design motifs; public spaces are enlivened with art deco flourishes, Persian rugs, and elaborate iron- and woodwork. ✉ *1 Ahwahnee Dr., Yosemite Village, CA* ☎ *888/413–8869* 🌐 *travelyosemite.com* $ *From $748.*

**AutoCamp Russian River.** Nestled amid the soaring redwood trees of Sonoma County's hip yet rustic Russian River region, this stylish glamping getaway consists of beautifully outfitted vintage Airstream and other trailers as well as nicely adorned canvas tents. ✉ *14120 Old Cazadero Rd., Guerneville, CA* ☎ *888/405–7553* 🌐 *autocamp.com/russian-river* $ *From $219.*

**Chateau de Vie.** With its creeper-covered walls, gardens of lavender and roses, lap pool, and views of a vineyard that produces the inn's own first-rate Cabernet Sauvignon, this lovely five-room retreat in northern Napa Valley captures the elegance and sophistication of this world-class wine country. ✉ *3250 Hwy. 128, Calistoga, CA* ☎ *877/558–2513* 🌐 *cdvnapavalley.com* $ *From $269.*

**Elk Meadow Cabins.** From the porches of these beautifully restored 1,200-square-foot former mill workers' cottages in the heart of Redwood National and State Parks, guests often see Roosevelt elk meandering in the meadows. ✉ *7 Green Valley Camp Rd., Orick, CA* ☎ *707/488–2222* 🌐 *elkmeadowcabins.com* $ *From $274.*

**Hotel del Coronado.** As much of a draw today as it was when it opened in 1888, the Victorian-style "Hotel Del" is always alive with activity, as guests—including U.S. presidents and celebrities—and tourists marvel at the fanciful architecture and ocean views. ✉ *1500 Orange Ave., San Diego, CA* ☎ *619/435–6611* 🌐 *hoteldel.com* $ *From $237.*

**Inn at Death Valley.** Built in 1927, this adobe brick–and–stone lodge in one of the park's greenest oases has been extensively renovated and offers Death Valley National Park's most luxurious accommodations, including 22 contemporary one- and two-bedroom casitas. ✉ *Hwy. 190, Death Valley, CA* ☎ *760/786–2345* 🌐 *oasisatdeathvalley.com* $ *From $509.*

**Madonna Inn.** From its rococo bathrooms to its pink-on-pink froufrou steak house, the Madonna Inn is a fabulous if incredibly kitschy getaway in the heart of the Central Coast wine country, and features some of the most playfully bizarre theme rooms in the state—the suites with rock-waterfall showers are especially fun. ✉ *100 Madonna Rd., San Luis Obispo, CA* ☎ *805/543–3000* 🌐 *madonnainn.com* $ *From $219.*

**Mark Hopkins InterContinental.** The circular redbrick drive of this towering 1926 Nob Hill architectural landmark leads to an opulent lobby, and the legendary rooftop lounge, the Top of the Mark, offers a breathtaking near-360-degree view of San Francisco. ✉ *999 California St., San Francisco, CA* ☎ *415/392–3434* 🌐 *intercontinentalmarkhopkins.com* $ *From $195.*

**Nick's Cove.** When you wake up in one of the smartly appointed cottages on stilts at this cool little compound on the border between Sonoma and Marin counties, through your picture window you'll see clear across Tomales Bay toward Hog Island (famous for its oysters) and the upper end of Point Reyes Peninsula. ✉ *23240 Hwy. 1, Marshall, CA* ☎ *415/663–1033* 🌐 *nickscove.com* $ *From $415.*

**Orbit In.** The fabulous mid-century modern architectural style of this hip inn on a quiet backstreet dates back to its 1955 opening—and nearly flat roofs, wide overhangs, glass everywhere—and the period feel continues inside. ✉ *562 W. Arenas Rd., Palm Springs, CA* ☎ *760/323–3585* 🌐 *orbitin.com* $ *From $150.*

**Palihotel.** Catering to young and hip budget travelers who crave style over space, this design-centric boutique property on Melrose Avenue is in the heart of Hollywood's best shopping and dining, including on-site hot spot Severance. ✉ *7950 Melrose Ave., Los Angeles, CA* ☎ *323/272–4588* 🌐 *palisociety.com* $ *From $163.*

**Queen Mary Hotel.** Experience the golden age of transatlantic travel without the seasickness: a 1936 art deco style reigns on the permanently docked *Queen Mary*, from the ship's mahogany paneling to its nickel-plated doors to the majestic Grand Salon. ✉ *1126 Queens Hwy., Long Beach, CA* ☎ *562/435–3511* 🌐 *queenmary.com* $ *From $121.*

**Treebones Resort.** Perched on a hilltop surrounded by national forest and stunning, unobstructed ocean views, this yurt resort provides a stellar back-to-nature experience along with creature comforts and the funky, tranquil vibe of Big Sur. ✉ *71895 Hwy. 1, South Big Sur, CA* ☎ *805/927–2390* 🌐 *treebonesresort.com* $ *From $340.*

# Hawaii

Hawaii overflows with natural beauty. Piercing the surface of the Pacific from the ocean floor, the Hawaiian Islands are garlanded with soft sand beaches and dramatic volcanic cliffs. Long days of sunshine and fairly mild year-round temperatures make this an all-season destination, and the islands' offerings—from urban Honolulu on Oahu to the luxury resorts of Maui to the natural wonders of Kauai and the Big Island—appeal to all kinds of visitors. Less-developed Lanai and Molokai are quieter, but all the islands are rich in Hawaiian culture.

## Bucket List Picks

The following boxes contain our picks for the top sights and experiences in Hawaii.

- ○ Waikiki
- ○ Honolulu's Kapahulu Avenue
- ○ Oahu's North Shore
- ○ Pearl Harbor
- ○ Molokai's Kalaupapa Peninsula
- ○ Old Lahaina Luau
- ○ The Road to Hana
- ○ Haleakala Summit
- ○ The Kohala and Kona Coasts
- ○ Kona Coffee Farms
- ○ Hawaii's Cowboy Country
- ○ Hawaii Volcanoes National Park
- ○ Kauai's Napali Coast
- ○ Waimea Canyon
- ○ Kauai's Waterfalls

# Waikiki

## Hawaii's Most Famous Beach

Hawaii's most famous 2-mile stretch of sand has an undeniable appeal, and it's a must when you visit Oahu. Waikiki's beach, capped at one end by the volcanic peak of Diamond Head, is gorgeous. You can visit historic palaces like the Moana Surfrider and the Royal Hawaiian, sip mai tais and nosh on pu pu platters at a slew of waterfront restaurants, take surfing lessons or ride in an outrigger canoe, or curl up on a beach blanket with that someone special (and thousands of others) while you enjoy the sunshine and soft ocean breezes. Waikiki is known for its wealth of nightspots, including the majority of Hawaii's LGBTQ hangouts.

## Don't Miss

The views from Diamond Head State Monument, a 760-foot extinct volcano, extend from Honolulu in one direction and Koko Head in the other, and even as far as Maui and Molokai on a clear day. Surfers and windsurfers are scattered like confetti on the cresting waves below. For this awesome view, drive to the crater and hike the ¾-mile trail to the top.

## Best Beach

An easy stroll from Waikiki's main drag, Fort DeRussy Beach Park is one of the finest beaches on the south side of Oahu. The soft, white sand and gently lapping waves makes it a family favorite. 🌐 *fortderussyhawaii.com.*

## When to Go

Waikiki is sunny and beautiful year-round, but is most crowded from mid-December to April.

## Getting Here and Around

On the southeastern side of Honolulu, Waikiki is easily reached from every-where town.

# Honolulu's Kapahulu Avenue

### The Best Old-School Hawaiian Food

Snaking northward from Waikiki Beach, Kapahulu Avenue isn't ready for its closeup and it's not at all trendy. But if you're looking to sample Hawaii's most famous treats, this is your go-to place. Sample plate lunches of loco moco or roast pork with gravy and generous sides at the Rainbow Drive-In, and ahi tuna poke bowls at Ono Seafood. And don't miss Leonard's Bakery for guava-filled Portuguese-style malasada doughnuts. At the Side Street Inn, you might spy some of Honolulu's most celebrated chefs getting their fix of lilikoi-glazed barbecue ribs.

### Don't Miss

Hope you saved room for dessert! Longtime local favorite Waiola Shave Ice specializes in the state's cherished frozen treat: powdery shave ice drizzled with syrup in flavors like lychee or haupia (coconut cream), and crowned with toppings like condensed milk and azuki beans.

### Best Breakfast

Diamond Head Market & Grill serves tantalizing, creative Hawaii fare all day long, but is especially great for breakfast dishes like coconut-macadamia pancakes. 🌐 *diamondheadmarket.com.*

### When to Go

Many of the restaurants along this strip keep very late hours, making Kapahulu Avenue lively and fun for an early lunch or a post-clubbing feast.

### Getting Here and Around

Most of the restaurants along Kapahulu are within a safe and easy walk or a short drive from Waikiki hotels.

**Kapahulu Avenue.** ✉ *Kapahulu Ave., between Kalakaua Ave. and I–H1, Honolulu, HI* 🌐 *gohawaii.com/islands/oahu.*

# Oahu's North Shore

## The Best Surfing Beaches in Hawaii

A relaxing respite from Honolulu's hustle and bustle, Oahu's North Shore is about roadside fruit stands and shrimp shacks, pretty parks and sandy shores, and endearing tourist traps. A beautiful bird sanctuary and a lush nature are among the dozens of reasons to stop between the plantation town of Kahuku and the surf meccas of Pupukea, Waimea Bay, and Haleiwa. Don't miss the sugary sands of Pupukea Beach Park, one of the best places in the state to watch world-class surfers.

## Don't Miss

As you make your way up the coast from Kaneohe, stop at Byodo-In Temple, where a meditation pavilion is set dramatically against the sheer, green cliffs of the Koolau Mountains. Tucked away in the back of the Valley of the Temples cemetery is a replica of the 11th-century Temple at Uji.

## Best Shrimp Truck

If you're looking to try the North Shore's favorite treat, you can't go wrong with the long-running Giovanni's Original in Haleiwa. You may have to wait in a long line, but all is forgiven when you're handed a platter of hot-and-spicy shrimp or garlicky scampi. 🌐 *giovannisshrimptruck.com.*

## When to Go

For catching the biggest surfing waves, November to February are best. But the North Shore is a beautiful drive all year.

## Getting Here and Around

The most enjoyable way to make this trip from Honolulu is via scenic Kamehameha Highway. Allow 90 minutes without stops. If time is short, it's a more direct 45-minute drive taking the H1 and H2 and then Highway 99 to Waialua.

**North Shore.** 🌐 *gohawaii.com/islands/oahu.*

# Pearl Harbor

## America's Most Poignant WWII Memorial

Just west of Honolulu, the World War II Valor in the Pacific National Monument preserves four different World War II sites at Pearl Harbor, including the USS *Arizona* Memorial. On December 7, 1941, the Japanese bombed Pearl Harbor, bringing the United States into World War II. The starting point for visitors is the Pearl Harbor Visitor Center, which contains moving exhibits featuring photographs and personal memorabilia from veterans. This is also where you start your tour of the USS *Arizona* Memorial, which was destroyed by a Japanese bomber and lies precisely where it sank. The USS *Bowfin* claimed to have sunk 44 enemy ships during World War II and now serves as the centerpiece of a museum honoring all submariners. Another key site is the Battleship *Missouri* Memorial, where the Japanese signed their Terms of Surrender after World War II.

## Don't Miss

The excellent Pearl Harbor Aviation Museum documents the history of aviation in the Pacific during World War II. It's in two hangars that survived the Japanese attack on Pearl Harbor. ⊕ *www.pearlharboraviation-museum.org.*

## Best Resort

About 20 miles west of Pearl Harbor at Oahu's Ko Olina resort, Aulani is Disney's first property in Hawaii. It melds the Disney magic with breathtaking vistas, white sandy beaches, and sunsets that even Mickey stops to watch. ⊕ *disneyaulani.com.*

## Getting Here and Around

Pearl Harbor is 3 miles northwest of the airport in Honolulu.

**Pearl Harbor National Memorial.** ✉ *1 Arizona Memorial Pl., Honolulu, HI* ☎ *808/422–3399* ⊕ *www.nps.gov/perl* 🎟 *Free.*

# Molokai's Kalaupapa Peninsula

## The Loneliest Place on Earth

One of the most remote areas in the Hawaiian Islands, the Kalaupapa Peninsula is a place of stunning natural beauty coupled with a tragic past. It's here on a strip of land hemmed in by the world's tallest sea cliffs that residents of Hawaii who displayed symptoms of Hansen's disease were permanently exiled between 1866 and 1969. A visit to Kalaupapa National Historical Park is a profound, once-in-a-lifetime experience. You must book a tour that arrives either by plane or—for a memorable experience—by descending on foot or by mule down (and later back up) a 2,000-foot cliff. Walking tours take you through the settlement and to several historic buildings and an excellent museum.

## Don't Miss

With its narrow rock walls arching out from the shoreline, Ali'i Fishpond is typical of the numerous such ponds that define southern Molokai.

## Best Restaurant

Close to the trailhead for Kalaupapa, the laid-back Kualapuu Cookhouse is a local favorite set in a refurbished green-and-white plantation house that's decorated with local photos and artwork and accented with a shady lanai.

## Getting Here and Around

There are flights to Molokai throughout the day from the neighboring islands of Maui and Oahu. Access to the park is by guided tour only, and visitation is capped at 100 people per day.

**Kalaupapa Peninsula.** ✉ *Kalaupapa National Historical Park, Molokai, HI* ☎ *808/567–6802* 🌐 *nps.gov/kala* 🎟 *Free.*

# Old Lahaina Luau

### Immerse Yourself in Hawaiian Culture

Considered the best luau on Maui, Old Lahaina is certainly among the most traditional. Before the show starts, immerse yourself in Hawaiian culture by watching a traditional *imu* (underground oven) being unearthed. Sitting either at a table or on a *lauhala* (mat made of leaves), you feast on such traditional Hawaiian cuisine as pork *laulau* (wrapped with taro sprouts in ti leaves), ahi poke (raw tuna salad), diced *lomilomi* salmon (a traditional Hawaiian side dish), and *haupia* (coconut-milk pudding). Talented performers will charm you with beautiful music, powerful chanting, and a variety of dances, from *kahiko* (the ancient way of communicating with the gods) to *auana* (the modern hula).

### Don't Miss

The capital of Hawaii from 1820 to 1845, when it was also one of the world's top whaling ports, Lahaina is a bustling waterfront town that, while filled with more than a few souvenir sellers, stands out for its historic architecture, excellent art galleries, and pretty harbor.

### Best Museum

Smack-dab in the center of colorful Front Street, the eye-catching Wo Hing Museum reflects the importance of Chinese immigrants to Lahaina. 🌐 *lahainarestoration.org.*

### When to Go

Old Lahaina Luau takes place daily, and this dry and pretty side of Maui enjoys pleasant weather year-round.

### Getting Here and Around

Lahaina is on Maui's northwest coast, off Highway 30, just south of the popular Kaanapali resort area.

**Old Lahaina Luau.** ✉ *1251 Front St., Lahaina, HI* ☎ *808/667–1998* 🌐 *oldlahainaluau.com.* 🎫 *$145.*

# The Road to Hana

## Hawaii's Most Thrilling Drive

The 55-mile Road to Hana is one of Hawaii's most exciting experiences—and arguably one of the most beautiful drives on the planet. It begins in the port town of Kahului and ends in the rustic village of Hana on the island's rain-gouged windward side. Many travelers venture further to Ohe'o Gulch, where you can cool off in basalt-lined pools and waterfalls. You'll want to slow the passage of time to take in foliage-hugged ribbons of road and roadside banana-bread stands, to swim beneath a waterfall, and to absorb the lush Maui tropics in all their glory.

## Don't Miss

A black-sand beach fringed with palms, Hana's gorgeous Waianapanapa State Park will remain in your memory long after your visit. Stairs lead through a tunnel of interlocking Polynesian hau (a native tree) branches to a cave pool. In the other direction, a dramatic 3-mile coastal path continues past sea arches and blowholes all the way to Hana.

## Best Restaurant

Fish kebabs and poke bowls are just a few of the always-changing choices at Hana Fresh. The organic produce comes from the restaurant's own farm. 🌐 *hanafresh.org*.

## Getting Here and Around

Without stops, Highway 360 takes a couple of hours, but give yourself at least twice that to enjoy the diversions along the way. A return option is to follow Highway 360 completely around the rugged southeast side of the island. This is a rough road in places, so allow at least three hours, but the stunning scenery as you climb through Maui's Upcountry makes this option very appealing, especially if you break up the trip with an overnight in Hana.

# Haleakala Summit

## The Most Beautiful Sunrise

Nowhere else on Earth can you drive from sea level to 10,023 feet in only 38 miles. And what's more shocking: in that short vertical ascent to the summit of the volcano Haleakala you'll journey from lush, tropical foliage to the stark, moonlike basin of the volcano's enormous crater. Established in 1916, Haleakala National Park covers an astonishing 33,222 acres, with the Haleakala Crater as its centerpiece. There's terrific hiking, but the most remarkable activity is viewing the sunrise or—if you're unable to secure a coveted reservation—the similarly stunning sunset.

## Don't Miss

The west-facing upper slope of Haleakala is Maui's Upcountry, and this picturesque region is responsible for most of the island's produce. Cowboys still work the fields of the historic 18,000-acre Ulupalakua Ranch and the 30,000-acre Haleakala Ranch, and the charming town of Makawao is famous for its *paniolo* (Hawaiian cowboy) culture.

## When to Go

Haleakala can have dramatic weather, and it's typically 30 degrees cooler up here than on the coast. Winter can be especially chilly, so call for the latest conditions before driving up.

## Getting Here and Around

The summit of Haleakala is reached via Highways 378, 377, and 37 from the island's largest town, Kahului. The drive takes about 45 minutes.

**Haleakala National Park.** ✉ *Haleakala Hwy., Kula, HI* ☎ *808/572–4400* 🌐 *nps.gov/hale* 🎟 *$30.*

# The Kohala and Kona Coasts

## The Big Island's Sunniest Beaches

The Big Island's—and some of the archipelago's—most beautiful beaches flank the lava-sculpted shores of the Kohala Coast. One of the best spots to explore is Kealakekua Bay State Historical Park, an underwater marine reserve with dramatic cliffs that surround super-deep turquoise water chock-full of stunning coral pinnacles and tropical fish. The Captain James Cook Monument, marking where the explorer died, stands at the northern edge of the bay. A gorgeous, expansive stretch of white sand fringed with coco palms, Anaehoomalu Bay fronts the Waikoloa Beach Marriott and is a perfect spot for swimming, windsurfing, snorkeling, and diving.

## Don't Miss

Puukohola Heiau National Historic Site is one of the most historic sites in all of Hawaii. It was here in 1810, on top of Puukohola (Hill of the Whale), that Kamehameha the Great built the war *heiau*, or temple, that would serve to unify the Hawaiian Islands, ending 500 years of almost continual warring chiefdoms. 🌐 *www.nps.gov/puhe/index.htm*.

## Best Beach Bar

The dining lanai at Huggo's overlooks the ocean's edge, and at night you can almost touch the marine life swimming below. Relax with cocktails and feast on fresh local seafood. On the Rocks, right next door, is a popular outdoor bar in the sand. 🌐 *huggos.com*.

## When to Go

The Big Island's Kona Coast is dry and sunny year-round. Resorts tend to be priciest during the mid-December to April high season.

## Getting Here and Around

The Big Island's biggest airport lies smack in the middle of the region, and Highways 19 and 11 hug the coastline.

# Kona Coffee Farms

### Hawaii's Richest Crop

Roughly 600 coffee farms dot the western Kona Coast of Hawaii's Big Island, each producing flavorful coffee grown in the rich, volcanic soil. You can learn about this storied industry at the Kona Coffee Living History Farm, a meticulously preserved farm that includes a 1913 farmhouse surrounded by coffee trees, a Japanese bathhouse, a *kuriba* (coffee-processing mill), and a *hoshidana* (traditional drying platform). Among the excellent coffee plantations open to visitors, Lions Gate Farms stands out for its spectacular ocean views. The coffee is processed in a mill that dates from 1942. Tours given by the friendly proprietors proudly show visitors how coffee beans and macadamia nuts are cultivated and harvested.

### Don't Miss

Much of the coffee scene is centered on the artsy village of Holualoa, which hugs the hillside along the Kona Coast, 3 miles up winding Hualalai Road from Kailua-Kona. Galleries here feature all types of artists—painters, woodworkers, jewelers, and potters.

### Best Coffeehouse

A fantastic stop before or after a morning of snorkeling at Kealakekua Bay, the Coffee Shack offers amazing views of the Honaunau Coast. 🌐 *coffeeshack.com.*

### When to Go

The Kona coffee region is pleasant year-round but tends to receive the driest weather from November (when the coffee festival takes place) through March.

### Getting Here and Around

Kona's coffee country is easily reached via Highway 11 just south of Kailua-Kona.

**Kona Coffee Farms.** 🌐 *gohawaii.com/islands/hawaii-big-island.*

# Hawaii's Cowboy Country

## Riding, Roping, and Rodeos

A half hour over the mountain from the Kohala Coast, Waimea offers a completely different experience than the rest of the Big Island. Lush green pastures dotted with cattle, men riding by on horseback, and signs advertising upcoming rodeos are common sights here in paniolo (cowboy) country. The spaces here are immense; for example, the 130,000-acre Parker Ranch is one of the largest privately held cattle ranches in the country. Paniolo Adventures offers horseback rides on a working cattle ranch, with spectacular views of three volcanoes and the coastline.

## Don't Miss

Near the birthplace of King Kamehameha, the charming towns of Hawi and Kapaau thrived during the sugar-plantation days. Both are full of lovingly restored vintage buildings housing fun and funky shops and galleries, as well as noteworthy eateries. A must-see is Pololu Valley Beach, which you reach via a 15-minute hike down a steep, rocky trail.

## Best Restaurant

This signature restaurant of Peter Merriman, one of the pioneers of Hawaii regional cuisine, Merriman's is the home of the original wok-charred ahi. 🌐 *www.merrimanshawaii.com/waimea*.

## When to Go

This sunny part of the island is beautiful year-round. Because Waimea is at a higher elevation, it's cooler than the coast, making it a pleasant retreat on hot days.

## Getting Here and Around

Waimea is at the northern end of the island, right at the junction of scenic Highways 19 and 190. From here, it's a beautiful, half-hour upcountry drive on Highway 250 to Hawi.

# Hawaii Volcanoes National Park

## See What Will Erupt

Sprawling over 520 square miles and encompassing Kilauea and Mauna Loa, two of the five volcanoes that formed the Big Island nearly half a million years ago, this fascinating national park is one of the world's best places to see an active volcano. Kilauea, youngest and most rambunctious of the Hawaiian volcanoes, has been flowing lava off and on over the past several decades. More than 150 miles of trail traverse the park's wide expanses of aa (rough) and pahoehoe (smooth) lava. The best way to explore the summit of Kilauea is to cruise along Crater Rim Drive to Kilauea Overlook, from which you can see all of Kilauea Caldera and Halemaumau Crater, an awesome depression in Kilauea Caldera measuring 3,000 feet across and nearly 300 feet deep.

## Don't Miss

One of the park's star attractions, the Thurston Lava Tube spans 600 feet underground. The massive tube, discovered in 1913, was formed by hot molten lava traveling through the channel. To reach the entrance of the tube, descend a series of stairs surrounded by lush foliage and the sounds of native birds.

## Best Drive

The park's coastal region is accessed via Chain of Craters Road, which descends 19 miles to sea level. The scenic road winds past ancient craters and modern eruption sites.

## Getting Here and Around

The park is on the southeast side of the island, off Highway 11, 30 miles from Hilo.

**Kilauea Visitor Center.** ✉ *1 Crater Rim Dr., Volcano, HI* ☎ *808/985–6011* 🌐 *nps.gov/havo* 🎫 *$30 per vehicle.*

# Kauai's Napali Coast

## Towering Sea Cliffs

After seeing the overwhelming beauty of the Napali Coast, many are at a loss for words. Kauai's northwestern coastline is cut by a series of small valleys, like fault lines, running to the interior, with the resulting cliffs seeming to bend back on themselves like an accordion-folded fan made of green velvet. More than 5 million years old, these sea cliffs rise thousands of feet above the Pacific. There are three ways to experience this coastline—by air, by water, or on foot. A helicopter tour is your best bet if you're strapped for time. Boat tours are great for family fun; and hiking is the most budget-friendly and potentially invigorating option. Hiking just the first 2 miles of the famed 11-mile Kalalau Trail offers a tremendous sense of the Napali Coast's grandeur.

## Don't Miss

A must-stop on the road to the Napali Coast, Hanalei offers a look at old-world Hawaii, including working taro farms, poi making, and evenings of throwing horseshoes at Black Pot Beach Park. The beach and river offer-snorkeling, surfing, and kayaking.

## Best Tour

Blue Hawaiian Helicopters flies some of Hawaii's roomiest choppers, each with space for six passengers, and offers unparalleled viewing of the Napali Coast and Manawaiopuna Falls, which appears famously in *Jurassic Park*. *bluehawaiian.com*.

## Getting Here and Around

The Napali Coast's Kalalau Trail starts at the end of Highway 560; the well-marked trailhead is at the west end of Kee Beach.

**Napali Coast State Wilderness Park.** *Hwy. 560, Kapaa, HI* *907/376–5155* *dlnr.hawaii.gov* *Free.*

# Waimea Canyon

## The Grand Canyon of the Pacific

Carved over countless centuries by the Waimea River and the forces of wind and rain, this dramatic gorge on Kauai's southwest side is one of the state's most remarkable sites. Trails wind through the canyon, which is 3,567 feet deep, 2 miles wide, and 10 miles long. Over the eons, the cliff sides have sharply eroded, exposing swatches of colorful soil. The deep red, brown, and green hues are constantly changing in the sun, and frequent rainbows and waterfalls enhance the natural beauty. A favorite hike is the Awaawapuhi Trail, with 1,600 feet of elevation gain, that ends with a dramatic descent along a spiny ridge to a perch overlooking the ocean.

## Don't Miss

Adjacent Kokee State Park contains 4,345 acres of wilderness park, including large tracts of native ohia and koa forest and many varieties of native plants.

## Best Sunset Sail

Offering several catamaran sails out of Port Allen, a 10-minute drive east of Waimea, Capt. Andy's Sailing Adventures offers a wonderful four-hour sunset tour that curves up along the Napali Coast. 🌐 *napali.com.*

## When to Go

The parks' higher elevation can translate to cool and wet weather, especially in winter and on the Kokee side, but even then it's pleasant.

## Getting Here and Around

Waimea Canyon lies at the southwest end of the island, on Highway 550, about 11 scenic miles north of the town of Waimea.

**Waimea Canyon State Park.** ✉ *Hwy. 550, Waimea, HI* 🌐 *dlnr.hawaii.gov/dsp/parks/kauai/waimea-canyon-state-park* 🎫 *$10.*

# Kauai's Waterfalls

### Splash Into Fantasy Island

Kauai's mighty Wailua River produces many dramatic waterfalls. Tucked away in the lush landscape near Lihue on the island's East Side, Wailua Falls is an impressive, cascading double-tiered waterfall best known from appearing in the opening sequences of the *Fantasy Island* television series. Kauai has plenty of other noteworthy waterfalls, but this one is especially gorgeous, easy to find, and easy to photograph.

### Don't Miss

Opaekaa (pronounced "oh-piekah-ah") Falls is just a short walk away. It plunges hundreds of feet to the pool below and can be easily viewed from scenic overlook Opaekaa Falls Lookout, with ample parking. Fun fact: Opaekaa means "rolling shrimp," which refers to tasty native crustaceans that were once so abundant they could be seen tumbling in the falls.

### Falls On Other Islands

While the Garden Island is home to many beautiful waterfalls, it's not the only place to check this bucket list item off your list. The Big Island is home to cascades like Manoa Falls and on Molokai, Oloupena Falls is Hawaii's tallest waterfall at more than 3,000 feet.

### While You're Here

It's a 40-minute drive to the South Shore from Wailua Falls, but herein, near Poipu, lies one of Kauai's other spectactular water features: Spouting Horn. The Old Faithful of Hawaii, this geyser created from a lava tube under the surface shoots water as high as 50 feet and legend has it was once guarded by a lizard.

### Getting Here and Around

To reach Wailua Falls, drive north from Lihue (Kauai's capital) following Maalo Road in Hanamaulu, then travel uphill for 3 miles.

# When in Hawaii

## KECK OBSERVATORY

Located at 13,796 feet on the sometimes snowy summit of Maunakea, the pair of 10-meter optical/infrared telescopes at W. H. Keck Observatory are used by leading astronomers to make astounding discoveries, thanks in part to their location far above the turbulence of the atmosphere. Because a four-wheel-drive vehicle is required to go beyond the 9,200-foot Onizuka Visitors Center, the best way to get here is by booking a stargazing tour. Several outfitters—Hawaii Forest and Trail and Mauna Kea Summit Adventures are a couple of excellent ones—offer these eight-hour trips, which include dinner, sunsets, and stargazing while you sip cocoa.

**Do This:** If you're not able to get to the summit, visit the W. M. Keck Observatory Headquarters Visitor Center in downtown Waimea. Renowned speakers present occasional free astronomy talks.

**W. M. Keck Observatory Visitor Center.** ✉ *65-1120 Mamalahoa Hwy., Waimea, HI* ☎ *808/885–7887* 🌐 *keckobservatory.org.*

## IAO VALLEY STATE MONUMENT

When Mark Twain saw this emerald expanse in the center of West Maui, he dubbed it the "Yosemite of the Pacific." An exaggeration perhaps, but this is a lovely valley with the curious Iao Needle, a natural stone pillar that rises some 1,200 feet above the park's junglelike topography. Ascend the stairs up to the Iao Needle for spectacular views of Central Maui. The park has some short strolls on paved paths where you can stop and meditate by the edge of a brook or marvel at the native plants. Mist often rises if it's rainy, which makes being here even more magical.

**Do This:** A repository of the largest and best collection of Hawaiian artifacts on Maui, Hale Hoikeike at the Bailey House contains objects from the sacred island of Kahoolawe. Erected in 1833 on the outskirts of Iao Valley on the site of the compound of Kahekili (the last ruling chief of Maui), the building was occupied by a family of missionary teachers until 1888. Surrounded by fragrant gardens, the museum contains missionary-period furniture that provide a snapshot of the island during his time. 🌐 *mauimuseum.org*

**Iao Valley State Monument.** ✉ *Iao Valley Rd., Wailuku, HI* ☎ *808/587–0300* 🌐 *hawaiistateparks.org* 🎟 *$10 per vehicle.*

## KANEMITSU'S BAKERY & COFFEE SHOP

Laid-back Molokai is perhaps the last island in Hawaii that you'd expect to find a James Beard–nominated restaurant. But here you'll find this quirky 1922 bakery, a veritable institution for morning coffee. During the day, regulars drop by for papaya bread, taro-glazed doughnuts, and cinnamon toast. But the real magic happens at night from 7:30 until 11 (midnight on weekends), when folks sniff their way down the alley to the hidden bakery window to pick up a loaf of hot bread, an insanely decadent confection that you can order with cream cheese, butter, strawberry and blueberry jam, sugar, or cinnamon. You can build your own with a combo of toppings or get "the works." One of these prodigious loaves is enough to share among several friends.

**Do This:** Built in 1877, the nicely restored R. W. Meyer Sugar Mill is a testament to Molokai's agricultural history. It is located next to the Molokai Museum and is usually included in the museum tour. Several interesting machines from the past are on display, including a mule-driven cane crusher. 🌐 *historichawaii.org/2014/03/03/r-w-meyer-sugar-mill.*

**Kanemitsu's Bakery & Coffee Shop.** ✉ *79 Ala Malama Ave., Kaunakakai, HI* ☎ *808/553–5855.*

## MAKENA BEACH STATE PARK

Locals successfully fought to turn Makena—one of Hawaii's most breathtaking beaches—into a state park. This southwestern Maui stretch of deep golden sand abutting sparkling aquamarine water is 3,000 feet long and 100 feet wide. It's sometimes referred to as Big Beach, but natives prefer its Hawaiian name, Oneloa. For a dramatic view of the beach, climb Puu Olai, the steep cinder cone near the park's first entrance. Continue on to discover Little Beach, which draws one of the more free-spirited crowds of any beach in the state, especially on Sundays, when there's a drumming circle and bonfire.

**Do This:** On your drive back from Makena Beach, arguably the best place for both oceanfront views and amazing food and drink is Morimoto, which turns out stellar Japanese fare with seating at the edge of the sleek Andaz Maui Resort's lagoon pool. 🌐 *www.morimotomaui.com.*

**Makena Beach State Park.** ✉ *4670 Makena Alanui, Kihei, HI* ☎ *808/587–0300* 🌐 *hawaiistateparks.org* 🎟 *$10 per car.*

## SHANGRI LA MUSEUM OF ISLAMIC ART, CULTURE & DESIGN

For more than 50 years, this home was a work in progress as heiress Doris Duke traveled the world, buying art and furnishings and picking up ideas for her Mughal Garden, for the Playhouse in the style of a 17th-century Irani pavilion, and for the water terraces and tropical gardens. At the time of her death in 1993, Duke stipulated that her home just southeast of Diamond Head become a public center for the study of Islamic art. The house is open only by guided tour, through the Honolulu Museum of Art. Book early, as tours fill up very quickly.

**Do This:** Downtown's excellent Honolulu Museum of Art is housed in a maze of courtyards, cloistered walkways, and quiet, low-ceiling spaces. There's an impressive permanent collection that includes an extensive collection of Hiroshige's ukiyo-e Japanese prints; Italian Renaissance paintings; and American and European art by Monet, van Gogh, and Whistler, among many others. 🌐 *honolulumuseum.org.*

**Shangri La Museum of Islamic Art, Culture & Design.** ✉ *4055 Papu Circle, Honolulu, HI* ☎ *808/532–3853* 🌐 *www.shangrilahawaii.org* 🎟 *$25.*

## SNORKELING ON LANAI

Snorkel trips are a great way to see the island of Lanai (the smallest inhabited Hawaiian Island), above and below the surface, and scuba divers can marvel at one of the top cave-dive spots in the Pacific. The best snorkeling on Lanai is at Hulopoe Beach and Manele Small Boat Harbor. Hulopoe, which is an exceptional snorkeling destination, has schools of manini that feed on the coral and coat the rocks with flashing silver. You can also easily view kala (unicorn fish), uhu (parrot fish), and papio (small trevally) in all their rainbow colors. Beware of rocks and surging waves. At Manele Harbor, there's a wade-in snorkel spot beyond the break wall. Enter over the rocks, just past the boat ramp. Do not enter if waves are breaking.

**Do This:** With an outfitter like Lanai Ocean Sports, you can take in the beauty of towering sea cliffs, playful spinner dolphins, and crystal-clear waters as you sail along Lanai's coastline, before arriving at Kaunolu, where King Kamehameha challenged his Hawaiian warriors to show their courage by cliff jumping. This intimate trip includes snorkel equipment, wet-suit tops, and stand-up paddleboards, plus a gourmet picnic lunch.

**Lanai Ocean Sports.** ✉ *Manele Small Boat Harbor, Manele Rd., Manele, Lanai City, HI* ☎ *808/866–8256* 🌐 *www.lanaioceansports.com* 🎟 *From $149.*

## Cool Places to Stay

**Falls at Reed's Island.** Overlooking a dramatic waterfall in the largest and most historic (although also rainiest) town on the Big Island, this tranquil three-bedroom vacation home surrounded by the lush rain forest is one of the region's most romantic accommodations. ✉ *286 Kaiulani St., Hilo, HI* ☎ *808/635–3649* 🌐 *reedsisland.com* 🎫 *From $398.*

**Hana-Maui Resort.** A destination in itself, this enchantingly remote and luxurious 75-room property at the end of the fabled Road to Hana still delivers the tropical Hawaii of your dreams. For additional peace and privacy, splurge with a stay in the Ocean Bungalows set on sprawling lawns overlooking the rugged coastline. ✉ *5031 Hana Hwy., Hana, HI* ☎ *808/400–1234* 🌐 *hyatt.com* [$] *From $559.*

**Lava Lava Beach Club.** Spend the day swimming at the beach just steps away from your private lanai and fall asleep to the sound of the ocean at one of four artfully decorated cottages on the sandy beach at Anaehoomalu Bay. ✉ *69-1081 Ku'uali'i Pl., Waikoloa Village, HI* ☎ *808/769–5282* 🌐 *lavalavabeachclub.com* 🎫 *From $299.*

**The Royal Hawaiian.** There's nothing like the iconic "Pink Palace of the Pacific," which sits on 14 acres of prime Waikiki Beach and has held fast to the luxury and grandeur that first defined it in the 1930s, when it became a favorite of the rich and famous. The Mai Tai Bar is Waikiki's most celebrated spot for sunset cocktails. ✉ *2259 Kalakaua Ave., Honolulu, HI* ☎ *808/923–7311* 🌐 *royal-hawaiian.com* [$] *From $332.*

**Sensei Lanai Four Seasons.** Among the five different Four Seasons resorts in Hawaii—and they're all incredible—this adults-only wellness retreat set among graceful pines at a crisp-aired elevation of 1,600 feet stands out for its blissful, utterly relaxing spa services, peaceful setting, and personalized service. ✉ *1 Keomoku Hwy., Lanai City, HI* ☎ *808/565–4500* 🌐 *fourseasons.com/sensei* 🎫 *From $650.*

**Volcano House.** Hawaii's oldest hotel—and the state's only national park lodge—is the ultimate destination if you want to spend the night on the edge of a volcanic crater. ✉ *1 Crater Rim Dr., Hawaii Volcanoes National Park, HI* ☎ *808/756–9625* 🌐 *hawaiivolcanohouse.com* 🎫 *From $189.*

**Waimea Plantation Cottages.** Originally built in the early 1900s, these one- to five-bedroom sugar-plantation cottages are tucked among coconut trees along a lovely, walkable stretch of beach on Kauai's sunny West Side. ✉ *9400 Kaumualii Hwy., Waimea, HI* ☎ *808/338–1923* 🌐 *coasthotels.com* 🎫 *From $199.*

# Oregon

Rugged beauty, locavore cuisine, and indie spirit are just some of Oregon's charms. The Pacific Northwest darling is home to hip Portland, whose happening foodie and arts scenes are anchored by an eco-friendly lifestyle. Smaller cities draw you in, too: you can sample microbrews in Bend, see top-notch theater in Ashland, and explore maritime history in Astoria. Miles of bike paths, hikes up Mt. Hood, and rafting in the Columbia River Gorge thrill outdoor enthusiasts. For pure relaxation, taste award-winning Willamette Valley wines and walk windswept Pacific beaches.

## Bucket List Picks

The following boxes contain our picks for the top sights and experiences in Oregon.

- ○ Portland's Washington and Forest Parks
- ○ Portland's East Side
- ○ The North Coast
- ○ Depoe Bay
- ○ Oregon Dunes National Recreation Area
- ○ The Willamette Valley
- ○ Historic Columbia River Highway
- ○ Mt. Hood
- ○ Bend
- ○ Crater Lake National Park
- ○ Oregon Shakespeare Festival
- ○ Wallowa Lake State Park
- ○ Astoria

# Portland's Washington and Forest Parks

### Lush Urban Spaces

One of the most unusual, and appealing, things about downtown Portland is its easy access to pristine nature. The city center fringes adjoining Forest Park and Washington Park, which contain several noteworthy attractions, including the Oregon Zoo, the World Forestry Center, and Hoyt Arboretum. The most glorious site of all is the International Rose Test Garden, which comprises three terraced gardens, where more than 10,000 bushes and some 550 varieties of roses flourish, peaking in June–July and again in September. Just a short stroll away, you can visit the serene Portland Japanese Garden, which unfolds over 12½ stunning acres and features five separate garden styles: Strolling Pond Garden, Tea Garden, Natural Garden, Sand and Stone Garden, and Flat Garden.

### Don't Miss

A local legend, and rightfully so, Powell's City of Books is the largest independent bookstore in the world, with more than 1.5 million new and used books along with a good selection of locally made gifts and goodies. 🌐 *powells.com*.

### Best Park

One of the nation's largest urban wildernesses, 5,157-acre Forest Park has more than 50 species of birds and mammals and more than 80 miles of trails through stands of Douglas fir, hemlock, and cedar. The 30-mile Wildwood Trail extends into adjoining Washington Park and to Pittock Mansion, with superb views of the skyline, rivers, and Mt. Hood and Mt. St. Helens.

### Getting Here and Around

You can reach Washington Park with a pleasant uphill stroll from downtown, or Bus 63.

## Portland's East Side

### Foodie Haven

To fully experience Oregon's largest city, you need to bike, stroll, and eat your way through its most lively and distinctive neighborhoods where you'll find the city's world-renowned food scene and a vast bounty of cool shops and galleries. A must-visit is the Alberta Arts District, an eclectic 1-mile stretch of indie arts spaces and cool bistros and bars. For the best people-watching, visit during a Last Thursday (of the month) art walk. Nearby are the similarly alluring North Mississippi and North Williams corridors, which buzz with sceney brewpubs, collectives, music venues, and an excellent food-cart pod, Mississippi Marketplace. Farther south, you'll find pockets of trendy food and retail in the Central East Side and Hawthorne.

### Don't Miss

A playground on top of a volcano cinder cone? You'll find it in the East Side's most magical swatch of greenery, 190-acre Mt. Tabor Park. Picnic tables and sports make it popular for outdoor recreation, but plenty of quiet, shaded trails and wide-open grassy lawns with panoramic views of the Downtown skyline appeal to sunbathers, hikers, and nature lovers.

### Best Food Carts

In a city famous for its distinctive food carts, Portland Mercado is a standout. This collection of some 40 businesses, including eateries as well as crafts vendors, is devoted to Latin culture and heritage. 🌐 *portlandmercado.org*.

### Getting Here and Around

These walkable East Side districts are easy to get to by bus or car, and it's usually easy to find street parking nearby.

# The North Coast

## Oregon's Most Stunning Beaches

From wide expanses of sand dotted with beach chairs to surf-shaped cliffs, Oregon's 300 miles of public coastline is the backdrop for thrills, serenity, rejuvenation, and romance. The pristine sections along the north coast, from Cannon Beach to Pacific City, are especially stunning. In the shadow of glorious 235-foot-tall Haystack Rock, family-friendly Cannon Beach is wide, flat, and perfect for exploring tide pools and taking romantic walks in the sea mist. Each June the town's sand-castle contest draws thousands of visitors. Nearby Ecola State Park is the place to spot whales during the twice-yearly migrations.

## Don't Miss

The Three Capes Loop, an enchanting 35-mile byway off U.S. 101, winds along the coast between Tillamook (take a tour, and grab a dish of marionberry ice cream, at the festive Tillamook Creamery) and Pacific City, passing three headlands: Cape Meares, Cape Lookout, and Cape Kiwanda.

## Best Hike

At Oswald West State Park, hike a half-mile trail to dramatic Short Sand Beach, a spectacular beach with caves and tidal pools that's famous for surfing. If you wish, continue with the arduous 5½-mile trek to the 1,680-foot summit of Neahkahnie Mountain for dazzling views south for many miles toward the surf, sand, and mountains.

## When to Go

Summer is high season and generally sunniest, but it's gorgeous here year-round, and storm-watching in winter is a highly popular pastime.

## Getting Here and Around

It's about a 90-minute drive from Portland via U.S. 26 the coast, which you can tour via stunning and rugged U.S. 101.

# Depoe Bay

## The West Coast's Best Whale-Watching

On Oregon's central coast, small but lively Depoe Bay is the whale-watching capital of the West Coast. With a narrow channel and deep water, its harbor is one of the smallest and most protected on the coast, making the charming beach town the place to spot massive whales migrating close to the shore. Get oriented at the small but excellent Whale, Sealife, and Shark Museum, whose marine biologist owner also operates the excellent Whale Research EcoExcursions tour company. The town's Whale Watching Center, perched on an oceanfront bluff, is a valuable resource. The observation deck offers fantastic views—you might see grays, humpbacks, and orcas along with a wide variety of seabirds and other sea mammals.

## Don't Miss

In nearby Newport, the 4½-acre Oregon Coast Aquarium brings visitors face-to-face with the creatures living in offshore and near-shore Pacific marine habitats: frolicking sea otters, colorful puffins, pulsating jellyfish, and even a several-hundred-pound octopus.

## Best Restaurant

At Local Ocean Seafood, retractable windows overlook Newport's picturesque Yaquina Bay. The operators purchase fish directly from the boats right outside. 🌐 *localocean.net*.

## When to Go

Any time of year you might spy resident gray whales off the Oregon Coast, but the winter (December) and spring (late March) migrations are the best periods for seeing other species.

## Getting Here and Around

Scenic U.S. 101 hugs the central Oregon shoreline.

**Depoe Bay.** 🌐 *discoverdepoebay.org*.

# Oregon Dunes National Recreation Area

## The Continent's Biggest and Wildest Sandbox

Along a 40-mile stretch of breathtaking, windswept coastline between Florence and Coos Bay, the largest expanse of coastal sand dunes in North America draws more than 1.5 million visitors annually. For those who just want to swim, relax, hike, and marvel at the amazing expanse of dunes against the ocean, there are spaces off-limits to motorized vehicles. About 25 miles south, there's also Bandon Dunes Golf Resort, one of the most vaunted links courses in America. But the area also contains some of the best ATV riding around. Honeyman Memorial State Park, 515 acres within the recreation area, is a base camp for dune-buggy enthusiasts, mountain bikers, and more.

## Don't Miss

The small but utterly enchanting town of Yachats (pronounced "yah-hots") lies at the mouth of the Yachats River, not far north of Oregon Dunes. Its rocky shoreline includes the highest vehicle-accessible lookout on the Oregon Coast, Cape Perpetua, which towers 800 feet above the rocky shoreline.

## Best Lighthouse

Some of the highest sand dunes surround Umpqua Lighthouse, a 65-foot tower near the small town of Reedsport. The Douglas County Coastal Visitors Center adjacent to the lighthouse can arrange tours. *oregonstateparks.org.*

## Getting Here and Around

U.S. 101 connects all of the Oregon Coast with roads that lead into the state's interior.

**Oregon Dunes National Recreation Area.** *855 U.S. 101, Reedsport, OR* *541/271–6000* *fs.usda.gov/siuslaw* *$5.*

# The Willamette Valley

## America's Acclaimed Pinot Noir Wine Region

The Willamette (pronounced "wil-LAM-it") Valley is a wine lover's Shangri-La, particularly in the northern Yamhill and Washington counties between Interstate 5 and the Oregon Coast, a region that is not only carpeted with vineyards but abounds with small hotels and inns, romantic restaurants, and casual wine bars. The valley divides two mountain ranges (the Cascade and Coast), and contains more than 500 wineries, the majority specializing in earthy, elegant Burgundy-style Pinot Noir, although white grapes like Pinot Gris, Riesling, and Chardonnay also thrive in this cool climate. You'll find particularly prolific concentrations of wineries and tasting rooms in the charming towns of Newberg, Dundee, Carlton, and McMinnville.

## Don't Miss

The Yamhill County seat, McMinnville lies in the center of Oregon's wine industry. The town's leafy and historic downtown area has a few shops and a growing number of tasting rooms set inside well-maintained 1890s–1920s buildings.

## Best Restaurant

You can dine in an actual underground wine cellar, with a fantastic list of local bottles, at Subterra. This smartly designed restaurant is known for creative comfort fare at lunch and seasonal prix-fixe three-course dinners. 🌐 *subterrarestaurant.com.*

## When to Go

July to October are the best times to wander the country roads in the Willamette Valley. Fall is spectacular, with leaves at their colorful peak in late October. Spring can be rainy, but wildflowers are in bloom.

# Historic Columbia River Highway

## The Northwest's Most Picturesque Gorge

Completed in 1922, the first planned scenic road in the country built expressly for automotive sightseers is a construction marvel. Serpentine U.S. 30 climbs to wooded bluffs, passes half a dozen waterfalls, and provides access to hiking trails leading to still more falls and gorgeous overlooks. Technically, the Historic Columbia River Highway extends the entire 74-mile length of the beautiful Columbia Gorge, but much of that is along the modern interstate. It's the 22-mile western segment that's the real draw.

## Don't Miss

The most famous attraction is Multnomah Falls, a 620-foot-high double-decker torrent, the second-highest year-round waterfall in the nation. Historic Multnomah Falls Lodge overlooks the cataract and contains a popular restaurant famous for its Sunday champagne brunches.

## When to Go

The gorge is always pretty to drive through, especially in spring when wildflowers and waterfalls are at their most magnificent.

## Getting Here and Around

The historic highway is accessed from the eastern edge of metro Portland as well as Interstate 84, the more direct path through the gorge. Note that across the river, Highway 14 is a similarly scenic drive along the Washington side of the gorge. From Portland, it's also easy to combine a drive through the gorge with a loop around Mt. Hood.

# Mt. Hood

## Oregon's Tallest Peak

Technically an active volcano that's had very minor, lava-free eruptive events as recently as the mid-1800s, this 11,250-foot mountain is known for the thrilling challenge it poses to climbers and for a dozen glaciers and snowfields that make skiing possible nearly year-round. A few small resort villages form a semicircle around the north side of the mountain, offering après-ski bars and rustic lodgings, the most famous and scenic being Timberline Lodge. Black bears, elk, and the occasional cougar share the space with humans who come to hike, camp, and fish in this quintessentially Pacific Northwest wild ecosystem.

## Don't Miss

Great fun after a day of hiking or skiing, the Timberline Lodge's inviting restaurant has views of neighboring mountains. Or, the atmospheric Ram's Head Bar overlooks a soaring 80-foot central fireplace and is popular for fondue and cocktails.

## Best Skiing and Snowboarding

The longest ski season in North America unfolds at Timberline Lodge & Ski Area, where the U.S. ski team conducts summer training. Thanks to the omnipresent Palmer Snowfield, it's the closest thing to a year-round ski area in the Lower 48. 🌐 *timberlinelodge.com*.

## When to Go

There can be snow on the ground outside Timberline Lodge even on the hottest summer days, and in winter, massive drifts of snow sometimes cover the building's entire first floor.

## Getting Here and Around

Mt. Hood is a 90-minute drive east of Portland via U.S. 26.

# Bend

### Oregon's Best Beer Town

A fast-growing former logging hub that's become one of the West's top recreational playgrounds, this largest city in central Oregon has several things going for it, including (sorry Portland and Seattle) the most impressive craft-beer scene in Pacific Northwest. And what better way to unwind after a day of skiing sunny Mt. Batchelor, mountain biking around Newberry National Volcanic Monument, rafting on the Deschutes River, or climbing in Smith Rock State Park, than to hoist a mug of crisp IPA or velvety stout on a brewpub patio? For a list of options, pick up a Bend Ale Trail brochure, or download the app. Once you've visited 10 locations, drop by the Bend Visitor Center to receive the prize: a durable silicone pint glass.

### Don't Miss

With so many notable options, it's hard to decide where to sip. Deschutes, 10 Barrel, Boneyard, Worthy Brewing are all worthy choices. But perhaps the most interesting spot is Crux Fermentation Project, an experimental brewery with an ever-changing variety of pale ales and other craft brews. On-site food carts and a patio add to the fun.

### Best Restaurant

Wild Rose serves some of the most authentic, and very spicy on request, Thai food in the state—and yes, there's an excellent craft beer list, too. 🌐 *wildrosethai.com*.

### When to Go

For patio drinking, spring through fall are best, but Bend offers plenty to see and do year-round, and it's one of the sunniest towns in the state.

### Getting Here and Around

Downtown Bend is at the junction of U.S. 97 and U.S. 20.

## Crater Lake National Park

### America's Deepest Lake

Whether you drive, bike, or hike around all or part of the rim, book a cruise on the surface of the water, or swim in a designated area, you're sure to be entranced by this extraordinarily deep-blue and clear lake inside a massive volcanic caldera that formed about 7,000 years ago, when Mt. Mazama blew its top. The park is also famed for its pitch-black night skies. It's an easy 33-mile drive around the lake, with numerous pullouts and trailheads.

### Don't Miss

At the regal log-and-stone Crater Lake Lodge, the lobby serves as a warm, welcoming gathering place where you can play games, socialize with a cocktail, or gaze out of the many windows to view spectacular sunrises and sunsets by a crackling fire.

### Best Tour

The most popular lake experience is on a two-hour ranger-led excursion aboard a 37-passenger launch. You can just cruise around the lake, but the best approach is to take one of the ferries that stops at Wizard Island, a 763-foot cinder cone whose summit you can hike. 🌐 *travelcraterlake.com.*

### When to Go

The park's high season is July and August. By mid-October until well into June, nearly the entire park closes due to heavy snowfall, but you can still get to Rim Village, as the South Entrance road is kept open.

### Getting Here and Around

The year-round southern entrance to the park is off Highway 62, 65 miles east of Medford and 44 miles north of Klamath Falls.

**Crater Lake National Park Visitor Center.** ✉ *Rim Visitor Center, Crater Lake, OR* ☎ *541/594–3000* 🌐 *nps.gov/crla* 🎫 *$30.*

# Oregon Shakespeare Festival

### The Granddaddy of Shakespeare Festivals

From mid-February to early November, more than 100,000 Bard-loving fans descend on the sunny and picturesque mountain town of Ashland for some of the finest Shakespearean productions you're likely to see outside of London— plus works by both classic (Ibsen, O'Neill) and contemporary playwrights, including occasional world premieres. Eleven plays are staged in repertory in three venues, the most famous of which is an atmospheric re-creation of the Fortune Theatre in London. The festival, which dates to 1935, generally operates close to capacity, so it's important to book ahead.

### Don't Miss

In the nearby wine country town of Jacksonville, the Northwest's oldest performing arts showcase—the Britt Music & Art Festival—features three midsummer weekends of concerts by some 90 international artists, offering everything from classical to bluegrass.

### Best Pre-Theater Stroll

The festival theaters overlook Lithia Park, a 93-acre jewel filled with picnickers, joggers, dog walkers, and theatergoers. 🌐 *ashland.or.us.*

### When to Go

The Shakespeare festival takes place in all but the dead of winter, and Ashland is sunny and lovely all year-round, popular for hiking, winery-hopping, and a great selection of restaurants and upscale inns, too.

### Getting Here and Around

Ashland is the last town in Oregon on Interstate 5 before you reach the California border, and downtown and the theater complex are perfect for strolling.

**Oregon Shakespeare Festival.** ✉ *15 S. Pioneer St., Ashland, OR* ☎ *541/482–4331* 🌐 *osfashland.org* 🎫 *Varies.*

# Wallowa Lake State Park

## America's Steepest Aerial Tram

Although it receives far fewer visitors than the rest of the state, northeastern Oregon is a land of astounding beauty that's framed by enormous mountain peaks and borders America's deepest river gorge, Hells Canyon. The perfect town for its mix of lively businesses and access to stunning natural scenery is Joseph. The peaks of the Wallowa Mountains, typically snow-covered until July, tower 5,000 feet above this community whose Main Street is speckled with shops, galleries, brewpubs, and cafés. At gorgeous Wallowa Lake State Park, you can ride the Wallowa Lake Tramway on a memorable journey that rises 3,700 feet in 15 minutes, rushing you up to the top of 8,150-foot Mt. Howard. There's great hiking, expansive views, and a casual patio restaurant at the top.

## Don't Miss

A relatively easy way to take in the natural splendor of the surrounding Eagle Cap Wilderness is by driving the Wallowa Mountain Loop. The three-hour trip from Joseph to historic Baker City, designated the Hells Canyon Scenic Byway, winds through the national forest and part of Hells Canyon Recreation Area, passing over forested mountains, creeks, and rivers.

## When to Go

The tramway is generally open May through September.

## Getting Here and Around

The most direct route to Joseph is Highway 82, a picturesque 70-mile journey from Interstate 5 in La Grande.

**Wallowa Lake Tramway.** ✉ *59919 Wallowa Lake Hwy., Joseph, OR* ☎ *541/432–5331* 🌐 *wallowalaketramway.com* 🎫 *$36.*

# Astoria

### The Goonies Town

It's hard not to get a little awestruck the first time you experience the beauty of Astoria, Oregon, in person. Located near the place where the Columbia River meets the Pacific Ocean, the city offers breathtaking views everywhere you turn. Once you gain your bearings, a new feeling creeps in—familiarity. No, it's not déjà vu. You know the tiny town of Astoria from the movies—lots of them. The town is famously the setting for *The Goonies* and *Kindergarten Cop*, but its relationship with Tinseltown doesn't stop there. *Short Circuit*, *Teenage Mutant Ninja Turtles 3*, *The Ring Two*, the *Free Willy* movies, *Benji the Hunted*, and more were filmed there, too.

### Don't Miss

The small but engaging Oregon Film Museum celebrates the state's long history of filmmaking and contains artifacts from productions, such as *One Flew Over the Cuckoo's Nest* and *Animal House*. The location is apt because it was featured prominently in the famous cult film *The Goonies*.

### Best Brewpub

One of the most acclaimed craft brewers on the coast, Buoy Beer has a warm and inviting taproom on Astoria's riverfront walk. 🌐 *buoybeer.com*.

### When to Go

Astoria is popular and interesting year-round, even during the rainy months. A one-day *Goonies* festival takes place each June.

### Getting Here and Around

Located at the junction of U.S. 101 and U.S. 30, just across the river from Washington's scenic Long Beach Peninsula, Astoria is a two-hour drive from Portland.

# When in Oregon

## EUGENE'S FOOD SCENE

At the southern end of the Willamette Valley Wine Country, Oregon's second-largest city and home of the University of Oregon is a lively, youthful place with a countercultural edge. Full of parks and oriented to the outdoors, Eugene is famously popular for biking and—as the birthplace of Nike—is known as the Running Capital of the World. On the north edge of downtown, the Market District and up-and-coming Whiteaker neighborhood both boast stellar food scenes rife with artisan food and drink producers. Downtown's bustling Fifth Street Public Market is a good place to start, with its font of boutiques and crafts shops; a large gourmet food hub, Provisions Market Hall; and a trendy boutique hotel, the Inn at the 5th. Make your way west stopping for a stroll through pretty Skinner Butte Park and a sip at Wildcraft Cider Works. At Blair Boulevard, you'll find the heart of Whiteaker's excellent eateries, among them El Buen Sabor Taqueria, Izakaya Meiji, and Territorial Vineyards & Wine Company.

**Do This:** Held every Saturday from April through mid-November, downtown's Eugene Saturday Market is a great place to browse for handicrafts, try out local food carts, or simply kick back and people-watch while listening to live music at the Market Stage.

**Eugene, Cascades & Coast Visitors Center.** ✉ *754 Olive St., Eugene, OR* ☎ *541/484–5307* 🌐 *eugenecascadescoast.org.*

## JOHN DAY FOSSIL BEDS NATIONAL MONUMENT

The geological formations that compose this peculiar monument cover hundreds of square miles and preserve a diverse record of plant and animal life spanning more than 40 million years of the Age of Mammals. The national monument is divided into three units: Sheep Rock, Painted Hills, and Clarno—each of which looks vastly different and tells a different part of the story of Oregon's history. If you only have time for one unit of the park, make it Painted Hills, where the namesake psychedelic mounds most vividly expose the region's unique geology.

**Do This:** If you can, come to the Painted Hills at dusk or just after it rains, when the colors are most vivid. If traveling in spring, the desert wildflowers are most intense between late April and early May. Take the steep, ¾-mile Carroll Rim Trail for a commanding view of the hills or sneak a peek from the parking lot at the trailhead, about 2 miles beyond the picnic area.

**John Day Fossil Beds National Monument.** ✉ *37375 Bear Creek Rd., Mitchell, OR* ☎ *541/987–2333* 🌐 *nps.gov/joda* 🎫 *Free.*

## OREGON CAVES NATIONAL MONUMENT

Marble caves, large calcite formations, and huge underground rooms shape this rare adventure in geology found in this massive cave network with 15,000 feet of passages. Offered late March through early November, the 90-minute half-mile tour is moderately strenuous, with low passageways, twisting turns, and more than 500 stairs. Aboveground, the surrounding valley holds an old-growth forest with some of the state's largest trees, and offers some excellent and generally uncrowded hiking.

**Do This:** You sleep among the leaves in the tree houses of the extraordinary Out 'n' About resort, about 25 miles south of the park. The highest unit is 37 feet from the ground—one has an antique claw-foot bath, and another has separate kids' quarters connected to the main room by a swinging bridge.

**Oregon Caves National Monument.** ✉ *19000 Caves Hwy., Cave Junction, OR* ☎ *541/592–2100* 🌐 *nps.gov/orca* 🎫 *Free.*

## PENDLETON ROUND-UP

More than 50,000 people roll into town in mid-September for one of the oldest and most prominent rodeos in the country. With its famous slogan of "Let 'er Buck," the Round-Up features eight days of parades, races, beauty contests, and children's rodeos, culminating in four days of rodeo competition. Vendors sell beadwork and curios, while country bands twang in the background. At the Round-Up Hall of Fame Museum, you can learn about the rodeo's history from the collection of photos and memorabilia that dates back to 1910.

**Do This:** Beyond the Round-Up, the town's most significant source of name recognition comes from Pendleton Woolen Mills, home of the instantly recognizable plaid wool shirts and colorful woolen Indian blankets. This location is the company's blanket mill; there's also a weaving mill in the Columbia Gorge town of Washougal, Washington. If you want to know more about the production process, take one of the engaging 20-minute tours. The mill's retail store stocks blankets and clothing, with good bargains on factory seconds.

**Pendleton Round-Up.** ✉ *1205 S.W. Court Ave., Pendleton, OR* ☎ *541/276–2553* 🌐 *pendletonroundup.com.*

## TILIKUM CROSSING BRIDGE

Downtown Portland's collection of striking bridges gained a new member in 2015 with the construction of this sleek, cable-stayed bridge a few steps from the superb and very family-friendly Oregon Museum of Science and Industry (OMSI). Nicknamed "the Bridge of the People," the Tilikum is unusual in that it's the largest car-free bridge in the country—it's open only to public transit (MAX light-rail trains, buses, and streetcars), bikes, and pedestrians. The 1,720-foot-long bridge connects Southeast Portland with the South Waterfront district and rewards those who stroll or cycle across it with impressive skyline views.

**Do This:** Portland is famously bike-friendly, with miles of dedicated bike lanes and numerous rental shops. Also, some great companies offer guided rides around the city, covering everything from eating and brewpub-hopping to checking out local parks and historic neighborhoods. Cycle Portland Bike Tours and Rentals is one of the best, offering tours with themes that include Essential Portland, Foodie Field Trip, and Brews Cruise. The well-stocked on-site bike shop serves craft beer on tap.

**Tilikum Crossing Bridge.** ✉ *Tilikum Crossing, Portland, OR.*

## TILLAMOOK

More than 100 inches of annual rainfall and the confluence of three rivers contribute to the lush green pastures around Tillamook, probably best known for its thriving dairy industry and cheese factory. The Tillamook County Cheese Factory ships about 50 million pounds of cheese around the world every year. The town itself lies several miles inland from the ocean, but it is the best jumping-off point for driving the dramatic Three Capes Loop, which passes over Cape Meares, Cape Lookout, and Cape Kiwanda and offers spectacular views of the ocean and coastline.

**Do This:** Cape Lookout State Park includes a moderately easy (though often muddy) 2-mile trail—marked on the highway as "wildlife viewing area"—that leads through giant spruces, western red cedars, and hemlocks, and ends with views of Cascade Head to the south and Cape Meares to the north. The section of the park just north of the trail comprises a long, curving stretch of beach with picnic areas and campsites.

## VOODOO DOUGHNUT

The long lines outside this Old Town 24/7 doughnut shop, marked by its distinctive pink-neon sign, attest to the fact that this irreverent bakery is almost as famous a Portland landmark as Powell's Books. The aforementioned sign depicts one of the shop's biggest sellers, a raspberry-jelly-topped chocolate voodoo-doll doughnut, but all of the creations here, some of them witty, some ribald, bring smiles to the faces of customers—even those who have waited 30 minutes in the rain.

**Do This:** Order the Loop (covered in Fruit Loops cereal), Grape Ape (vanilla frosting, grape dust, and lavender sprinkles), and Dirty Snowballs (marshmallow topping, dipped in coconut, with peanut butter center).

**Voodoo Doughnut.** ✉ *22 S.W. 3rd Ave. Portland, OR* ☎ *503/241–4704* 🌐 *www.voodoodoughnut.com*

## Cool Places to Stay

**Cannery Pier Hotel.** From every room in this captivating property there's a gorgeous view of the mighty Columbia River flowing toward the Pacific Ocean, and it's almost hypnotic to watch the tugboats shepherding barges to and fro. ✉ *10 Basin St., Astoria, OR* ☎ *503/325–4996* 🌐 *cannerypierhotel.com* *From $329.*

**Heceta Head Lighthouse Bed & Breakfast.** On a windswept promontory, this unusual late-Victorian property is one of Oregon's most remarkable bed-and-breakfasts; it's located at Heceta Head Lighthouse State Scenic Viewpoint and owned by a gifted chef who prepares an elaborate seven-course breakfast each morning, with seasonal offerings. ✉ *92072 Hwy. 1 South, Yachats, OR* ☎ *541/547–3696* 🌐 *hecetalighthouse.com* [$] *From $260.*

**KEX Portland.** Opened 2019, the first U.S. outpost of the hip and artful Reykjavík hotel–hostel has been developed expressly with the aim of encouraging travelers and locals to mix and mingle together, whether in the inviting lobby-restaurant or with friends in the cedar sauna. ✉ *100 N.E. Martin Luther King Jr. Blvd., Portland, OR* ☎ *971/346–2992* 🌐 *kexportland.com* [$] *From $169.*

**Suttle Lodge.** If the famously design-minded film director Wes Anderson built a wilderness lodge, it'd probably look something like this whimsically updated lakeside retreat in the Deschutes National Forest, where the vintage summer-camp vibes come with the finest craft cocktails you'll find between here and Portland. ✉ *13300 U.S. 20, Sisters, OR* ☎ *541/638–7001* 🌐 *thesuttlelodge.com* [$] *From $185.*

**Timberline Lodge.** Guest rooms are simple, rustic, and charming (a handful of them lack private baths), but don't expect a cushy experience—the reason for staying in this gorgeous lodge built by the CCC in the 1930s is the magnificent setting high on the southern slope of Oregon's most storied peak, Mt. Hood. ✉ *27500 E. Timberline Rd., Government Camp, OR* ☎ *503/272–3311* 🌐 *timberlinelodge.com* [$] *From $150.*

**Vintages Trailer Resort.** Just off the road that runs through the heart of the Willamette Valley Wine Country from Dundee to McMinnville, this quirky retro resort boasts 34 lovingly refurbished vintage trailers, most dating from the 1940s–60s, and each with a gas grill. ✉ *16205 S.E. Kreder Rd., Dayton, OR* ☎ *971/267–2130* 🌐 *the-vintages.com* [$] *From $99.*

# Washington

Whether you're looking for hip cities, beautiful hikes, or laid-back beaches, Washington State has it. In Seattle, you can sample farm-to-table treats at Pike Place Market and get a glimpse of the city lights at the top of the Space Needle, while outdoor adventurers can explore national parks like Olympic, North Cascades, and Mt. Rainier, as well hike up to Mt. St. Helens and the Cascade Mountains. Beach lovers will find their bliss here too, with the San Juan Islands and Long Beach Peninsula offering plenty of swimming, surfing, and whale-watching.

## Bucket List Picks

The following boxes contain our picks for the top sights and experiences in Washington.

- ○ Olympic National Park
- ○ North Cascades National Park
- ○ Mount Rainier National Park
- ○ Leavenworth
- ○ San Juan Islands
- ○ Spokane's Riverfront Park
- ○ Pike Place Market
- ○ The Space Needle
- ○ Lake Washington Ship Canal
- ○ Skydiving in Snohomish
- ○ Tacoma's Museum of Glass
- ○ Mt. St. Helens
- ○ Sequim Lavender Festival
- ○ Skagit Valley Tulip Festival

# Olympic National Park

## Beaches and Rain Forests

Covering nearly 1,500 square miles of the stunning peninsula for which it's named, Olympic National Park is home to some of the nation's most tranquil temperate rain forests, beautifully sculpted beaches, and dramatic coastal mountains. Beachcombers will discover miles of spectacular drift-wood-strewn coastline hemmed with sea stacks and tidal pools. A dip in Sol Duc's natural geothermal mineral pools offers a secluded spa experience in the wooded heart of the park, while hardy hikers and climbers will want to spend time in the park's meadowed foothill trails and frosty peaks.

## Don't Miss

Considered one of the quietest places in North America, the park's Hoh Rain Forest is a place of utter tranquility, and hiking here is suitable for all abilities.

## Best Camping

In addition to four beautiful, historic lodges, Olympic National Park is blessed with gorgeous campgrounds, but the most amazing place to pitch a tent is along one of the park's beaches. Rialto Beach is the most stunning with easy drive-in access, while up north among the park's alluring sea stacks is Shi Shi Beach. Remember to obtain a wilderness permit in advance.

## When to Go

The Olympic Peninsula is most appealing weather-wise, but also most crowded, in summer.

## Getting Here and Around

U.S. 101 nearly circumvents the entire park, and from this picturesque road, you can access all of its main areas.

**Olympic National Park.** ✉ *3002 Mount Angeles Rd., Port Angeles, WA* 🌐 *nps.gov/olym* 🎫 *$30 per vehicle.*

# North Cascades National Park

### The Most Glaciers in the Lower 48

Outside of Alaska, this remote and wild park at the Canadian border contains more glaciers than any place in the country. Other joys of visiting North Cascades National Park include the chance to see bald eagles, elk, and other wildlife along nearly 400 miles of hiking trails, to traipse meadows absolutely carpeted with colorful wildflowers in summer, and to raft and kayak on beautiful Lake Chelan, Ross Lake, and the Stehekin River. You can access this 1,070-square-mile wilderness most easily via the North Cascades Highway.

### Don't Miss

The only way to reach the Lake Chelan National Recreation Area portion of the park is by boat, and that's a big part of its appeal. A ferry and high-speed catamaran cruise between small waterfront villages along Lake Chelan, a pristine 55-mile-long fjord.

### Best Tour

On the shore of turquoise-hued Diablo Lake, North Cascades Environmental Learning Center offers outstanding guided tours. 🌐 *ncascades.org.*

### When to Go

Summer is peak season. North Cascades Highway closes from mid-November through mid-April, depending on snowfall.

### Getting Here and Around

The park is traversed by the North Cascades Highway during the warmer months, and Stehekin can be reached by ferry along Lake Chelan year-round. Bellingham to the west and Winthrop to the east are the best bases for exploring the park.

**North Cascades National Park.** ✉ *810 Hwy. 20, Sedro-Woolley, WA* 🌐 *nps.gov/noca* 🎫 *Free.*

# Mt. Rainier

## PNW's Highest Volcanic Peak

Some say Mt. Rainier is the most magical mountain in America. At 14,411 feet, it is a popular peak for climbing, with more than 10,000 attempts per year—nearly half of which are successful. But this land of superlatives also includes about 35 square miles of glaciers and snowfields, more than 100 species of wildflowers that bloom in the park's high meadows all summer, and absolutely dazzling hiking along 240 miles of trails through old-growth forest, river valleys, lakes, waterfalls, and rugged ridges. Take time to visit the historic Longmire Museum and the contemporary Jackson Memorial Visitor Center.

## Don't Miss

The 5-mile Skyline Trail loop, one of the highest trails in the park, beckons day-trippers with a vista of alpine ridges and, in summer, meadows filled with wildflowers and songbirds. At 6,800 feet is Panorama Point, the spine of the Cascade Range.

## Best Lodge

With its hand-carved Alaskan cedar logs, stone fireplaces, and glorious mountain views, the 1917 Paradise Inn is a classic example of a national park lodge. ⊕ *mtrainierguestservices.com*.

## When to Go

Mt. Rainier is the Puget Sound's weather vane: if you can see it, skies will be clear. You're most likely to see the summit July through September.

## Getting Here and Around

The park is relatively close to the Seattle–Tacoma Interstate 5 corridor, reached via a few different routes, the most direct being the 75-mile drive southeast on Highway 7 from Tacoma.

**Mount Rainier National Park.** ✉ *55210 238th Ave. E, Ashford, WA* ⊕ *nps.gov/mora* 🎟 *$30 per vehicle.*

# Leavenworth

### Where It's Always Festive

This charming (if a touch kitschy) Bavarian-style village thrives with both old-fashioned and surprisingly urbane restaurants and inns, and it's also a hub for winter skiing and summer hiking. Formerly a railroad and mining center, Leavenworth fell on hard times in the 1960s, and civic leaders, looking for ways to capitalize on the town's alpine setting, convinced shopkeepers to add Black Forest–style trim to their buildings. The pedestrian-friendly village center bustles with tourists year-round, but Leavenworth truly comes alive during the holidays. There's an intricate maypole dance during spring's Maifest, oompah bands and delicious German food and beer during autumn's three Oktoberfest weekends, and carriage rides, caroling, and performances by the Marlin Handbell Ringers during the Christkindlmarkt shopping season in December.

### Don't Miss

Nearly 7,000 modern and antique nutcrackers—some of them centuries old—are displayed in the two-story Nutcracker Museum and Shop. 🌐 *leavenworthmuseum.org.*

### Best Restaurant

Strolling accordion players set the mood at the Andreas Keller Restaurant, a festive eatery where the theme is "Germany without the Passport." 🌐 *andreaskellerrestaurant.com.*

### When to Go

Be sure to book hotel rooms well ahead for any of the holiday periods, and also for summer and ski-season weekends. Your best bet is shoulder season between big events.

### Getting Here and Around

From Seattle, the 120-mile drive to Leavenworth over the Cascades and dramatic Stevens Pass, via U.S. 2, is one of the prettiest in the state.

# The San Juan Islands

## The West Coast's Prettiest Archipelago

One of the most enchanting island getaways in the western United States, the mountainous and lush San Juan Islands sit in the middle of Puget Sound, just off the coast of British Columbia and within easy weekending distance of Seattle. These utterly peaceful islands, the three largest of which—San Juan, Orcas, and Lopez—have regular ferry service, are filled with enjoyable outdoorsy diversions, including great whale-watching, as well as plenty of urbane charms: think farm-to-table restaurants, exceptional art galleries, and cottages and B&Bs.

## Don't Miss

The top place to spot whales isn't Orcas Island but rather San Juan Island, especially Lime Kiln Point State Park, where a rocky coastal trail leads to lookout points and a little 1919 lighthouse. The best time to spot whales is from the end of April through September. Several tour companies also offer whale-watching expeditions, including Maya's Legacy. 🌐 *sanjuanislandwhalewatch.com.*

## When to Go

This part of Washington has a mild maritime climate, and while July and August are the most popular (and most expensive) times to visit, late spring or early fall can also be stunning.

## Getting Here and Around

Ferries serve the three main islands from the mainland town of Anacortes and, on a more limited basis, from Vancouver Island, Canada. A few local airlines also offer quick (but pricey) flights from Seattle and other Puget Sound communities.

**The San Juan Islands.** 🌐 *visitsanjuans.com.*

# Spokane's Riverfront Park

## Washington's Coolest Urban Green Space

This beautifully maintained 100-acre park is what remains of Spokane's Expo '74. Sprawling across several islands in the Spokane River, the striking park was developed from old railroad yards, where the stone clock tower of the former Great Northern Railroad Station still stands. The modernist Washington State Pavilion, built as an opera house, is now the excellent First Interstate Center for the Arts. A 1909 carousel, hand carved by master builder Charles I. D. Looff, is a local landmark. Another family favorite is the giant red slide shaped like a Radio Flyer wagon. The Pavilion at Riverfront hosts concerts, festivals, and an eye-catching light display on weekends. For a great view of the river and falls, walk across Post Street Bridge or take the sky ride over Spokane Falls.

## Don't Miss

On the grounds of the eclectic 1924 mansion, Arbor Crest Wine Cellars is a lovely place to sample wine, enjoy a fantastic view of the Spokane River, and meander through the impeccably kept grounds. 🌐 *www.arborcrest.com.*

## Best Restaurant

In a former flour mill with expansive Spokane River vistas, Clinkerdagger has been a Spokane favorite for decades. The seafood, steaks, and prime rib are excellent, but the setting is what really makes this spot special. 🌐 *clinkerdagger.com.*

## Getting Here and Around

Interstate 90 cuts through downtown Spokane, within a few blocks of Riverfront Park.

**Riverfront Park.** ✉ *507 N. Howard St., Spokane, WA* 🌐 *spokaneriverfront-park.com* 🎟 *Free.*

# Pike Place Market

## America's Iconic Market

This iconic structure with its famous neon red sign and a memorable setting overlooking Seattle's waterfront dates to 1907, when the city issued permits allowing farmers to sell produce from parked wagons. Today it buzzes with some 250 restaurants, bakeries, coffeehouses (including the flagship Starbucks), lunch counters, and ethnic eateries, plus crafts vendors, galleries, and cookery shops. A major expansion added artisanal-food purveyors, an on-site brewery, public art installations, seasonal pop-up vendors, and a 30,000-square-foot plaza and viewing deck overlooking Elliott Bay.

## Don't Miss

The Olympic Sculpture Park is a favorite destination for picnics, strolls, and quiet contemplation.

## Best Food

Attention foodies: for the best picnic supplies, head to DeLaurenti Specialty Food and Wine. This gourmet emporium has been doling out superb imported meats and cheeses and all sorts of other delicacies since 1972. Don't miss the excellent wine shop upstairs, too. 🌐 *delaurenti.com*.

## When to Go

The market is great fun year-round, and throughout the day. Mornings are a nice time for breakfast and seeing the fishmongers, flower sellers, and others set up their stalls before the crush of crowds descend. Later in the day, the plaza is a fantastic place to watch the sunset over the Olympic Mountains.

## Getting Here and Around

Pike Place is in the heart of downtown Seattle.

**Pike Place Market.** ✉ *85 Pike St., Seattle, WA* ☎ *206/682–7453* 🌐 *pikeplacemarket.org*.

# The Space Needle

### Washington's Most Famous Tower

The tallest building west of the Mississippi when it was constructed for the World's Fair in 1962, the 600-foot-tall Space Needle is as quirky and beloved as ever. A less-than-one-minute ride up to the observation deck yields 360-degree vistas of downtown Seattle, Elliott Bay, and the surrounding Olympic Mountains and Cascade Range through floor-to-ceiling windows, an open-air observation area, and a rotating glass floor. Below is the 74-acre Seattle Center, home to the kid-friendly Pacific Science Center, with more than 200 indoor and outdoor hands-on exhibits, two IMAX theaters, and a state-of- the-art planetarium.

### Don't Miss

For the best views of the Space Needle from afar, head to Kerry Park. And, while you're near the Space Needle, definitely spend time at MoPOP, a striking 140,000-square-foot complex designed by Frank Gehry with rock memorabilia from the likes of Bob Dylan and the grunge-scene heavies. 🌐 *www.mopop.org.*

### Best Art Installation

Just steps from the base of the Space Needle, fans of Dale Chihuly's glass works delight in exploring the artist's early influences at Chihuly Garden and Glass. 🌐 *chihulygardenandglass.com.*

### Getting Here and Around

The Seattle Center is on the northwest side of downtown, at the foot of Queen Anne Hill, and is easily reached on foot, bus, light-rail, and even monorail.

**The Space Needle.** ✉ *400 Broad St., Seattle, WA* ☎ *206/905–2100* 🌐 *spaceneedle.com* 🎟 *$35.*

## Lake Washington Ship Canal

### Seattle's Hippest Destination

For fantastic people-watching, scenic strolls through waterfront greenery, and hanging out at some of the city's hippest bars and eateries, check out the areas flanking this 8.6-mile canal that connects Lake Washington to Puget Sound. The top outdoor draws include 230-acre Washington Park Arboretum, with its rhododendrons, azaleas, and Japanese gardens; Gas Works Park, where the hulking remains of a 1907 gas plant lends quirky character to a green space overlooking Lake Union; and the Hiram M. Chittenden Locks, where you can see salmon and trout make the journey from saltwater to fresh each summer. Picnic beneath oak trees in the adjacent 7-acre Carl S. English Botanical Gardens.

### Don't Miss

Be sure to visit the Ballard Avenue Historic District. It's known for its lovely old buildings, fantastic shopping, and restaurant scene featuring standouts Staple & Fancy and the Walrus and the Carpenter. Every Sunday, Ballard hosts one of the best farmers' markets in town.

### Best Restaurant

At Agua Verde Cafe & Paddle Club, a festive establishment on Portage Bay, rent a kayak and paddle along the Lake Union shoreline and gawk at the hodgepodge of funky-to-fabulous houseboats. Afterward, take in the lakefront views. 🌐 *aguaverde.com*.

### Getting Here and Around

Several bridges and major roads cross the ship canal, and you can walk, jog, or ride a bike along the Burke-Gilman Trail, which fringes its northern banks.

**Lake Washington Ship Canal.** ✉ *701 Pike St., Seattle, WA* ☎ *206/461–5800* 🌐 *visitseattle.org*.

# Snohomish

## The West Coast's Best Skydiving Destination

In a scenic river valley just 20 miles northeast of Seattle, the town of Snohomish has earned a reputation as a top destination for skydiving. Once you begin your descent from between 8,000 and 14,000 feet, you're rewarded with eye-popping scenery in every direction: Mt. Baker to the north, the jagged Cascade Range to the east, Seattle's sleek skyline to the south, and Puget Sound, the San Juan Islands, the Olympic Mountains, and Victoria, British Columbia, to the west. The highly respected outfitter Skydive Snohomish caters to everyone from first-timers to those with plenty of experience.

## Don't Miss

Snohomish is a mere 10-minute drive from one of the loveliest towns in Washington. Woodinville contains more winery tasting rooms—some 130 in all—than any town in the Pacific Northwest.

## Best Restaurant

For the ultimate post–skydiving celebration, head to the Herbfarm in Woodinville's tony Spa at Willows Lodge, where prix-fixe-only nine-course dinners take place over a few hours and feature at least six wine pairings. ⊕ *theherbfarm.com.*

## When to Go

Skydive Snohomish offers jumps year-round, although your likelihood of blue skies and panoramic views are greatest in summer.

## Getting Here and Around

Skydive Snohomish is at Harvey Airfield, about 6 miles east of Interstate 5.

**Skydive Snohomish.** ✉ *9906 Airport Way, Snohomish, WA* ☎ *360/568–7703* ⊕ *skydivesnohomish.com* 🎫 *From $240.*

# Tacoma's Museum of Glass

## Clearly the Best Art

The showpiece of this spectacular complex of delicate and creative art-glass installations is the 500-foot-long Chihuly Bridge of Glass, a tunnel of glorious color and light that stretches above Interstate 705. Cross it from downtown to reach the museum's grounds, which sit above the Foss Waterway and next to a shallow reflecting pool dotted with large-scale sculptures. Inside, you can wander through quiet, light-filled galleries that present a fascinating and compelling array of rotating exhibits.

## Don't Miss

The Museum of Glass is part of a cluster of superb downtown Tacoma museums. A highlight is the Tacoma Art Museum and its stunning, light-filled Benaroya Wing—designed by Olson Kundig—with its hundreds of contemporary art-glass works, including pieces by artists trained at the prestigious Pilchuck Glass School. *www.tacomaartmuseum.org.*

## Best Bar

The offbeat McMenamins Elks Temple consists of several colorful bars and restaurants and a 44-room hotel inside a dramatically refurbished 1916 Renaissance Revival landmark adjacent to Tacoma's famous Spanish Steps. It's a memorable spot for drinks or a bite to eat after touring the city's museums. *mcmenamins.com.*

## Getting Here and Around

On the southern end of Puget Sound, about 30 miles south of Seattle, Tacoma is just off Interstate 5. The downtown museum district is quite pedestrian-friendly.

**Museum of Glass.** *1801 E. Dock St., Tacoma, WA* *253/284–4750* *museumofglass.org* *$17.*

# Mt. St. Helens

## America's Most Famous Volcano

The site of the most devastating volcanic eruption in recent U.S. history, Mount St. Helens National Volcanic Monument gives you an up-close look at this striking peak 55 miles northeast of Portland, Oregon. On May 18, 1980, the massive eruption of this 9,667-foot peak launched a 36,000-foot plume of steam and ash into the air, leveling a 230-square-mile area, and claiming 57 lives. The mountain now stands at 8,365 feet, and a horseshoe-shaped crater forms the scarred summit. The modern and scenic Spirit Lake Highway carries travelers to the outstanding Johnston Ridge Observatory, about 5 miles from the summit.

## Don't Miss

Located 6 miles southwest of the summit, Ape Cave is the longest continuous lava tube in the continental United States.

## Best Hike

Of the trails that lead to the summit of this legendary volcano, all of them requiring a permit, the most popular is the 10-mile round-trip Monitor Ridge Trail, which, though not for the faint of heart—it entails a 4,500-foot elevation gain—can be done in a day and requires no technical climbing. 🌐 *mshinstitute.org.*

## When to Go

It's best to visit from mid-May through late October; many roads are closed the rest of the year.

## Getting Here and Around

Johnston Ridge Observatory is at the end of the Spirit Lake Highway, 53 miles from Interstate 5. The trailhead for the Monitor Ridge Trail is Climbers Bivouac, a 14-mile drive from Cougar.

**Johnston Ridge Observatory.** ✉ *2400 Spirit Lake Hwy., Toutle, WA* 🌐 *fs.usda.gov/visit/destination/johnston-ridge-observatory* 🎫 *$8.*

# Sequim Lavender Festival

### Painting the Town Purple

Fragrant purple lavender flourishes in the fields of this endearing old mill town and farming center between the northern foothills of the Olympic Mountains and the southeastern stretch of the Strait of Juan de Fuca. About 30,000 people flock here over 10 days in mid-July to attend the Sequim Lavender Festival. Local farms are open for tours and "u-pick" gathering, and events include crafts sales, cooking demonstrations, and an afternoon lavender tea. Pronounced "skwim," this beautiful community has witnessed a boom in urbane eateries and hip boutiques in its walkable downtown.

### Don't Miss

Curving nearly 6 miles into the Strait of Juan de Fuca, Dungeness Spit is the country's longest natural sand spit and is situated in a wild section of shoreline. More than 30,000 migratory birds stop here each spring and fall.

### Best Lavender Farm

Purple Haze Organic Lavender Farm contains 12 acres of lavender fields as well as lawns for picnicking and a gift shop that carries bath and body products, honeys and jams, and other lavender-infused gifts. A little snack stand sells lavender ice cream and lemonade. 🌐 *purplehazelavender.com.*

### When to Go

The festival takes place in mid-July, but the region's lavender fields and Dungeness Spit are lovely for exploring from May through mid-September.

### Getting Here and Around

Sequim is on U.S. 101 at the northeastern end of the Olympic Peninsula, between Port Townsend and Port Angeles.

**Sequim Lavender Festival.** ✉ *Sequim, WA* ☎ *360/681–3035* 🌐 *lavenderfestival.com.*

# Skagit Valley Tulip Festival

## Tiptoe through the Tulips

Covering 1,200 acres, RoozenGaarde is the world's largest family-owned tulip-, daffodil-, and iris-growing business. Acres of greenhouses are filled with multicolored blossoms, and more than 200,000 bulbs are planted in the show gardens each fall. During April's monthlong Skagit Valley Tulip Festival, the flowers pop up in neat, brilliant rows across the flat landscape, attracting upwards of 400,000 visitors.

## Don't Miss

Just a 15-minute drive northwest of Mount Vernon, the twin villages of Bow-Edison have in just a short time become one of Washington's premier foodie destinations.

## Best Drive

Highway 11, also known as Chuckanut Drive, begins in the beautiful waterfront city of Bellingham, in the historic Fairhaven District, which is well worth exploring for its bounty of indie shops, galleries, and eateries. This 23-mile road winds along the cliffs and past the waterfalls above beautiful Chuckanut and Samish bays. Turnouts are framed by gnarled madrona trees and offer views of the San Juan Islands.

## When to Go

The Skagit Valley Tulip Festival takes place throughout April, but the area's farms, fields, and scenic roads are beautiful throughout summer and fall.

## Getting Here and Around

RoozenGaarde is 4 miles west of Interstate 5 in Mount Vernon. Bow-Edison and Chuckanut Drive are 12 miles northwest, via Highway 12.

**Skagit Valley Tulip Festival.** ✉ *15867 Beaver Marsh Rd., Mount Vernon, WA* ☎ *360/424–8531* 🌐 *tulips.com* 🎟 *Free.*

# When in Washington

## CAPE DISAPPOINTMENT STATE PARK

The cape and its treacherous neighboring sandbar—named in 1788 by an English fur trader who had been unable to find the Northwest Passage—has been the scourge of sailors since the 1800s. More than 250 ships have sunk after running aground on its ever-shifting sands. Now a 2,023-acre state park contained within the Lewis and Clark National Historical Park (which also has sections just across the Columbia River in Oregon), this dramatic cape with sheer sea cliffs and great stands of conifers offers 8 miles of trails leading to stunning beaches, two stately lighthouses, and the Lewis & Clark Interpretive Center, which sits atop a 200-foot cliff and has exhibits tracing the cape's human and natural history.

**Do This:** The adjacent Long Beach Peninsula consists of 28 continuous miles of broad, sandy beach bookended by two state parks and bounded by the Pacific Ocean and the Columbia River. This narrow stretch of land offers a series of oceanfront retreats, oyster farms, cranberry bogs, and beach after beach to comb. Kite flying, horseback riding, clam digging, and winter-storm watching are also popular pastimes.

**Cape Disappointment State Park.** ✉ *244 Robert Gray Dr., Ilwaco, WA* ☎ *360/642–3078* 🌐 *parks.state.wa.us/486/cape-disappointment* 🎫 *$10.*

## MARYHILL MUSEUM

A wonderfully eclectic collection—including the largest assemblage of Rodin works outside France; an impressive cache of Native American artifacts; furniture that belonged to Queen Marie of Romania; and posters, glasswork, and ephemera related to the modern-dance pioneer Loïe Fuller—is housed within the walls of a grandiose mansion built in the middle of nowhere by Sam Hill, the man who spearheaded the development of a scenic highway through the Columbia Gorge. The main Beaux Arts building dates to 1914, and a beautifully executed modern wing extends from the back, with a café and a terraced slope overlooking the Columbia River. The harmoniously landscaped grounds include a sculpture garden and pathways along the gorge.

**Do This:** The remarkable Stonehenge Memorial is a full-scale replica of England's legendary Neolithic stone creation. It was constructed in 1918 as the nation's first memorial to servicemen who perished in World War I. The memorial, a five-minute drive east of the Maryhill Museum, sits on a promontory with dramatic vistas overlooking the Columbia River.

**Maryhill Museum.** ✉ *35 Maryhill Museum of Art Dr., Goldendale, WA* ☎ *509/773–3733* 🌐 *maryhillmuseum.org* 🎫 *$12.*

## NORTHWEST MARITIME CENTER

The Olympic Peninsula's Port Townsend is one of only three Victorian-era seaports on the register of National Historic Sites, and you can learn all about its rich heritage at the handsome Northwest Maritime Center. You can launch a kayak or watch sloops and schooners gliding along the bay from the boardwalk, pier, and beach that fronts the buildings. It's the center of operations for the Wooden Boat Foundation, which stages the annual Wooden Boat Festival each September, during which hundreds of wooden boats sail into Port Townsend Bay for a weekend of presentations, tours, and sea shanties.

**Do This:** With beautifully restored Victorian-era officers quarters that you can tour, 432-acre Fort Worden State Park is a fascinating history lesson. There are also hidden bunkers and expansive parade grounds. A sandy beach leads to the graceful 1913 Point Wilson Lighthouse, and touch tanks at Port Townsend Marine Science Center offer an up-close look at sea anemones and other creatures. ⊕ *parks.state.wa.us/511/fort-worden.*

**Northwest Maritime Center.** ✉ *431 Water St., Port Townsend, WA* ☎ *360/385–3628* ⊕ *nwmaritime.org* 🎟 *Free.*

### WALLA WALLA WINE COUNTRY

Walla Walla's sunny, fertile slopes began attracting grape growers in the 1980s, and this attractive town with sweeping views of the Blue Mountains is now one of America's most exciting wine countries. You'll find more than 120 wineries and tasting rooms, many clustered among the attractive downtown's growing clutch of noteworthy bistros and bakeries—some musts include Kontos Cellars, Browne Family Vineyards, and House of Smith. It's also a treat to drive the region's back roads past acres of vines. Wineries with especially beautiful grounds and tasting rooms include Valdemar Estates, Revelry Vintners, Abeja, and Long Shadows.

**Do This:** Walla Walla's increasingly renowned food scene and growing number of vintners comes together at Waterbrook Winery, a 49-acre estate with an airy tasting room where you can sip on a spacious patio with an outdoor fireplace. Best of all, Waterbrook has a terrific locavore-driven restaurant overlooking a pond and the surrounding hills. ⊕ *waterbrook.com*

**Walla Walla.** ☎ *509/525–8799* ⊕ *wallawalla.org.*

## Cool Places to Stay

**The Finch.** A former motel has been reborn as this hip hotel that hopes to be your base for exploring all that's wonderful about Walla Walla and its gorgeous wineries. If offers helpful maps to help guide your discoveries. ✉ *325 E. Main St., Walla Walla, WA* ☎ *509/956–4994* ⊕ *finchwallawalla.com* [$] *From $119.*

**Inn at the Market.** From its heart-stopping views to the fabulous location just steps from Pike Place Market to its exceptional restaurants, this inviting boutique hotel is one you'll want to visit again and again. ✉ *86 Pine St., Seattle, WA* ☎ *206/443–3600* ⊕ *innatthemarket.com* [$] *From $197.*

**Kalaloch Lodge.** Overlooking an absolutely dazzling stretch of the Pacific Ocean in Olympic National Park, Kalaloch has cozy rooms with beach views, cabins along the bluff, and an inviting restaurant. ✉ *157151 U.S. 101, Forks, WA* ☎ *360/962–2271* ⊕ *thekalalochlodge.com* [$] *From $395.*

**Mountain Home Lodge.** This contemporary inn, where peeled-pine and vine-maple furniture fills the rooms, is built of sturdy cedar and redwood and sits on a 20-acre alpine meadow with breathtaking Cascade Mountains views and easy proximity to Leavenworth's Bavarian-style charms. ✉ *8201 Mountain Home Rd., Leavenworth, WA* ☎ *509/548–7077* ⊕ *mthome.com* [$] *From $260.*

**Salish Lodge & Spa.** The stunning, chalet-style lodge—which you may recognize from the opening credits of *Twin Peaks*—sits dramatically over Snoqualmie Falls and offers a slew of creature comforts, including plush rooms with gas fireplaces, window seats, and a first-rate spa with sauna, steam room, and soaking tubs. ✉ *6501 Railroad Ave., Snoqualmie, WA* ☎ *425/888–2556* ⊕ *salishlodge.com* [$] *From $299.*

**Society Hotel.** This stylish but unpretentious Scandinavian-inspired compound—a converted 1937 schoolhouse and a ring of sleek cabins set around a spa and bathhouse—is a perfect base for hiking, wine touring, and chilling out on the Washington side of the Columbia Gorge. ✉ *210 N. Cedar St., Cook, WA* ☎ *509/774–4437* ⊕ *thesocietyhotel.com* [$] *From $86.*

Chapter 8

# THE SOUTHWEST



Written by
Debbie Harmsen

# WELCOME TO THE SOUTHWEST

## TOP REASONS TO GO

★ **All-star parks:** The Southwest is home to a dozen national parks, including some of the most visited in the United States. Stand in wonder at the Grand Canyon, get away from it all at Great Basin—or even get underground at Carlsbad Caverns.

★ **Red rocks:** From Sedona's stunning formations to Bryce Canyon's hoodoos and Antelope Canyon's sweeping sandstone walls to Nevada's Valley of Fire State Park, this part of the country is awash in shades of ruby, red-orange, and maroon.

★ **Road trips:** From Route 66 to Utah's national parks, this part of the country begs for a good old American road trip, windows down and music up as you drive past nostalgia-inducing towns.

★ **Southwest cuisine:** Red hot chili peppers and Hatch green chilies bring the heat, but there's so much to love on every menu. You can find authentic Mexican food in border towns, and varieties, such as Tex-Mex, inland.

**1 Arizona.** With its deserts and canyons below and wide-open dark skies above, the Grand Canyon State is a place for both adventure and relaxation.

**2 Nevada.** The bright lights of Vegas get all the hype, but don't forget about the Hoover Dam, Reno, and so much more in the Silver State.

**3 New Mexico.** Known for its adobe architecture and abundance of Native American art, New Mexico attracts artistic types to its towns and mountains.

**4 Texas.** From boomtowns, beaches, and border towns to cityscapes, scenic spots, and historic sites, the second largest state (after Alaska) has it all.

**5 Utah.** With its five national parks, including Bryce and Zion, plus world-class skiing and mountain biking, the Beehive State is the place to be outdoors.

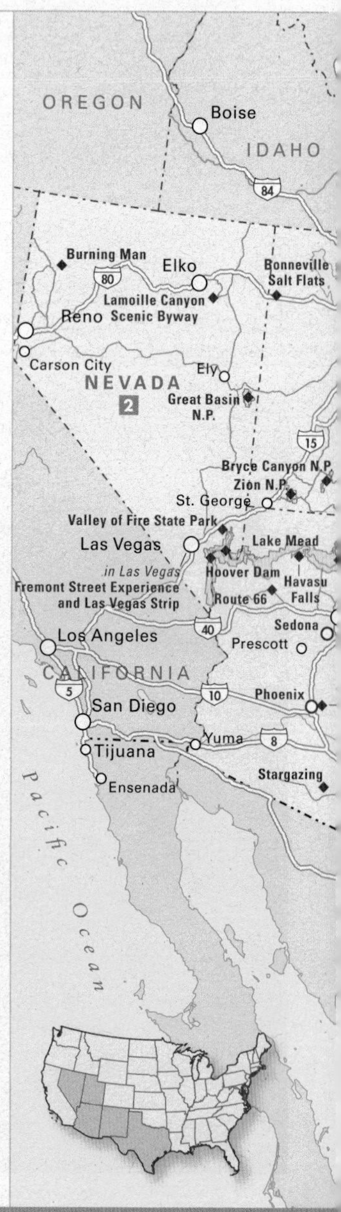

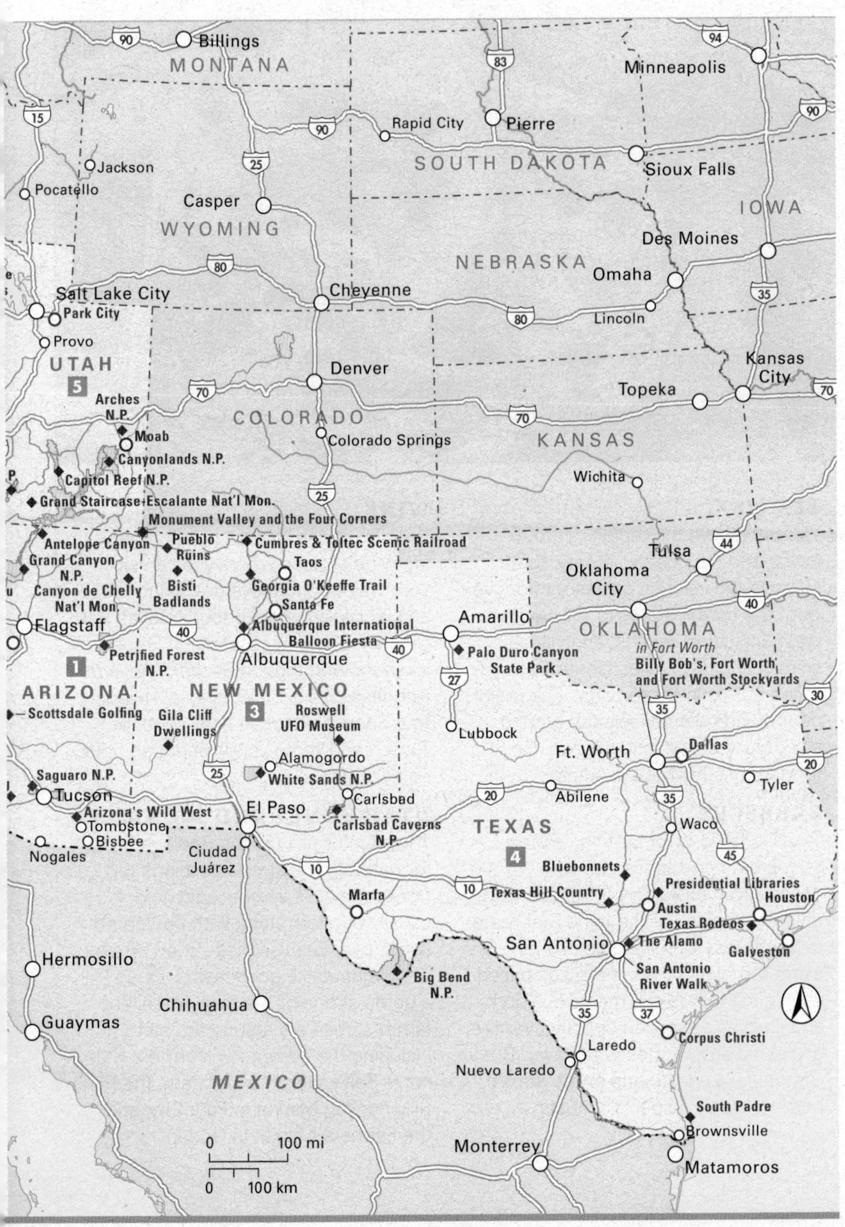
Billings
MONTANA
Minneapolis
Rapid City
Pierre
SOUTH DAKOTA
Sioux Falls
Jackson
Pocatello
Casper
WYOMING
IOWA
Des Moines
NEBRASKA
Omaha
Salt Lake City
Park City
Cheyenne
Lincoln
Provo
UTAH
5
Denver
Kansas City
Topeka
Arches N.P.
COLORADO
Moab
Colorado Springs
KANSAS
Canyonlands N.P.
Capitol Reef N.P.
Wichita
Grand Staircase-Escalante Nat'l Mon.
Monument Valley and the Four Corners
Antelope Canyon
Pueblo Ruins
Cumbres & Toltec Scenic Railroad
Tulsa
Grand Canyon N.P.
Taos
Oklahoma City
Canyon de Chelly Nat'l Mon.
Bisti Badlands
Georgia O'Keeffe Trail
Santa Fe
Flagstaff
Albuquerque International Balloon Fiesta
Amarillo
OKLAHOMA
Petrified Forest N.P.
Albuquerque
Palo Duro Canyon State Park
in Fort Worth
Billy Bob's, Fort Worth and Fort Worth Stockyards
1
ARIZONA
NEW MEXICO
3
Scottsdale Golfing
Gila Cliff Dwellings
Roswell UFO Museum
Lubbock
Ft. Worth
Dallas
Alamogordo
White Sands N.P.
Saguaro N.P.
Tucson
Carlsbad
Abilene
Tyler
El Paso
Arizona's Wild West
Tombstone
Bisbee
Carlsbad Caverns N.P.
TEXAS
Waco
Nogales
Ciudad Juárez
4
Bluebonnets
Presidential Libraries
Houston
Marfa
Texas Hill Country
Austin
Texas Rodeos
San Antonio
The Alamo
Galveston
San Antonio River Walk
Hermosillo
Big Bend N.P.
Chihuahua
Guaymas
Corpus Christi
Laredo
Nuevo Laredo
MEXICO
South Padre
Brownsville
0 100 mi
0 100 km
Monterrey
Matamoros

# WHAT TO EAT AND DRINK IN THE SOUTHWEST

Tex-Mex

## TEX-MEX

You can't leave the region without diving into the cheesy, meaty, totally-worth-the-calories dishes that derive from the border states of the Southwest, including nachos, enchiladas, chimichangas, burritos (sometimes called burros in these parts). The major pillar of ingredients includes ground beef, black beans, and cheese. Don't miss Pelons Tex Mex in Austin.

## BARBECUE

Texas is famous for putting its own stamp on the American favorite, especially in brisket, with variations in different regions of the Lone Star State. In South Texas, brisket and ribs are slathered with a thick molasses-based sauce. In West Texas, meats like pork and chicken are grilled directly over fire, giving it a smoky mesquite flavor. But Central Texas is the hub of the state's best barbecue, especially Austin.

## WINE

Both Texas and Arizona have burgeoning wine regions where you can sip your way through award-winning reds and whites. Start your tour in Texas Hill Country, centering yourself in Fredericksburg with trips to Becker Vineyards And Texas Wine Collective. In Arizona, tour Sonoita about an hour south of Tucson and Verde Valley, about an hour north of Phoenix.

## UTAH HONEY AND SCONES

They don't call Utah the Beehive State for nothing. The state's delicious wildflower honey is sweet liquid gold. It's usually drizzled, along with powdered sugar, over Utah scones—fried pillows of doughnut-like goodness. Pick up a bottle at one of the many excellent farmers' markets around the state, including the Downtown Farmers Market in Salt Lake's Pioneer Park, the Park Silly Sunday Market in Park City, and the Farmers Market in Ogden.

## PIÑON NUTS

This tasty variety of pine nuts is huge in New Mexico, Arizona, Utah, and Nevada and were traditionally harvested by the Navajo. They are sprinkled atop dishes like blue corn pancakes to give them texture and a rich nutty flavor. In Nevada's Great Basin National Park, you can fill three gunnysacks of piñon nuts you find in the park to take home. Piñon coffee is also popular.

## KOLACHES

Famous in Texas (especially the tiny town of West, Texas) kolaches are pastries made of sweet yeast dough stuffed with savory sausage or sweet fillings like jam. The pockets were brought over by Czech immigrants and have been a hit ever since, especially along the very busy Interstate 35 corridor where people stop and wait in long lines to buy them.

## TAMALES

Families order platters of this traditional Mexican dish by the dozen during the holidays, but you can enjoy them year-round. Much like burros or enchiladas, tamales feature a filling (usually meat but not always) surrounded by a shell. Tamales have a corn-based wrapper, and they're steamed in an actual corn husk, which you should unfold and discard before digging into the filling.

Tamales

Prickly Pear Margarita

## PRICKLY PEAR

The Southwest's many towering cacti are the source of several food specialities, including cholla, nopales, and prickly pear. The prickly pear cactus produces the wonderful, sweet fruit that's used to accent beverages, desserts, and even entrées. Try it in a prickly pear margarita. When you take your first sip of the bright, magenta-hued drink, you'll wonder how the original ever existed without it.

## TEXAS CHILI

The hearty classic is like a traditional chili save a few key ingredients. True Texans don't dare put beans or tomato sauce in chili ... it's beef, beef, and more beef. Try it in Tex-Mex restaurants across the state, especially at Texas Chili Parlor in Austin.

## WHATABURGER

California brought the country In 'N Out, Texas brought it Whataburger, a locally loved fast-food joint that serves up mouthwatering burgers and honey-butter chicken biscuits under an orange-and-white-striped triangular arch that evokes '50s-diner nostalgia. The original is in Corpus Christi, but you can find them across Texas.

# The Southwest Regional Snapshot

## Know Before You Go

### PLAN AHEAD FOR TRIBAL LAND VISITS

Arizona alone has 22 Native American tribes, each with its own government and culture. Most tribes have websites or phone information lines, and it's best to contact them before a trip. Many areas, like Antelope Canyon and Canyon de Chelly, require a guide from the tribe to take you on a tour; others require a permit for hiking, biking, taking photos, or filming in scenic areas. Always be respectful of individual cultures and traditions.

### RENT A CAR

Wide-open spaces mean there's a lot of territory to cover in these parts, and public transportation is sparse. Unless you are hunkering down at a resort or taking a guided tour, renting a car is the best way to explore the region. Many of the top sights are nature areas and archaeological sites in far-flung parts of the states. There are also long stretches of highway without gas stations or food services, so make sure to regularly top off your gas tank and bring snacks and water.

### BE PREPARED FOR EXTREMES

You can start your day in 90°F heat in Phoenix and end it in near-freezing temperatures at the rim of the Grand Canyon. Be sure to plan accordingly for the weather: if driving in the desert in summer, keep bottled water in the car; in winter in the high country, be prepared for icy roads. And remember that violent flash floods and dust storms can pepper the desert during the summer monsoons. Storms usually pass quickly.

### PREPARE FOR ALTITUDE SICKNESS

Altitude sickness can be a real downer on vacation. Breathtaking views and outdoor recreation lose appeal fast when you have trouble getting enough oxygen to breathe normally and feel dizzy, nauseous, weak, or get a headache. It happens because the level of oxygen gets lower the higher you go. Most of the ski resorts and many mountain trails are above the 8,000-foot altitude where the sickness begins to affect people. So it's best to take it slow and easy to get used to the mountain air and descend if you feel any symptoms rather than pushing on, as that can cause more severe problems. Stay well hydrated, too.

## Planning Your Time

Spring is a near perfect time to visit the region, when flowers bloom (bluebonnets in Texas and saguaro cacti in Arizona) and the weather isn't too hot yet. Alternatively, winter is a great time to hit the slopes in New Mexico and Utah (and the season in Park City coincides with the Sundance Film Festival). The region is vast, and any one of the states could be explored on a one-week road trip. Depending on your trip's focus, fly into the nearest major city (ex: Las Vegas, Phoenix, Dallas, Salt Lake City, or Santa Fe) and string together a few epic sights on a road trip from there.

## Road Trips

**3 Days:** Route 66

**3 Days:** Texas Hill Country

**5 Days:** Zion to Bryce to Grand Canyon National Park

## Big Events

**South by Southwest.** This huge festival with live music, film, and media brings people to Austin, Texas, each March.

**Albuquerque International Balloon Fiesta.** Colorful hot-air balloons fill the skies over New Mexico's largest city for a nine-day festival in October.

**Sundance Film Festival.** Presented by Robert Redford's Sundance Institute, the annual festival is on par with international festivals like Cannes and Toronto and attracts serious film buffs, locals, and plenty of celebrities to Park City and Salt Lake City at the end of January.

**Burning Man.** Thousands flock to the Nevada desert in late August to create the temporary town of Black Rock City, to party and to showcase their creative talents.

## What To ...

### READ

*The Bean Trees* by Barbara Kingsolver

*Laughing Boy: A Navajo Love Story* by Oliver La Farge

*Desert Solitaire* by Edward Abbey

*No Country for Old Men* by Cormac McCarthy

### WATCH

*Tombstone* (film set in Arizona)

*Friday Night Lights* (film set in Texas)

*Ocean's Eleven* (film set in Nevada)

*127 hours* (film set in Utah)

### BUY

Prickly pear candy and turquoise from Arizona

Stetson hat and cowboy boots from Texas

Native American art and Georgia O'Keeffe prints in New Mexico

## Contacts

### AIR

Major Airports

**Arizona.** PHX, TUS, PRC, FLG, GCN, BSQ

**Nevada.** LAS, RNO

**New Mexico.** ABQ, SAF, ROW, ALM

**Texas.** DFW, IAH, AUS, DAL, HOU, SAT, ELP

**Utah.** SLC

### VISITOR INFO

🌐 *visitarizona.com*

🌐 *travelnevada.com*, 🌐 *nv.gov/visit*

🌐 *newmexico.org*

🌐 *traveltexas.com*

🌐 *visitutah.com*

# Arizona

From the vastness of the Grand Canyon to Sedona's red rocks and the living Sonoran Desert, Arizona's landscapes are awe-inspiring. The state's spectacular canyons, blooming deserts, raging rivers, petrified forests, and scenic mountains enthrall lovers of the outdoors in pursuit of hiking, rafting, golf, or picturesque spots to watch the sunset. But there is more to Arizona than beautiful vistas. World-renowned spas in Phoenix provide plenty of pampering, while Native American cultures thrive throughout the state.

## Bucket List Picks

The following boxes contain our picks for the top sights and experiences in Arizona.

- ○ Grand Canyon National Park
- ○ Sedona
- ○ Petrified Forest National Park
- ○ Arizona's Wild West
- ○ Route 66
- ○ Phoenix
- ○ Antelope Canyon
- ○ Canyon de Chelly National Monument
- ○ Scottsdale Golfing
- ○ Havasu Falls
- ○ Stargazing
- ○ Saguaro National Park

# Grand Canyon National Park

## Geological Superstar

It's the big one, the bucket list topper, and what President Teddy Roosevelt called "the one great sight every American should see." The Grand Canyon draws millions each year, to river raft, camp, ride a mule, take a ranger-led tour, and see wildlife, but most of all, to be awed at one heck of a canvas Mother Nature has crafted. The statistics—the canyon measures an average width of 10 miles, length of 277 river miles, and depth of 1 mile—don't truly prepare you for that first impression.

## Don't Miss

White-water rafting down the Colorado River from the depths of the canyon is an experience you won't soon forget. Trips begin at Lee's Ferry near Page; sign up in advance.

## Best Hike

The Rim Trail runs along the edge of the canyon from Mather Point to Hermits Rest with several overlooks.

## Best Splurge

Get a bird's-eye view of the canyon with a splurge-worthy helicopter tour. Several carriers are based in Tusayan.

## Getting Here and Around

There are two main access points: the South Rim—the most popular and easily accessible—is 60 miles from Williams and 80 miles from Flagstaff. The less trodden North Rim is 220 miles from the South Rim and 265 miles from Las Vegas, and it's only accessible from mid-May to mid-October. Many choose to spend the night in nearby Tusayan, in the park's lodges (El Tovar, Bright Angel) or on park campgrounds (Mather, Bright Angel, or Desert View).

**Grand Canyon Visitor Center.** ✉ *450 Hwy. 64, Grand Canyon, AZ* 🌐 *www.nps.gov/grca* 🎫 *$35.*

# Sedona

## Good Views, Good Vibes

Surrounded by verdant pine forests and beautiful, rugged red rock formations, and filled with gourmet restaurants, art galleries, spas, boutiques, and wineries, Sedona is the ultimate place for outdoor adventure and a bit of desert sophistication. It also draws a New Age crowd looking for good vibes in the town's four major electromagnetic energy fields (or vortexes) said to be at Airport Mesa, Cathedral Rock, Bell Rock, and Boynton Canyon. Some locals say these spirals of energy make them feel energized and lighter. Of course, this also might be because they happen to afford some amazing, panoramic views of the red buttes. Regardless, you'll be in hiking heaven.

## Don't Miss

The showstopper is Cathedral Rock, a 1,200-foot-high butte with towering, variegated spires that looms dramatically over town. The butte is best seen toward dusk from a distance, but you can also hike the 1.5-mile trail.

## Best Tour

A jeep tour with Pink Adventure Tours is a popular choice for driving through the red rocks. Hang on as these seemingly gravity-defying vehicles clamber up and over boulders, giving you bursts of adrenaline in addition to panoramic views of the Coconino National Forest. 🌐 *www.pinkadventuretours.com* 🎫 *From $129.*

## Getting Here and Around

Sedona is about 30 miles from Flagstaff and about 120 miles from Phoenix. To explore on your own, rent a four-wheel-drive vehicle from an agency such as Barlow Adventures; most visitors opt for a jeep tour.

**Sedona Visitor Center.** ✉ *331 Forest Rd., Sedona AZ* ☎ *928/282–7722* 🌐 *visitsedona.com.*

# Petrified Forest National Park

## Rainbow Hills and Frozen Trees

Step into an otherworldly lunar landscape where ancient trees look like they're made of colorful stone. One of Arizona's most unusual sites, Petrified Forest National Park is home to fossilized trees that date back to the Triassic Period, plus a stretch of the famed Route 66 protected within park boundaries. It's worth the trip just to see the park's beautiful Painted Desert—especially if you catch the brilliant colors of the landscape at midday. You could easily spend half a day or more viewing petrified logs as well as Pueblo rock art, hiking various trails, and enjoying views from the many overlooks.

## Don't Miss

Old Faithful, a roughly 44-ton log, lies along Giant Logs, a half-mile loop that begins behind Rainbow Forest Museum near the park's south entrance.

## Scenic Drive

Winding 28 miles through the Painted Desert, the Painted Desert Scenic drive is a must for seeing the park's flora and fauna, plus Newspaper Rock, a large boulder with petroglyphs carved into it, and several cone-shaped teepees. The moderately steep 1-mile Blue Mesa trail loop can be accessed from the road.

## When to Go

The park is rarely crowded. The best time to visit is autumn, when nights are chilly but daytime temperatures hover near 70°F.

## Getting Here and Around

Situated between Interstate 40 and Highway 180, Petrified National Forest is closest to the town of Holbrook, Arizona, about 20 miles away.

**Petrified Forest National Park.** ✉ *1 Park Rd., Petrified Forest, AZ* ☎ *928/524–6228* 🌐 *www.nps.gov/pefo* 🎫 *$25.*

# Arizona's Wild West

### Wickedest Towns in the West

The Old West lives on in Arizona, especially in three towns: Jerome, Bisbee, and Tombstone. In these dusty Western towns, tours, shows, reenactments, and more bring legendary stories of sheriffs, saloons, and shootouts to life. If you're a movie buff, also visit Tucson's Old Tucson Studios, where 400 movies and TV shows were filmed, including *The Gambler*, *America's Most Wanted*, and *Little House on the Prairie*.

### Tombstone

Wyatt Earp and Doc Holliday made Tombstone famous with their quick draw near the O.K. Corral, and the town continues to re-create it among Allen Street's saloons and theaters.

### Bisbee

Explore the Bisbee Mining & Historical Museum and tour of the Copper Queen Mine, where you don a hard hat, headlamp, and yellow slicker and descend 1,500 feet under the surface.

### Jerome and Prescott

Once called the "wickedest town in the West," Jerome became a ghost town when its mine closed in 1953. Today popular attractions are the Douglas Mansion, the Gold King Mine Ghost Town, and ghost tours that include a stop at the supposedly haunted Jerome Grand Hotel. For a less touristy look at life during Holliday's heyday, visit nearby Prescott's Whiskey Row.

### Getting Here and Around

Tombstone is about an hour's drive southeast of Tucson near the southeastern corner of the state. Bisbee is a 25-minute drive from Tombstone on AZ 80 E, so it's easy to combine the two Old West towns into a single weekend trip. Jerome is 295 miles northwest of Tombstone, closer to Sedona, which is 27 miles away.

## Route 66

### Get Your Kicks

Created in 1926, the Mother Road still draws travelers on road trips through yesteryear. Although it's not a continuous route anymore and the number 66 was decertified as a U.S. highway designation in 1985, much of the road connecting Chicago to Los Angeles is still drivable and sprinkled with spots of Americana. Arizona communities along the route embrace the kitsch, with 1950s-style diners, neon signs, roadside art, and shops with memorabilia. The route partially follows Interstate 40 and traverses the Petrified National Forest and such communities as Winslow, Winona, Flagstaff, Williams, Seligman, Hackberry, Kingman, and Oatman.

### Don't Miss

Take your photo "standing on the corner of Winslow, Arizona," a mural that immortalizes the Eagles' hit song, and say cheese in front of the Wigwam Motel in Holbrook, the inspiration behind Cozy Cone Motel in the animated feature film *Cars*.

### Best Pit Stops

Near Winslow, stop at the Meteor Crater, where an enormous meteorite struck the ground thousands of years ago. In Seligman, stop at Delgadillo's Snow Cap Drive-In for its ice cream.

### Best Shops

The General Store in Hackberry and Angel & Vilma's Original Route 66 Gift Shop in Seligman are worthy stops.

### Good to Know

The Historic Route 66 Association of Arizona maintains a website with trip-planning information: 🌐 *www.historic66az.com.*

### Getting Here and Around

For those visiting Petrified National Forest, Holbrook is a convenient starting point. For those driving from the Grand Canyon, Williams is the closest access town.

# Phoenix

## Valley of the Sun

With 325-plus days of sunshine each year, the Valley of the Sun more than earns its nickname. But warm weather and stunning sunsets aren't the only appeal to Phoenix, the nation's fifth largest city. Year-round outdoor adventures, including hiking trails and world-class golf courses, plus world-class museums, spas, and renowned restaurants make it a true oasis in the desert. Whether you hike under the shadow of the towering Camelback Mountain or explore the Desert Botanical Garden, there's something for everyone here.

## Don't Miss

The Heard Museum is a treasure trove of art and artifacts from native tribes. It's especially good to visit during the Hoop Dance Contest in February or the annual Guild Indian Fair and Marketplace in March. 🌐 *heard.org* 🎫 *$18.*

## Best Hike

Named for its resemblance to a camel's hump, Camelback Mountain is not only Phoenix's most iconic natural landmark but also its most popular hiking destination. Two trails, Echo Canyon Trail and Cholla Trail, lead to stunning panoramic views.

## Best Spa

With its meditation garden and indoor-outdoor treatment rooms at the base of Camelback Mountain, the Sanctuary Spa at the five-star Sanctuary Camelback Mountain Resort is a favorite for rejuvenation. 🌐 *www.sanctuaryoncamelback.com.*

## Getting Here and Around

Fly into Phoenix Sky Harbor International Airport (PHX). It's best to rent a car to get around the sprawling town, although downtown Phoenix is served by the light rail or free DASH (Downtown Area Shuttle) bus service.

# Antelope Canyon

## Most Photogenic Canyon

Situated near the Utah-Arizona border, this narrow red-sandstone slot canyon stuns with its wondrous wavelike structure and convoluted corkscrew formations, dramtically illuminated by light streaming down from above. Like the steady hand of a master artist, wind and water carved the sandstone slot canyon over eons of time. The northern Arizona attraction is a sacred site of the Navajo, called Tsé bighánílíní (place where water runs through the rocks), and you can only visit as part of a guided tour.

## Don't Miss

Snapping photos of the canyon's natural formations (resembling a Navajo chief or a smiling shark, for example) is at the top of every photographer's bucket list. The best photos are taken at high noon, when light filters through the canyon surface.

## While You're Here

Combine a visit to Antelope Canyon with a trip to nearby Rainbow Bridge National Monument, Vermilion Cliffs National Monument, or Lake Powell.

## Good to Know

Because the canyon is on Navajo Nation grounds, the only way to experience it is through a guided tour with Antelope Canyon Navajo Tours. Note that the Navajo Nation observes daylight saving time while the surrounding areas of Arizona do not. *www.navajotours.com* *$80.*

## Getting Here and Around

Base yourself in nearby Page, or book with a touring company that will transport you to the canyon from Phoenix, Sedona, Flagstaff, or Las Vegas. Page is four hours' drive from either Phoenix or Las Vegas.

# Canyon de Chelly National Monument

## Ancient Home of the Navajo

This national monument located on the Navajo tribal lands of the Colorado Plateau is one of the longest continuously inhabited landscapes in the continent, not to mention one of the most breathtaking natural wonders of the Southwest. On a smaller scale, it rivals even the Grand Canyon in beauty, featuring dramatic red sandstone walls soaring to the sky, ancient pictographs dotting the cliffs, and 7,000 archaeological sites transporting you back in time. Among the features are White House Ruins and Mummy Cave, the remnants of ancient Pueblo villages. You can explore the canyon on your own, hike with a ranger, or sign up for a tour with a Navajo guide.

## Don't Miss

Spider Rock, a spectacular spire that rises more than 750 feet tall, can be viewed from an overlook on South Rim. The skinny needle of a rock is named for a character of Navajo legend, Spider Woman.

## Best Tour

The Navajo-led Jeep tour is the way to go. Take in the spectacular scenery with a knowledgeable guide and learn about the culture of the people who have lived there for thousands of years. 🌐 *www.canyondechellytours.com* 🎫 *From $247.*

## Good to Know

Canyon de Chelly is pronounced "Canyon d'Shay."

## Getting Here and Around

Located in northeast Arizona, the park entrance is 3 miles east of Chinle. The canyon is 222 miles east of the Grand Canyon and 167 miles from Page.

**Canyon de Chelly National Monument.** ✉ *Navajo Rte. 7, Chinle, AZ* ☎ *928/674–5500* 🌐 *www.nps.gov/cach* 🎫 *Free.*

# Scottsdale Golfing

## Tee Time in the Sunshine

The hot and dry climate of the Valley of the Sun, along with a wealth of high-end resorts, has made the upscale Phoenix suburb of Scottsdale an ideal playground for golfers. Scottsdale packs in 50 golf courses within its city limits and 200 more in its environs. Designed by such notable names as Robert Trent Jones, Phil Mickelson, Rees Jones, and Ben Crenshaw, Scottdale's sun-splashed courses provide golfers with a delightful cornucopia of Southwestern scenes, scents, and sounds—from rock formations, mountain vistas, and ribbonlike fairways lined with Sonoran Desert cacti to the aromas of eucalyptus, mesquite, and pine to the soft lullaby of cascading water.

## Don't Miss

Many of the courses have been ranked as top picks in the state and region by *Golf Magazine* and *Golf Digest*, including Boulders, Desert Forest, Estancia, We-Ko-Pa Golf Club (Saguaro), Scottsdale National (The Other Course), Desert Highlands, Whisper Rock (Upper and Lower), Talking Stick (O'odham), and Quintero.

## Good to Know

Staying at one of Scottsdale's golf resorts gives you access to a tee time at that property's private courses. For a directory of public courses, go to 🌐 *experiencescottsdale.com/golf*.

## While You're Here

After you've putted your way through Scottsdale's courses, retreat to one its many spas, pop into its art galleries, and visit Frank Lloyd Wright's winter home, Taliesin West.

## Getting Here and Around

Scottsdale is about a 15-minute drive from Phoenix Sky Harbor International Airport (PHX). Touring downtown is easily done on foot, but you'll want a car to explore further.

# Havasu Falls

## Land of Blue-Green Water

One of the most spectacular waterfalls in Arizona is Havasu Falls (literally, "blue-green waters") part of the Havasupai tribal land of the Grand Canyon. This breathtaking beauty is hidden to most of the world, but hikers with the resources to complete the multiday 19-mile hike—including stamina, initiative, and proper backcountry gear and experience—are rewarded by the glorious sight of the falls' turquoise waters cascading over rugged red rocks and crashing down 100 feet into Havasu Creek below, all of it tucked into a paradisical red-rock setting.

## Don't Miss

Camping at Havasupai Campground, located on Havasupai land between Havasu Falls and Mooney Falls, is a highlight of the hike.

## Planning Your Trip

This is not a last-minute trip. A hard-to-come-by permit is needed, so aspiring hikers must make a reservation well in advance. It is also not a day trip. The minimum commitment is a three-night stay at the rustic Havasupai Falls Campground ($100 to $125 a night) or at the basic lodge in the Supai Village ($660 per room per night up to four people per room); with either choice you will need to bring your own food. Permits are obtained at 🌐 *havasupaireservations.com* beginning February 1 each year.

## Getting Here and Around

The Hualapai Hilltop trailhead is a four-hour drive from the South Rim of Grand Canyon National Park. Peach Springs is the nearest town to the trailhead.

**Havasu Canyon.** 🌐 *havasupaireservations.com* 🎫 *From $100 per night.*

# Stargazing

## Diamonds in the Sky

The heavenly bodies shine bright in Arizona's "dark sky" destinations, specially designated places that are far enough from city light pollution that you can see uninterrupted swaths of twinkling constellations up above the world so high. You might even see a planet or two. This happens nearly every night, given Arizona's roughly 350 clear-sky nights each year. The Tucson-based International Dark Sky Association deems 16 places in Arizona official "dark sky" destinations, including Petrified Forest National Park, Oracle State Park, Flagstaff, Sedona, Camp Verde, the Village of Oak Creek, Kartchner Caverns State Park, and the Grand Canyon National Park. Find them all at 🌐 *www.darksky.org*.

## Don't Miss

To get a closer look with high powered telescopes, head to the Lowell Observatory in Flagstaff, where Pluto was discovered in 1930; and Kitt Peak National Observatory in Sells, home to the world's largest solar telescope.

## Stargazing Parties

In Tucson, Flandrau Science Center & Planetarium hosts a weekly astronomy program, and the Mt. Lemmon SkyCenter in Tucson holds nightly stargazing programs. Each June the Grand Canyon National Park hosts a weeklong affair with constellation tours, telescope viewing, and free nightly astronomy talks.

## Getting Here and Around

Stargazing is best in desert areas far from city light pollution. Flagstaff, Sedona, and the Grand Canyon are top places to stargaze. The Grand Canyon is a four-hour drive from Phoenix and its airport (PHX).

# Saguaro National Park

## USA's Largest, Oldest Cacti

The towering saguaro (pronounced sa–WAH–ro) cactus grows only in the Sonoran Desert, so naturally it symbolizes the American Southwest like nothing else. Two distinct sections of Saguaro National Park (East and West) flank either side of Tucson and preserve some of the densest stands of these revered desert giants, which can live to be 200 years old, grow up to 50 feet tall, and weigh a whopping 6 tons. In the spring, white flowers with yellow centers pop up along the cacti's trunk and arms—the official state flower of Arizona.

## Don't Miss

The park's West District (also called Tucson Mountain District) is smaller but more visited and has access to hiking trails, ancient petroglyphs, and Bajada Loop Drive, a scenic 6-mile drive through the densest growth in the park. The West entrance is near Tucson's Arizona–Sonora Desert Museum, so many visitors combine these two sites in one day.

## While You're Here

Saguaro National Park's East District (aka Rincon Mountain District) has more than 100 hiking trails, including the accessible Desert Ecology Trail.

## When to Go

Late April through June is when the saguaros bloom, with peak flowers in May. Fun fact: flowers only bloom on saguaros that are at least 35 years old.

## Getting Here and Around

Saguaro National Park is situated on both sides of Tucson. The East District (Saguaro East) is 16 miles from Tucson International Airport (TUS), while the West District (Saguaro West) is 22 miles from Tucson.

**Saguaro East.** ✉ *3693 S. Old Spanish Trail, Tucson, AZ* **Saguaro West.** ✉ *2700 N. Kinney Rd., Tucson, AZ* 🌐 *www.nps.gov/sagu* 🎫 *$25.*

# When in Arizona

## BEARIZONA

This 160-acre drive-through wildlife park within the Kaibab National Forest is home to more than two dozen animals, including the arctic wolf, bison, jaguars, pythons, javelinas, mini donkeys, prairie dogs, elk, raccoon, deer, porcupines, foxes, reindeer, goats, and of course black bears and grizzlies. You can see the animals in their natural habitat as you drive through the park on your own or via a bus tour. Animals here are in the wild, so on the drive-through portion you are not allowed to touch or feed the animals. However, at Fort Bearizona, the portion of the park that follows the drive-through area, there is a petting zoo.

**Do This:** Learn about the animals from a knowledgeable guide on the park's complimentary "Wild Ride" bus tour. The guide may stop to feed a couple of the tamer animals.

**Bearizona.** ✉ *1500 E. Rte. 66, Williams, AZ* ☎ *928/635–2289* 🌐 *bearizona.com* 🎫 *$25.*

## BISBEE ART SCENE

The independent spirit that once made Bisbee a rough-and-tumble kind of place in its old mining days now lends itself to artistic expression. Set in the Mule Mountains about 11 miles from the Mexico border and 90 miles south of Tucson, the town of just 5,000 has more than a dozen galleries. Among the creations displayed are paintings, sculptures, ceramics, handmade furniture, photographs, contemporary art, jewelry, and specially crafted toys. An art walk occurs every second Saturday. Visual art pairs with wine tastings, live music, and antiques shopping.

**Do This:** Walk along the alleyway of Brewery Gulch after grabbing a pint at Old Bisbee Brewing Company and be treated to an eclectic collection of art lining the exterior wall. The pieces have come from a variety of sources and been obtained in all manner of ways, including dumpster dives. If you feel so inclined, make your own contribution.

**Discover Bisbee.** ✉ *Bisbee, AZ* 🌐 *www.discoverbisbee.com.*

## LONDON BRIDGE

Remember the old nursery rhyme "London Bridge Is Falling Down"? Well, it was. In 1968, after about 150 years of constant use, the 294-foot-long landmark was sinking into the Thames. When Lake Havasu City founder Robert McCullough heard about this predicament, he set about buying London Bridge, having it disassembled, shipped more than 5,000 miles to northwestern Arizona, and rebuilt, stone by stone. The bridge was reconstructed on mounds of sand and took three years to complete. When it was finished, a mile-long channel was dredged under the bridge and water was diverted from Lake Havasu through the Bridgewater Channel. Today, the entire city is centered on this unusual attraction.

**Do This:** Ninety-minute walking tours include the bridge's history, items of interest, and a 51-stair climb to the top of the bridge. Stop and admire the antique lampposts. Lining the London Bridge, these historical structures were created from the cannons that the British took from Napoléon's army in 1815, spoils of war from the Battle of Waterloo.

**Visitor Center.** ✉ *422 English Village, Lake Havasu City, AZ* ☎ *928/855–5655* 🌐 *www.golakehavasu.com/london-bridge.*

## SPRING TRAINING

You can watch practices and exhibition games for several teams during Major League Baseball's spring training each March in the Phoenix area, when the weather is fantastic. The Arizona Cactus League is composed of 15 different MLB teams: the Arizona Diamondbacks, Chicago Cubs, Chicago White Sox, Cincinnati Reds, Cleveland Indians, Colorado

Rockies, Kansas City Royals, Los Angeles Angels, L.A. Dodgers, Milwaukee Brewers, Oakland Athletics, San Diego Padres, San Francisco Giants, Seattle Mariners, and the Texas Rangers. Venues include Goodyear Ballpark, Peoria Sports Complex, Sloan Park, Scottsdale Stadium, Tempe Diablo Stadium, Camelback Ranch–Glendale, and Surprise Stadium.

**Do This:** Bring a blanket and picnic on the sloped lawns of the outfield (the Royals/ Rangers, Indians/ Reds, Padres/Mariners, Angels, Giants, Cubs, and Diamondbacks/Rockies all have lawn seating) and let your kids collect any home-run balls that land nearby. And have your catcher's mitt at the ready, just in case.

**Arizona Cactus League.** *cactusleague.com* *Ticket prices vary.*

# Cool Places to Stay

**Grand Canyon lodges and campgrounds.** There are several options for sleeping at or near Grand Canyon National Park. Our three top picks are spending the night at Phantom Lodge after a hike or mule down to the canyon floor (or getting there via a guided rafting trip that drops you off there); sleeping right along the canyon's rim in the charming and historic El Tovar Lodge, where Theodore Roosevelt, Albert Einstein, and Zane Grey all stayed; and the Grand Canyon Railway & Hotel in Williams, where you can hop on a scenic and themed train ride to go to and from the canyon; bonus: the hotel has a pet resort for checking in furry friends. There also are many campgrounds and RV sites within and around the canyon as well as backcountry camping (permit required; see *nps.gov/grca*). **TIP→ Lodging in and near the park fills up quickly, so make your reservations far in advance.** *www.grandcanyonlodges.com.*

**Joshua Tree House Tucson.** Bordering Saguaro National Park, this posada takes advantage of its scenic and serene positioning with windows, patios, and rooftop balconies providing many glimpses of the flora and fauna as well as pleasant views of sunrises and star-filled nights. The desert-themed vacation rental home features five Spanish-styled suites that open into a shared living and dining area. Bookings by Airbnb only. *12051 W. Fort Lowell Rd., Tucson, AZ* *thejoshuatreehouse.com* $ *From $320.*

**Sanctuary Resort Camelback Mountain.** Step into luxury, comfort, and serenity at this 53-acre award-winning Scottsdale-area property, which has the scenic surroundings of Camelback Mountain as its backdrop. Enjoy a relaxing treatment at the Asian-inspired spa or a workout in the lap pool or fitness center, or satisfy your taste buds with the savory, seasonal dishes at the on-site restaurant overseen by chef Beau MacMillan, who has starred on the Food Network. Stay at a room or suite in the resort lodge or in a private mountainside villa. *5700 E. McDonald Dr., Paradise Valley, AZ* *855/245–2051* *www.sanctuaryoncamelback.com* $ *From $874.*

**Wigwam Motel.** Immerse yourself in the kitschy, 1950-era Americana vibes of Route 66 at this hard-to-miss village of concrete teepees along the Mother Road. Each cone-shaped structure comes equipped with pine log furniture and either two twin beds or a queen, and a small but full bathroom. There is also heat, air-conditioning, and cable TV. Pets are allowed at an additional charge. *811 W. Hopi Dr., Holbrook, AZ* *928/524–3048* *sleepinawigwam.com* $ *From $86.*

# Nevada

Nevada is a vast state with most of its population clustered in a certain Sin City in the southwest corner. Stark desert beauty and a bit of the Wild West is found in much of the rest of Nevada, particularly in Great Basin National Park, where high desert meets alpine forest. Straddling the California/Nevada state line is the Sierra Nevada resort region of Lake Tahoe and Reno, which beckons naturalists, campers, boaters, and those looking for similar action to Las Vegas in a more local setting.

## Bucket List Picks

The following boxes contain our picks for the top sights and experiences in Nevada.

- ○ Las Vegas Strip
- ○ Hoover Dam
- ○ Fremont Street Experience
- ○ Burning Man
- ○ Lake Mead National Recreation Area
- ○ Great Basin National Park
- ○ Valley of Fire State Park
- ○ Lamoille Canyon Scenic Byway

# Las Vegas Strip

## Entertainment Epicenter

A neon glow electrifies the 4.2 miles of 24/7 entertainment in the Las Vegas's strip, center of the action for the 37 million people a year who come for glittering casinos, theaters, restaurants, rides, shows, shops, and everything over-the-top. The Strip disorients and delights; when you're here, you're all-in, and the "real world" seems far out. More than a dozen hotel-casinos are on the strip, including the MGM Grand, Caesars Palace, and the Bellagio. There's a replica Eiffel Tower and a man-made volcano at the Mirage. Big-name musicians entertain crowds, but there are performers of all kinds, including acrobats, magicians, and comedians.

## Don't Miss

Take a gondola ride at the Venetian's rendition of Venice's Canalozzo. In addition to being serenaded on your boat ride, you can catch the gondoliers breaking out in song twice a day at the hotel. *From $29.*

## Best Tour

The Big Bus Open Top Las Vegas Night Tour, a three-hour excursion on a double-decker bus includes both the Strip and Fremont Street, takes riders by famous city landmarks. Guides narrate the tour, providing details about the buildings' history, architecture, and more. *www.bigbustours.com.*

## Getting Here and Around

Las Vegas's McCarran International Airport (LAS) is about 5 miles from the Strip, which is the portion of Las Vegas Boulevard that runs from Sahara Avenue in the north to Russell Road or near the Mandalay Bay Resort & Casino on the southern end. Free trams that connect casinos can help you get around the strip.

**Las Vegas Strip.** *S. Las Vegas Blvd., Las Vegas, NV.*

# Hoover Dam

## Industrial Wonder of the World

Straddling Nevada and Arizona, the Hoover Dam is an engineering feat that's been declared one of the industrial wonders of the world. The 6.6-million-ton, 724.6-foot-tall concrete dam was built as an arch-gravity dam, a type of barrier that uses an arch structure and the force of gravity to resist the pressure of the water against the dam—which, in the Hoover Dam's case, is 45,000 pounds per square foot at its base. Constructed by thousands of workers during the Great Depression between 1931 and 1936, the dam was built to control flooding and create a reservoir from the Colorado River that would supply water and electricity to the surrounding area. Today, the dam's stored water irrigates 2 million acres of farmland and goes to Los Angeles, Phoenix, and Tucson, while its power plant generates 4 billion kilowatt-hours of hydroelectric power to Nevada, Arizona, and California.

## Don't Miss

Learn about the dam's history and engineering through exhibits at the Hoover Dam Visitor Center ($10), the power plant tour ($15), or the guided dam tour ($30), which includes admission to the visitor center, the power plant tour, and an elevator ride to the top of the dam.

## While You're Here

Visit Boulder City, a community 7 miles away that was created for the workers erecting Hoover Dam. Inside the Boulder Dam Hotel is a free museum about the dam.

## Getting Here and Around

Hoover Dam is 30 miles from Las Vegas, off of Nevada State Route 172. Parking is $10.

# Fremont Street Experience

## Vegas On Full Blast

Not far from the northern terminus of the famous Strip, Fremont Street pulses with its own beat and slate of activities and entertainment. There's ziplining, live music, light shows, sports betting, the world's largest keno board, a 200,000-gallon shark tank, a microbrewery, and of course casinos. Unlike the casinos on the Strip, the casinos along Fremont Street are not the mammoth structures with over-the-top features but are more the classic casinos that first made Las Vegas the country's gaming capital—think Golden Nugget, Binion's Gambling Hall, and Golden Gate Hotel & Casino, which opened in 1906. Walk along Fremont Street's pedestrian walk and take it all in, or hop on and off of the open-air, double-decker bus that tours both Fremont Street and the Strip.

## Don't Miss

The Mob Museum shines a light on the seedy world of organized crime and law enforcement's response to it. Learn about the mob's history, the current state of organized crime, related court cases, and so much more. And if you love the era of Prohibition and the Roaring '20s, be sure to head downstairs to tour the underground and the speakeasy—you'll need the password to get inside. It's one of the best museums in all of Nevada. *themobmuseum.org* *$30.*

## Getting Here and Around

Fremont Street is about 5 miles from Las Vegas's McCarran International Airport (LAS) and is easily walkable.

**Fremont Street.** *Downtown Las Vegas, NV* *vegasexperience.com.*

# Burning Man

## Desert Playground for Creatives

What started as a bonfire on a San Francisco beach has transformed into a massive gathering that draws tens of thousands of people to Black Rock Desert every year, when the temporary city of Black Rock emerges from the dust. More like an experimental community than a festival, Burning Man draws adventurers, artists, and partiers to band together under principles like "self-expression, communal effort" and in true Western fashion, "self-reliance." Larger-than-life art installations, impromptu performances, and wild parties are the main attractions, but mostly, it's a spectacle you have to see to believe.

## Don't Miss

Unlike festivals like Coachella or Bonnaroo, the entertainment isn't booked in advance; instead, events are community driven. Theme camps are created in the "playa," or desert, based on groups with a common goal, whether that's to create neon art or creative ways to cool off in the desert—but there's always music or art to stumble upon.

## Good to Know

It's not cheap, and it's certainly not for everyone. Depending when you book, a ticket can cost more than $1,000, and you must bring all supplies—including food, water, and shelter for your campsite—for sticking it out in the desert. There's nothing to buy here.

## While You're Here

In the "Temple Burn" a giant temple structure is burned to the ground at the end of the event, said to be almost a spirtual experience.

## Getting Here and Around

Reno is the closest large city to Burning Man's Black Rock City. 🌐 *burningman.org*

# Lake Mead National Recreation Area

### Oasis in the Desert

Splash into 248 square miles of cool water at the nation's largest man-made lake and reservoir, Lake Mead, located in Lake Mead National Recreation Area. The area, which also includes Lake Mohave, has 1.5 million acres of playground away from the desert heat. The terrain is mixed, featuring beaches, mountains, valleys, and canyons. For water fun, there's houseboating, canoeing, kayaking, fishing, and swimming. You can even scuba dive in the fresh waters; underwater sights include white gypsum reef. On the shore you can hike, bike, camp, horseback ride, and even hunt in a designated area.

### Don't Miss

Rent a houseboat on Lake Mead and you can pull into coves and explore the shoreline, relax on the beach, or play in the calm waters by day and stargaze by night.

### While You're Here

Take a scenic drive along Lakeshore Road, which runs along a portion of Boulder Basin; Pearce Ferry Road, which winds through desert and Joshua trees near Grand Wash Cliffs; and 50-mile Northshore Road, which connects Callville Bay and Echo Bay.

### Getting Here and Around

Lake Mead National Recreation Area has eight main entrances: Boulder Beach, Lake Mead Boulevard, Lake Mead Parkway, Cottonwood Cove, Temple Bar, Northshore Road, Willow Beach, and Katherine Landing. It is 4 miles from Boulder City, which is 25 miles from Las Vegas's McCarran International Airport (LAS).

**Lake Mead National Recreation Area.** ✉ *Off U.S. 93* 🌐 *www.nps.gov/lake* 🎫 *$45.*

# Great Basin National Park

## Star-studded Solitude

One of the smallest and least visited of the national parks, Great Basin National Park is no less grand, and it's a place to be away from crowds. The 77,180-acre northern Nevada park occupies a small portion of the 200,000-square-mile Great Basin Desert, the largest desert in America, covering 75% of Nevada as well as portions of Utah, Idaho, and California. Within the park's desert terrain, there are some surprising gems: Lehman Caves, a limestone and marble cavern (explored by guided tour only, $12); groves of ancient and gnarly bristlecone pines, reached via Bristlecone Pine Trail, a moderate 1.5-mile hike to do solo or on a ranger-guided trek; and Wheeler Peak, best experienced by a scenic drive capped with panoramic views.

## Don't Miss

Great Basin is an International Dark-Sky Park, so it's a great place to stargaze. If you're here at night, check out the view from Mather Overlook.

## Best Tour

Take the stargazing a step further by booking a trip on the Nevada Northern Railway's Star Train, a ranger-led trip where the night sky is literally the star of the show. The three-hour trip departs just before sunset from Ely, an hour west of the park. Reservations are required.

## Good to Know

Each fall you can fill up to three gunnysacks of piñon nuts you find in the park.

## Getting Here and Around

The park is a 3¾-hour drive from Salt Lake City and a 4½-hour drive from Las Vegas.

**Great Basin National Park.** ✉ *Nevada State Rte. 488, Baker, NV* 🌐 *www.nps.gov/grba* 🎫 *Free.*

# Valley of Fire State Park

## Waves of Flame

Otherworldly rock formations and red Aztec sandstone highlight Valley of Fire State Park, a 40,000-acre state park in southern Nevada. Visitors can hike a 2-mile scenic loop, explore slot canyons, see petroglyphs from Native American communities from some 2,500 years ago, and marvel at structures like Arch Rock, Elephant Rock, Seven Sisters, Piano Rock, White Domes, Beehives, Silica Dome, Balanced Rock, and Atlatl Rock. Wildlife includes lizards, coyotes, and jackrabbits, as well as finches, sparrows, and roadrunners. Guided tours depart from Las Vegas.

## Don't Miss

Stop at Rainbow Vista for panoramic views or Fire Wave Trail for views of an incredible wavelike sandstone formation. To see colorful fossilized wood from ancient pines, head to Petrified Logs Loop in the park's southwest quadrant.

## Good to Know

The name of the park came from a visitor, who, when viewing the stunning scenery at sunset, proclaimed that the deep red color on the landscape made the valley look like it was on fire. View the park at sunset and see if you agree.

## When to Go

The sun-soaked, rocky landscape blooms in springtime with desert marigold, indigo bush, and desert mallow, and flourishes with burro bush, creosote brush, and a variety of cacti throughout the year.

## Getting Here and Around

Valley of Fire State Park is about 60 miles from Las Vegas's McCarran International Airport.

**Valley of Fire State Park.** ✉ *29450 Valley of Fire Hwy., Overton, NV* 🌐 *parks.nv.gov/parks/valley-of-fire* 🎫 *$10.*

# Lamoille Canyon Scenic Byway

## Dazzling Mountain Drive

This 12-mile drive through Humboldt National Forest might fool you into thinking you're no longer in Nevada. Climbing through 8,800 feet of a glacier-carved canyon, the paved road in the Ruby Mountains provides views of mountains and greenery in stark contrast to the desert scenery of much of the state and far from the bright lights of Las Vegas. Loosely following Lamoille Creek, the byway leads you past rock formations and through colorful alpine meadows filled with wildlife and wildflowers. You may see bighorn sheep, deer, and mountain goats.

## Don't Miss

Pull over to picnic and hike. Any of the hiking trails will lead you to more gorgeous scenery, including little lakes with beaver ponds, serene waterfalls, and trickling streams (where you can fish), as well as to camping spots.

## When to Go

Springtime, when the wildflowers are in bloom and the snow is melting, is an ideal time to make the drive. The fall, when the aspen trees turn yellow, is also especially beautiful for the drive. A portion of the road is closed in winter.

## Getting Here and Around

Lamoille Canyon Scenic Byway, also called FS Road 660, is about 1 mile from Lamoille, Nevada, and 22 miles from the town of Spring Creek. Reach it via Lamoille Highway or State Route 227. The scenic drive is not a loop; so when it ends, turn around and go back the way you came.

**Lamoille Canyon Scenic Byway.**
🌐 *www.fs.usda.gov.*

## When in Nevada

### AREA 51

Since the mid-1950s, at the height of the Cold War, a mystery has shrouded this highly classified U.S. Air Force base. Myths have circulated for decades of alien sightings within the highly secured area, and Nevada State Route 375 has even become known as the Extraterrestrial Highway. The official statement is that any flying saucers spotted are specially crafted spy planes, but that didn't stop a legend from forming about the military facility. Its ominous signs warning visitors to stay away only add to the speculation. The location is tightly sealed up, and trespassing should not be attempted.

**Do This:** Since you can't step inside Area 51, nearby towns entertain visitors looking for ET. Check out the Alien Research Center between Hiko and Alamo, where you can learn more related facts and fantasy, and the Little Ale-E-Inn in the tiny town of Rachel.

**Alien Research Center.** ✉ *100 Extraterrestrial Hwy., Hiko, NV.*

**Little Ale-E-Inn.** ✉ *9631 Old Mill St., Rachel, NV* 🌐 *www.littlealeinn.com.*

### NEON BONEYARD

Take a walk through the ghosts of Vegas signs past at the colorful 2-acre Neon Boneyard sitting behind the Neon Museum visitor center. You'll wind past walkways stacked with big, bold eye-popping signs that once dotted the Vegas landscape, from the iconic Golden Nugget and Stardust signs to the more modern guitar-shaped Hard Rock Cafe sign.

**Do This:** A guided tour of the boneyard, led by a historian, takes about one hour. The museum includes a North Gallery with signs from the 1930s to today.

**Neon Museum Visitor Center.** ✉ *770 Las Vegas Blvd. N, Las Vegas, NV* ☎ *702/387–6366* 🌐 *www.neonmuseum.org* 🎫 *Day tours, $19; night tours, $26.*

### RENO

Though sometimes called a smaller version of Las Vegas, Reno has its own personality that sets it apart from flashy Las Vegas. This "biggest little city in the world," as the Reno arch will announce when you arrive, has its share of casinos, shows, and museums, but the town also has some Old West attractions and the Nevada Museum of Art. Residents tend to gravitate to the outdoors and especially Lake Tahoe. Reno's rugged individualism also might have something to do with why Burning Man chose a location two hours away in Black Rock Desert.

**Do This:** Check out the National Automobile Museum, where you can see more than 200 classics, including those once driven by Elvis. ✉ *10 S. Lake St., Reno, NV* 🌐 *automuseum.org* 🎫 *$12.*

## Cool Places to Stay

**Bellagio Hotel & Casino.** Famously featured in *Ocean's 11*, the beautiful Bellagio, part of the MGM Resorts International chain of hotels, offers elegant rooms and suites with big-time views. Depending on which room you stay in, your window might frame mountain vistas, the Las Vegas Strip, or the famous Bellagio fountains. ✉ *3600 Las Vegas Blvd. S., Las Vegas, NV* ☎ *702/693–7111* 🌐 *bellagio.mgmresorts.com* [$] *From $239.*

**Houseboat on Lake Mead.** Just 30 miles from Las Vegas, Lake Mead is the largest man-made lake and reservoir in the country. You can rent a houseboat and enjoy gazing at the stars at night and at the surrounding cliffs, canyons, and mountains during the day. Explore the shore, hit the beach, and splash in the calm waters. 🌐 *houseboating.org* [$] *From $2,750 for 3 days.*

# New Mexico

Albuquerque is New Mexico's welcoming gateway, and its residents—like its food and art—reflect a confluence of Native American, Hispanic, and Anglo culture. Santa Fe is surrounded by mind-expanding mountain views and is filled with streets characterized by low-slung adobe architecture. Venture beyond New Mexico's cities and you'll discover a land of exceptionally diverse scenery, from the natural formations of Carlsbad Caverns to the towering dunes of White Sands National Park.

## Bucket List Picks

The following boxes contain our picks for the top sights and experiences in New Mexico.

- ○ White Sands National Park
- ○ Santa Fe
- ○ Albuquerque International Balloon Fiesta
- ○ Carlsbad Caverns National Park
- ○ Taos
- ○ Roswell UFO Museum
- ○ Georgia O'Keeffe Trail
- ○ Cumbres & Toltec Scenic Railroad
- ○ Gila Cliff Dwellings
- ○ Bisti Badlands
- ○ Pueblo Ruins

# White Sands National Park

## Endless Sand and Sky

Like a beach without an ocean, the towering dunes of gypsum sand in the Tularosa Basin of New Mexico extend for 275 square miles. A portion of this enormous stretch of sand is preserved at White Sands National Park, the world's largest gypsum dune field. People bring chairs and sit on the pristine sand, which glimmers hot and bright in the sunlight. The desert looks like a vast sea of snow, especially when people sled down the dunes on plastic boards. Visitors can also hike one of the five designated trails, participate in ranger-led activities, walk through a native plant garden, and bike on Dunes Drive.

## Don't Miss

Sunset is the most magical time to see White Sands. Hike a mile on the dunes in single file on a daily Sunset Stroll with a knowledgeable park ranger leading the way as the lowering sun sets the landscape aglow.

## Best Trail

Dune Life Nature Trail, a moderate 1-mile hike through sloping dunes and heavier vegetation than you'll see in much of the park, is a great bet for seeing wildlife such as kit foxes, badgers, reptiles, and birds.

## Good to Know

Drink plenty of water before hiking, and pack enough of it (and sunscreen) for the duration of your trip. This is the desert, after all. Pets are allowed on a leash.

## Getting Here and Around

White Sands is in the Chihuahuan Desert in south-central New Mexico, 52 miles northeast of Las Cruces. The park's entrance is 15 miles southwest of Alamogordo. The closest airport is in El Paso, Texas, 100 miles away.

**White Sands National Park.** ✉ *U.S. 70 between Alamogordo and Las Cruces* ☎ *575/479–6124* 🌐 *www.nps.gov/whsa* 🎫 *$25 per vehicle.*

# Santa Fe

### Oldest (and Artsiest) Capital

On a plateau at the base of the Sangre de Cristo Mountains—at an elevation of 7,000 feet—Santa Fe is both the highest and oldest capital city in the country. Its streets are brimming with reminders of four centuries of Spanish and Mexican rule, and of the Pueblo cultures that have been here for hundreds of years more. The town is perhaps best known for its adobe homes and art. Artists and writers—including Willa Cather and D. H. Lawrence—have been drawn to the rugged beauty and dry air of Santa Fe for centuries. During the Great Depression, FDR's New Deal hired more than 150 artists in New Mexico, including 30 Native American artists, to create artistic improvements on public property throughout the state. Santa Fe's New Mexico Museum of Art and Museum of Indian Arts & Culture contain some of these works.

### Don't Miss

More than one hundred art galleries line Canyon Road, a famous half-mile stretch of pavement that was once a dusty burro path. Called "the art and soul of Santa Fe," the road features adobes from the 18th century still serving as residences as well as others repurposed as shops, award-winning restaurants, and artists' studios.

### Adobe Houses

Many homes in Santa Fe are adobes, a style built with mud-and-straw bricks and thick walls in order to keep residents cool from the desert heat.

### When to Go

The weather is pleasant in fall; the Santa Fe Wine and Chile Fiesta takes place in September.

### Getting Here and Around

The Santa Fe Regional Airport (SAF) has daily nonstop flights to and from Dallas, Denver, and Phoenix.

# Albuquerque International Balloon Fiesta

### World's Largest Ballooning Event

More than 500 colorful hot-air balloons take to the skies of New Mexico's largest city each October. The event's signature two-hour Mass Ascension kicks off the nine-day festival at the 365-acre Balloon Fiesta Park. Most are powered by hot air (helium), while others use gas (hydrogen). Some whimsical creations—balloons shaped as a piggy bank, for example—don't fly but can be viewed during the Special Shape Rodeo. The event also includes fireworks and evening balloon "glows" when the balloons are lit up in the darkness.

### Don't Miss

The Rainbow Ryders are the only balloon ride company authorized to give rides at the event, and rides book up well in advance. A one-hour ride runs about $450. 🌐 *www.rainbowryders.com.*

### Where to Stay

Glamping in tents on the field of Balloon Fiesta Park outfitted with heated blankets, refrigerators, heaters, and queen beds at $1,500 for three nights is an epic (and convenient) location.

### Good to Know

If you're unable to snag a spot with Rainbow Ryders, pick up business cards as you interact with the balloon crews during the event and make plans for your own high-flying adventure after the festival.

### Getting Here and Around

Several major carriers fly into Albuquerque International Sunport (ABQ). Park & Ride shuttles run from select parking lots to Balloon Fiesta Park.

**International Balloon Fiesta.**
🌐 *balloonfiesta.com* 🎫 *$15 entry.*

# Carlsbad Caverns National Park

## Largest Cave Chamber

Tubular stalactites, soda straws, cave pearls, draperies, gypsum chandeliers, hydromagnesite balloons, subaqueous helictites, lily pads, stalagmites, and many more cave formations—known as speleothems—adorn the 119 caves in Carlsbad Caverns National Park. The impressive caves were created by sulfuric acid dissolving the limestone, with water and minerals then added to the mix. Exploring the underground maze of geological activity for most visitors begins 75 stories below the surface in what is known as the Big Room, thanks to a floor size equaling 14 football fields. The Big Room is also high, with a 255-foot ceiling, so it's no wonder actor Will Rogers said the cavern, the largest cave chamber in the United States, was "the Grand Canyon with a roof over it."

## Don't Miss

There are six ranger-led cave tours of varying difficulty, but for a truly bucket-list worthy challenge book the Hall of the White Giant tour, which requires belly crawling into tight spaces and climbing ladders. *$20.*

## While You're Here

While subterranean wonders are the main attraction, there are plenty of surface-level hiking trails leading to stunning views, including Guadalupe Ridge and Slaughter Canyon.

## When to Go

Under the surface, the temperatures are around 56°F year-round. If you want to see the bats, come between spring and late fall.

## Getting Here and Around

Carlsbad Caverns is about 27 miles southwest of Carlsbad and 35 miles north of Guadalupe Mountains National Park in Texas.

**Carlsbad Caverns National Park.** *727 Carlsbad Caverns Hwy., Carlsbad, NM* *www.nps.gov/cave* *$15.*

# Taos

## Epic Ski Town

Set in the Rocky Mountains, Taos draws visitors who want to sample its artsy side, but skiers and snowboarders know it as *the* place in New Mexico to embrace winter. With around 300 inches of snow a year, skiers shred serious powder at four ski areas within an hour's drive.

## Don't Miss

The largest of the Taos-area ski destinations is 1,294-acre Taos Ski Valley, sitting at a 9,200-foot elevation base and featuring a 3,281-foot vertical drop. It has options for snowboarders and plenty of runs for skiers of all levels, though 51% of its runs are black.

## Best Tour

With Mountain Skills Guided Backcountry Ski Tours, intermediate and advanced skiers can hire a guide to carve through snow on the ungroomed slopes of Taos's backcountry. *www.climbingschoolusa.com/backcountry-ski-tours* *$450 per 6-hour day.*

## More Great Skiing

Angel Fire has three terrain parks for snowboarding and more than 80 runs for downhill skiers, plus night skiing, ski tubing, cross-country skiing, snowshoeing, and kid's sledding. *www.angelfireresort.com.*

Red River Ski & Summer Area is a small mountain with terrain parks that have jumps and rails, along with ski runs and tubing trails. For something different, there's a snow coach tour that includes dinner on the mountain at 10,350 feet up. *redriverskiarea.com.*

## Getting Here and Around

About 70 miles away, Santa Fe Regional Airport (SAF) is the nearest commercial airport to Taos.

**Taos Skiing.** *www.skitaos.com.*

# Roswell UFO Museum

## Out of This World Exhibit

In the summer of 1947, a mysterious object crashed at a ranch near Roswell, New Mexico, and was retrieved by the U.S. military. Some believe it was a flying saucer, which is what the Roswell Army Air Field first reported, but the next day the RAAF said it was a weather balloon. Later, the U.S. government clarified that it was a nuclear test surveillance balloon. But the flying saucer theory still persists in this small central New Mexico town. Roswell's International UFO Museum and Research Center focuses on this Roswell incident. Exhibits at the small, nonprofit museum educate about various UFO sightings, crop circles, and supposed alien abductions.

## Don't Miss

The museum is open year-round, but plan your visit in July if you want to pair it with the Roswell UFO festival, Alien Fest. 🌐 *www.ufofestivalroswell.com.*

## Best Tour

Though not affiliated with the museum, Roswell UFO Tours will take you to 20 sites related to the 1947 UFO crash over the course of two hours. 🌐 *roswellufotours.com* 🎫 *$100 per tour, up to four people.*

## While You're Here

Walk through a blacklit path lined with kitschy spaceship and alien decor at the Roswell UFO Spacewalk to get in the UFO-spotting mood.

## Good to Know

The town has several fun UFO-related shops, including Alien Invasion, Alien Zone Area 51, and Roswell Landing.

## Getting Here and Around

The museum is about 6 miles from Roswell International Air Center (ROW).

**Roswell UFO Museum.** ✉ *114 N. Main St., Roswell, NM* 🌐 *www.roswellufomuseum.com* 🎫 *$5.*

# Georgia O'Keeffe Trail

### Follow a Southwest Icon

Trace the footsteps of the Southwest's most celebrated painter at the homes that inspired the desert scenes and floral blooms of her abstract modernist works. While the artist grew up in Wisconsin, attended the Art Institute of Chicago, then studied painting in New York, her Southwest connection is perhaps the most well known. After spending many summers in New Mexico, she settled there in 1949 and remained a resident until her death in 1986. At the several O'Keeffe attractions in the state, you'll see that scenes from her homes appear in her artwork.

### Don't Miss: Ghost Ranch

O'Keeffe's summer home, Rancho de los Burros, was on a dude ranch called Ghost Ranch a dozen miles from Abiquiú. She owned the house and 7 acres. The ranch offers art workshops and a handful of tours. 🌐 *www.ghostranch.org.*

### O'Keeffe Home and Studio

Georgia O'Keeffe's main New Mexico home was in the village of Abiquiú. Owned by the Georgia O'Keeffe Museum, the 5,000-square-foot home is a pueblo-style adobe. Tours begin at the O'Keeffe Welcome Center.

### Georgia O'Keeffe Museum

This collection in downtown Santa Fe features 150 of O'Keeffe's drawings and paintings as well as personal items and related photographs and documents. 🌐 *www.okeeffemuseum.org* 🎟 *$20.*

### Getting Here and Around

From Santa Fe make a side trip to Abiquiú, the town of O'Keeffe Home and Studio; it's about an hour drive north. From Abiquiú, it's a 15-minute drive to Ghost Ranch, so you can easily combine them in one trip. The nearest airport is Santa Fe Regional Airport (SAF).

# Cumbres & Toltec Scenic Railroad

## Ride Into the Rockies

Departing from Chama, New Mexico, a scenic train ride aboard the Cumbres & Toltec Scenic Railroad climbs into the Rocky Mountains in northeast New Mexico to begin a 64-mile journey through gorgeous changing scenery—from alpine meadows to mountain canyons to high desert landscape to thickets of conifers—to Osier, Colorado, for a lunch stop, and then on to Antonito, Colorado. Crossing Cascade Creek Trestle and snaking along Tanglefoot Curve, the powerful, coal-fired steam locomotive carries the train back and forth across the New Mexico and Colorado borders on this daylong escape to yesteryear. The train has been running since 1880 and is now a National Historic Landmark.

## Don't Miss

On your train ride, look out for Cumbres Pass. At 10,015 feet, it's the highest mountain pass in America traversed by train.

## When to Go

The train runs from early June through late October. Spring provides sprinklings of wildflowers, while late September and early October are the ideal times to see the aspen leaves change colors.

## Getting Here and Around

Chama is in north-central New Mexico, about two hours from the Santa Fe Regional Airport (SAF). At the end of your train ride, a bus takes you from Antonito back to Chama.

**Chama Depot.** ✉ *500 S. Terrace Ave., Chama, NM* ☎ *888/286–2737* 🌐 *cumbrestoltec.com* 🎟 *From $115.*

# Gila Cliff Dwellings

### Step Into the Past

Thousands of years ago, nomadic people of the Mogollon Culture created temporary cliff-side dwellings in what is today southwestern New Mexico. These stunning abandoned homes (talk about prime real estate) can be explored within the Gila Cliff Dwellings National Monument. Most people base themselves in Silver City to day-trip to the dwellings, though there are also four United States Forest Service campgrounds within a 10-minute drive of the park.

### Don't Miss

A moderately strenuous hike along a 1-mile Cliff Dweller Trail takes you up to the dwellings, caves cut into the rock with catwalks connecting them. This is one of the few parks that allows visitors to go inside the rooms, where you can imagine how the tribes must have lived.

### Best Base: Silver City

Forty-four miles away, Silver City, New Mexico, at the foothills of the Pinos Altos Mountains, also lets you step into a culture from the past—America's frontier days. The town was founded during the area's mining boom and contains the world's third-largest open-pit copper mine, Chino Mine (Santa Rita), which is still active.

### Getting Here and Around

Budget a full day for a day-trip to Gila Cliff Dwellings from Silver City. Gila Cliff Dwellings National Monument is 44 miles from Silver City, and driving along the mountainous road there takes about two hours. The nearest airport is El Paso International Airport (ELP), a 2½-hour drive from Silver City.

**Gila Cliff Dwellings.** ✉ *Off NM Hwy. 15* ☎ *575/536–9461* 🌐 *www.nps.gov/gicl* 🎟 *Free.*

# Bisti Badlands

## Hike Mars on Earth

"Unusual" and "surprising" don't even begin to describe this 45,000-acre wilderness in the Four Corners region of the San Juan Basin. Rocks twist and turn and appear to have tumbled onto a moonlike landscape out of nowhere. Get out and hike among the sandstone, shale, silt, and coal pinnacles, spires, cap rocks, and more, pinching yourself when you forget you're not actually on Mars. At one time, dinosaurs roamed here, including the "Bisti Beast," a 30-foot tyrannosaur that lived 34 million years ago and was excavated in 1998. Today among the wildlife are eagles, hawks, falcons, lizards, scorpions, snakes, and porcupines.

## Don't Miss

Spot rock formations including Conversing Hoodoos, the Alien Egg Hatchery, and Vanilla Hoodoos.

## Good to Know

This is wilderness land and there are no facilities or shade, so bring water and sun protection with you. You may choose to book a tour of the badlands with Journey Into the Past Tours.

## When to Go

Visit in spring or fall to avoid the extreme heat of summer, but be prepared for wind in the spring and rain in the fall.

## Getting Here and Around

The Bisti Access Parking Area is 36 miles south of Farmington, New Mexico, from the San Juan River crossing or 46 miles from Crownpoint. Within the wilderness area, use a compass or your phone GPS when hiking, because trails are not marked and it's easy to get turned around.

**Bisti Badlands.** ✉ *South of Farmington, NM* ☎ *505/564–7600* 🌐 *www.blm.gov/visit/bisti-de-na-zin-wilderness* 🎫 *Free.*

# Pueblo Ruins

## The "Village" Peoples

You haven't truly seen the Land of Enchantment until you've seen and appreciated it through the lens of its original inhabitants. New Mexico is home to 23 Native American tribes and sovereign nations from three groups: the Pueblos (or Village peoples), the Apache, and Navajo Nation. Most of the preserved sites in New Mexico relate to the rich Pueblo culture, including cliff dwellings, kivas (underground ceremonial chambers), and sacred symbols etched in rock.

## Don't Miss: Aztec Ruins National Monument

Ruins that are 900 years old highlight this national monument and UNESCO World Heritage site of the Ancestral Pueblos. There's a Great House with more than 400 rooms and a reconstructed kiva—look for T-shaped doorways. 🌐 *www.nps.gov/azru* 🎫 *Free.*

## Petroglyph National Monument

Designs and symbols were carved onto volcanic rocks with a stone chisel and a hammerstone 400 to 700 years ago by the Pueblo people as well as Spanish settlers. Three canyon trails let you see hundreds of petroglyphs: Boca Negra, Rinconada, and Piedras Marcadas. 🌐 *www.nps.gov/petr* 🎫 *$2.*

## Taos Pueblo

About 1,900 members of the Pueblo tribe live on the Taos Pueblo land, with 150 living within the multi-unit Taos Pueblo. 🌐 *taospueblo.com* 🎫 *$16.*

## Getting Here and Around

Petroglyph National Monument is a 15-minute drive from Albuquerque. From here, it's a three-hour drive to Aztec Ruins in far northwest New Mexico, nearest to Farmington. Taos Pueblo is outside of Taos, a four-hour drive from Aztec Ruins.

## When in New Mexico

### MEOW WOLF

Wander like Alice in Wonderland through 70 rooms filled with trippy, colorful, lights and immersive experiences at this arts collective, which can only be described as a feast for the senses. The arts complex and its permanent exhibition, the House of Eternal Return, have become some of Santa Fe's top attractions.

**Do This:** Give yourself at least a couple of hours to tour this sci-fi-inspired, 20,000-square-foot interactive exhibit in which you'll encounter hidden doorways, mysterious corridors, ambient music, and clever, surrealistic, and often slyly humorous artistic renderings. It's a strange experience, but it is absolutely family-friendly, and although occasionally eerie, the subject matter isn't at all frightening.

**Meow Wolf.** ✉ *1352 Rufina Cir., South Side Santa Fe, NM* ☎ *505/395–6369* 🌐 *www.meowwolf.com* 🎟 *$35*

### VERY LARGE ARRAY

The most versatile and widely used radio telescope in the world sticks out like a sore thumb with its large white radio dishes aimed at the sky of an otherwise remote area two hours from Albuquerque. It looks similar to a scene early in the movie *Contact,* and actress Jodie Foster, the female lead in that movie, provides the narration for an award-winning film about the location. The visitor center shows the film and features displays on radio astronomy and the Very Large Array telescope.

**Do This:** Take a guided tour when available, or a self-guided tour to the base of the dish antennas.

**Very Large Array.** 🌐 *public.nrao.edu/telescopes/vla* 🎟 *$6.*

## Cool Places to Stay

**Inn of the Five Graces.** In the heart of Santa Fe's historic downtown, near the tranquil Santa Fe River, this lovely adobe inn and Relais & Chateaux property has plush colorful rooms with wood-burning kiva fireplaces, deep soaking tubs, and hand-laid tile mosaics. Stone courtyards have fountains and flowering foliage, and there's a spa with a variety of treatments. Breakfast is included each morning. ✉ *150 E. DeVargas St., Santa Fe, NM* ☎ *505/992–0957* 🌐 *fivegraces.com* 💲 *From $700.*

**Kokopelli's Cave.** After exploring some of New Mexico's cliff dwellings, why not retire to a cliff of your own? Kokopelli's man-made cave is built into sandstone cliffs and gives you a breathtaking view of Shiprock Pinnacle and the Four Corners region. In your 1,700-square-foot room, enjoy views from your porches, a waterfall shower set within rock walls, and a constant pleasant temperature in the cave between 68°F and 73°F. The cave is 70 feet below the surface, so be prepared to walk down a slope to reach it once inside the cliff. ✉ *87 Rd. 1980, Farmington, NM* ☎ *505/860–3812* 🌐 *kokoscave.us.* 💲 From $290.

**Riverbend Hot Springs Resort.** Soak your cares away at this resort and spa's open-air hot springs on the banks of the Rio Grande, which were considered both healing and sacred by the Apache. The hotel rooms are done in either a delightful Southwestern motif or an upbeat Old West look, and RV sites are also available, and guests have complimentary access to the springs. If you're not staying overnight, the springs are $30 per hour. There is a two-night minimum stay on weekends. ✉ *100 Austin St., Truth or Consequences, NM* 🌐 *riverbendhotsprings.com* 💲 *From $183.*

# Texas

The Lone Star State is big and bold. Its sheer size allows you to craft a customized itinerary based on your personal preferences, time, and budget: outdoor adventures in more than 90 state parks, Wild West lifestyle experiences at dozens of guest ranches, and evolving Western art and culinary traditions in Texas's premier cities. Wherever you travel in the state's seven distinct regions, you'll find dramatic culture and a myriad of opportunities to explore Texas history and heritage.

## Bucket List Picks

The following boxes contain our picks for the top sights and experiences in Texas.

- The Alamo
- Big Bend National Park
- Houston
- Galveston
- Austin
- Dallas
- Billy Bob's, Fort Worth
- Palo Duro Canyon State Park
- Texas Hill Country
- Bluebonnet Season
- Presidential Libraries
- San Antonio River Walk
- Marfa
- Texas Rodeos
- South Padre and Corpus Christi
- Forth Worth Stockyards and Cattle Drive

# The Alamo

## Remembered Always

An icon of Texas freedom fighting, this mission church turned military fort is the most celebrated in Texas's military history. In 1836, Texas lost a major battle here against Mexico, and all inside died at the hands of Santa Anna's troops. Those slain included James Bowie, William Travis, and Davy Crockett. The defeat at the Alamo spurred Texans fighting in future battles for their independence to make sure they did not suffer the same fate. "Remember the Alamo" became the battle cry at San Jacinto, where Texas won its independence from Mexico with Sam Houston leading the charge.

## Don't Miss

The mission is just the beginning of the experience. Stroll through the gardens, see the encampment, artifacts, a 16-pound cannon, wall of history, statues of Alamo heroes, and—last but not least—Bella the Alamo cat, the official Alamo greeter and guard (at least from mice).

## Did You Know?

Rock star Phil Collins was a big-time collector of Alamo artifacts. He donated his private collection of weapons, relics, and original documents to Texas, and a museum for the objects is in the works for 2022.

## A Little History

Founded in 1718, the Alamo began as the Mission San Antonio de Valero, one of several churches in San Antonio created by Spain and the Catholic Church to further Spanish interests and to provide religious education.

## Getting Here and Around

The Alamo, 9 miles from the San Antonio International Airport (SAT), is easily explored on a self-guided tour.

**The Alamo.** ✉ *300 Alamo Plaza, San Antonio, TX* 🌐 *www.thealamo.org* 🎫 *Free, audio tours $7.*

# Big Bend National Park

## Backcountry Beauty

Set in the Chisos Mountains in West Texas, 1,252-square-mile Big Bend National Park has incredibly varied terrain, from desert landscape to bird-filled woods to natural hot springs to 8,000-foot-high mountains. The scenic and wild Rio Grande River cuts through the park and has carved out a number of canyons, including Boquillas Canyon, where the limestone walls rise up to 1,500 feet high along the river. Big Bend is a terrific place for hiking, wildlife viewing, scenic driving, and camping under dark and starry skies. You can view dinosaur fossils, caves with pictographs, and historic sites, including an abandoned mercury mine.

## Don't Miss

Hike the Santa Elena Canyon Trail near sunset; the setting sun turns the steep cliffs a beautiful red-chestnut color.

## Best Scenic Drive

Ross Maxwell Scenic Drive, a 30-mile drive that goes by heaps of volcanic ash from long-ago eruptions, ranches, and an old Army compound, has scenic overlooks that give you glimpses of Mule Ears and Tuff Canyon.

## Best Thrill

The Lower Canyons, with Class II, III, and IV rapids, is a multiday, 82-mile trip of a lifetime for experienced kayakers.

## When to Go

Summer is hot but ideal if you want to canoe or raft.

## Getting Here and Around

Big Bend is 39 miles south of Marathon, Texas, off U.S. 385. The nearest airport is in Midland, Texas, roughly 3½ hours' drive away.

**Big Bend National Park.** *www.nps.gov/bibe* *$30.*

# Houston

## Where Everything Is Bigger

The fourth-largest city in the country and, perhaps surprisingly, the country's most ethnically diverse metropolitan area, Houston is the Lone Star State's largest city, with 2.3 million residents within the city proper and 7.1 million when you include its suburbs. So it's no wonder that the city personifies the "everything is bigger" in Texas mentality, whether that's a 10-gallon hat worn to the Houston Rodeo or a megachurch with 52,000 attendees each Sunday (Joel Osteen's Lakewood Church, set in a former sports stadium). There's also the huge Galleria shopping complex, with 375 stores, 30 restaurants, and two hotels—plus a full-sized indoor ice-skating rink.

The city is known for sports, oil, commerce, and technology, as well as being a launching pad for exploring space. Just 25 miles south of downtown is NASA's Space Center Houston and the adjacent Johnson Space Center. Space aficionados can come here to learn about Apollo 13's mission and life with zero-gravity, and to explore Mission Control.

## Don't Miss

See world-class art in Houston's Museum District, including at the Menil Collection (🌐 *www.menil.org*) and at the enormous Museum of Fine Arts Houston (🌐 *www.mfah.org*).

## Fun Fact

John F. Kennedy gave his famous 1962 "Put a man on the moon" speech at Houston's Rice University.

## Getting Here and Around

Houston has two airports, George Bush Intercontinental Airport (IAH) and William P. Hobby Airport (HOU). A car is a necessity here.

# Galveston

## Texas' Victorian Seaside

The 32-mile-long island of Galveston, which lies along the Gulf of Mexico, has several beaches, a seaport museum, a popular shopping area called the Strand, a pier, a water park, and a cruise-ship terminal. But what it is best known for is its Victorian architecture. Several dozen of the city's buildings are listed on the National Register of Historic Places, and these beauties on Broadway are must-sees.

## Don't Miss

**Bishop's Palace.** Valued at $5.5 million today, this ornate building with stained-glass windows, painted ceilings, and marble columns was once home to railroad magnate Colonel Walter Gresham.

**Moody Mansion.** This 32-room limestone-and-brick home with gilded trim was first owned by one of the country's most wealthy men, W. L. Moody, an entrepreneur in the insurance industry. Many of the family's heirlooms are inside.

**Ashton Villa.** This 1859 Victorian Italianate home was the first on the island. It was built in large part by slave labor, and it served as headquarters for the Confederate Army. On June 19, 1865, however, Union general Gordon Granger stood on the balcony of Ashton Villa and declared all slaves to be free. Today June 19th is known as Juneteenth.

## Best Tour

The Galveston Historic Homes tour occurs the first two weekends in May. Step into homes from the 1800s that are owned by private residents.

## Getting Here and Around

Galveston is 50 miles from Houston. The nearest airport is Houston's William P. Hobby Airport (HOU).

# Austin

### Keeping It Weird

While Austin goes by many names—Live Music Capital of the World, Violet Crown City, Bat City, Hippie Haven—it's best known for its laid-back, individualistic, "keep it weird" vibe. Residents love their music, their outdoor pursuits, and the intellectual atmosphere of the behemoth University of Texas at Austin. The capital city continues to grow in both geographical size and population each year, drawing young professionals and adding even more chances to check out the music scene, eat delicious Southwestern food, snap photos next to artistic murals, and people-watch during bar hops.

### Don't Miss

Nightlife in Austin is always memorable. At popular downtown Sixth Street music spills out of clubs, and same goes for the hip South Congress district south of Lady Bird Lake.

### Best Murals

When you're on South Congress, stop by the famous "I love you so much" mural on 1300 South Congress Avenue before grabbing coffee and tacos at Jo's and the "Greetings From Austin" mural on 1720 South First Street for a life-size postcard.

### While You're Here

In Zilker Park, Barton Springs Pool is the place to enjoy a dip in spring-fed water.

### When to Go

South by Southwest (SXSW), a huge annual music and film event, occurs each March.

### Getting Here and Around

Centrally located in Texas, Austin is reached by car via the state's main north–south thoroughfare, Interstate 35. The Austin-Bergstrom International Airport (AUS) is 10 miles southeast of downtown, off Highway 71.

# Dallas

### Do It All in the Big D

Dallas is a city that has it all: arts and culture, professional sports, and trendy restaurants and bars. Whether you're strolling through the lovely Dallas Arboretum and Botanical Gardens, cheering on the Dallas Cowboys, or strolling through the Arts District, there's always something to do (and the oppurtunity to choose your own adventure) in the Big D. Take in the beautiful skyline studded with skyscrapers in this busy metropolis, and don't forget to order some Tex-Mex to fuel the adventures.

### Don't Miss

Art lovers should make a beeline to the Dallas Arts District, home to some the city's most notable attractions, including the Dallas Museum of Art, the Nasher Sculpture Center, The AT&T Performing Arts Center, Dallas Theater Center, and Winspear Opera House. 🌐 *www.dallasartsdistrict.org*.

### While You're Here

The Sixth Floor Museum at Dealey Plaza covers JFK's assassination. 🌐 *www.dallasartsdistrict.org* 🎫 *$18.*

### Good to Know

Southfork Ranch, where the TV show *Dallas* was filmed, is about an hour's trek north of Dallas in Parker, Texas. There are tours of the Ewing home as well as trail rides.

### Fun for All Ages

Great stops for those with kids in tow include the Dallas World Aquarium, Medieval Times, Six Flags Over Texas in Arlington, and the Ross Perot Museum of Nature and Science.

### Getting Here and Around

Two airports serve Dallas—Dallas/Fort Worth International Airport (DFW), just west of Dallas, and Love Field (DAL), near downtown Dallas.

## Billy Bob's, Fort Worth

### Line Dance at the World's Largest Honky-Tonk

When Texans want to go line dancing or two-stepping, they don their cowboy boots and head to Billy Bob's in Fort Worth, known as "the world's largest honky-tonk." Able to hold 6,000 people at a time, the more than 100,000-square-foot complex has a huge dance floor, pool tables, arcade games, a restaurant, multiple bars, a gift shop, and bull-riding area. Dancing inside Billy Bob's feels a lot like being in an enormous barn, and that could be because the facility was once an open-air barn where prized cattle were kept for the Fort Worth Stock Show. It has been used as a dance hall since 1981 with live entertainment by big-name artists like Alabama, Willie Nelson, and Garth Brooks—as well as ZZ Top, Marvin Gaye, and Ringo Starr.

### Don't Miss

There's a bull-riding area where professionals ride, but the rest of us can mount a fake bull and get our picture taken on it.

### Look the Part

Need a Stetson? Visit Fincher's White Front Western Wear 🌐 *www.fincherswhitefront.com*. Boots? Go with a pair of high-crafted leather ones from Lucchese Boot Company 🌐 *www.lucchese.com*. There's also Cavender's Boot City for boots, hats, belt buckles, and more 🌐 *www.cavenders.com*.

### Getting Here and Around

Billy Bob's is located in Fort Worth's Stockyards National Historic District, a little more than 30 miles west of Dallas via Interstate 30.

**Billy Bob's.** ✉ *2520 Rodeo Plaza, Fort Worth, TX* ☎ *817/624–7117* 🌐 *billybobstexas.com* 🎫 *$10.*

# Palo Duro Canyon State Park

### Grand Canyon of Texas

Dramatic vistas from far above the canyon floor as well as from within are the highlights of this canyon in Texas's Panhandle. Called by some the Grand Canyon of Texas, Palo Duro Canyon is 60 miles long and 800 feet deep and showcases layers of rock in varied hues along with hoodoos and other unusual rock formations. It is contained within the 16,402-acre Palo Duro Canyon State Park. People come to hike, bike, bird-watch, fish, and watch the summer musical *TEXAS!*, which is set in an amphitheater in the cleft of the canyon. Wildlife includes the diamondback rattlesnake, wild turkey, roadrunners, and wild pigs.

### Don't Miss

Take a scenic drive down the long, winding road into the canyon in the morning or evening to catch the gold colors the sun casts upon the ridges and pinnacles.

### Best Tour

Old West Stables leads visitors on one-hour guided horseback rides on trails through the canyon. ⊕ *www.oldweststables.com*.

### Good to Know

Meaning "hard wood" in Spanish, Palo Duro became the name for the canyon because of all of the mesquites growing among the canyon's rock formations.

### When to Go

Come in fall and early spring for the most pleasant weather.

### Getting Here and Around

Off Highway 217, Palo Duro Canyon State Park, which contains Palo Duro Canyon, is 14 miles from Canyon, Texas, and 25 miles from Amarillo.

**Palo Duro Canyon State Park.** ✉ *11450 Park Rd. 5, Canyon, TX* ☎ *512/389–8900* ⊕ *tpwd.texas.gov/state-parks/palo-duro-canyon* 🎟 *$8.*

# Texas Hill Country

## Wine Tasting With a View

Sitting atop the Edwards Plateau and the Balcones Escarpment, the Texas Hill Country begins in Austin and extends north to roughly Texas Highway 29, west to U.S. Highway 83, and south to northern San Antonio. The beautiful area is known for its rolling hills and the stunning vistas that come with the higher ground, in addition to vineyards in what's become the USA's fastest growing wine region. The joy of visiting is driving winding back roads that loop through farmlands, small towns with German culture, and state parks and ranches.

## Don't Miss

Fredericksburg, full of wineries, antiques shops, and German restaurants, is a charming and popular area. For tours and tastings, visitors rave about three wineries in particular: Becker Vineyards, Inwood Estates Vineyards Winery & Bistro, and Messina Hof Hill Country Winery. For hearty German fare, there's Otto's German Bistro.

## Scenic Stops

Pedernales Falls State Park is a great place to get out and stretch your legs on a hike to its waterfall. In the fall, Lost Maples State Park breaks out in red. There's also noteworthy scenery underground at Longhorn Caverns.

## Best Dancing

Country-western dancing is popular in Texas small towns, and the dance hall in Luckenbach or New Braunfels's Gruene Hall, the oldest dance hall in Texas, are the places to go for a little boot-scootin' boogie.

## Getting Here and Around

Austin and San Antonio are the region's gateway cities, and you can string along a few destinations on a weekend road trip. The area is especially pretty in spring when the bluebonnets dot the countryside.

# Bluebonnet Season

## Infinite Sea of Flowers

Late March and early April is the season to take scenic drives in the Lone Star State, because that's when beautiful violet-blue flowers carpet fields, yards, cemeteries, railroad tracks, even small patches of land along the interstate or medians in between lanes. The wildflower holds its own in the "truly gorgeous" category, but when it appears alongside pink Indian paintbrush (castilleja) and Texas yellow stars (part of the sunflower family), it's even more glorious to behold. If you've come across a great patch of them, you're sure to see cars pulled over for pictures. You'll easily see why the bluebonnet was chosen as the Texas state flower.

## Don't Miss

The bluebonnet can be found throughout the state, but some of the best places to see it are in central Texas towns like Brenham, north central Texas in Ennis, Big Bend National Park, and of course in the Hill Country—most notably in Austin, Burnet, Fredericksburg, Kingsland, Muleshoe Bend in Spicewood, and Turkey Bend Recreation Area.

## When to Go

The flowers are only around for a short window of time each spring, usually beginning in mid- to late March and peaking in early to mid-April.

## Good to Know

To get updates on where to see the bluebonnets, call the Texas Department of Transportation Wildflower Hotline at 800/452–9292.

## Getting Here and Around

Base yourself in Austin or San Antonio and drive through nearby Hill Country to combine a few bucket list destinations into one trip. La Cantera Resort & Spa is an excellent place to stay in San Antonio.

## Presidential Libraries

### Executive Paper Capital

If you're a fan of American history and learning about its commanders in chief, Texas is the place to be. The Lone Star State is home to official libraries and museums for three U.S. presidents—the 36th, the 41st, and the 43rd—more than any other state in the country. There are only 15 total presidential libraries across the country.

### LBJ Presidential Library

Located on the campus of the University of Texas at Austin, the library holds phone recordings Johnson made at the White House, more than 2,000 oral histories, and a large collection of photos and videos. ✉ *2313 Red River St., Austin, TX* 🌐 *lbjlibrary.org* 🎫 *$10.*

### George H. W. Bush Presidential Library & Museum

George Herbert Walker Bush chose Texas A&M as the setting for his library. ✉ *1000 George Bush Dr. W, College Station, TX* 🌐 *www.bush41.org* 🎫 *$9.*

### George W. Bush Presidential Library & Museum

Exhibits at this museum on the campus of Southern Methodist University recall the horror of 9/11 as well as artifacts about the 2000 election, legislation Bush signed, and policy initiatives his administration enacted. ✉ *2943 SMU Blvd., Dallas, TX* 🌐 *www.georgewbushlibrary.smu.edu.*

### Getting Here and Around

Make a road trip out of the libraries, perhaps starting in Dallas to see George W. Bush Presidential Library and Museum. Drive 195 miles south via Interstate 35 to reach Austin, where you'll see LBJ, and finally 107 miles east via TX 21 to College Station to see George H. W. Bush Presidential Library & Museum.

# San Antonio River Walk

## Best Urban Waterway

A whirl of colorful umbrellas, an array of tantalizing scents wafting from restaurants, and the sounds of mariachi bands blend together to make San Antonio's beautiful River Walk a feast for the senses. Winding 15 miles through the heart of the city, the pedestrian waterfront path is Texas's most visited attraction. Shops, restaurants, hotels, museums, and missions line the Paseo del Rio that in the south reaches La Villita Historic Arts Village and in the north connects to the Pearl, an entertainment district centered around an old brewery that churned out Pearl beer in the 1800s. With its below-street-level path, the River Walk is like a bonus, basement-level story of the city.

## Don't Miss

A narrated riverboat ride is a delightful way to see the river from a different perspective. Purchase tickets from the Rio San Antonio Cruise kiosk at the Rivercenter. ✉ *849 E. River Walk, San Antonio, TX* 🌐 *www.goriocruises.com.*

## While You're Here

The museums and missions along the route are excellent, from the family-friendly Witte Museum and culture-rich San Antonio Museum of Art to the four Spanish colonial missions.

## When to Go

For an extra dose of festivity, time your trip to coincide with Fiesta San Antonio in the spring or Las Posadas at Christmastime.

## Getting Here and Around

Fly into San Antonio International Airport (SAT). The River Walk can be accessed from multiple points in the city. To reach its northern points, like the museums and the Pearl, you can take a river shuttle from Lexington. For an area map, see 🌐 *www.thesanantonioriverwalk.com/maps.*

# Marfa

## End of the Earth Art

The serenity and laid-back nature of wide-open West Texas meets mystery, myth, and minimalist art in Marfa. Called by some a "hipster's paradise," this small town of 1,800 residents swells with tourists who come to see art, way-out-west architecture, and especially to see the famous Marfa lights, a mysterious phenomenon in which red, blue, and white lights sometimes appear at night for no particular reason. Visitors also gravitate toward the town's many art galleries, including the Chinati Foundation.

## Don't Miss

People have reported seeing strange, colorful lights glowing in the night here since the 1880s, long before cars were zipping around roads in the distance. They are seen on clear nights between Marfa and Alpine as you look west toward the Chinati Mountains. An official viewing area with built-in binoculars is off Highway 90, 9 miles outside of Marfa.

## While You're Here

Make like Beyoncé and strike a pose next to Prada Marfa, the sleekest piece of architecture you'll ever see in the middle of nowhere. Located 26 miles north of Marfa, the permanent art installation by artists Elmgreen and Dragset has become something of a pop culture legend and is particularly beautiful at sunset. ✉ *14880 U.S. 90, Valentine, TX.*

## Did You Know?

Marfa has been featured in several movies, including *Giant* (1956), *No Country for Old Men* (2007), and *There Will Be Blood* (2007).

## Getting Here and Around

At the junction of U.S. Highways 90 and 67, Marfa is 98 miles from Big Bend National Park. The nearest airports are in Midland or El Paso, both about three hours away by car.

# Texas Rodeos

### Official Lone Star Sport

While Texas has many popular professional and college sports teams, and even a big following of Friday night high school football—the inspiration behind *Friday Night Lights*— nothing compares to rodeo, the official state sport of Texas. Featuring barrel racing and bull riding paired with concerts, carnivals, and cowboys, rodeos are held throughout the state. Fort Worth has the oldest, while Houston has the largest and arguably most popular.

### Don't Miss: Houston

Drawing more than 65,000 people each night of the two-week affair in March, the Houston Livestock Show & Rodeo at NRG Stadium is the biggest of the big and the ultimate Texas rodeo experience with livestock exhibitions, parades, a chili cookoff, concerts, and competitions including calf roping, chuck wagon races, and more.

### Other Rodeos

In Fort Worth, catch the Fort Worth Stock Show & Rodeo; in San Antonio, head to the San Antonio Stock Show & Rodeo, and in Austin attend Rodeo Austin, featuring concerts by big-name artists, a livestock show, a carnival, and competitions by professional athletes.

### Getting Here and Around

Even if it *is* your first rodeo, wear your walking boots to these sprawling events like a pro. The Houston rodeo is located at NRG Stadium, closest to the William P. Hobby Airport, about 15 miles away. Buy tickets and parking in advance online. 🌐 *www.rodeohouston.com* 🎟 *From $20.*

# South Padre and Corpus Christi

## Best Beaches in Texas

Texas's eastern border is home to the only oceanfront beaches in the Southwest, and there are plenty of places to play in the sand and wade into sparkling Gulf water. Spring breakers have long known about Padre Island, and South Padre in particular, a popular beach town on Padre's southern end. The 100-mile-long island stretches from Corpus Christi down close to where the Rio Grande empties into the Gulf of Mexico. In both Corpus Christi and on South Padre you can choose beaches on the calm bay waters or set up your umbrella on the other side of Padre Island on a beach fronting the Gulf.

## Don't Miss

Gulf-facing beaches on South Padre are where the action is. In addition to swimming and suntanning, there's fishing, parasailing, surfing, snorkeling, scuba diving, kiteboarding, horseback riding, and more.

## While You're Here

Catch a dolphin training show and playful otters at the Texas State Aquarium in Corpus Christi as well as the hundreds of species of birds at Laguna Atascosa National Wildlife Refuge in the Rio Grande Valley.

## When to Go

March brings hundreds of college students on spring break, but most of the year Texas's coastline is relatively quiet, or at least less of a full-time party. For pleasant water temperatures, come April through October.

## Getting Here and Around

South Padre Island is 28 miles northeast of Brownsville. Corpus Christi is 181 miles north of South Padre via Highway 77. Airports include Brownsville South Padre International Airport (BRO) and Corpus Christi International Airport (CRP).

# Forth Worth Stockyards and Cattle Drive

### Calling All Cowboys

Want to see a real, authentic slice of Texas history? There's no better place than Fort Worth. From 1867 to 1884, drovers led longhorn cattle from Texas to Kansas on the Chisholm Trail, which began in South Texas and passed through Fort Worth. Though the route has long since been abandoned for such purposes, Fort Worth relives its cattle era twice a day—at 11:30 am and at 4 pm—with reenacted cattle drives down East Exchange Avenue in Fort Worth's Stockyards. The Stockyards is a historic district with an Old West ambience.

### Don't Miss

Each Saturday and Sunday in the summer from 1:30 to 2:30 pm at the Herd Observation Deck cowhands give free demonstrations. There's grooming, saddling horses, roping, and more.

### Best Restaurant

Joe T Garcia's is *the* place to eat in the area. There will be a line at this Mexican restaurant on North Commerce Street, and it's cash only but oh-so-worth the wait. 🌐 *joetgarcias.com.*

### While You're Here

About 5 miles away from the Stockyards, in Fort Worth's Cultural District, is the National Cowgirl Hall of Fame and Museum celebrating pioneering women trailblazers such as Sacagawea, Annie Oakley, and Laura Ingalls Wilder.

### Getting Here and Around

Dallas/Fort Worth International Airport (DFW) is Fort Worth's main airport, and it's about 27 miles away from the Stockyards.

**Forth Worth Stockyards.** ✉ *131 E. Exchange Ave., Fort Worth, TX* ☎ *817/624–4741* 🌐 *www.fortworthstockyards.org.*

# When in Texas

### AUSTIN'S EPIC BAT FLIGHT

In the middle of downtown Austin, 1.5 million Mexican free-tailed bats roost under the Ann Richards Congress Avenue Bridge. From April to October, people come from around the world to watch these winged mammals leave the bridge each night to take to the skies. There is a bat observation area on the southeast side of Congress Avenue, but you also can view their northwestward flight from a boat on Lady Bird Lake below or from along the sides of the bridge or even from a hotel room with windows that overlook the lake on the west side of the bridge. **■TIP➔ The bats will be gliding over your head, so wear a cap, just in case—unless you want an up-close experience with bat guano.**

**Do This:** Kayak at dusk to watch the bats flock overhead, or take a bat-watching boat ride to see the spectacle. 🌐 *www.capitalcruises.com* or 🌐 *www.lonestarriverboat.com*.

**Ann Richards Congress Avenue Bridge.** ✉ *305 S. Congress Ave., Austin, TX*.

### BLUE BELL CREAMERY

Vermont has Ben & Jerry's, but Texas has Blue Bell. The family-owned creamery in Brenham, Texas, is a fun place to visit, and a self-guided tour here is on the bucket list of many Texans. A museum tells about the creamery's beginnings in 1907 as a dairy that churned out butter that evolved into making homemade ice cream that it delivered by horse and buggy to each home on the delivery route, much like the old-school milkman. Bluebell still oversees all of its deliveries, only with grocery stores and supermarkets as the clients now.

**Do This:** In a separate building from the exhibits, the ice cream is made. Through big windows overhead you can watch the various flavors being made and packaged. Follow that, of course, with a dish of fresh ice cream at the adjacent parlor for only $1.

**Blue Bell Creamery.** ✉ *1101 S. Blue Bell Rd., Brenham, TX* ☎ *800/327–8135* 🌐 *www.bluebell.com/the-little-creamery*.

### BUDDY HOLLY CENTER

On February 3, 1959, a plane carrying musicians Buddy Holly, Ritchie Valens, and "The Big Bopper" J. P. Richardson crashed in Iowa, killing all aboard. In his hit song "American Pie," singer and songwriter Don McLean calls it the day the music died. Known for hit songs like "That'll Be the Day" and "Peggy Sue," Holly was just 22 years old. The rising star was from Lubbock, Texas, and his hometown recognizes his achievements and fame at the Buddy Holly Center. The small center, which has a guitar-shaped gallery, features a film on Holly along with a variety of his personal items, including photographs, record contracts, his famous eyeglasses, his record collection, one of his songbooks, his school records, and his guitars. Nearby is a Buddy Holly statue on the West Texas Walk of Fame.

**Do This:** Other Holly sites you can visit while in Lubbock are his childhood home at 1606 39th Street; Hutchinson Junior High, where he attended from 1949 to 1952 and sang in the choir; Lubbock High, where he graduated in 1955; and his grave at the City of Lubbock Cemetery.

**Buddy Holly Center.** ✉ *1801 Crickets Ave., Lubbock, TX* ☎ *806/775–3560* 🌐 *www.buddyhollycenter.org*.

### CADILLAC RANCH

If you've ever had the urge to spray-paint graffiti, but don't want to end up in court, this is the place for you. Kitschy to the core, this roadside attraction outside Amarillo is the site of 10 Cadillacs partially buried head first into the ground, their main bodies and back sides sticking up in the air. They have been spray-painted—and covered with Day-Glo fluorescent paint—over and over again each day throughout the years with bright colors, and some visitors say you can smell the paint a football-field's worth of distance away.

**Do This:** If you want to add to the graffiti already adorning the exhibit, bring some rubber gloves and a few cans of spray paint. Make sure to snap your picture next to your masterpiece, because it will undoubtedly be covered by the next visitor.

**Cadillac Ranch.** ✉ *13651 I–40 Frontage Rd., Exit 60, Amarillo, TX* 🎫 *Free.*

## CHIP & JOANNA'S WACO

HGTV's *Fixer Upper* stars Chip and Joanna Gaines put the central Texas town of Waco on the map, helping people see that there is so much more to this town than being near the former Branch Davidian site in the early 1990s. After filming multiple seasons of the reality TV show, the dynamic duo turned their sights toward expanding their entrepreneurial endeavors. They launched a home line, wrote several books, came out with a magazine, started a TV network, kicked off a new cooking show, and opened two restaurants and three shops. More than 2 million fans come to Waco each year to see sites related to the show and spend time and money at Magnolia properties, especially Magnolia Market at the Silo. In fact, the Dallas Morning News reported that Chip and Joanna draw more visitors to Waco each year than the Alamo draws people to San Antonio. Off Interstate 35, Waco is about 90 minutes south of the Dallas–Fort Worth metroplex and 90 minutes north of Austin.

**Do This:** Stay in one of Chip and Joanna's three renovated homes (two were featured on the show) that they turned into vacation rentals, including Magnolia House in MacGregor, about 20 miles away off U.S. Highway 84. While you're here, take the free trolley that leaves from the Silo District and makes several downtown Waco stops to see the sights. Waco is home to Baylor University, the Dr Pepper Museum, the Texas Ranger Hall of Fame & Museum, the Texas Sports Hall of Fame, the Waco Mammoth National Monument, and the Mayborn Museum.

**Magnolia properties.** ✉ *Waco, TX* ☎ *833/843–0590* 🌐 *magnolia.com.*

## TEXAS BOOMTOWNS

In East Texas, the famous Spindletop Well began gushing oil in 1901 near what is today the town of Beaumont, and in the 1930s the East Texas Oil Field near Kilgore started producing gratuitous amounts of oil, becoming for a time the largest oil field in the lower 48 states. Many hoping to strike it rich flooded into town. The oil was essentially all dried up by the 1960s, but while the drilling occurred, more than 5 billion barrels of oil were pumped from the land. Both Beaumont and nearby Port Arthur (where Janis Joplin grew up) are filled with oil refineries in use today, while Kilgore is a town time left behind—but the many abandoned derricks remain.

Meanwhile in West Texas, on what's known as the Permian Basin, oil was discovered in the 1920s near Midland and Odessa, bringing workers by the tens of thousands to the area. This region of the state has since had three big oil booms: in the 1950s, the 1970s, and the early 2000s. In Midland, Texas, the childhood hometown of George W. Bush, you could until recently see many pumpjacks still drawing "black gold" from the ground.

**Do This:** In West Texas, visit the 60,000-square-foot Petroleum Museum in Midland to learn about the state's oil history (🌐 *petroleummuseum.org* 🎫 *$8*). In East Texas, head to two spots: the Spindletop–Gladys City Boomtown

Museum in Beaumont at Lamar University to experience an old boomtown (🌐 *www.spindletop.org* 🎫 *$5*) and the East Texas Oil Museum on the campus of Kilgore College in Kilgore to ride an elevator down "to the center of the Earth" and step into the re-created town from its 1930s heyday (🌐 *www.easttexasoilmuseum.com* 🎫 *$10*).

## Cool Places to Stay

**Bloomhouse.** An unusual home resembling a dragon-shaped seashell is built into West Austin's hills, making it a great place to embrace the signature "weird" of Austin. The white Bloomhouse, which is made out of polyurethane foam and cement plaster, looks like something out of a fantasy novel. Inside the curvy structure there is one bedroom with a queen bed plus a full-size futon, one bathroom, and modern amenities including Wi-Fi, a dishwasher, and TV. ✉ *On High Rd. in Westlake Highlands, Austin, TX* ☎ *512/522–8747* 🌐 *bloomhouse.live* 💲 *From $650.*

**Dixie Dude Ranch.** Bandera is known as Texas's Cowboy Capital, and there are many cattle ranches in the area where you can immerse yourself in the experience. One of Bandera's oldest dude ranches, and still a working ranch, Dixie Dude Ranch invites overnighters to participate in trail rides, cookouts, and family-style dining in the lodge. Other activities include fishing, hiking, campfires with cowboy serenades, hayrides, volleyball, swimming, ping pong, and basketball. Lodging is in Western-style rooms in the lodge or in cabins, cottages, or a bunkhouse. Rates include two trail rides per day and three daily meals. There is a minimum two-night stay. ✉ *833 Dixie Dude Ranch Rd., Bandera, TX* ☎ *830/796–7771* 🌐 *www.dixieduderanch.com* 💲 *From $180.*

**La Cantera Resort & Spa.** Set in the foothills north of San Antonio, 20 minutes from the San Antonio airport, La Cantera Resort & Spa is all about relaxation amid Hill Country beauty. It attracts day spa visitors as well as overnighters who want to enjoy the panoramic views, the spa, the infinity pool, the golf, and spacious rooms. Private villas are also available. A free shuttle takes you into San Antonio for shopping and sightseeing, but if you're planning on doing a lot in downtown San Antonio, you may want to opt for a hotel like the Menger, the Emily Morgan, Havana, or Grand Hyatt San Antonio Riverwalk that's right downtown and within walking distance to major attractions—and then drive up to La Cantera for a day to unwind at the spa. ✉ *16641 La Cantera Pkwy., San Antonio, TX* ☎ *210/558–6500* 🌐 *www.lacanteraresort.com* 💲 *From $635.*

**Stockyards Hotel.** Open since 1907, this historical hotel in Fort Worth's Stockyards wrangles the cowboy theme well, with Western art and saddle seating in the hotel saloon. Rooms are named after famous Old West legends and include related artifacts, like the Butch Cassidy Suite, the Davy Crockett Room, and the Bonnie and Clyde Room, where the notorious couple actually stayed in 1933. Past guests also include Tanya Tucker, Trisha Yearwood, and Willie Nelson. ■ **TIP→ Because it's right in the Stockyards entertainment area, it can be loud on Saturday nights.** ✉ *109 E. Exchange Ave., Fort Worth, TX* ☎ *817/625–6427* 🌐 *www.stockyardshotel.com* 💲 *From $249.*

# Utah

From mountain biking on slickrock to hiking past dinosaur fossils, Utah has thrilling adventures for everyone. The world-class ski resorts of Park City are a haven for those seeking perfect powder, and national parks such as Arches and Zion offer colorful geology lessons with natural arches, hoodoos, and mesas in brilliant ocher and red. History lovers can ponder petroglyphs made by the earliest inhabitants or explore the Mormons' pioneer past in Salt Lake City. At the end of the day's activities, a hot tub and plush bed await.

## Bucket List Picks

The following boxes contain our picks for the top sights and experiences in Utah.

- O Moab
- O Park City
- O Arches National Park
- O Bonneville Salt Flats
- O Zion National Park
- O Bryce Canyon National Park
- O Monument Valley and the Four Corners
- O Capitol Reef National Park
- O Grand Staircase–Escalante National Monument
- O Canyonlands National Park

# Moab

## Moutain-Biking Capital of the World

Moab has earned a well-deserved reputation as the mountain-biking capital of the world, drawing riders of all ages onto rugged roads and trails. It's where the whole sport started, and the area attracts bikers from all over the globe to its red rocks and mountainous landscape. The towering cliffs and deep canyons can be intimidating and unreachable without the help of a guide. Fortunately, guide services are abundant in Moab.

## Don't Miss

One of the many popular routes is the Slickrock Trail, a stunning area of steep Navajo Sandstone dunes a few miles east of Moab.

## For Beginners

More moderate rides can be found on the Gemini Bridges or Monitor and Merrimac trails, both off U.S. 191 north of Moab. Klondike Bluffs, north of Moab, is an excellent novice ride.

## Best Outfitter

In a town of great bike shops, Poison Spider Bicylcles is one of the best. 🌐 *www.poisonspiderbicycles.com.*

## Best Tour

Head to Western Spirit Cycling Adventures for fully supported, go-at-your-own-pace, multiday mountain- and road-bike tours. 🌐 *westernspirit.com.*

## Good to Know

The Moab Information Center carries a free biking trail guide. Mountain-bike rentals range from $40 to $75 for a top-of-the-line workhorse.

## Getting Here and Around

Save a few days for your multiday mountain-bike adventure. From Moab, it's an easy drive to both Arches and Canyonlands national parks. The nearest large airport to southeastern Utah is Walker Field Airport in Grand Junction, Colorado, 110 miles from Moab.

# Park City

## Perfect Powder

Top-notch skiing and snowboarding are found in the winter wonderland of Park City. With an average snowfall of more than 300 inches and lots of "power days," Park City has two main ski areas: Deer Valley Resort and Park City Mountain Resort. Deer Valley is a step into luxury, where there are ski valets, upscale lodging options, gourmet dining, and vacation planners at the ready to make your stay perfect. Featuring a 3,000-foot vertical drop, Deer Valley has 103 runs, more than 2,000 skiable acres, and 21 lifts. It is a skiing-only mountain, catering to all levels of skiers. Meanwhile, Park City Mountain Resort features more than 7,300 skiable acres, 341 runs, six terrain parks, 43 lifts, and world-class half pipes. The largest ski resort in America, Park City Mountain Resort has 51% of its terrain for advanced skiers and snowboarders and only 8% for beginners. It is where the U.S. Ski and Snowboarding Team trains.

## Don't Miss

The 400-acre Utah Olympic Park, which hosted the 2002 Winter Olympics bobsled, skeleton, luge, and Nordic combined events, today contains the 2002 Olympic Games Museum and lets visitors don a helmet and take a bobsled ride ($175).

## Olympic History

During the 2002 Winter Olympics, Deer Valley hosted the slalom and freestyle ski competition, while Park City Mountain Resort held snowboarding competitions.

## While You're Here

Outside Park City but nearby are five other ski areas: Brighton, Solitude, Alta, Sundance, and Snowbird.

## Getting Here and Around

Park City is about 38 miles from the Salt Lake City airport (SLC).

# Arches National Park

## Nature's Windows

More than 1 million visitors come to Arches annually, drawn by the red rock landscape and its teasing wind- and water-carved rock formations. The park is named for the 2,000-plus sandstone arches—the largest collection of natural arches in the world—that frame horizons, cast precious shade, and nobly withstand the withering forces of nature and time. The park's longest is 306-foot, ribbonlike Landscape Arch, and there are fancifully named attractions like Tower of Babel, Three Gossips, and Sheep Rock to stir the curiosity. The best way to see the arches is to hike to them. The park's Windows area has trails to Turret Arch, North Window, South Window, and Double Arch (which had a cameo in *Indiana Jones and the Last Crusade*). Not far from the Windows is Balanced Rock, off the Main Park Road.

## Don't Miss

Explore a maze of orange spires that look like tongues of flame at Fiery Furnace either on your own or on a ranger-guided walk. It's about 14 miles from the park visitor center. Access the viewpoint to see the iconic 52-foot-tall Delicate Arch on the way.

## When to Go

The prettiest time in the park is spring, when wildflowers bloom, and fall has the best weather. If you want to explore in solitude, come in winter.

## Getting Here and Around

Arches National Park is in southeast Utah, 5 miles north of Moab on U.S. 191. It is 21 miles from Canyonlands. The nearest large airport is Walker Field Airport in Grand Junction, Colorado, 110 miles from Moab.

**Arches National Park.** ✉ *Moab, UT* ☎ *435/719–2299* 🌐 *www.nps.gov/arch* 🎫 *$30 per vehicle.*

# Bonneville Salt Flats

### Putting the "Salt" in Salt Lake

Did you know that the Great Salt Lake, the Western Hemisphere's largest saltwater lake, is saltier than the ocean? It's also part of what was once an ancient body of water that covered a third of Utah, Lake Bonneville. West of the lake is a souvenir from this ancient body of water: Bonneville Salt Flats. This mind-bending, barren, 30,000-acre stretch along Interstate 80 formed when most of Lake Bonneville dried up, leaving behind salt deposits that stretch for miles. The crusted, white, salty surface features sodium chloride (table salt) as well as magnesium, lithium, and potassium.

### Don't Miss

About 10 miles east of Wendover, Utah, is one of the best spots to view the salt flats. There's a rest stop here, where you can pause for a panoramic view and also walk onto the salt.

### While You're Here

About 90 miles to the east of Bonneville Salt Flats is Great Salt Lake State Park, where you can float in the salty waters of the Western Hemisphere's largest saltwater lake.

### When to Go

The flats are open year-round, but if it's solitude you seek come in early spring. In summer and fall, the flats draw car racers to its Bonneville Speedway to test their speeds and for the popular Speed Week each August. ⊕ *www.bonnevilleracing.com*.

### Getting Here and Around

Bonneville Salt Flats is in the northeastern part of Utah near the state's border with Nevada. The distance on Interstate 80 between Salt Lake City and Wendover is about 124 miles.

**Bonneville Salt Flats.** ✉ *I–80, Wendover, UT* ⊕ *www.blm.gov/visit/bonneville-salt-flats*.

# Zion National Park

### Land Before Time

The walls of Zion Canyon soar more than 2,000 feet above the valley below, but it's the character, not the size, of the sandstone forms that defines the park's splendor. Throughout the park, fantastically colored bands of limestone, sandstone, and lava in the strata point to the distant past. Stripes and spots of greenery high in the cliff walls create a "hanging garden" effect, and invariably indicate the presence of water seepage or a spring. Erosion has left behind a collection of domes, fins, and blocky massifs bearing the names and likenesses of cathedrals and temples, prophets and angels. Trails lead deep into side canyons and up narrow ledges to waterfalls, serene spring-fed pools, and shaded spots.

### Don't Miss

In addition to Zion Canyon, find three popular rock formations: Court of the Patriarchs; The Watchman; and the towering Great White Throne, one of the world's largest sandstone monoliths.

### Best Hike

One of the most difficult and rewarding hikes is a 4.4-mile trek up the 1,500-foot-tall Angels Landing.

### Good to Know

So diverse is this place that 85% of Utah's flora and fauna species are found here. Some, like the Zion snail, appear nowhere else on earth.

### When to Go

Visit in April, May, September, or October to avoid the extreme heat and the large summer crowds.

### Getting Here and Around

Zion National Park is in southern Utah off State Route 9 near Springdale. From April through October a free shuttle transports you within the park.

**Zion National Park.** ☎ *435/772–3256* 🌐 *www.nps.gov/zion* 🎫 *$35.*

# Bryce Canyon National Park

### Home of the Hoodoos

The world's highest concentration of hoodoos (tall, thin, weathered rock formations) can be found in this otherworldy national park, one of the most beloved in all of Utah. With its vivid colors, Bryce Canyon National Park is a feast for the eyes, especially when the light plays off the rocks and the brilliant colors pop. New hoodoos are continually formed as the rim of Bryce's amphitheater recedes, and old hoodoos affected by erosion eventually topple over, making this a living laboratory for geologists.

### Don't Miss

Sunrise Point, named for its stunning views at dawn, provides an overlook that's just a short walk from Bryce Canyon Lodge, 2 miles south of the park entrance. It's also the trailhead for the Queen's Garden Trail and the Fairyland Loop Trail.

### Best Tour

On a Full Moon Hike, park rangers lead guided hikes on the nights around each full moon (two per month May–October).

### Did You Know?

The park is named for Ebenezer Bryce, a pioneer cattleman and the first permanent settler in the area. His description of the landscape "not being hospitable to cows" has oft been repeated.

### Getting Here and Around

The nearest commercial airport to Bryce Canyon is 80 miles west in Cedar City, Utah, but many visitors fly into Las Vegas and road-trip the 265 miles from there. Many of the park's spectacular sights can be viewed from the 36-mile round-trip Main Park Road.

**Bryce Canyon National Park.** ✉ *Hwy. 63, Bryce, UT* 🌐 *www.nps.gov/brca* 🎫 *$35.*

# Monument Valley and the Four Corners

### Play Geographical Twister

Using two hands and two feet, you can be in Colorado, New Mexico, Arizona, and Utah all at once. The Four Corners is marked by a decorative cement and granite slab with a bronze disk in the middle noting where the state's borders touch. Because it's part of Native lands for the Navajo and Ute people, you can browse booths with arts and crafts from Native American artists as well as learn more about the tribes' culture at the visitor center. There are also pueblos and other former Native homes throughout the region. The Four Corners area offers horseback riding and hiking trails, hot-air balloon rides, Jeep tours, and glorious sights of red rocks in nearby Monument Valley—from buttes and mesas to arches and needlelike spires.

### Don't Miss

At the 30,000-acre Monument Valley, a Navajo Tribal Park, stop at the Monument Valley Visitor Center on U.S. 163 for hiking permits, to pick up information, and to view artifacts from the old trading post, then take a two- to three-hour scenic drive through the valley. If it looks familiar, it's likely because you've seen it on the big screen in old Westerns, *Forrest Gump*, and HBO's *Westworld*, to name a few. *$20 per vehicle.*

### Best Tour

The best way to travel through Monument Valley and the Four Corners area, viewing rock art, ancient dwellings, and more, is with a Navajo guide. Tour lengths and prices vary depending on the operator. Some even offer overnight trips. *navajonationparks.org*.

### Getting Here and Around

Monument Valley is 25 miles from Mexican Hat, Utah, and 51 miles from Bluff, Utah. The Four Corners Monument is off U.S. 160.

# Capitol Reef National Park

## Land of Sleeping Rainbow

A natural kaleidoscopic feast for the eyes, Capitol Reef National Park is saturated in colors that are more dramatic than anywhere else in the West. The dominant Moenkopi rock formation is a rich, red-chocolate hue. Deep blue-green juniper and pinyon stand out against it. Other sandstone layers are gold, ivory, and lavender. Sunset brings out the colors in an explosion of copper, platinum, and orange, then dusk turns the cliffs purple and blue. The texture of rock deposited in ancient inland seas and worn by subsequent erosion is pure art. It's no wonder the Fremont people, whose culture dating back a thousand years are written on rocks in the park, called this part of the country the "land of sleeping rainbow."

## Don't Miss

The park has a surprising feature tucked among its slot canyons, arches, and slickrock wilderness: orchards. See the cherry, apricot, peach, pear, and apple trees at Fruita Rural Historic District; you can eat as much of the fruit as you want.

## Best Hike

Hike Capitol Gorge Trail, beginning at the Pioneer Register (a wall where pioneers signed their names). The moderate, 2-mile round-trip jaunt includes the chance to view a natural bridge and petroglyphs.

## While You're Here

Formations like Temple of the Moon, Cathedral Valley, and the Bentonite Hills' (striking blue-and-red-tinged circular mounds) are all stunning.

## Getting Here and Around

Capitol Reef is 4½ miles from Torrey, Utah, via Utah State Route 24 East Highway 24 runs through the park.

**Capitol Reef National Park.** ✉ *South-central Utah, near Torrey* 🌐 *www.nps.gov/care* 🎟 *$20 per vehicle.*

# Grand Staircase-Escalante National Monument

## Remote Cliffs and Switchbacks

This national monument got its name from its series of rugged cliffs and terraces that look like a giant staircase stretching across the glorious terrain in this remote part of the state. The layers of cliffs show a variety of sediment in the rock formations. Its three distinct sections—the Grand Staircase, the Kaiparowits Plateau, and the Canyons of the Escalante—offer remote backcountry experiences hard to find elsewhere in the Lower 48. Highway 12, which straddles the northern border of the monument, is one of the most scenic stretches in the Southwest.

## Don't Miss

The showstopper is Jacob Hamblin Arch at Coyote Gulch, where you can splash in shallow water under a gigantic natural arch. The 2-mile Jacob Hamblin Trailhead is a relatively easy hike.

## Make It a Road Trip

The Scenic Byway 12 winds 124 miles through alpine forests and wild landscape as well as through Grand Staircase-Escalante National Monument.

## Getting Here and Around

Grand Staircase National Monument is 16 miles from Kanab, Utah. The small towns of Escalante and Boulder offer outfitters, lodging, and dining. Scenic Byway 12 runs from Torrey, Utah, in the north at the intersection with State Route 24 to just past Bryce Canyon in the south, intersecting with U.S. Route 89.

**Grand Staircase National Monument.** ✉ *69 S. Hwy. 89A, Kanab, UT* 🌐 *www.blm.gov* 🎫 *Free.*

# Canyonlands National Park

### Rugged Adventures

Spacious Canyonlands National Park in central Utah is a bit like walking on the moon thanks to its many mushroomlike rock formations in assorted shapes and colors. It's also so much more. Chocolate-brown canyons and deep-red mountains highlight the northern part of the park, while red and white needles stand soldier-like in the southern part of the park, where there are also red mesas and buttes and grassy meadows. The Maze, accessible only by four-wheel drive—or Butch Cassidy's horse back in the day—holds iconic Chimney Rock.

### Don't Miss

At Grand View Point, an overlook in the middle of the park, the panoramic view extends for miles. It's 12 miles from the Island in the Sky entrance and is serene in winter.

### Best Hike

The most popular trail is Mesa Arch Trail, a two-thirds mile loop that showcases a natural arch window sitting atop a cliff.

### Best Base: Moab

En route from Canyonlands National Park to Arches National Park is the picture-perfect-for-a-Jeep-commercial town of Moab. Outfitters here can set you up with mountain bikes or ATVs for exploring the slickrock and rock climbing gear for experienced scaling, or put you on a white-water rafting trip down the Colorado or Green rivers, where world-class rapids await. If you're a fan of adrenaline-inducing adventure, Moab is the place for you.

### Getting Here and Around

Canyonlands National Park's Island in the Sky area is 21 miles from Arches National Park and 32 miles from Moab on Route 313.

**Canyonlands National Park.**
☎ *435/719–2313* 🌐 *www.nps.gov/cany*
🎫 *$30 per vehicle.*

## When in Utah

### DINOSAUR NATIONAL MONUMENT

Just 7 miles from Jensen, Utah, crossing over the Utah-Colorado border, is Dinosaur National Monument. While the dinosaurs are long gone, *Jurassic Park* lovers come to see the more than 1,500 fossilized dinosaur bones captured in a cliff wall. View them in the Quarry Exhibit Hall on the Utah side. On the Colorado side of the monument, there are no dinosaur fossils, but you can hike through mountains and canyons. The 210,000-acre monument also includes Native American rock art, old-time cabins, and plenty of wildlife viewing. The entrance to the remote monument is roughly 16 miles from Vernal, Utah, where there are more than 200 dinosaur tracks at Red Fleet State Park. This area of the state has become known as Dinosaurland.

**Do This:** If time allows, do a guided one-day or multiday white-water rafting trip on the Green River, departing from the Gates of Lodores. Enjoy incredible views as well as thrills—rapid names like Disaster Falls and Hell's Half Mile give you an idea of the level of excitement on a high river run.

**Quarry Visitor Center.** ✉ *11625 E. 1500 S, Jensen, UT* ☎ *435/781–7700* 🌐 *www.nps.gov/dino* 🎫 *$25.*

### LAKE POWELL

The Glen Canyon Dam forms this ultimate water playground and reservoir in southern Utah and northern Arizona. With almost 2,000 miles of shoreline, the lake provides plenty of places to get on the water—whether you rent kayaks, paddleboards, and Jet Skis or swim or fish. There is also incredible hiking and delightful bird-watching around the lake.

**Do This:** To enjoy a multiday trip at the lake, camp at Lone Rock Beach, Bullfrog Basin Campground near Kanab, or Stanton Creek Campground. It's a great base for a trip to Rainbow Bridge National Monument.

**Lake Powell.** 🌐 *www.lakepowell.com.*

### SALT LAKE TEMPLE

In the mid-1800s, led by Brigham Young, a group of thousands of Mormons seeking religious freedom migrated west and settled in what today is the state of Utah. Young became the first governor of the territory. Today the religious group known also as the Church of Jesus Christ of Latter-day Saints has its headquarters in Salt Lake City. Built in the second half of the 1800s, the temple is considered holy by members of the Church of Jesus Christ of Latter-day Saints and is therefore not open to the general public. You can view the architecture from outside, walk through the grounds and gardens, and ask questions at the South Visitors' Center. Additional attractions related to the faith are in the area around Temple Square, and guided walking tours, which begin at the Conference Center, will enlighten you on the square's history and happenings. There are also tours of Brigham Young's home, the Beehive House.

**Do This:** Attend a free recital by the Tabernacle Choir each Sunday morning or listen to them rehearse on Tuesday evenings. Note that the temple and its grounds were closed in 2019 for major renovations and it's expected to open again in 2024.

**Salt Lake Temple.** ✉ *50 W. North Temple, Salt Lake City, UT* ☎ *801/240–2534* 🌐 *www.templesquare.com/explore/tabernacle.*

### SUNDANCE FILM FESTIVAL

The largest independent film festival in the United States draws 40,000 to 50,000 attendees to Park City each January for the unveiling of documentaries and dramatic features, among them an assortment of A-listers, independent filmmakers touting new releases and vying for recognition, and the general public. The showings take place in Park City, Salt Lake City, and Sundance Resort over a 10-day period. Founded in 1981 by Robert Redford, the Sundance Institute hosts the festival and encourages independence, risk-taking, and authentic voices. Past films that have debuted at the festival include *Little Miss Sunshine, An Inconvenient Truth, Brooklyn, Napoleon Dynamite,* and *Won't You Be My Neighbor.*

**Do This:** Insiders say the first week of the festival is focused on networking, while the second week is about sitting back and enjoying the shows. Whichever week you choose to go, book early and pack for winter weather in the mountains—designer but rubber-soled boots in, flimsy high heels out. Buy your tickets in advance and consider the festival pass.

**Sundance Institute.** ✉ *1500 Kearns Blvd. Suite B110, Park City, UT* ☎ *435/658–3456* 🌐 *www.sundance.org* 🎟 *$250–$600 for 10 screenings, depending on timing and availability.*

## Cool Places to Stay

**Amangiri.** Blending elegantly into its desert surroundings, this five-star resort is the place to find ultimate luxury in the desert and a good base for adventures to Page, Arizona. Everything about this resort respects the unique landscape of southern Utah, with its glowing swimming pool built into rock; walls of glass and outdoor decks for easy viewing of the mesas, deserts, and ancient rock formations; and extensive work with Navajo artists. ✉ *1 Kayenta Rd., Canyon Point, UT* 🌐 *www.aman.com.* $ From $2,000.

**Capitol Reef Resort.** If you love watching old *Little House on the Prairie* episodes, you may wonder what it's like to sleep in a covered wagon. Capitol Reef Resort lets you find out, sort of. The glamped-out Conestoga wagons here, which sleep up to six, do let you hear the night sounds, but they also include their own built-in bathrooms and bunk beds as well as modern-day amenities like air-conditioning. Other accommodation options at the resort are teepees, cabins, and Western-themed hotel rooms. ✉ *2600 E. Utah Hwy. 24, Torrey, UT* ☎ *435/425–3761* 🌐 *capitolreefresort.com* $ *From $305 per wagon.*

**The St. Regis Deer Valley.** Park City has several lodging options that are worthy of the stars, and if you're heading there for the Sundance Film Festival, you might be looking for just that. One is an upscale Marriott property on the mountain, the St. Regis Deer Valley, an especially good choice if you plan to ski while in Park City. At the Regis, temporary residents are pampered in posh surroundings and windows look out on Deer Valley ski area. Luxury suites include private balconies, fireplaces, and small kitchens. Accommodations book months in advance for the festival. ✉ *2300 Deer Valley Dr. E, Park City, UT* ☎ *435/940–5700* 🌐 *www.marriott.com* $ *From $1,000.*

**Talking Mountain Yurts.** Perfect for those on an adventure in Utah's La Sal Mountain Range, these three yurts, operated by a Moab-based company, are located at various spots in the backcountry. Each of the yurts can sleep up to eight in shared beds and futon or cots (bring your own linens or sleeping bags; no bedding is provided). Each has a kitchen with a wood-burning stove and cooking equipment and seating area. There is no electricity or plumbing in the yurts. Each has a nearby outhouse. No pets are allowed. ✉ *Moab, UT* ☎ *435/260–7601* 🌐 *talkingmountainyurts.com* $ *From $275.*

Chapter 9

# THE ROCKIES

Written by
Kyle Wagner

# WELCOME TO THE ROCKIES

## TOP REASONS TO GO

★ **Modern day Wild West:** Denver mixes Old West culture and big-city charm; Jackson Hole pairs ranching with glitz and glamour; Boise brings a thriving urban scene to life amid a wide-open landscape; and Cheyenne still feels like the frontier is alive and well.

★ **Outdoor adventures:** Getting into the backcountry is easier than ever, and activities abound, including skiing and other snow sports, rafting and other water sports, hiking, mountain biking, fishing, hunting, and more.

★ **National parks galore:** From Yellowstone and Grand Tetons in Wyoming to Rocky Mountain in Colorado and Glacier in Montana, there's no shortage of natural beauty to check off your list.

★ **Cool mountain towns:** Enjoy the chill vibes of towns like Grand Junction and Durango that are set among the most idyllic mountain backdrops.

★ **Go wild:** Spot elk, bison, and even Yogi bear in their natural habitat in the Wild West.

1 **Colorado.** The southernmost of the Rockies states, Colorado is known for Denver, its Mile High City, plus skiing mountains, and four national parks, including Rocky Mountain National Park and Mesa Verde National Park.

2 **Idaho.** The "Gem State" has its fair share of crown jewels for outdoor lovers, including the wild terrain of Owyhee Canyonlands, plus Hells Canyon, Shoshone Falls, and Sun Valley skiing.

3 **Montana.** Mountains and plains that beg to be explored are scattered all across Big Sky Country, known for Glacier National Park as well as epic trout fishing.

4 **Wyoming.** The Cowboy State is mountain country, where high peaks—some of which remain snowcapped year-round—tower above deep, glacier-carved valleys. Stunners include the Grand Tetons and Jackson Hole.

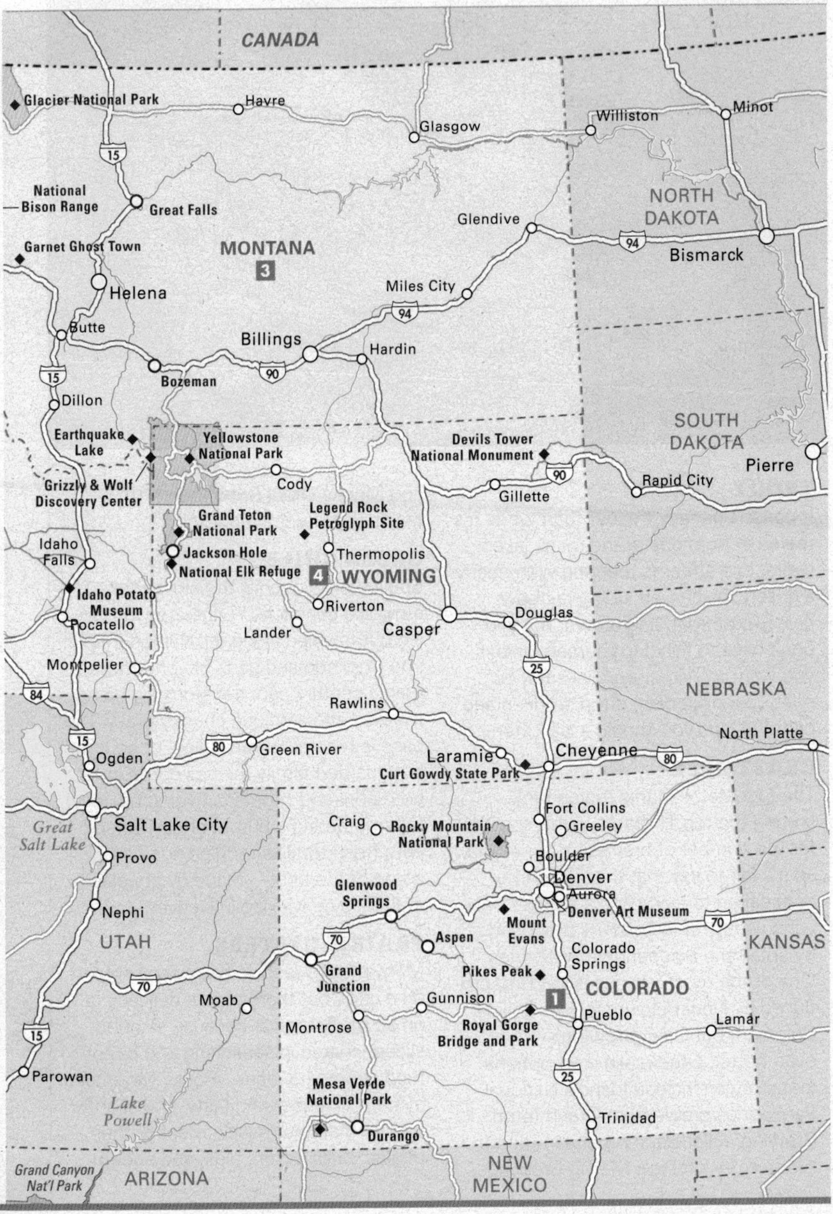

CANADA
Glacier National Park
Havre
Glasgow
Williston
Minot
15
National Bison Range
Great Falls
NORTH DAKOTA
Glendive
94
Bismarck
Garnet Ghost Town
MONTANA
3
Helena
Miles City
94
Butte
Billings
Hardin
Bozeman
90
15
Dillon
SOUTH DAKOTA
Earthquake Lake
Yellowstone National Park
Devils Tower National Monument
Pierre
90
Grizzly & Wolf Discovery Center
Cody
Gillette
Rapid City
Grand Teton National Park
Legend Rock Petroglyph Site
Idaho Falls
Jackson Hole
Thermopolis
National Elk Refuge
4
WYOMING
Idaho Potato Museum
Riverton
Pocatello
Lander
Casper
Douglas
Montpelier
25
84
NEBRASKA
Rawlins
15
80
Green River
North Platte
Ogden
Laramie
Cheyenne
80
Curt Gowdy State Park
Fort Collins
Salt Lake City
Craig
Rocky Mountain National Park
Greeley
Great Salt Lake
Provo
Boulder
Glenwood Springs
Denver
Aurora
Denver Art Museum
Nephi
Mount Evans
70
UTAH
70
Aspen
Colorado Springs
KANSAS
Grand Junction
Pikes Peak
70
1
COLORADO
Moab
Gunnison
Pueblo
Montrose
Royal Gorge Bridge and Park
Lamar
15
25
Parowan
Mesa Verde National Park
Lake Powell
Trinidad
Durango
Grand Canyon Nat'l Park
ARIZONA
NEW MEXICO

# WHAT TO EAT AND DRINK IN THE ROCKIES

Trout

## TROUT

It doesn't get any fresher than when it's reeled in from one of the many lakes, rivers, and streams teeming with nearly a dozen species, including rainbow, brook, cutthroat, and brown, but you don't have to fish it in yourself, unless you want to. Most regional eateries offer up a trout dish, often smoked and panfried, and you should avail, often.

## CRAFT BEER

The four states in this region rank among the top 11 states in the country for the number of breweries per capita, so it's fair to say that this is a prime destination for sampling a staggeringly wide variety of local beers produced by small and independent breweries. One of the most famous is Fat Tire, produced by New Belgium in Fort Collins, Colorado, but Odell Brewing's IPA is even better. Other solid craft options in the region include Idaho's National Park Series brews from Grand Teton Brewing; Killer Bees American Blonde Ale from Wyoming's Melvin Brewing; and Moose Drool Brown Ale from Montana's Big Sky Brewing Co.

## GREEN CHILE

Spelled chile or chili, the slow-cooked, stew-like concoction originated in Mexico but traveled along the Santa Fe Trail into Colorado and parts beyond more than a century ago, transforming along the way into a unique chunky gravy. The base is roasted green chiles, of course, but guarded family recipes come in both pork and vegetarian versions, ideal for smothering a burrito or served solo with fresh tortillas for dipping. Find some of the best— made by abuelas— at El Taco de Mexico in Denver.

## PRAIRIE OYSTERS

Many a bull's testicle has been eaten on a dare, but the Western delicacy is on so many menus because skinned, sliced, coated in seasoning and deep-fried, a properly done "Rocky Mountain oyster" is tender and tasty, and slightly gamier than the muscle meat of their origins: bulls, bison, pigs, and sheep.

Try them with a side of cocktail sauce at the Albany, a quintessential cowboy bar in a 1905 building in downtown Cheyenne, Wyoming.

### ROCKY MOUNTAIN HIGH

Colorado is famously the first state to have legalized cannabis, and the pot scene just continues to grow (pun intended). There's a dispensary on nearly every corner in most cities and towns—a few local favorites include Good Chemistry, Starbuds, Oasis Superstore, and Native Roots. To avoid couch coma from eating too much in edibles, start with 5 mg and wait four hours before adding more.

### PALISADE PEACHES

The banana-belt climate of Colorado's Grand Valley, which includes the orchard-filled wine country of Palisade, also produces a first-rate peach, so juicy and sweet that folks flock to the area come harvest time. Cling peaches are available in mid- to late summer, while the freestone varieties are ripe and ready around the state come August and September.

### ALL THE MEATS

The dark forms of cattle and bison dot nearly every landscape throughout the region—from the Rocky Mountain valleys out to the Great Plains—and area universities' meat labs continually focus on creating better marbling and more environmentally friendly resource management, which explains why exceptionally produced meat from cattle and bison can be found everywhere here as steaks (often chicken-fried), burgers, stews, chili, jerky, and more.

Moose meat

Palisade peaches

### POTATOES

The optimal climate in Idaho—hot days and cool nights through the summer together with the ashy volcanic soil—makes for a superior spud, fluffier when baked, crispier when fried, and not coincidentally, superb as a side for the mighty meats that also rule the region. When in Idaho …

### HUCKLEBERRY ANYTHING

Like a bigger, darker blueberry, the huckleberry has a similar sweetness when ripe, but also a tart edge that makes it perfect for pie, jams and jellies, wine and liqueur, ice cream, and other desserts. The official state fruit of Idaho, they're also native to Wyoming and Montana, and products containing huckleberries are so ubiquitous that you'll find them in gas stations.

# The Rockies Regional Snapshot

## Know Before You Go

### PLAN FOR ALL TYPES OF WEATHER

The Rocky Mountain West can be sunny, rainy, freezing cold, and searing hot—sometimes all in the same day. While most visitors set their sights on seasonal activities such as skiing, snowmobiling, mountain biking, hiking, or hunting, it's smart to have a backup plan, because the weather can change very fast. Temperatures and conditions can also be drastically different from lower elevations to higher altitudes, the latter of which can have snow in July. It is no exaggeration to say that not being prepared can be fatal out here.

### ALTITUDE MAKES A DIFFERENCE

The higher up you go, the easier it is to get dehydrated, so always carry water and watch your alcohol and cannabis intake, which can hit faster and harder. Bring layers, too, because temperatures can drop or rise 10–20 degrees from one locale to another.

### ROCKY MOUNTAIN HIGH

Nonresidents over 21 need an ID to purchase the same daily amount of cannabis as residents (1 ounce of flower or 800 milligrams of edibles). As with alcohol, cannabis can hit you faster here: the slogan is to start "low and slow" (start with 5 mg and wait four hours before adding more). Note: crossing state lines or flying with cannabis is illegal, as is driving under the influence or consuming in public. There are tour groups that will bus guests to dispensaries and grows, along with pot-friendly lodgings that allow on-site consumption.

## Planning Your Time

First-time visitors are often surprised by how far apart everything is in the Rockies—even from one end of a state to another. Add in constant construction, rush hour, and the ever-increasing popularity of the region, and delays are a given. Consider clustering your focus around a city or town to explore an area via day trips, and schedule longer excursions around rest days.

## Road Trips

**5 Days:** Denver to Rocky Mountain National Park to Aspen

**5 Days:** The national parks, Glacier to Yellowstone

**3 Days:** Boise to Sun Valley

## Big Events

**A Taste of Colorado.** Civic Center Park in Denver transforms into a giant sampler platter of favorite foods from around the state every Labor Day weekend. 🌐 *www.atasteofcolorado.com.*

**Telluride Bluegrass Festival.** The biggest names in bluegrass, along with a well-rounded roster of musicians from other genres, descend upon the picturesque former Colorado mining town over the annual summer solstice to pluck and harmonize for the masses. 🌐 *bluegrass.com/telluride.*

**Trailing of the Sheep Festival.** Every October, more than 1,500 sheep are paraded down the main drag in Hailey, Idaho, but first the town turns into a shrine to tasty lamb dishes and sheepdog trials. 🌐 *trailingofthesheep.org.*

**Cheyenne Frontier Days.** Since 1897, this part rodeo, part music festival for cowboys and cowboy wannabes has been held midsummer in Wyoming's capital. 🌐 *www.cfdrodeo.com.*

**Trout Creek Huckleberry Festival.** In a state that hosts multiple festivals devoted to the tart, blueberrylike fruit, the decades-old Trout Creek event each August is a down-home standout. 🌐 *www.huckleberryfestival.com.*

## What To ...

### READ

*Plainsong* by Kent Haruf

*On the Road* by Jack Kerouac

*A River Runs Through It* by Norman Maclean

*Colter's Run* by Stephen T. Gough

*The Whistling Season* by Ivan Doig

### WATCH

*South Park* (animated sitcom set in Colorado)

*Longmire* (television series set in Wyoming)

*Legends of the Fall* (movie set in Montana)

*Smoke Signals* (movie set in Idaho)

### LISTEN

*Lost Highways: Dispatches from the Shadows of the Rocky Mountains* (podcast)

"Rocky Mountain High" by John Denver (song)

"Montana" by Phish

"Wyoming and Me" by The Black Crowes

### BUY

Beer growlers from Colorado

Western shirts from Colorado

Huckleberry-infused pies, preserves, sauces, chocolates, and coffee from Montana, Wyoming, and Idaho

Sapphire jewelry from Montana

Cowgirl Chocolates from Idaho

Buffalo jerky from Wyoming

Cowboy boots from Wyoming

## Contacts

### AIR

Major Airports:

**Colorado:** COS, DIA

**Idaho:** BOI

**Montana:** BZN, BIL, FCA, MSO

**Wyoming:** CPR, JAC

### BUS

**Alpine Express.** ☎ *800/822–4844* 🌐 *alpine.letsride.co/contact-us.*

**Arrow Stage Lines.** ☎ *303/373–9119* 🌐 *arrowstagelines.com.*

**Jefferson Lines.** ☎ *858/800–8898* 🌐 *jeffersonlines.com.*

**Mountain Line.** 🌐 *mountainline.com.*

**National Charter Bus Denver.** ☎ *303/317–3208* 🌐 *nationalbuscharter.com/denver-charter-bus.*

**Northwestern Trailways.** ☎ *800/451–5333* 🌐 *www.northwesterntrailways.com.*

### TRAIN

**Amtrak.** ☎ *800/872–7245* 🌐 *www.amtrak.com.*

**Idaho Rail.** 🌐 *idahorail.com.*

**RTD Lightrail.** 🌐 *www.rtd-denver.com/services/rail.*

### VISITOR INFORMATION

🌐 *www.colorado.com*

🌐 *visitidaho.org*

🌐 *www.visitmt.com*

🌐 *www.nps.gov*

🌐 *travelwyoming.com*

# Colorado

A playground for nature lovers and outdoor enthusiasts, Colorado has majestic landscapes, raging rivers, and winding trails perfect for activities from biking to rafting. The heart of the Rocky Mountains has scores of snowcapped summits towering higher than 14,000 feet and trails from easy to challenging for exploring them—as well as roads offering spectacular drives. Skiers flock to the slopes here for the champagne powder and thrilling downhill runs. Need a break from the outdoors? Urban adventures await in cool cities like Denver, Boulder, and Aspen.

## Bucket List Picks

The following boxes contain our picks for the top sights and experiences in Colorado.

- ○ Rocky Mountain National Park
- ○ Royal Gorge Bridge and Park
- ○ Durango
- ○ Mt. Evans
- ○ Aspen
- ○ Denver Art Museum
- ○ Grand Junction
- ○ Pikes Peak
- ○ Glenwood Springs
- ○ Mesa Verde National Park

# Rocky Mountain National Park

## Astounding Scenery and Wildlife Viewing

With more than 350 miles of trails, 30 miles of the Continental Divide and 77 peaks jutting above 12,000 feet—including Longs Peak, the 14,259-foot flat-top monarch of the Front Range—Rocky Mountain National Park abounds with spectacular adventures for hard-core mountaineers, and incredible scenery for nature and wildlife lovers. Hike to high-alpine lakes, picnic in wide-open meadows of wildflowers, or just drive along Trail Ridge Road, viewing the abundant wildlife along the way. The gateway to RMNP's East Entrance is charming Estes Park, a quintessential mountain town with an abundance of souvenir shops and eateries.

## Don't Miss

The Alluvial Fan, a massive boulder field created by a 1982 flood, with the Roaring River running through it and a scenic trail to the top.

## Best Tour

Yellow Wood Guiding leads small groups for four to eight hours into the backcountry to find and learn to photograph wildlife. *ywguiding.com* *From $255.*

## When to Go

Late spring and early fall are the best times to visit, but they're also the busiest. Winter is considerably less crowded, but the main route through the park, Trail Ridge Road, often shuts down because of snow and ice.

## Getting Here and Around

Denver International Airport (DEN) is 78 miles and Denver is 67 miles from the East Entrance to RMNP.

**Rocky Mountain National Park.** *www.nps.gov/romo* *$25.*

# Royal Gorge Bridge and Park

### North America's Highest Zipline

The highest suspension bridge in America, the Royal Gorge Bridge also spans one of the country's most stunning canyons, carved by the Arkansas River, a white-water rafting destination 956 feet below. In addition to the walkable bridge, aerial gondolas that traverse the gorge, and a quaint kids Playland modeled after a mining town, the park also offers North America's highest zipline, the Cloudscraper ZipRider, which allows intrepid visitors to soar 1,200 feet above the Arkansas hands-free. Add rock climbing, the Skycoaster that swings you over the river at 50 miles per hour, and the feat of engineering that is the bridge, and you can see why this place takes visitors' breath away.

### Don't Miss

The Water Clock runs on power generated by water transferred from bucket to bucket.

### Best Tour

The Royal Gorge Route Railroad offers the best of both worlds by putting passengers at river level, while also running beneath the bridge and through the gorge for a 2- to 2½-hour trip. 🌐 *royalgorgeroute.com* 🎫 *From $54.*

### When to Go

Open year-round, the park is most easily explored in warmer months, but winter means fewer crowds.

### Getting Here and Around

Colorado Springs International Airport (COS) is 62 miles from the Royal Gorge Bridge and Park. Cañon City is the nearest city, 13 miles away.

**Royal Gorge Bridge.** ✉ *4218 County Rd. 3A, Cañon City, CO* 🌐 *royalgorgebridge.com* 🎫 *$23.*

# Durango

## Hollywood of the Rockies

Set against a scenic mountain backdrop with 2 million acres of wild national forest on its doorstep, Durango has served as a Hollywood go-to for Western movie sets, including *Butch Cassidy and the Sundance Kid, National Lampoon Vacation, A Ticket to Tomahawk,* and *City Slickers.* The small city and former mining town is surrounded by the San Juan Mountains and many remote areas once inhabited by Ancestral Puebloans—Chaco Canyon and Chimney Rock National Monument—as well as the Weminuche Wilderness, Colorado's largest wilderness area and a playground for outdoors enthusiasts. Professional skiers seek out Durango for its unrivaled terrain and spruce-lined trails, while fishermen flock to the many Gold Medal waters of the Animas River.

## Don't Miss

Nestled in the mountains, Vallecito Lake sits 18 miles outside the city. Once home to the Ute Indians, it now serves as a getaway at 8,000 feet for boaters, waterskiers, and the fishermen seeking the Kokanee salmon run.

## Best Tour

The Durango & Silverton Narrow Gauge Railroad offers a comfortable front-row seat to the San Juans during a five-hour excursion to remote and stunning Cascade Canyon, which is particularly scenic in winter. 🌐 *durangotrain.com* 🎫 *From $69.*

## Getting Here and Around

The regional Durango–La Plata County Airport (DRO) is 12 miles from Durango, while the nearest major airport, Albuquerque International Sunport (ABQ), sits 218 miles away.

**Durango.** 🌐 *durango.org* 🎫 *Free.*

# Mt. Evans

## The Highest Drive in North America

Colorado is famous for its Fourteeners, 58 mountains whose summits exceed 14,000 feet high. The most popular is Mt. Evans, partly because visitors can make the switchback-filled, 28-mile (round-trip) drive nearly to the top at 14,265 feet, although plenty of people park lower each year and hike up to "bag the peak." Plan to make your way up the highest paved road in North America slowly to wow over its sheer drop-offs and lakes along the way, and once at the parking area, join the other altitude-woozy walkers finding their way along the final few hundred feet to a literally breathtaking panoramic view of the Never Summer Range to the north and the Sangre de Cristo Mountains to the south. Get your reflexes and camera ready for the mountain goats and bighorn sheep that nimbly scramble all over the mountain.

## Don't Miss

Visit Echo Lake and Summit Lake on the way up, and try a meal of spicy buffalo chili and homemade pie at Echo Lake Lodge, which also sells kitschy souvenirs.

## Best Tour

The most relaxed way to get to the top of Mt. Evans is by tour shuttle, and the Colorado Sightseer makes it even more pleasant by offering a local guide, providing lunch in Idaho Springs, and including a tour of a gold mine. 🌐 *coloradosightseer.com* 🎫 *From $85.*

## Getting Here and Around

Idaho Springs is the nearest town, 56 miles from Denver International Airport (DEN).

**Mt. Evans.** ✉ *Idaho Springs, CO* 🌐 *www.colorado.com/byways/mount-evans* 🎫 *$10 per vehicle.*

# Aspen

### Legendary Après-Ski Scene

Forever honored in the lyrics of John Denver, the Roaring Fork Valley—and Aspen, its crown jewel—is the quintessential Rocky Mountain high. A rampart of the state's famed Fourteeners (peaks over 14,000 feet) guard this valley, but Glitter Gulch, as Aspen is also known, is just as famous for its celebrities, its skiing, its luxury ski resorts, and perhaps North America's best après-ski scene. From see-and-be-seen spots like Ajax Tavern to Maroon Bells views at the cozy Cloud 9 Bistro to hot-tub drinks with a DJ and views at the W Hotel's rooftop Wet Bar, Aspen's après scene serves up high-class post-ski debauchery like no other.

### Don't Miss

Two of the most photographed mountains in all of North America are the Maroon Bells, which sit about 12 miles west of town and serve as a backdrop for Maroon Lake and miles of hiking trails.

### When to Go

Anytime is a good time to be in Aspen—warmer seasons for hiking, biking, fishing, and other outdoor pursuits, winter for skiing and other snow sports. In June, crowds come for the annual Food & Wine Classic.

### Getting Here and Around

There are only two ways to drive in or out—over the precipitous Independence Pass (which closes in winter) or up the four-lane highway through the booming Roaring Fork Valley that stretches nearly 50 miles, from Glenwood Springs to Aspen. Aspen/Pitkin County Airport sits 3 miles outside of town, while Colorado Springs International Airport (COS) and Denver International Airport (DEN) are 117 and 124 miles away, respectively.

# Denver Art Museum (DAM)

## Epic Art and Atmosphere

The Mile High City boasts some of the best art collections in the country, but the DAM, as it's known by locals, is the alpha museum here, housing one of the most impressive collections of art between Chicago and the West Coast. Set in a striking building in the Golden Triangle neighborhood downtown—the newer part of which was designed by architect Daniel Libeskind—galleries showcase more than 70,000 works by famed artists such as Vincent van Gogh and Winslow Homer, although the dazzling mountain views through hallway windows often compete for your attention. Plan to spend most of the day wandering the unique displays of Asian, pre-Columbian, Spanish, colonial, and Native American art. The museum is known for its buzzing energy, generated by a creatives-in-residence program for local artists from a variety of disciplines.

## Don't Miss

The kid-friendly offerings, including backpacks filled with games and puzzles to enhance the experience, as well as hands-on art projects.

## Best Tour

As a counterpoint to First Fridays, the Denver Art Museum uses Final Fridays each month to team up with local creatives to offer late-night workshops, performances, and special tours. *denverartmuseum.org* *$13.*

## When to Go

Final Fridays, weekends, and free Colorado days can be packed, so plan your visit for midafternoon.

## Getting Here and Around

Denver International Airport (DEN) is 24 miles away.

**Denver Art Museum.** *100 W. 14th Ave. Pkwy., Denver, CO* *720/865–5000* *denverartmuseum.org* *$13.*

# Grand Junction

## The Perfect Rocky Mountain Town

The mountains meet the desert at the confluence of the mighty Colorado and Gunnison rivers—hence the name Grand Junction. And it really is a grand junction, with lakes and forests to the east, the Colorado National Monument to the west, fertile farmlands with world-famous peaches and prolific vineyards to the south, and the sandstone Book Cliffs to the north. The charming downtown is a certified creative district with cafés, galleries, and a year-round outdoor sculpture exhibit with more than 100 sculptures. The great Colorado River flows from the Rocky Mountains down through the city, so you can take mild to wild river-raft rides, with several areas on the river offering Class IV rapids. Nearby Rattlesnake Canyon is worth a trip to see spectacular red-sandstone arches.

## Don't Miss

Little Book Cliffs Wild Horse Range offers 36,113 acres of hiking in the canyons, as well as up to 150 mustangs wandering the sagebrush-covered hills.

## Best Tour

Visitors find fresh fossils all the time by joining the Museums of Western Colorado on half-day or one- to five-day Dino Digs around northwestern Colorado. *dinodigs.org* *From $100.*

## When to Go

Summer can be searing hot in this desert environment, and so fall and spring are best. Because Grand Junction sits in Colorado's banana belt, winters are mild.

## Getting Here and Around

Grand Junction Regional Airport (GJT) has direct flights to a few cities through several major airlines. Denver International Airport (DEN) is 269 miles away.

# Pikes Peak

### America's Mountain

Composed of granite and shaped by glaciers over millions of years, Pikes Peak mountain—the highest summit of the southern Front Range of the Rocky Mountains—is a stunning backdrop for Colorado's second-largest city, Colorado Springs. When Katharine Lee Bates arrived at the summit of Pikes Peak in 1893, she immortalized the majestic mountain in her beloved anthem "America the Beautiful." There are several ways to reach the summit of this iconic Fourteener yourself, including hiking—it's a slog, so consider camping halfway—biking, driving, and as a passenger on the comfortable 126-year-old Broadmoor Pikes Peak Cog Railway (🌐 *www.cograilway.com*).

### Don't Miss

Sitting at the foot of Pikes Peak, Colorado Springs offers mild weather year-round, clean air, and access to such geologic marvels as the hiking favorite Garden of the Gods, the seven waterfalls at the aptly named Seven Falls, and the stalactite- and stalagmite-packed Cave of the Winds. Man-made attractions include the charming Cheyenne Mountain Zoo (uniquely set against a mountain) and the U.S. Air Force Academy.

### Best Tour

The Colorado Springs Sunrise Balloon Ride through Rainbow Ryders offers a view of Pikes Peak and the Front Range that's hard to beat. 🌐 *rainbow-ryders.com* 🎫 *From $169.*

### Getting Here and Around

Colorado Springs International Airport (COS) is usually the cheapest option, with fewer flights but also fewer traffic jams on the way out than Denver International Airport (DEN) 88 miles away.

**Pikes Peak.** ✉ *Colorado Springs, CO* 🌐 *www.pikes-peak.com.*

# Glenwood Springs

## World's Largest Hot Springs Pool

The name Glenwood Springs is synonymous with hot springs in Colorado, because this town between Vail and Aspen sports the world's largest outdoor natural hot springs pool (the eponymous Glenwood Hot Springs), along with several other soaking options, including Iron Mountain Hot Springs and Yampah Spa's Vapor Caves where you will find naturally occurring mineral-steam baths. Originally inhabited by nomadic Ute Indian tribes, and known as Yampah, or literally "Big Medicine," the mineral-rich waters are a healing wonder after a day of skiing at Sunlight Mountain Resort, or biking the 20-mile round-trip paved path to Hanging Lake.

## Don't Miss

Family-friendly Glenwood Adventure Park is a marvelous mix of corny and cool—it's home to the Historic Fairy Caves' subterranean caverns and labyrinths, as well as a gravity-powered alpine slide.

## Best Tour

Out of the many tours Glenwood Adventure Company offers, the ATV excursions are the most fun, with two-hour or all-day treks on 6,000 acres of private land in Glenwood Canyon. *glenwoodadventure.com* *From $139 for ATV tour.*

## When to Go

Glenwood Springs comes into its own in the early summer, but there's a lot to be said for sitting in the springs as falling snow hits the steam.

## Getting Here and Around

Glenwood sits along Interstate 70, Colorado's main east–west highway, which leads right out of Denver International Airport (DEN) 182 miles away.

**Glenwood Springs.** *970/945–6580* *visitglenwood.com.*

# Mesa Verde National Park

### The Largest Archaeological Preserve in the U.S.

With more than 4,000 archaeological sites and 3 million found objects, UNESCO World Heritage site Mesa Verde National Park is the preeminent destination for all things related to the Ancestral Puebloan culture (precursor to the Hopi, Zuni, and Pueblo tribes) that flourished in the area between 700 and 1,400 years ago. The cliff dwellings are mind-blowing—some carved into the sandstone cliff walls, some sitting atop the mesa—and hikes throughout the 80 square miles range from effortless to hard-core. The big houses, such as Cliff Palace and Balcony House, require purchasing extra tickets, but they're well worth it to try to get a handle on an unfathomable ancient lifestyle.

### Don't Miss

The Chapin Mesa Archeological Museum, built in the 1920s, features artifacts and dioramas of Ancestral Puebloan life.

### Best Tour

Ranger-led hikes are the best way to fully appreciate how cliff dwellers navigated this unforgiving terrain. Hikes range from 90 minutes to eight hours and cover 1–8 miles to the lesser-visited and mostly unexcavated dwellings such as Mug House and Spring House. *nps.gov/meve* *From $25.*

### Getting Here and Around

Just 18 miles from the park, the closest airport is Cortez Municipal Airport (CEZ), which has connecting flights through Denver International Airport (DEN), which sits 392 miles away. Closer is the Albuquerque International Sunport (ABQ), a 249-mile drive.

**Mesa Verde National Park.** *Montezuma County, CO* *nps.gov/meve* *$20.*

## When in Colorado

### BISHOP CASTLE

Jim Bishop has been building his unusual and intriguing castle for more than 60 years, but he will tell you that it's still a work in progress. Purchased with paper route money in 1959, the property sits in the mountains west of Pueblo, surrounded by old-growth forest. The castle started as a one-room stone cottage, but is now 16 stories high, all designed without blueprints by Bishop himself—and he did most of the work, too. Wrought-iron walkways, a sculpture of a fire-breathing dragon, stained-glass windows, and just a general feeling of "what is going on here?" are among the highlights.

**Do This:** Bishop Castle sits just off the historic Frontier Pathways Scenic Byway, which is well worth continuing along as far as time allows. The paved, two-lane highway is 103 miles long, including the 16-mile spur to Westcliffe off the center of this horseshoe-shaped drive that climbs to 9,400 feet. Keep your eyes peeled for pronghorn.

**Bishop Castle.** ✉ *12705 CO 165, Rye, CO* ☎ *719/564–4366* 🌐 *bishopcastle.org* 🎫 *Free.*

### INTERNATIONAL CHURCH OF CANNABIS

Getting Rocky Mountain high can be hard for nonresidents, because it's illegal to consume cannabis in public anywhere in the state. While a handful of members-only social clubs have cropped up and dispensary tours come and go, the nondenominational International Church of Cannabis—located in an actual church in Denver—welcomes anyone over 21 with a professed devotion to community and, yes, the devil's lettuce, which is often enjoyed right in the pews as folks congregate. Instead of a pastor or hymns, most "services" are either chats with locals in the biz or low-key rap sessions. To join, sign up as a "member" on the website, and remember, no buying or selling on-premises—it's BYOC.

**Do This:** Check out the scene first by stopping by during one of the BEYOND guided meditations set to a laser light show ($25 per person), which happen at 20 minutes past the hour from noon–6 pm Friday–Monday and 1–3 pm Tuesday–Thursday.

**International Church of Cannabis.** ✉ *400 S. Logan St., Denver, CO* ☎ *303/800–5644* 🌐 *elevationists.org* 🎫 *Free.*

### THE WILD ANIMAL SANCTUARY

Being able to observe more than 500 wild animals from above is not something you get to do every day, which makes The Wild Animal Sanctuary special. These are rescues—bears (black, Syrian, Asiatic, and grizzly), lions, leopards, jaguars, tigers, wolves, coyotes, alpacas, and ostriches—who had previously been living on concrete pads or chained up in basements and garages. In fact, some of them had never been on grass until they arrived here. Situated on 789 acres, just 30 miles from Denver, the sanctuary allows you to observe the property from an elevated 1½-mile-long footbridge (it holds the Guinness World Record as the world's longest) that meanders around the property 20–30 feet above the animals as they play in pools, dig for bugs, wrestle, and just generally act like the wild creatures they are.

**Do This:** If you visit in the summer, plan around the popular Wild Nights, because as the sun starts to set, the animals leave their shady spots and romp around with abandon. Bring a picnic dinner and settle in to listen as the wolves howl to signal day's end. First thing in the morning is good in warmer months, too, before the animals hunker down away from the sun.

**The Wild Animal Sanctuary.** ✉ *2999 County Rd. 53, Keenesburg, CO* ☎ *303/536–0118* 🌐 *wildanimalsanctuary.org* 🎫 *$30.*

# Cool Places to Stay

**The Broadmoor.** The expansive complex that is The Broadmoor in Colorado Springs is one of those destination resorts that you never have to leave once you've settled in. The original dusty-rose-colored stucco buildings were constructed in 1918, but the 5,000-acre property has since grown to include three 18-hole golf courses, a full-service spa, dozens of cute little shops, a bowling alley, and multiple restaurants, including the AAA five-diamond Penrose (jacket required) overlooking it all from its penthouse location. Rooms are lavishly decorated (there are cottages and wilderness cabins available, as well), and the staff is exceptionally service-oriented. ✉ *1 Lake Ave., Colorado Springs, CO* ☎ *800/577–9718* 🌐 *broadmoor.com* [$] *From $340.*

**Dunton Hot Springs.** This transformation of a circa-1800s ghost town and then cattle ranch into a luxury resort tucked into the remote San Juan Mountains on 200 acres in southwest Colorado (near Telluride) is all about the property's inviting hot springs, as well as the 12 fully restored original cabins replete with modern amenities, plus private plunge pools and wood-burning stoves. Nearby Dunton River Camp features eight safari-style tents on the Dolores River, and the owners have 1,600 more acres for you to explore nearby for fly-fishing, hiking, and horseback riding. Rates include all meals and mountain bikes for getting around. ✉ *Dolores, CO* ☎ *877/288–9922* 🌐 *duntondestinations.com* [$] *From $1,275.*

**Vista Verde Guest Ranch.** A beautifully situated Western-style ranch 23 miles north of Steamboat Springs, Vista Verde is a top-notch destination for many activities, including honing your horseback riding skills with one of their pro wranglers, learning how to cross-country ski, snowmobile, mountain bike, or fly-fish (or vastly improve under the tutelage of the ranch's guides), or just wandering the 600-acre property that's surrounded by the 1.1 million-acre Routt National Forest. Rates are all-inclusive, including lodging in the secluded, well-stocked cabins (complete with private hot tubs and wood-fired stoves, along with snacks, wine, coffee, and pampering bath products), three exceptional meals daily, guided tours and instruction, activities, cooking and photography classes, round-trip shuttles to Steamboat Springs, and nightly entertainment (the staff is its own band). ✉ *58000 Cowboy Way, Clark, CO* ☎ *800/526–7433* 🌐 *vistaverde.com* [$] *From $1,795 for three nights.*

**Yogi Bear's Jellystone Park Estes Park.** Yogi Bear's Jellystone Park (aka "kid central") is just 10 minutes from the mountain town of Estes Park and offers a regular roster of family-friendly activities and room to roam. Lodging choices include campsites built into the hillside, for tents or with full hookups, along with a fire pit and a picnic table; cabins sleeping 5 to 14, either no-frills or fully stocked; and RVs that can be rented and delivered to stay in on-site. Activities included in your stay range from movies after dark, ice-cream-float nights, and minigolf, to two playgrounds, a game room, karaoke, and a seasonal heated swimming pool. For a small fee, campers can also participate in bingo, laser tag, ceramics, and mining for gems, and the campground's engaged staff hosts themed parties for all major holidays. The property also sports hiking trails, a basketball court, and horseshoe pits, and adults will appreciate the on-site laundry facility and sundries store. Yogi Bear or Boo Boo Bear visit on a daily basis. ✉ *5495 U.S. 36, Estes Park, CO* ☎ *970/586–4230* 🌐 *jellystoneofestes.com* *From $60.*

# Idaho

It's been said that "Idaho is as America was"—a western frontier with more wild land than developed, and only 1.5 million people scattered throughout our nation's 14th-largest state. Its big blue skies, pristine waters, and jagged snowcapped horizons have been largely untouched by the masses, making it an outdoors enthusiast's paradise. Rafters, kayakers, mountain climbers, backcountry skiers, and backpackers flock to Idaho's untamed wilderness.

## Bucket List Picks

The following boxes contain our picks for the top sights and experiences in Idaho.

- ○ Shoshone Falls
- ○ Owyhee Canyonlands Wilderness
- ○ Redfish Lake
- ○ Hells Canyon
- ○ Sun Valley
- ○ Route of the Hiawatha Trail
- ○ Morley Nelson Snake River Birds of Prey
- ○ Idaho Potato Museum

# Shoshone Falls

## Niagara of the West

As the Snake River makes its way through Twin Falls to join the Columbia River in Magic Valley, it pauses in the most beautiful way to tumble over a wide swath of basalt cliffs, creating the mesmerizing Shoshone Falls. The powerful movement of the water is so thunderous that most visitors report physically feeling the reverberations—it's not called the "Niagara of the West" for nothing. And at 212 feet high, it's taller than Niagara, too.

## Don't Miss

Most visitors just walk the 75 feet from the car to the observation deck, but there are other vantage points to be found if you keep going. Check out the Canyon Rim Trail, a mostly flat and moderately strenuous paved 12.6-mile out-and-back trail that is good for hiking or biking.

## Nearby Sights

After checking out Shoshone, stop by Caldron Linn, created by a slot canyon, and then head to the city's namesake Twin Falls. Auger Falls features extensive hiking and biking trails, and the extensive complex that comprises Thousand Springs sits in the state park of the same name. Bring a swimsuit, and end at one of the hot springs spots in Thousand Springs—Banbury, Miracle, or 1000 Springs Resort, all of which offer natural, private, and large swimming pools.

## When to Go

Spring is the best time because the snowpack melts, which pumps up the falls.

## Getting Here and Around

Boise Airport (BOI) sits 129 miles from the entrance to the falls.

**Shoshone Falls.** ✉ *4155 Shoshone Falls Grade Rd., Twin Falls, ID* 🌐 *tfid.org/309/shoshone-falls* 🎫 *$5 per car.*

# Owyhee Canyonlands Wilderness

## A Truly Wild Place

Spanning more than 2 million acres across northern Nevada, southwestern Idaho, and southeastern Oregon, the Owyhee Canyonlands Wilderness is one of the most remote, wild, and untouched places in the entire country. If solitude is what you seek, you'll find it here, with only the wind in the rushes, gently gurgling streams, antelope, golden eagles, red-tailed hawks, and the greater sage grouse for company. By day, explore stunning slot canyons, rocky spires, sagebrush-covered steppes, deep gorges, natural pools, and go white-water rafting on the Bruneau-Jarbidge-Owyhee river system. By night, enjoy stargazing in one of the least light-polluted areas in the Lower 48. Visitors are advised to bring a gas can, way more food and water than you think you'll need, tools for car repairs, and a good map. The nearest towns can be up to a hundred miles away and cell service is nonexistent.

## Don't Miss

The easiest dip into this vast wilderness is on the Perjue Canyon Trail, which offers a wildlife and wildflower-filled moderate trek of up to 8 miles.

## Best Tour

A three- to six-day rafting trip with glamping setup with Far and Away Adventures is an immersive experience through the far-flung canyons, with the chance to see eagles, antelope, bighorn sheep, and more. *far-away.com* *From $1,100.*

## When to Go

For river rafting, April through June offers the best water levels.

## Getting Here and Around

Boise Airport (BOI) is 203 miles from Bruneau. A four-wheel-drive vehicle is best.

# Redfish Lake

### Unspoiled Alpine Beauty

Situated at the headwaters of the Salmon River, the high-alpine Redfish Lake—about 60 miles north of Ketchum in the Sawtooth Mountains—is breathtaking, with crystal clear water, snowcapped mountain peaks, and pine trees bordering the lake shore. Named for the color of the sockeye salmon that once naturally proliferated, the lake is now the beneficiary of a local hatchery devoted to reestablishing the fish. Midsummer, swimmers brave what is still a frigid pool of crystal clear snowmelt. Lodging options include the vintage Redfish Lake Lodge and multiple campsites right on the water, as well as cabins for rent.

### Don't Miss

Hard-core hikers take a day to navigate the 17.5 miles all the way around the lake, a long but otherwise moderate trail that nets plenty of photo ops and the chance to see beavers building their dams, and elk and mule deer.

### Best Tour

Take a guided sunset cruise around the lake on a pontoon boat, complete with hearty appetizers, cocktails, and a chatty local captain. *redfishlake.com* *From $150 for the boat.*

### When to Go

Because the lake sits at 6,500 feet, June to September is the best time for comfortable temps, but spring brings wildflowers, and fall finds far fewer visitors. Lodging shuts down October to April.

### Getting Here and Around

Boise Airport (BOI) sits 148 miles away, but if you happen to be driving from Sun Valley, the 59-mile, switchback-packed drive is one of the most scenic in the country.

# Hells Canyon

## Raft Deeper than the Grand Canyon

Carved by the mighty Snake River, Hells Canyon in western Idaho is North America's deepest river gorge at 7,993 feet, almost 2,000 feet deeper than the Grand Canyon. Visitors usually find themselves with no one else around for miles, and tripping over mountain goats, bighorn sheep, mink, and otter, along with the occasional bobcat sighting. The recreation area encompasses more than 650,000 acres, 250,000 of which comprise the Hells Canyon Wilderness Area. More than a century ago, Native American tribes called Hells Canyon home (including the Nez Perce), and it's thrilling to happen upon pictographs and petroglyphs on the canyon walls, along with random abandoned homesteads. Hiking, rafting, fishing, hunting, and camping are the most popular pastimes in this vast geologic marvel.

## Don't Miss

The challenging 28-mile loop around Seven Devils offers forests, ridges, lakes, and incredible views and takes about three days.

## Best Tour

May through November, Canyon Outfitters drops guests off each morning to hike on their own along the shore and inland, as the boats continue on to meet hunters at day's end for dinner around the campfire. *canyonoutfitters.com* *From $1,450.*

## When to Go

Hells Canyon in the spring showcases colorful wildflower-covered slopes, while summer transforms the area into a desert. Fall can be cold, with early snows possible, but the area is navigable into November.

## Getting Here and Around

Boise Airport (BOI) sits 216 miles away from the nearest border of the canyon.

# Sun Valley

## America's Oldest Ski Resort

Sun Valley has long been a playground for celebrities, athletes, and ski bums, but it's more than just a ski town–it's one of the coolest small towns in the United States. The tiny town of just 5,000 people is full of surprises, from world-class music and arts to incredible dining and shopping to year-round outdoor adventures that showcase some of the most jaw-dropping scenery in the lower 48. Its famed Nordic skiing, mountain biking, angling, and backpacking has spawned a subculture of outdoors fanatics who call this place heaven.

## Don't Miss

Towering over the small town of Ketchum, the world-famous Bald Mountain ski resort (or "Baldy") is known for its 3,400 vertical feet of consistent pitch, sunny skies, and celebrity sightings.

## While You're Here

Stop into Sun Valley Lodge, a sprawling village-like resort with a few shops, restaurants, and two different hotels. In Ketchum, check out the Sun Valley Center for the Arts.

## More Great Skiing

With no lift lines, plenty of powder, two mountains (Kellogg Peak, at 6,297 feet high, and Wardner Peak, 6,205), and an average of 300 inches of snowfall annually, Silver Mountain is an often overlooked hidden gem of a ski area in far northwest Idaho.

## Getting Here and Around

Fly into Hailey's Friedman Memorial Airport (SUN), which is 14 miles from Sun Valley. The town is walkable and there is bus service to Ketchum and to Dollar and Bald mountains.

**Sun Valley.** ✉ *1 Sun Valley Rd., Sun Valley, ID* 🌐 *sunvalley.com*

## Route of the Hiawatha Trail

### Epic Rails-to-Trails

One of the country's best rails-to-trails rides—created from the former Intercontinental Railroad route that ran from Chicago to Seattle in the early 1900s—the Hiawatha is a 15-mile (one way) bike, hike, or horseback journey through nine train tunnels and over seven steel trestle bridges up to 230 feet high. The trail goes from Idaho into Montana, and the highlight for many visitors is the St. Paul Pass Tunnel, a 1½-mile dark tunnel that burrows under the state line. In Idaho, Lookout Pass Ski Area is the gateway to the route, where riders can rent gear, purchase a trail pass, and catch the shuttle for drop-off at the trailhead 12 miles away.

### Don't Miss

If you still long for more time in the saddle, check out the lift-served mountain-bike terrain at Lookout Pass, with its vertical drop of 1,150 feet and both single- and doubletrack.

### Best Tour

A five-day rails-to-trails trek hits the Trail of the Coeur d'Alenes and the Trail of the Hiawatha. Start and end in Spokane, Washington. 🌐 *rowadventures.com* 🎫 *From $1,795.*

### When to Go

The Hiawatha is open from late May to early October, weather permitting.

### Getting Here and Around

The nearest airport is Washington's Spokane International (GEG), 94 miles away. It takes about two to three hours to complete the trail one way, but plan to spend a whole day.

**Lookout Pass Ski Area.** ✉ *I–90 Exit 0, Mullan, ID* 🌐 *ridethehiawatha.com* 🎫 *$14.*

# Morley Nelson Snake River Birds of Prey

## Birder's Paradise

Bring the binoculars, because more than 800 pairs of hawks, owls, eagles and falcons, including up to 200 pairs of prairie falcons, nest in this 485,000-acre Birds of Prey National Conservation Area (NCA), most along an 81-mile stretch of the Snake River Canyon. Travel through the area by hiking, biking, or horseback riding, with views of the towering cliffs and river along the way. Camping and picnic spots are available in the Cove at CJ Strike Reservoir area of the NCA, or you can take a 56-mile loop driving tour beginning at the Kuna Visitor Center.

## Don't Miss

Nearby Bruneau Dunes State Park features the tallest single-structured sand dune in North America, and also enhanced wildlife viewing through its sagebrush desert and grassland flats, including a vast number of migratory ducks, bald eagles, blue herons, avocets, sandpipers, coyotes, jackrabbits, and a variety of lizards.

## Best Tour

The Birds of Prey float trip takes rafters from Swan Falls Dam to Celebration Park in Canyon County. The tour includes lunch and a short hike to petroglyphs. *idahoguideservice.com* *From $95.*

## When to Go

You can spot raptors in Snake River Canyon year-round, but mid-March–June, birds are in the nests teaching their young to fly. Eagles are most visible in March.

## Getting Here and Around

Road access to the eastern portion of the NCA can be found in the towns of Mountain Home, Grand View, and Bruneau. Boise Airport (BOI) sits 64 miles from Grand View.

# Idaho Potato Museum

## Ode to the Spud

Starting with the giant sour cream–filled potato sculpture outside, the Idaho Potato Museum is spud central in a state that is spud central to the universe. Kitschy and quirky, this shrine to all things tater sits in a building that was originally a train depot for the Oregon Short Line Rail Road, and it features not only the alleged largest collection of potato mashers in the world, but also the largest potato chip ever made (a 25-inch-long Pringle that's a Guinness Book of World Records holder). Visitors get a potato sack and a box of hash browns to commemorate their tuberous time, which most definitely should include a stop at the build-your-own Mr. Potato Head Station. At the end, all anyone wants to do is eat some potatoes, and so thankfully the attached Potato Station Café serves them up baked, fried, dipped in chocolate, and many other delicious ways.

## Don't Miss

At the Potato Lab, your inner scientist can perform experiments, participate in Mr. Potato Head races, and generally goof around.

## Try This

What goes well with potatoes? Meat, of course. At the Smokin' Gun BBQ, a side of Idaho potato skin-on fries can be had with falling-off-the-bone ribs, tender brisket, or juicy pulled pork just a mile from the museum. 🌐 *smokingunbbq.business.site.*

## When to Go

Open year-round; closed Sunday.

## Getting Here and Around

Idaho Falls Regional Airport (IDA) is 29 miles from the museum; Boise Airport (BIO) is 252 miles away.

**Idaho Potato Museum.** ✉ *130 N.W. Main St., Blackfoot, ID* ☎ *208/785–2517* 🌐 *idahopotatomuseum.com* 🎟 *$6.*

# When in Idaho

## BOISE

Boise is not a top tourist destination, which is a shame, because this laid-back city has a small-town feel and plenty of intriguing attractions, including historic architecture (the train depot, Hyde Park), Freak Alley (several blocks of offbeat shops and street art), and Camel's Back Park, with its hump-shaped hiking hill. But that also means fewer crowds and less competition for the fun. Low on chain eateries or shops, downtown Boise is easily navigated on foot, and noticeably cheaper than similarly sized cities. Bogus Basin is a mountain-biking hot spot in summer and a winter destination for skiing and snowboarding.

**Do This:** When summer temps hit triple digits, locals flock to float the Boise River. The easy, 6-mile stretch from Barber Park to Ann Morrison Park is fast but low-key and takes about two hours. Shuttle buses run between the put-in and take-out and cost $3, and inner tubes can be rented at Barber Park starting at $15.

**Boise.** ✉ *150 N. Capitol Blvd., Boise, ID* ☎ *208/608–7000* 🌐 *cityofboise.org.*

## BRUNEAU SAND DUNES

With killer views of the Snake River Canyon and the lake below and 4,800 acres to explore, Bruneau Sand Dunes features the tallest single-structure sand dune in North America, as well as many options for enjoying it. For instance, $25 nets two rented sandboards for carving the sand waves from top to bottom, or you can hike the 6-mile self-guided trail that showcases the varied terrain high and low. Camping, horseback riding around the base of the dunes, and fishing the lake or river are also cool ways to enjoy the endless sand. After the sun goes down (mid-March–October), head to the Observatory, which offers telescopes for crisp, clear stargazing in an area that's remarkably free of light pollution.

**Do This:** Just 30 minutes from the dunes, Bruneau Canyon Overlook feels like it's truly in the middle of nowhere. The 800-foot-deep desert canyon made of basalt and rhyolite is 1,300 feet wide and sports a breathtaking backdrop courtesy of the Owyhee Mountains, and the Bruneau River rumbles past below. It's also an ideal spot for sunrise or sunset viewing.

**Bruneau Sand Dunes.** ✉ *27608 Sand Dunes Rd., Bruneau, ID* ☎ *208/366–7919* 🌐 *parksandrecreation.idaho.gov/parks/bruneau-dunes* 🎟 *$7 per vehicle.*

## LIONHEAD NATURAL WATER SLIDES

Situated in the middle of a forest and found only by hiking in 1.5 miles from the little wooden sign at the end of the road, the natural waterslides near the Lionhead campground at Priest Lake make for a day of all-ages fun—just keep hiking back to the top to do it again. Go on a weekday to have the place to yourself, and bring a plastic bag or yoga mat to avoid shredding your bathing suit or shorts. To get to the campground—which sits 2½ hours north of Coeur d'Alene, Idaho, and the same distance from Spokane, Washington—take a right at the campground and follow the rutted gravel road for 5 miles to the trailhead, and then start hiking.

**Do This:** About 10 miles from the slides, Eightmile Island is 8 miles from the south end of Priest Lake in Coolin. This 100-acre island is accessible only by boat (you can rent at the marina) and was once inhabited by two brothers who built a little homestead cabin in 1897. It's now on the National Register of Historic Places, and anyone can tool up to the dock and come wander around—the current owners will usually take you around on a tour of the little museum, the funky nine-hole golf course, and the lovely forest that surrounds it all.

**Priest Lake.** ☎ *208/443–3191* 🌐 *priestlake.org* 💵 *Free.*

### MUSEUM OF CLEAN

In a world where sanitizing everything is now the norm, the 74,000-square-foot Museum of Clean is a shrine to the history of human attempts at controlling their environments. This laid-back place with plenty of spots for sitting down to contemplate what clean really means is designed to encourage interaction (you can touch everything) in a setting that doesn't take itself too seriously—don't miss the toilet collection, as well as the antique vacuum cleaners. There's also an art gallery with more than 200 pieces devoted to the clean theme, with some dating back to more than 2,000 years ago. The owner—who decades ago made millions with his own nationwide house-cleaning company—is usually on hand to give personal tours or share anecdotes about the exhibits.

**Do This:** Parents will appreciate Kid Planet—a three-story globe-shaped place to explore—and the other activities devoted to cleanliness (kids are usually shocked to try washing a sock on a washboard).

**Museum of Clean.** ✉ *711 S. Second Ave., Pocatello, ID* ☎ *208/236–6906* 🌐 *museumofclean.com* 💵 *$6.*

## Cool Places to Stay

**Black Swan Inn.** At the Black Swan Inn in Pocatello, you have your pick when it comes to room decor themes: pirate, Arabian, Egyptian, Mayan rain forest, Rocky Mountain cabin, Romeo and Juliet, tropical—to name a few. Each spacious suite is uniquely designed to evoke the theme (for instance, the Sea Cave room features a clam-shell bed and a jetted, heart-shaped tub for two with live fish in aquariums as a backdrop). ✉ *746 E. Center, Pocatello, ID* ☎ *208/233–3051* 🌐 *blackswaninn.com* [$] *From $99.*

**The Dog Bark Park Inn.** This cute inn has gone to the dogs—literally. Created and graciously run by a chainsaw artist and his wife, the lodging is in the belly of a 30-foot-tall replica of a beagle (named Sweet Willy), surrounded by handmade dog toys and other related little outbuildings (check out the fire hydrant with a bathroom inside). Dogs are welcome, of course. Note: two-night minimum stay required; open April to August. ✉ *2421 Business Loop 95, Cottonwood, ID* ☎ *208/962–3647* 🌐 *dogbarkpark.com* [$] *From $158.*

**Huckleberry Tent & Breakfast.** A 52-acre property 30 miles from Sandpoint, Huckleberry Tent & Breakfast offers three luxury tent experiences with a tasty breakfast every morning made from the property's extensive garden—the owners even welcome guests to pick their own strawberries or salad, and they'll provide a homemade dressing. Each tidy tent set far from the others and hidden by old-growth trees comes complete with a comfy queen bed, fully stocked campfire kitchen, woodstove, remarkably inviting outhouse (candlelit at night) and outdoor shower. Don't be surprised if deer and moose wander past at dawn and dusk. ✉ *180 Thunderbolt Dr., Clark Fork, ID* ☎ *208/266–0155* 🌐 *huckleberrytentandbreakfast.com* [$] *From $125.*

**Idaho Potato Hotel.** Is there anything cozier than a big, steamy-centered Idaho potato drenched in melted butter? Yes, there is: a big, steamy Idaho potato that you can sleep in! Billed as a farm stay on Airbnb, this one-of-a-kind lodging that sits 20 minutes outside of Boise was once a marketing tool for the Idaho Potato Commission, but now its home is 400 acres of farmland with views of the Owyhee Mountains, complete with a sweet Jersey cow keeping guests company. ✉ *Orchard, ID* 🌐 *idahopotato.com/big-idaho-potato-hotel* [$] *From $165.*

# Montana

Big Sky Country is more than just a nickname: Montana has huge expanses of rugged country. It's a place to discover how beautiful the night sky can be and what "dark" truly is with limited city lights. But in addition to the natural beauty—stunning glaciers and ski slopes, trout-filled streams and high plains—you'll also find a welcoming place full of locals who love to share their state's natural beauty, mining history, and thriving cultural communities with others.

## Bucket List Picks

The following boxes contain our picks for the top sights and experiences in Montana.

- ○ Glacier National Park
- ○ National Bison Range
- ○ Great Falls
- ○ Bozeman
- ○ Kootenai Falls
- ○ Garnet Ghost Town
- ○ Earthquake Lake
- ○ Grizzly & Wolf Discovery Center

# Glacier National Park

## The Crown of the Continent

With its 1 million acres of glacier-carved peaks and valleys, pristine turquoise lakes and streams, and dense ancient forests, Glacier National Park—a designated UNESCO Biosphere Reserve and World Heritage site—is a true ecological wonder. It's also one of the few national parks that still offers a true wilderness experience, with more than 700 miles of hiking trails and the chance to spot grizzly bears, cougars, gray wolves, moose, and bighorn sheep, among many other animals. Rivers and lakes provide cooling waters to lounge by or play in, and there are plentiful camping options. Hiking options range from an easy 1-mile stroll on a boardwalk through a cedar forest to 10-milers that gain more than 2,000 feet in elevation.

## Don't Miss

Rent a boat and glide around a glacier-fed lake.

## Best Tour

Experience the park as first visitors to Glacier would have—on horseback. Opt for an easy one-hour ride into less-traveled sections of the park or go for an overnighter complete with cowboy cookout and the chance to sleep under the stars. 🌐 *swanmountainglacier.com* 🎟 *From $50.*

## Getting Here and Around

The west entrance, near West Glacier, is 19 miles east of Columbia Falls via U.S. 2; the east entrance, in St. Mary, is 22 miles northwest of Browning via U.S. 89. The closest airport is Glacier Park International Airport (FCA) in Kalispell, 25 miles from the west entrance.

**Glacier National Park.** ✉ *64 Grinnell Dr., West Glacier, MO* 🌐 *nps.gov/glac/index.htm* 🎟 *$20.*

# National Bison Range

### Bison in the Wild

One of the West's best icons, bison were slated for extinction until, ironically, Theodore Roosevelt started hunting them. He later realized that they needed to be saved and joined the American Bison Society in New York in 1905, followed by actively committing three major chunks of land around the country for a reintroduction—among them the National Bison Range in the Mission Valley of northwest Montana. This 18,800-acre property, part of the Mission Mountain Range, is home to a herd of 350–500 bison, the descendants of the original 40-member herd. Drive the 19-mile, one-way loop that passes through four different habitats (grasslands, riparian, wetlands, and montane), or park and hike one of the four short (less than a mile each) trails, but always maintain a safe distance from the wild animals.

### Don't Miss

The bison rut occurs from June to September, and bison calves are born in the early spring and can be seen romping about among the adults.

### Good to Know

More than 110 years after this land was seized to create a wildlife refuge, management of the 18,800 acres of grassland, woodland, and wildlife that comprise the National Bison Range have been returned to the Confederated Salish and Kootenai Tribes.

### When to Go

The range is open year-round, with periodic closures on some roads in winter due to weather.

### Getting Here and Around

The closest airport is Missoula International (MSO), 50 miles away.

**National Bison Range.** ✉ *58355 Bison Range Rd., Charlo, MT* 🌐 *fws.gov/refuge/national_bison_range* 🎫 *$5.*

# Great Falls

## Epic Lewis and Clark Pit Stop

The third-largest city in Montana, but one of the least-visited, Great Falls boasts Montana's first ski hill (Showdown), the most museums in the state, and yes, some great falls: Great Falls, Crooked Falls, Rainbow Falls, Colter Falls, and Black Eagle Falls. It was these falls that slowed down the explorers Lewis and Clark for a month in 1805, when their equipment and supplies, including canoes, had to be carried by hand or in makeshift wagons overland for 18 miles. Today, the famed portage route can be followed as part of the legacy left by the famed expedition. Surrounded by endless outdoors opportunities and plenty of Old West attractions and artifacts, Great Falls is an ideal base for present-day explorers of the Great Plains. Take a themed walking tour to learn about the area's railroad history and architecture, see the collection of cowboy artist Charles M. Russell at the C. M. Russell Museum, and learn everything there is to know about early exploration of the West at the Lewis and Clark Interpretive Center.

## Don't Miss

The Sip 'n Dip Lounge at the circa-1962 O'Haire Motor Inn has a giant glass wall through which patrons can watch mermaids and mermen swimming.

## Best Trail

The 60-mile River's Edge Trail connects many of Great Falls' signature attractions, but with public art, scenic overlooks, and events, the trail is also an attraction in itself.

## Getting Here and Around

Great Falls International Airport (GTF) sits just 5 miles outside of downtown Great Falls.

**Great Falls.** 🌐 *visitgreatfallsmontana.org* 🎫 *Free.*

# Bozeman

## The Gateway to Yellowstone

Culture meets nature at this bustling university town in southern Montana, set in a valley at the foot of four different mountain ranges, and a little over an hour from Yellowstone National Park. Often topping lists of best places to live in the United States, Bozeman's bustling Main Street is filled with trendy cafés and restaurants, and locals who enjoy easy access to hiking, mountain biking, fly-fishing, hot springs, skiing, and a variety of other snow sports. The Custer Gallatin National Forest surrounds the town, providing over 3 million acres of forest to explore throughout the year, and it's just an hour to Big Sky Resort where you'll find internationally acclaimed downhill skiing and snowboarding and nearly 6,000 acres of rideable terrain. It's the perfect base camp to explore the great outdoors.

## Don't Miss

Look up to see the "M," a 250-foot-high letter made from rocks that stands for Montana State University and marks the spot for the summit of two short but steep hiking trails that afford panoramic views of the city.

## Best Tour

Montana Wilderness Outfitters has guests covered when it comes to hunting during rifle and archery seasons or fishing for trout the blue-ribbon mountain streams. *montanawildernessoutfitter.com.*

## Getting Here and Around

Bozeman Yellowstone International Airport (BZN) sits just 10 miles outside the city.

**Bozeman Chamber of Commerce.** *2000 Commerce Way, Bozeman, MT* *bozemancvb.com* *Free.*

# Kootenai Falls

### Scenic Swinging Bridge

Located between the cities of Libby and Troy in northwestern Montana, Kootenai Falls is the largest undammed falls in the state and is not only a spectacular reward for hikers in the Kootenai National Forest, but also a premiere white-water play area for kayakers. Famously serving as a setting for the movies *The Revenant* and *The River Wild*, the area is sacred to the Kootenai tribe as it is a meeting place for convening with the spirits. The hike to the falls is only a mile round-trip, but it includes a unique 210-foot-long swinging bridge that sits 100 feet over the water and offers stunning views of the rapids and the falls as well as the many bird species along the river, including bald eagles, ospreys, and many types of waterfowl.

### Don't Miss

If you kayak, check out the left ledge, aka the Main Falls, along with the other great play and huck waves in this river section.

### Best Tour

Fishing the Kootenai usually means holding on for dear life, because the trout here run Big Sky big, upwards of 16 inches long. Kootenai Canyon Anglers takes anglers out to find the hidden caches of prized rainbow trout. Guides bring all the gear needed for full- or half-day trip. 🌐 *kcanglers.com* 🎫 *From $375.*

### Getting Here and Around

The hike to the falls sits just off U.S. 2. Glacier Park International Airport (FCA) in Kalispell is closest at 116 miles away.

**Kootenai Falls.** ✉ *31374 U.S. 2, Libby, MT* 🌐 *fs.usda.gov/kootenai* 🎫 *Free.*

# Garnet Ghost Town

## Montana's Best Preserved Ghost Town

Most abandoned mining towns have a story, and pretty Garnet Ghost Town, tucked away in the heavily forested Garnet Mountains east of Missoula, is no exception. In the 1890s, more than a thousand people lived in this thriving little gold town. There were four stores, four hotels, three livery stables, two barber shops, a union hall, a school, a doctor's office, and 13 saloons, but a series of unfortunate events caused the town to be deserted not once, but twice, and now all that remains are hints of what was clearly an austere existence—and tales of sounds of music and laughter at the former saloon. Wander around the 30 remaining buildings, which are in various stages of disrepair but are continually being restored for posterity.

## Don't Miss

Several moderate trails leave from the ghost town's parking lot, each between 2 and 3 miles round-trip. History buffs will love the Sierra Mine Loop Trail.

## Best Place to Stay

The especially adventurous can rent one of two off-the-grid cabins in winter by contacting the Bureau of Land Management.

## Get on Your Bike

Mountain bikers will find 30 miles of backcountry roads and trails in the Garnet Range, climbing up to about 7,000 feet.

## Getting Here and Around

Missoula International Airport (MSO) is 40 miles away.

**Garnet Ghost Town.** ✉ *Drummond, MT* 🌐 *garnetghosttown.org* 🎫 *$3.*

# Earthquake Lake

## The Power of Nature

Named for a one-minute earthquake which, on a full-moon night in 1959, blew 80 million tons of rock in the way of the Madison River as it flowed through the canyon, "Quake Lake," as locals call it, is a 5-mile-long, third-of-a-mile-wide lake. The quake had a magnitude of 7.5, shaking loose rocks, trees, and earth at the western end of the canyon to form a massive landslide. The slide went three-quarters of a mile north and spread a mile east to west, burying 19 people and killing nine more later. Situated 27 miles northwest of West Yellowstone, the peaceful alpine lake is known for some of the best fly-fishing for cutthroat and browns around due to timber clogging the bottom, which creates ideal feeding and hiding spots. It's also surrounded by hiking trails, world-renowned ice climbing areas, and horse camps.

## Don't Miss

Take the short hike to the Memorial Boulder, a massive slab that not only offers scale for the force of the quake, but also features a plaque of the 28 who died.

## Tip

Earthquake Lake is located in the 3-million-acre Custer Gallatin National Forest, which offers an extensive rental cabin system. Built in the 1920s and 1930s, the cabins all have wood or electric stoves.

## Getting Here and Around

Yellowstone Airport (WYS) is regional and sits just 2 miles from the lake. Bozeman Yellowstone International Airport (BZN) is 89 miles away.

**Earthquake Lake Visitor Center.** *317 U.S. 287, Cameron, MT* *406/682–7620* *fs.usda.gov/main/custergallatin/home* *Free.*

# Grizzly & Wolf Discovery Center

### See Yogi Bear

Set on the edge of Yellowstone National Park, this not-for-profit wildlife park and rehabilitation and educational facility is dedicated to giving visitors the opportunity to observe magnificent wild animals while learning how to coexist with them. The priority is placed on not stressing out the animals, so they are rotated in and out of enclosures on a regular schedule. Most people come for the bears and the wolves, but there's also a Birds of Prey exhibit with eagles, as well as an otter habitat that offers the most consistent activity. Plan to spend an hour or two here before heading into Yellowstone (the West Entrance is mere blocks away), where you might see them out wandering, minus the fencing.

### Don't Miss

The Grizzly & Wolf Discovery Center is an active participant in product testing to determine how bear-proof products are. It's a hoot to see how the bears try to puzzle or muscle their way in. If after 60 minutes, the bears are defeated, the item gets a coveted "bear-resistant" designation.

### Good to Know

On theme, the Running Bear Pancake House is just a few blocks from the center, and is known for its decadent cinnamon roll pancake. 🌐 *runningbearph.com.*

### Getting Here and Around

Just one block from the West Entrance to Yellowstone, the center is a little more than 2 miles from the regional Yellowstone Airport (WYS) and 91 miles from Bozeman Yellowstone International Airport (BZN).

**Grizzly & Wolf Discovery Center.** ✉ *201 South Canyon, West Yellowstone, MT* ☎ *800/257–2570* 🌐 *grizzlydiscoveryctr.org* 🎫 *$15.*

# When in Montana

## HAVRE BENEATH THE STREETS

When a fire burned down the railroad town of Havre in 1904, the residents came up with a unique way to rebuild: underground. Built mostly by the Chinese workers who had constructed the railroad tracks, this six-block mini town was a bustling collection of the shops needed for day-to-day life a century ago—a meat market, a saloon, a bordello, a saddlery, a blacksmith, a smokehouse, a bakery, an ice cream shop, a laundry, a pharmacy, a funeral parlor, and an opium den. After everyone moved aboveground again and Prohibition began, the tunnels were used to smuggle and store liquor. How anyone lived in such dimly lit close quarters is hard to fathom, but wandering around this beautifully preserved piece of history, looking as though everyone just left for a few minutes, is a fascinating way to try to imagine it.

**Do This:** On the same block as Havre Beneath the Streets, the Palace Bar has a back bar built in 1912 and genteel feel, and echoes the old-timey atmosphere of the underground town, but with welcome modern "amenities," such as pool, beer pong, shuffleboard, and darts.

**Havre Beneath the Streets.** ✉ *120 3rd Ave., Havre, MT* ☎ *406/265–8888* 🌐 *havrechamber.com* 🎫 *$17.*

## MEDICINE ROCKS STATE PARK

Named for the "big medicine" practiced in the area by Native Americans, the 320-acre Medicine Rocks State Park in southeastern Montana features unique sandstone formations that have taken on a "Swiss cheese" look, turning them into perfect hand- and footholds for scrambling to the tops of some of the larger formations—many of which have transformed into spires, caves, and arches—to get a better look at the surrounding peaceful plains. Amid the holes, thousands of petroglyphs were carved by the Sioux and Northern Cheyenne tribes that once camped here.

**Do This:** Visitors can also camp in one of the free designated sites, keeping an eye out for the golden eagles, antelope, mule deer, and sharp-tailed grouse that call the park home. Because of its far-flung locale, the park is usually nearly empty, so climb up a pockmarked boulder, close your eyes, and listen to the piercing cries of a falcon and the whisper of the prairie winds.

**Medicine Rocks State Park.** ✉ *1141 MT 7, Ekalaka, MO* 🌐 *fwp.mt.gov/stateparks/medicine-rocks* 🎫 *$8.*

## MIRACLE OF AMERICA MUSEUM

Nicknamed the "Smithsonian of the West," the massive complex that comprises the nonprofit Miracle of America Museum in Polson contains 42 buildings across 4½ acres, filled with more than 340,000 items unique to the USA—the result of decades of collecting by the museum's owners. Most impressive in this astoundingly diverse assemblage is the exhibit of more than 3,000 motorcycles, as well as military vehicles, race cars and aircraft that guests can climb into, and a coin-operated section of vintage arcade games and hundreds of other hands-on items will keep kids occupied for hours. The best time to visit is during Live History Days, held every third weekend in July, when reenactors demonstrate day-to-day life through the country's history.

**Do This:** One of the best burgers in the state can be had at The Shoe—Lakeview Dining and Spirits (✉ *820 Shoreline Dr.* ☎ *406/883–1425* 🌐 *lakeviewshoe.com*), a casual and reasonably priced locals joint that sits at the edge of pretty Polson Bay.

**Miracle of America Museum.** ✉ *36094 Memory La., Polson, MT* ☎ *406/883–6804* 🌐 *miracleofamericamuseum.org* 🎫 *$10.*

## Cool Places to Stay

**Izaak Walton Inn.** Built by the Great Northern Railroad to house the work crews, and 30 minutes from either the East or West entrances of Glacier National Park, this inn offers six types of lodging on one property, all anchored by a 1939 alpine lodge (with rustic, Montana-themed rooms). In keeping with the theme, the most popular stays are in fact the train cabooses and luxury railcars, all of which have been converted into comfortable cabins with heated floors, stocked kitchenettes, and decks with views of the mountains and the railroad tracks. The property also offers a Finnish sauna and game room, and snow-sports gear and guides can be rented on-site. ✉ *290 Izaak Walton Inn Rd., Essex, MT* ☎ *800/847–4868* 🌐 *izaakwaltoninn.com* [$] *From $109.*

**McGinnis Meadows Cattle & Guest Ranch.** If your inner cowboy or cowgirl longs to hit the open range and improve your horsemanship while wrangling some cattle, McGinnis Meadows is the working ranch to visit. Each stay lasts 10 days—in one of the cozy cabins, each of which has a gas fireplace, sitting area, private bath, mini-refrigerator, coffeepot, and private deck, or in a lodge room, all decorated in Western style—and during that time, guests (no more than 19 at a time) drive and sort cattle based on their horseback-riding experience level, from beginner to advanced. During rest time or for nonriders, there are mountain bikes for exploring this gorgeous part of northwest Montana, as well as inner tubes and fishing gear for the pristine lake, and a game room and hot tub. ✉ *6220 McGinnis Meadows Rd., Libby, MT* ☎ *406/293–5000* 🌐 *mmgranch.net* [$] *From $2,316.*

**The Resort at Paws Up.** A destination resort for celebs—the likes of Gwyneth Paltrow, Leonardo DiCaprio, and the Rolling Stones have stayed here—the Paws Up is also famously the first place to have used the term "glamping," which in this case means giant, secluded, one- to three-bedroom safari-style tents with hardwood and (heated) slate floors, fancy linens on beds with heated mattresses, oversized showers, Wi-Fi, and heat and a/c, along with a massive list of additional amenities, and chef-created meals. ✉ *40060 Paws Up Rd., Greenough, MT* ☎ *877/580–6343* 🌐 *pawsup.com* [$] *From $1,155.*

**The Shire of Montana.** The owners of the Shire of Montana took the line, "In a hole in the ground, there lived a hobbit" to heart, creating their own version of the dwelling described in J. R. R. Tolkien's beloved books—yes, underground—and it's so charming and comfortable that even non-fans will be delighted. This adults-only lodging requires a two-night-minimum stay, but that gives guests extra time to explore the surrounding Cabinet National Forest, where hikers, bikers, kayakers, and fly-fishermen will find plenty to do, including casting for the cutthroat trout in the guests-only pond and bass fishing in the Clark Fork and Thompson rivers. At night, the Hobbit Village comes to life as lights strung everywhere illuminate the Whimsical Village of wooden mushrooms and tiny abodes, along with a grill, outdoor fire pit, and picnic deck with views of Cougar Peak and the forest. ✉ *9 Hobbit La., Trout Creek, MT* ☎ *406/827–7200* 🌐 *theshireofmontana.com* [$] *From $395.*

# Wyoming

While the days of the Wild West seem like history to many of us, Wyoming is still a land of cowboys and ranches. Even in high-end Jackson Hole, Western attire mixes with ski gear. True to that frontier spirit, it's a land perfect for exploration. The world's oldest national park, Yellowstone, brings scores of visitors to the state every year for the geothermal features and abundant wildlife. But don't miss out on the Grand Tetons, atmospheric towns like Cody and Jackson, and vast stretches of wide-open plains.

## Bucket List Picks

The following boxes contain our picks for the top sights and experiences in Wyoming.

- ○ Yellowstone National Park
- ○ Grand Teton National Park
- ○ Devils Tower National Monument
- ○ Curt Gowdy State Park
- ○ Jackson Hole
- ○ Legend Rock Petroglyph Site
- ○ National Elk Refuge

# Yellowstone National Park

### The World's First National Park

The country's first designated national park, the 2.2-million acre Yellowstone National Park is home to more geysers and hot springs than any other place on earth with about 10,000 hydrothermal features, including active geysers like Old Faithful and many far less famous gushers. More than a thousand miles of trails offer plenty of opportunities to struggle to maintain the mandatory distance between yourself and bison, bighorn sheep, elk, grizzly and black bears, moose, wolves, pronghorn, and trumpeter swans—because the wildlife is everywhere, especially in the less trafficked parts of the park (as in, away from the geysers). Fishing, canoeing and boating, horseback riding, and bus touring are also options.

### Don't Miss

During a winter visit, hop on a snowcoach or snowmobile tour—the park allows only reduced-noise machines—which can you get you out to the lesser-known mudpots and fumaroles.

### Best Tour

A sunset paddle through an active geyser basin is just as cool as it sounds in areas few will ever see, because they can only be accessed by kayak. Day and overnight trips are offered and all gear is provided. *geyserkayak.com* *From $125.*

### Getting Here and Around

The West Entrance can be accessed by flying into West Yellowstone Airport. In winter fly into Jackson Hole Airport (JAC) and then arrange for a snowcat or other over-snow means of entering the park's South Entrance, 57 miles north.

**Yellowstone National Park.** *307/344–7381* *nps.gov/yell* *$35 per vehicle.*

# Grand Teton National Park

## Wild Wonderland

Featuring some of the country's most dramatic scenery, Grand Teton National Park boasts 310,000 acres of lush valley floors, mountain meadows, alpine lakes, and the magnificent Teton Range. Hiking and climbing are top activities, and photographers flock here to catch iconic shots such as the old barn on Mormon Row (a remnant from the homesteaders who settled here in 1890). The melt from the stunning snowcapped peaks feeds the popular Jenny and Jackson lakes where you can rent a canoe or kayak for the day. Just looking? Drive the 42-mile road through the park—with optional spurs to Jenny Lake and the panoramic valley views at the summit of Signal Mountain—for a sense of the park and likely some bison, bear, and moose sightings. Towering above it all is the Grand Teton, dotted with climbers tackling the daunting peak.

## Don't Miss

The best hike in the park leads to both Inspiration Point, overlooking Jenny Lake, and Hidden Falls. Take the shuttle across the lake ($18 round-trip) to access the trail, which is 2 miles out and back.

## Best Tour

Jackson Hole Wildlife Safaris will help you cover way more of the park in one day than you could ever see on your own in a week, and guides are in constant communication with park rangers, so they know where the grizzlies are. *jacksonholewildlifesafaris.com* *From $145.*

## Getting Here and Around

Jackson Hole Airport (JAC) is just under 10 miles from the entrance.

**Grand Teton National Park.** *Jackson, WY* *307/739–3399* *nps.gov/grte* *$35 per vehicle.*

# Devils Tower National Monument

### Craggiest Climb

The country's first national monument, the 867-foot-high Devils Tower in northeastern Wyoming is a unique butte formed when cooling lava formed the columns of rock—although Native Americans have a much more interesting creation story for it involving two girls being chased by bears. Climbers flock here from around the world to sample the excellent routes to the top and for the hundreds of parallel cracks that make it one of the finest traditional crack climbing areas in North America. Hiking trails offer different vantage points and range from an easy two-thirds-mile stroll to a moderately strenuous 2.8-miler.

### Don't Miss

Look for signs pointing to overlooks along Highway 110 where you can stop to watch the many inhabitants of Prairie Dog Town pop in and out of their homes.

### Take This Side Trip

A scenic 28-mile drive from Devils Tower, the town of Sundance Kid was named for the place where he successfully stole a lot of horses from a nearby ranch.

### When to Go

Devils Tower is open year-round, but winter can bring unexpected blizzards and ice storms. Throughout June, the park asks visitors to refrain from climbing on the tower out of respect for area tribes.

### Getting Here and Around

The closest airport is the Northeast Wyoming Regional Airport (GCC) in Gillette, Wyoming, 65 miles away. The closest major airport is Rapid City Regional Airport (RAP), 119 miles away.

**Devils Tower National Monument.** ☎ *307/467–5283* 🌐 *nps.gov/deto* 🎫 *$25 per vehicle.*

## Curt Gowdy State Park

### Mountain-Biking Mecca

Sometimes state parks are just, well, another great park, but not Curt Gowdy (named for the beloved sportscaster who was born and raised in Green River) which sits halfway between Cheyenne and Laramie and offers endless recreational opportunities. With more than 35 miles of single- and doubletrack trails, four mountain-bike terrain playgrounds, and a skills area, the park was awarded the designation of "epic" by the International Mountain Biking Association (IMBA), and its log jumps, vertical drops, slab cruising, and meandering dirt paths draw bicyclists of all levels. Boaters and fishermen also love the three reservoirs which offer a variety of fish, and in spring, bird-watchers flock here to catch sight of the many migrating, non-native birds who make stops here. In June, the Stone Temple Mountain Bike Camp allows teens to spend four days honing their fat-tire skills.

### Don't Miss

The park's 19.2-mile loop track wends through alpine and meadow settings and around the reservoirs, with moderately challenging technical sections and plenty of downhill to shake up those quads.

### Insider Tip

The four cabins in the Sherman Hills Campground have views of the Granite Springs Reservoir.

### Getting Here and Around

From Laramie or Laramie Regional Airport (LAR), take Interstate 80 to Wyoming 210 (Happy Jack Road) to County Road 106; from Cheyenne or Cheyenne Regional Airport (CYS), take Happy Jack Road straight from town.

**Curt Gowdy State Park.** ✉ *1264 Granite Springs Rd., Cheyenne, WY* 🌐 *wyoparks.wyo.gov/index.php/places-to-go/curt-gowdy* 🎫 *$7 per vehicle.*

# Jackson Hole

## The Big One

The gateway to Grand Teton National Park and one of the primary gateways to Yellowstone National Park, the ruggedly beautiful Jackson Hole is also a winter wonderland for skiers as home to Snow King Mountain Resort, Grand Targhee Resort, and Jackson Hole Mountain Resort—"the Big One," which has the longest continuous vertical rise of any ski area in the United States, rising 4,139 feet from the valley floor to the top of Rendezvous Mountain. With the Snake River winding through it all, Jackson Hole is, not surprisingly, gorgeously and obsessively outdoors-oriented. But the valley (Jackson Hole) and the town (Jackson) also offer a remarkably cultured experience, with one of the country's most famous and popular annual fine-arts festivals, noteworthy dining, and lots of Western-themed shopping.

## Don't Miss

The National Wildlife Museum 2½ miles north of town features more than 5,000 noteworthy artworks depicting animals from artists such as Georgia O'Keeffe and Andy Warhol. The building is inspired by the ruins of a castle in Scotland. A sculpture trail outside overlooks the National Elk Refuge.

## Best Tour

There are many outfitters rafting the 8 exhilarating miles of whitewater through the Snake River Canyon, but none as fun as hopping in a 13-foot self-bailer with Lewis & Clark River Expeditions. 🌐 *lewisandclarkriverrafting.com* 🎫 *From $88.*

## Getting Here and Around

Jackson Hole Airport (JAC) is just under 10 miles from downtown Jackson.

**Jackson Hole.** 🌐 *visitjacksonhole.com.*

# Legend Rock Petroglyph Site

## The Original Instagram

Located 23 miles west of Thermopolis, Legend Rock Petroglyph Site is a 1,312-foot-long cliff that features 92 panels with more than 300 petroglyphs, some of which were carved nearly 10,000 years ago. The site is probably best known for its large, elaborate, and highly abstract anthropomorphic petroglyphs. There are also depictions of humans as well as birds and animals such as elk, deer, bighorn sheep, horses, and buffalo. Trails with informative placards lead visitors around the rock walls, which helps to identify and offer the best interpretations of the figures and symbols incised and etched into the rock.

## Don't Miss

Thermopolis boasts the world's largest mineral hot springs, which can be enjoyed at the Hot Springs State Park Bath House, one of several family-friendly mineral springs–fed swimming pools in town.

## While You're Here

Rocks, minerals, and gems (jade, agate, petrified wood, and geodes, to name a few) cover every surface inside and outside at Ava's Silver and Rock Shop. There are also dinosaur-themed souvenirs, locally made jewelry, and books on rockhounding in the area. ☎ *307/864–3800.*

## Getting Here and Around

The site is located 29 miles northwest of Thermopolis, which has the regional Hot Springs County Airport (THP). The closest major airport is Casper–Natrona County International Airport (CPR) 123 miles away.

**Legend Rock Petroglyph Site.** ✉ *2861 W. Cottonwood Rd., Thermopolis, WY* ☎ *307/864–2176* 🌐 *wyoparks.wyo.gov/index.php/places-to-go/legend-rock* 🎟 *Free.*

# National Elk Refuge

## Largest Migrating Elk Herd in North America

Just a mile from Jackson's Town Square, the National Elk Refuge spans 27,000 acres and is home to one of the world's largest elk herds every winter. The refuge was established in 1912 to protect the grazing grounds of elk herds who begin migrating down from the high country in early November in search of food, with their numbers growing to up to 7,000 by February. Later in the spring, the elk begin to make their journey back up to higher elevation to graze in Grand Teton National Park, Gros Ventre, Yellowstone National Park, and the Teton Wilderness. While elk are the primary wildlife species occupying the National Elk Refuge, bison, bighorn sheep, bald eagles, and gray wolves (especially when large numbers of wintering elk populate the landscape) can be observed in this incredibly scenic winter habitat.

## Don't Miss

Wildlife observation decks at the Flat Creek turnout north of the visitor center on Highway 26/191 and at the visitor center offer good opportunities for waterfowl, bird, and wildlife photography.

## Best Tour

From mid-December through early April, horse-drawn sleigh rides are available at the refuge. Rides take you across the refuge and into a herd of thousands of elk. 🌐 *www.nersleighrides.com* 🎟 *From $27.*

## Getting Here and Around

The refuge is located just northeast of the town of Jackson. Jackson Hole Airport (JAC) is just under 10 miles from downtown Jackson.

**National Elk Refuge.** ✉ *675 E. Broadway Ave., Jackson, WY* 🌐 *www.fws.gov/refuge/national_elk_refuge* 🎟 *Free.*

## When in Wyoming

### COWGIRLS OF THE WEST MUSEUM

Located in a storefront and staffed by passionate historians, the Cowgirls of the West Museum in downtown Cheyenne offers a welcome overview of the women who won the West just as handily as their cowboy counterparts. Photos, newspaper clippings, clothing, and other artifacts are displayed with well-researched placards explaining their significance, and although this is a small place, a lot has been packed in. The rodeo and women's suffrage sections are extensive—Wyoming was the first state to give women the right to vote, by the way, and its pride in those who tamed the Wild West is palpable here.

**Do This:** Next door to the museum is the Emporium (203 W. 17th St.), a shop that sells women's Western wear, cowgirl boots, silver and turquoise jewelry and cowgirl-centric gifts and souvenirs, most locally made, and some vintage items, too.

**Cowgirls of the West Museum.** ✉ *205 W. 17th St., Cheyenne, WY* ☎ *307/638–4994* 🌐 *cowgirlsofthewestmuseum.com* 🎫 *Free.*

### FOSSIL BUTTE NATIONAL MONUMENT

Once covered in lakes, Fossil Butte—which sits about 9 miles west of Kemmerer—is now covered for 8,198 acres with the fossilized remains of extraordinary plant and animal fossil specimens, some up to 56 million years old. You'll find originals and replicas of prehistoric fish species, as well as those of alligators, stingrays, and other sea creatures at the visitor center. Follow 4 miles of moderate to strenuous hiking trails for a close-up of a fossil quarry and scenic, rolling hills with their unique lake-bed-spawned flora and fauna.

**Do This:** Fishing in the surrounding Fossil Basin of southwestern Wyoming is a unique treat for the rich landscape and generously stocked reservoirs, including Fontenelle and Viva Naughton, as well as on the Hams Fork and Green rivers. In winter, ice fishing the reservoirs can yield some monster fish.

**Fossil Butte National Monument.** ☎ *307/877–4455* 🌐 *nps.gov/fobu/index.htm* 🎫 *Free.*

### HELL'S HALF-ACRE

Don't let the name fool you: Hell's Half-Acre isn't a half acre—it's actually more than 320 acres of colorful canyons and rock formations, and it's not hellacious at all. In fact, this longtime Wyoming Geological Survey study area is a type of badlands, a moonscape of sandstone and shale that makes for a great sunset stop. Adding to the confusion is that this isn't even the original Hell's Half-Acre, but instead got its name because a wrangler wandering around Casper thought he had stumbled upon the one in Idaho and the name stuck.

**Do This:** Famously the setting for the campy movie *Starship Troopers,* the area offers no hiking or amenities (it's fenced off, and the restaurant there shut down years ago), but it's a cool roadside stop right off the highway for its shocking stark landscape in the middle of miles of sagebrush as you travel between Casper and Thermopolis. Just west of Casper in the little town of Mills right off the Yellowstone Highway on the way to Hell's Half-Acre is a good stop for food: G-Ma's Diner.

**Hell's Half-Acre.** ☎ *307/766–2286* 🌐 *wsgs.wyo.gov/public-info/tour-hells-half-acre* 🎫 *Free.*

### OLD TRAIL TOWN

Pulling up to the assemblage of authentic Old West buildings that is Old Trail Town—just outside Cody along the Yellowstone Highway—is a surreal step back in time, a peek at what it must have been like in the late 1800s to hitch your horse outside the cabin where Butch Cassidy and the Sundance Kid were staying, or the saloon where they and they rest of the Hole in the Wall gang did shots of whisky and planned their escapades. The buildings were moved from their original locations around Wyoming and Montana and reassembled here in the form of a tiny town, in the spot that Buffalo Bill Cody originally surveyed for a "Cody City" in 1895.

**Do This:** If Old Trail Town spurs a longing for more from the Old West, the Buffalo Bill Center of the Wild West sits just 2 miles away and is home to five museums: The Buffalo Bill Museum, Whitney Western Art Museum, Draper Natural History Museum, Cody Firearms Museum, and Plains Indian Museum each showcase a different aspect of the country's Native American and pioneering history.

**Old Trail Town.** ✉ *1831 Demaris Dr., Cody, WY* ☎ *307/587–5302* 🌐 *oldtrailtown.org* 🎟 *$10.*

## Cool Places to Stay

**Brush Creek Ranch.** It's hard to imagine the term "elegant" applying to a working cattle ranch, but that's the best way to describe sprawling Brush Creek Ranch, a 30,000-acre resort in south-central Wyoming's stunning North Platte River Valley, tucked between the Sierra Madres and the Medicine Bow National Forest. Three properties in one, the all-inclusive Brush Creek's lodging options include spacious, Western-themed rooms in The Lodge and Spa, and luxury cabins and cabin suites at Magee Homestead and the French Creek Sportsmen's Club. Activities include horseback riding (including cattle drives), fly-fishing the properties' lakes, rivers, and streams, hunting, rock climbing, ATV riding, golf, mountain biking, hiking, and trail running in warm months. Skiing at the ranch's own Green Mountain ski area is available in winter, along with snowshoeing, tubing, ice-skating, and snowmobiling. ✉ *66 Brush Creek Ranch Rd., Saratoga, WY* ☎ *307/327–5284* 🌐 *brushcreekranch.com* $ *From $2,000.*

**Terry Bison Ranch.** Laid-back and ideal for families, Terry Bison Ranch sits just over the state line between Colorado and Wyoming, right off the highway outside of Cheyenne. The rustic cabins (some dog-friendly) feature large decks looking out onto the wetland meadows teeming with wildlife and portions of the 2,500-head bison herd, and although they have kitchens, it's BYO cookware. The second-largest bison ranch in the country, Terry Bison built a train to take guests out across the 27,500-acre property to get an up-close look at the herd, and you can even feed the animals. ✉ *51 I–25 Service Rd. W, Cheyenne, WY* ☎ *307/634–4171* 🌐 *terrybisonranch.com* $ *From $115.*

**The Wort.** Charming and individually decorated, the comfortable rooms at The Wort, situated just off the famous Town Square in the heart of Jackson, are each uniquely decorated using custom-made furniture and original Western art. This shrine to the Wild West was built in Tudor Revival style in 1941 and has such an authentic feel that you're forgiven for expecting to see frontier folk climbing the grand staircase as you enter the front door. The hotel's raucous Silver Dollar Saloon features live music and dancing most nights, and the Silver Dollar Grill is famous for its smoky pheasant soup and buffalo burgers. ✉ *50 N. Glenwood St., Jackson, WY* ☎ *800/322–2727* 🌐 *worthotel.com* $ *From $389.*

Chapter 10

# THE GREAT LAKES



Written by
Amy Cavanaugh

# WELCOME TO THE GREAT LAKES

## TOP REASONS TO GO

★ **Lake life:** Whether you visit Lake Michigan, Erie, Huron, Ontario, or Superior, there are plenty of activities to try, from swimming to ice-skating to watching a sunrise or sunset over the water.

★ **Must-see cities:** In Chicago, Indianapolis, and Detroit, there are a wealth of standout museums, exceptional restaurants, stunning architecture, and buzzing nightlife.

★ **Spectator sports:** No need to travel far for good games in this region: Packers games are a big deal in Wisconsin, Ohio has the Cavaliers and Browns, and Chicago draws baseball fans to Wrigley Field.

★ **Winter wonders:** From ice fishing and exploring frozen falls to snow tubing and searching for the northern lights, the Great Lakes offer plenty of outdoor fun.

★ **Diverse cultures:** The region is home to lots of people originally from the Middle East, Somalia, Mexico, and many other places, which is reflected in the culture and excellent cuisine.

**1 Illinois.** Thanks to Chicago, the biggest city in the region, it's at the center of the Midwest action.

**2 Indiana.** From NCAA football to racing, there's always an event to catch in this sports-obsessed state.

**3 Michigan.** With tons of idyllic towns and lakefront, it's a prime place to hit the beach and explore natural attractions.

**4 Minnesota.** With hiking, skiing, ice fishing, and more, the "Land of 10,000 Lakes" has plenty of outdoor adventures in store.

**5 Ohio.** The gateway to the Midwest has a number of midsize cities to explore and is beloved for its spectator sports and Rock & Roll Hall of Fame.

**6 Wisconsin.** Beers, brats, the Packers, and cheese give America's Dairyland a culture all its own.

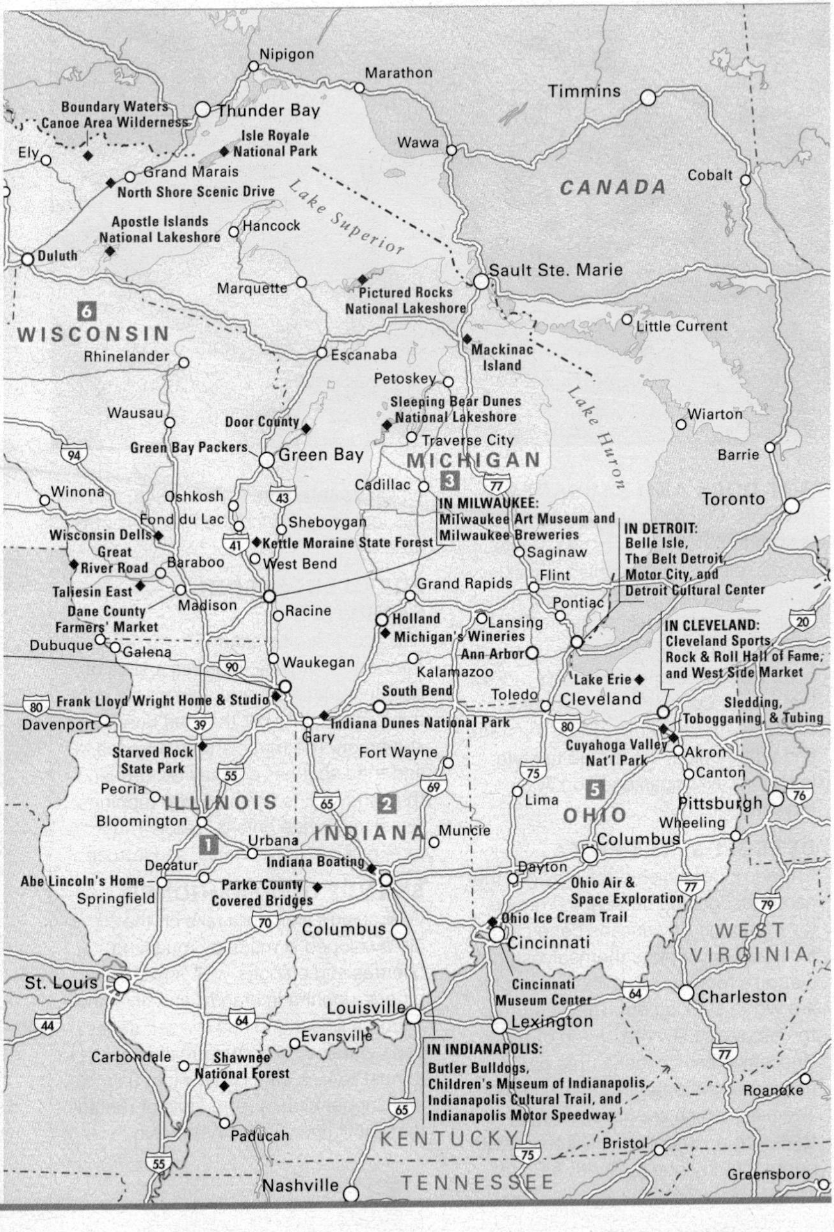

Nipigon
Marathon
Timmins
Boundary Waters Canoe Area Wilderness
Thunder Bay
Isle Royale National Park
Wawa
Ely
Grand Marais
North Shore Scenic Drive
CANADA
Cobalt
Lake Superior
Apostle Islands National Lakeshore
Hancock
Duluth
Sault Ste. Marie
Marquette
Pictured Rocks National Lakeshore
6
WISCONSIN
Little Current
Rhinelander
Escanaba
Mackinac Island
Petoskey
Lake Huron
Sleeping Bear Dunes National Lakeshore
Wausau
Door County
Wiarton
Traverse City
Green Bay Packers
Green Bay
MICHIGAN
Barrie
94
Cadillac
3
77
Winona
Oshkosh
43
Toronto
IN MILWAUKEE:
Milwaukee Art Museum and
Milwaukee Breweries
Fond du Lac
Sheboygan
IN DETROIT:
Belle Isle,
The Belt Detroit,
Motor City, and
Detroit Cultural Center
Wisconsin Dells
41
Kettle Moraine State Forest
Saginaw
Great River Road
Baraboo
West Bend
Flint
Taliesin East
Grand Rapids
Dane County Farmers' Market
Madison
Pontiac
Racine
Holland
Lansing
IN CLEVELAND:
Cleveland Sports,
Rock & Roll Hall of Fame,
and West Side Market
20
Michigan's Wineries
Dubuque
Galena
Ann Arbor
Waukegan
90
Kalamazoo
Lake Erie
South Bend
Toledo
Cleveland
80
Frank Lloyd Wright Home & Studio
Sledding, Tobogganing, & Tubing
Davenport
39
Indiana Dunes National Park
80
Gary
Cuyahoga Valley Nat'l Park
Akron
Starved Rock State Park
Fort Wayne
55
75
Canton
Peoria
69
Lima
5
ILLINOIS
65
2
Pittsburgh
76
OHIO
Bloomington
Wheeling
1
INDIANA
Muncie
Columbus
Urbana
Decatur
Indiana Boating
Dayton
Abe Lincoln's Home
Springfield
Parke County Covered Bridges
Ohio Air & Space Exploration
77
79
70
Ohio Ice Cream Trail
Columbus
Cincinnati
WEST VIRGINIA
St. Louis
Cincinnati Museum Center
64
Charleston
Louisville
64
Lexington
44
Evansville
IN INDIANAPOLIS:
Butler Bulldogs,
Children's Museum of Indianapolis,
Indianapolis Cultural Trail, and
Indianapolis Motor Speedway
Carbondale
Shawnee National Forest
77
Roanoke
65
Paducah
KENTUCKY
75
Bristol
55
Nashville
TENNESSEE
Greensboro

# WHAT TO EAT AND DRINK IN THE GREAT LAKES

Chicago-style hot dog

### HOT DOGS AND SAUSAGES

In Illinois, Chicago-style hot dogs come dressed with yellow mustard, white onions, electric-green relish, a pickle spear, tomatoes, sport peppers, and a sprinkle of celery salt, while in Wisconsin, bratwursts are cooked in beer with onions before being grilled and tucked into a bun. Coney dogs, hot dogs topped with beef chili, yellow mustard, and white onion, are the go-to style in Detroit, Michigan and Fort Wayne, Indiana.

### DETROIT-STYLE PIZZA

Chicago's deep-dish pizza may get the name recognition outside the region (even though Chicagoans generally opt for tavern-style pizza themselves), but Detroit's rectangular, thick, crispy pies are worth seeking out. They feature tomato sauce layered on top of the Wisconsin brick cheese (that order helps give the edges a cheesy crunch). The pies, which are baked in steel trays, are most commonly served with pepperoni. Try one at Buddy's Pizza, which invented the style in 1946, and has locations around the Detroit metro area.

### PORK TENDERLOIN SANDWICH

This monster of a sandwich, found throughout Indiana, features a slice of pork loin that's pounded out so it's very thin but much larger than the bun it's served on. The meat is then breaded and fried so it has a crispy texture, and the sandwich is finished with toppings like sliced white onions, yellow mustard, pickles, mayonnaise, and lettuce.

### BRANDY OLD-FASHIONED

Wisconsin's signature take on the old-fashioned is made by muddling cherries and oranges with sugar and bitters, pouring in brandy, and finishing it with a splash of soda (sweet, sour, soda water, or half sweet/half soda). It's a must to kick off a Friday-night fish fry at a supper club, a retro style of restaurant you'll find all over Wisconsin.

### HORSESHOE

Springfield, Illinois, is home to the horseshoe, an open-faced sandwich made by piling two slices of Texas toast with meat (a hamburger patty and sliced ham are common, but you'll also see chicken and pork tenderloin versions). Cheese sauce is poured over it all, and crispy French fries finish the dish.

### JUICY LUCY

Minnesota's Juicy Lucy is a twist on the cheeseburger: two patties are formed around a slice of cheese, creating a burger with a gooey center. Two bars in Minneapolis claim to have invented it, Matt's Bar (where it's stuffed with American cheese and finished with pickles) and 5-8 Club (where you can opt for cheeses like blue or Swiss and your choice of garnishes).

### CINCINNATI CHILI

Cincinnati chili, made with ground beef mixed with warm spices like cinnamon and cloves, is served over spaghetti (or hot dogs). Order it "three-way" and it comes with a mound of shredded cheddar, while "four-way" adds on chopped white onions or beans, and "five-way" adds both.

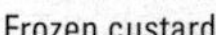

Frozen custard

Detroit-style pizza

### SHAWARMA

Dearborn, Michigan, has a large Middle Eastern population, and you'll find shawarma, beef and lamb or chicken roasted on a spit, then shaved off (some spots grill the meat instead) at restaurants there and in Detroit. Try it at Tuhama's or Hamido in Dearborn.

### FROZEN CUSTARD

Made with milk, cream, and egg yolks (the latter ingredient sets it apart from ice cream), thick, rich frozen custard is the definitive icy treat in the Great Lakes region. At spots like Scooter's Frozen Custard in Chicago, you can get it with mix-ins or turned into shakes.

### SUGAR CREAM PIE

The filling in this Indiana-favorite pie is a mixture of pantry staples: sugar, butter, cornstarch, and milk, and flavored with vanilla and nutmeg. The result is a creamy, custardy pie that never goes out of season. Grab a slice at Wick's Pies in Winchester.

### KRINGLE

Kringle is a round, flaky Danish pastry stuffed with fillings like almond or raspberry and finished with icing. It's popular in Racine, Wisconsin, where there's a large Danish-American population. Pick one up at O&H Danish Bakery.

# The Great Lakes Regional Snapshot

## Know Before You Go

### TAKE ADVANTAGE OF THE COLD

The region can get quite cold and snowy between November and February, but the chill means smaller crowds at popular locations and lower prices at hotels. Plus, you can take part in epic winter activities, like skating and snowshoeing.

### GET ON THE LAKE

No matter which state they're in, locals are all about spending time on or near the Great Lakes. Swimming, fishing, boating, and even surfing are typical summer pastimes, while skating and ice fishing are popular winter activities.

### CONSIDER RENTING A CAR

Chicago is the only city in the Great Lakes with dedicated subway service. Light-rails and metros exist in other big cities like Minneapolis and Indianapolis, but cars are the preferred way to get around the rest of the region.

## Planning Your Time

The Great Lakes states may be large, but most major cities are within a days' drive of each other, so you can easily hit destinations in two states in one day. If you base yourself in Chicago, the biggest city in the region, you can visit parts of Wisconsin, Michigan, and Indiana for day trips and knock some items off your bucket list.

## Road Trips

**3 days:** Chicago to Door County, Wisconsin

**3 days:** Detroit to Traverse City

**4 days:** Cleveland to Columbus to Cincinnati

## Big Events

**St. Patrick's Day.** March 17 is a big deal in Chicago, with multiple parades and the river dyed bright green.

**Indianapolis 500.** Each Memorial Day weekend "The Greatest Spectacle in Racing" is a 500-mile race around the track.

**Minnesota State Fair.** The massive celebration caps off summer with shows, agricultural events, shopping, and fun things to eat and drink.

## What To ...

### READ

*Electric Arches* by Eve Ewing

*Kitchens of the Great Midwest* by J. Ryan Stradal

*The Fault in Our Stars* by John Green

*Little Fires Everywhere* by Celeste Ng

### WATCH

*Ferris Bueller's Day Off* (movie set in Chicago)

*Blues Brothers* (movie set in Chicago)

*Parks and Recreation* (show set in Indiana)

### LISTEN TO

*Where Did Our Love Go* by The Supremes (album)

*Yankee Hotel Foxtrot* by Wilco (album)

### BUY

A Packers jersey from Wisconsin

Garrett's Popcorn from Chicago

Stadium Mustard from Cleveland

Dried cherries from Michigan

## Contacts

### AIR

**Indiana:** IND

**Michigan:** DTW, GRR

**Illinois:** ORD, MDW

**Ohio:** CLE, CMH, DAY

**Wisconsin:** MKE, MSN

### BUS

**Megabus.** ☎ *877/462–6342* 🌐 *us.megabus.com*

**Greyhound.** ☎ *800/231–2222* 🌐 *www.greyhound.com*

**Barons Bus.** ☎ *888/378–3823* 🌐 *baronsbus.com*

### TRAIN

**Amtrak.** ☎ *800/872–7245* 🌐 *www.amtrak.com*

### TAXI

**Yellow Cab.** ☎ *312/829–4222* 🌐 *yellowcabchicago.com*; **Flash Cab.** ☎ *773/561–4444* 🌐 *flashcab.com*

**Checker.** ☎ *313/963–7000* 🌐 *www.checkerdetroit.com*

**Taxi Milwaukee.** ☎ *414/220–5000* 🌐 *taximke.com*

**Ace Taxi.** ☎ *216/361–4700* 🌐 *acetaxi.com*

**Transportation Plus.** ☎ *612/888–8888* 🌐 *www.tplusride.com*

**zTrip.** ☎ *317/487–7777* 🌐 *www.ztrip.com/indianapolis*

**Columbus Yellow Cab.** ☎ *614/444–4444* 🌐 *yellowcabofcolumbus.com*

**Union Cab.** ☎ *608/242–2000* 🌐 *www.unioncab.com*

### METRO/SUBWAY

**Chicago Transit Authority.** ☎ *888/968–7282* 🌐 *www.transitchicago.com*

**Metro Transit (Minneapolis).** ☎ *612/373–3333* 🌐 *metrotransit.org*

**Greater Cleveland Regional Transit Authority.** ☎ *216/621–9500* 🌐 *www.riderta.com*

**IndyGo.** ☎ *317/635–3344* 🌐 *www.indygo.net*

**Detroit Department of Transportation.** ☎ *313/933–1300* 🌐 *detroitmi.gov/departments/detroit-department-transportation*

**Milwaukee County Transit System.** ☎ *414/344–6711* 🌐 *www.ridemcts.com*

**Madison Metro.** ☎ *608/266–4466* 🌐 *www.cityofmadison.com/metro*

**Central Ohio Transit Authority.** ☎ *614/228–1776* 🌐 *www.cota.com*

### VISITOR INFORMATION

🌐 *www.enjoyillinois.com*

🌐 *www.michigan.org*

🌐 *www.exploreminnesota.com*

🌐 *ohio.org*

🌐 *www.travelwisconsin.com*

🌐 *visitindiana.com*

# Illinois

Home to Chicago and therefore the de facto capital of culture for the Midwest, Illinois is much more than its most famous city. Yes, of course, many visitors flock here for the Windy City and its art museums, architecture, blues clubs, comedy shows, and deep-dish pizza, but the rest of the state offers plenty in terms of history, culture, and the great outdoors. Explore the charms of smaller towns like Galena, see the houses designed by Frank Lloyd Wright in Oak Park, and learn what makes this the "Land of Lincoln" in Springfield.

## Bucket List Picks

The following boxes contain our picks for the top sights and experiences in Illinois.

- ○ Wrigley Field
- ○ Starved Rock State Park
- ○ Abe Lincoln's Home
- ○ Chicago's Museum Campus
- ○ Skydeck Chicago
- ○ Frank Lloyd Wright Home and Studio
- ○ Shawnee National Forest
- ○ Millennium Park
- ○ Art Institute of Chicago
- ○ Chicago's Theater Scene
- ○ Chicago Speakeasies

# Wrigley Field

### Root for the Home Team

Few ballparks are quite as iconic (and historic) as Wrigley Field, home of the beloved Chicago Cubs. The team famously won the 2016 World Championship after decades of being "cursed." Their North Side park was built in 1914 as Weeghman Park, making it one of the oldest ballpark stadiums in MLB. Between innings, appreciate the park's retro touches, including ivy-covered brick walls and a manually updated scoreboard, and participate in all the traditions: order a hot dog, sing along to a celebrity-led rendition of "Take Me Out to the Ballgame" in the seventh-inning stretch, and on game days, check for victory by spotting the "W" or "L" flag waving over the stadium.

### Don't Miss

Statues of Cubs icons outside the park include famed announcer Harry Caray, located by the bleachers.

### Best Tour

The off-season tour is the way to go, as a game-day tour is more limited. During the 60-minute off-season tour, you'll visit the Cubs' dugout, visitors' clubhouse, and go out onto the field. *cubs.com/tours* *$25.*

### Good to Know

Most Cubs games take place during the day with a 1 pm Central start time, so get there early to grab a Chicago-style hot dog or fancy sausage from the Hot Doug's kiosk for lunch before the first pitch.

### Getting Here and Around

From Chicago's Midway Airport (MDW), it's an 18-mile drive to the park; from O'Hare International Airport (ORD), it's 13 miles. On the El, the Addison Red Line stop is a one-minute walk from the park.

**Wrigley Field.** *1060 W. Addison St., Chicago, IL* *773/404–2827* *www.mlb.com/cubs/ballpark.*

# Starved Rock State Park

## Eagles, Waterfalls, and Canyons

In a state with no national parks, Illinois's state parks pull their weight in beauty. Located in central Illinois between Chicago and Peoria, Starved Rock State Park is a destination for its glacier-formed sandstone canyons, waterfalls, and beautiful hiking trails as well as the chance to spot America's national bird, the bald eagle. There are 13 miles of trails and 18 canyons in the park, so it's impossible to see everything in a day—take a free guided hike, offered on weekends throughout the year.

## Don't Miss

French Canyon, which features a striking waterfall, is located less than half a mile from the visitor center. And if you're searching for eagles, keep your eyes peeled across from the park at Plum Island, home to a bald eagle sanctuary.

## Best Hotel

The historic property Starved Rock Lodge includes a log lodge with wood-paneled hotel rooms as well as cozy cabins. All rooms come with modern amenities, and the lodge also offers a swimming pool and a great room with a fireplace. 🌐 *starvedrocklodge.com.*

## When to Go

The park is open year-round and winter is especially beautiful—besides activities like ice fishing and winter hiking, the waterfalls can freeze.

## Getting Here and Around

From Chicago's Midway Airport (MDW), it's a 90-mile drive to the park; Chicago's O'Hare International Airport (ORD) is 95 miles. General Wayne A. Downing Peoria International Airport (PIA) is 70 miles away.

**Starved Rock State Park.** ✉ *2678 E. 875th Rd., Oglesby, IL* 🌐 *starvedrock.org* 🎟 *Free.*

# Abe Lincoln's Home

## Welcome to Springfield

The president who preserved the Union during the Civil War and made history with the Emancipation Proclamation resided in Springfield from 1844 to 1861 with his wife, Mary, and three children—and you can take a tour of his home. Run by the National Park Service, the home tour includes the reception rooms and bedrooms. Take a stroll around the neighborhood, noticing how the surrounding four blocks are restored to their 1860 appearance. Springfield also includes other must-visit Lincoln attractions, including the Abraham Lincoln Presidential Museum & Library. The Lincoln's New Salem State Historic Site is 20 miles away and features a reconstruction of the village where Lincoln lived from 1831 to 1837.

## Don't Miss

Lincoln is buried in Oak Ridge Cemetery; visit the elaborate tomb, which includes an obelisk, sculptures, and interior rooms with statues and plaques with Lincoln's speeches. ✉ *1500 Monument Ave. Cemetery, W. Oak Ridge St.* 🌐 *www.lincolntomb.org.*

## Good to Know

Tickets to the Lincoln Home are first come, first served and go quickly March through November. The house is open year-round, so plan a visit during the off-season for a quieter tour. If you don't manage to snag tickets, you can still peruse self-guided exhibits and explore the area.

## Getting Here and Around

Abraham Lincoln Capital Airport (SPI) is located 4 miles from the Lincoln Home. An Amtrak station is located about a half mile from the home.

**Lincoln Home.** ✉ *413 S. 8th St., Springfield, IL* ☎ *217/492–4241* 🌐 *www.nps.gov/liho* 🎫 *Free.*

# Chicago's Museum Campus

### Acres of World-Class Institutions

Many of Chicago's best museums and institutions are clustered in a 57-acre park nestled along Lake Michigan just south of downtown. There, you'll find the Adler Planetarium, Shedd Aquarium, and Field Museum of Natural History, along with Soldier Field (home of the Chicago Bears football team), and the Lakeside Center of McCormick Place (a convention center). The area also features walking paths and parks, so stop for a picnic between museums.

### Don't Miss

Máximo, a titanosaur at the Field Museum, is modeled off fossils from the largest dino that ever lived.

### Good to Know

If you're planning to visit multiple museums during your trip, opt for the CityPass, which saves you almost 50% on admission to the Shedd, Field, and Adler, among other museums, or a Go Chicago card that offers deals on tickets to more than 25 attractions.

### Best Lunch Options

Chinatown is located one stop away on the CTA Red Line, so hop on the train and head to spots like Qing Xiang Yuan Dumplings for dumplings, Tous Les Jours for pastries and sandwiches, or Moon Palace for Shanghainese favorites.

### Getting Here and Around

Chicago's Midway Airport (MDW) is 11 miles from the campus, while O'Hare International Airport (ORD) is 20 miles. Within the city, the best way to reach the campus is via the CTA to the Roosevelt Red Line. From there, it's a 10- to 20-minute walk depending on which attraction you're heading to see. You can also take the 146 bus from Roosevelt out to the campus

**Chicago Museums.** ✉ *1400 S. Lake Shore Dr. Chicago, IL* ☎ *312/409–9696* 🎟 *Varies by museum.*

# Skydeck Chicago at Willis Tower

## The Highest Observation Deck in the U.S.

At 110 stories and 1,451 feet high, the tallest building in Chicago's skyline—and third-tallest building in the Western Hemisphere—is the Willis Tower. The tower mostly houses offices, but you can visit the Skydeck on the 103rd floor to take in a 360-degree view of the city and its architecture. If you're feeling especially brave, go out onto the Ledge, an observation deck—the highest one in the United States—with a glass floor to walk out onto, and peer below. In addition to an unparalleled bird's eye view of Chicago, you'll see three states besides Illinois from the Skydeck: Indiana, Wisconsin, and Michigan.

## Best Tour

If you want to see the city's architecture from the ground level (and by water), the best tour is a river cruise from the pros at the Chicago Architecture Foundation. The 90-minute tour will tell you about the major architects who contributed to Chicago's world-class skyline, and you'll get a new perspective on the Willis Tower. *architecture.org/tours* *$46.29.*

## Good to Know

Don't be surprised if you ask a Chicagoan for directions to Willis Tower and they don't know: many city residents still refer to it by its previous name, the Sears Tower.

## Getting Here and Around

Chicago's Midway Airport (MDW) is an 11-mile drive to the tower, while Chicago's O'Hare International Airport (ORD) is 18 miles. At about a four-minute walk, Quincy is the closest CTA stop.

**Willis Tower.** *233 S. Wacker Dr., Chicago, IL* *312/875–9447* *theskydeck.com* *$26.*

# Frank Lloyd Wright Home and Studio

### Mecca for Modernist Architecture

The city of Oak Park, located just outside Chicago, has more Frank Lloyd Wright buildings than anywhere in the world, making it a must-stop for architecture buffs. Wright, who completed work on the building in 1889, lived with his family for 20 years in the home, which showcases open spaces and Japanese artwork. He designed many of his Prairie-style works in the adjoining studio space, and these homes and buildings are a short walk away.

### Don't Miss

Visit Unity Temple, a Wright-designed building that was commissioned by the Oak Park Unity Church in 1905. It's available for tours, but you can also attend a weekly Sunday service.

### Best Spot for Lunch

Grab an Italian beef and a lemon ice at Johnnie's Beef, an iconic cash-only stand located less than 2 miles away. ✉ *7500 W. North Ave., Elmwood Park, IL*

### Best Tour

**Home and Studio Guided Interior Tour + Outdoor Historic Neighborhood Audio Walking Tour.** You can take each of these tours separately, but sign up for the combined 90-minute tour to get to know Wright's work and appreciate his artistic vision. 🎫 *$35.*

### Getting Here and Around

Chicago's Midway Airport (MDW) and O'Hare International Airport (ORD) are both about 10 miles from the Home and Studio. The CTA Green Line has an Oak Park stop that is a 15- to 20-minute walk away.

**Frank Lloyd Wright Home.** ✉ *951 Chicago Ave., Oak Park, IL* ☎ *312/994–4000* 🌐 *flwright.org/visit/homeandstudio* 🎫 *Starts at $15.*

# Shawnee National Forest

### Stunning Hikes and Rock Formations

A hiking destination located in southern Illinois, Shawnee National Forest offers 403 miles of equestrian and hiking trails. The forest is set between the Mississippi and Ohio rivers, and serious hikers can trek the River to River Trail, a 160-mile route that stretches between the two and can take weeks to complete. There are plenty of shorter hikes as well, like the 3-mile Little Grand Canyon Trail, plus swimming and fishing at Pounds Hollow Lake, and more.

### Don't Miss

Shawnee Forest's best-known attraction is Garden of the Gods, a part of the park with high sandstone cliffs, views of the hills, and striking rock formations, including Anvil Rock, Devil's Smoke Stack, and others. There's a ¼-mile hiking path you can walk along, as well as horseback riding trails.

### While You're Here

Make sure to snap a photo with the Shawnee National Forest Big Foot statue and join the hundreds of other visitors who upload photos to her Facebook page. She's located near the Garden of the Gods. 🌐 *facebook.com/ShawneeForestBigFoot*

### Best Hotel: Willowbrook Cabins

Camping is available, but for digs that are a little more luxe, the cozy Willowbrook Cabins offer amenities like Wi-Fi and laundry. 🌐 *www.willowbrookcabins.com.*

### Getting Here and Around

St. Louis Lambert International Airport (STL) is about 90 miles from the western edge of the forest, while Evansville Regional Airport (EVV) is about 60 miles from the eastern edge.

**Shawnee National Forest.** ✉ *Herod, IL* 🌐 *www.shawneeforest.com* 🎫 *Free.*

# Millennium Park

## Chicago's Iconic Bean

The crown jewel of downtown Chicago, Millennium Park is best known as the home of Anish Kapoor's sculpture Cloud Gate (aka "the Bean"), but it also offers plenty of activities year-round, from movie screenings, festivals, and concerts in the summer to ice-skating in the winter. The park, which opened in 2004 (it was built to commemorate the start of a new millennium), also features artistic installations, such as the Crown Fountain video sculpture.

## Don't Miss

The 2½-acre Lurie Garden, located at the southern end of the park, features changing flora throughout the year, including colorful bulbs in the spring and ornamental grasses in the winter.

## Best Activity

The Frank Gehry–designed Pritzker Pavilion hosts the Grant Park Music Festival, a series of evening concerts from the Grant Park Symphony Orchestra throughout the summer, and locals gather on the lawn to listen over elaborate picnics. 🌐 *www.grantparkmusicfestival.com.*

## Good to Know

For a beautiful view of the park from above, head to Cindy's at the Chicago Athletic Association; the outdoor patio space overlooks the park, giving you a bird's eye view. It's also a good spot to meet for a drink after the Grant Park Music Festival.

## Getting Here and Around

From Chicago's Midway Airport (MDW), it's 12 miles to the park; Chicago's O'Hare International Airport (ORD) is 18 miles. From the CTA, take the Red Line to Lake, Blue Line to Washington, or Pink, Green, Brown, Orange, or Purple Lines to Washington/Wabash.

**Millennium Park.** ✉ *201 E. Randolph St., Chicago, IL* 🌐 *chicago.gov* 🎟 *Free.*

# Art Institute of Chicago

### 5,000 Years of World-Class Art

You could easily spend your entire Chicago visit exploring the Art Institute's 300,000 works. The museum, which was founded in 1879, is one of the oldest and largest art museums in the United States, and features holdings that span 5,000 years, with art from Southeast Asia, ancient Greece and Rome, and the European Renaissance, with a particularly strong impressionist program. The airy adjoining Modern Wing features 20th- and 21st-century artworks. There's also an outdoor sculpture garden; food trucks frequently post up outside the park, so pick up lunch and eat among the statues.

### Don't Miss

Three of the most famous works in the collection are Grant Wood's *American Gothic*, Edward Hopper's *Nighthawks*, and Georges Seurat's *A Sunday on La Grande Jatte.*

### Best Exhibit

The Deering Family Galleries of Medieval and Renaissance Art, Arms, and Armor has an almost universal appeal. With armored knights and horses, jewelry, paintings, and treasures dating from from 1200 to 1600, there's plenty to see for kids and adults alike.

### Getting Here and Around

From Chicago's Midway Airport (MDW), it's a 12-mile drive; Chicago's O'Hare International Airport (ORD) is 18 miles. On the CTA, you can take the Red Line to Monroe or the Pink, Green, Brown, Orange, or Purple Lines to State/Lake.

**Art Institute of Chicago.** ✉ *111 S. Michigan Ave., Chicago, IL* ☎ *312/443–3600* 🌐 *www.artic.edu* 🎫 *$25.*

# Chicago's Theater Scene

## The Broadway of the Midwest

With more than 250 theaters in Chicago (including five Tony award–winning companies), you can see everything from splashy Broadway performances to indie shows at storefront theaters. The main theater district is in the Loop, where you'll find Broadway theaters like James M. Nederlander Theatre, but smaller options are scattered all across the city. The Goodman Theatre, the oldest and largest nonprofit theater, consistently stages excellent shows, while Steppenwolf Theater (which launched Nick Offerman's career) includes three stages and offers a regular series of plays geared toward young adults. For a real Chicago experience, see a show at an offbeat storefront theater, like Victory Gardens, a former movie theater in Lincoln Park.

## Don't Miss

The Neo-Futurists is a lively, inventive experimental theater group that presents a number of short plays in a short amount of time (such as *45 Plays for America's First Ladies*). ✉ *5153 N. Ashland Ave., Chicago, IL* 🌐 *neofuturists.org*.

## While You're Here

Improv and comedy are also huge parts of Chicago's cultural scene, and no one leads the way like Second City, the comedy company that launched the careers of Tina Fey, Stephen Colbert, and many others. Catch nightly shows at the Chicago Main Stage, or, sign up for a class to learn from the pros. ✉ *1616 N. Wells St., 2nd fl., Chicago, IL* 🌐 *secondcity.com*.

## Getting Here and Around

Chicago's Midway Airport (MDW) and O'Hare International Airport (ORD) are your best bet for landing you in the city. Most theaters and shows will be accessible via the CTA.

# Chicago Speakeasies

### Drink Like a Mob Boss

Chicago has a storied mob history, thanks to Al Capone and his Chicago Outfit. There are plenty of historical sites around the city with ties to the mob, but none are more fun than the speakeasies, which featured tunnels and secret entrances so patrons could enter them during Prohibition and get a drink. You can still drink in many of these speakeasies today—a local favorite is the Drifter, which is located behind a door in the basement of the Green Door Tavern. Nowadays, you don't need to hide your drinking—order an excellent cocktail from the tarot card menu, and watch a nightly performance, such as a burlesque show.

### Don't Miss

The Green Mill Lounge, located in Uptown, is an iconic jazz club that offers nightly shows. The more-than-100-year-old bar has mob ties—it was a favorite spot of Capone, who had his own booth at the bar, and there are tunnels underneath to facilitate secretive comings and goings. 🌐 *greenmilljazz.com*.

### Best Tour

The Original Chicago Prohibition Tour, an energetic 3½-hour bus tour, transports you to four different speakeasies, including Capone favorite the 226 Club (today it's the Exchequer Restaurant & Pub), and imparts knowledge about both the bars and the drinks of the era. A shorter downtown walking tour is also available, as is a group cocktail-making class. 🌐 *www.prohibitiontours.com* 🎫 *$55*.

### Getting Here and Around

Chicago's Midway Airport (MDW) and O'Hare International Airport (ORD) will land you in the city; from there, most places are accessible by CTA trains and buses.

## When in Illinois

### BAHÁ'Í HOUSE OF WORSHIP

The oldest surviving Bahá'í temple, this striking, towering white structure opened in 1953. Designed to serve North America, the temple offers space for quiet prayer and reflection. The Bahá'í faith teaches the unity of all people, and the structure's design emphasizes the Bahá'í conception of oneness. Located just north of Chicago, it's an easy, safe ride out of the city along bike paths and makes for an excellent photo op.

**Do This:** Visit the nine gardens that surround the temple. The gardens feature plants and foliage in a variety of colors and scents to help further the idea of unity. The gardens include both Eastern and Western design influences, such as fountains and reflecting pools.

**Bahá'í House of Worship.** ✉ *100 Linden Ave., Wilmette, IL* ☎ *847/853–2300* 🌐 *www.bahai.us/bahai-temple.*

### CALUMET FISHERIES

Smoked fish was popular in Chicago in the mid-20th century, and although many of the smokehouses have since closed, you can still find some excellent ones. Calumet Fisheries, which was founded in 1948, was named a James Beard Foundation's America's Classic recipient in 2010. Located along the Calumet River next to the 95th Street bridge, the fishery smokes seafood over oak wood on-site.

**Do This:** The restaurant is take-out only, so spread out a picnic on your trunk. The smoked shrimp and pepper and garlic salmon are the restaurant's specialties, but you won't go wrong with anything.

**Calumet Fisheries.** ✉ *3259 E. 95th St., Chicago, IL* ☎ *773/933–9855* 🌐 *calumet-fisheries.com.*

### GALENA COUNTRY

Galena Country comprises 11 different towns, from the historic city of Galena, which features a downtown composed of 19th-century architecture to Hanover, where you'll find several wineries. The area is also a draw for shopping and antiquing, hiking or biking the 8-mile Galena River Trail, and exploring nature at the Valley of Eden Bird Sanctuary, a 400-acre preserve. In the winter, it's a destination for Midwestern skiing—stay at the Chestnut Mountain Resort, which features slopes for skiers of all levels.

**Do This:** Ulysses S. Grant, the 18th president and Civil War general, moved to Galena before the war, and you can visit his Italianate-style home. The U.S. Grant Home State Historic Site features original furnishings; the house has been restored to look as it did in 1868.

**Galena Country.** ✉ *123 N. Commerce St., Galena, IL* ☎ *815/776–9200* 🌐 *www.visitgalena.org.*

## Cool Places to Stay

**Chicago Athletic Association.** This chic hotel, located right across the street from Chicago's Millennium Park, is as much a draw for tourists as locals, thanks to delicious food and beverage offerings. Located in an old athletic association building, the hotel has a vintage sports vibe, from the pommel horses in guest rooms to a sprawling Game Room bar with bocce, billiards, and shuffleboard. ✉ *12 S. Michigan Ave., Chicago, IL* ☎ *312/940–3552* 🌐 *www.chicagoathletichotel.com* [$] *From $135.*

**The Has Bin Guest House.** Who can say they've slept in a recycled grain bin? You can if you stay at this bed-and-breakfast. It's located on a working farm, so your choice of sweet or savory breakfast delivery will be fresh and local. ✉ *2 Chicago St., Alvin, IL* ☎ *217/304–0108* 🌐 *www.thehasbinguesthouse.com* [$] *From $100.*

# Indiana

With its feet firmly planted in the heartland, Indiana is like one big small town, where locals take pride in their "Hoosier hospitality." The state is a healthy mix of rural and urban. Indianapolis, the state's largest city, features big-city culture like an opera and symphony orchestra, yet still retains charm and character. Stop and ask for directions and chances are you'll also receive a tip on where to have dinner that night.

## Bucket List Picks

The following boxes contain our picks for the top sights and experiences in Indiana.

- ○ Indiana Dunes National Park
- ○ Indianapolis Motor Speedway
- ○ Indianapolis Cultural Trail
- ○ The Children's Museum of Indianapolis
- ○ Parke County Covered Bridges
- ○ Butler Bulldogs
- ○ South Bend
- ○ Boating in Indiana

# Indiana Dunes National Park

## Towering Sand Dunes

Stretching 15 miles along Lake Michigan in northern Indiana, the Indiana Dunes may be best known as a pretty beach escape from Chicago, but the dune-filled national park (one of the newest in the country) offers plenty of chances to get active as well. There are more than 50 miles of hiking trails over rugged dunes, including the Cowles Bog Trail, which takes you along wetlands. Bring your binoculars—there are notable bird-watching opportunities; you can spot more than 350 species, including sandhill cranes that migrate here in fall. Make sure to catch the sunset over Lake Michigan—you'll get to see the Chicago skyline set against the orange-hued sky.

## Don't Miss

To get your heart racing, the Three Dune Challenge is a 1.5-mile-long trail that loops you around to the three tallest dunes in the state park. Those three—Mt. Tom, Mt. Holden, and Mt. Jackson—are the equivalent of climbing 552 vertical feet (or 55 stories), so it's not a stroll for the fainthearted.

## When to Go

Summer is the best time to visit, when you can take advantage of all the trails and beaches. In winter, you can cross-country ski, snowshoe, and look for animal tracks in the snow.

## Getting Here and Around

From Chicago's Midway Airport (MDW), it's a 50-mile drive to the park, while Chicago's O'Hare International Airport (ORD) is 70 miles. From Indianapolis International Airport (IND), it's about 170 miles to the park.

**Indiana Dunes National Park.** ✉ *1050 N. Mineral Springs Rd., Chesterton, IN* ☎ *219/395–1882* 🌐 *www.nps.gov/indu* 🎟 *From $6.*

# Indianapolis Motor Speedway

## The Greatest Spectacle in Racing

The Indianapolis Motor Speedway is the venue for the Indianapolis 500, the famous race where 33 drivers zip 500 miles (200 laps) around the track, so it's a must for racing fans. But the 500 isn't the only time to soak up the excitement of the race and learn about its history. Visit the grounds for free on non-event days, or head to the museum ($12 admission) and take a tour of the grounds. You can also catch other races and practices, including for the 500, on the track.

## Don't Miss

The Indianapolis Motor Speedway Museum's collection includes more than 300 vehicles, including vintage race cars, along with a Hall of Fame.

## Best Tour: "Kiss the Bricks" Tour

The most popular tour, "Kiss the Bricks" is a 30-minute narrated bus trip through the property, including a lap around the race track and a visit to the Yard of Bricks, the start and finish line of the Indy 500 race (winners typically bend down to "kiss the bricks," hence the name). 🌐 *indyracing-museum.org* 🎫 *$22*

## When to Go

The Indianapolis 500 is held annually on Memorial Day weekend, making it the most exciting time to visit (but also the busiest, so be sure to book tickets in advance). The museum and grounds are open year-round.

## Getting Here and Around

Indianapolis International Airport (IND) is located 12 miles from the race track.

**Indianapolis Motor Speedway.** ✉ *4790 W. 16th St., Indianapolis, IN* ☎ *317/492–8500* 🌐 *www.indianapolis-motorspeedway.com* 🎫 *From $15.*

# Indianapolis Cultural Trail

### Miles of Midwest Treasures

The Indianapolis Cultural Trail is an 8-mile path that connects all six of the city's cultural districts, which means you can see many of Indy's highlights in a single afternoon. Walk or bike along the path, which stretches from White River State Park to the Fountain Square neighborhood and covers many downtown attractions. The path will take you past the Soldiers' and Sailors' Monument, NCAA Hall of Champions, and the Eiteljorg Museum of American Indians and Western Art, and also includes nine commissioned art installations.

### Don't Miss

Fountain Square is a neighborhood packed with great places to eat and drink, including Bluebeard, a small-plates restaurant, and sister spot Amelia's Bread for pastries.

### Best Tour

Active Indy Tours offers walking, biking, and running tours of the city. Book the bike tour, and you'll see the highlights of the Cultural Trail along with some of the city's historic neighborhoods, like the cobblestone streets of Lockerbie Square, all at a casual pace. 🌐 *activeindytours.com.*

### Good to Know

Many downtown hotels, such as the Conrad, offer complimentary cruisers and 10-speed bikes, or you can rent Indiana Pacers Bikeshare wheels at more than 50 stations around the city. 🌐 *indyculturaltrail.org/bikeshare.*

### Getting Here and Around

Indianapolis International Airport (IND) is located 12 miles from White River State Park, where you can rent a Pacers bike and pick up the trail.

**Indianapolis Cultural Trail Office.** ✉ *132 W. Walnut St., Indianapolis, IN* 🌐 *indyculturaltrail.org.*

# The Children's Museum of Indianapolis

### The World's Largest Kid's Museum

The Children's Museum of Indianapolis is more than just a museum. It's an action-packed education center with five floors of exhibits and galleries, plus a planetarium, a theater with live shows, and room for outdoor sports activities. There's truly something for every kid, whether they're interested in dinosaurs (you'll spot some on the facade of the building and can visit the Dinosphere, complete with skeletons and an archaeological dig), pop culture, sports, puzzles, or travel (on Earth or in space). The museum's playscape is ideal for younger kids; it includes a padded climbing area and a water table.

### Don't Miss

The Power of Children exhibit teaches kids about the lives of Anne Frank, Ruby Bridges, and Ryan White, and the contributions they made to the world through replica rooms and theatrical performances.

### Best Exhibit

*Beyond Spaceship Earth* gives kids a chance to learn about the history of space exploration, see astronaut artifacts, try on space-walk costumes, and sit in a Soyuz spacecraft. There's also the Indiana Astronaut Wall of Fame, which honors state residents who have made notable contributions of astronomy.

### Getting Here and Around

Indianapolis International Airport (IND) is located 22 miles from the museum.

**The Children's Museum of Indianapolis.** ✉ *3000 N. Meridian St., Indianapolis, IN* ☎ *317/334–4000* 🌐 *childrensmuseum.org* 🎟 *From $16.*

# Parke County Covered Bridges

## The Covered Bridge Capital of the World

Indiana is proud of its charming covered bridges, and they're more than just a photo op—they bring the community together for festivities like the state's largest festival, the Covered Bridge Festival. Parke County, located in western Indiana, is home to the state's most covered bridges (31 to be exact) that were built from 1856 to 2006. Some bridges are drive-through, while others are walk-through; download a map of the bridges on the county website to help plan your route. Biking and motorcycling are also popular ways to see the bridges.

## Don't Miss

The Jackson Covered Bridge, built in 1861, is the longest single-span covered bridge in Indiana.

## Best Restaurant

Mecca Tavern, in Mecca, IN, has been serving bar fare since 1899 (it's the oldest bar in the county). Offerings include burgers and steak sandwiches, but you're going for the pork tenderloin sandwich, which is hand-pounded to order.

## When to Go

The annual Covered Bridge Festival, held over 10 days in October, is the largest festival in the state. Nine communities in the county come together to offer arts and crafts vendors, plant sales, pig roasts, and more, all amid fall foliage.

## Getting Here and Around

Indianapolis International Airport (IND) is about 50 miles from Parke County; University of Illinois-Willard Airport (CMI), which is 75 miles from the county, has shuttle flights from Chicago, Dallas-Fort Worth, and Charlotte.

**Parke County Covered Bridges.** 🌐 *www.coveredbridges.com.*

# Butler Bulldogs

## Slam Dunk for Basketball Fans

Basketball is a way of life in Indiana, and Butler University's Hinkle Fieldhouse is one the oldest college arenas still in use. The brick fieldhouse, designed by Indianapolis architect Fermor Spencer Cannon, was built in 1928 and its design inspired gymnasiums for decades. Named for longtime coach Tony Hinkle, the 9,100-seat arena has played host to the championship game in the movie *Hoosiers* as well as Butler University's basketball and volleyball games and is a National Historic Landmark. Seeing the crammed fieldhouse during a game is the best time to visit, but the building is also open during the week and on weekends for free, self-guided tours.

## Don't Miss

The Bulldogs' English bulldog mascot, Butler Blue IV, attends each men's basketball game.

## Best Restaurant

Head to nearby Chatham Tap before or after a game. The British-inspired pub is an easygoing spot to grab a pint of beer or fish-and-chips. ✉ *4702 Sunset Ave., Indianapolis, IN* 🌐 *chathamtap.com/butler-university.*

## When to Go

The Bulldogs' women's volleyball season runs August to November, while the men's and women's basketball season runs November to March. Tickets are available for all sports at 🌐 *butlersports.com.*

## Getting Here and Around

Indianapolis International Airport (IND) is 20 miles from the fieldhouse. You can find parking a few blocks away, or take the IndyGo bus from downtown.

**Hinkle Fieldhouse.** ✉ *510 W. 49th St., Indianapolis, IN* ☎ *305/242–7700* 🌐 *butlersports.com.*

# South Bend

## Touchdown Jesus and an Epic Ice Trail

Best known as the home of the University of Notre Dame, South Bend is a city of 100,000 people that offers plenty of ways to get active. Start by taking a free tour of the Notre Dame campus, where you'll see the Grotto, Basilica of the Sacred Heart, the Golden Dome, and the "Touchdown Jesus" statue. Besides touring the university, you can visit the red pandas at the Potawatomi Zoo and see the vintage cars at the Studebaker National Museum. Save time for wandering downtown, where you can dine at favorite local restaurants like fine-dining spot Café Navarre and modern Southern restaurant Fatbird.

## Don't Miss

The Ice Trail at Howard Park, a unique 16,000-square-foot ice-skating loop, draws winter revelers to its gentle hills and curves. Its smaller side pond is a good spot to practice. There are free drop-in skating classes on Monday evenings, a DJ plays on Friday nights from 8–10 on the trail, and you can also sign up to play broomball (for the uninitiated, that's like hockey but with brooms and balls, and without skates). *visithowardpark.com/ice-skating* *From $7.*

## Good to Know

The South Bend Cubs, a minor league team for the Chicago Cubs, play at Four Winds Field. Grab a hot dog and cheer on the team throughout the summer months.

## Getting Here and Around

South Bend International Airport (SBN) offers flights from 13 cities, including Chicago, Las Vegas, and Detroit.

**South Bend.** *visitsouthbend.com*

# Boating in Indiana

## Lakes for Days

Indiana has 100,000 acres of public lakes (not counting the Great Lakes shoreline in Indiana Dunes National Park), which makes boating a top Indiana summertime activity. Among the many lakes worth seeking out are Patoka Lake, the second largest in the state, which has 10 launch ramps along with notable fishing and migratory bird-watching opportunities (including bald eagles!), as well as Indianapolis's Geist Reservoir, where you can rent pontoon boats at the marina for the day or evening.

## Don't Miss

Clear Lake, so named for its crystal clear waters, is an 800-acre lake that was formed by a glacier. Rent a rowboat and peer down at turtles and other wildlife in the lake.

## Best Lake for Boating

Monroe Lake, built in 1965 in Bloomington, is the state's largest inland lake. Bring your own boat, or there are plenty of options to rent one there (including Lake Monroe Boat Rental, which you can book online) like a pontoon or double-decker boat for a group, a fishing boat if you're hoping to catch dinner, or a canoe or kayak for a leisurely option that allows for bird-watching and soaking up nature.

## Good to Know

If you bring your own boat to a state park, you'll need a permit to put it on the water. Yearly permits are $25 for motorized boats and $5 for nonmotorized vehicles. See which lakes require permits and learn where to get them at 🌐 *www.in.gov/dnr*.

## Getting Here and Around

Indianapolis International Airport (IND) is a good central location; it's located 58 miles from Monroe Lake and just over 110 miles from Patoka Lake.

## When in Indiana

### EITELJORG MUSEUM OF AMERICAN INDIANS AND WESTERN ART

The downtown Indianapolis museum is one of only two museums east of the Mississippi to focus on art from both the American West and the Indigenous peoples of North America. It's also one of the best for its cultural programs and presentation of the continent's complex history. The Western holdings, which range from from the 1820s to the present, include paintings of landscapes by Georgia O'Keeffe and cowboys by Frederic Remington, while the Native American collection includes clothing, jewelry, carvings, and more. There's also a substantial collection of contemporary Native art. Tours of the collection are free with museum admission (but must be booked three weeks in advance), and private tours can also be arranged for groups.

**Do This:** The museum's annual fine-art market and cultural festival (held each June on the weekend following Father's Day) brings together more than 100 Native artists from across the country who work in disciplines such as painting, pottery, and weaving. It also includes Native American music and dance performances.

**Eiteljorg Museum.** ✉ *500 W. Washington St., Indianapolis, IN* ☎ *317/636–9378* 🌐 *eiteljorg.org* 🎫 *$15.*

### ST. ELMO'S STEAKHOUSE

This downtown Indianapolis restaurant has been serving classic steak-house fare since 1902, but nothing about the experience feels dated. Grab a seat at the bar and order a shrimp cocktail, which comes with a cocktail sauce absolutely loaded with sinus-clearing horseradish, and an Elmo Cola, cherry-vanilla-infused bourbon served alongside a glass bottle of Coke. Move on to a full steak dinner with all the classics in the retro wood-paneled dining room.

**Do This:** If you like the cocktail sauce, take home a bottle. St. Elmo's also offers a line of bottled sauces and seasonings, including steak house seasoning, creamy horseradish (to serve alongside steak or on roast beef sandwiches), root beer glaze (they use it on thick-cut bacon at the restaurant), and truffle dijonaise dipping sauce.

**St. Elmo's Steakhouse.** ✉ *127 Illinois St., Indianapolis, IN* ☎ *317/635–0636* 🌐 *www.stelmos.com.*

## Cool Places to Stay

**The Alexander Hotel.** With rain showers, mini refrigerators, and extended-stay suites, the Alexander is a luxe spot to stay in downtown Indy. The design is sleek and artsy, with a coffee and cocktail bar that offers views of the skyline (and a rooftop deck) and an Italian restaurant, all walking distance from top destinations, including the Colts' Lucas Oil Stadium. ✉ *333 S. Delaware St., Indianapolis, IN* ☎ *317/624–8200* 🌐 *thealexander.com* [$] *From $180.*

**Graduate Hotel Bloomington.** The Indiana University–themed hotel isn't just a draw for returning alumni—the cute, cozy lodging is located close to campus and other downtown spots, like Cardinal Spirits. The pet-friendly rooms are decked out in plaid and include work stations and references to IU's Little 500 (a notable bike race). ✉ *210 E. Kirkwood Ave., Bloomington, IN* ☎ *812/994–0500* 🌐 *graduatehotels.com/bloomington* [$] *From $95.*

# Michigan

Flanked by four Great Lakes and with 2,000 miles of shoreline (even more than California), Michigan is divided into two peninsulas—the Lower, which resembles a mitten and is the more densely populated, and the Upper, which is more rugged and rural. The state is graced with dramatic topography, including waterfalls in the Upper Peninsula and towering dunes near Lake Michigan. Growing wine-country regions exist near Traverse City and Grand Rapids. Lovely resort towns, from Traverse City to Saugatuck, overflow with lakeside inns and boutiques. Yet Michigan has its share of big cities, too, including Detroit.

## Bucket List Picks

The following boxes contain our picks for the top sights and experiences in Michigan.

- ○ Mackinac Island
- ○ Detroit's Cultural Center
- ○ Holland
- ○ The Belt
- ○ Belle Isle
- ○ Ann Arbor
- ○ Sleeping Bear Dunes National Lakeshore
- ○ Motor City
- ○ Michigan's Wineries
- ○ Pictured Rocks National Lakeshore
- ○ Isle Royale National Park

# Mackinac Island

### Explore a Car-Free Island

Mackinac Island, located in Lake Huron in northern Michigan, is a classic Midwest summertime destination. Cars aren't allowed, so the island has a leisurely pace. Spend your days biking around the island, riding horses, or exploring Mackinac Island State Park. With striking limestone bluffs and Arch Rock (a natural rock bridge), the park is a beautiful spot to hit the beach, or go hiking, kayaking, or sailing.

### Don't Miss

Mackinac is known for fudge—13 shops on the island make 5 tons a day during high season from May to October, and there's even a Fudge Festival in August.

### Best Attraction

Fort Mackinac, an American and British fort located in Mackinac Island State Park, was founded in 1780, and control passed back and forth between the two countries until after the War of 1812. In operation until the late 19th century, the fort has been restored to its appearance from that era. 🌐 *www.mackinacparks.com* 🎫 *$13.50.*

### When to Go

While you can visit year-round, winter is more challenging as ferries can't travel through frozen waters and many restaurants and hotels close for the season. There are year-round air taxis starting at $35 through Mackinac County Airport in St. Ignace.

### Getting Here and Around

You'll need to take a ferry over to the island; the ride takes about 18 miles from either Mackinaw City (the closest airport is Pellston Regional Airport [PLN], 15 miles to the south), or St. Ignace (the closest airport is Chippewa County International Airport [CIU], 35 miles to the north). Get around the island by walking, biking, or taking a horse-drawn carriage.

# Detroit's Cultural Center

## Heart and Soul of the City

Detroit has a vibrant arts and culture scene, and many of the city's museums are clustered in the Cultural Center District, including the Charles H. Wright Museum of African American History, Michigan Science Center (a kid-friendly museum and planetarium), Detroit Institute of Arts (a standout art museum with 65,000 works), the Detroit Historical Museum, and the Museum of Contemporary Art. The Motown Museum (two houses devoted to telling the history of the famous record label) is just a couple of miles away.

## Don't Miss

*And Still We Rise: Our Journey Through African American History and Culture*, a long-term exhibit at the Wright Museum, powerfully traces the African American experience.

## Best Tour

You'll need to sign up for a tour to visit the Motown Museum, aka Hitsville U.S.A., which you can do in advance of your visit. On the lively, music-filled tour of the houses that formed Berry Gordy's original Motown offices and studio, you'll see costumes and photos, and visit Studio A, where artists like Marvin Gaye and the Supremes recorded music from 1959 to 1972. *motownmuseum.org* *$15.*

## Good to Know

Sign up for the free D Discount Pass and you'll save 20% on many of the museums and attractions in the city, including the Motown Museum, Wright Museum, and Science Center. *visitdetroit.com/discount.*

## Getting Here and Around

From Detroit Metropolitan Wayne County Airport (DTW), it's 20 miles to the Charles H. Wright Museum. Most of the museums are within walking distance of each other, or a quick cab ride away.

# Holland

## Tulip City USA

Rows of radiant blooms and a traditional Dutch windmill in Holland, Michigan, could have anyone believing they're actually in the Netherlands. The aptly named town, which is set along Lake Michigan, was founded by Dutch immigrants in the mid-19th century, and its distinctive Dutch feel is still undeniable. Numerous attractions explore the city's Dutch heritage, from the Holland Museum, which focuses on its history, to De Zwaan, an 18th-century windmill (the only functioning Dutch windmill in the United States) that was brought over from the Netherlands in 1964. It's set in Windmill Island Gardens, a 36-acre park near downtown Holland.

## Don't Miss

The colorful Veldheer Tulip Garden has more than 6 million tulips and 800 different varieties. It comes alive in the spring, especially during Tulip Time.

## Best Activity

Nelis' Dutch Village is one part history, one part kids' theme park. The Dutch Village is based on life in the Netherlands over 150 years ago and features cheese-making demos, wooden shoe–carving demos, hands-on *stroopwafel* making, and more. The theme park includes a carousel, a windmill-inspired Ferris wheel, and a petting zoo. *www.dutchvillage.com* *$14.*

## When to Go

Tulip Time, the annual celebration of all things tulip, starts the first Saturday in May and runs for eight days.

## Getting Here and Around

Holland is a 35-mile drive from Grand Rapids' Gerald R. Ford International Airport (GRR).

**Holland.** *www.holland.org*

# The Belt

## America's Coolest Alley

A downtown alley tucked between two parking garages in Detroit's former garment district has transformed into one of the most exciting art and cocktail scenes in the United States. It's decked out with vibrant murals and rotating large-scale paintings from local, national, and international artists (like Jammie Holmes from Texas and Cleon Holmes from L.A.) as well as lively restaurants and bars, shopping, and nightclubs that invite you to linger. The public art is curated by Library Street Collective, which also has a permanent gallery space in the alley. There are contemporary art galleries, such as Louis Buhl & Co., while events, such as Alley Flea, a flea market organized by the Skip, are also held there. The alley is adjacent to the Z, a 10-story parking garage that features 27 murals.

## Don't Miss

The Skip is an open-air, tropical-inspired cocktail bar that serves bar snacks like Wagyu beef hot dogs and collard grilled cheese, frozen slushies, and other cocktails. Grab a seat at the picnic tables in the alleyway, or sit at the bar. 🌐 *www.theskipdetroit.com.*

## Best Restaurant

Standby, the sister restaurant to the Skip, is a sleek spot that focuses on American and comfort food dishes, like double cheeseburgers and Sichuan fried chicken and waffles, served alongside excellent cocktails. 🌐 *www.standbydetroit.com*

## Getting Here and Around

From Detroit Metropolitan Wayne County Airport (DTW), it's about 20 miles to the Belt. Detroit Amtrak Station is about 3 miles away; you can take a QLine streetcar from the station to the Belt.

# Belle Isle

## Cutest Urban Picnic Spot

An island located in the middle of the Detroit River, Belle Isle is a 987-acre state park that's both larger and older than New York's Central Park (though both were at least partially designed by the landscape architect Frederick Law Olmsted). The island's woodsy spaces are ideal for picnicking away from the hustle and bustle of the city, but the park also includes top-notch attractions such as the Belle Isle Aquarium, Dossin Great Lakes Museum, a half mile of beachfront, and wooded walking trails. The Anna Scripps Whitcomb Conservatory is a notable spot for plant lovers; it features an outdoor lily pond, tropical house, cactus house, and more.

## Don't Miss

From Belle Isle, you'll have great views of the Detroit and Windsor, Ontario, skylines. It's also an excellent spot to see the Detroit fireworks on the Fourth of July.

## Best Attraction

With an extensive collection of air-breathing fish (one of the largest in the world), Belle Isle Aquarium is housed in a Beaux Art–style building that dates back to 1904 (it was the third-largest aquarium in the world when it opened). The aquarium closed in 2005, but reopened in 2012; the collection now includes species from all over the world, as well as the Great Lakes. *www.belleisleconservancy.org* *Free.*

## Getting Here and Around

From Detroit Metropolitan Wayne County Airport (DTW), Belle Isle is a 25-mile drive. You can get there by walking or biking across MacArthur Bridge, which is less than half a mile. You can also take the No. 12 Conant bus, which stops in front of the aquarium.

**Belle Isle Park.** *www.belleisleconservancy.org* *$12 per car (good for the year); free for walkers and cyclists.*

# Ann Arbor

## The Quintessential College Town

Best known as the home of the University of Michigan, Ann Arbor is a classic college town, filled with museums, art galleries, shopping, great restaurants, and a favorite football team that plays in the largest stadium in the country. The best time to visit is the fall, when you can catch a game and see peak foliage, but there's plenty to do year-round. The Ark, a music venue that's been operating since 1965, is always a draw; in summer, go floating down the Argo Cascades. The food scene is led by restaurants like Cuban street-food spot Frita Batidos, legendary sandwich shop Zingerman's Deli, and quirky Krazy Jim's Blimpy Burger.

## Don't Miss

The University of Michigan Museum of Art is a must-see free museum with cutting-edge exhibitions and a collection that includes African, Asian, and contemporary art.

## Best Tour: Michigan Stadium Tour

Michigan Stadium, aka "the Big House," is the home turf for the University of Michigan's Wolverines football team. Sixty- to ninety-minute tours take you onto the field and through the locker room and press box. 🌐 *umich.edu* 🎫 *$20.*

## Good to Know

You're never too far from a great pint in Ann Arbor; top local breweries include Arbor Brewing Company, Grizzly Peak, Blue Tractor, and Jolly Pumpkin. The latter three are located downtown within walking distance.

## Getting Here and Around

From Detroit Metropolitan Wayne County Airport (DTW), Ann Arbor is a 25-mile drive. There's an Amtrak station located at 325 Depot Street, and a Greyhound station at 115 E. William Street.

# Sleeping Bear Dunes National Lakeshore

## Dunes You Can See From Space

Located in northwest Michigan along 65 miles of Lake Michigan, Sleeping Bear Dunes National Lakeshore is part of the largest freshwater dune system in the world—so large they're visible from space. The expansive, awe-inspiring lakeshore park is known for its stretches of sandy beaches and bluffs that rise 450 feet, along with 100 miles of hiking trails, canoeing and kayaking opportunities (including 21 lakes within the park boundaries), and the Sleeping Bear Heritage Trail, a 27-mile paved bike path.

## Don't Miss

A chain of islands off the coast of the dunes, Manitou Islands' two main islands are North and South Manitou Island, which you can reach by ferry. With old-growth cedar forests and small villages, the islands are ideal for hiking and camping.

## Best Base

If you aren't camping at the park, you may want to stay in Traverse City to soak up its culture scene (it hosts a major summer film festival) and have some memorable meals and drinks. Sample suds from the strong craft-beer community, and stop by The Cooks' House for a local, sustainable menu, or Grand Traverse Pie Company for an epic slice of Grand Traverse cherry crumb pie.

## Getting Here and Around

Sleeping Bear Dunes is 30 miles from Traverse City's Cherry Capital Airport (TVC). To reach the Manitou Islands, you'll need to take a ferry from Leland. The ferry is offered seasonally and can be booked through Manitou Island Transit. 🌐 *manitoutransit.com.*

**Sleeping Bear Dunes National Lakeshore.** ✉ *9922 Front St., Empire, MI* 🌐 *www.nps.gov/slbe* 🎟 *$25.*

# Motor City

### America Runs on Detroit

The Detroit area is home to the "Big Three" automakers (Ford, General Motors, and Chrysler)—and the city itself is nicknamed the "Motor City"—which means there's no better place to visit to understand the history of automotives, as well as its present and future. You can spend several days visiting all the attractions, including Fair Lane, Home of Clara and Henry Ford; GM World, with displays of the latest GM vehicles at the GM Renaissance Center; the Ford Piquette Plant, the birthplace of the Model T; and the world's first concrete mile on Woodward Avenue, which was built in 1909.

### Don't Miss

The Automotive Hall of Fame traces the history of cars and motorcycles, from their debut to today, and how that's allowed for personal exploration and travel. On view are permanent and changing exhibits as well as vintage cars and memorabilia. ⊕ *www.automotivehalloffame.org* 🎫 *$10.*

### Best Tour

The Ford Rouge Factory Tour gives you an overview of Ford in the Henry Ford Museum of American Innovation, including a look at some vintage autos (like the 1929 Model A), several films, and, the highlight, a walking tour along an elevated walkway at the Dearborn Truck Plant, where you'll get to see a Ford F-150 truck being assembled. ⊕ *www.thehenryford.org* 🎫 *$19.*

### Getting Here and Around

Flying into Detroit Metropolitan Wayne County Airport (DTW) will land you in Detroit; from there, all locations are a quick drive or cab away from each other.

# Michigan's Wineries

### The Country's Best (and Only) Ice Wine

Michigan has more than 13,000 acres of vineyards, 140 wineries, and 30 varieties of wine grapes grown. The state holds annual wine festivals and offers trails that group wineries into easy-to-travel routes. For instance, the Leelanau Peninsula Wine Trail features 24 wineries clustered around Traverse City. Michigan has five different appellations, Fennville and Lake Michigan Shore in the southern half of the state, and the Leelanau and Old Mission Peninsulas and Tip of the Mitt, located in the northern half. That the state's wine is so good is thanks to Lake Michigan: it helps warm the air, which protects grapes during spring and fall, and also helps insulate the grapevines.

### Don't Miss

Ice wine is only made in a few places in the world; Michigan is one. Try the sweet dessert wine from producers like Fenn Valley Vineyards, paired with cheese.

### Best Tour: Fruitful Vine Tours

This southwest Michigan tour operator offers tours through the region, which include visits to three wineries, tasting fees, and lunch as well as a wine-expert tour guide. *fruitfulvinetours.com* *From $139.*

### Getting Here and Around

If you're looking to visit wineries in the Fennville or Lake Michigan Shore areas, fly into Grand Rapids' Gerald R. Ford International Airport (GRR). If you're planning to visit wineries in the northern part of the state, fly into Traverse City's Cherry Capital Airport (TVC).

**Michigan Wineries.** *www.michigan.org/wineries*

# Pictured Rocks National Lakeshore

## Colorful Cliffs

Located on Lake Superior in the Upper Peninsula, Pictured Rocks National Lakeshore, the country's first national lakeshore, is an all-season destination for nature lovers. Named for the brightly colored sandstone cliffs (the colors are due to minerals in the rocks), the park also offers 100 miles of hiking trails, waterfalls, and the Au Sable Light Station, a working 19th-century lighthouse that you can tour and climb up for a view of Lake Superior, forests, and the Grand Sable Dunes.

## Don't Miss

The striking Munising Falls features a 50-foot drop over a sandstone cliff and is accessible via a paved walking trail. In winter, the falls transform into stunning ice formations.

## Best Tour

The best way to see the rocks is by boat, and from May through October, Pictured Rocks Cruises offers daily 2½- to 3-hour tours that take you along the cliffs. On the classic cruise, you'll see sights like the rock arch Lover's Leap and rock formation Miner's Castle, while tours that add on the Spray Falls waterfall at sunset are also available. 🌐 *picturedrocks.com* 🎫 *From $40.*

## When to Go

Summer is the best time to take advantage of the beaches and activities like kayaking and camping, but in winter you can go ice climbing at Sand Point, where the ice columns are 20 to 50 feet high.

## Getting Here and Around

The closest airport is Sawyer International Airport (SAW), which has daily flights from Detroit. You'll need to rent a car; from the airport, it's about 45 miles to the entrance to the park.

**Pictured Rocks National Lakeshore.** 🌐 *www.nps.gov/piro* 🎫 *Free.*

# Isle Royale National Park

## Explore Remote Wilderness

Accessible only by seaplane or boat, the secluded Isle Royale National Park consists of a main island, Isle Royale, and hundreds of smaller islands where solitude is king. The park, located in Lake Superior near mainland Michigan, Minnesota, and Ontario, Canada, has a rich population of wildlife (moose and wolves are in abundance), and offers activities like kayaking, hiking, boat tours, and camping (there are 36 campgrounds on the main island). Or, go scuba diving and see shipwrecks; there are 10 registered in the national park, which date back to the 19th century.

## Don't Miss

Rock Harbor Lighthouse, which was built in 1855, is inactive, but you can tour it, see the view from the top, and learn about the park and its shipwrecks at a small museum.

## Best Hotel

Rock Harbor Lodge offers a few different types of rooms, a main lodge, cottages with kitchenettes, and cabins without indoor plumbing. The hotel also books fishing charters and water taxis. *rockharborlodge.com.*

## When to Go

The park is open April 16 through October 31, and closed the remainder of the year. Mosquitoes and black flies are worst in late June and early July.

## Getting Here and Around

Reach Isle Royale through either Michigan or Minnesota. Ferries, seaplanes, or private boats are available. You can't bring your car (or any vehicle, including bikes) to Isle Royale, so plan to get around by hiking, canoe, or kayak.

**Isle Royale National Park.** *www.nps.gov/isro* *$7 per day.*

# When in Michigan

## CHICKEN DINNER IN FRANKENMUTH

Family-style chicken dinners are an iconic meal in Frankenmuth, a town located in the eastern part of the state that has a long German heritage and Bavarian-style architecture. There are two spots for this meal, which features fried chicken, mashed potatoes with gravy, buttered egg noodles, bread stuffing, bread, and a choice of ice cream (vanilla, chocolate, orange, or orange swirl).

**Do This:** Zehnder's of Frankenmuth, which was named a James Beard American Classic in 2020, and Bavarian Inn Restaurant are the spots to go. They're located across the street from each other, and though both meals are similar, they feature little twists (a reason to try both!).

**Zehnder's of Frankenmuth.** ✉ *730 S. Main St., Frankenmuth, MI* ☎ *844/802–8323* 🌐 *zehnders.com* **Bavarian Inn Restaurant.** ✉ *713 S. Main St., Frankenmuth, MI* ☎ *989/652–9941* 🌐 *bavarianinn.com.*

## DETROIT EASTERN MARKET

This large 19th-century market (it was founded in 1841) is a one-stop shop for picking up fresh ingredients, prepared foods, and more. The main market is held year-round on Saturdays and features more than 225 vendors, food trucks, and more. Two other markets are held June to September. The Sunday market includes local artists and musicians, and the smaller Tuesday market includes yoga and Zumba classes.

**Do This:** Wander the market, then stop by one of the many nearby restaurants for lunch. Bert's Marketplace is all about the soul food (dishes include the Aretha Franklin World Famous Fried Chicken), Supino Pizzeria for a quick slice, or Zeff's Coney Island for breakfast anytime (and Coney dogs, of course).

**Eastern Market.** ✉ *1445 Adelaide St., Detroit, MI* ☎ *313/833–9300* 🌐 *easternmarket.org.*

## GRAND RAPIDS FREDERIK MEIJER GARDENS & SCULPTURE PARK

Founded in 1995, this park is a draw for both art and garden lovers. The park includes numerous gardens, including a Japanese garden, farm garden, and annual butterfly garden, as well as nature trails to wander. There are about 300 sculptural works on display throughout the indoor and outdoor gardens, including art from Auguste Rodin, Edgar Degas, Alexander Calder, Louise Bourgeois, and Ai Weiwei.

**Do This:** Spend time exploring at the Lena Meijer Tropical Conservatory, which is the largest tropical conservatory in Michigan. It features 500 species from five continents, and includes an orchid wall, cacao and breadfruit trees, and birds, such as the turquoise tanager.

**Frederik Meijer Gardens & Sculpture Park.** ✉ *1000 E. Beltline Ave. NE, Grand Rapids, Michigan* ☎ *616/957–1580* 🌐 *meijergardens.org.*

## GREAT LAKES SHIPWRECK MUSEUM

Lake Superior has more than 500 shipwrecks, with about 200 along Lake Superior's Shipwreck Coast, an 80-mile stretch of shoreline along the Upper Peninsula. A museum dedicated to these wrecks is located at the tip of Whitefish Point, which is near where the wreck of the *Edmund Fitzgerald,* a freighter that sank in 1975, lies. The museum covers this tragedy and others through exhibits and artifacts, such as the *Edmund Fitzgerald*'s bell.

**Do This:** Take a tour of the 1861 light-keepers quarters, which are part of the Whitefish Point Light Tower, the oldest operating lighthouse on Lake Superior. The home features period furnishings, exhibits, and artifacts from the families who kept the lighthouse working and those who rescued ships.

**Great Lakes Shipwreck Museum.** ✉ *18335 N. Whitefish Point Rd., Paradise, MI* ☎ *906/492–3747* 🌐 *www.shipwreckmuseum.com*

### ZINGERMAN'S DELICATESSEN

An iconic Ann Arbor deli, Zingerman's opened in 1982 and is a destination for sandwiches as well as specialty grocery offerings, from olive oils to teas to spices. In the decades since Ari Weinzweig and Paul Saginaw opened the deli, Zingerman's has expanded its tasty empire across the city to include a bakery, a creamery, a coffee company, a full-service restaurant (Zingerman's Roadhouse), and more.

**Do This:** Having a corned beef Reuben at the deli is an Ann Arbor rite of passage, but you can put together a food crawl and try bites and sips from all their establishments, such as tangy pimiento cheese from Zingerman's Creamery, a latte at Zingerman's Coffee Company, sour cream coffee cake from Zingerman's Bakehouse, and a gelato-topped doughnut sundae at Zingerman's Roadhouse.

**Zingerman's Delicatessen.** ✉ *422 Detroit St., Ann Arbor, MI* ☎ *734/663–3354* 🌐 *zingermansdeli.com.*

## Cool Places to Stay

**Lake Shore Resort.** When Andrew Milauckas took over his family's lakefront mid-century motel, he added a dose of hipster cool. Rooms feature lake views (perfect for seeing the incredible sunsets), custom-made rugs, succulents, and solar shades for privacy. The rate includes continental breakfast along the lake, adult bikes to take and explore the town, kayaks, yoga classes, and more. ✉ *2885 Lakeshore Dr., Saugatuck, MI* ☎ *269/857–7121* 🌐 *www.lakeshoreresortsaugatuck.com* [$] *From $175.*

**Mackinac Island Grand Hotel.** The place to stay on Mackinac Island, this 1887-built hotel has an old-world vibe with 400 rooms that are all uniquely decorated (stay in one of the "named rooms," which are designed to match a historic figure's tastes; the First Lady rooms include rooms named for Jacqueline Kennedy and Laura Bush). Even if you don't stay here, you can pay $10 to spend time relaxing on the porch (it's the world's longest porch at 660 feet and has 1,500 geraniums) and exploring the grounds. ✉ *286 Grand Ave., Mackinac Island, MI* ☎ *800/334–7263* 🌐 *www.grandhotel.com* [$] *From $413.*

**Mushroom Houses.** "Mushroom" houses, a quirky design from architect Earl Young, are perfect for fans of *The Hobbit* (or anyone who wants an unexpected experience). The four houses, each entirely different in design, resemble hobbit abodes or mushrooms due to their roofs. The houses, which are located near the beach, include multiple bedrooms (they range from accommodating 6 to 12 people) and amenities such as heated floors, grills, and washer-dryers. ✉ *Charlevoix, MI* ☎ *713/624–2544* 🌐 *www.mushroomhouses.com* [$] *From $200.*

**The Siren.** Located in downtown Detroit in the 1926 art deco Wurlitzer Building, the Siren is a glamorous hotel—think potted palms, fringed and leopard-print furniture, and cozy nooks in the public areas. The rooms are decked out with vintage and custom furniture and terrazzo-tiled bathrooms, and while the hotel is walking distance to lots of great spots, there are plenty of reasons to not leave: there's an on-site barber shop, an elegant shop, and a candy-pink cocktail bar, appropriately named Candy Bar. ✉ *1509 Broadway St., Detroit, MI* ☎ *313/277–4736* 🌐 *www.thesirenhotel.com* [$] *From $179.*

# Minnesota

Minnesota's 11,842 lakes offer more shoreline than Florida, California, and Hawaii combined. One out of every six people in Minnesota owns a boat, the highest ratio in the country. If you travel all of Minnesota's 406 miles, from Canada to Iowa, you'll see three distinct kinds of terrain. To the west and south you'll find grassland plains and prairies. The eastern part of the state, once known as the "Big Woods," is the natural home of hardwood forests.

## Bucket List Picks

The following boxes contain our picks for the top sights and experiences in Minnesota.

- ○ The Northern Lights
- ○ Voyageurs National Park
- ○ Ice Fishing
- ○ Minnehaha Regional Park
- ○ Weisman Art Museum
- ○ Boundary Waters Canoe Area Wilderness
- ○ North Shore Scenic Drive
- ○ Mall of America

# The Northern Lights

## Nature's Big Show

While your chances of seeing the otherworldly and enchanting northern lights dramatically increase the farther north you go, you don't have to travel to the Arctic to cross this off your bucket list. Far northern Minnesota, away from bright lights and big cities, is an incredible spot to see the skies dance with swirls of greens, blues, purples, and yellows. Boundary Waters Canoe Area Wilderness, Voyageurs National Park, and Northwest Angle, the northernmost spot in the continental United States, are prime viewing locations, but if the conditions are right (that means no cloud cover) and magnetic activity is strong, you can see the charged solar particles in much of the state.

## Don't Miss

Keep an eye on the Kp index, which tracks geomagnetic activity—it's on a scale of 1 and 10, and 6 is strong enough to see the aurora as far south as the Twin Cities.

## Best Hotel

For guidance viewing the aurora, book the Northern Lights package at Gunflint Lodge, a Northwoods resort in Grand Marais. The booking includes a guided night hike. 🌐 *gunflint.com/northern-lights-package.*

## When to Go

Though strong light displays are possible during any phase of the moon, lighter displays can be washed out by moonlight. Visit during the new moon phase for better visibility. The lights can appear year-round but fall and winter are most common.

## Getting Here and Around

Ontario's Thunder Bay International Airport (YQT) is the closest airport to Grand Marais; Duluth International Airport (DLH) is 150 miles away.

# Voyageurs National Park

## Watery Wonderland

Choose your own water adventure at Voyageurs National Park, a water-based national park located at the very top of Minnesota near the Canadian border. Boating, paddling, fishing, swimming, camping, sitting on the shore; Voyageurs has water activities to spare with 84,000 acres of water. Named for the French Canadians who traveled the waterways to trade furs, this untrafficked national park has no roads but does have 30 lakes and 1,200 miles of canoe routes, which you can explore with your own vehicle or on a tour through 🌐 *recreation.gov* (tours sell out, so be sure to book in advance).

## Don't Miss

The impressive Ellsworth Rock Gardens were designed by Jack Ellsworth, an artist and carpenter from Chicago, who created a terraced garden with 62 flower beds and more than 200 sculptures.

## Best Hotel

Historic Kettle Falls Hotel offers a saloon and screened-in veranda, along with both hotel rooms and villas with kitchens. It also offers boat, canoe, and kayak rentals. 🌐 *www.kettlefallshotel.com.*

## When to Go

The park is open year-round, but the summer months are usually best for exploring the lakes. Snowfall averages 55 to 70 inches, so it's also a prime winter destination for snowmobiling, snowshoeing, or ice fishing.

## Getting Here and Around

International Falls Airport (INL) is the closest airport; it offers flights to and from Minneapolis/St. Paul International Airport (MSP) daily. The park is a five-hour drive from the Twin Cities and a three-hour drive from Duluth.

**Voyageurs National Park.** ✉ *360 MN 11 E, International Falls, MN* 🌐 *www.nps.gov/voya* 🎫 *Free.*

# Ice Fishing

### The North's Great Pastime

Whether you're a seasoned fisherman or just want to try your hand at jigging with a spring bobber, Minnesota's many lakes make it a good spot to hit the ice and fish for walleye (the state fish) plus perch and northern pike. Lake of the Woods and Lake Mille Lacs are two of the top destinations, but you can find great ice fishing nearly anywhere in the state. If you're new to Minnesota ice fishing, book a guide, such as Grand Rapids Guide Service, to help steer you to the best fishing holes.

### Don't Miss

If you're visiting the Twin Cities, try ice fishing at nearby Lake Minnetonka or Lake Phalen—either are close enough for a day trip.

### Best Hotel

Lake of the Woods, located in northwest Minnesota near the Canadian border, is a particularly good destination for ice fishing and is one of the largest freshwater lakes in the United States. Here, Ballards Resort offers ice fishing packages that include cabin lodging and meals, transportation to the lake, two holes in a fishing house, bait, and more. Guides track the best spots to fish each day. ⊕ *ballardsresort.com* [$] *From $385.*

### Good to Know

Ice fishing season runs from early December through late March. You'll need to get a license (required if you're over 16), and check the Minnesota Department of Natural Resources (⊕ *www.dnr.state.mn.us/fishing*) to verify how many of each fish you're allowed to catch at a given time.

### Getting Here and Around

International Falls Airport (INL) is the closest airport to Lake of the Woods, and Ballards Resort is 80 miles away.

# Minnehaha Regional Park

### See an Urban Waterfall

One of the nation's first state parks, Minnehaha Regional Park is a must-visit for its beautiful Minnehaha Falls, a 53-foot rushing waterfall surrounded by limestone bluffs. While there are grander, taller waterfalls in the United States, few can match Minnehaha's accessibility (you can reach it by Minneapolis's light-rail) as well as its beauty in winter, when the falls freeze. Plus, the 167-acre park features Mississippi River overlooks, sprawling gardens, hiking trails, an off-leash dog park, and a bike path. The park's Princess Depot was on the first railroad line west of the Mississippi River, and the Stevens House was the first wood frame house in Minnesota.

### Don't Miss

In winter the Minnehaha Falls can freeze, creating a stunning ice cave that makes for a striking photo op.

### Good to Know

Minnehaha is sometimes incorrectly referred to as the "laughing waters" though its direct translation is "waterfall" in the Dakota language.

### Best Activity

The park has a trio of gardens, Song of Hiawatha Garden, Minnehaha Falls Pergola Garden, and Longfellow Gardens, which feature woodland areas, prairie flowers like goldenrods, and other perennials.

### Getting Here and Around

The park is located 3 miles from Minneapolis–St. Paul International Airport (MSP). Take the light-rail to 50th Street/Minnehaha Park.

**Minnehaha Regional Park.** ✉ *4801 S. Minnehaha Dr., Minneapolis, MN* 🌐 *www.minneapolisparks.org/parks* 🎫 *Free.*

# Weisman Art Museum

## A Museum That's A Work of Art

Located on the University of Minnesota, Twin Cities campus in a striking Frank Gehry–designed building, this teaching museum has more than 25,000 works. The collection has strong holdings in ceramics, Korean furniture, and early-20th-century and contemporary American art, with works by painters such as Marsden Hartley and Milton Avery. Besides the permanent collection, the Weisman features rotating special exhibits, a student art showcase, gallery talks, and other events that allow you to engage with art. The museum also runs a Public Art on Campus program, which installs sculptures around the campus.

## Don't Miss

Gehry's abstract architectural genius is on display before you even enter the museum. Take a moment to admire the building's brick facades and curved stainless steel sheets that resemble tin cans. Gehry added a brick addition to the building in 2011 to significantly increase the gallery space.

## Best Collection

The museum has an exceptional collection of traditional Korean furniture, with works from the Choson and Silla dynasties, as well as folk arts. The collection, a bequest from Dr. Edward Reynolds Wright Jr. in 1988, features works that encompass a range of woods, styles, and types of items, such as desks, rice storage chests, and tray tables.

## Getting Here and Around

The museum is located 13 miles from Minneapolis–St. Paul International Airport (MSP). The East Bank stop on the Green Line light-rail is about a half mile from the museum.

**Weisman Art Museum.** ✉ *333 E. River Pkwy., Minneapolis, MN* ☎ *612/625–9494* 🌐 *wam.umn.edu* 🎫 *Free.*

# Boundary Waters Canoe Area Wilderness

## Paddler's Paradise

Located in the northern reaches of northeastern Minnesota's Superior National Forest along the Canadian border, Boundary Waters is a canoer's dream. The huge preserve spans more than 1 million acres with 1,200 miles of canoe routes, 12 hiking trails, plus opportunities for camping, dog sledding, and other outdoor activities. There's ample wildlife to spot, from black-and-white loons on the water to wolves in the forest and eagles and falcons in the sky. You'll need a permit for a specific entry point to visit as well as border permits if you plan to explore the Canadian side (find them at *recreation.gov*).

## Don't Miss

Dog sledding is a popular winter activity in the preserve. Book a day trip to try it yourself or watch the area's John Beargrease Sled Dog Marathon, the longest sled dog race in the Lower 48.

## Best Tour

Since it's so remote, a trip to Boundary Waters requires a ton of planning. Leave the work to the pros by booking either a single day canoeing trip or group overnight camping trip through the Boundary Waters Guide Service out of Ely. The experienced guides plan the itinerary, provide sleeping bags and gear, and cook all the meals, so you can focus on soaking up nature and taking great shots. *elyoutfitting-company.com* *From $295.*

## Getting Here and Around

Fly into Duluth International Airport (DLH), which is 115 miles from Ely, a good home base for exploring the region.

**Boundary Waters Canoe Area Wilderness.** *www.fs.usda.gov* *$16.*

# North Shore Scenic Drive

## Explore an All-American Road

Stretching from Duluth to Grand Portage on the Canadian border, this 154-mile drive hugs Lake Superior and offers buckets of beautiful scenery and an array of activities along the way. You can stick to the road and drive north, admiring the wooded lakefront scenery and cliffs, and stop for lunch (try Betty's Pies, an iconic 1956 diner in Two Harbors that specializes in pasties as well as slices of pie). Or, visit one of seven state parks along the route, such as Gooseberry Falls State Park and Temperance River State Park, and go boating, fishing, hiking, or swimming.

## Don't Miss

Split Rock Lighthouse, located in Split Rock Lighthouse State Park, opened in 1910 after a ferocious storm wrecked more than two dozen ships a few years earlier. Today, the decommissioned lighthouse is a National Historic Landmark that is open for guided tours.

## Best Stop

Artsy Grand Marais is a great village to spend the night since the town is filled with restaurants and bars, including local favorites World's Best Donuts and Voyageur Brewing Company. You can also spend time hiking up Eagle Mountain to take in an amazing view, or sit by the water and admire the sunrise or sunset. 🌐 *www.visitcookcounty.com.*

## Getting Here and Around

If you're starting at the southern end of the road, fly into Duluth International Airport (DLH); from the other direction, fly to Thunder Bay International Airport (YQT) in Ontario, which is located 43 miles from Grand Portage.

**Explore Minnesota.** 🌐 *exploreminnesota.com.*

## Mall of America

### America's Mega Mall

With more than 500 stores, from Apple to Zara, the Mall of America is the biggest in the United States, clocking in at more than 96 acres in size (that could fit seven Yankee Stadiums!) and more than 4.3 miles of storefront. It's anchored by Nordstrom and Macy's department stores, but also includes plenty of specialty shops for gifts, books, and more. The Lego Store is fun for kids of all ages, thanks to play tables, cool models, and a wall with dozens of different specialty Lego pieces to purchase. But there's much more to do than just shop: the mall includes Sea Life Minnesota Aquarium, Minnesota's largest aquarium, with sharks, seahorses, and other creatures; an amusement park with rides; and an escape room.

### Don't Miss

Nickelodeon Universe, an amusement park with more than two dozen rides, is your chance to ride a roller coaster *inside* the mall.

### Best Activity

The Crayola Experience features more than two dozen hands-on activities, including naming and wrapping a custom crayon and coloring page. *crayolaexperience.com/mall-of-america* *From $20.99.*

### Good to Know

The mall's food options are a step up from your standard food court pizza; try Korean fried chicken at Bonchon, scoops of cookie dough at Dough Dough, and burgers at Shake Shack.

### Getting Here and Around

From Minneapolis-St. Paul International Airport (MSP), the mall is about a 7-mile drive.

**Mall of America.** *60 E. Broadway, Bloomington, MN* *952/883–8800* *www.mallofamerica.com.*

# When in Minnesota

## FIND YOUR VIKING ROOTS IN DULUTH

Located on the shores of Lake Superior, Duluth is a waterfront city with tons to see and do, from the Great Lakes Aquarium to the Duluth Art Institute to the annual Bob Dylan Fest held each May (the rocker was born here). There are plenty of outdoor activities, including sailing, watching ships pass under the turn-of-the-century Aerial Lift Bridge from Canal Park, and strolling through gardens at Leif Erickson park. You may notice Erickson isn't the only Viking connection here; there's a strong sense of Nordic heritage throughout Minnesota (think: Minnesota Vikings football, and Duluth's own aquavit distillery), no wonder since the state has the largest population of Norwegians and Swedes outside of Scandinavia.

**Do This:** Sip aquavit, that favorite Minnesota spirit, at Vikre Distillery; visit the Nordic Center for cultural exhibits; and grab breakfast at Vanilla Bean Cafe, serving Scandinavian breakfast dishes such as Norwegian crepes and Swedish pancakes.

## MINNEAPOLIS SCULPTURE GARDEN

A partnership between the Walker Art Center and the Minneapolis Park and Recreation Board, this 11-acre sculpture garden has about 60 sculptures, the most famous of which is Claes Oldenburg and Coosje van Bruggen's *Spoonbridge and Cherry,* a fountain sculpture. The free garden is open 6 am to midnight every day of the year.

**Do This:** Take a self-guided tour of the sculptures; you can download a pdf onto your phone and see six of the most important sculptures in the park. Besides providing background information on the artwork, the guide asks thought-provoking questions (starting with: What is sculpture?) and gives you artistic and creative writing prompts.

**Minneapolis Sculpture Garden.** ✉ *725 Vineland Pl., Minneapolis, MN* ☎ *612/375–7600* 🌐 *walkerart.org/visit/garden.*

## THE NORTH AMERICAN BEAR CENTER

Meet black bears and learn about their northern Minnesota habitat at this one-of-a-kind educational center, which features tours and exhibits showcasing mounted bears (including extinct species). The Northwoods Ecology Hall explores the animals with which black bears share their habitat and features aquariums, a reptile terrarium, mounted moose, and more.

**Do This:** See the four black "ambassador bears" that make the center home; they live in a 2½-acre forested enclosure. Spot them from the viewing windows indoors or the outdoor balcony. Hourly tours highlight at least one of the bears with the chance for an up-close viewing.

**The North American Bear Center.** ✉ *1926 MN 169, Ely, MN* ☎ *218/365–7879* 🌐 *bear.org.*

## PAISLEY PARK

Prince left behind a stunning estate and production studio outside the Twin Cities when he died in 2016; it's been turned into a museum that you can visit and is also a spot for concerts, music festivals, and other events. The sprawling Paisley Park, which is as colorful and eclectic as the musician's wardrobe (you'll see his bright suits, hats, and jewelry on display as well) is a must for Prince fans, but a fun tour even if you're a newcomer to his music. For the most die-hard Prince fans, book a three-hour tour for an in-depth exploration of the property. You'll have access to special archives, a private video screening, and studio tours, plus see Prince's concert wardrobe, instruments, motorcycles, and more. Food and beverages are provided after the tour; it often sells out, so be sure to book in advance of your visit ($160).

**Do This:** Each tour includes a stop at Studio A recording studio. Besides all the recording equipment, you can see the lyrics on a stand to the last song Prince was working on when he died.

**Paisley Park.** *www.paisleypark.com* *From $45.*

### THE SOMALI MUSEUM OF MINNESOTA

Minnesota has the largest population of Somalians in the United States, and this museum, the only one of its kind in North America, explores Somali culture. The museum has more than 700 items on display, including nomadic huts, kitchen tools, woven textiles, and contemporary paintings from local artists. The museum also has a dance troupe that performs around the city and offers free dance lessons on Saturdays at Tapestry Folkdance Center.

**Do This:** After visiting the museum, have lunch at Afro Deli, which has four locations around Minneapolis and St. Paul. The menu features Somali classics like chicken fantastic, chicken and vegetables in a Parmesan cream sauce served with saffron rice. *afrodeli.com.*

**The Somali Museum of Minnesota.** *1516 E. Lake St. No. 011, Minneapolis, MN* *612/234–1625* *www.somalimuseum.org.*

## Cool Places to Stay

**Alma.** A must for food-loving travelers, Alma is an elegant seven-room hotel attached to the James Beard Award–winning Alma Restaurant. Each room is uniquely designed with queen or king beds with natural linens, flat-screen TVs with AppleTV and streaming services, vintage rugs, walk-in showers, and custom-made desks. Continental breakfast is provided each morning, as is complimentary wine and antipasti upon arrival. *528 University Ave. SW, Minneapolis, MN* *612/379–4909* *www.almampls.com* $ *From $250.*

**Hewing Hotel.** This hip hotel in Minneapolis' North Loop neighborhood combines Scandinavian inspiration with Minnesota touches, including artwork from Minnesota artists and photographers, pine timber beams, and Faribault woollen blankets. Set in a historic building in a former farm implement warehouse, the hotel includes pet-friendly rooms that have an outdoorsy vibe, and an all-season rooftop lounge featuring city views. *300 Washington Ave. N, Minneapolis, MN* *651/468–0400* *www.hewinghotel.com* $ *From $179.*

**Lutsen Resort.** The oldest continuously operating hotel in Minnesota (it's been open since 1885), Lutsen Resort is a Scandinavian-inspired lodge on Lake Superior that's set along a pebbled beach. The beach and woodsy setting make it an ideal spot for swimming, kayaking, and bonfires in summer, and ice-skating and snowshoeing in winter. You can stay in the lodge, cabins, condos, or town homes; the lodge includes an indoor pool and game room. *5700 W. Hwy. 61, Lutsen, MN* *800/218–8589* *www.lutsenresort.com* $ *From $129.*

**Whistle Stop BNB.** For "I spent the night somewhere wild" bragging rights, seek out this bed-and-breakfast, which features five restored train cars transformed into rooms. The cars, which are decorated with turn-of-the-20th-century antiques, include Murphy beds, whirlpool tubs, refrigerators, and fireplaces. The woodsy acre of property also includes a cottage and house with rooms, all of which include full breakfast each day. *107 E. Nowell St., Mills, MN* *800/328–6315* *whistlestopbedandbreakfast.com* $ *From $125.*

# Ohio

Known as the "Gateway to the Midwest," the Buckeye State is a beautifully balanced blend of not only everything Midwestern but also everything American. From college and pro sports to ballet and theater, Ohio's got a lot to entice folks from out of town. There are history, science, art, and children's museums; and water parks north and south. Food lovers relish the many ethnic eateries. Indoor and outdoor concerts pull in the biggest names around, while natural attractions and outdoor activities can be found in parks and along lakes and rivers throughout the state.

## Bucket List Picks

The following boxes contain our picks for the top sights and experiences in Ohio.

- ○ Rock & Roll Hall of Fame
- ○ Cuyahoga Valley National Park
- ○ Lake Erie
- ○ Cleveland Sports
- ○ Cincinnati Museum Center
- ○ Tobogganing, Sledding, and Tubing
- ○ Ohio Ice Cream Trail
- ○ Ohio Air and Space Exploration
- ○ Cleveland's West Side Market

# Rock & Roll Hall of Fame

## Greatest Hits

A must-visit for music fans, the Rock & Roll Hall of Fame is loaded with memorabilia, photographs, costumes, instruments, and much more from artists like Elvis Presley, Whitney Houston, and the Beatles. As you'd expect from a museum dedicated to music, the exhibits are packed with films, interactive kiosks, and videos, so you can watch and listen to iconic performances. The museum includes the main exhibit hall, which traces the beginnings and evolution of rock and roll, and the Hall of Fame level, with panels honoring each inductee. The architecture of the building itself is worth a look: the geometric structure, designed by I. M. Pei, features pyramids and a tower—it's meant to look like a record player from above.

## Don't Miss

In the Garage, pick up an instrument and jam like your favorite rockers.

## Best Tour

The Hall of Fame has curated some tours, from Women Who Rock to an instrument-focused tour, but to see the best of the artifacts and memorabilia on display, follow the Staff Picks tour, which takes 2½ hours and leads you to all the highlights, from Joey Ramone's black leather jackets to Run DMC's Adidas sneakers.

## Just Nearby

The Great Lakes Science Center, home to the NASA Glenn Visitor Center and kid-friendly science exhibits, is a few minutes' walk away.

## Getting Here and Around

From Cleveland Hopkins International Airport (CLE), the Hall of Fame is a 15-mile drive.

**Rock & Roll Hall of Fame.** ✉ *1100 E. 9th St., Cleveland, OH* ☎ *216/781–7625* 🌐 *www.rockhall.com* 🎫 *$28.*

# Cuyahoga Valley National Park

## Go Chasing Waterfalls

Located halfway between Cleveland and Akron, the 33,000-acre Cuyahoga Valley National Park is an easy day trip from both cities. Known for its waterfalls (there are about 100 in the park), Cuyahoga also offers 140 miles of trails for hiking, biking, and horseback riding; the Ohio & Erie Towpath Trail is a notable path that traces the route of the Ohio & Erie Canal. Paddling and picnicking are also popular activities, and the park is also a good spot to stargaze and see Mercury, nebulae, eclipses, and the aurora borealis.

## Don't Miss

Brandywine Falls, a striking 60-foot waterfall, is the most popular location in the park. Get there by parking nearby and walking along the boardwalk, or hiking in from the Boston Mill Visitor Center, about a 5-mile hike.

## Best Activity

The best way to see the park is by rail on the Cuyahoga Valley Scenic Railroad. This leisurely train trip through the park goes through the Cuyahoga Valley and along the rushing Cuyahoga River. You'll see wildlife like eagles and deer. Sit in the upper dome panoramic observation car for the best view. 🌐 *www.cvsr.org* 🎫 *From $15.*

## Getting Here and Around

From Cleveland Hopkins International Airport (CLE), the park is 22 miles; from Akron-Canton Airport (CAK), the park is about 28 miles.

**Boston Mill Visitor Center.** ✉ *5793 Boston Mills Rd., Peninsula, OH* 🌐 *www.nps.gov/cuva* 🎫 *Free.*

# Lake Erie

### Where the Water Is Just Right

Much of Ohio's northern border is on Lake Erie, a major summer destination for beaches and water activities like kayaking. The shallowest of the Great Lakes, Lake Erie is also the warmest, which means it's perfect for swimming. Visit sandy spots like East Harbor State Park in Lakeside-Marblehead and Headlands Beach State Park in Geneva. From here you can also check out the Merry-Go-Round Museum in Sandusky; the highlight is a restored working carousel with a collection of animals dating back to 1915.

### Don't Miss

Try a Lake Erie Monster IPA, produced by Great Lakes Brewing Co. of Cleveland; it's named after Lake Erie's mythical lake monster, Bessie.

### Best Day Trip

Kelleys Island, located off the coast, showcases the effects of glaciers on the rocks and land; you can reach it by ferry. Head over to visit the 677-acre state park and go swimming, boating, and fishing, or in winter, cross-country skiing or ice fishing. Grab lunch at The Village Pump, a popular spot for Lake Erie perch and brandy alexanders. Book a ferry at 🌐 *kelleysislandferry.com*.

### Best Tour

Rent a kayak, paddleboard, canoe, or hydrobike and hit the water on your own, or book a Harbor Yak Kayak Tour. For $20, you can take a 90-minute sunset kayak tour, a quiet way to admire the beauty of the lake. 🌐 *www.harboryak.com/guided-tours*.

### Getting Here and Around

Cleveland Hopkins International Airport (CLE) is located at about the Lake Erie midpoint, while Toledo Express Airport (TOL) is located at the western edge; you can fly into either depending on your lake destination.

## Cleveland Sports

### Cheer for O-H-I-O

Spectator sports reign supreme in Ohio, home to iconic professional teams—and good ones at that—in all major leagues. A few of the greats are conveniently clustered together in downtown Cleveland, including the Cavaliers NBA team, Browns NFL team, Indians MLB team, and Monsters AHL team. That means no matter the season, it's easy to catch a game or two. The Cavs and Monsters share the Rocket Mortgage Field-House arena, while the Browns play at FirstEnergy Stadium, and the Indians make their home at Progressive Field. Elsewhere in Ohio, Cincinnati prizes the Bengals and Reds, and Columbus is home to the Ohio State University's often top-ranking college football team.

### Don't Miss

The Pro Football Hall of Fame is located in Canton, about 60 miles south of downtown Cleveland. Visit to see the Hall of Fame Gallery, with bronze busts of each enshrined player, Super Bowl rings, the Lombardi Trophy for Super Bowl LV, and a gallery devoted to exploring contemporary issues in the National Football League. 🌐 *profootballhof.com*.

### Best Activity

Tailgate a Cleveland Browns game: hours before the game kicks off, Browns fans bedecked in orange and brown gather for a time-honored tradition: tailgating at the Muni Lot, the Pit, and elsewhere in the area.

### Getting Here and Around

Fly into Cleveland Hopkins International Airport (CLE); it's 12 miles from the airport to Progressive Field. From Progressive, FirstEnergy Stadium is a mile away, and Rocket Mortgage Field-House is ¼ mile. The Pro Football Hall of Fame is 60 miles from the airport.

## Cincinnati Museum Center

### Culture Hub

With three museums, an archives collection, an IMAX theater, and traveling exhibits, the Cincinnati Museum Center is a jam-packed spot for all things art, history, and science. Located in the 1933 art deco Union Terminal, a former train station, the building is a National Historic Landmark and includes the Cincinnati History Museum, the Duke Energy Children's Museum, the Cincinnati History Library and Archives, and the Museum of Natural History and Science. With more than 1.8 million artworks and artifacts, the collection offers something of interest for all kinds of museumgoers.

### Don't Miss

Visit the Rookwood Ice Cream Parlor, a tiled art deco café where you can get locally made Graeter's ice cream.

### Best Activity

Train lovers should visit Tower A, the original Union Terminal control tower. Run by the Cincinnati Railroad Club, it gives you a view of Queensgate Yard, where you can see arriving and departing trains. There are also train-related books to peruse and train tables for kids to play on.

### Good to Know

The National Underground Railroad Freedom Center, which is located 2 miles from the Museum Center, explores the concept of freedom, from the history of the Underground Railroad to figures fighting for freedom today. 🌐 *freedomcenter.org*.

### Getting Here and Around

Cincinnati/Northern Kentucky International Airport (CVG) is about 12 miles from the Museum Center. Parking is $6, and there's a Cincinnati Metro Route 49 bus stop at the entrance.

**Cincinnati Museum Center.** ✉ *1301 Western Ave., Cincinnati, OH* 🌐 *www.cincymuseum.org* 🎟 *$14.50.*

# Tobogganing, Sledding, and Tubing

### Winter Thrills

No winter visit to Ohio is complete without taking to the snow with a sled, inner tube, or toboggan; there are opportunities all over the state to take a quick zip down a hill. Go sledding at state parks, like Punderson State Park in Newbury Township, which has a lighted sledding hill with a tow rope, or the Wright Brothers Memorial Park in Dayton, which has a 40-degree hill with multiple sledding trails.

### Don't Miss

Ohio's tallest and fastest toboggan chutes at Cleveland Metroparks' Mill Stream Run Reservation have been operating since 1967; the two chutes are 70 feet high and 700 feet long, and as you zip down, you can reach speeds of up to 50 mph. The chutes operate from the day after Thanksgiving through the first weekend in March. *www.clevelandmetroparks.com* *$12.*

### Best Snow Tubing

Snow Trails in Mansfield is Ohio's oldest ski resort, and it also offers seven lanes for vertical descent tubing plus glow tubing at night. No prior experience is required to hop on a tube—it's also an all-ages activity, since you can link tubes and go down the hill together. Tubes are provided, and a conveyor belt will bring yours back up to the top of the hill. *snowtrails.com.*

### Getting Here and Around

From Cleveland Hopkins International Airport (CLE), Mill Stream Run Reservation is 8 miles, Punderson State Park is 35 miles, and Snow Trails is 72 miles. From John Glenn Columbus International Airport (CMH), Snow Trails is 60 miles, and Wright Brothers Memorial Park is 72 miles.

## Ohio Ice Cream Trail

### I Scream, You Scream

With more than 2,200 dairy farms, it's only natural that Ohio has become such an ice cream destination—the state even has its own ice cream trail, which guides you to 15 top spots for a scoop. Jeni's Splendid Ice Creams, which started in Columbus, and Graeter's, which started in Cincinnati, are two of the best-known purveyors, but you'll find many other worthy spots to try the frozen treat. Toft's in Sandusky is Ohio's oldest dairy, churning out flavors like black sweet cherry and Cedar Point cotton candy, while Tom's Ice Cream Bowl in Zanesville is the go-to for giant sundaes.

### Don't Miss

Graeter's, which started in 1870 when Louis Graeter began selling his ice cream at Cincinnati street markets, is arguably the most famous producer in Ohio and has dozens of shops across the state. It's famous for its chocolate chip ice creams, like mocha, mint, and black raspberry filled with thick, yet pliable, chocolate chunks.

### Best Tour

The Utica-based company Velvet Ice Cream has been a family-run business since 1914, and you can go behind the scenes to see how their dessert is made. The 30-minute walking tour will give you a look at the ice cream production facility; end by trying the Buckeye Classic, inspired by the Ohio-favorite peanut butter and chocolate candies. 🌐 *velveticecream.com* 🎫 *Free.*

### Getting Here and Around

Ice cream makers are located all across the state, but flying into John Glenn Columbus International Airport (CMH) will give you a good home base. Velvet's factory is located about 35 miles from the airport, Tom's is 55 miles away, and Toft's is just over 100 miles to the north.

**Ice Cream Trail.** 🌐 *trails.ohio.org/wps/portal/gov/trails/home.*

# Ohio Air and Space Exploration

## The Birthplace of Aviation

Ohio is full of museums and sites that honor the state's contributions to space exploration because the Wright brothers, who invented the airplane, hail from Dayton, and more NASA astronauts are from Cleveland than any other city. John Glenn and Neil Armstrong are both Ohioans as well. You can visit the John & Annie Glenn Museum (Glenn's boyhood home) in New Concord to learn about their lives, or the Armstrong Air & Space Museum in Wapakoneta to see artifacts like space suits and full-size aircraft flown by Armstrong. You can also learn about the space race and how Ohio has influenced space travel.

## Don't Miss

The Neil Armstrong Space Exploration Gallery at the Cincinnati Museum Center is a permanent exhibition that explores the Apollo 11 mission, during which Armstrong and Buzz Aldrin walked on the moon (that's one small step for man, one giant leap for Ohio). The exhibit includes a replica of Armstrong's space suit from the mission and a moon rock he collected.

## Best Stargazing

Stare into infinity and beyond with a close-up view of the night sky at Nassau Astronomical Station in Observatory Park, the only dark-sky park in Ohio (there are only 39 the United States). The 36-inch deep-sky telescope is open for viewing nightly; consult a map on the website before your visit to ensure it'll be clear. 🌐 *geaugaparkdistrict.org/park/observatory-park* 🎫 *Free.*

## Getting Here and Around

From John Glenn Columbus International Airport (CMH), the Armstrong Air & Space Museum is 90 miles away and the John & Annie Glenn Museum is 70 miles. Nassau Astronomical Station is 55 miles from Cleveland Hopkins International Airport (CLE).

# Cleveland's West Side Market

### Midwest Melting Pot

Cleveland's historic West Side Market, which got its start as an open-air market in 1840, is a living embodiment of America's diverse tapestry of cultures. More than 100 vendors—including many family-owned businesses—showcase cuisines from Polish to Cambodian to French and more, all under one roof. Aisles are packed with stalls selling items like spices, produce, cheeses, meats, baked goods, and candy, with a mix of ingredients and ready-to-eat dishes. The market has been modernized since the brick building (with its iconic 137-foot clock tower) opened in 1912, but its vintage feel remains.

### Don't Miss

Pierogi Palace is a longtime market favorite; the Polish stall sells stuffed cabbage, latkes, sauerkraut balls, and more than 200 types of large frozen pierogies, from classic flavors like potato-cheese and cabbage to inventive offerings like bourbon chicken, taco, or Philly cheesesteak.

### Best Restaurant

Frank's Bratwurst, which has been slinging sausages since 1970, serves a quick and tasty lunch.

### Good to Know

Put together a picnic by hitting vendors like Sebastian's Deli for smoked meats, the Cheese Shop for domestic and imported cheeses, and Mediterra Bakehouse for freshly baked bread. There are some benches outside; or, take your lunch to the Market Square park across the street or a lakefront spot like Edgewater Park.

### Getting Here and Around

The Market is located 11 miles from Cleveland Hopkins International Airport (CLE).

**West Side Market.** ✉ *1979 W. 25th St., Cleveland, OH.*

## When in Ohio

### *A CHRISTMAS STORY* HOUSE

The famous house from *A Christmas Story* is located in Cleveland; take a tour of the home, which looks just as it did in the movie, right down to the leg lamp. Visit the A Christmas Story Museum across the street to see costumes and memorabilia from the film, including Randy's snowsuit and the family's car.

**Do This:** Die hard fans of the movie can spend the night at the house for $595; the top floor features a private loft, and you have access to the entire house from an hour after closing until 9 am the next day. The Bumpus House, where the next-door neighbors live in the film, has two suites available for rent.

***A Christmas Story* House** ✉ *3159 W. 11th St., Cleveland, OH* ☎ *216/298–4919* 🌐 *www.achristmasstoryhouse.com.*

### CEDAR POINT

Sandusky's Cedar Point, the second-oldest operating amusement park in the United States (it opened in 1870), packs in the rides: it has 72 in total, including 18 roller coasters, the second most of any park. It's set along Lake Erie, and includes a mile-long beach, as well as a water park with waterslides and wave pools.

**Do This:** With so many coasters, there's a ride for everyone, but the record-breaking Steel Vengeance is beloved among thrill-seekers. It's the longest hybrid coaster in the world and includes a 90-degree 200-foot drop and three inversions.

**Cedar Point.** ✉ *1 Cedar Point Dr., Sandusky, OH* ☎ *419/627–2350* 🌐 *www.cedarpoint.com*

### CLEVELAND'S WADE OVAL

Wade Oval, a 7-acre park on the east side of the city, is lined with attractions like the Cleveland Museum of Art, Cleveland Natural History Museum, Museum of Contemporary Art, Severance Hall (where the Cleveland Orchestra plays), and the Cleveland Botanical Garden. This larger area is called University Circle, and it's also home to Case Western Reserve University, several libraries, historic homes, and more. Pick up a CirclePass, which gets you 25% off admission to the History Museum, botanical garden, and Museum of Natural History. The Museum of Contemporary Art is free.

**Do This:** WOW! Wade Oval Wednesdays, held Wednesday evenings from June to August, features live-music performances, food trucks, local beer, and more. In the winter, the oval turns into a skating rink. 🌐 *www.universitycircle.org*

## Cool Places to Stay

**The Casa at Gervasi Vineyard.** Located on a 55-acre estate, this elegant hotel features 24 suites, with fireplaces and covered verandas, as well as continental breakfast with fresh croissants and fruit delivered each morning. The vineyard has several dining and drinking options, and 5 acres of vines; they grow three different types of grapes suited to the Ohio climate. ✉ *1700 55th St. NE, Canton, OH* 🌐 *www.gervasivineyard.com/stay/the-casa* $ *From $199.*

**Getaway Beaver Creek.** These tiny cabins encourage unplugging for the weekend—stocked with cell-phone lockboxes, a queen bed, a bathroom, a tiny kitchenette, and big windows to peer into nature, they have everything you need for a cozy break. Located 90 minutes from Cleveland, this outpost is near hiking trails as well as grocery stores if you're cooking for yourself (and restaurants if not). ✉ *45529 Middle Beaver Rd., Lisbon, OH* 🌐 *getaway.house/pittsburgh-cleveland* $ *From $119.*

# Wisconsin



Welcome to America's Dairyland, famous for its cheese, beer, the beloved Green Bay Packers, and some stunning natural attractions. From Door County's shoreline and Kettle Moraine's glacial forest to the Wisconsin Dells' water parks and Milwaukee's cool neighborhoods, there's truly something for every visitor. Most of Wisconsin's landscape was formed some 10,000 years ago by a great glacier that left in its wake 15,000 lakes, 12,624 rivers and streams, pristine prairies, and some of America's finest examples of glacial topography.

## Bucket List Picks

The following boxes contain our picks for the top sights and experiences in Wisconsin.

- ○ Door County
- ○ Apostle Islands National Lakeshore
- ○ Milwaukee Art Museum
- ○ Dane County Farmers' Market
- ○ Green Bay Packers
- ○ Wisconsin Dells
- ○ Taliesin East
- ○ The Great River Road
- ○ Milwaukee Breweries
- ○ Kettle Moraine State Forest

# Door County

## Coastal Bliss

Door County, the long, narrow peninsula that juts out from Green Bay into Lake Michigan, is a year-round destination for exploring the outdoors, whether that's hiking to take in the foliage at Peninsula State Park or visiting beaches (and quaint ice cream shops) during the summer. The small towns that dot the peninsula, like Sister Bay and Ephraim, each have their own feel, and there's a growing food and drink scene led by places like Wickman House and Island Orchard Cider.

## Don't Miss

A fish boil, in which big pots full of whitefish and red potatoes are set aflame, is as much a show as a meal. Catch it at the White Gull Inn, among other spots on the peninsula.

## Best Day Trip

A 30-minute ferry ride from Ellison Bay's Northpoint Pier, the 22-square-mile Washington Island is known for its large Icelandic community. Check out School House Beach, a beautiful stretch made of gray stones, and Stavkirke Church, a striking wooden church modeled after a Scandinavian design.

## When to Go

Summer draws families to the beaches, while autumn draws leaf-peepers, but they both draw crowds, so plan ahead if you're visiting in either season. Winter is an underrated time to visit; while some spots are closed, you'll have the run of the little towns, plus the Sister Bay Cherry Drop is a festive way to spend New Year's Eve.

## Getting Here and Around

Green Bay's Austin Straubel International Airport (GRB) is located at the base of the peninsula. From there, it's 99 miles to Gills Rock, at the very tip of the peninsula. You'll need a car to get around between towns.

## Apostle Islands National Lakeshore

### Sea Caves and Dramatic Cliffs

The Apostle Islands National Lakeshore, a remote destination on Lake Superior in northern Wisconsin, consists of a stretch of shoreline on the mainland with walking trails, along with 21 islands that are only accessible by water, where you can see rock formations, ice caves, and 19th-century lighthouses. Wildlife is a draw, with bald eagles and black bears in abundance, and camping is available on 18 of the islands for adventurous souls who prefer to spend the night.

### Don't Miss

The sea caves, striking arches, and cutouts in the cliffs on Devil's Island are a must-see by boat.

### Best Tour

Book a tour with Apostle Islands Cruises, which offers multiple options for seeing the islands from the water. The Grand Tour ($47.95), a 55-mile scenic narrated tour, takes you past lighthouses, sea caves, and wildlife. The company also offers kayaking tours ($149), which include a power-boat ride and kayaking around the cliffs for two hours. 🌐 *www.apostleisland.com.*

### When to Go

Summer is the easiest time to visit and offers the most activities, although the islands are open year-round. In the winter, you can visit the ice caves.

### Getting Here and Around

Gogebic–Iron County Airport (IWD) is the closest airport; access it by flying Boutique Air from Chicago O'Hare (ORD) or Minneapolis–St. Paul (MSP). From the airport, it's 66 miles to Bayfield, where you can catch a shuttle boat, take your own vessel, or even rent a kayak to reach the islands.

**Apostle Islands National Lakeshore.** 🌐 *www.nps.gov/apis* 🎫 *Free.*

# Milwaukee Art Museum

## Wings of Wisconsin

Founded in 1888 as Milwaukee's first art gallery, the museum includes more than 30,000 works, spanning from ancient Mediterranean sculpture to contemporary painting. Areas of particular focus include American decorative arts, German Expressionism, and Haitian art, but the museum's winged architecture is often considered one of its showstoppers. Spread across three distinctive buildings (designed by Eero Saarinen, David Kahler, and Santiago Calatrava), the museum, which is located right on Lake Michigan, also includes a geometrically designed garden.

## Don't Miss

The Burke Brise Soleil, the striking, white, 217-foot architectural "wings" on the building's exterior, were designed by Santiago Calatrava (the architect of New York's Oculus). They open and close each day at 10 am, noon, and 5 pm; make sure you head outside to catch the show.

## Best Collection

The collection of art from painter and Wisconsin native Georgia O'Keeffe is among the largest holdings of her work in the country.

## Getting Here and Around

General Mitchell International Airport (MKE) is located 10 miles from the museum. From the Milwaukee Intermodal Station, where Amtrak operates, it's just over a mile to the museum. From Chicago's O'Hare International Airport (ORD), it's an 80-mile drive.

**Milwaukee Art Museum.** ✉ *700 N. Art Museum Dr., Milwaukee, WI* ☎ *414/224–3200* 🌐 *mam.org* 🎫 *$19.*

# Dane County Farmers' Market

## Sample America's Dairyland

The Dane County Farmers' Market, held outdoors at the Wisconsin State Capitol building every Saturday morning from mid-April to early November, is America's largest producers-only farmers' market, with more than 100 vendors. That means you'll find an unparalleled selection of locally grown fruits and vegetables, plus jams, baked goods, meats, eggs, fresh beans, maple syrup, popcorn, and Wisconsin's famous cheese. Pick up prepared foods, like Stella's hot and spicy cheese bread, to snack on as you walk around the square.

## Don't Miss

You can't go to Wisconsin without trying the cheese (it is America's Dairyland after all). Dairy vendors at the market frequently bring samples of their sharp cheddars, creamy spreads, and squeaky curds, so you can find your favorite. Hook's Cheese, which makes exceptional cheddars and blue cheeses, is a standout.

## While You're Here

The market is held surrounding the Wisconsin State Capitol, so be sure to admire the architecture. You can also go inside for a free tour, and, during the summer, you can walk up to the sixth floor observation deck to get a view of the city.

## Good to Know

The market is held year-round, but it moves indoors in mid-November to the Garver Feed Mill (✉ *3241 Garver Green, Madison, WI*).

## Getting Here and Around

The Dane County Regional Airport (MSN) will get you to Madison; from there, it's just under 5 miles to the capitol building.

**Capitol Square.** ✉ *2 E. Main St., Madison, WI* 🌐 *www.dcfm.org* 🎫 *Free.*

## Green Bay Packers

### The People's Team

Of all the major league professional sports teams in the United States, there's only one that's community-owned, by its loyal fans—the Green Bay Packers. The third-oldest team in the National Football League, Green Bay is also dubbed "Titletown" for its NFL wins (including four Super Bowl championships). The best way to experience the big small-town love is by visiting the team's home turf at Lambeau Field. While season tickets are hard to come by, you can take a tour that brings you onto the field or visit the Hall of Fame to see artifacts and exhibits devoted to the team's history. The Hall of Fame is self-guided and includes the fan-favorite replica office of legendary coach Vince Lombardi. Even if you can't make it to the field, make like a local and head to the corner bar to watch the game any Sunday in season.

### Don't Miss

The Packers Heritage Trail highlights locations around the city that represent key moments in Packers history, from the Packers practice fields to team founder Curly Lambeau's grave site. A trolley tour of the trail is available as well. Hungry along the way? Stop by Al's Hamburgers, a vintage 1934 diner, for classic burgers and shakes.

### Getting Here and Around

Green Bay's Austin Straubel International Airport (GRB) is about 4 miles from Lambeau Field. The Heritage Trail features walkable sections, and they're a quick drive away from each other.

**Lambeau Field.** ✉ *1265 Lombardi Ave., Green Bay, WI* 🌐 *packers.com/lambeau-field* 🎫 *Tours from $15.*

## Wisconsin Dells

### Water Park Capital of the World

Wisconsin Dells is both the name of a city along the Wisconsin River, the state's largest, and a 5-mile gorge that cuts through it. For Wisconsinites though, "the Dells" is a family-friendly summer destination packed with water parks, pancake restaurants, minigolf, and boat tours through the gorge. Get up close to the towering sandstone cliffs of the gorge by taking to the water in a kayak, canoe, or tube. Those who prefer a less active way to enjoy the scenery can stroll down the quarter-mile walking path that offers views of the cliffs.

### Don't Miss

The largest and arguably the most popular water park in the Dells is Noah's Ark Water Park, with 70 acres of waterslides, surfing, minigolf, restaurants, and more. 🌐 *www.noahsarkwaterpark.com.*

### Best Tour

The Original Wisconsin Ducks, the oldest duck-boat operator in the Wisconsin Dells (they debuted in 1946), offers hour-long tours of the Wisconsin River and Lake Delton, plus woodsy trails. They'll zip you through Red Bird Gorge, and give you a great view of the sandstone cliffs. The company also runs nighttime ghost boat tours for the truly adventurous. 🌐 *www.wisconsinducktours.com* 🎫 *From $32.*

### When to Go

Summer is the time to visit the Dells, as all the restaurants and outdoor water parks are open for the season.

### Getting Here and Around

Dane County Regional Airport (MSN) in Madison is just over 50 miles from the Wisconsin Dells. You can also take Amtrak or Greyhound from Chicago, which takes 3½ hours by train and 5½ hours by bus.

# Taliesin East

## Frank Lloyd Wright's Summer Home

Taliesin, renowned architect Frank Lloyd Wright's summer home and studio, features buildings he designed from the 1890s to the 1950s. A World Heritage site, Taliesin is set on an 800-acre estate on a hill in the Wisconsin River valley. There's plenty to explore, from Wright's 37,000-square-foot house to Hillside Home, a school run by his aunts, to the rolling landscape, which helped inspire some of his designs.

## Don't Miss

The Riverview Terrace Cafe is Wright's only restaurant design, and the menu features local cuisine made with ingredients grown on-site or from neighboring farms.

## Best Tour

Taliesin offers a number of different tours, but for true Frank Lloyd Wright fans, the Estate Tour is the only way to go. The four-hour tour takes you to the Romeo and Juliet Windmill Tower, Hillside Home, and the studio. You'll also get to relax on the terrace with provided snacks. *$95.*

## While You're Here

Combine a trip to Taliesin with a show at American Players Theatre. Located a mile from Taliesin, the outdoor amphitheater is set in a wooded meadow and focuses on Shakespeare's plays. *americanplayers.org.*

## Getting Here and Around

The Dane County Regional Airport (MSN) in Madison is just over 40 miles from Taliesin. From General Mitchell International Airport (MKE) in Milwaukee, Taliesin is about 120 miles away.

**Taliesin East.** *5481 County Rd. C, Spring Green, WI* *877/588–7900* *www.taliesinpreservation.org* *From $25.*

# The Great River Road

### Wine, Dine, and Hike the Mississippi

Wisconsin's stretch of the Great River Road runs 250 miles alongside the Mississippi River in the western part of the state. The road, which you can drive or bike, features beautiful mountains and views of the river, and offers plenty of opportunities to hike, fish, and camp at five state parks, including Wyalusing State Park. The road stops in 33 towns, so there are many options for shopping and dining. La Crosse is home to an outpost of the University of Wisconsin and has some memorable pit stops, including Pearl Ice Cream Parlor, which dates back to the 1930s.

### Don't Miss

The Great River Road Wine Trail features 10 wineries set along the Mississippi River. Stops are mostly located in Wisconsin and just across the river in Minnesota. Visit Maiden Rock Winery & Cidery, which offers wine and cider tastings, as well as a river wine cruise, where you can also admire the cliffs of the coastline. 🌐 *www.greatriverroadwinetrail.org.*

### Good to Know

Birders should head to the Trempealeau National Wildlife Refuge along the Mississippi River to spot warblers, pelicans, eagles, and more.

### When to Go

While summer offers the most activities (and means snow-free driving) and autumn offers vibrant foliage, winter allows for activities like ice fishing, cross-country skiing, and winter camping at the state parks.

### Getting Here and Around

Minneapolis–St. Paul Airport (MSP) is just under 30 miles from the northern start of the road in Prescott, Wisconsin. Dubuque Regional Airport is 16 miles from the southern edge of the road in Kieler, Wisconsin.

# Milwaukee Breweries

## Superior Suds

Beer is in Milwaukee's DNA—the city has been a brewing destination since the mid-19th century, when European settlers to the region began making beer. It became home to Pabst, Schlitz, and Miller, and even as other cities' beer scenes have surpassed it in size, the association has endured (the city's baseball team is called the Brewers, after all). Plenty of excellent new breweries have joined the lineup in recent years, from 1840 Brewing Co., where you can get farmhouse beers, to Hacienda Beer Co., where the food is a perfect pairing to the beer (try a Guava Milkshake IPA with a habanero-honey hot chicken sandwich).

## Don't Miss

Miller Brewery's tour includes a visit to the underground beer caves where beer baron Frederick Miller used to chill beer in the 1880s.

## Best Tour

The more-than-30-year-old Lakefront Brewery is known for its laid-back 45-minute tour that focuses on the samples (four to be exact), so it's especially fun if you aren't there for all the technical details about how beer is made (and if you are, there's a separate, three-hour tour for that!). Bonus: you'll also get a coupon for a free pint of Lakefront at a nearby bar on the day of your tour. 🌐 *lakefront-brewery.com* 🎫 *From $10.*

## Getting Here and Around

General Mitchell International Airport (MKE) or Milwaukee Intermodal Station (Amtrak) are easy jumping-off points for exploring the beer scene. You'll want to skip a rental car, of course, but it's easy to take rideshares between breweries.

**Brewery Map.** 🌐 *www.visitmilwaukee.org/plan-a-visit/food-drink/official-brew-city-beer-map.*

# Kettle Moraine State Forest

### Wonders From the Ice Age

The big geographic feature of this 56,000-acre forest is a large moraine (basically, what's left after a significant glacier moved through the area many thousands of years ago). The resulting landscape consists of hills, lakes, and prairies, which means the forest is a prime location for swimming, hiking, cross-country skiing, and fishing. The terrain is also a draw for equestrians, and an equestrian campground is available, as are RV campgrounds. Prefer to take in the sights from your car? The 115-mile Kettle Moraine Scenic Drive winds through the forest and offers scenic stops to picnic along the way.

### Don't Miss

Parnell Observation Tower, the highest elevation in Kettle Moraine, offers a 25-mile panoramic view of the surrounding forest. ✉ *W7876 County Hwy. U, Plymouth, WI.*

### Best Canoe Trail

The 17-acre lake doesn't allow motorized boats, which makes it a calm, clear lake for a quiet paddling adventure. The Ottawa Lake Canoe Trail takes 30 to 40 minutes to complete, and you can pick up a pamphlet on-site that will guide you to numbered buoys and highlight the natural features of the lake. There's also excellent fishing, with walleye, muskie, trout, bass, and other species in the waters.

### Getting Here and Around

Dane County Regional Airport (MSN) in Madison is 61 miles to the west of the forest's Southern Unit, while Milwaukee's General Mitchell International Airport (MKE) is 37 miles to the east. MKE is 50 miles to the south of the forest's Northern Unit, while MSN is 75 miles to the southwest.

**Kettle Moraine State Forest.** ✉ *S59 W36530 County ZZ, Dousman, WI* 🌐 *dnr.wisconsin.gov* 🎫 *From $8.*

## When in Wisconsin

### HOUSE ON THE ROCK

Spring Green may be best known for Frank Lloyd Wright's Taliesin, but Alex Jordan's House on the Rock is another worthy pilgrimage. Like something from Zillow Gone Wild, the home, which opened in 1959, has a seemingly endless array of themed rooms, which have expanded over the years to include a massive carousel, rooms filled with model airplanes and doll houses, a Titanic display, Japanese gardens, and more.

**Do This:** You'll want your camera out as much as possible, but save the selfie for the Infinity Room, a long corridor made of tiny glass windows that extends out over the forested valley below.

**House on the Rock.** ✉ *5754 WI 23, Spring Green, WI* ☎ *608/935–3639* 🌐 *thehouseontherock.com* 🎫 *$29.95.*

### MILWAUKEE PUBLIC MUSEUM

This natural- and human-history museum, located in downtown Milwaukee, opened in 1884 and has been teaching residents about the world around them ever since. Exhibits include a Costa Rican rain forest with a tree-top walkway, a Wisconsin woodlands exhibit that focuses on archaeology and birds, and Asian decorative arts.

**Do This:** Go back in time and visit the *Streets of Old Milwaukee* exhibit, where you'll be transported back to Milwaukee at the turn of the 20th century for a glimpse of restaurants, shops, homes, and more, all represented at about three-quarters of their original size.

**Milwaukee Public Museum.** ✉ *800 W. Wells St., Milwaukee, WI* ☎ *414/278–2702* 🌐 *mpm.edu* 🎫 *$18.*

### PIZZA FARMS

Wisconsin has many culinary claims to fame, but none are more offbeat than pizza farms, a tradition in the western part of the state. As the name implies, the experience includes eating pizza on a working farm, but it's more than that: it's a summertime weekend tradition in which friends and neighbors can gather for a casual evening over pizzas made with fresh ingredients straight from the farm, like house-made fennel-maple sausage.

**Do This:** Stoney Acres Farm hosts pizza nights April to November. They also have a beer and wine garden with suds and ciders from their own brewery, as well as a farmstand to stock up on produce to take home with you.

**Pizza Farms.** ✉ *7002 Rangeline Rd., Athens, WI* ☎ *715/432–6285* 🌐 *stoneyacresfarm.net/pizza-on-the-farm* 🎫 *Pizzas start at $15.*

## Cool Places to Stay

**The Iron Horse Hotel.** Motorcycle aficionados can ride up to this downtown Milwaukee hotel, which is located a half mile from the Harley-Davidson Museum and features covered on-site parking for your wheels and gear storage. Built into a 100-year-old warehouse, the rooms are spacious and dog-friendly, with views of the city, and there's a spa for those days you'd rather stay in. ✉ *500 W. Florida St., Milwaukee, WI* ☎ *414/374–4766* 🌐 *theironhorsehotel.com* [$] *From $119.*

**Seth Peterson Cottage.** Spend the night in a Frank Lloyd Wright–designed cabin in Mirror Lake State Park. The one-bedroom cabin has huge windows with views of the forest, a full kitchen, stone walls, and a large fireplace you can cozy up next to in the winter. In summer, take advantage of the canoe that goes along with the property. ✉ *400 Viking Dr., Reedsburg, WI* ☎ *877/466–2358* 🌐 *sethpeterson.org* [$] *From $325.*

# Index

## A



## B

## C

## N



## O

## T



## U



## V



## W

## Y



## Z

# Photo Credits

**Front Cover:** Kris Wiktor / Alamy [Description: Woman enjoying cup of coffee at Sunrise Reflection Canyon, Lake Powell, Utah, USA.]. **Back cover, from left to right:** sunsinger/Shutterstock, FloridaStock/Shutterstock, Sean Pavone/Shutterstock. **Spine:** Lorcel/Dreamstime. **Interior, from left to right:** Reinhard Dirscherl/agefotostock (1). OverlandTheAmericas/Shutterstock (2). **Chapter 1: Experience Bucket List USA:** Songquan Deng/Shutterstock (6). bluejayphoto/iStockphoto (10). Stuart Monk/Shutterstock (10). f11photo/Shutterstock(10). SL_Photography/iStockphoto (10). Ugo Lora/iStockphoto (11). R.C. Bennett/Shutterstock(11). dibrova (11). Ingus Kruklitis/Shutterstock (11). Skreidzeleu/Shutterstock. (12). kan_khampanya/Shutterstock. (12). TRphotos/Shutterstock. (12). Sara Winter/Shutterstock. (12). Dan Sedran/Shutterstock. (13). Don Mammoser/Shutterstock (13). Biolifepics | Dreamstime.com (13). BlueBarronPhoto/Shutterstock (13). Saro17/iStockphoto (14). lembi/Shutterstock (14). ablokhin/iStockphoto (14). Joakim Lloyd Raboff/Shutterstock (15). Jim Mallouk/Shutterstock (15). F11photo | Dreamstime.com (16). Jorgeantonio | Dreamstime.com (16). Konstantin L/Shutterstock (16). RomanSlavik.com/Shutterstock (16). RodClementPhotography/Shutterstock (17). Dononeg | Dreamstime.com (17). Meunierd | Dreamstime.com (17). Dbvirago | Dreamstime.com (17). Zack Frank/Shutterstock (18). Matthew Connolly/Shutterstock (18). Larrymetayer | Dreamstime.com (18). zrfphoto/iStockphoto (18). Wirestock | Dreamstime.com (19). Bloodua | Dreamstime.com (20). Ritu Manoj Jethani/Shutterstock (20). LnP images/Shutterstock (20). f11photo/Shutterstock (20). Negro Leagues Baseball Museum, Inc. (21). Georgia O'Keeffe Museum (21). Phagenaars | Dreamstime.com (21). stock_photo_world/Shutterstock (21). Brendamunsterman | Dreamstime.com (22). Mia2you/Shutterstock (22). Adeliepenguin | Dreamstime.com (22). Jimmy W/Shutterstock (23). Hoover Tung/Shutterstock (23). James Zandecki/Shutterstock (24). Kirkikis/iStockphoto (24). Jefflindeman | Dreamstime.com (24). Margaret619 | Dreamstime.com (25). Copyright (c) 2014 f11photo/Shutterstock (25). Mikericci | Dreamstime.com (26). Copyright (c) 2020 Michael Gordon/Shutterstock (26). Tbintb | Dreamstime.com (26). IN Dancing Light/Shutterstock (26). Zhukova Valentyna/Shutterstock (27). Wangkun Jia/Shutterstock (27). Adeliepenguin | Dreamstime.com (27). F11photo | Dreamstime.com (27). Tiago_Fernandez/iStockphoto (28). Nagel Photography/Shutterstock (28). northlight/Shutterstock (28). Grossinger/Shutterstock (28). Susan Vineyard/iStockphoto (29). marekuliasz/Shutterstock (29). Stanislavskyi/Shutterstock (29). Edgar Lee Espe/Shutterstock (29). lev radin/Shutterstock (30). trekandshoot/iStockphoto (30). r_drewek/iStockphoto (30). Steve Broer/Shutterstock (31). Alexey Stiop/Shutterstock (31). WilshireImages/iStockphoto (32). PureRadiancePhoto/Shutterstock (32). Jarretera | Dreamstime.com (32). Courtesy Black Star Farms (33). Karenfoleyphotography | Dreamstime.com (33). Shriver's (34). JHVEPhoto/Shutterstock (34). Mitten Crate (34). Peterboro Basket Company (34). Amana Society, Inc (35). Green Mountain Exposure/Shutterstock (36). Evan Austen/Shutterstock (37). Ancha Chiangmai/Shutterstock (38). Joe Hendrickson/Shutterstock (39). **Chapter 2: Great Itineraries:** trekkerimages LLC/iStockphoto (43). **Chapter 3: New England:** Mike Ver Sprill/Shutterstock (83). Brent Hofacker/Shutterstock (86). AnastasiaKopa/Shutterstock (87). Magdalena Kucova/Shutterstock (87). cvrestan/Shutterstock (91). Max Moraga/Shutterstock (92). Sean Pavone/Shutterstock (93). Malley Photography/Shutterstock (94). Shanshan0312/Shutterstock (95). Ian Dagnall / Alamy Stock Photo (96). Try Media/iStockphoto (100). Sean Pavone/iStockphoto (101). Jonathan A. Mauer/Shutterstock (102). Esposito Photography/Shutterstock (103). Wangkun Jia/Shutterstock (104). CNMages / Alamy Stock Photo (105). alekseystemmer/iStockphoto (106). Seacoastmountainphoto/iStockphoto (107). Pat (108). Sandi Cullifer/Shutterstock (109). Jackschultz50 | Dreamstime.com (110). Sean Pavone/Shutterstock (114). f11photo/Shutterstock (115). LnP images/Shutterstock (116). Mbastos | Dreamstime.com (117). Jay Yuan/Shutterstock (118). Georgios Antonatos/Shutterstock (119). Alexander Sviridov/Shutterstock (120). Allan Wood Photography/Shutterstock (121). Jon Bilous/Shutterstock (122). mauritius images GmbH / Alamy Stock Photo (123). T photography/Shutterstock (124). T photography/Shutterstock (125). Heidi Besen/Shutterstock (126). Harmony Waldron/Shutterstock (127). Appalachianviews | Dreamstime.com (131). J. S. Wolf Photography/Shutterstock (132). YuziS/Shutterstock (133). JMP Traveler/iStockphoto (134). Patrick Herlihy/Shutterstock (135). Dan Lewis/Shutterstock (136). Edward Fielding/Shutterstock (137). Ryan Garrett/Shutterstock (138). Carl Beust/Shutterstock (142). Danita Delimont / Alamy Stock Photo (143). WFProvidence/WikimediaCommons (144). MollieGPhoto/Shutterstock (145). randydellinger/iStockphoto (146). Kirkikisphoto | Dreamstime.com (147). Wangkun Jia/Shutterstock (148). FashionStock.com/Shutterstock (152). AlbertPego/iStockphoto (153). Eric Dale/Shutterstock (154). dbimages / Alamy Stock Photo (155). James Casil/Shutterstock (156). Ken Lund/Flickr, [CC by 2.0] (157). Andrei Medvedev/Shutterstock (158). Jay Yuan/Shutterstock (159). Doug Kerr/Flickr, [CC by 2.0] (160). **Chapter 4: The Mid-Atlantic:** Tomas1111 | Dreamstime.com (163). Rawf8/iStockphoto (166). MSPhotographic/iStockphoto (167). Hihitetlin/Shutterstock (167). Jon Bilous/Shutterstock (171). Cmoulton | Dreamstime.com (172). Randy Duchaine / Alamy Stock Photo (173). TOLBERT PHOTO / Alamy Stock Photo (174). Jpcat012 | Dreamstime.com (177). Vito Palmisano/iStockphoto (178). Debramillet | Dreamstime.com (179). Kruck20/iStockphoto (180). Thomas Marchessault / Alamy Stock Photo (181). Lunamarina | Dreamstime.com (182). Wilsilver77/iStockphoto (183). nathaniel gonzales/Shutterstock (184). abriggs21/iStockphoto (185). Sorbis/Shutterstock (188). EQRoy/Shutterstock (189). Kirkikis/iStockphoto (190). D. Pimborough/Shutterstock (191). Gary C. Tognoni/Shutterstock (192). EleanorAbramson/Shutterstock (193). Aoldman | Dreamstime.com (194). Brian Logan Photography/Shutterstock (195). Mandritoiu | Dreamstime.com (196). MargaretW/iStockphoto (200). spyarm/Shutterstock (201). Roman Babakin/Shutterstock (202). duha127/iStockphoto (203). Sepavo | Dreamstime.com (204). Saletomic | Dreamstime.com (205). Felix Lipov/Shutterstock (206). Tinnaporn Sathapornnanont/Shutterstock (207). haveseen/Shutterstock (208). Leonard Zhukovsky/Shutterstock (209). Alessio Catelli/Shutterstock (210). bukharova/iStockphoto (211). anderm/Shutterstock (212). Michael Urmann/Shutterstock (213). Anita Warren-Hampson/Shutterstock (214). Somsubhrachatterjee | Dreamstime.com (215). Melissa Kopka/iStockphoto (216). Joseph Sohm/Shutterstock (217). rarrarorro/iStockphoto (218). Sean Pavone/Shutterstock (223). Appalachianviews | Dreamstime.com (224). MontenegroStock/Shutterstock (225). Nagel Photography/Shutterstock (226). MH Anderson Photography/Shutterstock (227). Vadim 777/Shutterstock (228). Zack Frank/Shutterstock (229). Olivier Le Queinec/Shutterstock (230). Desha Utsick/Shutterstock (231). Gscott54 | Dreamstime.com (232). Jon Bilous/Shutterstock (236). studiodr/iStockphoto (237). Kristi Blokhin/Shutterstock (238). Sean Pavone/Shutterstock (239). Sherry V Smith/Shutterstock (240). Andrew Repp/Shutterstock (241). Bob Pool/Shutterstock (242). Sean Pavone/Shutterstock (245). Steve Heap/Shutterstock (246). turtix/Shutterstock (247). Mihai_Andritoiu/Shutterstock (248). moretown/Shutterstock (249). Sean Pavone/Shutterstock (250). Appalachianviews | Dreamstime.com (251). Pat (255). Steveheap | Dreamstime.com (256). PT Hamilton/Shutterstock (257). MarkVanDykePhotography/Shutterstock (258). Breck P. Kent/Shutterstock (259)

# Photo Credits



Tristanbnz | Dreamstime.com (260). **Chapter 5: The Southeast:** Steve Bower/iStockphoto (263). bhofack2/iStockphoto (266). Stockimo/Shutterstock (267). Olyina/Shutterstock (267). Mrolands | Dreamstime.com (271). Phagenaars | Dreamstime.com (272). Sean Pavone/Shutterstock (273). Alpha Stock / Alamy Stock Photo (274). James Kirkikis/Shutterstock. (275). Michael Gordon/Shutterstock (276). Peter Pajor/Flickr, [CC BY 2.0] (277). Jennifer Lynn/Flickr, [CC BY 2.0] (280). Mia2you/Shutterstock (281). Vito Palmisano/iStockphoto (282). littleny/iStockphoto (283). Suncoast Aerials/Shutterstock (284). Florida's Historic Coast (285). Andriy Blokhin/Shutterstock (286). Courtesy of Visit South Walton (287). Thierry Eidenweil/Shutterstock (288). Parick Farrell and Peter W. Cross (289). NaughtyNut/Shutterstock (290). William Rodrigues Dos Santos | Dreamstime.com (291). Michael Marko/Ball & Chain (292). Rafal Michal Gadomski/Shutterstock (293). Sean Pavone/Shutterstock (294). Felix Mizioznikov/Shutterstock (298). Nicole Kibert/Flickr, [CC BY 2.0] (299). elan7t50/iStockphoto (300). Hanny1224/Shutterstock (301). csfotoimages/iStockphoto (302). f11photo/Shutterstock (303). Brandy Wright/Shutterstock (304). Michael Gordon/Shutterstock (305). B Cruz/Shutterstock (306). Jshanebutt | Dreamstime.com (307). Irina Mos/Shutterstock (311). Alexey Stiop/Shutterstock (312). Bill Brine/Wikimedia Commons (313). Phil Denton/Flickr, [CC BY 2.0] (314). Joe Hendrickson/Shutterstock (315). Zack Frank/Shutterstock (316). PEO ACWA/Wikimediacommons, [CC BY 2.0] (317). Roman Zaiets/Shutterstock (318). Oliclimb/Shutterstock (319). Steve Robinson/Shutterstock (322). lazyllama/Shutterstock (323). Brent Hofacker/Shutterstock (324). RIRF Stock/Shutterstock (325). Brian Lauer/Flickr, [CC BY 2.0] (326). GTS Productions/Shutterstock (327). William A. Morgan/Shutterstock (328). Alisa_Ch/Shutterstock (329). Page Light Studios/Shutterstock (330). Tiago Lopes Fernandez / Peek Creative Collective/iStockphoto (334). James Kirkikis/Shutterstock (335). Sean Pavone/Shutterstock (336). The best photo is earned/iStockphoto (337). James Kirkikis/Shutterstock (338). Sean Pavone/iStockphoto (339). All Stock Photos/Shutterstock (340). magraphy/Shutterstock (341). Sean Board/iStockphoto (344). LEVAI/Shutterstock (345). Nolichuckyjake/Shutterstock (346). anthony heflin/Shutterstock (347). Toribio93/Shutterstock (348). Coralimages2020 | Dreamstime.com (349). Kmm7553 | Dreamstime.com (350). Denis McDonough/Shutterstock (351). skiserge1/iStockphoto (354). digidreamgrafix/Shutterstock (355). Cfarmer | Dreamstime.com (356). Jon Bilous/Shutterstock (357). Warren LeMay/Flickr, [CC by 2.0] (358). Izibns | Dreamstime.com (359). Susanne Pommer/Shutterstock (360). alex grichenko/iStockphoto (361). Sean Pavone/Shutterstock (362). Nicholas Lamontanaro/Shutterstock (365). Rolf_52/Shutterstock (366). dwhob/iStockphoto (367). jejim/Shutterstock (368). Alizada Studios/Shutterstock (369). f11photo/Shutterstock (370). Jonathan Ross/iStockphoto (371). Sean Pavone/Shutterstock (372). **Chapter 6: The Great Plains:** Cavan Images/iStockphoto (375). Glenn Price/Shutterstock (378). Courtesy of Travel South Dakota (379). Bhofack2 | Dreamstime.com (379). Niwat panket/Shutterstock (383). nishav/Shutterstock (384). Doug Fox/Shutterstock (385). Damon Shaw/Shutterstock (386). Eric Urquhart/Shutterstock (387). Itsadream | Dreamstime.com (388). Tony Webster/Flickr, [CC by 2.0] (389). Iowa Tourism Office (393). Jacob Boomsma/Shutterstock (394). Riverboat Twilight (395). Harvestville Farm (396). David Papazian/Shutterstock (397). Iowa Tourism Office (398). Judidthann59 | Dreamstime.com (399). Bruce Leighty / Alamy (400). Iowa Tourism Office (401). Camerashots | Dreamstime.com (402). Sue Smith/Shutterstock (405). RaksyBH/Shutterstock (406). CLP Media/Shutterstock (407). Brent Coulter/iStockphoto (408). Vincent Parsons/Flickr, [CC by 2.0] (409). Dave Drum/iStockphoto (410). APN Photography/Shutterstock (411). Sean Pavone/iStockphoto (414). TGC Photography (415). Water Street/Shutterstock (416). Visit KC (417). STLJB/Shutterstock (418). Missouri Division of Tourism (419). ZUMA Press, Inc. / Alamy Stock Photo (420). marekuliasz/Shutterstock (423). Aspects and Angles/Shutterstock (424). Kent Weakley/Shutterstock (425). marekuliasz/iStockphoto (426). Nattapong Assalee/Shutterstock (427). Ken Schulze/Shutterstock (428). drewthehobbit/Shutterstock (429). Martin Hobelman/Shutterstock (430). Randall Runtsch/Shutterstock (434). Bob Pool/Shutterstock (435). Pjworldtour | Dreamstime.com (436). Sharon Lumpkin/Shutterstock (437). Americanspirit | Dreamstime.com (438). northlight/Shutterstock (439). Plains Art Museum (440). hlopex/Shutterstock (441). Joshua McDonough/iStockphoto (444). Ridetheremuda | Dreamstime.com (445). SuperStock / Alamy Stock Photo (446). Ehrlif | Dreamstime.com (447). zrfphoto/iStockphoto (448). Allison Meier/Flickr, [CC by 2.0] (449). Evan Sloyka/Shutterstock (453). Joseph Sohm/Shutterstock (454). Ashmephotography | Dreamstime.com (455). Crazy Horse Memorial Foundation (456). Sopotnicki/Shutterstock (457). Chaden Roggow/iStockphoto (458). ThePonAek/Shutterstock (459). Photostravellers/Shutterstock (460). Jacob Boomsma/Shutterstock (461). Fiskness | Dreamstime.com (462). **Chapter 7: The West Coast and the Pacific:** NKneidlphoto/Shutterstock (465). FloridaStock/Shutterstock (468). Guajillo studio/Shutterstock (469). Thejamez | Dreamstime.com (469). Denemiles | Dreamstime.com (473). Image Source Trading Ltd/Shutterstock (474). Troutnut | Dreamstime.com (475). Npgal77 | Dreamstime.com (476). Glebtarro | Dreamstime.com (477). Jim Lambert/Shutterstock (478). Rex Lisman/Shutterstock (479). Ivaphotos7 | Dreamstime.com (480). Michael Rosebrock/Shutterstock (481). Sekarb | Dreamstime.com (482). Gentilcore | Dreamstime.com (483). Jefwod | Dreamstime.com (484). Stephen Moehle/Shutterstock (488). ESB Professional/Shutterstock (489). Stephanie Braconnier/Shutterstock (490). Francesco Ferrarini/Shutterstock (491). Michael Urmann/Shutterstock (492). Brian Swanson/Shutterstock (493). Rumata7 | Dreamstime.com (494). Gary C. Tognoni/Shutterstock (495). Marcorubino | Dreamstime.com (496). Dan Sedran/Shutterstock (497). Dancestrokes/Shutterstock (498). Engel Ching/Shutterstock (499). bannosuke/Shutterstock (500). CSNafzger/Shutterstock (501). Checubus | Dreamstime.com (502). Viewapart | Dreamstime.com (503). BlueBarronPhoto/Shutterstock (504). Dancestrokes/Shutterstock (505). mikechapazzo | Dreamstime.com (506). Kit Leong/Shutterstock (507). Andrew Zarivny/Shutterstock (508). Tryder | Dreamstime.com (509). Jimekstrand | Dreamstime.com (510). Benny Marty/Shutterstock (511). randy andy/Shutterstock (512). Bennymarty | Dreamstime.com (519). rusty426/Shutterstock (520). Gnagel | Dreamstime.com (521). Pung/Shutterstock (522). Vipersniper/iStockphoto (523). Hiroyuki Saita/Shutterstock (524). Linda Bair/iStockphoto (525). Pierre Leclerc/Shutterstock (526). Damienverrier | Dreamstime.com (527). janaph/iStockphoto (528). Big Island Visitors Bureau (BIVB)/Nancy Erger (529). George Burba/Shutterstock (530). Maridav/Shutterstock (531). Art Boardman/Shutterstock (532). Demerzel21 | Dreamstime.com (533). Paula Cobleigh/Shutterstock (538). ARTYOORAN/Shutterstock (539). tusharkoley/Shutterstock (540). Kelly vanDellen/Shutterstock (541). Nadia Yong/Shutterstock (542). Chiyacat | Dreamstime.com (543). Cgardinerphotos | Dreamstime.com (544). Victoria Ditkovsky/Shutterstock (545). Joshuaraineyphotography | Dreamstime.com (546). Zhukova Valentyna/Shutterstock (547). Kim Budd (548). Unclejay | Dreamstime.com (549). William Downs Photography/Shutterstock (550). Laurens Hoddenbagh/Shutterstock (555). Galyna Andrushko/Shutterstock (556). Galyna Andrushko/Shutterstock (557). Strekoza2 | Dreamstime.com (558). Monika Wieland Shields/Shutterstock (559). Kirk Fisher/Shutterstock (560).

# Photo Credits

Mlharrisphotography | Dreamstime.com (561). Sean Pavone/Shutterstock (562). bpperry/iStockphoto (563). Skydive Snohomish (564). Irina88w | Dreamstime.com (565). Roman Khomlyak/Shutterstock (566). City of Sequim (567). Pierre Leclerc/Shutterstock (568). **Chapter 8: The Southwest:** francesco ricca iacomino/iStockphoto (571). zoryanchik/Shutterstock (574). Rose Ressner/Shutterstock (575). Msphotographic | Dreamstime.com (575). Pat Tr/Shutterstock (579). Neilld | Dreamstime.com (580). Cheri Alguire/Shutterstock (581). CrackerClips Stock Media/Shutterstock (582). Jon Chica/Shutterstock (583). Likephotography | Dreamstime.com (584). NaughtyNut/ Shutterstock (585). Zack Frank/Shutterstock (586). BCFC/iStockphoto (587). Anirav | Dreamstime.com (588). raphoto/iStockphoto (589). Nate Hovee/Shutterstock (590). randy andy/Shutterstock (594). Sean Pavone/iStockphoto (595). Sean Pavone/Shutterstock (596). Duncan Rawlinson/Flickr, [CC by 2.0] (597). CrackerClips Stock Media/Shutterstock (598). Beth Ruggiero-York/Shutterstock (599). Filip Fuxa/ Shutterstock (600). "Gerald Corsi "/iStockphoto (601). sunsinger/Shutterstock (604). amadeustx/Shutterstock (605). Zhukova Valentyna/ Shutterstock (606). Name_Thats_Not_Taken/iStockphoto (607). Blake Jorgensen/Taos Ski Valley (608). Steve Lagreca/Shutterstock (609). Adam-Springer/iStockphoto (610). Brianwelker | Dreamstime.com (611). Traveller70/Shutterstock (612). harryhayashi/iStockphoto (613). Traveller70/Shutterstock (614). Sean Pavone/Shutterstock (617). zrfphoto/iStockphoto (618). Tom Durr/Shutterstock (619). Fotoluminate LLC/ Shutterstock (620). Rolf52 | Dreamstime.com (621). Sean Pavone/Shutterstock (622). Antonello Marangi/Shutterstock (623). Zrfphoto | Dreamstime.com (624). Terri Butler Photography/Shutterstock (625). Brian Luke/Shutterstock (626). Jfortner2015 | Dreamstime.com (627). Sean Pavone/Shutterstock (628). anitatakespictures/Shutterstock (629). corlaffra/Shutterstock (630). RoschetzkyIstockPhoto/iStockphoto (631). Paulbradyphoto | Dreamstime.com (632). VisualCommunications/iStockphoto (637). Irene Skvorzowa/iStockphoto (638). Fyletto/ iStockphoto (639). Hotaik Sung/iStockphoto (640). evenfh/Shutterstock (641). dibrova/Shutterstock (642). Stefano Borsa/Shutterstock (643). TomKli/Shutterstock (644). kojihirano/Shutterstock (645). Colin D. Young/Shutterstock (646). **Chapter 9: The Rockies:** aphotostory/ Shutterstock (649). Goskova Tatiana/Shutterstock (652). Phillip Rubino/Shutterstock (653). Saastaja | Dreamstime.com (653). JFunk/ Shutterstock (657). Mile High Aviator/Shutterstock (658). WorldPictures/Shutterstock (659). Hikeflyshoot/Shutterstock (660). CSNafzger/ Shutterstock (661). gnagel (662). marekuliasz/Shutterstock (663). John Hoffman/Shutterstock (664). Jon Arnold Images Ltd / Alamy Stock Photo (665). Sopotnicki/Shutterstock (666). Benny Marty/Shutterstock (670). chasehunterphotos/Shutterstockn (671). CSNafzger/Shutterstock (672). Danita Delimont/Shutterstock (673). CodyHaskell/iStockphoto (674). Seattle.roamer/Flickr, [CC by 2.0] (675). Bureau of Land Management/Flickr, [CC by 2.0] (676). Michael Vi/Shutterstock (677). Dan Breckwoldt/Shutterstock (681). Debraansky/iStockphoto (682). varkdvr (683). Jeremy Janus/Shutterstock (684). TheBigMK/Shutterstock (685). Sue Smith/Shutterstock (686). stellalevi/iStockphoto (687). Dennis Stogsdill/iStockphoto (688). Lorcel/Shutterstock (692). Chase Dekker/Shutterstock (693). Hale Kell/Shutterstock (694). Jayme Burney/ Shutterstock (695). Kevin Cass/Shutterstock (696). Larry Porges/Shutterstock (697). Green Mountain Exposure/Shutterstock (698). **Chapter 10: The Great Lakes:** Alexey Stiop/Shutterstock (701). Brent Hofacker/Shutterstock (704). Korsar1 | Dreamstime.com (705). Andy's Frozen Custard (705). FiledIMAGE/Shutterstock (709). Jason Patrick Ross/Shutterstock (710). Grindstone Media Group/Shutterstock (711). photo.ua/ Shutterstock (712). Hollandog | Dreamstime.com (713). Thomas Barrat/Shutterstock (714). Eddie J. Rodriquez/Shutterstock (715). STLJB/ Shutterstock (716). Tupungato/Shutterstock (717). Sepavo | Dreamstime.com (718). Anthony Farinas (719). Delmas Lehman/Shutterstock (722). Grindstone Media Group/Shutterstock (723). Sean Pavone/iStockphoto (724). James Kirkikis/Shutterstock (725). Keifer | Dreamstime. com (726). Zach Bolinger/Butler Athletics (727). Chuck W Walker/Shutterstock (728). NCSchneider_Images/Shutterstock (729). Mikesdeemer | Dreamstime.com (732). Smontgom65 | Dreamstime.com (733). Yochika photographer/Shutterstock (734). Alessandra Ferrara/The artist and Library Street Collective (735). Sean Pavone / Alamy Stock Photo (736). Paul Brady Photography/Shutterstock (737). John McCormick/ Shutterstock (738). Monica Wells / Alamy Stock Photo (739). Jeffrey Isaac Greenberg 6+ / Alamy Stock Photo (740). Adeliepenguin | Dreamstime.com (741). Steven Schremp/Shutterstock (742). BlueBarronPhoto/Shutterstock (746). Steven Schremp/Shutterstock (747). Dan Thornberg/Shutterstock (748). Ken Wolter/Shutterstock (749). Sophie James/Shutterstock (750). Wildnerdpix/Shutterstock (751). Lonnie Paulson/Shutterstock (752). Jeffreyjcoleman | Dreamstime.com (753). Sean Pavone/Shutterstock (757). Michael Shake/Shutterstock (758). Sara Winter/Shutterstock (759). Droopydogajna | Dreamstime.com (760). Alexey Stiop/Shutterstock (761). Jennifer Stone/Shutterstock (762). Flickr.com, [CC by 2.0] (763). David Davis Photoproductions / Alamy Stock Photo (764). Sean Pavone/Shutterstock (765). Nejdet Duzen/ Shutterstock (768). Apostle Islands Cruises (769). Noodle2007 | Dreamstime.com (770). MarynaG/Shutterstock (771). Roger Gerbig/Flickr, [CC by 2.0] (772). Charles821 | Dreamstime.com (773). Boscophotos1 | Dreamstime.com (774). Ferrerphoto | Dreamstime.com (775). Raymond Maiden/Shutterstock (776). Adamwineke | Dreamstime.com (777). **About Our Writers:** All photos are courtesy of the writers except for the following: Cameron Roberts, courtesy of Jim Roberts.

*Every effort has been made to trace the copyright holders, and we apologize in advance for any accidental errors. We would be happy to apply the corrections in the following edition of this publication.

# Notes

# Notes

# Notes

# Notes

# Notes

# Fodor's BUCKET LIST USA

**Publisher:** Stephen Horowitz, *General Manager*

**Editorial:** Douglas Stallings, *Editorial Director*; Jill Fergus, Amanda Sadlowski, Caroline Trefler, *Senior Editors*; Kayla Becker, Alexis Kelly, *Editors*

**Design:** Tina Malaney, *Director of Design and Production*; Jessica Gonzalez, *Graphic Designer;* Mariana Tabares, *Design & Production Intern*

**Production:** Jennifer DePrima, *Editorial Production Manager*; Elyse Rozelle, *Senior Production Editor;* Monica White, *Production Editor*

**Maps:** Rebecca Baer, *Senior Map Editor*; Mark Stroud (Moon Street Cartography), Cartographer

**Photography:** Viviane Teles, *Senior Photo Editor;* Namrata Aggarwal, Ashok Kumar, *Photo Editors;* Rebecca Rimmer, *Photo Intern*

**Business & Operations:** Chuck Hoover, *Chief Marketing Officer*; Robert Ames, *Group General Manager*; Devin Duckworth, *Director of Print Publishing*; Victor Bernal, *Business Analyst*

**Public Relations and Marketing:** Joe Ewaskiw, *Senior Director of Communications & Public Relations*

**Fodors.com:** Jeremy Tarr, *Editorial Director;* Rachael Levitt, *Managing Editor*

**Technology:** Jon Atkinson, *Director of Technology;* Rudresh Teotia, *Lead Developer*; Jacob Ashpis, *Content Operations Manager*

---

**Writers:** Amy Cavanaugh, Andrew Collins, Debbie Harmsen, Cameron Roberts, Mark Sullivan, Kyle Wagner, Carson Walker, Jillian Wilson

**Editors:** Jacinta O'Halloran, Kayla Becker, Mark Sullivan

**Production Editor:** Elyse Rozelle

---



1st Edition

ISBN 978-1-64097-456-2

ISSN 2768–3974



PRINTED IN THE UNITED STATES OF AMERICA

10 9 8 7 6 5 4 3 2 1

# About Our Writers

**Amy Cavanaugh** is a Chicago-based food and drink writer and the dining editor at *Chicago* magazine. She has recently written for publications such as *Condé Nast Traveler, Monocle,* and *Plate Magazine*. She is originally from Holyoke, Massachusetts. Amy wrote the Great Lakes chapter.

Former Fodor's staff editor **Andrew Collins** is based in Mexico City but spends a good bit of the year both in New Hampshire's Lake Sunapee region and in different parts of Oregon and Washington. He wrote the New England and the West Coast and Pacific chapters. A longtime contributor to more than 200 Fodor's guidebooks, including *Pacific Northwest, National Parks of the West, Utah, Santa Fe, Inside Mexico City,* and *New England,* he's also written for dozens of mainstream and LGBTQ publications—*Travel + Leisure, New Mexico Magazine, AAA Living, The Advocate,* and *Canadian Traveller* among them. Additionally, Collins teaches travel writing and food writing for New York City's Gotham Writers Workshop. You can find more of his work at AndrewsTraveling.com, and follow him on Instagram at TravelAndrew.

**Debbie Harmsen**, a longtime writer and editor based in Dallas, loves a good road trip, whether she's traveling for work or for pleasure. She was the lead editor of the award-winning first edition *Fodor's National Parks of the West* guidebook and has written and edited for numerous magazines and websites. Debbie wrote the Southwest chapter.

**Cameron Roberts** has written about travel and entertainment for Fodors.com, Tripsavvy.com, and Fodor's and Michelin guidebooks. An eager road tripper, she splits her time between New Orleans and the Blue Ridge Mountains of North Carolina, and loves to explore everything weird and wonderful in between. Cameron wrote the Southeast chapter.

**Mark Sullivan** has edited or contributed to more than 200 travel books. His latest, *Best Weekend Road Trips,* was published in October by Fodor's Travel. His work (appearing regularly in publications like TripAdvisor and Zagat) has been nominated for a prestigious Lowell Thomas Prize. Mark wrote the Experience and Great Itineraries chapters.

**Kyle Wagner** was the travel editor for *The Denver Post* for nine years; for the 15 years prior to that, she reviewed restaurants for the *Post, Denver's Westword,* and the *Naples Daily News* in Florida. She has been to 72 countries (and counting). She currently writes and edits for multiple magazines and newspapers on a freelance basis, and has updated the *Fodor's Guide to Colorado* for more than a decade. When she's not "working," she races mountain bikes and rafts the rivers of the West in her packraft. Kyle updated the Rockies chapter.

**Carson Walker** worked in radio, television, newspaper, and at the Associated Press as a multiplatform reporter and photojournalist, editor, and manager. While at the AP, he had numerous stories and photos published

# About Our Writers

in major online news platforms and national newspapers. He also has experience in media relations, internal communications, and currently leads crowdsourcing at the largest rural health care organization in the United States. You can follow him on Twitter at @carsonjw and at *linkedin.com/in/carsonwalker*. He wrote the Great Plains chapter.

**Jillian Wilson** is a writer and editor based in Philadelphia. She specializes in writing about Philadelphia, travel, restaurants, health, and wellness. She wrote the Mid-Atlantic chapter of *Bucket List USA*. Her work has also appeared in *HuffPost, The Philadelphia Inquirer, Eater Philly, cupcakes and cashmere, visitphilly.com,* and more. When she isn't writing, Jillian enjoys traveling, exploring Philly, and spending time with loved ones. Jillian is a proud graduate of Temple University. See more of her work at *www.jillian-wilson.com.*